SAP MM I[nventory] Management

Technical Reference and Learning Guide

P. K. AGRAWAL

Formerly Program Manager
Tata Technologies Limited
Pune

PHI Learning Private Limited

Delhi-110092

2014

₹ 795.00

SAP MM INVENTORY MANAGEMENT: Technical Reference and Learning Guide
P. K. Agrawal

Warning and Disclaimer
While every precaution has been taken in the preparation of this book, the author and the publisher do not guarantee the accuracy, adequacy, or completeness of any information contained in this book. Neither is any liability assumed by the author and the publisher for any damages or loss to your data or your equipment resulting directly or indirectly from the use of the information or instructions contained herein.

Trademark Acknowledgements
SAP, SAPconnect, SAPNet, SAPoffice, SAPscript, ABAP, Basis, ECC are registered or unregistered trademark of SAP AG.

All product and service names mentioned in this book are registered or unregistered trademarks or service marks of their respective companies. Use of any product or service name in this book should not be regarded as affecting the validity of any trademark or service mark.

ISBN-978-81-203-4976-6

The export rights of this book are vested solely with the publisher.

Published by Asoke K. Ghosh, PHI Learning Private Limited, Rimjhim House, 111, Patparganj Industrial Estate, Delhi-110092 and Printed by Rajkamal Electric Press, Plot No. 2, Phase IV, HSIDC, Kundli-131028, Sonipat, Haryana.

This book is dedicated to
SAP consultants and users
who deserve to understand SAP much better

Table of Contents

Each chapter is rated for its importance and relevance for functional consultants (FC), users (US), business process owners (PO) and senior managers (SM). In MR, you can keep your own rating and in UL, your understanding level. These ratings are repeated at the beginning of each chapter, so that at the beginning of each chapter you know whether to read it, or skip it, without having to go back to the Table of Contents.

SAP Menu

Sequence number	SAP Menu (ECC 6)	Where covered	Why not covered
	▽ 🗁 SAP menu		
1	▷ 🗀 Office		OoS
2	▷ 🗀 Cross-Application Components		OoS
3	▷ 🗀 Collaboration Projects		OoS
4	▽ 🗁 Logistics		
4.1	▽ 🗁 Materials Management		
4.1.1	▷ 🗀 Purchasing		OoS
4.1.2	▽ 🗁 Inventory Management		
4.1.2.1	▽ 🗁 Goods Movement		
4.1.2.1.1	⬡ MIGO - Goods Movement (MIGO)	5.1	
4.1.2.1.2	▽ 🗁 Goods Receipt		
4.1.2.1.2.1	▽ 🗁 For Purchase Order		
4.1.2.1.2.1.1	⬡ MIGO_GR - GR for Purchase	5.1	
4.1.2.1.2.1.2	⬡ MIGO - PO Number Known	5.1	
4.1.2.1.2.1.3	⬡ MIGO - PO Number Unknow	5.1	
4.1.2.1.2.2	⬡ MIGO_GO - GR for Order (MIGO)	5.8	
4.1.2.1.2.3	⬡ MB31 - For Order	5.8	
4.1.2.1.2.4	⬡ MIGO_GI - Other (MIGO)	6.1	
4.1.2.1.2.5	⬡ MB1C - Other	5.7	
4.1.2.1.3	⬡ MIGO_GI - Goods Issue (MIGO)	6.1	
4.1.2.1.4	⬡ MB1A - Goods Issue	6.1	
4.1.2.1.5	⬡ MIGO_TR - Transfer Posting (MIGO)	8.1	
4.1.2.1.6	⬡ MB1B - Transfer Posting	11.2	
4.1.2.1.7	▽ 🗁 Subsequent Adjustment		
4.1.2.1.7.1	⬡ MIGO_GS - Subcontracting (MIG	11.4	
4.1.2.1.7.2	⬡ MB04 - Subcontracting	11.4	
4.1.2.1.8	▷ 🗀 Goods Movement of Handling Units		HUM

Sequence number	SAP Menu (ECC 6)	Where covered	Why not covered
4.1.2.5	▽ ⬦ Environment		
4.1.2.5.1	▽ ⬦ List Displays		
4.1.2.5.1.1	⬡ MB51 - Material Documents	22.3.1	
4.1.2.5.1.2	⬡ MR51 - Accounting Document for Material	23.2	
4.1.2.5.1.3	⬡ MBAL - Archived Material Documents	33.9	
4.1.2.5.1.4	⬡ MBSM - Cancelled Material Documents	22.3.2	
4.1.2.5.1.5	⬡ MBGR - Reason for Movement	22.3.3	
4.1.2.5.2	▽ ⬦ Stock		
4.1.2.5.2.1	⬡ MB5T - Stock in Transit (Company Code)	4.3.9	
4.1.2.5.2.2	⬡ /CWM/STOCK - Stock Balance Display		Xn not Ex
4.1.2.5.2.3	⬡ /CWM/STOCK_CHECK - Check Stock Vari		Xn not Ex
4.1.2.5.2.4	⬡ MMBE - Stock Overview	4.3.3	
4.1.2.5.2.5	⬡ MD04 - Stock/Requirements List	8.7.3, 28.3.3	
4.1.2.5.2.6	⬡ MB53 - Plant Stock Availability	4.3.5	
4.1.2.5.2.7	⬡ CO09 - Availability Overview	21.3.10	
4.1.2.5.2.8	⬡ MB52 - Warehouse Stock	4.3.7	
4.1.2.5.2.9	⬡ MB5M - Expiration Date List	21.5.9	
4.1.2.5.2.10	⬡ MB5B - Stock for Posting Date	4.3.8	
4.1.2.5.2.11	⬡ MB5T - Stock in Transit	4.3.9	
4.1.2.5.2.12	⬡ MBBS - Valuated Special Stock	14.1.11, 15.1.11	
4.1.2.5.2.13	⬡ MBLB - Stock with Subcontractor	11.1.5	
4.1.2.5.2.14	⬡ J3RFLVMOBVED - Stock Overview (Russia	4.3.12	
4.1.2.5.3	▷ ☐ Information		OoS
4.1.2.5.4	▽ ⬦ Balances Display		
4.1.2.5.4.1	⬡ MB5S - List of GR/IR Balances	4.3.13	
4.1.2.5.5	▽ ⬦ Consignment		
4.1.2.5.5.1	▽ ⬦ Consignment from Vendor		
4.1.2.5.5.1.1	⬡ MB54 - Stock	12.1.10	
4.1.2.5.5.1.2	⬡ MRKO - Liability	12.1.11	
4.1.2.5.5.2	⬡ MB58 - Consignment at Customer	13.1.11	
4.1.2.5.6	▷ ☐ Batch Where-Used List		OoS
4.1.2.5.7	▷ ☐ Batch Search Strategy		OoS
4.1.2.5.8	▽ ⬦ Inventory Controlling		
4.1.2.5.8.1	⬡ O4J3 - Tracking Report		Xn not Ex
4.1.3	▷ ☐ Excise Duty		OoS
4.1.4	▷ ☐ Logistics Invoice Verification		OoS

SAP Customizing Implementation Guide

Sequence number	SAP Customizing Implementation Guide (ECC 6)	Where covered	Why not covered
	SAP Customizing Implementation Guide		
1	Activate SAP ECC Extensions		OoS
2	SAP NetWeaver		OoS
3	Enterprise Structure		OoS
4	Cross-Application Components		OoS
5	Auto-ID Infrastructure		OoS
6	SAP xApp Resource and Portfolio Manageme		OoS
7	Financial Accounting		OoS
8	Financial Accounting (New)		OoS
9	Financial Supply Chain Management		OoS
10	Strategic Enterprise Management/Business		OoS
11	Controlling		OoS
12	Investment Management		OoS
13	Enterprise Controlling		OoS
14	Real Estate		OoS
15	Flexible Real Estate Management (RE-FX)		OoS
16	Logistics - General		OoS
17	Environment, Health & Safet		OoS
18	Sales and Distribution		OoS
19	Materials Management		
19.1	General Settings for Materials Manageme		OoS
19.2	Consumption-Based Planning		OoS
19.3	Purchasing		OoS
19.4	External Services Management		OoS
19.5	Inventory Management and Physical Inver		
19.5.1	Plant Parameters	1.3.5	
19.5.2	Define Attributes of System Messages	21.7	
19.5.3	Number Assignment		
19.5.3.1	Define Number Assignment for Ac	23.3	
19.5.3.2	Define Number Assignment for M;	22.4	
19.5.3.3	Define Number Assignment for R	28.5	
19.5.3.4	Define Number Assignment for G	21.8	
19.5.4	Field Selection for Goods Movements	20.3	

Reasons for 'why not covered'

Reason	Description
CS	Country specific functionality is out of scope of this book.
HUM	Handling Unit Management is out of scope of this book.
OoS	Out of scope.
Retail	SAP Retail is out of scope of this book.
W/o Wizard	This configuration is covered under individual nodes without wizard.
Xn not Ex	These transactions are not executing.

Preface

If you are a consultant or a user of SAP and feel frustrated because SAP seems impossible to master, this book is for you. It shows that SAP is finite, can be understood well, and that the task is not as daunting as it appears. Moreover, you do not have to worry about forgetting things; you can always find them again, and fairly with ease.

This book has evolved from the difficulty that each one of us experiences in 'Managing SAP'. As I constantly struggled, trying to understand the concepts of SAP and explore their linkages with other concepts, I found memory to be a major handicap. So I started taking notes. Before long, I could not find what I had written. Then I started reorganizing my notes, and finally, I started feeling more comfortable. I knew where to write when I learnt something new, and I could find things conveniently which I was looking for.

The notes improved continuously, and then came the desire to share them with others; hence I decided to write a series of books on SAP MM. While writing this book, I have tried to be clear, crisp and comprehensive as much as possible.

This book is meant for the SAP users, business process owners and senior managers of companies, who have implemented, or are in the process of implementation, or are planning to implement, or are evaluating modules of SAP MM. Their need to understand the subject is not as comprehensive as that of functional consultants. How all these category of readers should use this book is described below.

How to use this book

There are two ways in which you can use this book. You can use it as a learning guide, or else it can be used as a technical reference. When you use this book as a learning guide, you have to cover it in several iterations. Each iteration is designed to enhance your knowledge and prepare you for the next iteration.

In terms of job roles one can classify the readers as senior managers, business process owners, users, and functional consultants. Senior managers need to know only the important concepts, and what SAP can do for them. BPOs need to know more of SAP concepts and have a good idea of how to perform different tasks in SAP. Users need to have a thorough understanding of different tasks they have to perform in SAP and the concepts underlying them. Functional consultants need to know everything, or at least everything important.

In the table of contents, each topic is classified in terms of relevance and importance for each category of user. Each topic is given an A, B, C, or X rating for each category of user. During each iteration, you can decide the role and importance level you intend to cover. You can select the role you are going to refer to in an iteration, based on your job role, but that is not essential. For example, if you are going to be a user of SAP, but do not know anything about SAP, you may select senior manager role in your first iteration. Having learnt important concepts, you may select BPO role in the next iteration. Finally, you may select the user role. Also, once you become a proficient user, you may go through the book from the perspective of a functional consultant. These ratings are repeated at the beginning of each section so that you can decide whether to read it, or skip it without going back to the Table of Contents.

In addition to the suggested ratings, I have left two blank columns. Although I have given an importance rating to each topic, you can decide the importance based on your requirements. For example, if Account Assignment is not applicable to you, you may mark it as not relevant for you. Similarly, you can decide the importance rating. There is nothing sacrosanct about the rating given by me. You may note this rating in the blank column 'MR—My Rating'. As you read a topic, you will achieve a level of understanding. You can record it in the column 'UL—Understanding Level'. You may use A/B/C/X, or any other rating scale. After you complete an iteration, these columns will help you decide, which topics to revisit.

When you are reading this book, you will need to work on the system. When you are reading only the important concepts as a senior manager, it may be possible to read the book without hands-on experience. However, as you go deeper and deeper, working on the system will become more and more necessary.

If you are using this book as a technical reference, apart from the table of contents and index, you can also locate the relevant material by using 'SAP Menu', and 'SAP Customizing Implementation Guide (IMG)'. Expanded tree of both the SAP menu and IMG (ECC 6.0) is given after the Table of Contents. Once you find the node in these structures, you will be guided to the relevant chapter. If any node is not covered in the book, the reason for not covering it is also mentioned. In such cases you may have to look for other sources; this book may not be of help to you.

You can also use the structure of this book to keep your findings and observations in an organized way. You can maintain a Word or an Excel document where you record your findings and observations either against page numbers or chapter numbers.

You can also use the structure of this book for documenting your discussion with the users and recording their input, which will finally become the configuration manual.

Acknowledgements

I am deeply indebted to Mr. D.V. Prasad, Mr. Hemant Khedkar, and my family, who contributed in different ways to make this book possible. I express my sincere gratitude to my publisher, PHI Learning, for putting their trust in me and for improving the presentation of this book.

Individual social responsibility

There is no doubt that we must excel in our chosen profession, but our responsibility does not end there. Indeed, we have a greater responsibility of making the world a better place to live in—to address the challenges the world faces, to analyze, to find solutions, to share, to network, and to make a difference. You may have wondered about the diagram on the cover page; it is a plan for a City without Traffic Lights. There are four articles at the end of this book. You will perhaps find them interesting to read. In particular, think about Samay Daan to make a difference. It is our Individual Social Responsibility.

P.K. AGRAWAL

Enterprise Structure

1.1 ENTERPRISE STRUCTURE

Functional Consultant	User	Business Process Owner	Senior Management	My Rating	Understanding Level
A	A	A	A		

1.1.1 Organizational Levels

Client

Many customers of SAP are corporate groups having one or more companies. Whereas each company is an independent financial entity, consolidation of financial data is required for the entire enterprise. SAP permits this by keeping data of all the companies in the same set of tables on a single server from which it can be extracted as required.

Apart from the production server, which contains real-life business data, you also need a server for Quality Assurance, Training, etc. While many customers of SAP maintain separate servers for each of these purposes, there are some customers who would like to keep all these data on a single server. To meet this requirement, SAP allows division of a server in multiple clients. The data stored in one client is invisible in other clients. When you log on to SAP, you log on to a client. This determines the data you will see.

Company code

Your business may consist of one or more company codes. A company code is a legal entity having its own balance sheet and profit and loss statement.

Plant

In common parlance, a plant is a manufacturing facility. In SAP, it has a wider meaning. Any place of work, be it a manufacturing facility or an office, is called a plant. All goods movements take place in a plant and, therefore, in a company code.

Storage location

A storage location is a physical location where you receive, store and issue materials. You also periodically check the quantity of material stored and compare it with book inventory.

1.1.2 Enterprise Structure

Company code, plant, storage location

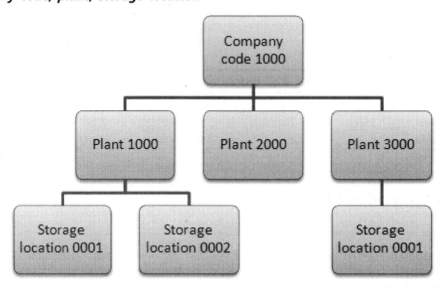

The figure above shows the relationships between company codes, plants and storage locations, which may be summarized as under:

➢ A client may have one or more company codes.

➢ A company code may have zero, one, or many plants.

➢ A plant belongs to one and only one company code.

➢ Plant ids are unique in the entire implementation. The same plant id cannot exist in another company code.

➢ A plant may have zero, one, or many storage locations.

➢ A storage location belongs to one and only one plant.

➢ A storage location is identified by the combination of the plant id and storage location id. Therefore, the same storage location id can exist in another plant, but it is a different storage location.

1.2 COMPANY CODE

Functional Consultant	User	Business Process Owner	Senior Management	My Rating	Understanding Level
A	A	A	A		

1.2.1 Purpose

Your business may consist of one or more company codes. A company code is a legal entity having its own balance sheet and profit and loss statement.

1.2.2 IMG Node

SM30 ➤ V_T001

1.2.3 Screen

Company Code	1000
Company Name	IDES AG

Additional data	
City	Frankfurt
Country	DE
Currency	EUR
Language	EN

1.2.4 Primary Key

Company Code

1.3 PLANT

Functional Consultant	User	Business Process Owner	Senior Management	My Rating	Understanding Level
A	A	A	A		

1.3.1 Overview

Plant

In common parlance, a plant is a manufacturing facility. In SAP, it has a wider meaning. Any place of work, be it a manufacturing facility or an office, is called a plant. All Inventory Management transactions take place in a plant and, therefore, in a company code.

Relationship of plant with company code

Each plant belongs to one and only one company code. A company code can have zerc, one, or many plants.

Relationship of plant with storage locations

Each storage location belongs to one and only one plant. A plant can have zero, one, or many storage locations.

1.3.2 IMG Node

SM30 ➤ V_T001W

1.3.3 Screen

Plant	1000
Name 1	Werk Hamburg
Name 2	

Detailed information

Language Key	EN	English
House number/street	Alsterdorfer Strasse 13	
PO Box		
Postal Code	22299	
City	Hamburg	
Country Key	DE	Germany
Region	02	Hamburg
County code		
City code		
Tax Jurisdiction		
Factory calendar	01	Factory calendar Germany standard

1.3.4 Primary Key

Plant

1.3.5 Plant Parameters

Plant parameters control different aspects related to a plant. These are discussed along with related functionality. They can also be configured in view V_159L.

Plant	1000	Werk Hamburg

Goods movements

Create SLoc. automat.	☑	BBD/Prod. Date	☑
Del. compl. default	☑	BOM Usage	☐
Miss. parts active	☑	BOM Application	PP01
Summarize miss.parts	☑	Trans./Event Type	WV
BaWU deactivated	☐	GR/GI slip number	☐
BaWU synchron.postng	☑	BchNo.auto.GR AcAsst	☐

Physical inventory

Stock type	1
Alternative Unit	☑
Batch in Background	☑
Change document	☐
Adj. Book Inventory	☐
Reason f. difference	

Reservations

Movement Allowed	☑
Days mvt. allowed	10
Retention period	30

Negative stocks

Vendor consignment gds	☐	Customer Consignment	☐
RTP stocks	☐	Return.pack.at cust.	☐
Stcks of mat. w. vendor	☐	Sales order stock	☐
		Project stock	☐

1.3.6 Assignment of Plant to Company Code

After you create a plant, you can assign it to a company code in view V_T001K_ASSIGN, or using transaction OX18.

CoCd	Plnt	Name of Plant	Company Name	Status
0001	0001	Werk 0001	SAP A.G.	
0005	0005	Hamburg	IDES AG NEW GL	
0006	0006	New York	IDES US INC New GL	
0007	0007	Werk Hamburg	IDES AG NEW GL 7	
0008	0008	New York	IDES US INC New GL 8	
1000	0099	Werk für Customizing-Kurse SCM	IDES AG	
1000	1000	Werk Hamburg	IDES AG	

A plant is assigned to a company code through valuation area (not seen in this view). A plant has a valuation area, and a valuation area has a company code. Thus, a plant has a company code.

1.3.7 Factory Calendar for a Plant

A plant usually have non-working days, e.g. weekly offs. These are specified in a factory calendar. Factory calendar for a plant can be specified in view V_001W_F.

Plnt	Name 1	Cal	Text
0001	Werk 0001	01	Factory calendar Germany standard
0005	Hamburg	01	Factory calendar Germany standard
0006	New York	US	Factory calendar US standard
0007	Werk Hamburg	01	Factory calendar Germany standard
0008	New York	US	Factory calendar US standard
0099	Werk für Customizing-Kurse SCM	01	Factory calendar Germany standard
1000	Werk Hamburg	01	Factory calendar Germany standard

Factory calendar for a plant can also be maintained in view V_T001W.

1.4 STORAGE LOCATION

Functional Consultant	User	Business Process Owner	Senior Management	My Rating	Understanding Level
A	A	A	A		

1.4.1 Purpose

A storage location is a physical location where you receive, store and issue materials. You also periodically check the quantity of material stored and compare it with book inventory. There may be zero, one or more storage locations within a plant. Storage locations are always created for a plant. Storage location ids are unique within a plant. The same storage location id in another plant is a different storage location.

1.4.2 IMG Node

SM34 ➤ VC_T001L

1.4.3 Storage Locations

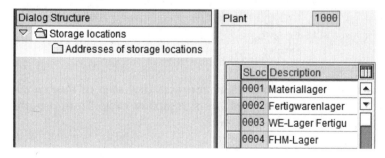

Dialog Structure
▽ 🗀 Storage locations
🗀 Addresses of storage locations

Plant	1000

SLoc	Description	
0001	Materiallager	▲
0002	Fertigwarenlager	▼
0003	WE-Lager Fertigu	
0004	FHM-Lager	

1.4.4 Addresses of Storage Locations

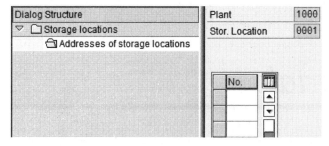

A storage location can have multiple addresses. You can create an entry and maintain address details. This is useful if a storage location has multiple entry and exit gates and their postal addresses are not the same.

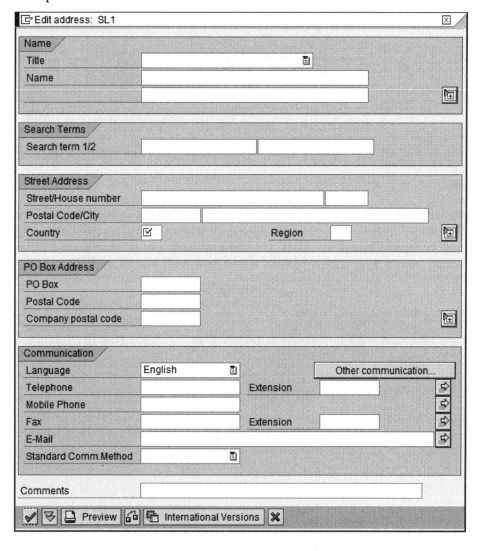

Material

2.1 MATERIAL MASTER

Functional Consultant	User	Business Process Owner	Senior Management	My Rating	Understanding Level
A	A	A	A		

2.1.1 Purpose

The material master comprising all the individual material master records stored in the system contains descriptions of all materials that an enterprise procures, produces, and keeps in stock. It is the central repository of information on materials for the enterprise. Materials can be procured and used without a material master record, but they cannot be stocked or produced.

2.1.2 Initial Screen

When you run transaction MM01 to create a material, the system gives the following initial screen.

Create Material (Initial Screen)

Select view(s)	Organizational levels	Data

Material	
Industry sector	
Material Type	

Change Number	

Copy from...	
Material	

Material

Material number

Each material is assigned a unique material number, which identifies the material. Although it is called material number, it is actually an 18-digit alphanumeric string.

Old material number

If you want to use your pre-SAP material numbers in SAP, you can do so by using external number range. Alternatively, you can use old material number field for linking pre-SAP material number to the SAP material number.

Internal material number

When you create a material in the system, you identify it through a material number. SAP can automatically assign number from a running serial to the material you create. Further, you can have multiple running serials, called internal number ranges, and different materials may be assigned numbers from different number ranges, depending on their material types.

External material number

➤ Some companies follow a numbering system which can tell you what kind of material it is. For example, you can tell from the material number that it is a raw material, that it is steel, that it is a cold rolled steel, etc. Although this sounds very useful, you may often run out of numbers in your numbering scheme.

➤ Some companies want to retain their pre-SAP material numbers.

In both these, and other scenarios, a company may decide that the user creating the material will specify the material number.

Number ranges

Numbers can be assigned to different materials from different number ranges. For more details, see Section 2.6.

Industry Sector

SAP is used by different industries worldwide as shown in the following screenshot.

The material data that the mechanical engineering industry needs to maintain would be different from the material data that the pharmaceutical industry needs to maintain. Hence, when you create material data, you specify the industry sector, and the system adjusts the data screens accordingly.

Default Industry Sector

You can set a default value for industry sector by clicking Defaults ➤ Industry sector... . The system gives the following dialog box.

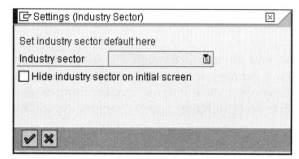

Industry sector

If you set the industry sector here, it is proposed as the default value when you create a material.

Hide industry sector on initial screen

If you set the industry sector and select this checkbox, the system uses this industry sector when you create a material, and does not even show it on the initial screen. This facility is useful for those users who operate in a single industry sector.

Material Type

A material type is a group of materials with similar attributes. The material type allows the management of different materials in a uniform manner. There are different types of materials. A material is assigned a type when you create the material master record. The data you maintain for a material also depends on the type of material. For example, the data needed for manufactured parts would be different from the data needed for perishables.

IBAU	Maintenance assembly
HERS	Manufacturer parts
MPO	Material Planning Object
NLAG	Non-stock material
UNBW	Non-valuated material
NOF1	Nonfoods
HIBE	Operating supplies
VERP	Packaging
FRIP	Perishables
PIPE	Pipeline material

For details of control functions of material type, see Section 2.7.

Change Number

In your company you can implement engineering change management, and control changes through change master records. If you are using the engineering change management system, you can enter the change number here.

Screen Layout

The screen you get for maintaining a material can be customized to your requirement. You can get different screens based on material type, industry sector, user and transaction.

2.1.3 Views

Selecting the Views

SAP maintains material data in a large number of views. When you change or display a material, you need to select the views you are going to work with. This is because each view has associated organizational levels, and the system prompts you to specify them. By selecting the views, you need to specify only those organizational levels that are needed by the selected views. If you click Select view(s) , the system shows you the available views and you can select the views you want to maintain.

View
Basic Data 1
Basic Data 2
Classification
Sales: Sales Org. Data 1
Sales: Sales Org. Data 2
Sales: General/Plant Data
Foreign Trade: Export Data
Sales Text
Purchasing
Foreign Trade: Import Data
Purchase Order Text
MRP 1
MRP 2
MRP 3
MRP 4
Forecasting
Work Scheduling
Production Resources/Tools
General Plant Data / Storage 1
General Plant Data / Storage 2
Warehouse Management 1
Warehouse Management 2
Quality Management
Accounting 1
Accounting 2
Costing 1
Costing 2
Plant Stock
Storage Location Stock

Default Views

You can set default views by clicking Defaults ➢ Views.... The system gives the following dialog box.

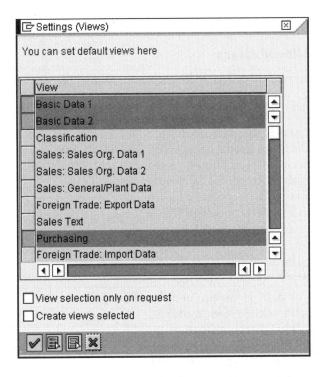

View

Select the views you want to be selected by default.

View selection only on request

If you select the views and also this checkbox, the system directly displays the material without showing the select view(s) dialog box. Of course, you can always click Select view(s) , and select more or less views to work on.

Create views selected

If this indicator is set, all selected views are created, with the exception of the Sales Text view, the Purchase Order Text view, and the Classification view, when you save the material master record. As a result, you do not have to access and confirm each screen individually. This function is particularly useful when creating a material master record with a reference.

2.1.4 Organizational Levels

Material Data at Different Organizational Levels

The data in the material master is maintained at different levels as illustrated below.

Level	*Table and primary key*	*Description*	*Example view*
Client - general data	MARA Material Number	General data is the data applicable to all individual group companies, all plants, and all warehouses/stores belonging to an enterprise (corporate group). Examples of general data are details on a material's design (CAD drawings, for instance) and storage conditions (temperature range, whether the material is explosive or perishable, and so on).	Basic Data 1
Plant	MARC Material Number Plant	Plant level data is maintained for each plant where the material is used. The data important to Purchasing is stored at this level. Examples of this data are the maximum and minimum order quantities of a material and the reorder point.	Purchasing
Storage location	MARD Material Number Plant Storage Location	Storage location level data is data specific to a storage location. Stock levels are an example of the data maintained for each storage location.	Storage Location Stock

Specifying Organizational Levels

You need to specify organizational levels depending on the views you select. If you select all the views and click Organizational levels , the system gives the following dialog box.

If you do not select all the views, you may not see some of the fields in the above dialog box.

Default Organizational Levels

You can set default values for organizational levels by clicking Defaults ➤ Organizational levels... . The system gives the following dialog box.

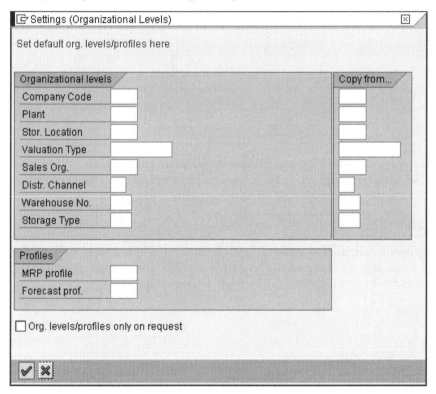

Organizational levels

If you usually work with a set of organizational levels, you can specify them here and save. If you do so, when you enter the material number and click ✅, the system proposes these organizational levels by default.

Copy from

Here you enter the organizational levels you want to use as a reference during creation.

Profiles

Here you specify the MRP and Forecast profiles that the system uses by default.

Organizational levels/profiles only on request

If you select the organizational levels and also this checkbox, the system directly displays the material without showing the organizational level dialog box. Of course, you can always click ⎾ Organizational levels ⏌, and change the organizational levels.

2.1.5 Basic Data 1

Material

Basic data 1	Basic data 2	Classification	Sales: sales org. 1	Sales:

Material	400-510	Ball bearing	

Material number

Each material is uniquely identified by an 18-character alphanumeric code. When you create a material, the material number may be assigned internally by the system, or externally by the user creating the material.

Material description

The material description explains the material and is entered when a user creates the material for the first time. It is a good practice to define a policy for describing materials. Abbreviations and standard wordings should be used wherever possible.

General Data

General data			
Base Unit of Measure	PC piece(s)	Material Group	001
Old material number		Ext. Matl Group	
Division	01	Lab/Office	
Product allocation		Prod.hierarchy	
X-plant matl status		Valid from	
☐ Assign effect. vals		GenItemCatGroup	

Base unit of measure

The base unit of measure is the unit in which stocks of the material are managed. The system converts all the quantities you enter in other units of measure (alternative units of measure) to the base unit of measure. The base unit of measure is the unit satisfying the highest necessary requirement for precision.

Material group

The material group classifies your materials, and thereby helps you locate a particular material. Examples of material groups are steel, non-ferrous metals, fasteners, and lubricants. Material group is an important filtering and aggregating criterion in reporting on materials.

You can also maintain purchasing info record for non-stock material at vendor, material group level. For example, this facility can be used to identify vendors of Stationery items.

You need to differentiate between material type and material group. Material types have a large number of properties associated with them and you generally use material types predefined by SAP. Material groups do not have associated properties but you use them for analysis, e.g. total inventory of steels. Material groups also help in searching for a material.

Old material number

When you implement SAP, you may transfer data from existing systems. If you assign the material numbers in SAP independently, you can keep the old material number here. You can use the old material number to systematically search for material master records via matchcodes.

External material group

Sometimes there are material groups defined by external bodies, e.g. CCG material group or the Nielsen material group. Here you can specify an external material group for this material. The master list of external material groups is maintained in view V_TWEW.

Ext. Material Group	Ext. matl grp descr.

Division

Division is a way of grouping materials, products, or services from the point of view of Sales and Distribution. The system uses divisions to determine the sales areas and the business areas for a material, product, or service.

Laboratory/office

Here you can specify the design office, laboratory, or laboratory worker who is responsible for this material. This field is used mostly in chemical industry. The master list of laboratory/engineering office is maintained in view V_024L.

Lab/Office	Text: Lab./engineering office
001	Laboratory 1
002	Laboratory 2
G01	Lab Group 01

Product allocation

The product allocation determination procedure determines how product allocation is carried out.

Product hierarchy

The product hierarchy is used in the Sales and Distribution area for analyses and price determination. It is used to depict the competitive materials of competitor 1 in relation to those of competitor 2. Here, your own company is also regarded as a competitor and its materials as competitive materials. You can use this representation as a basis for market analysis.

Cross-plant material status, valid from

If you do not want the material to be purchased after a certain date, you can set the material status to Blocked for Purchasing with the date from which the blocking is effective. This can be done for all the plants in the Basic data 1 tab or for individual plants in the Purchasing tab.

Assign effectivity parameter values

Here you indicate whether you can assign values to the effectivity parameters or override the date when you explode an assembly or a finished product.

General item category group

Here you can specify the material grouping that helps the system determine item categories during sales document processing. The master list is maintained in view V_TPTM and configured in Sales and Distribution.

Dimensions/EANs

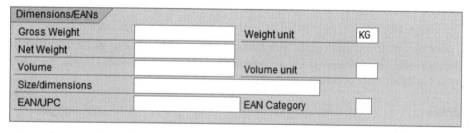

Dimensions/EANs			
Gross Weight		Weight unit	KG
Net Weight			
Volume		Volume unit	
Size/dimensions			
EAN/UPC		EAN Category	

Gross weight, net weight, weight unit

This information can be used to check storage bin capacity in Warehouse Management. It is also used in the Goods Receipt Forecast report generated by transaction ME2V.

Volume and unit

This information can be used to plan storage and transportation. It is also used in the Goods Receipt Forecast report generated by transaction ME2V.

Size/dimensions

Here you can specify the size or dimensions of the material along with unit of measure. The data you enter is merely for information and is not used by the system.

EAN/UPC, EAN category

The European Article Number (EAN) is assigned by the manufacturer of the particular material. The EAN identifies the manufacturer uniquely. In the USA, the equivalent to the EAN is the Universal Product Code (UPC). With internal number assignment, you enter the EAN category but not an EAN. With external number assignment, you enter the EAN but not an EAN category. In this case, the EAN is checked for correctness and the EAN category is determined by the system automatically.

Packaging Material Data

Packaging material data	
Matl Grp Pack.Matls	
Ref. mat. for pckg	

Material group of packing materials

If this material uses packaging material, here you specify the material group of packaging materials. This information can be used to find all materials that require similar packaging materials. Material groups of packing materials are maintained in view V_TVEGR.

Reference material for packaging

If this material is packed in the same way as another material, for which you have specified detailed packing instructions, you can enter the number of that material here.

Basic Data Texts

Basic Data Texts				
Languages Maintained	0	Basic Data Text	Language:	

Basic data texts

You maintain detailed description of the material in different languages in the Basic data text tab, which you access by clicking Basic Data Text . The system shows the number of languages in which the text is maintained.

2.1.6   Basic Data 2

Material

🖉 Basic data 1	ᵒ̄ Basic data 2	Classification	Sales: sales org. 1	Sales:

Material	400-510	Ball bearing	ⓘ
	✎ ☐		

Other Data

Other Data			
		Ind. Std Desc.	
	☐ CAD Indicator		
Basic material			

Industry standard description

Here you can store description of the material in accordance with the appropriate industry standard (such as ANSI or ISO). This field is purely for information.

CAD indicator

The CAD indicator shows that the material was transferred to SAP from a CAD system. This indicator is only for information but can also be used as a search criterion to find a material.

Basic material

Here you can maintain the basic constituent of the material. The master list of basic material is maintained in view TWSPR.

Basic matl
C 60
CR25
CRNIMO2
Edelstahl / stainless steel
Grauguß 25
Metall / Metal
SPHAEROGUSS
St60
Stahl / Steel
Steel 50 / Stahl 50
Titan / Titanium

Environment

Environment		
DG indicator profile	☐	Environmentally rlvt
☐ Highly viscous		☐ In bulk/liquid

Dangerous goods indicator profile

If a material is dangerous, you can assign it a profile here. The profiles are maintained in view DGV_TDG41. A profile specifies whether the material is dangerous or not and whether it is relevant for dangerous goods checks, dangerous goods documents, template materials and one-time materials.

Environmentally relevant

Here you can specify that this is an environmentally relevant material. This indicator is used in the Sales and Distribution module.

Highly viscous

You can use this indicator to identify highly viscous materials. This indicator can be used to control data output on transport documents.

In bulk/liquid

This indicator shows if the goods are to be transported in bulk. You can use this indicator to control data output on transport documents.

Design Documents Assigned

Design documents assigned
☑ No link

No link

This checkbox indicates if design documents are linked to this material.

Design Drawing

Design Drawing					
Document			Document type		Doc.vers.
Page number		Doc.ch.no.		Page format		No. sheets

Document number, document type and document version

A document has a number and a version. When creating a document, you specify a document type, which controls field selection and the available statuses for a document info record.

Page number

Here you specify the page number of the document on which the material can be found.

Document change number

Document change number indicates the change status of the drawing.

Page format

Here you can store the page size of the technical document of this material.

Number of sheets

Here you can store the number of pages that the technical document contains.

Client-Specific Configuration

Client-specific configuration		
Cross-plant CM		☐ Material is configurable
☐ Variant		🖾 Configure variant

Cross-plant configurable material

Unlike the plant-specific configurable material, the cross-plant configurable material is valid for all plants.

Material is configurable

Here you can specify that the material is configurable. For example, if you buy envelopes of various sizes, colors, with or without an address window, etc., instead of creating separate material master records for every possible combination (e.g. C5 with window, C6 without window), you can use a configurable material. For a configurable material, you create characteristics, class, material, and configuration profile.

Variant

This specifies that the material is a variant of a configurable material.

Configure variant

Click [🖾 Configure variant] to configure variant of this material.

Additionals

```
┌─────────────────────────┐
│       Additionals       │
└─────────────────────────┘
```

You can assign additionals to articles to ensure their effective presentation at sale. Price tickets, security tags, clothes hangers, and shipping materials are all examples of additionals. Click [Additionals] to enter additionals for the material.

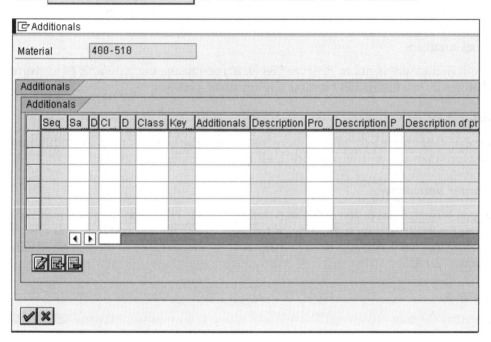

2.1.7 Purchasing

Material, Plant

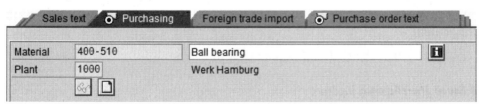

Not all data in this view is at plant level. Some data is at material level. These are discussed separately. If a material exists in one plant and you want to create it in another plant, use transaction MM01 (Create), not transaction MM02 (Change).

Material Level General Data

General Data					
Base Unit of Measure	PC	piece(s)	Order Unit		Var. OUn
			Material Group	001	
			Qual.f.FreeGoodsDis.		
Batch management					

Base unit of measure

The base unit of measure is not at the plant level. If you change the base unit of measure here, it changes in the Basic data 1 tab and applies to all plants.

Order unit

Order unit can differ from base unit of measure because the vendors may use a different unit of measure than the unit of measure used by the company internally.

Variable order unit active

Normally you buy material in the order unit defined above. However, for some materials you want the flexibility to buy in different order units from different vendors. You can do so by activating this field. You also need to maintain conversion ratios in the Units of measure tab (see Section 2.1.8).

Material group

Here you specify the material group. The material group is also displayed in the Basic data 1 tab.

Qualifies for free goods discount

Here you can specify whether, and for which areas, the material qualifies for a discount in kind. This indicator is presently used only in Purchasing.

Batch management

Here you can specify that the material is managed in batches.

Material Level Purchasing Values

Purchasing values					
Purchasing value key	1		Shipping Instr.		
1st Rem./Exped.	10	days	Underdel. Tolerance	0.0	percent
2nd Reminder/Exped.	20	days	Overdeliv. Tolerance	0.0	percent
3rd Reminder/Exped.	30	days	Min. Del. Qty in %	0.0	percent
StdValueDelivDateVar	0	days	Unltd Overdelivery		Acknowledgment Reqd

Purchasing value key

In the purchasing documents you specify a number of characteristics: reminder days, tolerance limits, shipping instructions, order acknowledgment, etc. These characteristics are combined in a purchasing value key in customizing and assigned to a material here. In the purchasing documents, this data is proposed from the purchasing info record or, in its absence, from the material master record.

Reminder 1, 2, 3

These fields indicate the time interval in days at which reminders are to be issued to the vendor before (if the number is negative) or after the due date. The due date depends on the purchasing document. For example, for RFQ it is receipt of quotation.

Standard value for delivery time variance

Is one week delay in delivery too much, or too less? The answer depends on the material. In this field, the value in days specifies how many days variance from the planned delivery date is to count as a 100% variance. If the actual delivery is 2 days after the planned delivery date and this field contains 10, then the variance is 20%.

Shipping instructions

This field specifies the packaging and shipping instructions for the item. Shipping instructions are configured in view cluster VC_T027A, which is discussed in Section 2.11.

Under-delivery tolerance

This field specifies the percentage (of the order quantity) up to which an under-delivery of this item will be accepted.

Over-delivery tolerance

This field specifies the percentage (of the order quantity) up to which an over-delivery of this item will be accepted.

Minimum delivery quantity in %

This is the minimum percentage of the purchase order quantity that must be delivered for the goods receipt to be included in the vendor evaluation. In this way, you can prevent a vendor from receiving a good score for a punctual delivery, where the quantity delivered was insufficient.

Unlimited over-delivery

This field specifies whether unlimited over-delivery can be accepted for the item.

Acknowledgement required

This field indicates whether the vendor is required to acknowledge the receipt of purchasing document, e.g. purchase order, outline purchase agreement, etc.

Material Level Manufacturer Data

Other data / manufacturer data

Mfr Part Profile

Mfr Part Number

Manufact.

Manufacturer part profile

This field contains a profile if you work with MPN materials. The profile then applies to all MPN materials that are assigned to this firm's own, inventory-managed material.

Manufacturer part number and manufacturer

This field contains the number used by the manufacturer, or by the vendor, to manage a material. If there is just one manufacturer part number for your firm's own inventory-managed material, the manufacturer is specified. In that case, there is no need to create an MPN material. In order to use manufacturer part numbers, it must be enabled in view V_130S.

Plant level General Data

General Data

Base Unit of Measure	PC	piece(s)	Order Unit		Var. OUn
Purchasing Group	001		Material Group	001	
Plant-sp.matl status			Valid from		
Tax ind. f. material			Qual.f.FreeGoodsDis.		
Material freight grp			☐ Autom. PO		
			OB Management		
☐ Batch management			OB ref. matrial		

Purchasing group

Purchasing group is a buyer or a group of buyers. Here you specify the purchasing group that is responsible for buying this material for this plant.

Plant specific material status, valid from

If you do not want the material to be purchased after a certain date, you can do so by specifying the material status Blocked for Purchasing with the date from which the blocking is effective. This can be done for all the plants in the Basic data 1 tab or for individual plants in the Purchasing tab.

Tax indicator for material

The tax indicator is used in the automatic determination of the tax code in Purchasing. The tax code can be determined automatically by price determination using purchasing conditions.

Material freight group

Material freight group determines freight codes and classes in a freight code set. The freight code set is used to determine freight costs. Configuration of the freight groups and codes is in Sales and Distribution.

Automatic PO

Here you can specify that purchase orders can be generated automatically from purchase requisitions using transaction ME59N. To make the generation automatic, a further indicator must be set in the vendor master record of the vendor associated with the purchase order.

Original batch management, original batch reference material

The concept of original batch is used in batch management.

Plant Level Other Data

Other data / manufacturer data			
GR Processing Time	1 days	☐ Post to insp. stock	☐ Critical Part
Quota arr. usage		☐ Source list	JIT Sched. Indicator
			Mfr Part Profile
Mfr Part Number			Manufact.

GR processing time

This field specifies the number of workdays required for inspection of material after its receipt.

Post to inspection stock

By default a material is received in unrestricted use stock. However, if you want the material to be received in quality inspection stock by default, set this indicator. This indicator is copied to purchase order items and when goods are received quality inspection stock is proposed by default.

Critical part

This field specifies that this is a critical material, and during stock taking, it should be counted completely.

Quota arrangement usage

Quota arrangement determines which vendor or plant should get the next order. This decision is based on the quantity ordered on the vendor, or the plant, and its share of business. The key question here is what purchasing documents should be included in determining the quantity ordered. Quota arrangement usage determines the purchasing documents that are included in determining how much quantity has been ordered. SAP provides the following preconfigured options.

Q	PO	SLn	PlOr	PReq	MRP	Ord
1	☑	☑	☐	☐	☐	☐
2	☑	☑	☑	☑	☐	☐
3	☑	☑	☑	☑	☑	☐
4	☑	☑	☑	☑	☑	☑

Source list

If this indicator is set for a plant, a source of supply must be entered in the source list before the material can be ordered.

JIT schedule indicator

This indicator determines whether it is possible to generate JIT delivery schedules in addition to forecast schedules for a material specified in a purchase scheduling agreement.

2.1.8   Units of Measure

Sometimes, for a material, you use different units of measures for different purposes. You need to convert quantities from one unit to another. You can maintain this conversion in the material master. If you click ⇒ Additional data in the material master, you get additional tabs in which you can enter data about a material. One of these tabs is the Units of measure.

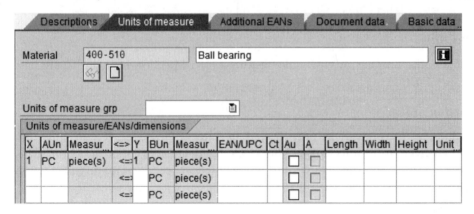

Material

You specify units of measures and their conversion to each other for this material.

Units of measure group

In the tab above, either you can maintain the data yourself, or you can copy sets of predefined conversions, by specifying Units of measure grp. Units of measure groups are defined in view V_006M. If you enter a Units of measure grp in the tab above, all entries for that Units of measure group are copied in the tab.

Unit group	Alt. Unit	Measurement unit text	Counter	Denominat.
LAMP	PAC	Pack	50	1
LAMP	PAL	Pallet	1,000	1
LAMP	PC	piece(s)	1	1

Conversion

Here you specify the ratios for converting a quantity of this material from one unit to another.

2.1.9 Material Texts

In the material master you can maintain the texts specified in view V_TTXIDI.

Object	ID	Meaning
MATERIAL	BEST	Purchase order text
MATERIAL	GRUN	Basic data text
MATERIAL	IVER	Internal note
MATERIAL	PRUE	Inspection text

Purchase order text can be entered in the `Purchase order text` tab. For the other three texts, click `⇒ Additional data` and go to the appropriate tab. In all these tabs you can enter the texts in multiple languages.

Texts in the material master can be copied in the items of purchasing documents using copying rules. In a copying rule you specify the source object, source text, target object and target text. You also specify whether copying takes place automatically or is decided by the user. Copying rules defined by SAP allow the users to copy purchase order text of the material master in the items of the following documents.

Source object	Source text	Target object	Target text
Material master	Purchase order text	RFQ	Material PO text
Material master	Purchase order text	Purchase order	Material PO text
Material master	Purchase order text	Purchasing info record	Purchase order text
Material master	Purchase order text	Contract	Material PO text
Material master	Purchase order text	Scheduling agreement	Material PO text

2.1.10 Plant Data/Storage 1

Material, Plant, Storage Location

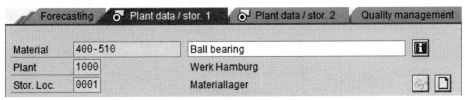

Forecasting	Plant data / stor. 1	Plant data / stor. 2	Quality management

Material	400-510	Ball bearing
Plant	1000	Werk Hamburg
Stor. Loc.	0001	Materiallager

Not all data in this view is at storage location level. Some data is at material level, some at plant level, and some at storage location level. These are discussed separately. If you do not specify the plant and the storage location, you will see the material level data in this tab.

Material Level General Data

General data			
Base Unit of Measure	PC	piece(s)	
Temp. conditions		Storage conditions	
Container reqmts		Haz. material number	
		Number of GR slips	
Label type		Lab.form	☐ Appr.batch rec. req.
☐ Batch management			

Base unit of measure

The base unit of measure is the unit in which stocks of the material are managed. The system converts all the quantities you enter in other units of measure (alternative units of measure) to the base unit of measure. The base unit of measure is the unit satisfying the highest necessary requirement for precision.

Temperature conditions

Some of your materials may require storage at certain temperatures. In view V_143 you maintain the master list of temperature conditions.

Temp. conditions	Description
20	20° Fahrenheit
30	30° Fahrenheit
40	40° Fahrenheit

Storage conditions

Some of your materials may require special storage conditions. In view V_142 you maintain the master list of storage conditions.

SC	Description
HU	Controlled humidity
RA	Radioactive material
RE	Refrigerator
SU	No sunlight

Container requirements

Some of your materials may require certain containers for storage and transport. In view V_144 you maintain the master list of container requirements.

Container reqmts	Description
B1	Bin 2' x 2' x 1'
B2	Bin 3' x 3' x 2'
P3	Pallet 3' x 3'
P4	Pallet 4' x 4'

Hazardous material number

The hazardous material number indicates that the material is dangerous, making special precautions necessary for its storage and shipment.

Number of goods receipt slips

You may print goods receipt slips that accompany the goods during storage and movement. The goods receipt slip usually has information on the material, vendor, purchase order, goods receipt date, plant, and storage location. The base unit of material is usually a small unit, e.g. pieces. However, the material is usually stored and moved in larger units, e.g. cartons. You need a goods receipt slip per carton, not per piece. In this field you can maintain the ratio. During goods receipt, you will specify the number of pieces received, and the system will determine the number of goods receipt slips to be printed. If you enter nothing in this field, only one goods receipt slip is printed.

Label type

You may also print goods labels. One label is printed for each unit of goods. Labels may be of different types. Master list of label types is maintained in view V_6WP3.

Label type	Text
ST	Sticker
TG	Tag

Label form

Label form determines the size and layout of the label. Master list of label forms is maintained in view V_6WP4.

Label form	Text
E1	Label quantity in order quantity
E2	Label quantity in stock quantity
E3	Label quantity in order price quantity

For more information on label printing, see Section 24.7.

Approved batch record required

In process industry, you may approve batches before they can be stored for unrestricted use. For such materials, select this indicator.

Batch management

Here you can specify that the material is managed in batches.

Material Level Shelf Life Data

Shelf life data			
Min. Rem. Shelf Life		Total shelf life	
Period Ind. for SLED	D	Rounding rule SLED	
Storage percentage			

The Shelf life data is used for checking shelf life expiration in Inventory Management. For more details, see Section 21.5.4.

Plant Level General Data

General data				
Base Unit of Measure	PC	piece(s)	Unit of issue	
Temp. conditions			Storage conditions	
Container reqmts			Haz. material number	
CC phys. inv. ind.		☐ CC fixed	Number of GR slips	
Label type		Lab.form	☐ Appr.batch rec. req.	
		OBManagmnt	OB Ref. Material	
☐ Batch management				

Unit of issue

Here you enter the unit that the system proposes for goods issues, transfer postings, other goods receipts, and reservations. You should enter a value in this field only if you want to use a unit of measure differing from the base unit of measure.

Cycle counting physical inventory indicator, cycle counting fixed

See Section 29.34.3 for cycle counting.

Original batch management, original batch reference material

The concept of original batch is used in batch management.

Storage Location Level Data

Storage Bin		Picking area	

Storage bin

Here you specify the storage bin within a storage location where the material is stored. The storage bin is only significant if you do not use SAP Warehouse Management. It appears on goods receipt/issue slips.

Picking area

The picking area groups together storage bins from the standpoint of picking strategies; that is, the storage bins are arranged in a strategically advantageous manner for the task of picking.

2.1.11   Plant Data/Storage 2

Material, Plant, Storage Location

Plant data / stor. 1	Plant data / stor. 2	Quality management	Accounting

Material	400-510	Ball bearing	
Plant	1000	Werk Hamburg	
Stor. Loc.	0001	Materiallager	

Not all data in this view is at storage location level. Some data is at material level, some at plant level, and some at storage location level. These are discussed separately. If you do not specify the plant and the storage location, you will see the material level data in this tab.

Material Level Weight/Volume Data

Weight/volume			
Gross Weight	3	Weight unit	KG
Net Weight	3		
Volume		Volume unit	
Size/dimensions			

Here you maintain the weight, volume and size of the material. This data can also be maintained in Basic data 1 tab.

Material Level General Plant Parameters

General plant parameters	
SerLevel	☐

Serialization level

Serialization level	Short text
	Serialization within the stock material number
1	Keep equipment number and serial number synchronous

You may give a serial number to each item of a material, e.g. a car, or an engine. The serial numbers uniquely identify an item within a material number. These materials are assigned Serialization level blank. However, for plant and machinery, you want the serial number to be synchronous with equipment. These materials are assigned Serialization level 1.

Plant Level General Plant Parameters

General plant parameters			
☐ Neg. stocks in plant		Log. handling group	
Serial no. profile	SerLevel ☐	Distr. profile	
Profit Center	1010	Stock determ. group	

Negative stocks allowed in plant

Here you specify whether negative stocks are allowed for the material in the plant. For more information on allowing negative stocks, see Section 4.2.2.

Logistics handling group

The logistics handling group is used in the calculation of working loads such as placement into stock and picking. Master list of logistics handling group is maintained in view V_TLOG.

Serial number profile

A serial number profile must be assigned to each material that is to be serialized. This assignment at plant level is made here.

Distribution profile

Here you can assign a control profile for merchandise distribution. Materials can be distributed among the individual recipients in a plant. Master list of distribution profiles is maintained in view V_TMFPF.

Profit center

The profit center you specify here is used in cost accounting.

Stock determination group

Stock determination groups classify materials for stock determination. Here you can specify the stock determination group of a material in a plant. For more information on stock determination, see Chapter 27.

Storage Location Level Data

There is no storage location level field in this tab.

2.1.12   Plant Stock

See Section 4.3.2.

2.1.13   Storage Location Stock

See Section 4.3.1.

2.1.14   Accounting 1

Material, Plant, Valuation Type

Quality management	⦶ Accounting 1	Accounting 2	Plant stock	Stor. loc...

Material	100-302	Hollow shaft	**i**
Plant	1000	Werk Hamburg	
Val. type	EIGEN_HALB		

Valuation area

The data in this tab is for a valuation area, not a plant. If you change any data in this tab, it is changed for all plants that have the same valuation area as the plant specified here.

Material with split valuation

If the material has a split valuation, the valuation type field also appears and the data is at material, valuation area, valuation type level.

General Data

General data			
Base Unit of Measure	PC piece(s)	Valuation Category	B
Currency	EUR	Current period	12 2013
Division	01	Price determ.	☐ ML act.

Base unit of measure

The base unit of measure is the unit in which stocks of the material are managed. The system converts all the quantities you enter in other units of measure (alternative units of measure) to the base unit of measure. The base unit of measure is the unit satisfying the highest necessary requirement for precision.

Valuation category

You can do split valuation only if the material has a valuation category. If the valuation category for a material is blank, you cannot do split valuation.

ValCat	Description
B	Inhse/ext.proc.
C	Status
H	Origin

In the case of split valuation, the valuation category also determines which valuation types are allowed.

Currency

The system shows the currency for all the values on this tab.

Current period

The system shows the current posting period.

Division

Division is a way of grouping materials, products, or services from the point of view of Sales and Distribution. The system uses divisions to determine the sales areas and the business areas for a material, product, or service.

Price determination

The indicator is only of use if the material ledger is active.

Material ledger active

This checkbox indicates whether material ledger valuation is active for the material.

Current Valuation

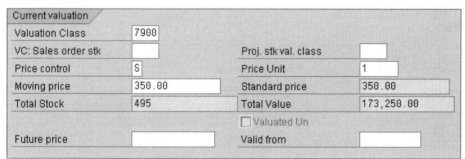

Valuation class

You can specify valuation class for a material in a plant. Valuation classes possible for a material are restricted by the account category reference of the material type of the material.

Valuation class: sales order stock

If you want to post sales order stock of a material to an account different from the account to which the standard stock is posted, you can specify a valuation class here. Valuation classes possible for a material are restricted by the account category reference of the material type of the material.

Valuation class: project stock

If you want to post project stock of a material to an account different from the account to which the standard stock is posted, you can specify a valuation class here. Valuation classes possible for a material are restricted by the account category reference of the material type of the material.

Price control

Inventory of a material may be managed at standard price, or at moving average price.

Price control	Short text
S	Standard price
V	Moving average price/periodic unit price

This parameter affects the accounting of goods receipt for storage.

Price unit

Normally the price is for one unit, but sometimes it may be for a number of units.

Moving price

When goods are received, the system calculates the moving average price automatically by dividing the total value of the material in the plant by the total stock in the plant.

Standard price

You can maintain inventory of a material in a plant at standard price that you specify here. Difference in the value of the material received and that calculated at standard price is charged to the Income from price difference account.

Total stock

Here the system shows the stock of the material in the plant, or if applicable, for the valuation type.

Total value

Here the system shows the value of the material in the plant, or if applicable, for the valuation type.

Valuated unit

Here you can indicate that the valuation is based on batch-specific unit of measure.

Future price, valid from

If you want to change the material's price on a future date, you specify the price and the date.

Previous Valuation, Standard Cost Estimate

Previous period/year

Click   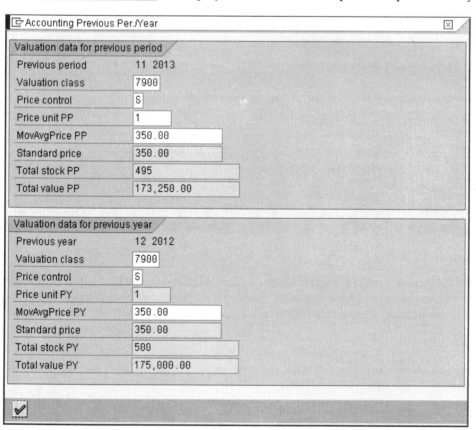 to display valuation data for previous period and year.

Accounting Previous Per./Year	
Valuation data for previous period	
Previous period	11 2013
Valuation class	7900
Price control	S
Price unit PP	1
MovAvgPrice PP	350.00
Standard price	350.00
Total stock PP	495
Total value PP	173,250.00
Valuation data for previous year	
Previous year	12 2012
Valuation class	7900
Price control	S
Price unit PY	1
MovAvgPrice PY	350.00
Standard price	350.00
Total stock PY	500
Total value PY	175,000.00

Standard cost estimate

Click | Std cost estimate | to see the standard cost estimate.

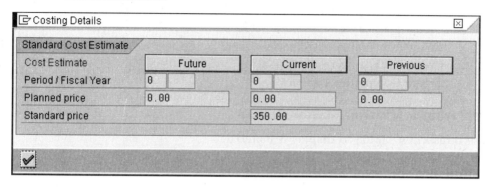

2.2 MATERIAL MASTER PROCESSES

Functional Consultant	User	Business Process Owner	Senior Management	My Rating	Understanding Level
A	A	A	B		

2.2.1 Creating a Material Master Record

You can use transaction MM01 to create a material. If a material exists in one plant and you want to create it in another plant, use transaction MM01 (Create), not transaction MM02 (Change).

2.2.2 Creating Material with Predefined Material Types

You can use special material creation transactions in which the material type is predefined. These transactions are useful if you want to authorize a person to create materials only of specific types.

Transaction	Description
MMB1	Create Semi-finished Product
MMF1	Create Finished Product
MMG1	Create Returnable Packaging
MMH1	Create Trading Goods
MMI1	Create Operating Supplies
MMK1	Create Configurable Material
MML1	Create Empties
MMN1	Create Non-Stock Material

(Contd.)

Transaction	Description
MMP1	Create Maintenance Assembly
MMR1	Create Raw Material
MMS1	Create Service
MMU1	Create Non-Valuated Material
MMV1	Create Packaging
MMW1	Create Competitor Product

2.2.3 Displaying a Material Master Record

You can use transaction MM03 to display a material.

2.2.4 Changing a Material Master Record

You can use transaction MM02 to change a material. The system logs the changes made. You can see the changes made to a material by selecting Environment ➤ Display changes .

2.2.5 Changing Material Type

If you want to change the material type, use transaction MMAM and specify the new material type because the screen you get depends on the material type.

2.2.6 Mass Maintenance of Material Master

If you want to make similar changes in several materials, use transaction MM17. Here you can select the tables and fields you want to maintain.

Object Type	BUS1001	Materials (industry)
Variant Name		

Tables | Fields

Short Description	Table Name
General Material Data	MARA
Material Descriptions	MAKT
Plant Data for Material	MARC
Material Valuation	MBEW
Storage Location Data for Material	MARD
Units of Measure for Material	MARM
Sales Data for Material	MVKE
Forecast Parameters	MPOP
Planning Data	MPGD_MASS
Tax Classification for Material	MLAN
Material Data for Each Warehouse Number	MLGN
Material Data for Each Storage Type	MLGT

In this transaction, you can make changes for several materials in a single screen.

2.2.7 Displaying Change Documents

You can use transaction MM04 to view the changes that have taken place in a material.

2.2.8 Deleting a Material Master Record

Flagging a material for deletion

You can use transaction MM06 to flag a material for deletion. You may not delete the material data completely. You can delete it for a plant, storage location etc. If you want to review materials that are without stock, in the initial screen you can select Extras ➢ Proposal list... to generate the proposed deletion list. You can select a combination of material, plant and storage location from this list, which is then transferred to the initial screen for deletion.

Deleting a material

To actually delete a material, run transaction MM71.

Removing deletion flag

Transaction MM06 can also be used to remove the deletion flag if transaction MM71 has not been run to actually delete the material. Run transaction MM06, remove the tick, and save.

2.2.9 Scheduling Material Creation, Change, Deletion

You can schedule creation, change or deletion of a material. Specify the date when the change would come in effect.

Transaction	Description
MM11	Schedule Creation of Material
MM12	Schedule Changing of Material
MM16	Schedule Material for Deletion

The planned changes do not take effect until you run transaction MM13.

2.2.10 Displaying Scheduled Changes

You can display planned changes and how a material would look on a given date.

Transaction	Description
MM14	Display Planned Changes
MM19	Display Material at Key Date

2.2.11 Activating Planned Changes

If you schedule creation, change or deletion of a material, you need to activate the changes using transaction MM13. You can use this facility to create a two step material maintenance process. Several persons may schedule material creation, change or deletion. A higher level person would periodically review the planned changes and activate them.

2.2.12 Extending a Material to Storage Locations

You can run transaction MMSC to extend a material in a plant to one or more storage locations.

Material	400-510	Ball bearing
Plant	1000	Werk Hamburg
Base Unit	PC	

Storage locations

SLoc	Copy from	Bin	MRP	Reorder Point	Fixed lot size	SPT
0001						

2.2.13 Loading Material Data from a File

You can use program RMDATIND to transfer material master records to SAP for test purposes. Production data is transferred with program RBMVSHOW (transaction BMV0). Program RMMMDE00 can be used to delete all material data in the current client.

2.3 MATERIAL MASTER REPORTS

Functional Consultant	User	Business Process Owner	Senior Management	My Rating	Understanding Level
A	A	A	B		

2.3.1 Materials List

Run transaction MM60 to display the list of materials.

Material	Plant	Material Description	MTyp	Matl Group	Unit	ABC	Pr.	Price	Crcy	PGr
817	1000	Paint	HAWA	004	PC		V	10.00	EUR	
819	1000	Wallpaper	HAWA	00107	PC		S	350.00	EUR	
820	1000	Door	HAWA	00107	PC		S	600.00	EUR	
1157	1000	170DS55001C-184M	HALB	00101	EA		V	4,190.38	EUR	001
100-100	1000	Casing	HALB	001	PC		S	113.76	EUR	100

2.4 MATERIAL MASTER SCREEN

Functional Consultant	User	Business Process Owner	Senior Management	My Rating	Understanding Level
A	C	C	C		

2.4.1 Screen Sequence Determination

Purpose

The screen that you get for maintaining the material master is technically called a screen sequence, and can depend on the transaction, the user, the material type and the industry sector. In this view cluster you define how the screen sequence is determined.

IMG Node

SM34 ➤ V_CM2

Screen Sequence Control

The screen sequence used for maintaining material master can depend on the following:

- ☐ Transaction screen reference
- ☐ User screen reference
- ☐ Material type screen reference
- ☐ Industry sector screen reference

For each combination of these four variables, the screen sequence is defined here.

Dialog Structure		SRef. trans.	SRef. user	SRef. matl type	SRef. industry	SSq	Screen seq. description
🗂 Screen sequence control		01	*	*	*	21	Std ind.(short) tab pages
📁 Transaction screen reference		01	*	HERS	*	12	Manufacturer Parts
📁 User screen reference		01	*	PLM	*	PL	Std ind.(short) tab pages
📁 Material type screen reference		01	*	ROH	B	ZB	Excise Duty + VSO
📁 Industry sector screen reference		01	*	ROH	C	EH	Std (short) w/EH&S tabs

Transaction Screen Reference

You can group your transactions in transaction screen references, which are used for determining screen sequence.

Dialog Structure		TCode	Transaction Text	SRef. trans.
📁 Screen sequence control		MAL1	Create material via ALE	01
🗂 Transaction screen reference		MAL2	Change material via ALE	01
📁 User screen reference		MM01	Create Material &	01
📁 Material type screen reference		MM02	Change Material &	01
📁 Industry sector screen reference		MM03	Display Material &	01

User Screen Reference

You can group your users in user screen references, which are used for determining screen sequence.

Dialog Structure		Name	SRef. user
📁 Screen sequence control		ALBAT	
📁 Transaction screen reference		ASCHE	EH
🗂 User screen reference		BAESSLER	BA
📁 Material type screen reference		BATIPPS	EB
📁 Industry sector screen reference		BLUMOEHR	

Material Type Screen Reference

You can group your material types in material type screen references, which are used for determining screen sequence.

Dialog Structure		MTyp	Material type description	SRef. matl type
📁 Screen sequence control		ABF	Waste	ROH
📁 Transaction screen reference		AEM	Samples	ROH
📁 User screen reference		BLG	BLG Empties External	ROH
🗂 Material type screen reference		BLGA	BLGA Empties Fixed assets	ROH
📁 Industry sector screen reference		CH00	CH Contract Handling	ROH

Industry Sector Screen Reference

You can group your industry sectors in industry sector screen references, which are used for determining screen sequence.

Dialog Structure		I	Industry description	SRef. industry
☐ Screen sequence control		1	Retail	M
☐ Transaction screen reference		2	Aerospace & Defense	M
☐ User screen reference		3	Service Provider	M
☐ Material type screen reference		A	Plant Engin./Construction	M
☐ Industry sector screen reference		B	Beverage	B

2.4.2   Screen Sequence Definition

Purpose

When you maintain material master, you get a screen. This screen is defined here.

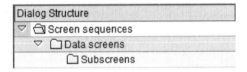

A screen, technically called a Screen sequence:, consists of several Data screens (tabs in the material master). Each Data screen in turn consists of Subscreens, whose sequence can be changed. The screen sequence used is determined based on transaction, user, material type and industry sector.

IMG Node

SM34 ➢ V_CM1

Screen Sequences

When you maintain material master, you get a screen. This screen can be customized to your requirement. There are multiple levels in defining this screen. The highest level is the screen sequence. Although SAP provides many preconfigured screen sequences, screen sequence 21 is default. This book also uses screen sequence 21. In this screen sequence, data is grouped in tabs.

Dialog Structure		SSq	Screen seq. description
▽ ☐ Screen sequences		01	Std industry sequence
▽ ☐ Data screens		03	Standard retail sequence
☐ Subscreens		11	Std industry: small scrns
		12	Manufacturer Parts
		21	Std ind.(short) tab pages

Data Screens

The tabs that you see while maintaining material master are defined as data screens here. Screen sequence 21 has the following data screens.

SSq	Scrn	Screen description	T	SC	M	GUI status	TT	R	Alt. screen descrip.
21	07	Basic Data 1	1	4004	K	DATE00	2		Basic data 1
21	08	Basic Data 2	1	4004	K	DATE00	2		Basic data 2
21	09	Sales: Sales Org. Data 1	1	4000	V	DATE00	2		Sales: sales org. 1
21	10	Sales: Sales Org. Data 2	1	4000	V	DATE00	2		Sales: sales org. 2
21	11	Sales: General/Plant Data	1	4000	V	DATE00	2		Sales: General/Plant

Subscreens

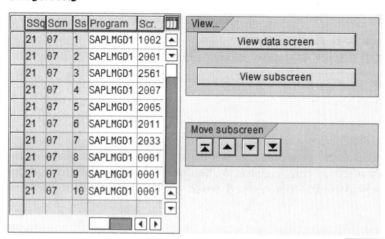

A data screen consists of several subscreens. If you click [View data screen], you see the entire tab, but if you click [View subscreen], you see only a part of the tab. If you change the sequence of subscreens, the sequence of the fields in the tab changes. You can move a subscreen up or down using ⤒ ▲ ▼ ⤓.

Creating Your Own Subscreens

If you want to create your own subscreens, you can create a function group of your own by copying function group MGD1 (for industry) or function group MGD2 (for retail) using transaction OMT3C. The subscreens are not copied, except for two subscreens which are copied for technical reasons. You can use this copy to create subscreens of your own.

2.4.3 Additional Screens

Purpose

In the material master, apart from the main screens, you can go to additional screens by clicking ⇨ Additional data. Here you can specify that a secondary screen appears as an additional screen or is accessed by pushbutton from another main screen or additional screen.

IMG Node

SM30 ➤ V_T133S_ZUORD

Screen

Screen sequence [21]   Std ind.(short) tab pages

Scr	Screen description	FCode			Additional			Processing routine
40	Descriptions		🗋	🗑	1	🗋	🗑	OKCODE_KURZTEXTE
41	Units of Measure		🗋	🗑	2	🗋	🗑	OKCODE_MENGENEINHEITEN
42	Basic Data Text	PB26	🗋	🗑	5	🗋	🗑	OKCODE_BDT
48	Consumption	PB09	🗋	🗑	8	🗋	🗑	OKCODE_VERBRAUCH

2.4.4   Sequence of Main and Additional Screens

Purpose

If you want to change the sequence of tabs in the material master, you can do that here.

IMG Node

SM30 ➤ V_T133S_REIHF

Screen

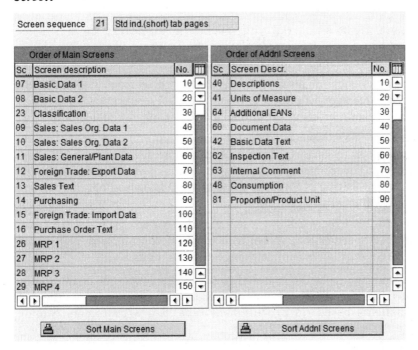

Screen sequence [21] Std ind.(short) tab pages

Order of Main Screens				Order of Addnl Screens		
Sc	Screen description	No.		Sc	Screen Descr.	No.
07	Basic Data 1	10	▲	40	Descriptions	10 ▲
08	Basic Data 2	20	▼	41	Units of Measure	20 ▼
23	Classification	30		64	Additional EANs	30
09	Sales: Sales Org. Data 1	40		60	Document Data	40
10	Sales: Sales Org. Data 2	50		42	Basic Data Text	50
11	Sales: General/Plant Data	60		62	Inspection Text	60
12	Foreign Trade: Export Data	70		63	Internal Comment	70
13	Sales Text	80		48	Consumption	80
14	Purchasing	90		81	Proportion/Product Unit	90
15	Foreign Trade: Import Data	100				
16	Purchase Order Text	110				
26	MRP 1	120				
27	MRP 2	130				
28	MRP 3	140 ▲				▲
29	MRP 4	150 ▼				▼

🖶 Sort Main Screens   🖶 Sort Addnl Screens

You get the main screens when you create, change or display material. You go to additional screens by clicking  .

2.4.5 Data Entry Properties of a Field

Overview

Data entry property of a field

In the material master, a field can have one of the following data entry properties.

Hide	Display	Reqd Entry	Opt. entry

Factors affecting data entry property of a field

The data entry property of a field is determined by the following factors.

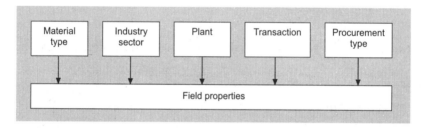

Factor	Determination of the factor and relevance
Material type	When you create a material, you specify the Material Type . Certain fields may not be relevant for certain material types. For example, CAD Indicator may not be relevant for raw materials.
Industry sector	When you create a material, you specify the Industry sector . Certain fields may not be relevant for certain industry sectors. For example, Highly viscous may be relevant for chemical industry, but not for mechanical industry.
Plant	For entering plant specific data for a material, you specify the plant. Depending on the nature of your plant, certain fields may or may not be relevant. For example, if one of your plants does not use the Quota arrangement feature of SAP, the Quota arr. usage field may not be relevant for that plant.
Transaction	You create, change, or display a material using a transaction. Using this factor, SAP specifies that all fields in transaction MM03 will be display only. SAP's customers cannot change these settings.
Procurement type	You specify whether the material is externally procured, or internally produced in the MRP 2 tab of a material. SAP specifies properties of certain fields based on procurement type. SAP's customers cannot change these settings.

Grouping of factors affecting field property (Field reference groups)

If material type influences data entry property of a field, you need to define data entry property of each field for each material type. The same is true for industry sector, plant, transaction and procurement type. This design would require considerable effort in initial configuration and maintenance of the same. It is also prone to inconsistencies. SAP, therefore, lets you group the factor influences in Field reference groups.

Grouping of fields having identical field properties (Field selection groups)

There are certain fields which have identical data entry properties. You can group them in Field selection group.

Fields (Field selection group 87)	
Field name	Short Description
MARA-BEHVO	Container requirements
MARA-RAUBE	Storage conditions
MARA-STOFF	Hazardous material number
MARA-TEMPB	Temperature conditions indicator

Field properties for a combination of field reference group and field selection group

For each combination of field reference group and field selection group, you specify field property.

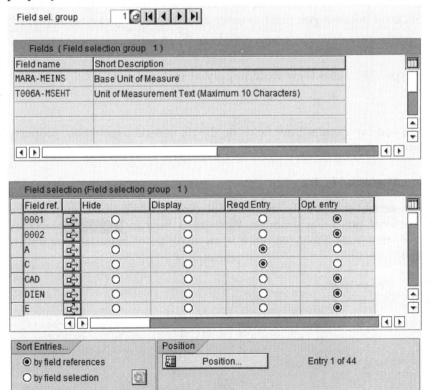

Determination of field property

Field reference groups represent factor influences. Each factor can give you one field reference group. So, you may have five field reference groups, each of which will have a data entry property. The system will use the field property as per the following priority.

Setting	Priority
Hide	1
Display	2
Required entry	3
Optional entry	4

Guidelines for determining properties of a field reference

It might seem daunting to adjust three variables to get the right field property; the other two are predetermined by SAP. But if you can evolve clear policy guidelines, it may be possible to tackle this complex task.

Industry sector

At the highest level is industry sector. A client will usually have one, or at the most a few, industry sectors. At this level, you can decide which fields you do not want at all, and hide them. For some fields you may specify required entry. It is unlikely that you would specify display at this level because you need to enter a value before it can be displayed.

Material type

The next is material type. The same logic would apply at material type level.

Plant

The next is plant. Here you can decide about fields on the plant level page whose property might vary from plant to plant.

Field References for Material Types

When you create a material, you specify the material type. Certain fields may not be relevant for certain material types. For example, CAD Indicator field in Basic data 2 tab may not be relevant for raw materials. Field reference is an attribute of material type and is specified in view T134.

Material Type	FERT	Finished product
General data		
Field reference		FERT

Field References for Industry Sectors

A group may operate in multiple industry sectors, e.g. Automobiles, Chemical and Steel. There are certain fields that will not be relevant to each of these sectors. For example, the field `Highly viscous` in `Basic data 2` tab may be relevant for Chemical industry, but not for Automobile industry. You may, therefore, decide to hide the field `Highly viscous` in the material master screen in the Automobile companies. Field references for industry sectors are defined in view V137. Industry sectors are also maintained through this view.

Industry sector	Industry description	Field reference
1	Retail	A
2	Aerospace & Defense	A
3	Service Provider	A
A	Plant Engin./Construction	A
B	Beverage	A
C	Chemical Industry	C
F	Food and Related Products	P
M	Mechanical Engineering	M
P	Pharmaceuticals	P
W	Retailing	A

It is recommended that you do not change the field references for industry sectors defined by SAP. By doing so, you will be able to use the field properties defined by SAP. You may change the field properties if you want to. If you define your own field reference for an industry sector, you must define the properties of all fields. If you change the field reference for an industry sector, you must review the properties of all fields.

Field References for Plants

You can use this feature for implementing plant-specific influence on field properties. For example, if one of your plants does not use the Quota arrangement feature of SAP, the `Quota arr. usage` field in the `Purchasing` tab may not be relevant for that plant. Field references for plants are defined in view V_130W. These are applicable only for plant level fields.

Plant	Name 1	Maintenance status	Field reference
1000	Werk Hamburg	KDEVALBPQSZXCFG	0001
1100	Berlin	KDEVALBPQSZXCFG	0001
1200	Dresden	KDEVALBPQSZXCFG	0001
1300	Frankfurt	KDEVALBPQSZXCFG	0001
1400	Stuttgart	KDEVALBPQSZXCFG	0001

Field References for Transactions

Field references for transactions are predefined in table T130M by SAP. There is no maintenance view for maintaining this field.

Transaction Code	Field reference
MM01	MM01
MM02	MM02
MM03	MM03
MM06	
MM11	MM11
MM12	MM12
MM16	
MM18	MM02
MM19	MM03
MM41	MM01
MM42	MM02
MM43	MM03

Field References for Procurement Types

Procurement type for a material

Each material has a procurement type in the MRP 2 view of the material.

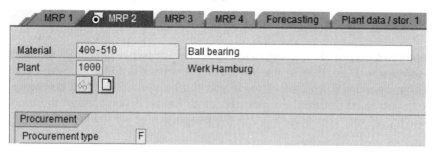

The master list of procurement types

The procurement type field can have the following values.

Procurement type	Short text
E	In-house production
F	External procurement
	No procurement
X	Both procurement types

Field references for procurement types

For each procurement type, the field reference is given below:

Procurement type	Field reference
E	E
F	F
Blank	No field reference
X	No field reference

Field Selection Groups

Fields are grouped in field selection groups. A field selection group is a logical grouping of fields that should have the same data entry property. Fields are assigned to a field group in view V_130F. A field can belong to only one field selection group.

Field name in full	Short Description	Sel. group	
CALP-AUFSG	Actual Markup in Sales Price Calculation	177	⇨
CALP-EKORG	Purchasing Organization	176	⇨
CALP-ENDPR	Final price	180	⇨
CALP-KZPBL	Indicates that prices at plant level are to be deleted	194	⇨
CALP-LIFNR	Vendor Account Number	176	⇨

Field Properties

Field properties are defined for each combination of field selection group and field reference group in view V_T130A_FLREF (transaction OMS9).

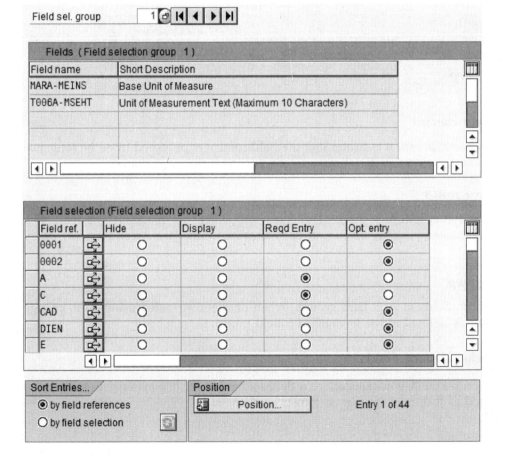

Field references with prefix SAP are valid client-wide and must not be changed. Field reference KB is also valid client-wide, but may be changed.

2.4.6   Field Attributes

Apart from data entry properties of a field, some other field attributes are also defined in view V_130F.

Field name	EINE-EKGRP
	Purchasing Group

Field attributes (industry and retail)
- ☐ Propose field cont.
- Maint. status   E
- ALE field group   GR_E

Field attributes (retail only)
- Restrict matl cat.   Default for all material categories
- ☑ Copy field content
- ☐ Incl. initial values

Propose field content

If this checkbox is ticked, it indicates that the field content is proposed from the reference material when creating a material master record using a reference material.

Maintenance status

Maintenance status indicates the user departments which can maintain this field. If a field has maintenance status BE, it can be maintained either by Accounting (B) or by Purchasing (E).

ALE field group

You can group fields in ALE field groups. When data is distributed using ALE, change authorization is defined at the level of ALE field group.

2.4.7   Lock-Relevant Fields

In transaction OMSFIX you can declare a field lock-relevant. If a material is locked, the fields flagged as lock-relevant can no longer be changed.

Field name	Short Description	Lock-rel.
CALP-AUFSG	Actual Markup in Sales Price Calculatio	☐
CALP-EKORG	Purchasing Organization	☐
CALP-ENDPR	Final price	☐
CALP-KZPBL	Indicates that prices at plant level are to	☐

2.5 MATERIAL MASTER COMPLETENESS

Functional Consultant	User	Business Process Owner	Senior Management	My Rating	Understanding Level
A	C	C	X		

2.5.1 Maintenance Status

Since a material master record has so many views, ensuring completeness of material data is a challenging task. SAP provides a method of checking completeness and maintaining the missing data. This method is based on the concept of maintenance status. The data in the material master is divided in 15 functional areas or user departments. Each user department is given a one-character code.

User department	Maintenance status
Basic data	K
Classification	C
Sales	V
Purchasing	E
MRP	D
Forecasting	P
Work scheduling	A
Storage	L
Warehouse management	S
Quality management	Q
Accounting	B
Costing	G
Plant stocks	X
Storage location stocks	Z
Production resources/tools	F

Plant stock and storage location stocks are for display purpose only.

2.5.2 User Departments which have Maintained Data for a Material

When a user department creates its data for a material, the material master record acquires the corresponding maintenance status. The maintenance status is stored in a 15-character field in material master tables, e.g. MARA, MARC, MARD, etc. These fields are not maintained by users; they are updated by the system automatically. Table MARC contains the following data for material 400–510.

Material	Plant	Maint. status
☐ 400-510	1000	VEDPLQBG
☐ 400-510	3000	EDPLBGVXQ

This shows that sales data, `Maint. status` V, has been maintained for plant 1000, but not for plant 3000.

2.5.3 User Departments which are Required to Maintain Data for Materials of a Material Type

In view T134 (see Section 2.7.8), for a material type you specify the user departments which are required to maintain data for a material. This is used for checking completeness of data for a material.

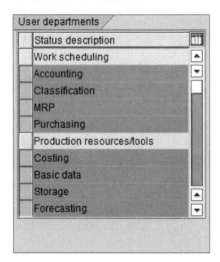

2.5.4 Checking and Completing Material Data

SAP provides transaction MM50 to identify incomplete data. In the initial screen you limit the range of checking data completeness. For example, you may be interested in completing data for Purchasing department for plant 1000. In that case, you enter E in the Maintenance status field and 1000 in the Plant field in the initial screen. When you execute, you get the following result.

	S	Created	Material	MTyp	I	CoCd	Plnt	SLoc	SOrg	DC	WhN	Material Description
☐	E	21.12.2005	RX_5129	HALB	M		1000					Bolt
☐	E	21.12.2005	RX_5170	HALB	M		1000					Drive
☐	E	21.12.2005	RX_5210	HALB	M		1000					Booster Frame
☐	E	21.12.2005	RX_5214	HALB	M		1000					Drive Unit
☐	E	21.12.2005	RX_5221	HALB	M		1000					Rotation Column
☐	E	21.12.2005	RX_5270	HALB	M		1000					Drive
☐	E	18.01.2006	GTS-N2-013	HALB	M		1000					Engine Block
☐	E	16.02.2006	GTS-RES02	HAWA	1		1000					milk powder

You can select one or more lines in this list and click Maintain materials . The system takes you to the material master screen where you can update and save the data. In this way you can ensure completeness of the material data.

2.5.5 Maintenance Status of a Field

In view V_130F you can see the maintenance status of a field.

Field name	EINE-EKGRP
	Purchasing Group

Field attributes (industry and retail)

☐ Propose field cont.

Maint. status	E
ALE field group	GR_E

Field attributes (retail only)

Restrict matl cat.	Default for all material categories

☑ Copy field content

☐ Incl. initial values

Maintenance status of a field indicates the user departments that can maintain the field. If a field has maintenance status BE, it can be maintained either by Accounting (B) or by Purchasing (E).

2.5.6 Maintenance Status Determination in Data Transfer

When you transfer material data, how do you determine maintenance status? Do you take into account all fields? You can select from the following options.

1	All fields are considered
2	All are considered except general fields for client/plant
3	Only single status fields are used as far as possible

You specify the value of this key for each screen sequence in view V_T133S.

SSq	Screen seq. description		Determination type
01	Std industry sequence	3	Only single status fields are used as far as possible
11	Std industry: small scrns	3	Only single status fields are used as far as possible
12	Manufacturer Parts	3	Only single status fields are used as far as possible
21	Std ind.(short) tab pages	3	Only single status fields are used as far as possible

This setting is required only for data transfer, and only if you have not specified which maintenance statuses are to be created or changed during data transfer.

2.5.7 Maintenance Status for Plants

Maintenance statuses for plants are defined in view V_130W. In this view you can restrict the maintenance statuses allowed for each plant.

Plant	Name 1	Maintenance status	Field reference
1000	Werk Hamburg	KDEVALBPQSZXCFG	0001
1100	Berlin	KDEVALBPQSZXCFG	0001
1200	Dresden	KDEVALBPQSZXCFG	0001
1300	Frankfurt	KDEVALBPQSZXCFG	0001
1400	Stuttgart	KDEVALBPQSZXCFG	0001

2.6 NUMBER RANGES

Functional Consultant	User	Business Process Owner	Senior Management	My Rating	Understanding Level
A	C	C	C		

2.6.1 Purpose

Here you define number ranges and link them to materials.

2.6.2 IMG Node

Transaction MMNR—Define Material Master Number Ranges

2.6.3 Overview

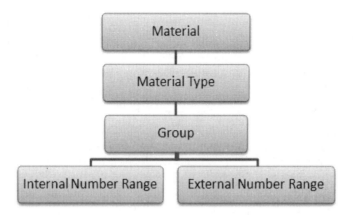

Number ranges in a group

A material can get number from the internal number range, or the external number range, which are accessed via material type and group. A group can be assigned at the most one internal number range, and at the most one external number range.

Internal material number

When you create a material, you have the option of using internal or external number range. If you do not specify a number, the system assigns the next number from internal number range. If an internal number range is not assigned to the group, it gives error.

External material number

If you specify a number or alphanumeric string, the system proceeds as follows:

➢ Checks that the number is not already used.

➢ Checks if ☐ External no. assignment w/o check field is selected for the material type in table T134.

  ➢ If the above field is selected, the system not to check the material number entered on the screen against the number range. In this case, the material number assigned must contain at least one letter, and not consist only of figures.

  ➢ If the above field is not selected, the system checks that the number is within the external number range assigned to the group.

External material number for unassigned material types

If you have not assigned a particular material type to a group, you can create materials of that type only if the ☑ External no. assignment w/o check field is selected for the material type in table T134. For materials of that type you can use only the external material numbers.

2.6.4 Groups

Groups

Material types are grouped in Groups. All material types in a group are assigned material numbers from the same number ranges.

Materials in a group

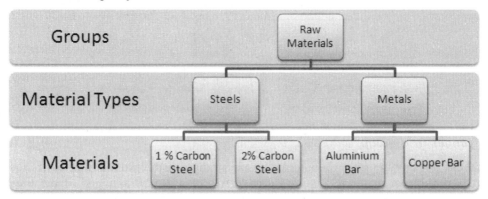

Groups are linked to material types as described below. All material types that are not assigned to a group belong to the group Not assigned. When a material is created in the material master, its material type is specified.

Through these linkages, each material belongs to a group.

Number ranges for a group

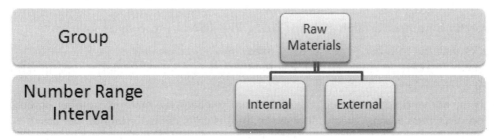

2.6.5 Creation of a Group

Click ⌐ Groups ⌐ to maintain groups. You can create one or more groups. To create a group and to assign number ranges to it, click Group ➤ Insert .

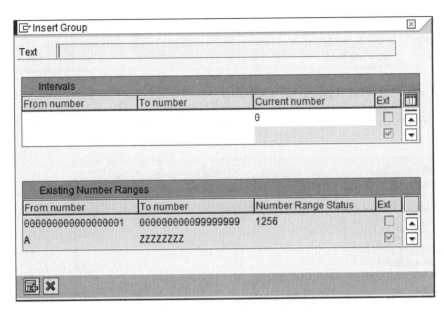

Enter the group name. Enter the range of numbers for internal and external number ranges. Press 'Enter' or click 🔁 to add the group.

2.6.6   Renaming a Group

You can rename a group by selecting the group and clicking Gr_oup ➢ M_aintain text .

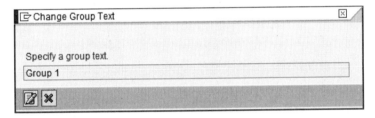

2.6.7   Material Types in a Group

You can assign a material type to a group. A material type can belong to only one group. When a material type is created, it is automatically put in the group Not assigned. A material type in the Not assigned group, or in any group, can be assigned to another group. Place cursor on a material type and click 🔍 to select it. Then place the cursor on a group and click 🔳 Element/Group to assign the material type to the new group. The old assignment is automatically deleted.

2.6.8   Number Range Intervals for a Group

You should maintain number range intervals only for a group. Click 🖉 Groups and select a group ☑ Foods and Beverages . Click Interval ➢ M_aintain .

To a group you can assign only one internal number range interval and only one external number range interval. If both internal and external number ranges are assigned, you cannot add a number range interval.

2.6.9 Overview of Material Types in a Group

You can click 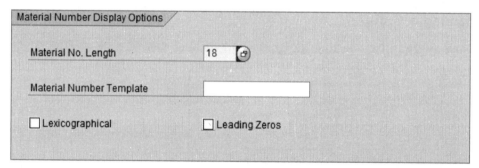 to see material types in a group and the number ranges assigned to the group.

Subobj.val	No Year	From number	To number	Number Range Status	Ext P
Element		No No P			
	01	000000000000000001	000000000099999999	1256	
ABF		01 02			
AEM		01 02			
BLG		01 02			
BLGA		01 02			

2.6.10 Output Format of Material Numbers

You can define the output format of the material numbers in view V_TMCNV. There can be only one format.

Material Number Display Options	
Material No. Length	18
Material Number Template	
☐ Lexicographical	☐ Leading Zeros

Material number length

Here you can specify the maximum length of the material numbers in your organization. The material number length cannot be more than 18, but you can specify shorter lengths.

Material number template

You can specify a template for the material numbers, consisting of editing characters and selection characters; an underscore (_) denotes a selection character that is replaced by a significant character in the material number. For example, the material number 12345678 (significant characters) with template __-_____-_ is stored as 12-34567-8. The length of the material number includes the editing characters, and is 10 in this case.

Lexicographical

This indicator is relevant only for numeric material numbers. Alphanumeric material numbers are stored as entered and are left justified.

Indicator	Assignment	Storage	Justification	Examples
Not set	Internal as well as external	The material number is padded with leading zeros to the defined length.	Right-justified	123 is stored as 0000000123 (if length is 10 characters).
Set	Internal	The material number is padded with leading zeros to the defined length.	Left-justified	123 is stored as 0000000123 (if length is 10 characters).
Set	External	The material number is not padded with leading zeros. Leading zeros, if entered, are stored too.	Left-justified	The material numbers 123 and 0123 are two different material numbers.

Leading zeros

If you tick this checkbox, a numeric material number is shown with leading zeros to fill up its defined length. If the ☐ Lexicographical indicator is set, then this indicator is ignored by the system.

2.7 MATERIAL TYPE

Functional Consultant	User	Business Process Owner	Senior Management	My Rating	Understanding Level
A	C	C	C		

2.7.1 Purpose

A material type is a group of materials with similar attributes. The material type allows the management of different materials in a uniform manner. The material type defines certain attributes of a material, which have important control functions, including screen layout determination, number range assignment and material valuation.

2.7.2 IMG Node

SM34 ➤ MTART (view T134)

2.7.3 Material Type

Material Type	FERT	Finished product

Material type and description

SAP provides a number of predefined material types.

MTyp	Material type description
ABF	Waste
AEM	Samples
BLG	BLG Empties External
BLGA	BLGAEmpties Fixed assets
CH00	CH Contract Handling
COMP	Prod. alloc., purchased
CONT	KANBAN Container
COUP	Coupons
DIEN	Service
DOCU	documentary batch
EPA	Equipment Package
ERSA	Spare parts
FERT	Finished product

Select a material type and click 🔍 to see and change its properties. You can also create your own material types.

2.7.4 General Data

General data			
Field reference	FERT	X-plant matl status	☐
SRef. material type	ROH	Item category group	NORM
Authorization group		☑ With Qty Structure	
☑ External no. assignment w/o check		☐ Initial Status	

Field reference

On the material master screen you see a number of fields. Properties of these fields can be set as per your requirement based on five parameters as explained in Section 2.4.5. Material type is one of the parameters. For a material type, you define the field reference here which is used in setting field properties.

Cross-plant material status

The cross-plant material status restricts the usability of the material for all plants.

01	Blocked for Procmnt/Whse
02	Blocked for task list/BOM
BP	Blocked for Purchasing
KA	Blocked for Costing
OB	Obsolete Materials
PI	Free for Pilot Phase

When you create a material of this type, the value specified in this field is proposed in the X-plant matl status field of Basic data 1 tab by default. You can change the value there.

Screen reference: material type

Screen layout of materials master can differ for different material types. For more information, see Section 2.4.1.

Item category group

When you create a material of this type, the value specified in this field is proposed in the GenItemCatGroup field of Basic data 1 tab by default. You can change the value there.

Authorization group

You can give authorization to maintain material master record based on authorization group using authorization object M_MATE_MAT. You can specify authorization group at material type level here. If no authorization group is entered, no specific authorization check is carried out for materials of this material type.

With quantity structure

The value in this field provides the default value in the field With Qty Structure in the Costing 1 tab of the materials master.

External number assignment without check

Internal and external number ranges are assigned to material types via group. If a material type is not assigned to any group, it has no internal or external number range assigned to it. You can tick this field to allow external number assignment without a check against the number range. In this case, the material number assigned must contain at least one letter, and should not consist only of figures.

Initial status

This indicator specifies that the initial status of a batch is "restricted".

2.7.5 Special Material Types

Special material types
- [ ] Material is configurable
- [ ] Material f. process
- [ ] Pipeline mandatory
- [ ] Manufacturer part

Material is configurable

If you tick this field and create a material of this type, the `Material is configurable` indicator in the material master is automatically set and you can't change it. If you mark a material configurable, you should not be allowing quantity and value updating.

Material for process

This indicator allows materials of this type to be defined as materials for a process in which there may be co-products.

Pipeline mandatory

This indicator makes pipeline handling mandatory for materials of this type. Neither external nor internal purchase orders are possible for pipeline materials. In addition, neither quantities nor values are updated for these materials.

Manufacturer part

This indicator identifies materials of this type as manufacturer parts. In Purchasing, you can create a material master record for each manufacturer part number and assign it to your company's own material. Only a restricted amount of material master data can be maintained for manufacturer parts. In particular, plant-specific data cannot be maintained.

2.7.6 Internal/External Purchase Orders

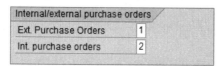

Internal/external purchase orders
| Ext. Purchase Orders | 1 |
| Int. purchase orders | 2 |

External purchase orders

Here you can specify whether external purchase orders are allowed, not allowed, or allowed with a warning.

Internal purchase orders

Here you can specify whether internal purchase orders, i.e. in-house production of the material, are allowed, not allowed, or allowed with a warning.

Both these indicators together decide which procurement types are available in the `MRP 2` view of a material.

2.7.7   Classification

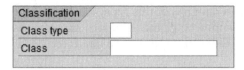

Class type and class

You can use class to extend the industry material master to include a subscreen on which you can maintain the characteristics of the class as additional fields.

2.7.8   User Departments

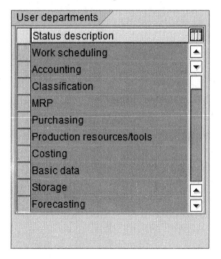

User departments

Here you specify the user departments which are expected to maintain data for material of this type. The system uses this information to identify the user departments which are yet to maintain data for a material. For more information, see Section 2.5.3.

2.7.9   Valuation

Valuation		
Price control	Standard price	
Acct cat. reference	0009	☐ Price ctrl mandatory

Price control

In the Price control field of the Accounting 1 tab of the material master you can specify whether the stock is valuated using standard price or moving average price/periodic unit price. The value in this field provides the default value for that field.

Price control mandatory

If you tick this checkbox, when you create or change a material of this type, the `Price control` defined on this screen applies to the material and cannot be changed. If this checkbox is not ticked, the `Price control` defined on this screen is defaulted but can be changed.

Account category reference

In the `Accounting 1` tab of the material master, you specify a valuation class. Valuation classes are grouped in account category references. Here you specify the account category reference. The system then lets you select from valuation classes of that account category reference only.

2.7.10 Quantity/Value Updating

Quantity/value updating	
Quantity updating	**Value updating**
○ In all valuation areas	○ In all valuation areas
○ In no valuation area	○ In no valuation area
◉ By valuation area	◉ By valuation area

Quantity/value updating

When a goods movement takes place, usually the quantity and the value of the material is updated. However, for certain material types, you may not want the quantity or the value to be updated. This decision is specified at valuation area level in view VT134M (see Section 2.7.12). The fields shown above present a summary of that decision.

2.7.11 Retail-Specific Fields

Retail-specific fields	
Material type ID	General material type
Time till deleted	
☐ Display material	☐ Print price

SAP Retail is outside the scope of this book.

2.7.12 Quantity/Value Updating for Valuation Areas

In view cluster MTART (view VT134M), you define properties of a valuation area for a given material type.

Val.	Matl	Qty updating	Value Update	Pipe.mand.	PipeAllowd
0001	FERT	☑	☑	☐	☐
0005	FERT	☑	☑	☐	☐
0006	FERT	☑	☑	☐	☐
0007	FERT	☑	☑	☐	☐

Valuation area and material type

For a given material type, quantity and value updating properties can differ for different valuation areas.

Quantity updating

If you specified quantity updating in certain valuation areas but not in others in the main screen, here you specify the valuation areas for which quantity updating is allowed.

Value updating

If you specified value updating in certain valuation areas but not in others in the main screen, here you specify the valuation areas for which value updating is allowed.

Pipeline mandatory

Here you specify whether a material assigned this material type is subject to mandatory pipeline handling for this valuation area.

Pipeline allowed

Here you specify whether a material assigned this material type is allowed to be subject to pipeline handling for this valuation area.

2.7.13 Material Creation Transactions for Specific Material Types

For creating material master record, you can use special create transactions which are used to create specific material types. In view V_134K you assign material types to transaction groups. Transaction groups are linked to transactions in table T130M by SAP. There is no maintenance view for maintaining this field. Both the view V_134K and relevant entries from table T130M are given in the screenshot below.

Grp	MTyp	Material type description		Transaction grp	Transaction Code
B	HALB	Semi-finished product		B	MMB1
F	FERT	Finished product		F	MMF1
G	LEIH	Returnable packaging		G	MMG1
H	HAWA	Trading goods		H	MMH1
I	HIBE	Operating supplies		I	MMI1
K	KMAT	Configurable material		K	MMK1
L	LEER	Empties		L	MML1
N	NLAG	Non-stock material		N	MMN1
P	IBAU	Maintenance assembly		P	MMP1
R	ROH	Raw material		R	MMR1
S	DIEN	Service		S	MMS1
U	UNBW	Non-valuated material		U	MMU1
V	VERP	Packaging		V	MMV1
W	WETT	Competitive product		W	MMW1

2.8 MATERIAL GROUP

Functional Consultant	User	Business Process Owner	Senior Management	My Rating	Understanding Level
A	C	C	X		

2.8.1 Material Group

Material groups are defined in view V023. For a material group you can specify an authorization group, and thereby control authorization to maintain a material using the authorization object M_MATE_MAT. You can also specify a default unit of weight, which is proposed when a material is created. If nothing is specified, the default unit of weight is kg. You can create a hierarchy of material groups by appropriately numbering the material groups, which is evident in the screenshot below:

Matl Group	Material Group Desc.	Grp.	DUW	Description 2 for the material group
001	Metal processing			
00101	Steels			
00102	Steel sheets			
00103	Electronics			
00104	Mechanics			
001041	Fasteners			Mechanical fasteners

You may use the United Nations Standard Products and Services Code (UNSPSC) for configuring your material groups.

2.8.2 Entry Aids for Items without a Material Master

Sometimes you place order for a material group instead of a specific material. In view V023_E you can assign a purchasing value key and a valuation class to a material group.

Mat. Grp	Mat. Grp Descr.	ValCl	PurValK
001	Metal processing		
00101	Steels		
00102	Steel sheets		
00103	Electronics		
00104	Mechanics		
001041	Fasteners		

2.8.3 Distinction between Material Group and Material Type

You need to differentiate between material type and material group. Material types have a large number of properties associated with them and you generally use material types predefined by SAP. Material groups do not have associated properties but you use them for analysis, e.g. total inventory of steels. Material groups also help in searching for a material.

2.9 MATERIAL STATUS

Functional Consultant	User	Business Process Owner	Senior Management	My Rating	Understanding Level
A	C	C	X		

2.9.1 Purpose

The material status determines how a material is handled in purchasing, materials planning etc. For a material in a plant you can set a material status in the corresponding material master record. If a material has a material status, the system will issue either a warning or an error message if the material is used.

2.9.2 IMG Node

Transaction OMS4—Define Material Statuses

2.9.3 Material Status List

Material Status	Description
01	Blocked for Procmnt/Whse
02	Blocked for task list/BOM
BP	Blocked for Purchasing
KA	Blocked for Costing
OB	Obsolete Materials
PI	Free for Pilot Phase

2.9.4 Screen

Material Status	01	Blocked for Procmnt/Whse

Plant-specific settings

Purchasing

Purchasing msg.	B

Production resources/tools

PRT message	

BOMs

BOM header msg.	
BOM item message	

Plant maintenance

Plant maint. message	

Inventory management

Inventory mgmt msg.	B

Routing/recipe

Routing/master recipe message	

Warehouse management

Transfer requirement msg.	
Transfer order message	

Material requirements

Ind. reqmt msg.	
Forecasting message	B
MRP message	B
LT planning message	

Cost estimate with quantity structure

Mat. Cost Estimate Procedure	

Production

POrder header msg.	
PO/network item msg.	

Cross-plant settings

ALE distribution

Distr. lock	
Profile Name	

For each activity, you can assign one of the following:

	No message
A	Warning
B	Error message

In ALE distribution, you can lock distribution of object data for the Integrated Distributed PDM Solution. If you want a material with this status to be distributed, enter a profile that controls change authorizations in ALE systems.

2.9.5 Material Status at Plant Level

The material status can be assigned at plant level in the `Purchasing` tab of the material master.

2.9.6 Material Status for all Plants

You can also set `X-plant matl status` in the `Basic data 1` tab, which applies restrictions to all plants.

2.10 PURCHASING VALUE KEYS

Functional Consultant	User	Business Process Owner	Senior Management	My Rating	Understanding Level
A	C	C	X		

2.10.1 Purpose

In the `Purchasing` view of the material master record, you can store rules governing the following:

➢ The issue of reminders with respect to nearly due and overdue deliveries

➢ The admissibility of over- and under-deliveries

➢ Order acknowledgment requirements for purchase order items

➢ Shipping/packaging instructions

You stipulate these rules in a purchasing value key. In the purchasing documents, the purchasing value key is taken from the purchasing info record. If the purchasing info record is not used, or the purchasing value key is not found there, it is taken from the material master.

2.10.2 IMG Node

SM30 ➢ V_405

2.10.3 Screen

Pur.Val.Key	1

Deadline monitoring

1st Reminder/Exped.	10
2nd Reminder/Exped.	20
3rd Reminder/Exped.	30
☐ Acknowledgment Reqd	

GR/IR control

Tol. Underdelivery	
Tol. Overdelivery	
☐ Unlimited Overdel.	
Shipping Instr.	

Vendor evaluation

Min.Del.Qty %	
StdDelDtVar	

2.10.4 Primary Key

Purchasing Value Key

2.10.5 Important Fields

Reminders 1, 2, 3

These reminders specify the number of days representing the time interval at which reminders are to be issued to the vendor before (if the number is negative) or after the due date. The due date depends on the purchasing document. For example, for RFQ it is the receipt of quotation.

In the case of purchasing documents, the time intervals are defaulted from the purchasing info record or, if the purchasing info record does not exist, from the material master record. In the event of several reminder levels, the days must be set out in ascending order of time, without gaps.

Acknowledgement required

If you want vendors to acknowledge purchase orders, contracts, scheduling agreements, etc., you specify that here.

Under-delivery tolerance

This specifies the percentage (of the order quantity) up to which an under-delivery of this item will be accepted.

Over-delivery tolerance

This specifies the percentage (of the order quantity) up to which an over-delivery of this item will be accepted.

Unlimited over-delivery

This indicator specifies that unlimited over-delivery can be accepted for the item.

Shipping instructions

Here you specify the packaging and shipping instructions for the item.

Minimum delivery quantity in %

This is the minimum percentage of the purchase order quantity that must be delivered in order for the goods receipt to be included in the vendor evaluation. In this way, you can prevent a vendor from receiving a good score for a punctual delivery, where the quantity delivered was insufficient.

Standard value for delivery date variance

The number in this field represents the number of days that will be counted as 100% variance. The difference between actual and planned delivery in days is divided by this number to give actual variance. If the actual delivery is 2 days after the planned delivery date and this field contains 10, then the variance is 20%.

2.11 SHIPPING INSTRUCTIONS

Functional Consultant	User	Business Process Owner	Senior Management	My Rating	Understanding Level
A	C	C	X		

2.11.1 Purpose

In the purchasing value key, you specify shipping instructions. When you assign a purchasing value key to a material, the shipping instructions embedded in the purchasing value key are applicable to that material.

In the purchasing documents, the purchasing value key is taken from the purchasing info record. If the purchasing info record is not used, or the purchasing value key is not found there, it is taken from the material master. As a constituent of the purchasing value key, the shipping instructions become a part of the purchasing document.

When the relevant goods receipts are entered, the extent to which the vendor has complied with these instructions can be noted.

2.11.2 IMG Node

SM34 ➤ VC_T027A

2.11.3 Shipping Instructions

Dialog Structure		Shipping Instr.	Dsc. Ship.Instr.	Print Ship.Instr.
▽ 🗁 Shipping instructions		V1	Shipping instruction 1	☑
📁 Compliance with		V2	Shipping instruction 2	☑

Print shipping instructions

If you set this indicator, the shipping instructions will also be printed out on the form when purchasing documents are outputted as messages.

2.11.4 Compliance with Shipping Instructions

Shippg Instr.	V1	Shipping instruction 1

	Comp	Text Compl. w. Shipping Instr.	Pts	Default	Sh. Text GR	Long Txt GR	Text Key
	01	Instruction complied with	100	◉	☑	☑	
	02	Instruction not complied with		○	☑	☑	

Compliance key

When the goods are received, you may check the vendor's compliance with the shipping and packaging instructions. You may give him a score which is used in vendor evaluation and may want to print the compliance or non-compliance of the shipping and packaging instructions on the goods receipt slip. All these are encapsulated in the compliance key. When you assign compliance key to a goods receipt slip, all the features described here automatically apply.

Text

You assign a compliance key to a goods receipt slip. You select the key, whose text best describes the compliance with the shipping and packaging instructions.

Points for compliance with shipping instructions

When you assign a compliance key to a goods receipt slip, the vendor gets the points specified here for that compliance key.

Default value indicator

You can specify one of the compliance keys as the default key. This key appears in the goods receipt slip by default, and the user can change it.

Short text indicator

If you tick this checkbox, the short description is printed on the goods receipt slip.

Long text indicator

If you tick this checkbox, the long description is printed on the goods receipt slip.

Text key for compliance with shipping instructions

If you specify a standard text here, it is printed on the goods receipt slip.

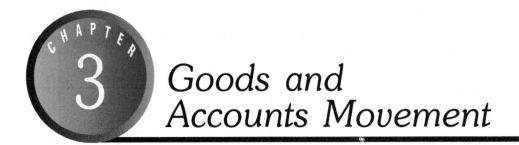

Goods and Accounts Movement

3.1 GOODS MOVEMENT

Functional Consultant	User	Business Process Owner	Senior Management	My Rating	Understanding Level
A	A	A	A		

3.1.1 Goods Movement

Whenever you receive goods, or issue goods, you are performing goods movement. Goods movement includes both "external" movement (goods receipts from external procurement, goods issues for sales orders) and "internal" movement (goods receipts from production, withdrawals of material for internal purposes, stock transfers, and transfer postings). Some of the goods movements are listed below.

3.1.2 Categories of Goods Movement

Category	Description
Goods receipt	A goods receipt (GR) is a goods movement with which the receipt of goods from a vendor or from production is posted. A goods receipt leads to an increase in warehouse stock.
Goods issue	A goods issue (GI) is a goods movement with which a material withdrawal, a material issue, a material consumption, or a shipment of goods to a customer is posted. A goods issue leads to a reduction in warehouse stock.
Stock transfer	A stock transfer is the removal of material from one storage location and its transfer to another storage location. Stock transfers can occur either within the same plant or between two plants (belonging to the same company code or different company codes).
Transfer posting	A transfer posting is a general term for stock transfers and changes in stock type or stock category of a material. It is irrelevant whether the posting occurs in conjunction with a physical movement or not. Examples of transfer postings are: ➤ Transfer postings from one material to another material ➤ Release from quality inspection stock ➤ Transfer of consignment material into company's own stock

3.1.3 Effects of Goods Movement

When you enter a goods movement, you start the following chain of events in the system.

➢ A material document is generated, which is used as a proof of the goods movement and as a source of information for any other applications involved.

➢ If the movement is relevant for Financial Accounting, one or more accounting documents are generated.

➢ The stock quantities of the material are updated.

➢ The stock values in the material master record are updated, as are the stock and consumption accounts.

➢ You can print goods receipt/issue slips to facilitate physical movements.

Depending on the movement type, additional updates are carried out in participating applications. All updates are based on the information contained in the material document and the financial accounting document. For example, in the case of a goods issue for a cost center, the consumption values of the items are also updated.

3.1.4 Documents in Goods Movement

When posting a goods movement in the SAP System, the following documents are created.

Document	Description
Material document	When a goods movement is posted in the Inventory Management system, a material document is generated that serves as a proof of the movement and as a source of information for any applications that follow.
	A material document consists of a header and at least one item. The header contains general data about the movement (for example, its date). Each item describes one movement.
Accounting documents	If the movement is relevant for Financial Accounting (that is, if it leads to an update of the General Ledger accounts), an accounting document is created parallel to the material document.
	In some cases, several accounting documents are created for a single material document. This might be the case, for example, if you have two material document items with different plants that belong to different company codes.
	The G/L accounts involved in a goods movement are determined through an automatic account assignment.

3.1.5   Checks in Goods Movement

When posting a goods movement, the system performs the following checks.

Check	Description
Dynamic availability check	You can issue a material only if it is in stock. Such a check by the system is called availability check. In Inventory Management, availability checks are carried out automatically. The availability check prevents the book inventory balance of various physical stock types (for example, unrestricted-use stock) from becoming negative.
Missing part check	In MRP, if requirement of a material exceeds the available quantity, that material is called a missing part. If the missing parts check function is active in the plant, the system checks whether the material posted as a receipt is a missing part. If it is a missing part, the system issues a warning message and sends an e-mail to the MRP controller responsible in the plant.
Shelf life expiration check	You can check the shelf life of a material when you enter a goods receipt. You thereby ensure that you store only materials that are still usable. This functionality is possible only if the material is managed in batches.

3.1.6   Movement Type

When you enter a goods movement, you must always enter the movement type. The movement type has important control functions in Inventory Management. It determines what you can or cannot do. It also determines what happens internally in the system.

To determine which movement type you should use in a given scenario, look at the description of the movement type. The descriptions are in business language and you should understand them easily. In case of doubt, ask a knowledgeable colleague, or the consultant supporting your installation. In the course of time, you will remember important movement types, and will need to look for movement types only rarely.

Movement type determines screen layout.

3.1.7   Reversal Movement Type

You can reverse the action of a goods movement, by another goods movement using reversal movement type. The reversal movement type is the original movement type + 1 (reversal of movement type 101 is movement type 102).

3.1.8 Goods Movement Reports

Goods movements by movement type

Run transaction MB51 to generate a report of goods movements based on movement types. For more details, see Section 22.3.1.

Goods movements by movement reason

Run transaction MBGR to generate a report of goods movements based on movement reason. For more details, see Section 22.3.3.

3.2 ACCOUNTS MOVEMENT

Functional Consultant	User	Business Process Owner	Senior Management	My Rating	Understanding Level
A	A	A	A		

3.2.1 Goods Movement and Accounts Movement

When goods are received or issued, the inventory changes, both in terms of quantity and value. The event is recorded in a material document and associated accounting documents. The material document records the movement of goods that lead to change in stock quantity. The accounting document records the accounts movements that lead to change in the value of stock in appropriate G/L accounts.

3.2.2 General Ledger Accounts

The account of the money raised and deployed by a company is maintained in G/L accounts. One area where the company deploys money is inventory of material. The value of material held by the company is usually maintained in several G/L accounts, each G/L account having the value of a specific type of material, e.g. raw material, finished goods, spare parts, etc.

3.2.3 Debit and Credit

Credit

You get credit for giving.

Debit

You get debit for receiving.

3.2.4   Double Entry Book Keeping

In double entry book keeping, debits and credits are always matched. Money always gets transferred, from one account to another; it is never lost or gained. Therefore, in a goods receipt, when the inventory account is debited, the GR/IR clearing account is credited. Later when an invoice is received from the vendor and settled, the GR/IR clearing account is debited and vendor account is credited.

3.2.5   Chart of Accounts

Chart of accounts

A chart of accounts is a list of G/L accounts. For each G/L account, the chart of accounts contains the account number, account name, and control information, e.g. whether the account is a balance sheet account, or a P&L account.

Chart of accounts for a company code

Each company code is assigned one and only one chart of accounts. It may use some or all of the G/L accounts in the chart of accounts. Another company code may use the same chart of accounts, or a different chart of accounts.

Chart of accounts for a group of companies

Use of the same chart of accounts by several group companies helps in consolidation of the group's financial information.

3.2.6   Company Code

Company code

Inventory management takes place for a plant. The plant belongs to a company code. All financial transactions take place in a company code. Balance sheet and Profit and Loss (P&L) statement is published for each company code. Company code used in this book is 1000.

G/L accounts for a company code

Each company code is assigned one and only one chart of accounts. It may use some or all of the G/L accounts in the chart of accounts. Some properties of a G/L account, e.g. whether the account is a balance sheet account, or a P&L account, is specified at the level of the chart of accounts, and must remain the same for all company codes that use that G/L account. However, there are some properties of a G/L account that can vary from company code to company code.

3.2.7 Accounts Relevant to Inventory Management

Inventory management transactions result in posting to various accounts, e.g.

➤ Stock accounts

➤ GR/IR clearing account

➤ Price difference account

Stock accounts

When goods are received, inventory goes up. Inventory may be classified in several G/L accounts, e.g. raw material, parts for assembly, finished goods etc. Collectively these G/L accounts are called stock accounts.

GR/IR clearing account

Most companies do not credit the vendor on goods receipt. They credit a GR/IR clearing account. When invoice is received and settled, the GR/IR clearing account is debited and the vendor is credited.

Price difference account

Sometimes a company uses standard price for a material for internal purposes. When such a material is received, there may be difference between the procurement price and the standard price. Such difference is debited or credited to a price difference account.

Other accounts

Depending on the business scenario, several other types of accounts may be posted to, e.g. asset, tax, etc.

3.2.8 Account Determination

SAP does not require you to manually specify G/L accounts every time. It determines them automatically based on logic specified by you at the time of configuration. However, you can also specify G/L accounts manually in certain situations that are permitted by your company.

3.2.9 Financial Statements

Balance sheet

A balance sheet is a statement of the company's assets and liabilities. Each company is required by law to publish its balance sheet periodically.

P&L statement

A P&L statement is a statement of the company's revenues and expenses for a period. Each company is required by law to publish its P&L statement periodically.

3.2.10   Accounting Period

Accounting divides the financial year into several accounting periods. Accounting periods may be open for posting, or closed for posting. If you try to post a transaction in a period that is closed, you will get an error message.

3.2.11   Price Control

Moving average price

When you receive a material, you pay for it at certain price. You also have the same material, purchased earlier, perhaps at a different price. Usually, companies determine a moving average price by dividing the total value of the material by total quantity. This is the rate charged when goods are issued to a cost object.

Standard price

Some companies do not want the material price to keep changing all the time. They specify the price of a material, which is used for all internal purposes. This is called standard price. SAP supports standard price. You can change the standard price if required. You can also use standard price for some materials, and moving average price for others.

Price control for a material

You can decide whether a material will be valuated at moving average price or standard price. This is specified in the material master at plant level in the `Price control` field.

Quality management	Accounting 1	Accounting 2	Costing 1	Costi

Material	100-100	Casing		
Plant	1000	Werk Hamburg		
Price control	S	Price Unit	1	
Moving price	104.65	Standard price	113.76	
Total Stock	1,156	Total Value	131,506.56	

The `Price control` field has the following options.

Price control	Short text
S	Standard price
V	Moving average price/periodic unit price

Periodic unit price

Periodic unit price is used in Product Cost Controlling. It is out of scope of this book.

3.2.12 Controlling Area

Controlling area

Several company codes may belong to a controlling area. Company code 1000 used in this book belongs to controlling area 1000.

Controlling area documents

Along with documents for financial accounting, the system also produces controlling documents.

Stock

4.1 STOCK

Functional Consultant	User	Business Process Owner	Senior Management	My Rating	Understanding Level
A	A	A	A		

4.1.1 Stock in a Storage Location

When you receive goods, you store it in a storage location which belongs to a plant. When you issue goods, you do so from a storage location. All these transactions are performed in the system, and at any point of time you can view the stock of material available in a storage location.

4.1.2 Stock Types

You may have different types of stock, e.g.

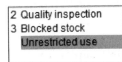

4.1.3 Batch

For some materials you maintain batch-wise inventory. Information about batch is particularly important in Pharmaceutical, Chemical and Food industries.

4.1.4   Special Stocks

Special Stock Indicators

Special stock indicators are used to distinguish one type of stock from the other. In SAP you have the following special stock indicators.

E	Orders on hand
K	Consignment (vendor)
M	Ret.trans.pkg vendor
O	Parts prov. vendor
P	Pipeline material
Q	Project stock
V	Ret. pkg w. customer
W	Consignment (cust.)
Y	Shipping unit (whse)

Properties of Special Stock Indicators

Table T148 gives properties of special stock indicators. This table is specified in Domain SOBKZ (Special Stock Indicator) itself.

Cl.	S	S	S	S	Special stock descr.
800	E			E	Orders on hand
800	K	K			Consignment (vendor)
800	M	M			Ret.trans.pkg vendor
800	O		O		Parts prov. vendor
800	P	P			Pipeline material
800	Q			Q	Project stock
800	V		V		Ret. pkg w. customer
800	W		W		Consignment (cust.)
800	Y				Shipping unit (whse)

Special stock indicator

Special stock indicators are used to distinguish one type of stock from the other.

Accounting/bookkeeping assignment

Special stock indicators K, M and P are materials owned by vendors but kept with you. These are not a part of your inventory value.

Logistics assignment

Special stock indicators O, V and W are materials owned by you but kept with your vendors and customers. These Materials are not available for in-house use. Their physical inventory also has to take place at the site of the vendor or the customer.

Transaction assignment

Special stock types E and Q are materials owned by you but committed for a purpose. These materials are not available for other uses. Physical inventory has to take place separately.

Special Stocks in Stock Overview

Stock overview shows both the standard stock of a material as well as its special stocks.

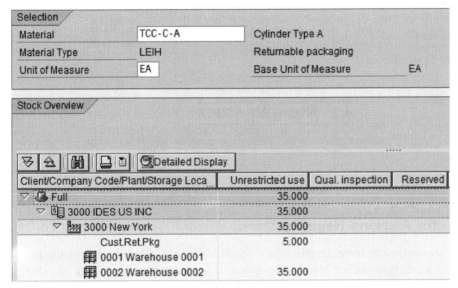

4.1.5 Account Assignment Objects

You do not maintain stock for projects, or sales orders; you maintain stock for a specific project, or a specific sales order item. Therefore, along with special stock indicator, you also specify the specific project or sales order item to which the material belongs.

4.1.6 Stock Management Unit

Stocks are maintained for a combination of all the above parameters. This combination is called a stock management unit. All items within a stock management unit can be used interchangeably. In transaction MI23 the inventory is reported at the level of stock management unit.

Material	Material Description		
Plnt Name 1			
SLoc Batch	S Special stock descr. Assignmnt		STy
100-100	Casing		
1000 Werk Hamburg			
0001			1
0001			2
0001			4

As you can see, a stock management unit is a unique combination of the following:

➢ Material
➢ Plant
➢ Storage location
➢ Batch
➢ Special stock indicator
➢ Account assignment object for special stock, e.g. project, sales order etc.
➢ Stock type
➢ Properties of Special Stock Indicators

4.2 NEGATIVE STOCK

Functional Consultant	User	Business Process Owner	Senior Management	My Rating	Understanding Level
A	B	B	B		

4.2.1 Reason for Allowing Negative Stocks

Negative stocks are necessary, for example, when goods issues are entered for organizational reasons prior to the corresponding goods receipts and the material is already physically located in the warehouse.

Once the goods receipts have been posted, the book inventory balance must again correspond to the physical stock, that is, the book inventory balance may no longer be negative. Negative stocks are always a sign that physical movements must be entered in the system at a later stage.

In transaction OMJ1 you specify whether negative stocks are allowed for unrestricted-use stock in the valuation area, in the plant, and in the storage location.

4.2.2 Control of Negative Stocks

You can control whether negative stocks are allowed or not in the following manner. You can have negative balances in stocks of the types "unrestricted-use" and "blocked".

Type of stock	Level	Method of allowing negative stock
Special stocks	Type of special stock in a plant	Allow negative stocks for a valuation area (see Section 4.2.3) Allow negative stocks for each type of special stock at plant level area (see Section 4.2.4) If the stock is at storage location level, allow negative stock at storage location level (see Section 4.2.5).
General stock	Material in a plant	Allow negative stocks for a valuation area (see Section 4.2.3) Allow negative stocks for a material in a plant in the ☐ Neg. stocks in plant field in the ⚙ Plant data / stor. 2 tab in the material master. If the stock is at storage location level, allow negative stock at storage location level (see Section 4.2.5).

4.2.3   Negative Stocks Allowed for a Valuation Area

In transaction OMJ1 you set the Neg. stocks allowed indicator for the valuation areas. A valuation area can be a plant or a company code, depending on the configuration.

	ValA	= plant	Neg. stocks allowed
Dialog Structure			
▽ 🗂 Valuation area	0001	Werk 0001	☐
▽ 🗂 Plant	0005	Hamburg	☐
🗂 Storage location	0006	New York	☐
	0007	Werk Hamburg	☐
	0008	New York	☐
	0099	Werk für Customizing	☐
	1000	Werk Hamburg	☐
	1100	Berlin	☑

4.2.4   Negative Special Stocks Allowed for a Plant

In view V_159L_NEG you specify the special stocks for which negative stocks are allowed for a plant.

Dialog Structure	Valuation Area 1100		
▽ 🗂 Valuation area			
▽ 🗂 Plant	Plant 1100 Berlin		
🗂 Storage location			
	Negative special stocks		
	Vendor consignment gds	☑	Customer Consignment ☐
	RTP stocks	☐	Return.pack.at cust. ☐
	Stcks of mat. w. vendor	☐	Project stock ☑
			Sales order stock ☑

Note that you cannot allow negative stock for Pipeline material from vendor (P) and Shipping unit (Y).

4.2.5 Negative Stocks Allowed for Storage Locations

In view V_T001L_N you specify the storage locations of the plant for which negative stocks are allowed.

Dialog Structure		
▽ ☐ Valuation area	Plant	1100 Berlin
▽ ☐ Plant		
☐ Storage location		

SLoc	Neg.stocks
0001	☑
0002	☑
0003	☑
0004	☐
0005	☐
0088	☐
0100	☐
0101	☐

4.3 STOCK REPORTS

Functional Consultant	User	Business Process Owner	Senior Management	My Rating	Understanding Level
A	A	A	A		

4.3.1 Storage Location Stock

You can see the stock of a material in a storage location using transaction MM02 or MM03.

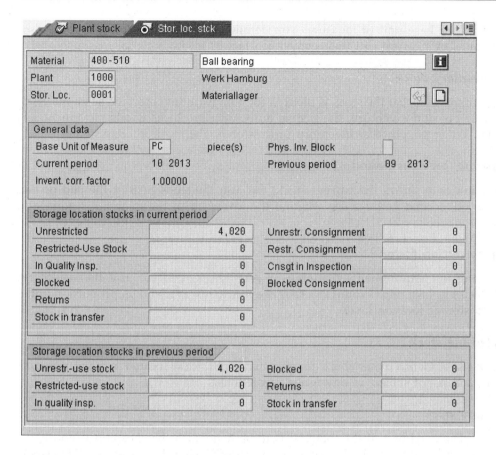

Material

SAP allows you to buy and use a material without a material number, but you cannot stock or produce a material without a material number. You can stock a material only if it has a material number.

Plant, storage location

Normally a material is stocked in a storage location of a plant. Exceptions to this rule are:

➢ Stock held with a vendor, e.g. in the case of subcontracting
➢ Stock held with a customer, e.g. in the case of consignment
➢ Stock in transit
➢ In transfer (Plant)

These stocks are held directly at plant level, not at storage location level.

Base unit of measure

Base unit of measure is the unit in which stocks of the material are managed. The system converts all the quantities you enter in other units of measure (alternative units of measure) to the base unit of measure. You define the base unit of measure and also alternative units of measure and their conversion factors in the material master record.

Physical inventory block

This indicator specifies that the stock is blocked for a physical inventory. When a material is selected for physical inventory, the system automatically blocks goods movement for the material. When the physical inventory process ends, the block is lifted.

Current period, previous period

The system not only shows the current stock, but also the stock held at the end of the previous period, so that you can see whether the inventory of the material is going up or down.

Inventory correction factor

When carrying out requirements planning or ATP check, you can use the inventory correction factor to take into account stocks that are actually available in proportion units at plant and storage location level.

Unrestricted-use stock

Unrestricted-use stock of a material is a quantity that is physically located in the warehouse, is valuated, and is not subject to any usage restrictions.

Restricted-use stock

This stock is displayed only if the material is to be handled in batches and if you have flagged the stock as restricted in the batch master record using the status key. This stock is regarded as available in materials planning.

Stock in quality inspection

This field shows the quantity of material in quality inspection.

Blocked stock

This stock is only shown if the material is managed in batches. This means that you need to have identified the stock with the appropriate batch status key in the batch's master segment. This stock is considered as unavailable for the purposes of material requirements planning.

Returns (blocked stock)

This field shows customer returns. Because returns from customers normally have to be inspected, they are posted initially to the blocked stock returns where they are not subject to valuation or unrestricted use. If the result of the inspection is that the stock can be released for unrestricted use, you enter this conclusion as a separate step. Valuation then takes place for the goods received.

Stock in transfer (from one storage location to another)

This field shows the quantity that has already been withdrawn from the issuing storage location but has not yet arrived at the receiving storage location. Until its arrival, the system manages this material as stock in transfer of the receiving storage location. This does not include the quantity being transferred on the basis of stock transport orders.

Consignment fields

Some of your vendors may stock their own material at your premises. You pay for the material only after you use it. This is called consignment. Although the material belongs to the vendor, you are responsible for its safe-keeping and accounting. These fields contain quantity of material with you under consignment. Unrestricted-use, blocked, etc., have the same meaning as your own material.

Previous period fields

These fields display quantities at the end of the previous period. This information is useful in knowing whether the inventory is going up or down.

4.3.2   Plant Stock

You can see the stock of a material in a plant using transaction MM02 or MM03.

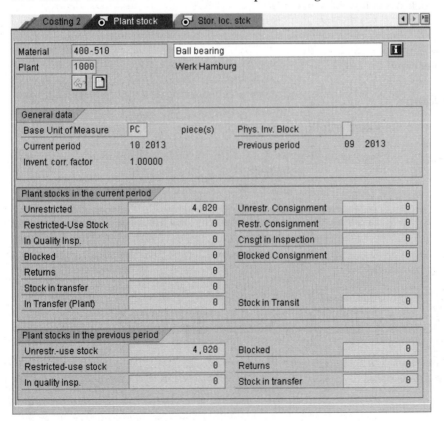

The fields in this tab are the same as the stock fields for a storage location. For stock in transfer and stock in transit, the storage location is not known until they are received in the receiving plant. Hence, they are shown at the receiving plant level.

In transfer (plant)

This field shows the quantity that has already been withdrawn from the issuing plant but has not yet arrived at the receiving plant. Until the material arrives at the receiving plant, the system manages it as stock in transfer belonging to the receiving plant. This does not include the quantity being transferred on the basis of stock transport orders.

Stock in transit

This field shows the quantity of a material that has already been withdrawn from stock in the issuing plant, but not yet arrived at the receiving plant when stock is transferred using a stock transport order. Stock in transit is managed in the valuated stock of the receiving plant. However, its use is not yet unrestricted.

4.3.3 Stock Overview

Purpose

You can see the stock overview of a material.

Transaction

MMBE—Stock Overview

Stock Overview Report

The stock overview looks like the following.

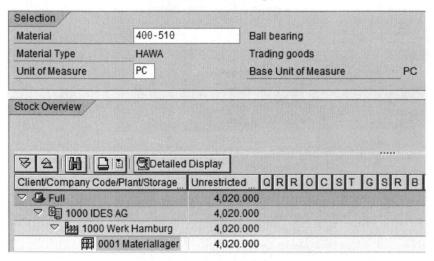

Rows

The stock is shown at various levels. You can specify the level of detail you want to see in the selection screen.

Columns

The report shows the stock in various columns. These columns depend on the Display version specified in the selection screen.

Detailed display

If you select a row and click ⌖Detailed Display , you see the breakup of the stock.

Stock Type	Stock
Unrestricted use	4,070.000
Qual. inspection	0.000
Returns	0.000
On-Order Stock	0.000

The detailed display can be configured as per your requirement in view V_136V.

Stock line	Spec.Stock	LNo	Field name	Description
1		1	LABST	Unrestricted use
1		2	INSME	Qual. inspection
1		3	RETME	Returns
1		4	MENGE	On-Order Stock

The Stock line refers to the level of the line in the report and has values from 1 to 6 as shown below.

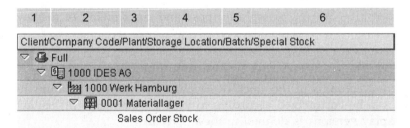

Selection Screen

The selection screen gives an insight into various concepts that make the report more user-friendly. These are discussed below.

Database selections

Database selections			
Material	=		
Plant		to	
Storage location		to	
Batch		to	

The report is for one material. You can restrict the data selected by specifying one or more plant, storage location and batch.

Stock type selection

Stock Type Selection
☑ Also Select Special Stocks
☑ Also Select Stock Commitments

You can specify whether you want the report to show stock of special stock types, e.g. project stock. You can also specify whether you want to show stock commitments, e.g. reservation.

Special stock indicator

In `Special Stock Indicator` `to` you can choose one or more special stock indicators and select data only for those indicators.

Display version

Selecting a display version

You can select a `Display version` `1`. Purpose and customizing of display versions is explained below.

Master list of display versions

You see stock under different columns in the stock overview report. Which columns to show, and in what order, can be customized according to your requirements in display versions. Master list of display versions is defined in view V_136A.

Display Version	Description
1	All stock types
2	W/o stck transfer/SD
3	SD only
13	Batches
14	Batches with status
24	In-Transit Inv
51	Version SCM510

Columns in a display version

For each display version, you define the columns in view V_136.

Vers	Window	Column no.	Field name	Description
1	1	1	LABST	Unrestricted use
1	1	2	INSME	Qual. inspection
1	1	3	BDMNG	Reserved
1	2	1	BDMNS	Rcpt reservation

Master list of fields

Master list of fields you can choose from, is defined in database table T136F.

Display unit of measure

Sometimes, for a material, you use different units of measures for different purposes. You need to convert quantities from one unit to another. You can maintain this conversion in the material master. If you click ⇨ Additional data in the material master, you get additional tabs in which you can enter data about a material. One of these tabs is the Units of measure. If you have maintained different units of measure for a material, you can choose the Display Unit of Measure here.

No zero stock lines

If you select ☑ No Zero Stock Lines, the system shows only those lines where there is stock. If a plant does not have stock, that plant is not shown. If some storage locations in a plant do not have stock, those storage locations are not shown.

Decimal place as per unit

Stock values in the stock overview are normally displayed with a fixed number of 3 decimal places. However, by setting ☐ Decimal Place as per Unit indicator, you can display them with the number of decimal places defined for each unit of measure in transaction CUNI.

Selection of display levels

Selection of Display Levels
- ☑ Company Code
- ☑ Plant
- ☑ Storage Location
- ☑ Batch
- ☑ Special Stock

The stock can be displayed at various levels. The total stock is always displayed.

Additional selection criteria

Additional Selection Criteria				
MRP Area		to		⇨

You can restrict the selection further by specifying the MRP Area for which you want to run the report.

4.3.4 Stock/Requirements List

Run transaction MD04 to compare stock with requirements of one or more materials. It helps you determine which materials to order.

Material	400-510			Ball bearing			
MRP area	1000		Hamburg				
Plant	1000	MRP type	PD	Material Type	HAWA	Unit	PC

Σ	A	Date	MRP	MRP element data	Rescheduling	Exception	Rec./reqd.qty	Available qty
		10.02.2014	Stock					4,020
		01.09.1996	---->	Effective-out date				

4.3.5 Plant Stock Availability

Run transaction MB53 to display an overview of the stock of a given material in selected plants. You can specify that materials stocked in the storage locations of the plant, but having zero stock currently, also be displayed. You cannot display stock of multiple materials using this report.

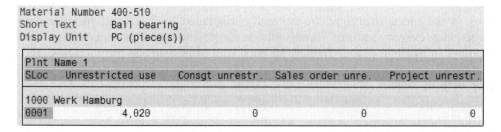

```
Material Number 400-510
Short Text     Ball bearing
Display Unit   PC (piece(s))

Plnt Name 1
SLoc   Unrestricted use   Consgt unrestr.   Sales order unre.   Project unrestr.

1000 Werk Hamburg
0001          4,020              0                 0                   0
```

4.3.6 Availability Overview

Run transaction CO09 to view the availability of a material in a plant.

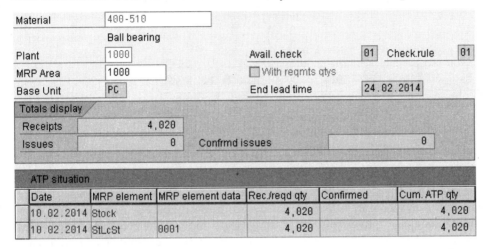

4.3.7 Warehouse Stock

Run transaction MB52 to display the total stock quantity and value of a material at plant and storage location level. If transit stocks or stock transfer stocks exist at plant level, the system totals these stocks and displays them in the column `Stock in transfer` in a stock line without a storage location. Note that in this report, the stock value of the warehouse is calculated using a simplified formula and does not represent the actual stock value.

Material	Material Description		Plnt Name 1			
SLoc SL	Unrestricted Unit	Stock in transfer	In Quality Insp.	Restricted-Use	Blocked	Returns
	Total Value Crcy	Total Value	Total Value	Total Value	Total Value	Total Value
400-510	Ball bearing		1000 Werk Hamburg			
0001	4,020 PC	0	0	0	0	0
	41,107.87 EUR	0.00	0.00	0.00	0.00	0.00
• Total						
	41,107.87 EUR	0.00	0.00	0.00	0.00	0.00

4.3.8 Stock for Posting Date

Run transaction MB5B to display stock at the beginning of the period, transactions during the period, and stock at the end of the period. The list has many columns, which you can choose from, by clicking ⬚.

```
Plant            1000
Material         100-100
Description      Casing

Stock on 01.10.2013              1,169  ST
  Total Receipts                    10  ST
  Total Issues                      15- ST
Stock on 31.12.2013              1,164  ST
```

SLoc	MvT	S	Mat. Doc.	Item	Pstng Date	Quantity	BUn	MTyGr
0001	101		5000000050	1	05.10.2013	10	PC	REST
0001	502		4900000070	1	06.10.2013	8-	PC	REST
0001	122		5000000051	1	06.10.2013	2-	PC	REST
0001	201		4900000080	1	05.12.2013	5-	PC	REST

Grouping the movements

You can analyze the movements of a material by grouping them. For example, you may group the movements by movement types and create movement type wise subtotals. SAP also lets you group movement types into movement type groups. You may create movement type groups, e.g. Purchase, Production, Sales etc., and display movements grouped by movement type groups with subtotals.

Movement type groups

You can create your own movement type groups in view V_156S_GR.

Mvmt Type	Spec.Stock	Mvmt Ind.	Receipts	Consumpt.	MTy Group
101		B			
101		B		A	
101		B		E	
101		B		P	

4.3.9 Stock in Transit

Run transaction MB5T to output a list with all stocks that are located in a plant's stock in transit. These can be stock transport orders or cross-company-code stock transport orders. On the selection screen, you can choose the types of orders that are to be displayed. You can also include purchase orders that are flagged with the `Del.Completed` Ind. or flagged for deletion. If you enter a special stock indicator, you can select explicitly for stock transfers of sales order stock, for example.

Material		Material Description		Plnt Name 1					
Purch.Doc.	Item SPlt S		Quantity BUn	Amount in LC Crcy	Order Quantity OUn	Net Order Value Crcy			
R100000		Yoghurt all natural		R110 SB Warenhaus R110					
4500010291	10 R100		13,770 PC	0.00 EUR	1,377 CAR	0.00 EUR			
4500011867	10 R100		1,100 PC	0.00 EUR	110 CAR	0.00 EUR			
4500012902	10 R100		11,610 PC	0.00 EUR	1,161 CAR	0.00 EUR			
R100000		Yoghurt all natural		R310 GM Store R310					
4500009935	10 R300		3,840 PC	0.00 USD	384 CAR	0.00 USD			
4500014580	10 R300		12,930 PC	0.00 USD	1,293 CAR	0.00 USD			

4.3.10   Valuated Special Stock

Run transaction MBBS to see valuated sales order stock (E) and valuated project stock (Q).

Material	ValA	Val. Type	S	WBS Element	Total Stock	BUn	Total Value	Crcy
P-2002	1000	C1	Q	I/5000-1-2-1	2	PC	3,067.76	EUR
T-20100	1300		Q	T-20301	0	PC	0.00	EUR
T-20210	1300		Q	T-20301	0	PC	0.00	EUR
T-20220	1300		Q	T-20301	0	PC	0.00	EUR
T-20230	1300		Q	T-20301	0	PC	0.00	EUR
T-20300	1300		Q	T-20301	0	PC	0.00	EUR
T-20400	1300		Q	T-20301	0	PC	0.00	EUR
T-20500	1300		Q	T-20301	0	PC	0.00	EUR
T-20600	1300		Q	T-20301	0	PC	0.00	EUR
T-20610	1300		Q	T-20301	0	PC	0.00	EUR
T-20620	1300		Q	T-20301	0	PC	0.00	EUR
T-20630	1300		Q	T-20301	0	PC	0.00	EUR
T-20810	1300		Q	T-20301	0	M	0.00	EUR
T-20820	1300		Q	T-20301	0	M	0.00	EUR

If you have defined that valuated sales order stock is to be valuated together with the anonymous warehouse stock in one valuation class (indicator KZBWS=A), you can no longer use this report to display the value of this stock.

4.3.11   Stock with Subcontractor

Run transaction MBLB to see the stock lying with subcontractors.

Vendor	Name 1		City				
Material	Plnt	Unrestricted	Qual.Insp.	Restricted	BUn	Total Value	Crcy
1000	C.E.B. BERLIN		Berlin				
100-120	1000	190	0	0	PC	2,236.97	EUR
100-130	1000	420	0	0	PC	0.00	EUR
101-100	1000	190	0	0	PC	7,307.40	EUR

4.3.12 Stock Overview (Russia)

Run transaction J3RFLVMOBVED to see the stock overview.

```
Stock Overview
from 01.02.2014 to 28.02.2014
List prepared on 10.02.2014 17:27:53
   1
```

Material Val	Plnt	SLoc	S	Ord/WBS/V	BUn	StockOnSt	StockOnEn	Cost begin	Cost end
ValC G/L		Price	Description		GoodReceip	GoodSIssue	ReceiValue	IssueValue	
100-100	1000	####			PC	21	21	2,388.96	2,388.96
7900 0		113.76	Casing						
100-100	1000	0001			PC	1,142	1,142	128207.52	128207.52
7900 0		112.27	Casing						
100-100	1000	0001	Q	T-20301	PC	3	3	341.28	341.28
7900 0		113.76	Casing						
100-100	1000	0002			PC	12	12	1,365.12	1,365.12
7900 0		113.76	Casing						
100-100	1000	0088			PC	10	10	1,137.60	1,137.60
7900 0		113.76	Casing						

Unlike transaction MMBE, material number is not a mandatory selection condition in this transaction. This is a very powerful transaction and it also needs long processing time.

4.3.13 List of GR/IR Balances

Run transaction MB5S to generate a list of GR/IR balances. The report compares the GR quantities and values relating to a purchase order with the invoice quantities and values for the same PO. The report can thus be used to check goods and invoice receipts when the purchasing documents show some discrepancy.

POrg PGr Vendor								
Purch.Doc.	Item	Received	invoiced	OUn		GR value	Invoice amount	LC Crcy
1000 000 111								
4500017104	10	2-	0	PC		10.60-	0.00	EUR
4500017105	10	4-	0	PC		21.20-	0.00	EUR
1000 000 1000								
4500012884	10	100	0	PC		500.00	0.00	EUR
4500012885	10	100	0	PC		500.00	0.00	EUR
4500012885	20	100	0	PC		500.00	0.00	EUR
4500012885	30	100	0	PC		500.00	0.00	EUR
4500014492	10	100	0	PC		5,000.00	0.00	EUR

If the invoice quantity is greater than the GR quantity both quantities are displayed in red; in the opposite case, these are displayed in green.

4.3.14   Consignment Stock of Vendor

Run transaction MB54 to see the consignment stocks.

Material		Material Description				Plnt Name 1				
Vendor	SLoc Batch		Unrestr. Consgt	BUn	Cnsgt price Curre		per	Total Value	Curre
99-130		Hexagon head screw M10				1000 Werk Hamburg				
1000	0001		800	PC	0.26 EUR		1	208.00	EUR

4.3.15   Consignment and Pipeline Settlement

Run transaction MRKO to display the consignment and pipeline withdrawals that are not yet settled and are therefore a liability.

	CoCd	Vendor	Mat. Doc.	MatYr	Item	Doc. Date	Plant	Material	Qty Withdr	Un	Amount	Crcy
	1000	1000	4900000036	2013	1	09.09.2013	1000	1300-550	10	PC	63.65	EUR
	1000	1000	4900000037	2013	1	09.09.2013	1000	1300-550	5	PC	31.82	EUR
	1000	1000	4900000038	2013	1	09.09.2013	1000	1300-550	4	PC	25.46	EUR
	1000	1000	4900000043	2013	1	10.09.2013	1000	1300-800	10	L	7.22	EUR

You can also settle them by choosing the ⦿ Settle option in the selection screen of this report.

4.3.16   Consignment at Customer

Run transaction MB58 to generate a list of consignment stocks and stocks of returnable packaging at customer's site.

Customer	Name 1					
Material		Batch	Unrestricted	In Quality Insp.	Restricted-Use	BUn
1171	Hitech AG					
L-120			89	0	0	PC
1175	Elektromarkt Bamby					
L-120			1,334	0	0	PC

Goods Receipt

5.1 GOODS RECEIPT IN WAREHOUSE

Functional Consultant	User	Business Process Owner	Senior Management	My Rating	Understanding Level
A	A	A	A		

5.1.1 Scenario

This chapter describes in detail the receipt of goods in warehouse against a purchase order. Other goods movement processes work in much the same way. In subsequent chapters these are discussed only for their unique features.

5.1.2 Transaction

MIGO—Goods Movement (MIGO)
MIGO_GR—GR for Purchase Order (MIGO)

5.1.3 Enjoy Screen

Enjoy Screen

In the original design, SAP had header and items of a goods movement on different screens and you were required to switch from one to the other. Now SAP has introduced screens, which are divided into sections, and everything is accommodated on one screen. The screens of goods movements are designed to have uniform look, feel and functionality.

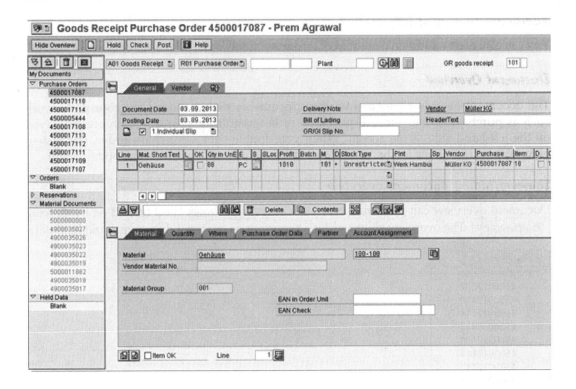

Sections of Screen

The screen is divided in five sections:

	Selection
	Header
Document Overview	Item Overview
	Item Detail

Each of these sections is discussed below in detail.

Closing and opening sections

These sections can be closed by clicking 🗗 or opened by clicking 🗗, so that you can get more space where you need it. In many fields you can double-click to see the relevant master record or document.

Additional sources of information

You can also access additional sources of information through the menu item, 'Environment'.

Document Overview

The document overview contains various documents that you need for your daily work such as purchase orders, etc. All purchase orders requiring your attention are displayed on the left-hand side of the screen. When you double-click a purchase order, the system gives appropriate lines in the right hand side, which you may use for goods receipt.

Showing/hiding document overview

Document overview can be turned off by clicking ⸢ Hide Overview ⸥ and turned on by clicking ⸢ Show Overview ⸥. The overview shows orders, reservations, material documents and held data.

My Documents
▽ Purchase Orders
4500017087
4500017118
4500017114
4500005444
4500017108
4500017113
4500017112
4500017111
4500017109
4500017107
▽ Orders
Blank
▷ Reservations
▷ Material Documents
▽ Held Data
Blank

Expand or collapse the nodes

In the document overview, you can expand or collapse all nodes by clicking ▽△. You can also expand an individual node by clicking ▷ and collapse one by clicking ▽.

Delete nodes

In the document overview, you can delete the nodes you do not need by clicking 🗑.

Hide document overview

In the document overview, you can hide the document overview by clicking .

Copying a document

You can double-click on a document in the document overview to copy its content on the right hand side.

5.1.4 Selection

Executable action

In the field [A01 Goods Receipt], you specify what you want to do, e.g. goods receipt, goods issue, etc. Depending on the transaction, the system limits your options (view cluster MIGO_LISTBOX). In transaction MIGO you get the full list given below.

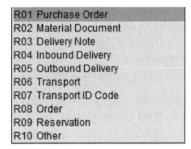

A01 Goods Receipt
A02 Return Delivery
A03 Cancellation
A04 Display
A05 Release GR Blocked Stock
A06 Subsequent Delivery
A07 Goods Issue
A08 Transfer Posting
A09 Remove from Storage
A10 Place in Storage
A11 Subsequent Adjustment

Reference document type

In the field [R01 Purchase Order], you specify the type of reference document with respect to which you are creating the material document. This list is also restricted based on transaction and action (view cluster MIGO_LISTBOX). The full list is given below.

R01 Purchase Order
R02 Material Document
R03 Delivery Note
R04 Inbound Delivery
R05 Outbound Delivery
R06 Transport
R07 Transport ID Code
R08 Order
R09 Reservation
R10 Other

Reference document details

Depending on the context set by reference document category, the system gives you fields. For a purchase order, the system gives fields for purchase order number, item number and plant. In these fields you specify information about reference document. You can also double-click the reference document in the document overview. Information from reference documents is defaulted in the items.

Movement type and special stock indicator

Movement type and special stock indicators are at item level. In the selection subscreen, the value comes from Settings ➤ Default Values , and is used to default in items of this document. However, it can be changed in the items and different items can have different movement types and special stock indicators.

Copying a reference document from the overview

You can also copy the contents of a document in the document overview to the right hand side.

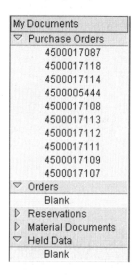

If you are receiving goods for a purchase order, you can double-click on the purchase order, and the system will transfer the data to the goods receipt screen. Before selecting a document from the overview, you should have selected the Action, and Reference document type.

Entering reference document manually

If you select purchase order as the type of reference document, you specify the purchase order number and item number. The system inserts the specified item. If you do not specify any item, the system inserts all the items. After inserting items from one purchase order, you can also select another item from another purchase order and insert. You can also insert an unordered item by clicking ▣.

Finding a reference document

You can click ▣ to find a document.

5.1.5 Header

The header has context sensitive multiple tabs which depend on the executable action and the type of reference document. It contains information that is relevant to the whole document, e.g. document date, posting date, etc.

General

| General | Vendor | 🛍 |

Document Date	03.09.2013	Delivery Note		Vendor	Müller KG
Posting Date	03.09.2013	Bill of Lading		HeaderText	
🖨 ☑ 1 Individual Slip 📄		GR/GI Slip No.			

If you have selected a reference document, the header data from that document is copied here.

Document date

Document date is the date of creation of the original document.

Posting date

Posting date is the date of accounting entries. The fiscal year and the period for which an update of the accounts specified in the document or cost elements is made, are derived from the posting date. When entering documents, the system checks whether the posting date entered is allowed by means of the posting period permitted. The posting date can differ from both the entry date (day of entry into the system) and the document date (day of creation of the original document).

Printing active/inactive

🖨 indicates the status of output determination. By setting the Print via output control indicator ☑, you can activate the printing of goods receipt/issue slips.

Print via output control

You set this indicator ☑ if you wish to print a goods receipt/issue slip. This indicator is preselected if the parameter NDR has been set to X in your user parameters (System ➤ User Profile ➤ Own Data). Even if this indicator is set, output generation is controlled by Output Determination (see Chapter 24).

You cannot set this indicator manually for movements that are posted from other applications. This means that in this case you have to set the indicator through the user parameter NDR.

In configuration it is specified whether the goods receipt slip is to be printed immediately, or in a separate step executed by the user.

Printing GR/GI slip

1 Individual Slip
2 Individual Slip with Inspection Text
3 Collective Slip

In the first case, one GR/GI slip is printed for each item. In the second case also, one GR/GI slip is printed for each item but the slip also contains the quality inspection text if there is one in the material master record. In the last case, one GR/GI slip is printed containing all the items.

Delivery note

Usually a vendor supplies the material with a delivery note, which has a number for identification. Here you can enter that delivery note number.

Bill of lading

Here you can enter the number of bill of lading at the time of goods receipt.

GR/GI slip number

The GR/GI slip number has been designed for use in those countries whose legislation requires specification of this number for goods that leave the plant and are transported on public roads. In other countries, the material document number printed on the GR/GI slip is usually sufficient. Both the GR/GI slip number and the material document number uniquely identify the document. The GR/GI slip number can be assigned both internally and externally.

Header text

Here you can enter the text that applies to the document as a whole.

Vendor

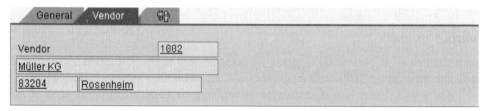

If you select a purchase order or a purchase order item, the vendor details are automatically copied from the purchase order. Otherwise, you can enter the vendor data.

Employees

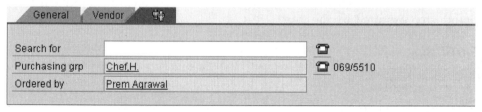

If you select a purchase order or a purchase order item, the purchasing group and the orderer's details are automatically copied from the purchase order. Otherwise, you can enter them in this tab. You can also search for a user by entering partial name in the `Search for` field.

List is sorted by	Last name		Number of hits		2
Last name	**First name**	**Company**	**Department**	**Telephone**	
Dalsegno	Tony	IDES			
GOLYNKIN	TONY	IDES			

5.1.6 Header Functions

Show overview

You can click `Show Overview` to show data relevant for adopting in a goods receipt. On the left hand side, the system shows the following panel.

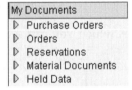

Restart

You can click ▢ to remove the existing data and starting afresh.

Hold

If you have entered incomplete data, you may click `Hold` to hold it. You can fetch the held data either from the overview or by choosing `Goods Receipt` ➢ `Held Data`.

Check

After entering goods receipt data, you can check it by clicking `Check`. The system will show data problems if any.

Post

After the goods receipt is entered, post it by clicking `Post`. When you post a goods receipt, a material document and an accounting document (if required) is created.

Help

If you click `🛈 Help`, the system opens a panel on the right side of the main screen, showing help.

Posting Goods Receipts

You can use the transaction (MIGO) to post the following goods movements:

- Goods receipts from external procurement
- Goods receipts for orders
- 'Other' goods receipts
- Return deliveries and subsequent deliveries
- Goods issues
- Transfer postings and stock transfers
- Subsequent adjustment for subcontracting

Default values

If you choose Settings ➤ Default Values, the system shows default values which you can set according to your requirements so that data entry effort is reduced.

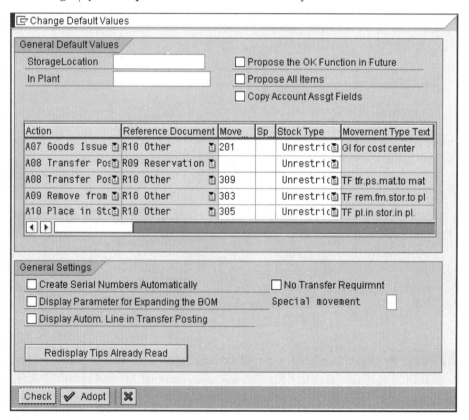

Here you can specify default movement type, special stock, and stock type based on Action and Reference Document . You can also set other default values and functionalities.

5.1.7   Item Overview

Line	Mat. Sho	Linked	OK	Qty in UnE	E	S	SLoc	M	D	Stock Type	Plnt	Sp
1	Gehäuse		☐	200	PC			101	+	Unrestricted	Werk Hamb	

Items

When you select a purchase order, the system inserts appropriate items in items overview. These items depend on the movement type currently being processed.

Items for goods receipt movement types

In the case of goods receipt movement types, the items are the items of the purchase order. The quantities proposed are the balance quantities in the purchase order. Usually the system does not insert items with zero or negative balance quantity, but if you want even these items to be inserted in item overview you can specify your choice in Settings ➤ Default Values ➤ ☑ Propose All Items .

Items for reversal/return movement types

In the case of reversal movement types, the items are the original movement type which is being reversed. However, you cannot reverse the following goods movements.

➤ Goods movements that have already been reversed.

➤ Goods that have been returned to the vendor.

➤ Goods that have been moved further, e.g. from GR blocked stock to warehouse.

If the above has happened for partial quantity, you can reverse the balance quantity.

Coordination between item overview and item detail

The item you select in item overview is shown in item detail. For the selected item, you can change the data only in item detail, not in item overview.

5.1.8   Item Detail

In the item detail, you can enter detailed data on a particular item. It contains multiple tabs, each containing a logical group of data. The tabs and the data fields can differ depending on the movement type.

Material

| Material | Quantity | Where | Purchase Order Data | Partner | Account Assignment |

Material	Gehäuse	100-100	
Vendor Material No.			
Material Group	001		
		EAN in Order Unit	
		EAN Check	

Material number and description

If you are creating goods receipt from a reference document, material number and description are displayed, otherwise you can enter them. You can receive materials which do not have a material number. Such materials cannot be stocked. They are given to the orderer on receipt, and their cost charged to appropriate accounts.

Vendor material number

If the vendor has his own number for the material supplied by him, that number is displayed here, usually from the purchasing document.

Material group

The group of the material is displayed here.

EAN in order unit

Here you can enter the international article number (EAN or UPC) of the material in the purchase order unit. The system suggests the EAN/UPC of the purchase order item. If you enter a different number, the system checks whether this number already exists in the material master record in the unit of measure. If not, the system reacts as follows:

➤ In the case of external number assignment, the new EAN or UPC is created (provided it is valid)

➤ In the case of internal number assignment, you get an error message

EAN check and unit of measure

In addition to the EAN/UPC in the order unit, you can enter another EAN/UPC in a different unit of measure for control purposes. If the EAN/UPC does not yet exist, it will be created in the material master record in the event of external number assignment.

Display linked documents

You can click 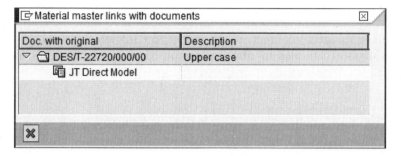 to display documents linked to this material.

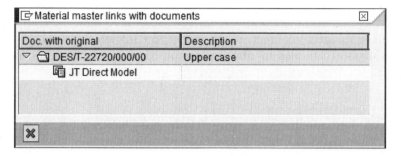

Quantity

Material	Quantity	Where	Purchase Order Data	Partner	Account Assignment

Qty in Unit of Entry	10	PC	
Qty in SKU	10	PC	
Qty in Delivery Note			
Quantity Ordered	200	PC	
Quantity Received	113		No. Containers

Quantity in unit of entry, unit

Here you specify the quantity to be moved (received) in the unit of entry, along with the unit of entry.

Quantity in SKU, unit

SAP manages a material in stock keeping unit (base unit of measure). This stock keeping unit is shown in the unit field here. If the unit of entry is same as the stock keeping unit, the quantity in unit of entry is copied in the quantity in SKU. If they are different, the quantity in unit of entry is converted in the quantity in SKU. This conversion is specified in the material master record in tab Units of measure accessed by clicking ➡ Additional data in Basic data 1 or Basic data 2 tab.

Quantity in delivery note, unit

The goods received from a vendor is usually accompanied by a delivery note. Here you can enter that quantity. It is then used by Invoice Verification in the processing of differences.

Quantity ordered, received, unit

These fields show the quantity ordered and received along with unit.

Number of containers, unit

Here you specify the number of lot containers in the inspection lot which is used to determine the number of physical samples in physical-sample drawing in the Quality Management system.

Stock determination

You can click 📠 to do stock determination. For more details, see Chapter 27.

Where

| Material | Quantity | Where | Purchase Order Data | Partner | Account Assignment |

Movement Type	101	☐ + GR goods receipt	Stock type	Unrestricted use 🖫
Plant	Werk Hamburg		1000 🖾	
Storage Location				
Goods recipient				
Unloading Point				
Text				

Movement type

Movement type determines the type of goods movement, e.g. goods receipt or goods issue. In certain cases, it further characterizes the goods movement, e.g. whether the received goods are placed in the warehouse and are fit to be used or whether they are placed in the blocked stock and are not fit to be used.

Special stock indicator

Certain stocks are managed as special stocks.

E	Orders on hand
K	Consignment (vendor)
M	Ret.trans.pkg vendor
O	Parts prov. vendor
P	Pipeline material
Q	Project stock
V	Ret. pkg w. customer
W	Consignment (cust.)
Y	Shipping unit (whse)

Wherever applicable, you select the special stock indicator along with the movement type.

Direction

The direction indicator indicates receipts (+), issues (–), or neither (blank). This is displayed based on the movement type selected.

Stock type

When you receive the material, you specify one of the following.

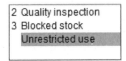

```
2 Quality inspection
3 Blocked stock
  Unrestricted use
```

Plant, storage location, goods recipient and unloading point

These fields specify the destination of the material. You can set default values of plant and storage location in `Settings` ➤ Default Values ➤ StorageLocation / In Plant .

Text

Line item texts can be used internally and externally. To be able to distinguish between these, you must begin texts for external use with "*". These texts can then be printed on all correspondence, dunning notices, payment advice notes, etc. The asterisk is removed when the text is printed.

Stock overview

You can click ⬚ to see the overview of the material's stock. The stock overview report is discussed in more detail in Section 4.3.3.

Purchase Order Data

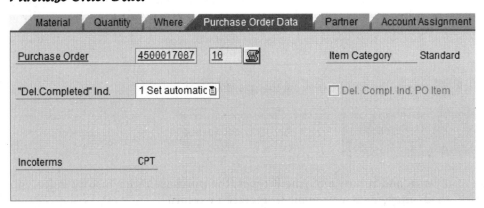

Purchase order, item, item category

This information is displayed from the purchase order item selected for goods receipt.

Delivery completed indicator

For each purchase order item, both the company and the vendor need to know whether delivery of the item is completed, or more material is expected against the purchase order item. If the supplied quantity is more than or equal to the ordered quantity, delivery is completed. But, if the supplied quantity is less than the ordered quantity, delivery may not be completed if the vendor is going to supply the remaining quantity. However, sometimes the difference may be small and both the company and the vendor may not be keen on supply of the remaining quantity. You can set the `Del.Completed Ind.` to one of the following values.

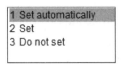

If a delivery lies within the under/over-delivery tolerances, you can have the system set the `Del.Completed Ind.` automatically by choosing the first option.

Delivery completed indicator PO item

This checkbox indicates whether the delivery completed indicator is already set for this item in the corresponding purchase order.

Incoterms

This field displays the incoterms specified in the purchase order. Incoterms specify certain internationally recognized procedures that the shipper and the receiving party must follow for the shipping transaction to be successfully completed. For example FOB specifies that the material is delivered 'Free on Board'. For certain incoterms, you can also specify a second part, e.g. FOB Mumbai.

PO history

You can click 🖳 to see the PO history of this purchase order item.

S	M	Material Do	Ite	Posting Date	☐ Quantity	O	☐ Amount in LC	L.cur
WE	101	5000000001	1	28.06.2013	4	PC	240.00	EUR
WE	101	5000000000	1	28.03.2013	1	PC	60.00	EUR

In the case of reversal and return movement types, the purchase order history helps you decide which goods movement you want to reverse or return.

Partner

In this tab you can see the partners involved in the purchasing process. The partners need to receive appropriate information about the activities taking place in your organization.

Account Assignment

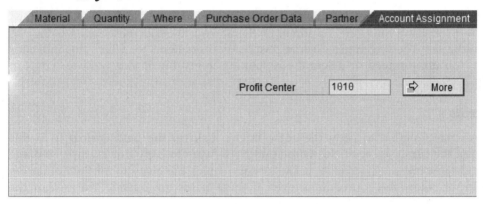

This tab contains many fields if account assignment exists for an item.

Item OK

Item OK

When you select a purchase order, the system inserts many items in the item overview. You may be processing only one, or some, of them. You identify these items using the ☑ Item OK indicator. The system checks and posts only those items for which this indicator is selected. You do not need to delete the remaining items, but if you want to, you can click 🗑 Delete . You can decide whether this indicator is set or unset by default. You specify your choice in Settings ➤ Default Values ➤ ☐ Propose the OK Function in Future .

Line

You can move to the previous line by clicking 🔼, or to the next line by clicking 🔽. For creating a new item, you should be on the last line, and click 🔽. You can also move to any line by specifying the line number in Line ⎯⎯⎯⎯⎯ 1 and clicking 📊. You can also select a line by clicking on the line number in the items overview.

5.1.9 Item Functions

Sort items in item overview

You can select a field and click 🔼 to sort the items in ascending order and 🔽 to sort the items in descending order.

Search item overview

You can search for text in item overview using ⎯⎯⎯⎯⎯⎯⎯⎯⎯⎯ 🔍🔍.

Delete

When you select a purchase order, the system inserts many items in the item overview. You may be processing only one, or some, of them. You identify these items using the ☑ Item OK indicator. The system checks and posts only those items for which this indicator is selected. You do not need to delete the remaining items, but if you want to, you can click 🗑 Delete .

Copy contents

You can use this function to copy the entry in this field to the fields below it in this column. Place the cursor on the field whose entry you want to copy (for example, storage location) and then press 📋 Contents . The system copies the entry to all fields that are ready for input below the source item, even if these fields are outside the area of the item overview that is currently visible.

Distribute quantity

You can click 🔲 to distribute the total quantity of an item between different stock types, movement types, and storage locations.

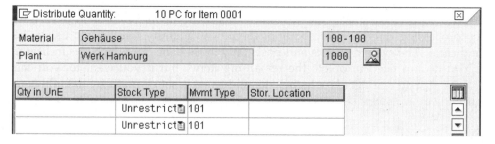

Stock determination for all

You can perform stock determination for a single item in the quantity tab for the item. If you want to perform stock determination for all items, click 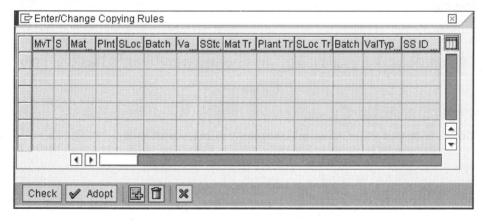 below item overview. Stock determination is explained in Chapter 27.

Non-ordered item

To reduce data entry, the system lets you enter the purchase order number as a reference document and copies its data in goods receipt. However, your goods receipt document may contain data from more than one purchase orders. Remember, purchase order data is maintained at item level, and the purchase order number you enter in reference document is only to reduce data entry. So, if you want to add an item from another purchase order, or a non-ordered item, you may do so by clicking 📝.

Transport equipment

You may click 🖳 to indicate that an item is a transport equipment. Transport equipment is a category of vehicle representing moveable equipment containing goods. It is towed by a means of transport and can then be detached from it.

Copying rules

In a MIGO transaction, you can select `Settings` ➤ `Copying Rule Transfer Posting`. In the following 'ialog box, you can determine which fields from the current item are copied when you execute the Copy to new item function.

MvT	S	Mat	Plnt	SLoc	Batch	Va	SStc	Mat Tr	Plant Tr	SLoc Tr	Batch	ValTyp	SS ID	

Enter/Change Copying Rules

Check ✓ Adopt

If, after copying to the new item, primary posting fields that are maintained under `Settings` ➤ `Default Values` for the transaction but are not filled, these values are adopted, if possible (for example, plant and storage location).

5.1.10 Holding a Goods Receipt

If you have entered incomplete data, you may click Hold to hold it. You can fetch the held data either from the overview, or by choosing Goods Receipt ➤ Held Data .

5.1.11 Checking a Goods Receipt

After entering goods receipt data, you can check it by clicking Check . The system shows data problems if any. Only the items with ☑ Item OK indicator are checked.

5.1.12 Posting a Goods Receipt

After the goods receipt is entered, post it by clicking Post . The system posts only those items for which ☑ Item OK indicator is set. When you post a goods receipt, stock is updated and a material document is created. Accounting documents are created if appropriate. A goods receipt slip is also generated and message for missing part (see Section 24.11) is sent.

5.1.13 Goods Receipt Slip

Goods Receipt Slip Generation

A goods receipt slip is generated automatically when you receive goods. Generation of goods receipt slip is controlled by Output Determination (see Chapter 24).

Message Display

Transaction

You can see the attributes of a goods receipt slip in material document transaction MB02 or MB03.

Selection screen

In the selection screen you enter material document number and year.

Item overview

Click 🔳 to see item overview.

Details from item

Select an item and click 🔳 Details from Item to display item details.

Messages

Click [🖼 Messages] to see the message (output) generated for the goods movement.

Material Document... 5000000010 0001

Output											
Out	Description	Medium	Fu	Partner	L	C	Processin	Time	Date/Time	Sa	
WE01	GR Note Vers.	1 Print output 🗒			EN	☐	03.09.2013	17:10	4		☑
WEE1	GR Label Vers	1 Print output 🗒			EN	☐	03.09.2013	17:10	4		☑

Further message details

You can see more details of the message and perform various functions by clicking [🖳 Communication method] [🖩 Processing log] [Further data] [Repeat output] [Change output] .

Print

Transaction

MB90—Process output

Selection screen

Enter the material document year and material document number. Choose [Processing mode] [2] for Repeat processing .

Message list

Mat. Doc.	Item	Out.	Med	Material	Descr.	Plnt	SLoc
☐ 5000000010	1	WE01	1	100-100	Casing	1000	0001
☐ 5000000010	1	WEE1	1	100-100	Casing	1000	0001

Print preview

Select the line and click [🖨] to see the print preview.

Print

Select the line and click [🖨] to print the goods receipt slip.

Goods Receipt Slip

```
G O O D S   R E C E I P T   S L I P       5000000010/0001
----------------------------------------------------------------
Goods receipt date : 03.09.2013
Current date        : 03.09.2013
----------------------------------------------------------------
Plant        : 1000
Description : Werk Hamburg

Vendor       : 0000001002        Delivery note:
Name         : Müller KG
PO           : 4500017087/00010
Pur. group  : 000   Chef,H.      Telephone    : 069/5510
----------------------------------------------------------------
Material     : 100-100
Batch        :
Description : Gehäuse

Quantity     :                   10   PC
----------------------------------------------------------------
W A R E H O U S E   I N F O R M A T I O N

Storage loc.: 0001
Storage bin :
----------------------------------------------------------------

Issued by    : SAPUSER   S I G N A T U R E
```

Stock type not mentioned in the goods receipt slip

The standard goods receipt slip does not indicate the stock type. This information may be crucial for the vendor, particularly if the material is put in blocked stock. You may want to modify the goods receipt slip, if you want to include this information.

Number of Goods Receipt Slips

Sometimes you may want multiple goods receipt slips, one per pallet for example. SAP lets you do that. To print multiple goods receipt/goods issue slips, you do the following.

Maintain the multiple indicator

In view V_159P maintain the Multiple indicator for the printer.

Printer	Location	B.code	Multiple
LP01	Beispieldrucker. Mit SPAD anpassen.	☐	☑
$LT4F		☐	☑

Number of goods receipt slips

In the material master, maintain the Number of GR slips field. One goods receipt slip is printed for the quantity entered here.

Enter print version

Select print version 1 (individual slip), or 2 (individual slip with quality inspection text), while entering the goods movement.

Number of goods receipt slips

The system divides the quantity moved by the figure in the Number of GR slips field, and rounds up to determine the number of goods receipt slips to be printed.

5.1.14 Goods Receipt Labels

You can see/print the GR/GI slip and labels using transaction MB90. Choose Processing mode 2 for Repeat processing. If GR/GI slip and/or labels are not generated, print indicator may not have been set in the goods movement screen, or printing may not be enabled in Output Determination (see Chapter 24).

```
Material: 100-100            Material: 100-100
Vendor: Müller KG            Vendor: Müller KG
Plant/SL: 1000 0001          Plant/SL: 1000 0001
GR/ GI Number: 5000000010    GR/ GI Number: 5000000010
GR/ GI Date: 03.09.2013      GR/ GI Date: 03.09.2013
```

```
Material: 100-100            Material: 100-100
Vendor: Müller KG            Vendor: Müller KG
Plant/SL: 1000 0001          Plant/SL: 1000 0001
GR/ GI Number: 5000000010    GR/ GI Number: 5000000010
GR/ GI Date: 03.09.2013      GR/ GI Date: 03.09.2013
```

5.1.15 Material Document

The material document can be displayed using transaction MB02 or MB03. You can click 🔍 Details from Item to see the movement type and reference document number among other things.

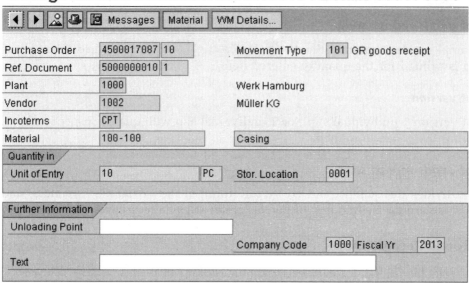

Change Material Document 5000000010 : Details 0001 / 0001

5.1.16 Accounting Documents

List of documents in accounting

In transaction MB02 or MB03 click Accounting Documents... in the item overview of the material document to see the accounting documents.

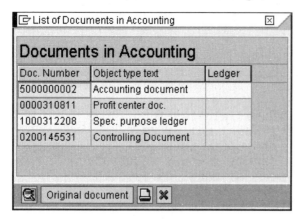

Accounting entries

Double-click the | Accounting document | to open it.

Data Entry View						
Document Number	5000000002	Company Code	1000		Fiscal Year	2013
Document Date	03.09.2013	Posting Date	03.09.2013		Period	9
Reference		Cross-CC no.				
Currency	EUR	Texts exist	☐		Ledger Group	

CoCd	Itm	PK	S	Account	Description	Amount	Curr.	Tx	Cost Ctr	Assignment
1000	1	89		790000	Unfinished products	1,137.60	EUR			
	2	96		191100	Goods Rcvd/Invoice R	600.00-	EUR			450001708700010
	3	93		281500	Income from price di	537.60-	EUR		1000	20130903

Income/loss from price difference arises during goods receipt if the material is valuated at standard price and not at moving average price.

5.1.17 Stock Overview

Run transaction MMBE to see the stock overview of a material. It shows the received quantity in appropriate column.

Client/Company Code/Plant/Storage Location/Batch	Unrestricted use	Qual. inspection	Blocked
▽ 🗄 Full	1,105.000	25.000	15.000
▽ 🏢 1000 IDES AG	1,105.000	25.000	15.000
▽ 🏭 1000 Werk Hamburg	1,105.000	25.000	15.000
🏬 0001 Materiallager	1,085.000	25.000	15.000

5.1.18 Purchase Order History

Run transaction ME22N or ME23N to see the purchase order history.

Sh...	MvT	Material Document	Item	Posting Date	Σ Quantity	OUn	Σ Amount in LC	L.cur
WE	101	5000000010	1	03.09.2013	10	PC	600.00	EUR
WE	101	5000000001	1	28.06.2013	4	PC	240.00	EUR
WE	101	5000000000	1	28.03.2013	1	PC	60.00	EUR

The purchase order history for goods receipt shows that both quantity and amount have positive values.

5.2 GOODS RECEIPT FOR A MATERIAL WITHOUT MATERIAL NUMBER

Functional Consultant	User	Business Process Owner	Senior Management	My Rating	Understanding Level
A	A	B	X		

5.2.1 Scenario

In SAP, you can order and receive a material without a material number. However, you cannot store a material without material number. Hence, it must be consumed on receipt.

5.2.2 Transaction

MIGO—Goods Movement (MIGO)

5.2.3 Selection

5.2.4 Prerequisite

You must have a purchase order for a material without material number. The item must have price and account assignment.

5.2.5 Item Detail

Material

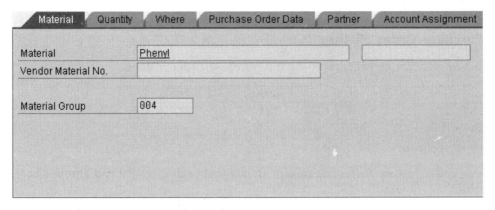

Note that there is no material number.

Purchase Order Data

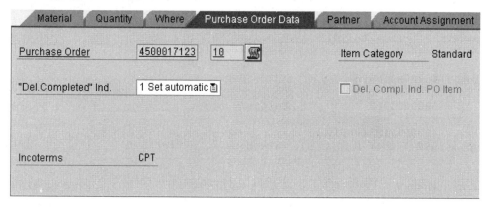

Account Assignment

Since material without a material number cannot be stored, the goods receipt must have an account assignment so that it is consumed on receipt.

5.2.6 Posting Goods Receipt

After the goods receipt is entered, post it by clicking [Post]. The system posts only those items for which ☑ Item OK indicator is set.

5.2.7 Goods Receipt Slip

You can see/print the GR/GI slip and labels using transaction MB90. Choose [Processing mode 2] for Repeat processing. If GR/GI slip and/or labels are not generated, print indicator may not have been set in the goods movement screen, or printing may not be enabled in Output Determination (see Chapter 24).

```
G O O D S   R E C E I P T   S L I P        5000000014/0001
------------------------------------------------------------
Goods receipt date : 04.09.2013
Current date       : 04.09.2013
------------------------------------------------------------
Plant        : 1000
Description  : Werk Hamburg

Vendor       : 0000001002          Delivery note:
Name         : Müller KG
PO           : 4500017123/00010
Pur. group   : 000   Chef,H.        Telephone   : 069/5510
------------------------------------------------------------
Material     :
Description  : Phenyl

Quantity     :                10  L
------------------------------------------------------------
C O N S U M P T I O N / U S A G E   I N F O R M A T I O N

Recipient     :
Unloadg. point:
Cost center   : 0000001000
------------------------------------------------------------

Issued by   : SAPUSER   S I G N A T U R E
```

5.2.8 Material Document

The material document can be displayed using transaction MB02 or MB03.

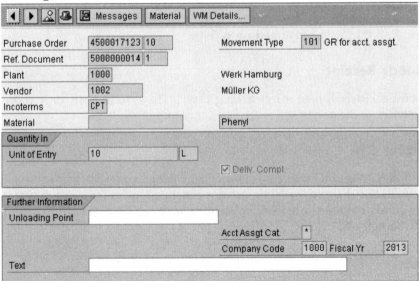

Change Material Document 5000000014 : Details 0001 / 0001

Note the absence of material number in the material document.

5.2.9 Accounting Documents

List of documents in accounting

In transaction MB02 or MB03 click | Accounting Documents... | in the item overview of the material document to see the accounting documents.

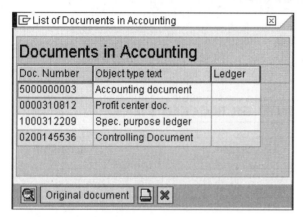

Accounting entries

Double-click the | Accounting document | to open it.

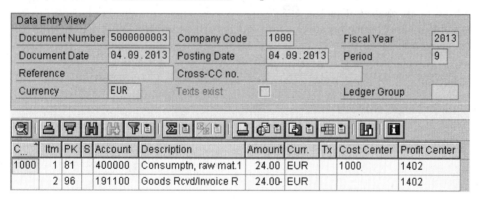

Usually goods receipt debits a stock account, but in this case the consumption account is debited, instead.

5.2.10 Stock Overview

Material without a material number cannot be stocked.

5.2.11 Purchase Order History

Run transaction ME22N or ME23N to see the purchase order history.

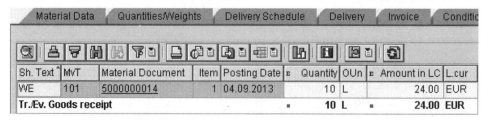

Sh. Text	MvT	Material Document	Item	Posting Date	Σ	Quantity	OUn	Σ	Amount in LC	L.cur
WE	101	5000000014	1	04.09.2013		10	L		24.00	EUR
Tr./Ev. Goods receipt					▪	10	L	▪	24.00	EUR

5.3 GOODS RECEIPT INTO GR BLOCKED STOCK

Functional Consultant	User	Business Process Owner	Senior Management	My Rating	Understanding Level
A	A	B	X		

5.3.1 Scenario

If you receive the goods in blocked stock, it cannot be used, but it becomes a part of your inventory and accounting entries are generated. If the material has been supplied wrongly, or is damaged, you can receive it in the GR blocked stock. These materials continue to be owned by the vendors and hence no accounting entries are generated. You use movement type 103 for such goods receipts.

5.3.2 Transaction

MIGO—Goods Movement (MIGO)

5.3.3 Selection

5.3.4 Item Overview

When you select a purchase order, the system inserts appropriate items in items overview. In the case of goods receipt movement types, the items are the items of the purchase order. The quantities proposed are the balance quantities in the purchase order.

5.3.5 Item Detail

Where

Material	Quantity	Where	Purchase Order Data	Partner	Account Assignment

Movement Type	103 [ ] [+]	GR into blocked stck
Plant	Werk Hamburg	1000 [⚲]

<u>Goods recipient</u>	
<u>Unloading Point</u>	
<u>Reason for Movement</u>	
Text	

Movement type

You use movement type 103.

No stock type

When you receive goods in GR blocked stock, there is no stock type.

No storage location

When you receive goods in GR blocked stock, there is no storage location. The stock is at plant level.

Reason for movement

You can select from the reasons for movement configured for this movement type. Configuration for a movement type also specifies whether reason for movement is mandatory, or optional, or whether the field is hidden.

5.3.6 Posting Goods Receipt

After the goods receipt is entered, post it by clicking [Post]. The system posts only those items for which [✓] Item OK indicator is set.

5.3.7 Goods Receipt Slip

You can see/print the GR/GI slip and labels using transaction MB90. Choose `Processing mode` `2` for `Repeat processing`. If GR/GI slip and/or labels are not generated, print indicator may not have been set in the goods movement screen, or printing may not be enabled in Output Determination (see Chapter 24).

```
G O O D S   R E C E I P T   S L I P      5000000011/0001
----------------------------------------------------------
Goods receipt date : 03.09.2013
Current date       : 03.09.2013
----------------------------------------------------------
Plant         : 1000
Description : Werk Hamburg

Vendor        : 0000001002        Delivery note:
Name          : Müller KG
PO            : 4500017087/00010
Pur. group    : 000    Chef,H.    Telephone     :069/5510
----------------------------------------------------------
Material      : 100-100
Batch         :
Description : Gehäuse

Quantity      :              5  PC
----------------------------------------------------------
W A R E H O U S E   I N F O R M A T I O N

Storage loc.:
Storage bin :
----------------------------------------------------------

Issued by    : SAPUSER    S I G N A T U R E
```

GR blocked stock not mentioned in the goods receipt slip

The goods receipt slip does not indicate that the item has been received in GR blocked stock, nor the reason for doing so. You may want to modify the goods receipt slip to include these.

5.3.8 Material Document

The material document can be displayed using transaction MB02 or MB03. You can click 🔍 Details from Item to see the movement type and reason for movement among other things.

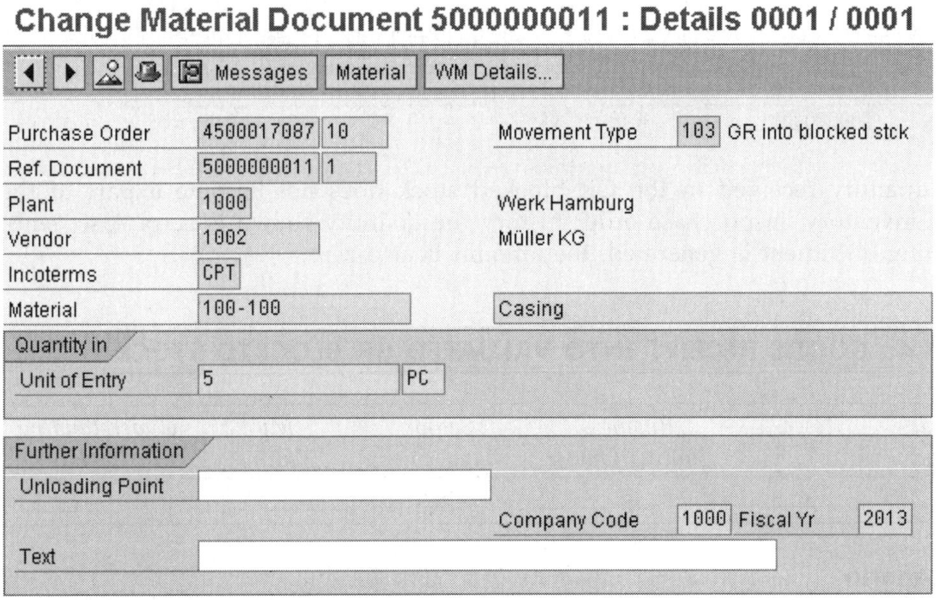

Change Material Document 5000000011 : Details 0001 / 0001

◀ ▶ 🔲 🗐 🗐 Messages | Material | WM Details...

Purchase Order	4500017087 10	Movement Type	103 GR into blocked stck
Ref. Document	5000000011 1		
Plant	1000	Werk Hamburg	
Vendor	1002	Müller KG	
Incoterms	CPT		
Material	100-100	Casing	

Quantity in
Unit of Entry	5	PC

Further Information
Unloading Point		
	Company Code	1000 Fiscal Yr 2013
Text		

5.3.9 Accounting Documents

List of documents in accounting

In transaction MB02 or MB03 click Accounting Documents... in the item overview of the material document to see the accounting documents. GR blocked stock are not valuated and they do not become a part of your inventory. Hence, the system gives the message ⓘ Material document 5000000011 does not include an accounting document .

5.3.10 Stock Overview

Run transaction MMBE to see the stock overview of a material. The GR blocked quantity shows in the stock overview at plant level.

Client/Company Code/Plant/Storage Location/	Unrestricted use	Qual. inspection	GR Blocked Stock
▽ � Full	1,105.000	25.000	6.000
▽ 🖳 1000 IDES AG	1,105.000	25.000	6.000
▽ 🏭 1000 Werk Hamburg	1,105.000	25.000	6.000
🎛 0001 Materiallager	1,085.000	25.000	
🎛 0002 Fertigwarenlager	10.000		
🎛 0088 Zentrallager WM	10.000		

Note that the GR blocked stock does not belong to any storage location.

5.3.11 Purchase Order History

Run transaction ME22N or ME23N to see the purchase order history.

Since the quantity received in the GR blocked stock does not become a part of the company's inventory, in purchase order history the quantity shown is zero. Also, since no accounting document is generated, the amount is also zero.

5.4 GOODS RECEIPT INTO VALUATED GR BLOCKED STOCK

Functional Consultant	User	Business Process Owner	Senior Management	My Rating	Understanding Level
A	A	B	X		

5.4.1 Scenario

Valuated GR blocked stock is a special type of stock. When material is received in valuated GR blocked stock (movement type 107), the stock is not increased, but liability is created. Consequently, when material is moved from valuated GR blocked stock to standard stock (movement type 109), the stock is increased, but accounting entries are not passed.

5.4.2 Transaction

MIGO—Goods Movement (MIGO)

5.4.3 Selection

5.4.4 Item Overview

When you select a purchase order, the system inserts appropriate items in items overview. In the case of goods receipt movement types, the items are the items of the purchase order. The quantities proposed are the balance quantities in the purchase order.

5.4.5   Item Detail

Where

Material	Quantity	Where	Purchase Order Data	Partner	Account Assignment

Movement Type   `107` ☐ `+` GR to Val. Bl. Stock

Plant   Werk Hamburg   `1000` 🔲

<u>Goods recipient</u>   _____

Unloading Point   _____

Text   _____

Movement type

You use movement type 107.

No stock type

When you receive goods in valuated GR blocked stock, there is no stock type.

No storage location

When you receive goods in valuated GR blocked stock, there is no storage location. The stock is at plant level.

Reason for movement

For movement type 107, this field is suppressed. However, if you want you can enable this field, decide whether the field is mandatory or optional, and configure possible values for this field.

5.4.6   Posting Goods Receipt

After the goods receipt is entered, post it by clicking Post . The system posts only those items for which ☑ Item OK indicator is set.

5.4.7 Goods Receipt Slip

You can see/print the GR/GI slip and labels using transaction MB90. Choose `Processing mode` `2` for `Repeat processing`. If GR/GI slip and/or labels are not generated, print indicator may not have been set in the goods movement screen, or printing may not be enabled in Output Determination (see Chapter 24).

```
G O O D S    R E C E I P T    S L I P     5000000015/0001
-----------------------------------------------------------
Goods receipt date : 04.09.2013
Current date       : 04.09.2013
-----------------------------------------------------------
Plant       : 1000
Description : Werk Hamburg

Vendor      : 0000001002        Delivery note:
Name        : Müller KG
PO          : 4500017087/00010
Pur. group  : 000   Chef,H.     Telephone    : 069/5510
-----------------------------------------------------------
Material    : 100-100
Batch       :
Description : Gehäuse

Quantity    :                3  PC
-----------------------------------------------------------
W A R E H O U S E    I N F O R M A T I O N

Storage loc.:
Storage bin :
-----------------------------------------------------------
Issued by   : SAPUSER    S I G N A T U R E
```

Valuated GR blocked stock not mentioned

Note that the goods receipt slip does not indicate that the item has been received in valuated GR blocked stock. You may want to modify the goods receipt slip to include these.

5.4.8 Material Document

The material document can be displayed using transaction MB02 or MB03. You can click ⟨ Details from Item ⟩ to see the movement type among other things.

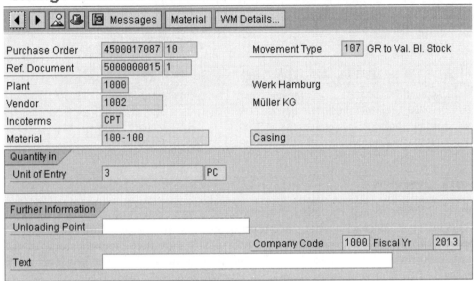

Change Material Document 5000000015 : Details 0001 / 0001

Purchase Order	4500017087 10	Movement Type 107 GR to Val. Bl. Stock
Ref. Document	5000000015 1	
Plant	1000	Werk Hamburg
Vendor	1002	Müller KG
Incoterms	CPT	
Material	100-100	Casing

Quantity in

Unit of Entry	3	PC

Further Information

Unloading Point	
	Company Code 1000 Fiscal Yr 2013
Text	

5.4.9 Accounting Documents

List of documents in accounting

In transaction MB02 or MB03 click ⟨ Accounting Documents... ⟩ in the item overview of the material document to see the accounting documents.

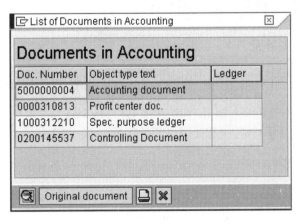

Documents in Accounting

Doc. Number	Object type text	Ledger
5000000004	Accounting document	
0000310813	Profit center doc.	
1000312210	Spec. purpose ledger	
0200145537	Controlling Document	

Original document

Accounting entries

Double-click the |Accounting document| to open it.

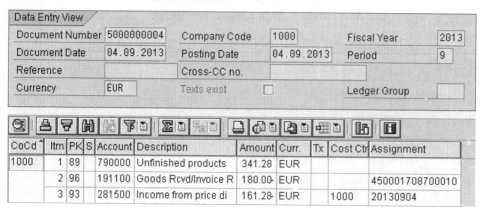

5.4.10 Stock Overview

Run transaction MMBE to see the stock overview of a material. Valuated GR blocked stock is a special type of stock, where accounting entries are passed but the material does not become a part of the company's inventory. The valuated blocked stock is not shown in any column and added in total. To see this quantity, select a line and click |Detailed Display|. You will find this quantity in |Val. GR Bl. Stock   3.000|.

5.4.11 Purchase Order History

Run transaction ME22N or ME23N to see the purchase order history.

Valuated GR blocked stock is a special type of stock. When material is received in valuated GR blocked stock (movement type 107), the stock is not increased, but liability is created. Consequently, when material is moved from valuated GR blocked stock to standard stock (movement type 109), the stock is increased, but accounting entries are not passed.

5.5 GOODS RECEIPT WITHOUT A PURCHASE ORDER

Functional Consultant	*User*	*Business Process Owner*	*Senior Management*	*My Rating*	*Understanding Level*
A	A	B	X		

5.5.1 Scenario

If you are not using the purchasing function in SAP, or want to allow receipt of goods without a purchase order, you can use the following movement types.

Movement type	*Type of stock created*
501	Unrestricted use
503	Quality inspection
505	Blocked stock

5.5.2 Transaction

MIGO—Goods Movement (MIGO)

5.5.3 Selection

Goods Receipt	Other		GI receipt w/o PO	501

5.5.4 Item Detail

Material

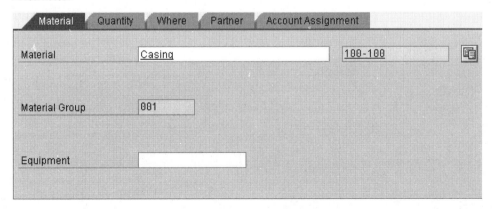

Since the goods receipt does not refer to a purchase order item, the material number must be entered.

Quantity

Material	Quantity	Where	Partner	Account Assignment

Qty in Unit of Entry	8	PC
Qty in SKU	8	PC

No. Containers

Since the goods receipt does not refer to a purchase order item, the quantity cannot be defaulted from it.

Where

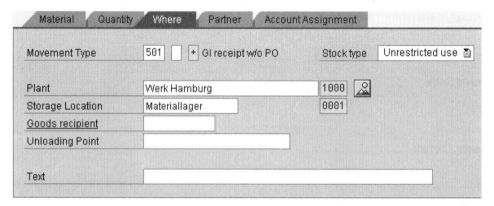

Material	Quantity	Where	Partner	Account Assignment

Movement Type	501	+ GI receipt w/o PO	Stock type	Unrestricted use
Plant	Werk Hamburg	1000	
Storage Location	Materiallager	0001	
Goods recipient			
Unloading Point			
Text			

Partner

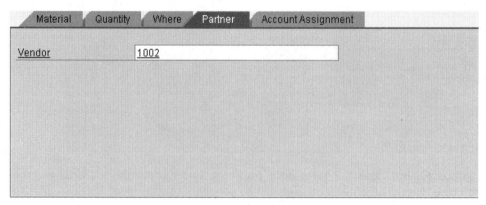

Material	Quantity	Where	Partner	Account Assignment

Vendor	1002

Since the goods receipt does not refer to a purchase order item, the vendor must be entered.

Account Assignment

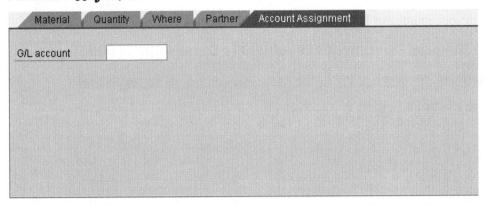

You can specify a G/L account.

5.5.5 Posting Goods Receipt

After the goods receipt is entered, post it by clicking Post . The system posts only those items for which ☑ Item OK indicator is set.

5.5.6 Goods Receipt Slip

You can see/print the GR/GI slip and labels using transaction MB90. Choose Processing mode 2 for Repeat processing . If GR/GI slip and/or labels are not generated, print indicator may not have been set in the goods movement screen, or printing may not be enabled in Output Determination (see Chapter 24).

```
G R / G I   S L I P                      4900000000/0001
-----------------------------------------------------
Posting date  : 04.09.2013
Current date  : 04.09.2013

Plant         : 1000
Description   : Werk Hamburg
-----------------------------------------------------
Material      : 100-100
Batch         :
Description   : Casing

Quantity      :                8   PC
-----------------------------------------------------

Storage loc.  : 0001
Storage bin   :
```

5.5.7   Material Document

The material document can be displayed using transaction MB02 or MB03.

Change Material Document 4900000000 : Details 0001 / 0001

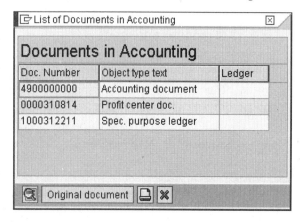

Movement Type	501 GI receipt w/o PO
Material	100-100 Casing

Quantity in

Unit of Entry	8	PC	Plant	1000	Stor. Loc. 0001

Account Assignment

G/L Account	893025
	Goods recipient
Vendor	1002
Text	

5.5.8   Accounting Documents

List of documents in accounting

In transaction MB02 or MB03 click Accounting Documents... in the item overview of the material document to see the accounting documents.

List of Documents in Accounting

Documents in Accounting

Doc. Number	Object type text	Ledger
4900000000	Accounting document	
0000310814	Profit center doc.	
1000312211	Spec. purpose ledger	

Original document

Accounting entries

Double-click the Accounting document to open it.

Data Entry View						
Document Number	4900000000	Company Code	1000		Fiscal Year	2013
Document Date	04.09.2013	Posting Date	04.09.2013		Period	9
Reference		Cross-CC no.				
Currency	EUR	Texts exist	☐		Ledger Group	

CoCd	Itm	PK	S	Account	Description	Amount	Curr.	Tx	Cost Center	Profit Center
1000	001	89		790000	Unfinished products	910.08	EUR			1010
	002	91		893025	Inventory change	910.08-	EUR			1010

If you post a goods receipt without a purchase order, the goods receipt is valuated on the basis of the valid price in the material master record. Thus, the price in the material master record is not changed by the transaction; the stock quantity and the stock value increase proportionally.

A goods receipt without a purchase order is posted to the stock account; the offsetting entry is made to a "stock change" account.

5.5.9 Stock Overview

Run transaction MMBE to see the stock overview of a material.

Client/Company Code/Plant/Storage Location/Batch/	Unrestricted use	Qual. inspection	Blocked
▽ 🗄 Full	1,113.000	25.000	15.000
▽ 🗄 1000 IDES AG	1,113.000	25.000	15.000
▽ 🗄 1000 Werk Hamburg	1,113.000	25.000	15.000
🗄 0001 Materiallager	1,093.000	25.000	15.000
🗄 0002 Fertigwarenlager	10.000		
🗄 0088 Zentrallager WM	10.000		

5.6 GOODS RECEIPT WITH AUTOMATIC PURCHASE ORDER CREATION

Functional Consultant	User	Business Process Owner	Senior Management	My Rating	Understanding Level
A	A	B	X		

5.6.1 Scenario

To meet urgent requirements, sometimes you receive goods for which purchase order has not been issued. SAP provides the functionality of creating purchase order automatically for such goods receipts, provided this facility is enabled.

5.6.2 Enabling Automatic Purchase Order for a Movement Type

In view V_156_AB you can enable creation of automatic purchase orders for movement type 101 that is used for entering goods receipts for purchase orders.

MvT	Movement Type Text	Automatic PO
101	GR goods receipt	☑
102	Reversal of GR	☐

5.6.3 Default Purchasing Organization

You need to specify the price of the material in the purchase order you create. This price comes from the purchasing info record. But, price information is specified at purchasing organization level. The system determines the default purchasing organization for a plant from view V_001W_E.

Plnt	POrg	Plant description
0001	0001	Werk 0001
0005	1000	Hamburg
0006	3000	New York
0007	1000	Werk Hamburg
0008	3000	New York
0099	1000	Werk für Customizing-Kurse SCM
1000	1000	Werk Hamburg

5.6.4 Transaction

MIGO—Goods Movement (MIGO)

5.6.5 Selection

Movement type may be 101 or 161. Do not enter the purchase order number and item number.

5.6.6 Item Overview

Click [icon] to add a non-ordered item.

5.6.7 Item Detail

Material

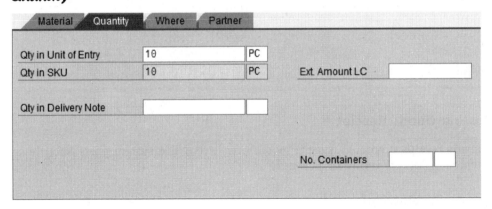

Quantity

Purchasing info record

The price of the material comes from the purchasing info record. Check whether a purchasing info record exists for the vendor material combination using transaction ME13. You will be entering the vendor in the **Partner** tab.

Externally entered posting amount in local currency

The value of the movement is calculated automatically by the system. However, it is possible to manually enter the amount of the document item in the local currency of the company code if the item is to be valuated at a different price.

Where

Material	Quantity	Where	Partner

Movement Type	101	+ GR goods receipt	Stock type	Unrestricted use
Plant	Werk Hamburg	1000
Storage Location	Materiallager	0001
Goods recipient		
Unloading Point		
Text		

Partner

Material	Quantity	Where	Partner

Vendor	KBB Schwarze Pumpe	111
Customer		

5.6.8 Posting Goods Receipt

After the goods receipt is entered, post it by clicking ⟨Post⟩. The system posts only those items for which ☑ Item OK indicator is set.

5.6.9 Goods Receipt Slip

You can see/print the GR/GI slip and labels using transaction MB90. Choose Processing mode 2 for Repeat processing . If GR/GI slip and/or labels are not generated, print indicator may not have been set in the goods movement screen, or printing may not be enabled in Output Determination (see Chapter 24).

```
G O O D S   R E C E I P T   S L I P        5000000017/0001
-----------------------------------------------------------------
Goods receipt date : 05.09.2013
Current date       : 05.09.2013
-----------------------------------------------------------------
Plant        : 1000
Description  : Werk Hamburg

Vendor       : 0000000111          Delivery note:
Name         : KBB Schwarze Pumpe
PO           : 4500017124/00010
Pur. group   : 000   Chef,H.       Telephone    : 069/5510
-----------------------------------------------------------------
Material     : 100-100
Batch        :
Description  : Gehäuse

Quantity     :                10   PC
-----------------------------------------------------------------
W A R E H O U S E   I N F O R M A T I O N

Storage loc.: 0001
Storage bin :
-----------------------------------------------------------------

Issued by    : SAPUSER    S I G N A T U R E
```

5.6.10 Material Document

The material document can be displayed using transaction MB02 or MB03.

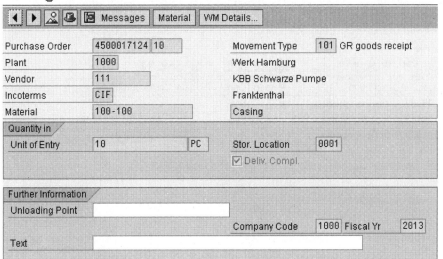

Note that no purchase order was specified during goods receipt. The purchase order has been created automatically.

5.6.11   Accounting Documents

List of documents in accounting

In transaction MB02 or MB03 click | Accounting Documents... | in the item overview of the material document to see the accounting documents.

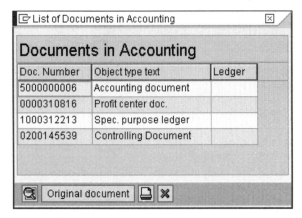

Accounting entries

Double-click the | Accounting document | to open it.

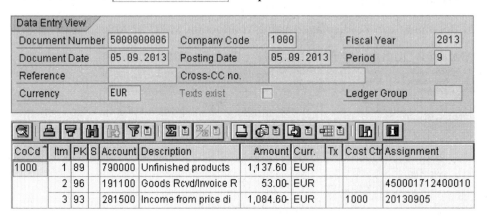

5.6.12   Stock Overview

Run transaction MMBE to see the stock overview of a material. The received quantity is shown in the appropriate column.

Client/Company Code/Plant/Storage Location/Batch/	Unrestricted use	Qual. inspection	Blocked
▽ 🗔 Full	1,125.000	25.000	15.000
▽ 🗔 1000 IDES AG	1,125.000	25.000	15.000
▽ 🗔 1000 Werk Hamburg	1,125.000	25.000	15.000
🗔 0001 Materiallager	1,105.000	25.000	15.000
🗔 0002 Fertigwarenlager	10.000		
🗔 0088 Zentrallager WM	10.000		

5.6.13   Automatic Purchase Order Creation

The system automatically created purchase order number 4500017124. You may display it using transaction ME23N.

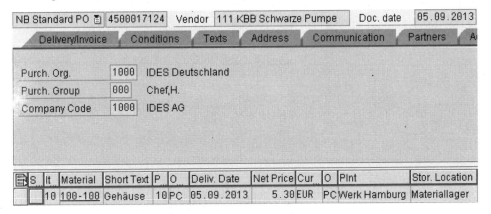

5.6.14   Purchase Order History

Run transaction ME22N or ME23N to see the purchase order history.

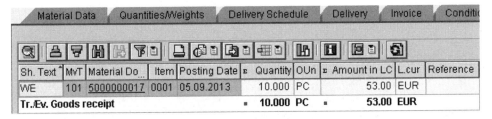

5.7 GOODS RECEIPT FOR FREE GOODS

Functional Consultant	User	Business Process Owner	Senior Management	My Rating	Understanding Level
A	A	B	X		

5.7.1 Scenario

If you receive free goods from your vendors, you can use movement type 511 to receive it in your warehouse.

5.7.2 Transaction

MB1C—Goods Receipt Other

5.7.3 Initial Screen

Document Date	05.09.2013	Posting Date	05.09.2013
Material Slip			
Doc.Header Text		GR/GI Slip No.	

Defaults for Document Items

Movement Type	511	Special Stock	
Plant	1000	Reason for Movement	
Storage Location	0001	☐ Suggest Zero Lines	

GR/GI Slip

☑ Print

◉ Individual Slip
○ Indiv.Slip w.Inspect.Text
○ Collective Slip

5.7.4 Item

Movement Type	511	GI deliv. w/o charge
Material	100-120	

Quantity in

Unit of Entry	7		Plant	1000	Stor. Loc. 0001
			Batch		

Account Assignment

	Goods recipient
Vendor	1002
No. Containers	
Text	Year-end Sale

5.7.5 Posting Goods Receipt

After the goods receipt is entered, post it by clicking 🖫.

5.7.6 Goods Receipt Slip

You can see/print the GR/GI slip and labels using transaction MB90. Choose Processing mode 2 for Repeat processing. If GR/GI slip and/or labels are not generated, print indicator may not have been set in the goods movement screen, or printing may not be enabled in Output Determination (see Chapter 24).

5.7.7 Material Document

The material document can be displayed using transaction MB02 or MB03. You can click 🔍 Details from Item to see the movement type among other things.

Change Material Document 4900000001 : Details 0001 / 0001

◀ ▶ 🔏 🕮 🖾 Messages	Material	WM Details...

Movement Type	511	GI deliv. w/o charge			
Material	100-120		Flat gasket		

Quantity in

Unit of Entry	7	PC	Plant	1000	Stor. Loc.	0001

Account Assignment

		Goods recipient	
Vendor	1002		
Text	Year-end Sale		

5.7.8 Accounting Documents

List of documents in accounting

In transaction MB02 or MB03 click Accounting Documents... in the item overview of the material document to see the accounting documents.

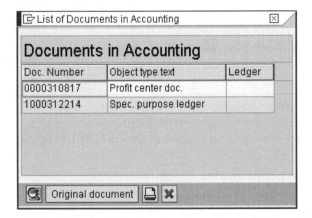

For free goods there are no accounting and controlling documents.

5.7.9 Stock Overview

Run transaction MMBE to see the stock overview of a material. The received quantity is shown in appropriate column.

Client/Company Code/Plant/Storage Location/Batch/...	Unrestricted use	Qual. inspection	Blocked
▽ 🏭 Full	1,479.000		
▽ 🏢 1000 IDES AG	1,479.000		
▽ 📊 1000 Werk Hamburg	1,479.000		
Stock Provided to Vendor	200.000		
🏛 0001 Materiallager	1,474.000		

5.8 GOODS RECEIPT FOR A PRODUCTION ORDER

Functional Consultant	User	Business Process Owner	Senior Management	My Rating	Understanding Level
A	A	B	X		

5.8.1 Scenario

You receive goods for a production order.

5.8.2 Transaction

MB31—Goods Receipt for Order
MIGO_GO—GR for Order (MIGO)

5.8.3 Initial Screen

Document Date	04.09.2013	Posting Date 04.09.2013
Delivery Note		
Doc. Header Text		

Defaults for Document Items

Movement Type	101	
Order	60003225	
Plant	1000	Reason for Movement
Stor. Location		☐ Suggest Zero Lines

GR/GI Slip

☑ Print

    ○ Individual Slip
    ◉ Indiv.Slip w.Inspect.Text
    ○ Collective Slip

5.8.4 Item Detail

Order	60003225	Movement Type 101 Goods receipt
Plant	1000 Werk Hamburg	
Material	100-100	Casing
Ordered	10 PC	Material Group 001
Received	0	

Quantity in

Unit of Entry	2 PC	Stor. Location 0001

Further Information

☐ Deliv. Compl.		No. of GR Slips 5
Unloading Point		No. Containers
Text		
Company Code	1000	Fiscal Year 2013

5.8.5 Posting Goods Receipt

After the goods receipt is entered, post it by clicking 🖫.

5.8.6 Goods Receipt Slip

You can see/print the GR/GI slip and labels using transaction MB90. Choose Processing mode 2 for Repeat processing . If GR/GI slip and/or labels are not generated, print indicator may not have been set in the goods movement screen, or printing may not be enabled in Output Determination (see Chapter 24).

5.8.7 Material Document

The material document can be displayed using transaction MB02 or MB03.

Change Material Document 5000000016 : Details 0001 / 0001

◀ ▶ ⅗ ⎙ 📧 Messages	Material	WM Details...

Order	60003225		Movement Type	101	Goods receipt
Plant	1000	Werk Hamburg			
Material	100-100		Casing		

Quantity in

Unit of Entry	2	PC	Stor. Location	0001

Further Information

		No. of GR Slips	1
Unloading Point			
Text			
Company Code	1000	Fiscal Year	2013

5.8.8 Accounting Documents

List of documents in accounting

In transaction MB02 or MB03 click Accounting Documents... in the item overview of the material document to see the accounting documents.

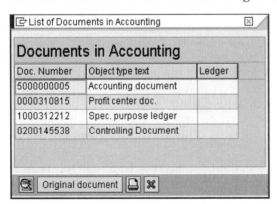

Accounting entries

Double-click the `Accounting document` to open it.

Data Entry View					
Document Number	5000000005	Company Code	1000	Fiscal Year	2013
Document Date	04.09.2013	Posting Date	04.09.2013	Period	9
Reference		Cross-CC no.			
Currency	EUR	Texts exist	☐	Ledger Group	

CoCd	Itm	PK	S	Account	Description	Amount	Curr.	Tx	Cost Center	Profit Center
1000	1	89		790000	Unfinished products	227.52	EUR			1010
	2	91		895000	Factory output of pr	227.52-	EUR			1010

5.8.9   Stock Overview

Run transaction MMBE to see the stock overview of a material.

Client/Company Code/Plant/Storage Location/Batch/..	Unrestricted use	Qual. inspection	Blocked
▽ 📦 Full	1,115.000	25.000	15.000
▽ 🏢 1000 IDES AG	1,115.000	25.000	15.000
▽ 🏭 1000 Werk Hamburg	1,115.000	25.000	15.000
🏬 0001 Materiallager	1,095.000	25.000	15.000
🏬 0002 Fertigwarenlager	10.000		
🏬 0088 Zentrallager WM	10.000		

5.9   GOODS RECEIPT WITHOUT A PRODUCTION ORDER

Functional Consultant	User	Business Process Owner	Senior Management	My Rating	Understanding Level
A	A	B	X		

5.9.1   Scenario

If you are not using the Production Planning module of SAP, you need to receive goods from your production lines in your warehouse without referring to a production order in SAP. You can use the following movement types for this purpose.

Movement type	Type of stock created
521	Unrestricted use
523	Quality inspection
525	Blocked stock

5.9.2 Transaction

MB1C—Goods Receipt Other

5.9.3 Initial Screen

Document Date	05.09.2013		Posting Date	05.09.2013
Material Slip				
Doc.Header Text			GR/GI Slip No.	

Defaults for Document Items

Movement Type	521		Special Stock	☐
Plant	1000		Reason for Movement	
Storage Location	0001		☐ Suggest Zero Lines	

GR/GI Slip

☑ Print

- ◉ Individual Slip
- ○ Indiv.Slip w.Inspect.Text
- ○ Collective Slip

5.9.4 Item

Movement Type	521	GI receipt w/o PrOrd
Material	100-100	

Quantity in

Unit of Entry	20	PC	Plant	1000	Stor. Loc.	0001
			Batch			

Account Assignment

		Order	
		Goods recipient	
No. Containers			
Text			

5.9.5 Posting Goods Receipt

After the goods receipt is entered, post it by clicking 💾.

5.9.6   Goods Receipt Slip

You can see/print the GR/GI slip and labels using transaction MB90. Choose Processing mode 2 for Repeat processing. If GR/GI slip and/or labels are not generated, print indicator may not have been set in the goods movement screen, or printing may not be enabled in Output Determination (see Chapter 24).

```
G R / G I   S L I P                        4900000002/0001
-----------------------------------------------------------
Posting date  : 05.09.2013
Current date  : 05.09.2013

Plant         : 1000
Description   : Werk Hamburg
-----------------------------------------------------------
Material      : 100-100
Batch         :
Description   : Casing

Quantity      :                    20   PC
-----------------------------------------------------------

Storage loc.  : 0001
Storage bin   :

Prod. order   :
```

5.9.7   Material Document

The material document can be displayed using transaction MB02 or MB03. You can click Details from Item to see the movement type among other things.

Change Material Document 4900000002 : Details 0001 / 0001

| | | | | Messages | Material | WM Details... |

Movement Type	521	GI receipt w/o PrOrd		
Material	100-100		Casing	

Quantity in

| Unit of Entry | 20 | PC | Plant | 1000 | Stor. Loc. | 0001 |

Account Assignment

| G/L Account | 895000 |

Order

Goods recipient

Text

5.9.8 Accounting Documents

List of documents in accounting

In transaction MB02 or MB03 click ⌈ Accounting Documents... ⌉ in the item overview of the material document to see the accounting documents.

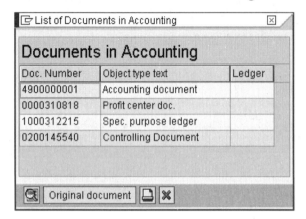

Accounting entries

Double-click the ⌈ Accounting document ⌉ to open it.

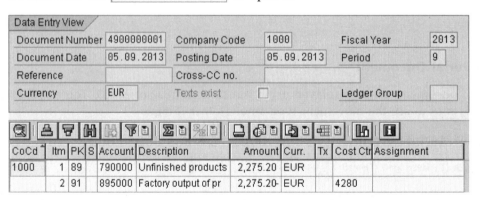

5.9.9 Stock Overview

Run transaction MMBE to see the stock overview of a material. The received quantity is shown in appropriate column.

Client/Company Code/Plant/Storage Location/Batch/	Unrestricted use	Qual. inspection	Blocked
▽ 🥤 Full	1,145.000	25.000	15.000
▽ 📇 1000 IDES AG	1,145.000	25.000	15.000
▽ 🏭 1000 Werk Hamburg	1,145.000	25.000	15.000
🎴 0001 Materiallager	1,125.000	25.000	15.000

5.10 GOODS RECEIPT OF BY-PRODUCTS

Functional Consultant	User	Business Process Owner	Senior Management	My Rating	Understanding Level
A	A	B	X		

5.10.1 Scenario

If your production process creates by-products, you can use movement type 531 to receive it in your warehouse.

5.10.2 Transaction

MB1C—Goods Receipt Other

5.10.3 Initial Screen

Document Date	05.09.2013	Posting Date	05.09.2013
Material Slip			
Doc.Header Text		GR/GI Slip No.	

Defaults for Document Items

Movement Type	531	Special Stock	
Plant	1000	Reason for Movement	
Storage Location	0001	☐ Suggest Zero Lines	

GR/GI Slip

☑ Print

- ◉ Individual Slip
- ○ Indiv.Slip w.Inspect.Text
- ○ Collective Slip

5.10.4 Item

Movement Type	531	GI by-product
Material	100-890	

Quantity in

Unit of Entry	5	KG	Plant	1000	Stor. Loc.	0001
			Batch		

Account Assignment

	Order	
	Goods recipient	
No. Containers		
Text		

5.10.5 Posting Goods Receipt

After the goods receipt is entered, post it by clicking 🖫.

5.10.6 Goods Receipt Slip

You can see/print the GR/GI slip and labels using transaction MB90. Choose `Processing mode` `2` for `Repeat processing`. If GR/GI slip and/or labels are not generated, print indicator may not have been set in the goods movement screen, or printing may not be enabled in Output Determination (see Chapter 24).

```
G R / G I   S L I P                    4900000003/0001
-----------------------------------------------------------
Posting date  : 05.09.2013
Current date  : 05.09.2013

Plant         : 1000
Description   : Werk Hamburg
-----------------------------------------------------------
Material      : 100-890
Batch         :
Description   : Filler

Quantity      :                   5   KG
-----------------------------------------------------------

Storage loc.  : 0001
Storage bin   :

Prod. order   :
```

5.10.7 Material Document

The material document can be displayed using transaction MB02 or MB03. You can click ▣ `Details from Item` to see the movement type among other things.

Change Material Document 4900000003 : Details 0001 / 0001

| ◀ | ▶ | 👤 | 📇 | 🗐 Messages | Material | WM Details... |

| Movement Type | 531 | GI by-product |
| Material | 100-890 | | Filler |

Quantity in

| Unit of Entry | 5 | KG | Plant | 1000 | Stor. Loc. | 0001 |

Account Assignment

| G/L Account | 895000 |

| Order | |
| Goods recipient | |

| Text | |

5.10.8 Accounting Documents

List of documents in accounting

In transaction MB02 or MB03 click Accounting Documents... in the item overview of the material document to see the accounting documents.

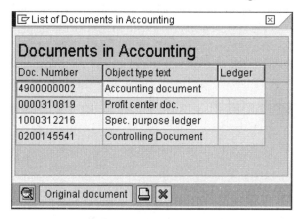

Accounting entries

Double-click the Accounting document to open it.

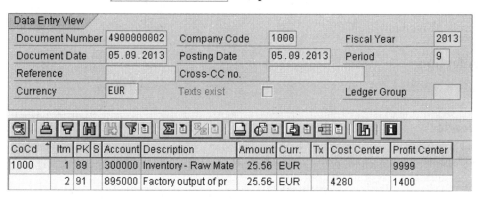

Note that even goods receipt of a by-product increases inventory.

5.10.9 Stock Overview

Run transaction MMBE to see the stock overview of a material. The received quantity is shown in appropriate column.

Client/Company Code/Plant/Storage Location/Batch/...	Unrestricted use	Qual. inspection	Blocked
▽ 📇 Full	5,005.000		
▽ 🖥 1000 IDES AG	5,005.000		
▽ 🏭 1000 Werk Hamburg	5,005.000		
🗄 0001 Materiallager	5,005.000		

5.11 INITIAL ENTRY OF INVENTORY

Functional Consultant	User	Business Process Owner	Senior Management	My Rating	Understanding Level
A	A	B	X		

5.11.1 Scenario

When you implement SAP, you need to create stock of existing material in SAP. You can use the following movement types for this purpose.

Movement type	Type of stock created
561	Unrestricted use
563	Quality inspection
565	Blocked stock

Apart from warehouse, you can also receive material in various special stocks. You can do initial entry of inventory only against a material number.

5.11.2 Transaction

MIGO—Goods Movement (MIGO)

5.11.3 Selection

A01 Goods Receipt ⬦ R10 Other ⬦   GI entry of st. bals   561

5.11.4 Header

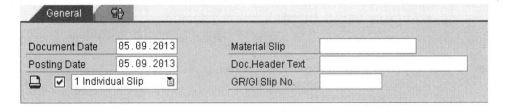

5.11.5 Item Detail

Material

Material	Quantity	Where

Material	Casing	100-100

Equipment	

Quantity

Material	Quantity	Where

Qty in Unit of Entry		
	0.000	Ext. Amount LC

For a material valued at a standard price, the initial entry of inventory data is valuated on the basis of the standard price. If you enter an alternative value during the initial entry of inventory data, the system posts the difference to a price difference account.

For a material valued at a moving average price, the initial entry of inventory data is valuated as follows:

➢ If you enter a value when entering initial data, the quantity entered is valuated at this price. If the quotient of the value and the quantity of the initial data differs from the moving average price, the moving average price changes when initial data is entered.

➢ If you do not enter a value when entering initial data, the quantity entered is valuated at the moving average price. In this case, the moving average price does not change.

Where

Material	Quantity	Where

Movement Type	561 + GI entry of st. bals	Stock type Unrestricted use 🔲
Plant	Werk Hamburg 1000 🔍	
Storage Location	Materiallager 0001	
Unloading Point		
Text		

5.11.6   Posting Goods Receipt

After the goods receipt is entered, post it by clicking Post . The system posts only those items for which ☑ Item OK indicator is set.

5.11.7   Goods Receipt Slip

You can see/print the GR/GI slip and labels using transaction MB90. Choose Processing mode 2 for Repeat processing . If GR/GI slip and/or labels are not generated, print indicator may not have been set in the goods movement screen, or printing may not be enabled in Output Determination (see Chapter 24).

5.11.8   Material Document

The material document can be displayed using transaction MB02 or MB03.

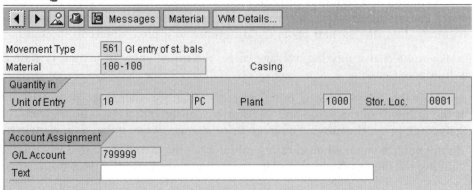

Change Material Document 4900000004 : Details 0001 / 0001

◀	▶	🔍	🖨	📋 Messages	Material	WM Details...

Movement Type	561 GI entry of st. bals	
Material	100-100	Casing

Quantity in

Unit of Entry	10 PC	Plant	1000	Stor. Loc.	0001

Account Assignment

G/L Account	799999
Text	

5.11.9 Accounting Documents

List of documents in accounting

In transaction MB02 or MB03 click Accounting Documents... in the item overview of the material document to see the accounting documents.

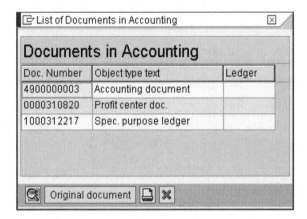

Accounting entries

Double-click the Accounting document to open it.

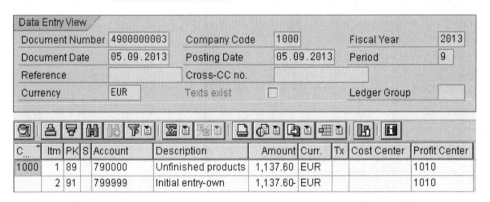

An account meant specifically for initial entry of stock is credited.

5.11.10 BDC

You may use transaction MB1C to upload initial inventory using a BDC. Usually you create a session in transaction SM35 after recording the steps required. But SAP provides transaction MBBM in which it is already done.

5.12 GOODS RECEIPT FOR NON-VALUATED MATERIAL

Functional Consultant	User	Business Process Owner	Senior Management	My Rating	Understanding Level
A	A	B	X		

5.12.1 Scenario

You receive goods for a non-valuated material. Whether a material is valuated or not is determined from its material type and valuation area in view VT134M. For a non-valuated material, there is no Accounting 1 view.

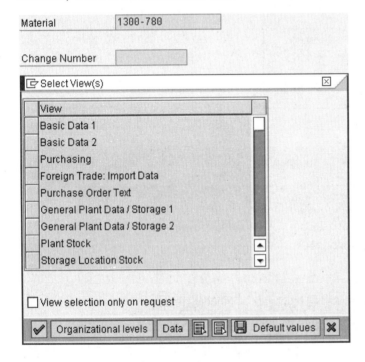

5.12.2 Transaction

MIGO—Goods Movement (MIGO)

5.12.3 Selection

5.12.4 Item Detail

Material

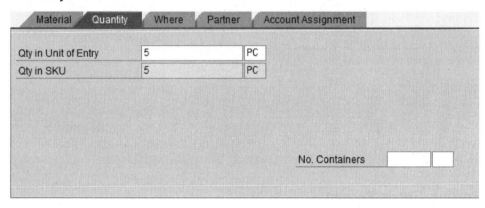

| Material | Quantity | Where | Partner | Account Assignment |

| Material | Operating instructions HD-1300 | 1300-780 |

| Material Group | 009 |

| Equipment | |

Quantity

| Material | Quantity | Where | Partner | Account Assignment |

| Qty in Unit of Entry | 5 | PC |
| Qty in SKU | 5 | PC |

No. Containers

Where

| Material | Quantity | Where | Partner | Account Assignment |

| Movement Type | 501 | + | GI receipt w/o PO | Stock type | Unrestricted use |

Plant	Werk Hamburg	1000
Storage Location	Materiallager	0001
Goods recipient	
Unloading Point	

| Text | |

Partner

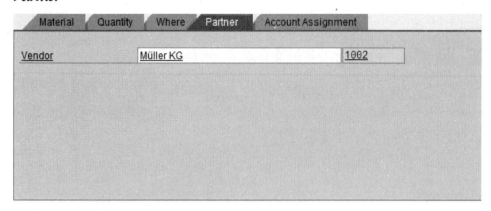

Account Assignment

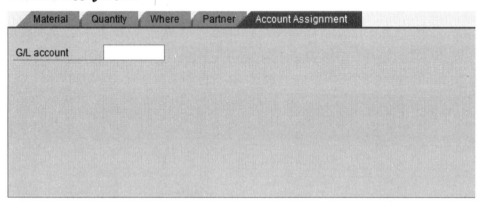

5.12.5 Posting Goods Receipt

After the goods receipt is entered, post it by clicking Post . The system posts only those items for which ☑ Item OK indicator is set.

5.12.6 Goods Receipt Slip

You can see/print the GR/GI slip and labels using transaction MB90. Choose Processing mode 2 for Repeat processing . If GR/GI slip and/or labels are not generated, print indicator may not have been set in the goods movement screen, or printing may not be enabled in Output Determination (see Chapter 24).

```
G R / G I   S L I P                    4900000005/0001
-------------------------------------------------------
Posting date  : 05.09.2013
Current date  : 05.09.2013

Plant         : 1000
Description   : Werk Hamburg
-------------------------------------------------------
Material      : 1300-780
Batch         :
Description   : Operating instructions HD-1300

Quantity      :                    5   PC
-------------------------------------------------------

Storage loc.  : 0001
Storage bin   :
```

5.12.7   Material Document

The material document can be displayed using transaction MB02 or MB03.

Change Material Document 4900000005 : Details 0001 / 0001

| ◀ | ▶ | 👤 🖨 | 🖼 Messages | Material | WM Details... |

| Movement Type | 501 | GI receipt w/o PO |
| Material | 1300-780 | Operating instructions HD-1300 |

Quantity in

| Unit of Entry | 5 | PC | Plant | 1000 | Stor. Loc. | 0001 |

Account Assignment

		Goods recipient	
Vendor	1002		
Text			

5.12.8   Accounting Documents

List of documents in accounting

In transaction MB02 or MB03 click ⎡ Accounting Documents... ⎦ in the item overview of the material document to see the accounting documents. No accounting document is generated as the material is non-valuated.

5.12.9 Stock Overview

Run transaction MMBE to see the stock overview of a material.

Client/Company Code/Plant/Storage Location/Batch/...	Unrestricted use	Qual. inspection	Blocked
▽ 🛢 Full	10.000		
▽ 🗐 1000 IDES AG	10.000		
▽ 🏭 1000 Werk Hamburg	10.000		
🗄 0001 Materiallager	10.000		

5.13 GOODS RECEIPT FOR CONSUMPTION

Functional Consultant	User	Business Process Owner	Senior Management	My Rating	Understanding Level
A	A	B	X		

5.13.1 Scenario

Sometimes you receive material which is directly provided to the user of the material, e.g. cost center, project etc. For material so received, the account assignment must be specified in the purchase order. The material does not enter the warehouse and the inventory of the storage location and plant does not go up. The cost of the material is charged to the cost object to which the material is issued.

5.13.2 Transaction

MIGO—Goods Movement (MIGO)

5.13.3 Selection

5.13.4 Item Overview

When you select a purchase order, the system inserts appropriate items in items overview. In the case of goods receipt movement types, the items are the items of the purchase order. The quantities proposed are the balance quantities in the purchase order.

5.13.5 Item Detail

Account Assignment

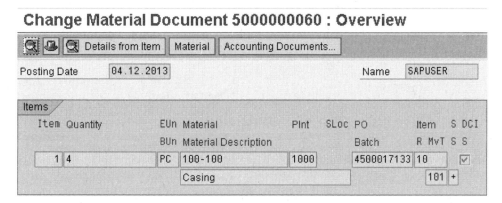

| Material | Quantity | Where | Purchase Order Data | Partner | Account Assignment |

G/L account	890000
Business Area	9900
Cost Center	1000	Corporate Services
Profit Center	1402	Administration
Functional Area	0400		⇨ More

Note that the account assignment is copied from the purchase order.

5.13.6 Posting Goods Receipt

After the goods receipt is entered, post it by clicking | Post |. The system posts only those items for which ☑ Item OK indicator is set.

5.13.7 Goods Receipt Slip

You can see/print the GR/GI slip and labels using transaction MB90. Choose Processing mode 2 for Repeat processing. If GR/GI slip and/or labels are not generated, print indicator may not have been set in the goods movement screen, or printing may not be enabled in Output Determination (see Chapter 24).

5.13.8 Material Document

The material document can be displayed using transaction MB02 or MB03.

Change Material Document 5000000060 : Overview

| Details from Item | Material | Accounting Documents... |

| Posting Date | 04.12.2013 | | Name | SAPUSER |

Items

Item	Quantity		EUn	Material		Plnt	SLoc	PO		Item	S	DCI
			BUn	Material Description				Batch		R	MvT	S	S
1	4		PC	100-100		1000		4500017133	10		☑
				Casing						101	+

5.13.9 Accounting Documents

List of documents in accounting

In transaction MB02 or MB03 click Accounting Documents... in the item overview of the material document to see the accounting documents.

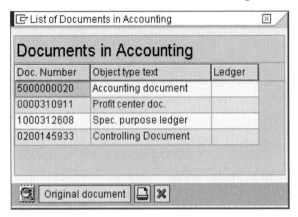

Accounting entries

Double-click the Accounting document to open it.

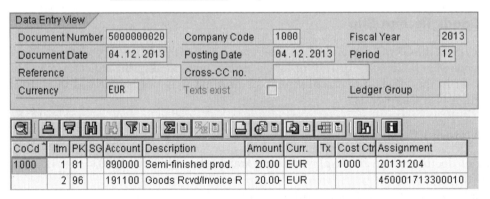

Note that the cost center is debited by the value of the goods receipt, not inventory.

5.13.10 Stock Overview before Goods Receipt

Run transaction MMBE to see the stock overview of the material before goods receipt.

Client/Company Code/Plant/Storage Location/...	Unrestricted use	Qual. inspection	Blocked
▽ 🔶 Full	1,131.000	23.000	15.000
▽ 🗐 1000 IDES AG	1,131.000	23.000	15.000
▽ 🏭 1000 Werk Hamburg	1,131.000	23.000	15.000
▽ 🏢 0001 Materiallager	1,109.000	23.000	15.000
Sales Order Stock	5.000		
Project Stock	3.000		
🏢 0002 Fertigwarenlager	12.000		
🏢 0088 Zentrallager WM	10.000		

5.13.11 Stock Overview after Goods Receipt

Run transaction MMBE to see the stock overview of the material after goods receipt.

Client/Company Code/Plant/Storage Location/...	Unrestricted use	Qual. inspection	Blocked
▽ 🔶 Full	1,131.000	23.000	15.000
▽ 🗐 1000 IDES AG	1,131.000	23.000	15.000
▽ 🏭 1000 Werk Hamburg	1,131.000	23.000	15.000
▽ 🏢 0001 Materiallager	1,109.000	23.000	15.000
Sales Order Stock	5.000		
Project Stock	3.000		
🏢 0002 Fertigwarenlager	12.000		
🏢 0088 Zentrallager WM	10.000		

Note that there is no change in the inventory of the material.

Goods Issue

6.1 GOODS ISSUE TO A COST CENTER

Functional Consultant	User	Business Process Owner	Senior Management	My Rating	Understanding Level
A	A	B	X		

6.1.1 Scenario

You issue goods to a cost center.

6.1.2 Transaction

MIGO_GI—Goods Issue (MIGO)
MB1A—Goods Issue

6.1.3 Selection

A07 Goods Issue	R10 Other		GI for cost center	201

6.1.4 Item Detail

Material

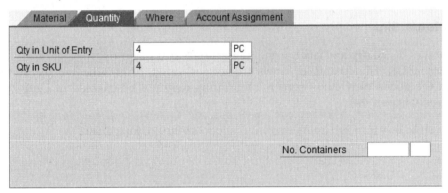

In goods receipt you can receive a material which does not have material number. But such material cannot be stored, and hence cannot be issued. Therefore, for goods issue, the material field is mandatory.

Quantity

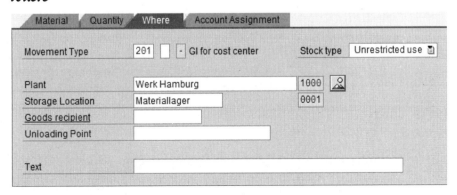

For goods issue, quantity and unit fields are mandatory.

Where

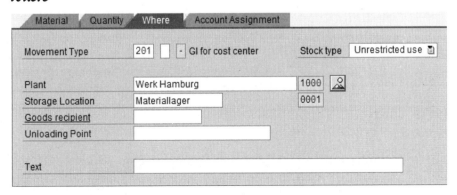

Account Assignment

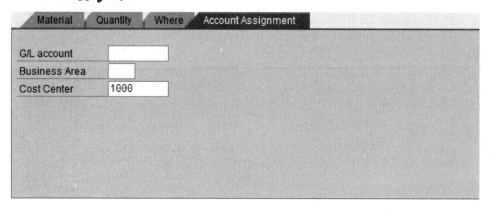

For goods issue to cost center, this tab shows the cost center field, which is mandatory.

6.1.5 Posting Goods Issue

After the goods issue is entered, post it by clicking [Post]. The system posts only those items for which ☑ Item OK indicator is set.

6.1.6 Goods Issue Slip

You can see/print the GR/GI slip and labels using transaction MB90. Choose Processing mode [2] for Repeat processing. If GR/GI slip and/or labels are not generated, print indicator may not have been set in the goods movement screen, or printing may not be enabled in Output Determination (see Chapter 24).

```
G R / G I   S L I P                        4900000006/0001
-----------------------------------------------------------------
Posting date  : 05.09.2013
Current date  : 05.09.2013

Plant         : 1000
Description   : Werk Hamburg
-----------------------------------------------------------------
Material      : 100-100
Batch         :
Description   : Casing

Quantity      :                    4   PC
-----------------------------------------------------------------

Storage loc.  : 0001
Storage bin   :

Cost center   : 0000001000
```

6.1.7 Goods Issue Labels

```
Material: 100-100          Material: 100-100
Vendor:                    Vendor:
Plant/SL: 1000 0001        Plant/SL: 1000 0001
GR/ GI Number: 4900000006  GR/ GI Number: 4900000006
GR/ GI Date: 05.09.2013    GR/ GI Date: 05.09.2013
```

```
Material: 100-100          Material: 100-100
Vendor:                    Vendor:
Plant/SL: 1000 0001        Plant/SL: 1000 0001
GR/ GI Number: 4900000006  GR/ GI Number: 4900000006
GR/ GI Date: 05.09.2013    GR/ GI Date: 05.09.2013
```

6.1.8 Material Document

The material document can be displayed using transaction MB02 or MB03.

Change Material Document 4900000006 : Details 0001 / 0001

◄ ► 🗒 🗊 📋 Messages | Material | WM Details...

Movement Type	201	GI for cost center		
Material	100-100		Casing	

Quantity in

Unit of Entry	4	PC	Plant	1000	Stor. Loc.	0001

Account Assignment

G/L Account	890000	
Business Area	9900	
Cost Center	1000	Corporate Services

Goods recipient [   ]

Text [   ]

6.1.9   Accounting Documents

List of documents in accounting

In transaction MB02 or MB03 click | Accounting Documents... | in the item overview of the material document to see the accounting documents.

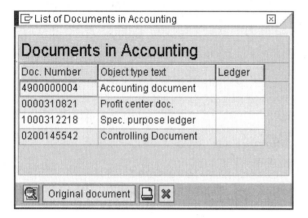

Accounting entries

Double-click the | Accounting document | to open it.

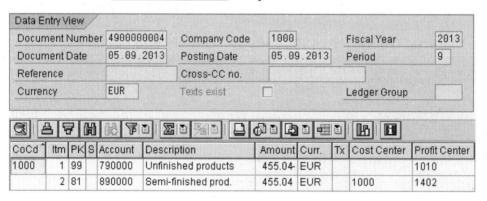

The cost center account is debited and inventory account is credited. For both materials valuated at a standard price and materials valuated at a moving average price, goods issues are always valuated at the current price. Consequently, a goods issue reduces the total value and the total quantity in relation to the price and the price remains unchanged.

6.2 GOODS ISSUE FOR A PROJECT

Functional Consultant	User	Business Process Owner	Senior Management	My Rating	Understanding Level
A	A	B	X		

6.2.1 Scenario

You issue goods to a project.

6.2.2 Transaction

MIGO_GI—Goods Issue (MIGO)

6.2.3 Selection

| Goods Issue 📄 | Other 📄 | | GI for project | 221 |

6.2.4 Item Detail

Account Assignment

| Material | Quantity | Where | **Account Assignment** |

G/L account   [_____]
Business Area   [__]

WBS Element   T-20301   Network   [_____] [__]

6.2.5 Posting Goods Issue

After the goods issue is entered, post it by clicking [Post]. The system posts only those items for which ☑ Item OK indicator is set.

6.2.6 Goods Issue Slip

You can see/print the GR/GI slip and labels using transaction MB90. Choose Processing mode 2 for Repeat processing . If GR/GI slip and/or labels are not generated, print indicator may not have been set in the goods movement screen, or printing may not be enabled in Output Determination (see Chapter 24).

```
G R / G I   S L I P                          4900000007/0001
--------------------------------------------------------------
Posting date  : 05.09.2013
Current date  : 05.09.2013

Plant         : 1000
Description   : Werk Hamburg
--------------------------------------------------------------
Material      : 100-100
Batch         :
Description   : Casing

Quantity      :                        2   PC
--------------------------------------------------------------

Storage loc.  : 0001
Storage bin   :

Project       : T-20301
```

6.2.7 Goods Issue Labels

```
Material: 100-100                    Material: 100-100
Vendor:                              Vendor:
Plant/SL: 1000 0001                  Plant/SL: 1000 0001
GR/ GI Number: 4900000007            GR/ GI Number: 4900000007
GR/ GI Date: 05.09.2013              GR/ GI Date: 05.09.2013
```

6.2.8 Material Document

The material document can be displayed using transaction MB02 or MB03.

Change Material Document 4900000007 : Details 0001 / 0001

◀	▶	🔍 🖨	🗎 Messages	Material	WM Details...	

Movement Type	221	GI for project
Material	100-100	Casing

Quantity in

Unit of Entry	2	PC	Plant	1000	Stor. Loc.	0001

Account Assignment

G/L Account	890000
Business Area	2000
WBS Element	T-20301
Network	
Goods recipient	
Text	

6.2.9   Accounting Documents

List of documents in accounting

In transaction MB02 or MB03 click | Accounting Documents... | in the item overview of the material document to see the accounting documents.

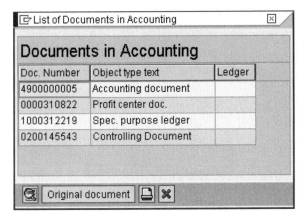

Accounting entries

Double-click the | Accounting document | to open it.

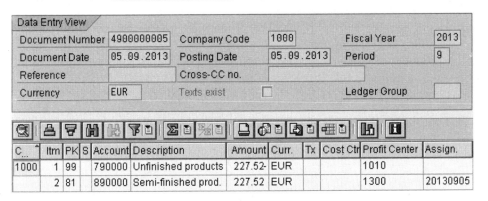

The project account is debited and inventory account is credited.

6.3   GOODS ISSUE FOR A SALES ORDER

Functional Consultant	User	Business Process Owner	Senior Management	My Rating	Understanding Level
A	A	B	X		

6.3.1   Scenario

You issue goods to a sales order.

6.3.2   Transaction

MIGO_GI—Goods Issue (MIGO)

6.3.3   Selection

Goods Issue	▤	Other	▤		GI for sales order	231

6.3.4   Item Detail

Account Assignment

Material	Quantity	Where	Account Assignment

G/L account [ ]

Business Area [ ]
Sales Order [5014] [10] [ ]

6.3.5   Posting Goods Issue

After the goods issue is entered, post it by clicking Post . The system posts only those items for which ☑ Item OK indicator is set.

6.3.6   Goods Issue Slip

You can see/print the GR/GI slip and labels using transaction MB90. Choose Processing mode 2 for Repeat processing. If GR/GI slip and/or labels are not generated, print indicator may not have been set in the goods movement screen, or printing may not be enabled in Output Determination (see Chapter 24).

```
G R  /  G I    S L I P                           4900000008/0001
-----------------------------------------------------------------
Posting date  : 05.09.2013
Current date  : 05.09.2013


Plant         : 1000
Description   : Werk Hamburg
-----------------------------------------------------------------
Material      : 100-100
Batch         :
Description   : Casing


Quantity      :                        1   PC
-----------------------------------------------------------------

Storage loc.  : 0001
Storage bin   :

Sales order   : 0000005014000010000
```

6.3.7 Goods Issue Labels

```
Material: 100-100
Vendor:
Plant/SL: 1000 0001
GR/ GI Number: 4900000008
GR/ GI Date: 05.09.2013
```

6.3.8 Material Document

The material document can be displayed using transaction MB02 or MB03.

Change Material Document 4900000008 : Details 0001 / 0001

| ◀ | ▶ | ⚇ | ⎙ | 🕮 Messages | Material | WM Details... |

| Movement Type | 231 | GI for sales order |
| Material | 100-100 | Casing |

Quantity in

| Unit of Entry | 1 | PC | Plant | 1000 | Stor. Loc. | 0001 |

Account Assignment

| G/L Account | 893010 |

Business Area	1000
Sales Order	5014	10	0
Goods recipient	

| Text | |

6.3.9   Accounting Documents

List of documents in accounting

In transaction MB02 or MB03 click `Accounting Documents...` in the item overview of the material document to see the accounting documents.

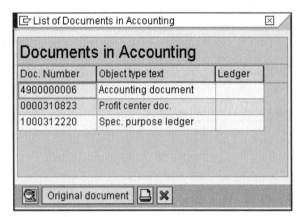

Accounting entries

Double-click the `Accounting document` to open it.

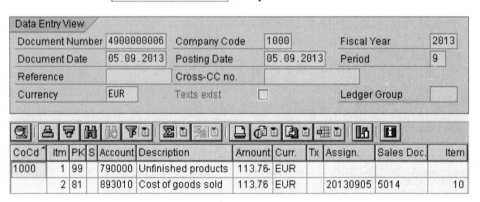

The sales order account is debited and inventory account is credited.

6.4 GOODS ISSUE FOR ASSET

Functional Consultant	User	Business Process Owner	Senior Management	My Rating	Understanding Level
A	A	B	X		

6.4.1 Scenario

You issue goods for asset.

6.4.2 Transaction

MIGO_GI—Goods Issue (MIGO)

6.4.3 Selection

| Goods Issue ▤ | Other ▤ | GI for asset | 241 |

6.4.4 Item Detail

Account Assignment

6.4.5 Posting Goods Issue

After the goods issue is entered, post it by clicking | Post |. The system posts only those items for which ☑ Item OK indicator is set.

6.4.6 Goods Issue Slip

You can see/print the GR/GI slip and labels using transaction MB90. Choose Processing mode 2 for Repeat processing. If GR/GI slip and/or labels are not generated, print indicator may not have been set in the goods movement screen, or printing may not be enabled in Output Determination (see Chapter 24).

```
G R / G I   S L I P                          4900000009/0001
---------------------------------------------------------------
Posting date  : 05.09.2013
Current date  : 05.09.2013

Plant         : 1000
Description   : Werk Hamburg
---------------------------------------------------------------
Material      : IT1007
Batch         :
Description   : IT Office Software License

Quantity      :                 10   PC
---------------------------------------------------------------

Storage loc.  : 0002
Storage bin   :

Asset         : 0000000033730000
```

6.4.7 Material Document

The material document can be displayed using transaction MB02 or MB03.

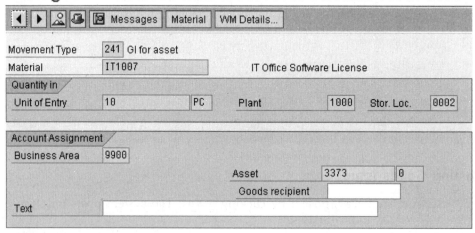

Change Material Document 4900000009 : Details 0001 / 0001

6.4.8 Accounting Documents

List of documents in accounting

In transaction MB02 or MB03 click ☐ Accounting Documents... in the item overview of the material document to see the accounting documents. Since this is a non-valuated material, there is no accounting document.

6.5 GOODS ISSUE FOR SALES

Functional Consultant	User	Business Process Owner	Senior Management	My Rating	Understanding Level
A	A	B	X		

6.5.1 Scenario

You issue goods for sales.

6.5.2 Transaction

MIGO_GI—Goods Issue (MIGO)

6.5.3 Selection

| Goods Issue | 🗒 | Other | 🗒 | | GI for sales | 251 |

6.5.4 Item Detail

Account Assignment

Material	Quantity	Where	Account Assignment

G/L account	
Business Area	
Cost Center	1000

6.5.5 Posting Goods Issue

After the goods issue is entered, post it by clicking ☐ Post . The system posts only those items for which ☑ Item OK indicator is set.

6.5.6 Goods Issue Slip

You can see/print the GR/GI slip and labels using transaction MB90. Choose Processing mode 2 for Repeat processing . If GR/GI slip and/or labels are not generated, print indicator may not have been set in the goods movement screen, or printing may not be enabled in Output Determination (see Chapter 24).

```
G R / G I   S L I P                          4900000010/0001
--------------------------------------------------------------
Posting date  : 05.09.2013
Current date  : 05.09.2013

Plant         : 1000
Description   : Werk Hamburg
--------------------------------------------------------------
Material      : 100-100
Batch         :
Description   : Casing

Quantity      :                    4   PC
--------------------------------------------------------------

Storage loc.  : 0001
Storage bin   :

Cost center   : 0000001000
```

6.5.7 Goods Issue Labels

```
Material: 100-100              Material: 100-100
Vendor:                        Vendor:
Plant/SL: 1000 0001            Plant/SL: 1000 0001
GR/ GI Number: 4900000010      GR/ GI Number: 4900000010
GR/ GI Date: 05.09.2013        GR/ GI Date: 05.09.2013
```

```
Material: 100-100              Material: 100-100
Vendor:                        Vendor:
Plant/SL: 1000 0001            Plant/SL: 1000 0001
GR/ GI Number: 4900000010      GR/ GI Number: 4900000010
GR/ GI Date: 05.09.2013        GR/ GI Date: 05.09.2013
```

6.5.8   Material Document

The material document can be displayed using transaction MB02 or MB03.

Change Material Document 4900000010 : Details 0001 / 0001

| ◀ | ▶ | 👤 | 🖨 | 🗒 Messages | Material | WM Details... |

Movement Type	251	GI for sales
Material	100-100	Casing

Quantity in						
Unit of Entry	4	PC	Plant	1000	Stor. Loc.	0001

Account Assignment		
G/L Account	890000	
Business Area	9900	
Cost Center	1000	Corporate Services
		Goods recipient
Text		

6.5.9   Accounting Documents

List of documents in accounting

In transaction MB02 or MB03 click Accounting Documents... in the item overview of the material document to see the accounting documents.

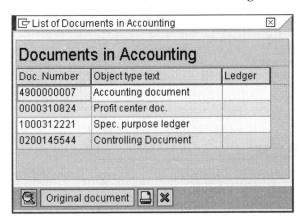

> ☞ List of Documents in Accounting   ☒
>
> ## Documents in Accounting
>
> | Doc. Number | Object type text | Ledger |
> |---|---|---|
> | 4900000007 | Accounting document | |
> | 0000310824 | Profit center doc. | |
> | 1000312221 | Spec. purpose ledger | |
> | 0200145544 | Controlling Document | |
>
> | 🔍 | Original document | 🖨 | ☒ |

Accounting entries

Double-click the Accounting document to open it.

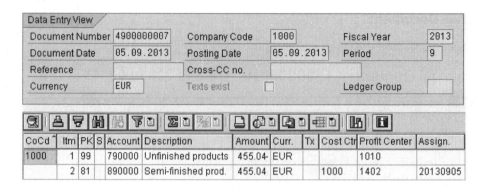

6.6 GOODS ISSUE FOR ORDER

Functional Consultant	User	Business Process Owner	Senior Management	My Rating	Understanding Level
A	A	B	X		

6.6.1 Scenario

You issue goods for an order.

6.6.2 Transaction

MIGO_GI—Goods Issue (MIGO)

6.6.3 Selection

A07 Goods Issue	R10 Other		GI for order	261

6.6.4 Item Detail

Account Assignment

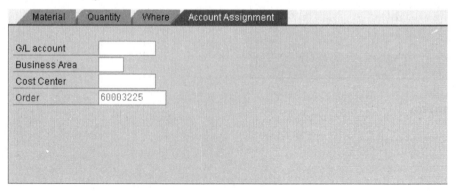

6.6.5 Posting Goods Issue

After the goods issue is entered, post it by clicking Post . The system posts only those items for which ☑ Item OK indicator is set.

6.6.6 Goods Issue Slip

You can see/print the GR/GI slip and labels using transaction MB90. Choose Processing mode 2 for Repeat processing . If GR/GI slip and/or labels are not generated, print indicator may not have been set in the goods movement screen, or printing may not be enabled in Output Determination (see Chapter 24).

```
G R / G I   S L I P                    4900000011/0001
--------------------------------------------------------------
Posting date  : 05.09.2013
Current date  : 05.09.2013

Plant         : 1000
Description   : Werk Hamburg
--------------------------------------------------------------
Material      : 100-110
Batch         :
Description   : Slug for spiral casing

Quantity      :                    5   PC
--------------------------------------------------------------

Storage loc.  : 0001
Storage bin   :

Prod. order   : 000060003225
```

6.6.7 Material Document

The material document can be displayed using transaction MB02 or MB03.

Change Material Document 4900000011 : Details 0001 / 0001

| ◀ | ▶ | ☒ | 🖨 | 🗐 Messages | Material | WM Details... |

Movement Type	261	GI for order
Material	100-110	Slug for spiral casing

Quantity in

| Unit of Entry | 5 | PC | Plant | 1000 | Stor. Loc. | 0001 |

Account Assignment

G/L Account	400000
Business Area	1000
Cost Center	
Order	60003225	Casing
	Goods recipient
Text	

6.6.8 Accounting Documents

List of documents in accounting

In transaction MB02 or MB03 click [Accounting Documents...] in the item overview of the material document to see the accounting documents.

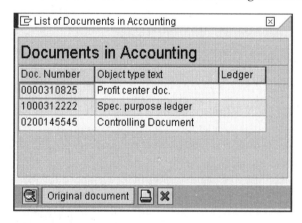

Accounting entries

This material is valuated at moving average price [Price control [V]]. Also, its moving average price is zero [Moving price [0.00]]. Hence, the system did not create any accounting document for this transaction.

6.7   GOODS ISSUE FOR NETWORK

Functional Consultant	User	Business Process Owner	Senior Management	My Rating	Understanding Level
A	A	B	X		

6.7.1   Scenario

You issue goods for a network.

6.7.2   Transaction

MIGO_GI—Goods Issue (MIGO)

6.7.3   Selection

| Goods Issue | 📄 | Other | 📄 | | GI for network | 281 | |

6.7.4   Item Detail

Account Assignment

| Material | Quantity | Where | **Account Assignment** |

G/L account   [ ]
Business Area   [ ]

Network   [902799] [1000]

6.7.5   Posting Goods Issue

After the goods issue is entered, post it by clicking [Post]. The system posts only those items for which ☑ Item OK indicator is set.

6.7.6   Goods Issue Slip

You can see/print the GR/GI slip and labels using transaction MB90. Choose Processing mode [2] for Repeat processing. If GR/GI slip and/or labels are not generated, print indicator may not have been set in the goods movement screen, or printing may not be enabled in Output Determination (see Chapter 24).

```
G R / G I   S L I P                              4900000012/0001
-----------------------------------------------------------------
Posting date  : 05.09.2013
Current date  : 05.09.2013

Plant         : 1000
Description   : Werk Hamburg
-----------------------------------------------------------------
Material      : 100-100
Batch         :
Description   : Casing

Quantity      :                     2   PC
-----------------------------------------------------------------

Storage loc.  : 0001
Storage bin   :

Network       : 000000902799/1000
```

6.7.7 Goods Issue Labels

```
Material: 100-100                   Material: 100-100
Vendor:                             Vendor:
Plant/SL: 1000 0001                 Plant/SL: 1000 0001
GR/ GI Number: 4900000012           GR/ GI Number: 4900000012
GR/ GI Date: 05.09.2013             GR/ GI Date: 05.09.2013
```

6.7.8 Material Document

The material document can be displayed using transaction MB02 or MB03.

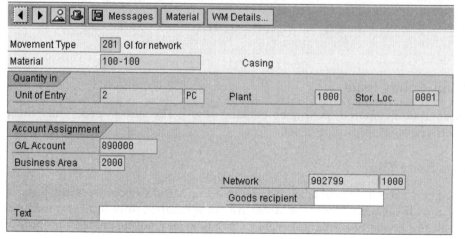

Change Material Document 4900000012 : Details 0001 / 0001

6.7.9 Accounting Documents

List of documents in accounting

In transaction MB02 or MB03 click Accounting Documents... in the item overview of the material document to see the accounting documents.

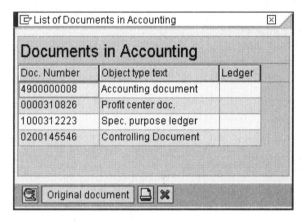

Accounting entries

Double-click the Accounting document to open it.

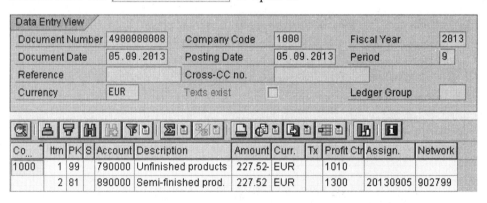

The network account is debited and inventory account is credited.

6.8 GOODS ISSUE FOR ALL ACCOUNT ASSIGNMENTS

Functional Consultant	User	Business Process Owner	Senior Management	My Rating	Understanding Level
A	A	B	X		

6.8.1 Scenario

You can use movement type 291 for making any account assignment for the goods issue.

6.8.2 Transaction

MIGO_GI—Goods Issue (MIGO)

6.8.3 Selection

| Goods Issue 🗎 | Other 🗎 | | GI all acc. assigmts | 291 |

6.8.4 Item Detail

Account Assignment

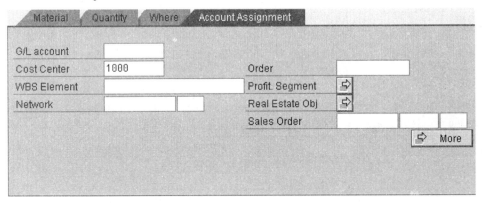

6.8.5 Posting Goods Issue

After the goods issue is entered, post it by clicking Post . The system posts only those items for which ☑ Item OK indicator is set.

6.8.6   Goods Issue Slip

You can see/print the GR/GI slip and labels using transaction MB90. Choose Processing mode 2 for Repeat processing. If GR/GI slip and/or labels are not generated, print indicator may not have been set in the goods movement screen, or printing may not be enabled in Output Determination (see Chapter 24).

```
G R / G I   S L I P                      4900000013/0001
-------------------------------------------------------
Posting date  : 05.09.2013
Current date  : 05.09.2013

Plant         : 1000
Description   : Werk Hamburg
-------------------------------------------------------
Material      : 100-100
Batch         :
Description   : Casing

Quantity      :                 5  PC
-------------------------------------------------------
Storage loc.  : 0001
Storage bin   :

Cost center   : 0000001000
```

6.8.7   Goods Issue Labels

```
Material: 100-100            Material: 100-100
Vendor:                      Vendor:
Plant/SL: 1000 0001          Plant/SL: 1000 0001
GR/ GI Number: 4900000013    GR/ GI Number: 4900000013
GR/ GI Date: 05.09.2013      GR/ GI Date: 05.09.2013
```

6.8.8 Material Document

The material document can be displayed using transaction MB02 or MB03.

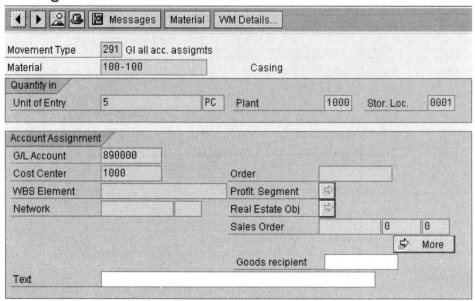

6.8.9 Accounting Documents

List of documents in accounting

In transaction MB02 or MB03 click [Accounting Documents...] in the item overview of the material document to see the accounting documents.

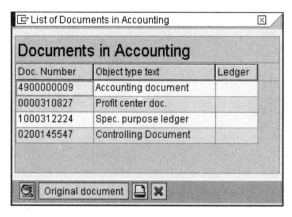

Accounting entries

Double-click the [Accounting document] to open it.

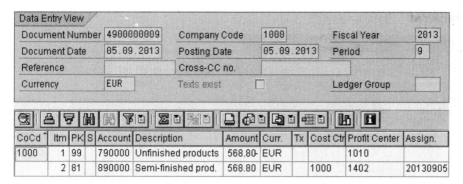

The cost center account is debited and inventory account is credited.

6.9 GOODS ISSUE FOR SAMPLING

Functional Consultant	User	Business Process Owner	Senior Management	My Rating	Understanding Level
A	A	B	X		

6.9.1 Scenario

You issue goods for sampling.

6.9.2 Transaction

MIGO_GI—Goods Issue (MIGO)

6.9.3 Selection

Goods Issue	Other		GI to sampling unre.	333

6.9.4 Item Detail

Where

Material	Quantity	Where	Account Assignment

Movement Type	333	- GI to sampling unre.	Stock type	Unrestricted use
Plant	Werk Hamburg	1000
Storage Location	Materiallager	0001
Goods recipient		
Unloading Point		
Text		

Account Assignment

Material	Quantity	Where	Account Assignment

G/L account	
Business Area	
Cost Center	1000

6.9.5 Posting Goods Issue

After the goods issue is entered, post it by clicking [Post] . The system posts only those items for which ☑ Item OK indicator is set.

6.9.6 Goods Issue Slip

You can see/print the GR/GI slip and labels using transaction MB90. Choose Processing mode [2] for Repeat processing . If GR/GI slip and/or labels are not generated, print indicator may not have been set in the goods movement screen, or printing may not be enabled in Output Determination (see Chapter 24).

6.9.7 Material Document

The material document can be displayed using transaction MB02 or MB03.

Change Material Document 4900000014 : Details 0001 / 0001

◀ ▶ 🔒 🐷 🗐 Messages | Material | WM Details...

Movement Type	333	GI to sampling unre.
Material	100-100	Casing

Quantity in

Unit of Entry	2	PC	Plant	1000	Stor. Loc.	0001

Account Assignment

G/L Account	237000	
Business Area	9900	
Cost Center	1000	Corporate Services
		Goods recipient

Text	

6.9.8   Accounting Documents

List of documents in accounting

In transaction MB02 or MB03 click [Accounting Documents...] in the item overview of the material document to see the accounting documents.

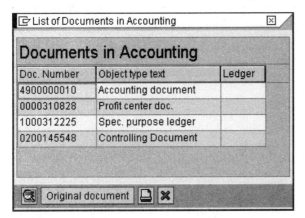

Accounting entries

Double-click the [Accounting document] to open it.

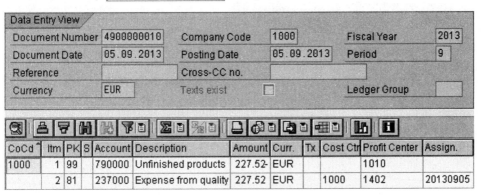

The quality expense account is debited and inventory account is credited.

6.10 GOODS ISSUE FOR SCRAPPING

Functional Consultant	User	Business Process Owner	Senior Management	My Rating	Understanding Level
A	A	B	X		

6.10.1 Scenario

You issue goods for scrapping.

6.10.2 Transaction

MIGO_GI—Goods Issue (MIGO)

6.10.3 Selection

| Goods Issue ▤ | Other ▤ | | GI scrapping | 551 | |

6.10.4 Item Detail

Where

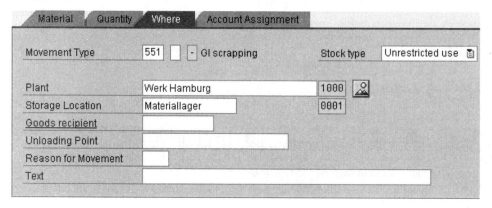

Account Assignment

| Material | Quantity | Where | Account Assignment |

G/L account [ ]
Business Area [ ]
Cost Center [1000]

6.10.5   Posting Goods Issue

After the goods issue is entered, post it by clicking [Post]. The system posts only those items for which ☑ Item OK indicator is set.

6.10.6   Goods Issue Slip

You can see/print the GR/GI slip and labels using transaction MB90. Choose Processing mode [2] for Repeat processing. If GR/GI slip and/or labels are not generated, print indicator may not have been set in the goods movement screen, or printing may not be enabled in Output Determination (see Chapter 24).

6.10.7   Material Document

The material document can be displayed using transaction MB02 or MB03.

Change Material Document 4900000015 : Details 0001 / 0001

| ◄ | ► | | | Messages | Material | WM Details... |

Movement Type [551] GI scrapping
Material [100-100]   Casing

Quantity in
Unit of Entry [3]   PC   Plant [1000]   Stor. Loc. [0001]

Account Assignment
G/L Account [890001]
Business Area [9900]
Cost Center [1000]   Corporate Services
                              Goods recipient [ ]
Text [ ]

6.10.8 Accounting Documents

List of documents in accounting

In transaction MB02 or MB03 click | Accounting Documents... | in the item overview of the material document to see the accounting documents.

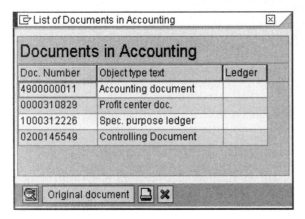

Accounting entries

Double-click the | Accounting document | to open it.

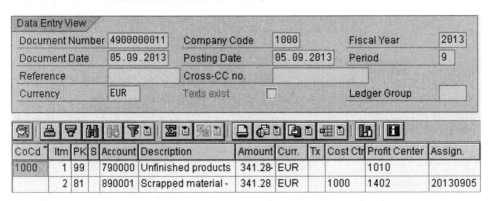

The scrapped material account is debited and inventory account is credited.

Goods Return

7.1 GOODS RETURN TO VENDOR

Functional Consultant	User	Business Process Owner	Senior Management	My Rating	Understanding Level
A	A	B	X		

7.1.1 Scenario

You want to return material to the vendor.

7.1.2 Transaction

MIGO—Goods Movement (MIGO)

7.1.3 Selection

Enter the purchase order number (and item) here, or double-click on the purchase order number in the document overview.

7.1.4 Selecting the Goods Receipt of Return Item

Possible candidates

When you select a purchase order, the system inserts appropriate goods receipts in the item overview.

Line	Mat. Sho	OK	Qty	E	SLoc	M	D	Plnt	Sp	Vendor	Purchase	Item	Ref. Doc.
16	Gehäuse	☐	1	PC		122	-	Werk		Müller KG	4500017087	10	5000000000
17	Gehäuse	☐	4	PC		122	-	Werk		Müller KG	4500017087	10	5000000001
18	Gehäuse	☐	10	PC		122	-	Werk		Müller KG	4500017087	10	5000000010

Selecting the goods receipt whose material is being returned

Out of these you need to select the goods receipt whose material is being returned. Usually the selection is based on the reference document (material document number under which the material was received). Click in the OK column of that item to ☑ it. Click 🗑 Delete button to delete items where OK column is ☐.

7.1.5 Item Detail

Quantity

Quantity and unit

Enter the quantity and the unit. You may return the full quantity received, or partial quantity. But you cannot return more goods than received under the reference document.

Where

Movement type

Movement type should be 122.

Stock type

Enter the stock type.

Storage location

Enter the storage location.

Reason for movement

You can select from the reasons for movement configured for this movement type. Configuration for a movement type also specifies whether reason for movement is mandatory, or optional, or whether the field is hidden.

Purchase Order Data

Material	Quantity	Where	Purchase Order Data	Partner	Account Assignment

Purchase Order	4500017087	10		Item Category	Standard
Reference Document	5000000001	1			
"Del.Completed" Ind.	1 Set automatic			☐ Del. Compl. Ind. PO Item	
Incoterms	CPT				

Purchase order

The system shows the purchase order number against which the goods were received, which is now being returned to the vendor.

Reference document number

Note that the reference document number refers to the material document number of the goods receipt.

7.1.6 Posting Goods Return

After the goods return is entered, post it by clicking Post . The system posts only those items for which ☑ Item OK indicator is set.

7.1.7 Goods Return Slip

You can see/print the GR/GI slip and labels using transaction MB90. Choose Processing mode 2 for Repeat processing. If GR/GI slip and/or labels are not generated, print indicator may not have been set in the goods movement screen, or printing may not be enabled in Output Determination (see Chapter 24).

```
R E T U R N   D E L I V E R Y   S L I P   5000000018/0001
------------------------------------------------------------
Goods receipt date : 06.09.2013
Current date       : 06.09.2013
------------------------------------------------------------
Plant       : 1000
Description : Werk Hamburg

Vendor      : 0000001002          Delivery note:
Name        : Müller KG
PO          : 4500017087/00010
Pur. group  : 000   Chef,H.       Telephone    : 069/5510
------------------------------------------------------------
Material    : 100-100
Batch       :
Description : Gehäuse

Quantity    :                2  PC
------------------------------------------------------------
W A R E H O U S E   I N F O R M A T I O N

Storage loc.: 0001
Storage bin :
------------------------------------------------------------
Reas./ret. del. : Poor quality

Issued by   : SAPUSER   S I G N A T U R E
```

7.1.8 Goods Return Labels

```
Material: 100-100            Material: 100-100
Vendor: Müller KG            Vendor: Müller KG
Plant/SL: 1000 0001          Plant/SL: 1000 0001
GR/ GI Number: 5000000018    GR/ GI Number: 5000000018
GR/ GI Date: 06.09.2013      GR/ GI Date: 06.09.2013
```

7.1.9 Material Document

The material document can be displayed using transaction MB02 or MB03.

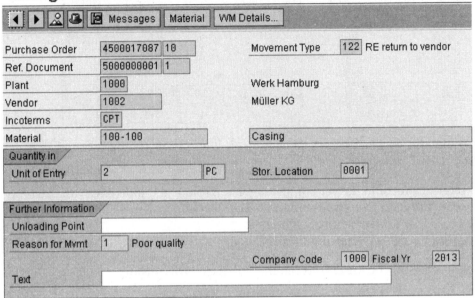

7.1.10 Accounting Documents

List of documents in accounting

In transaction MB02 or MB03 click [Accounting Documents...] in the item overview of the material document to see the accounting documents.

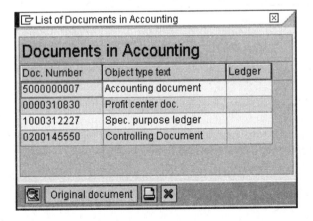

Accounting entries

Double-click the Accounting document to open it.

Data Entry View						
Document Number	5000000007	Company Code	1000		Fiscal Year	2013
Document Date	06.09.2013	Posting Date	06.09.2013		Period	9
Reference		Cross-CC no.				
Currency	EUR	Texts exist	☐		Ledger Group	

C...	Itm	PK	S	Account	Description	Amount	Curr.	Tx	Cost Ctr	Profit	Assignment
1000	1	99		790000	Unfinished products	227.52-	EUR			1010	
	2	86		191100	Goods Rcvd/Invoice F	120.00	EUR			1010	450001708700010
	3	83		281500	Income from price di	107.52	EUR		1000	1402	20130906

When you return material to the vendor, the invoice account, and if necessary the income/ loss from price difference account is credited. The GR/IR account is debited.

7.1.11 Purchase Order History

Run transaction ME22N or ME23N to see the purchase order history.

Sh. Text	MvT	Material Document	Item	Posting Date	∑ Quantity	OUn	∑ Amount in LC	L.cur
WE	122	5000000018	0001	06.09.2013	2.000-	PC	120.00-	EUR

The purchase order history for return delivery to vendor shows that both quantity and amount have negative values because the goods receipt had positive values.

7.2 GOODS RETURN FROM GR BLOCKED STOCK

Functional Consultant	User	Business Process Owner	Senior Management	My Rating	Understanding Level
A	A	B	X		

7.2.1 Scenario

If you receive material in GR blocked stock, you can return it to vendor. This process cannot be used for returning material received in valuated GR blocked stock.

7.2.2 Transaction

MIGO—Goods Movement (MIGO)

7.2.3 Selection

| A01 Goods Receipt 🗓 | R01 Purchase Order🗓 | | | Plant | | ⊕ 🖩 | 🔲 | GR rtrn blocked stck | 124 |

7.2.4 Item Overview

When you select a purchase order, the system inserts goods receipts of movement type 103 as possible candidates for returning goods to vendor from GR blocked stock. However, you cannot move goods if

➢ The original goods movement has been reversed using movement type 104.

➢ The goods have already been moved earlier using movement type 105.

➢ The material received has been returned to the vendor using movement type 124.

If the above has happened for partial quantity, you can reverse the balance quantity. The system should not give you valuated GR blocked stock in the item overview. Even if it does, you will not be able to post them.

7.2.5 Item Detail

Quantity

Material	Quantity	Where	Purchase Order Data	Partner	Account Assignment

Qty in Unit of Entry	4	PC 🖫
Qty in SKU	4	PC
Qty in Delivery Note		
Quantity Ordered	200	PC
	No. Containers	

Quantity and unit

Enter the quantity and the unit. You may return the full quantity received, or partial quantity. But you cannot return more goods than received under the reference document.

Where

Material	Quantity	Where	Purchase Order Data	Partner	Account Assignment

Movement Type [124] ☐ [-] GR rtrn blocked stck

Plant Werk Hamburg [1000] 🔲

Goods recipient ☐

Unloading Point ☐

Reason for Movement [1] Poor quality

Text ☐

Movement type

Movement type should be 124.

No stock type

Material in GR blocked stock does not have any stock type. Hence, you do not specify the stock type from which inventory is to be reduced.

No storage location

Material in GR blocked stock is stored at plant level, not at storage location level. Hence, when returning the material to vendor, you do not specify storage location.

Reason for movement

You can select from the reasons for movement configured for this movement type. Configuration for a movement type also specifies whether reason for movement is mandatory, or optional, or whether the field is hidden.

Purchase Order Data

Material	Quantity	Where	Purchase Order Data	Partner	Account Assignment

Purchase Order [4500017087] [10] 🔲 Item Category Standard
Reference Document [5000000011] [1]

☐ Del. Compl. Ind. PO Item

Incoterms CPT

Purchase order

The system shows the purchase order number against which the goods were received, which is now being returned to the vendor.

Reference document number

Note that the reference document number refers to the material document number of the goods receipt in GR blocked stock.

No delivery completion indicator

When you return material to the vendor, you do not set delivery completion indicator.

7.2.6 Posting Goods Return

After the goods return is entered, post it by clicking Post . The system posts only those items for which ☑ Item OK indicator is set.

7.2.7 Goods Return Slip

You can see/print the GR/GI slip and labels using transaction MB90. Choose Processing mode 2 for Repeat processing . If GR/GI slip and/or labels are not generated, print indicator may not have been set in the goods movement screen, or printing may not be enabled in Output Determination (see Chapter 24).

```
R E T U R N   D E L I V E R Y   S L I P   5000000019/0001
-----------------------------------------------------------------
Goods receipt date : 06.09.2013
Current date       : 06.09.2013
-----------------------------------------------------------------
Plant       : 1000
Description : Werk Hamburg

Vendor      : 0000001002          Delivery note:
Name        : Müller KG
PO          : 4500017087/00010
Pur. group  : 000   Chef,H.       Telephone    : 069/5510
-----------------------------------------------------------------
Material    : 100-100
Batch       :
Description : Gehäuse

Quantity    :              4   PC
-----------------------------------------------------------------
W A R E H O U S E   I N F O R M A T I O N

Storage loc.:
Storage bin :
-----------------------------------------------------------------
Reas./ret. del. : Poor quality

Issued by   : SAPUSER   S I G N A T U R E
```

Return to vendor from GR blocked stock not mentioned

Note that the goods receipt slip does not indicate that the item returned to the vendor is from the GR blocked stock. You may want to modify the goods receipt slip to include this.

7.2.8   Goods Return Labels

```
Material: 100-100            Material: 100-100
Vendor: Müller KG            Vendor: Müller KG
Plant/SL: 1000              Plant/SL: 1000
GR/ GI Number: 5000000019    GR/ GI Number: 5000000019
GR/ GI Date: 06.09.2013     GR/ GI Date: 06.09.2013
```

7.2.9   Material Document

The material document can be displayed using transaction MB02 or MB03.

Change Material Document 5000000019 : Details 0001 / 0001

| ◄ | ► | 👤 | 🖨 | 🗐 Messages | Material | WM Details... |

Purchase Order	4500017087	10	Movement Type	124	GR rtrn blocked stck
Ref. Document	5000000011	1			
Plant	1000		Werk Hamburg		
Vendor	1002		Müller KG		
Incoterms	CPT				
Material	100-100		Casing		

Quantity in

Unit of Entry	4	PC

Further Information

Unloading Point		
Reason for Mvmt	1	Poor quality
		Company Code 1000 Fiscal Yr 2013
Text		

7.2.10   Accounting Documents

List of documents in accounting

In transaction MB02 or MB03 click │ Accounting Documents... │ in the item overview of the material document to see the accounting documents. When the material is received in the GR blocked stock, it does not become a part of your inventory and no accounting documents are created. Hence, when the material is returned to vendor from the GR blocked stock no accounting documents are created.

7.2.11 Purchase Order History

Run transaction ME22N or ME23N to see the purchase order history.

Sh. Text	MvT	Material Document	Item	Posting Date	Σ Quantity	OUn	Σ Amount in LC	L.cur
WE	124	5000000019	0001	06.09.2013	0.000	PC	0.00	EUR

The purchase order history for return delivery to vendor shows that both quantity and amount have zero values because the goods receipt in GR blocked stock had zero values.

7.3 GOODS RETURN WITH AUTOMATIC PURCHASE ORDER CREATION

Functional Consultant	User	Business Process Owner	Senior Management	My Rating	Understanding Level
A	A	B	X		

7.3.1 Scenario

Sometimes you may return goods to a vendor. If you have the material document number of goods receipt for that item, you can use the return processes described earlier. If you do not have the material document number, you can create a purchase order with return items and return the goods. SAP simplifies this process further. It can automatically create the purchase order when you return the goods.

7.3.2 Enabling Automatic Purchase Order for a Movement Type

In view V_156_AB you can enable creation of automatic purchase orders for movement type 161 that is used for returning the goods to vendors.

MvT	Movement Type Text	Automatic PO
161	GR returns	☑
162	GR rtrns reversal	☐

7.3.3 Default Purchasing Organization

A purchase order is created for a purchasing organization. Therefore, in order to create a purchase order automatically, the system must determine the purchasing organization.

Purchasing organization is also needed for determining the price. You need to specify the price of the material in the purchase order you create. This price comes from the purchasing info record. But, price information is specified at purchasing organization level.

The system determines the default purchasing organization for a plant from view V_001W_E.

Plnt	POrg	Plant description
0001	0001	Werk 0001
0005	1000	Hamburg
0006	3000	New York
0007	1000	Werk Hamburg
0008	3000	New York

7.3.4 Transaction

MIGO—Goods Movement (MIGO)

7.3.5 Selection

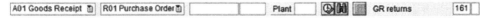

Do not enter the purchase order number and item number.

7.3.6 Item Overview

Click ![icon] to add a non-ordered item.

7.3.7 Item Detail

Material

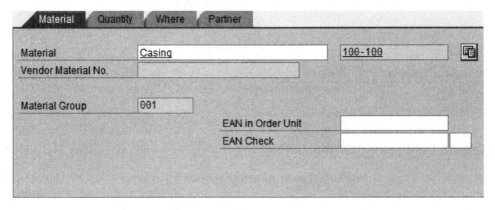

Quantity

Material	Quantity	Where	Partner

Qty in Unit of Entry	2	PC	
Qty in SKU	2	PC	Ext. Amount LC
Qty in Delivery Note			

No. Containers

Purchasing info record

The price of the material comes from the purchasing info record. Check whether the purchasing info record exists for the vendor material combination using transaction ME13.

Externally entered posting amount in local currency

The value of the movement is calculated automatically by the system. However, it is possible to manually enter the amount of the document item in the local currency of the company code if the item is to be valuated at a different price.

Where

Material	Quantity	Where	Partner

Movement Type	161	– GR returns	Stock type	Unrestricted use
Plant	Werk Hamburg	1000		
Storage Location	Materiallager	0001		
Goods recipient				
Unloading Point				
Reason for Movement				
Text				

Partner

Material	Quantity	Where	Partner

Vendor	KBB Schwarze Pumpe	111
Customer		

7.3.8   Posting Goods Return

After the goods return is entered, post it by clicking Post . The system posts only those items for which ☑ Item OK indicator is set.

7.3.9   Goods Return Slip

You can see/print the GR/GI slip and labels using transaction MB90. Choose Processing mode 2 for Repeat processing . If GR/GI slip and/or labels are not generated, print indicator may not have been set in the goods movement screen, or printing may not be enabled in Output Determination (see Chapter 24).

7.3.10   Material Document

The material document can be displayed using transaction MB02 or MB03.

Change Material Document 5000000020 : Details 0001 / 0001

◀ ▶ 🔍 🖨 🗗 Messages | Material | WM Details...

Purchase Order	4500017125 10	Movement Type	161 GR returns
Plant	1000	Werk Hamburg	
Vendor	111	KBB Schwarze Pumpe	
Incoterms	CIF	Franktenthal	
Material	100-100	Casing	

Quantity in			
Unit of Entry	2	PC	Stor. Location 0001
			☑ Deliv. Compl.

Further Information			
Unloading Point			
		Company Code 1000	Fiscal Yr 2013
Text			

Note that no purchase order was specified during goods return. The purchase order has been created automatically.

7.3.11 Accounting Documents

List of documents in accounting

In transaction MB02 or MB03 click Accounting Documents... in the item overview of the material document to see the accounting documents.

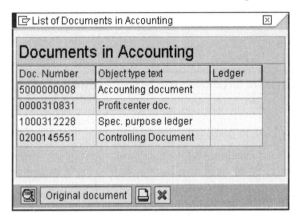

Accounting entries

Double-click the Accounting document to open it.

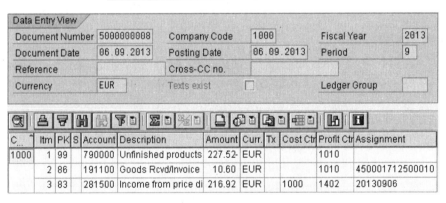

C...	Itm	PK	S	Account	Description	Amount	Curr.	Tx	Cost Ctr	Profit Ctr	Assignment
1000	1	99		790000	Unfinished products	227.52-	EUR			1010	
	2	86		191100	Goods Rcvd/Invoice	10.60	EUR			1010	450001712500010
	3	83		281500	Income from price di	216.92	EUR		1000	1402	20130906

7.3.12 Automatic Purchase Order Creation

The system automatically created the purchase order number 4500017125. You may display it using transaction ME22N.

S	Itm	Material	Short Text	P	O	Deliv. Date	Net Price	Curr	O	Returns Item	Fr	T	P
	10	100-100	Gehäuse	2	PC	06.09.2013	5.30	EUR	PC	☑	☐		

Note that the quantity shown is 2, but the return item indicator is ticked.

7.3.13 Purchase Order History

Run transaction ME22N or ME23N to see the purchase order history.

Sh. Text	MvT	Material Document	Item	Posting Date	∑ Quantity	OUn	∑ Amount in LC	L.cur
WE	161	5000000020	1	06.09.2013	2-	PC	10.60-	EUR
Tr./Ev. Goods receipt				■	**2- PC** ■		**10.60- EUR**	

Note that here the quantity shown is –2.

7.4 GOODS RETURN WITH PURCHASE ORDER HAVING RETURN ITEMS

Functional Consultant	User	Business Process Owner	Senior Management	My Rating	Understanding Level
A	A	B	X		

7.4.1 Scenario

Sometimes you may return goods to a vendor. If you have the material document number of goods receipt for that item, you can use the return processes described earlier. If you do not have the material document number, you can create a purchase order with return items and return the goods.

7.4.2 Purchase Order

You can return material to a vendor directly by creating a goods movement in Inventory Management. If you want to be more formal, you issue a purchase order, showing returns item.

S	Itm	A	I	Material	Short Text	PO Quantity	OUn	Plnt	Stor. Location	Returns Item
	10			100-100	Gehäuse	4	PC	Werk Hamburg	Materiallager	☑

7.4.3 Transaction

MIGO—Goods Movement (MIGO)

7.4.4 Selection

Use movement type 101. The system will automatically convert it to 161 for return items.

7.4.5 Item Overview

When you select a purchase order, the system inserts appropriate goods receipts in the item overview. For this process use purchase order having return items.

7.4.6 Item Detail

Material

Material,	Quantity	Where	Purchase Order Data	Partner	Account Assignment

Material	Gehäuse	100-100	
Vendor Material No.			
Material Group	001		
		EAN in Order Unit	
		EAN Check	

Quantity

Material	Quantity	Where	Purchase Order Data	Partner	Account Assignment

Qty in Unit of Entry	4	PC
Qty in SKU	4	PC
Qty in Delivery Note		
Quantity Ordered	4	PC
		No. Containers

Where

Material	Quantity	Where	Purchase Order Data	Partner	Account Assignment

Movement Type	161	- GR returns	Stock type	Unrestricted use

Plant	Werk Hamburg	1000
Storage Location	Materiallager	0001
Goods recipient		
Unloading Point		
Reason for Movement		
Text		

Purchase Order Data

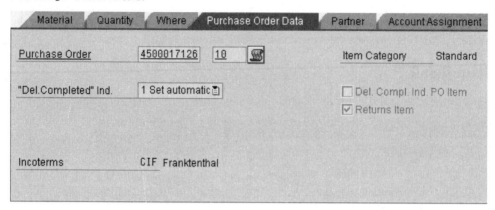

Partner

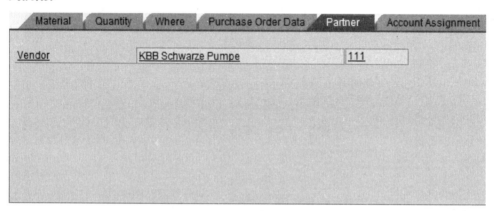

Account Assignment

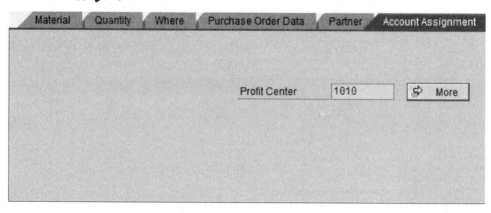

7.4.7 Posting Goods Return

After the goods return is entered, post it by clicking `Post`. The system posts only those items for which ☑ Item OK indicator is set.

7.4.8 Goods Return Slip

You can see/print the GR/GI slip and labels using transaction MB90. Choose `Processing mode` `2` for `Repeat processing`. If GR/GI slip and/or labels are not generated, print indicator may not have been set in the goods movement screen, or printing may not be enabled in Output Determination (see Chapter 24).

```
R E T U R N   D E L I V E R Y   S L I P   5000000021/0001
-----------------------------------------------------------.
Goods receipt date : 06.09.2013
Current date       : 06.09.2013
-----------------------------------------------------------.
Plant       : 1000
Description : Werk Hamburg

Vendor      : 0000000111        Delivery note:
Name        : KBB Schwarze Pumpe
PO          : 4500017126/00010
Pur. group  : 000   Chef,H.     Telephone    : 069/5510
-----------------------------------------------------------
Material    : 100-100
Batch       :
Description : Gehäuse

Quantity    :                4  PC
-----------------------------------------------------------.
W A R E H O U S E   I N F O R M A T I O N

Storage loc.: 0001
Storage bin :
-----------------------------------------------------------.

Issued by   : SAPUSER   S I G N A T U R E
```

7.4.9 Goods Return Labels

```
Material: 100-100              Material: 100-100
Vendor: KBB Schwarze Pumpe     Vendor: KBB Schwarze Pumpe
Plant/SL: 1000 0001            Plant/SL: 1000 0001
GR/ GI Number: 5000000021      GR/ GI Number: 5000000021
GR/ GI Date: 06.09.2013        GR/ GI Date: 06.09.2013
```

7.4.10 Material Document

The material document can be displayed using transaction MB02 or MB03.

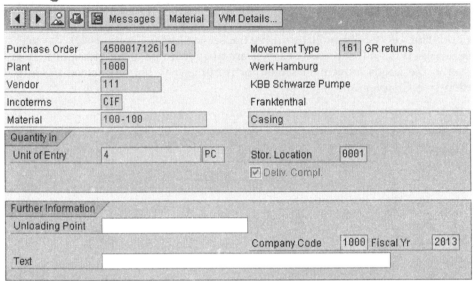

Change Material Document 5000000021 : Details 0001 / 0001

7.4.11 Accounting Documents

List of documents in accounting

In transaction MB02 or MB03 click Accounting Documents... in the item overview of the material document to see the accounting documents.

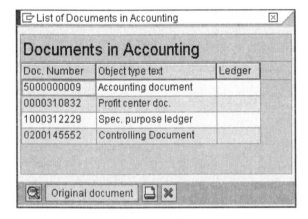

Accounting entries

Double-click the [Accounting document] to open it.

Data Entry View						
Document Number	5000000009	Company Code	1000	Fiscal Year		2013
Document Date	06.09.2013	Posting Date	06.09.2013	Period		9
Reference		Cross-CC no.				
Currency	EUR	Texts exist	☐	Ledger Group		

C...	Itm	PK	S	Account	Description	Amount	Curr.	Tx	Cost Ctr	Profit Ctr	Assignment
1000	1	99		790000	Unfinished products	455.04-	EUR			1010	
	2	86		191100	Goods Rcvd/Invoice	21.20	EUR			1010	450001712600010
	3	83		281500	Income from price di	433.84	EUR		1000	1402	20130906

7.4.12 Purchase Order History

Run transaction ME22N or ME23N to see the purchase order history.

Sh. Text	MvT	Material Document	Item	Posting Date	Σ Quantity	OUn	Σ Amount in LC	L.cur
WE	161	5000000021	1	06.09.2013	4-	PC	21.20-	EUR
Tr./Ev. Goods receipt					**4- PC**		**21.20- EUR**	

Note that here the quantity shown is –4.

Stock Transfer

8.1 STOCK TRANSFER WITHIN A PLANT

Functional Consultant	User	Business Process Owner	Senior Management	My Rating	Understanding Level
A	A	B	X		

8.1.1 Scenario

You transfer material from one store to another within a plant.

8.1.2 Transaction

MIGO_TR—Transfer Posting (MIGO)

8.1.3 Selection

| A08 Transfer Posting ▤ | R10 Other ▤ | | TF tfr. within plant | 311 | |

8.1.4   Item Detail

Transfer Posting

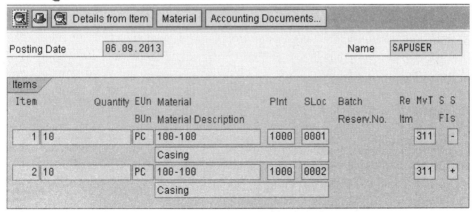

8.1.5   Posting Goods Transfer

After the goods transfer is entered, post it by clicking [Post].

8.1.6   Material Document

The material document can be displayed using transaction MB02 or MB03.

Change Material Document 4900000016 : Overview

[🔍] [🖨] [🔍] Details from Item | Material | Accounting Documents...

Posting Date 06.09.2013   Name SAPUSER

Item	Quantity	EUn	Material	Plnt	SLoc	Batch	Re	MvT	S	S
		BUn	Material Description			Reserv.No.	Itm			FIs
1	10	PC	100-100	1000	0001			311	-	
			Casing							
2	10	PC	100-100	1000	0002			311	+	
			Casing							

You can see that the storage location from which the goods are transferred is credited, and the storage location which has received the goods is debited.

8.1.7 Accounting Documents

List of documents in accounting

In transaction MB02 or MB03 click [Accounting Documents...] in the item overview of the material document to see the accounting documents. No accounting document is generated because the material remains within the same plant.

8.2 STOCK TRANSFER BETWEEN PLANTS IN ONE STEP

Functional Consultant	User	Business Process Owner	Senior Management	My Rating	Understanding Level
A	A	B	X		

8.2.1 Scenario

You transfer material from one plant to another in a single step.

8.2.2 Transaction

MIGO_TR—Transfer Posting (MIGO)

8.2.3 Selection

| A08 Transfer Posting 🖺 | R10 Other 🖺 | | TF tfr.plnt.to plnt. | 301 |

8.2.4   Item Detail

Transfer Posting

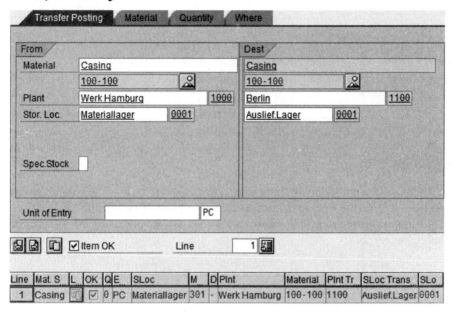

8.2.5   Posting Goods Transfer

After the goods transfer is entered, post it by clicking Post .

8.2.6   Goods Issue Slip

You can see the goods issue slip using transaction MB90. Choose Repeat processing for Repeat processing .

```
G R / G I   S L I P                        4900000017/0001
-----------------------------------------------------------------
Posting date   : 06.09.2013
Current date   : 06.09.2013

Plant          : 1000
Description    : Werk Hamburg
-----------------------------------------------------------------
Material       : 100-100
Batch          :
Description    : Casing

Quantity       :                5  PC
-----------------------------------------------------------------

Storage loc.   : 0001
Storage bin    :
```

Note that the plant number is 1000, which is the issuing plant.

8.2.7 Goods Issue Labels

You can see the goods issue labels using transaction MB90. Choose `Processing mode` `2` for Repeat processing.

```
Material: 100-100            Material: 100-100
Vendor:                     Vendor:
Plant/SL: 1000 0001         Plant/SL: 1000 0001
GR/ GI Number: 4900000017   GR/ GI Number: 4900000017
GR/ GI Date: 06.09.2013     GR/ GI Date: 06.09.2013
```

Note that the plant number is 1000, which is the issuing plant.

8.2.8 Goods Receipt Slip

You can see/print the GR/GI slip and labels using transaction MB90. Choose `Processing mode` `2` for Repeat processing. If GR/GI slip and/or labels are not generated, print indicator may not have been set in the goods movement screen, or printing may not be enabled in Output Determination (see Chapter 24).

```
G R / G I   S L I P                       4900000017/0002
-----------------------------------------------------------------
Posting date  : 06.09.2013
Current date  : 06.09.2013

Plant         : 1100
Description   : Berlin
-----------------------------------------------------------------
Material      : 100-100
Batch         :
Description   : Casing

Quantity      :                    5   PC
-----------------------------------------------------------------

Storage loc.  : 0001
Storage bin   :
```

Note that the plant number is 1100, which is the receiving plant.

8.2.9 Goods Receipt Labels

```
Material: 100-100            Material: 100-100
Vendor:                     Vendor:
Plant/SL: 1100 0001         Plant/SL: 1100 0001
GR/ GI Number: 4900000017   GR/ GI Number: 4900000017
GR/ GI Date: 06.09.2013     GR/ GI Date: 06.09.2013
```

Note that the plant number is 1100, which is the receiving plant.

8.2.10   Material Document

The material document can be displayed using transaction MB02 or MB03.

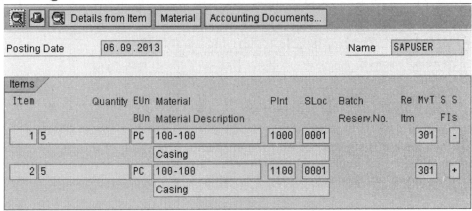

You can see that the goods are transferred from one plant to another.

8.2.11   Accounting Documents

List of documents in accounting

In transaction MB02 or MB03 click | Accounting Documents... | in the item overview of the material document to see the accounting documents.

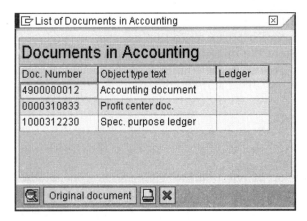

Accounting entries

Double-click the | Accounting document | to open it.

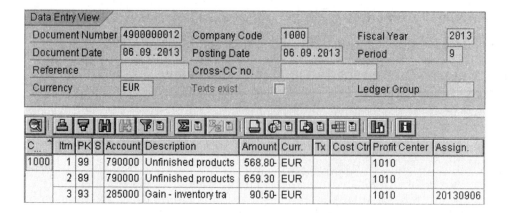

The material may have different prices in different plants. The value of transfer is equal to the value of stock in the issuing plant. Difference is posted in the receiving plant as gain or loss from inventory transfer.

8.3 STOCK TRANSFER BETWEEN PLANTS IN TWO STEPS

Functional Consultant	User	Business Process Owner	Senior Management	My Rating	Understanding Level
A	A	B	X		

8.3.1 Scenario

When you transfer material from one plant to another in one step, the receiving plant has no control over the transaction. Some companies prefer to do this transfer in two steps. In the first step the supplying plant transfers the material out of his plant and storage location into In Transfer (Plant) of the receiving plant. In the second step, the receiving plant moves the material from In Transfer (Plant) to his plant and storage location.

8.3.2 Transfer Out

Process Step

You transfer material from a storage location of one plant to In Transfer (Plant) of another plant.

Transaction

MIGO_TR—Transfer Posting (MIGO)

Selection

A08 Transfer Posting   R10 Other   TF rem.fm.stor.to pl   303

Item Detail

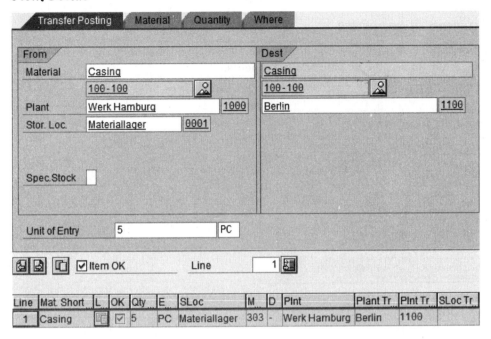

Posting Goods Transfer Out

After the goods transfer is entered, post it by clicking | Post |.

Material Document

The material document can be displayed using transaction MB02 or MB03.

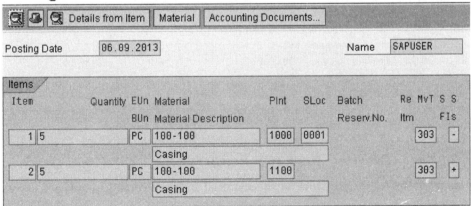

Note that the system automatically creates an item for receiving plant because it has to put the material in In Transfer (Plant) in that plant.

Accounting Documents

List of documents in accounting

In transaction MB02 or MB03 click [Accounting Documents...] in the item overview of the material document to see the accounting documents.

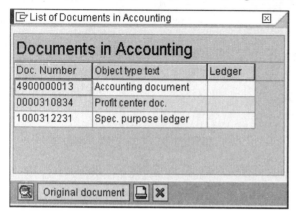

Accounting entries

Double-click the [Accounting document] to open it.

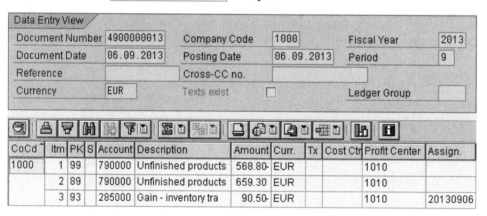

The material may have different prices in different plants. The value of transfer is equal to the value of stock in the issuing plant. Difference is posted in the receiving plant as gain or loss from inventory transfer.

Stock of Material in Receiving Plant after Transfer Out

Run transaction MM02 to see the stock of the material in the receiving plant.

Stock of the material in the receiving plant shows the transferred stock in the field In Transfer (Plant).

8.3.3   Transfer In

Process Step

You transfer material from In Transfer (Plant) to a storage location.

Transaction

MIGO_TR—Transfer Posting (MIGO)

Selection

| A08 Transfer Posting | R10 Other | | TF pl.in stor.in pl. | 305 |

Item Detail

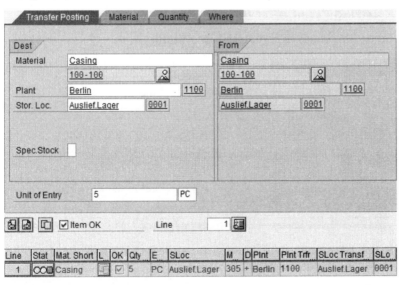

Note that you can also transfer the material to a special stock.

Posting Goods Transfer In

After the goods transfer is entered, post it by clicking Post.

Material Document

The material document can be displayed using transaction MB02 or MB03.

Change Material Document 4900000019 : Overview

		Details from Item	Material	Accounting Documents...		

Posting Date   06.09.2013   Name   SAPUSER

Items

Item	Quantity	EUn	Material	Plnt	SLoc	Batch	Re	MvT	S	S
		BUn	Material Description			Reserv.No.	Itm			FIs
1 5		PC	100-100	1100	0001			305	+	
			Casing							

Accounting Documents

List of documents in accounting

In transaction MB02 or MB03 click Accounting Documents... in the item overview of the material document to see the accounting documents. Since accounting entries are already passed during transfer out process, there are no accounting entries now.

Stock of Material in Receiving Plant after Transfer In

Run transaction MM02 to see the stock of a material in a plant.

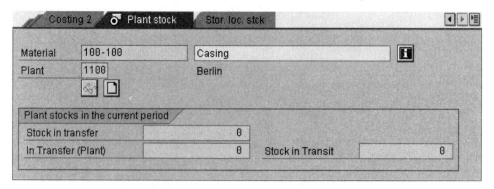

Stock of the material in the receiving plant shows the transferred stock in the field In Transfer (Plant). After transfer in, the stock becomes zero.

8.4 STOCK TRANSFER USING STO OR PURCHASE ORDER

Functional Consultant	User	Business Process Owner	Senior Management	My Rating	Understanding Level
A	B	C	X		

8.4.1 Scenario

Sometimes companies want to transfer material from one plant to another using a formal process. The supplying plant is the vendor, and the receiving plant the customer. The receiving plant raises a stock transport order or a purchase order. The supplying plant creates a delivery, issues goods, and if necessary, raises an invoice. The receiving plant receives goods and processes invoice. This section explains the prerequisites necessary for this process to work. Subsequent sections demonstrate the process.

8.4.2 Stock Transport Order

A stock transport order is a purchase order with following differences.

Purchase order: vendor

When you raise a purchase order using transaction ME21N, you specify a vendor.

| 🛒 | NB Standard PO | 🗐 | | Vendor | | | Doc. date | 07.09.2013 |

A stock transport order is a purchase order that you create using transaction ME21N.

Stock transport order: supplying plant

If you select 🛒 UB Stock transport ord.🗐, the screen changes, and instead of specifying the vendor, you specify the supplying plant.

| 🛒 | UB Stock transport ord. 🗐 | | | Supplying Plant | 1100 Berlin | Doc. date | 07.09.2013 |

Stock transport order: item category

In the item category field, you select U.

🗓📝	S	It.	A	I	Material	Short Text	PO Qua	O	C	Deliv. Date	C	Plnt	Stor. Location
		10		U	100-100	Gehäuse	4	PC	D	17.09.2013	EUR	Werk Hamburg	Materiallager

8.4.3 Stock Transfer Scenarios

Scenario	STO/PO	Delivery	Invoice	Goods issue	Goods receipt	Section
Stock transfer using STO without delivery	STO	No	No	Yes	Yes	8.5
Stock transfer using STO with delivery via shipping	STO	Yes	No	Yes	Yes	8.6
Stock transfer using purchase order	PO	Yes	Yes	Yes	Yes	8.7
Stock transfer between storage locations using STO	STO	Yes	No	Yes	Yes	8.8

In a purchase order you specify the vendor; hence the supplying plant must be created as a vendor. In an STO, you specify the supplying plant; hence you do not need a vendor number for the supplying plant.

If the process involves creation of a delivery, a customer must be created for the plant. It should also be possible to determine the delivery type, the sales area and the shipping point.

8.4.4 Material Master

Purpose

The material master record for the material must exist in both the supplying and the receiving plants so that the supplying plant can supply the material and the receiving plant can receive it.

Transaction

MMBE—Stock Overview

Stock Overview

The screenshot below shows the stock of the material (1300-260) in both the receiving plant (1000) and the supplying plant (2000).

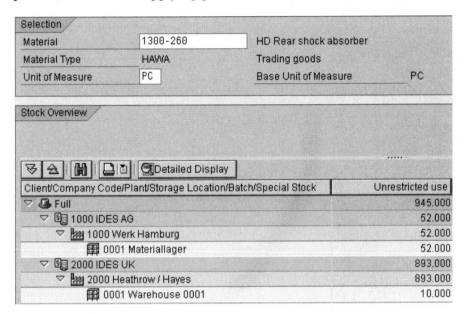

8.4.5 Vendor

Purpose

If a plant supplies material to other plants against purchase orders, it must be created as a vendor.

Transaction

XK01—Create Vendor
XK02—Change Vendor
XK03—Display Vendor

Initial Screen

Vendor	4444
Company Code	1000	IDES AG
Purch. Organization	1000

General data
- ☐ Address
- ☐ Control
- ☐ Payment transactions

Company code data
- ☐ Accounting info
- ☐ Payment transactions
- ☐ Correspondence
- ☐ Withholding tax

Purchasing organization data
- ☑ Purchasing data
- ☐ Partner functions

Purchasing Data

Vendor	4444	London Supplying Plant	London
Purchasing Org.	1000	IDES Deutschland	

Conditions

Order currency	EUR	Euro (EMU currency as of 01/01/1999)
Terms of paymnt	ZB00	
Incoterms	EXW	Ex Works
Minimum order value		
Schema Group, Vendor		Standard procedure vendor
Pricing Date Control		No Control
Order optim.rest.		

Additional Purchasing Data

Click Extras ➤ Add.purchasing data to see the plant assigned to this vendor.

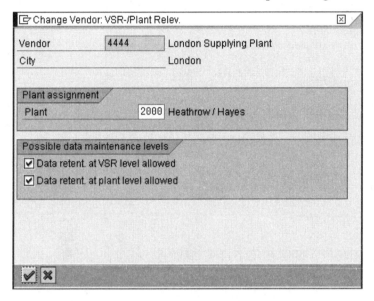

Is the Vendor Number for a Plant Unique?

The vendor number for a plant is stored in the vendor master table LFA1.

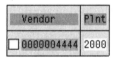

This means that the vendor number for a plant is the same for all company codes and purchasing organizations. The process of assigning a plant number to a vendor may give an impression that the plant is assigned to a vendor at purchasing organization level, but that is not the case.

8.4.6 Customer

Purpose

In Sales and Distribution, you maintain customer related information, e.g. customer number, sales area (sales organization, distribution channel and division), and shipping point. When you sell to another plant in your company or group, you maintain this information for each receiving plant.

IMG Node

SM30 ➤ V_001W_IV

Screen

| Plant | 1000 | Werk Hamburg |

Detailed information

| Customer no. - plant | 1185 | Werk Hamburg 1000 |

Hamburg

SlsOrg.Int.B.	1000	Germany Frankfurt
DistChannelB	10	Final customer sales
Div.Int.Billing	00	Cross-division

Language for stock transport order texts

| Language Key | EN | English |

Customer Number

If an inter plant stock transfers involves billing, the system must be able to determine a customer for the receiving plant. You specify that here.

Sales Area

Sales organization, distribution channel and division are collectively referred as sales area. If an inter plant stock transfers involves creation of a delivery, the system must be able to determine a sales area for the receiving plant. You specify that here.

Shipping Point

If an inter plant stock transfers involves creation of a delivery, the system must be able to determine a sales area and a shipping point for the receiving plant. You specify that in view V_T001W_L.

Plnt	Sales Org.	Distrib. Channel	Shipping Point	Division
0001	0001	01		01
0005	1000	10	1000	00
0006	3000	10		00
0007	1000	10	1000	00

8.4.7 Delivery

Delivery Type

In the scenarios that require a delivery to be created, the delivery type is determined from the supplying plant and the document type of the purchase order in view VV_161V_VF.

Ty.	DT Dscr.	SPl	Name 1	DlTy.	Description	CRl	Description of	Sh	R
NB	Standard PO	1100	Berlin	NLCC	Replen.Cross-c	B	SD delivery	☑	☐

Shipping Tab

If a delivery type is specified here, you will get a ▆Shipping▆ tab when you create the item in the purchase order. If no delivery type is specified here, you will not get a ▆Shipping▆ tab when you create the item in the purchase order and delivery cannot be created in the supplying plant.

8.5 STOCK TRANSFER USING STO WITHOUT DELIVERY

Functional Consultant	User	Business Process Owner	Senior Management	My Rating	Understanding Level
A	B	C	X		

8.5.1 Scenario

Some companies prefer a mechanism wherein the ordering plant raises a formal stock transport order on the supplying plant. This method can be used even if the supplying plant and receiving plants are in different company codes.

8.5.2 Prerequisite

In order for this mechanism to work, the document type should not have a delivery type in view VV_161V_VF.

Ty.	DT Dscr.	SPl	Name 1	DlTy.	Description
UB	Stock transport ord.	1100	Berlin		

If a delivery type is specified here, you will get a ▆Shipping▆ tab when you create the item in the purchase order. If you try to transfer out material with respect to this purchase order item, you will get the following error.

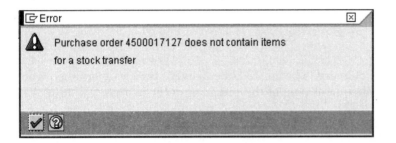

8.5.3 Stock Transport Order

Process Step

The ordering plant orders the material on the supplying plant using a stock transport order (a type of purchase order). This method can be used even if the supplying plant and receiving plants are in different company codes.

Transaction

ME21N—Create Purchase Order

Screen

🚚	UB Stock transport ord. 🗐		Supplying Plant	1100 Berlin	Doc. date	07.09.2013
📂 Header						

🗀	S	It	A	I	Material	Short Text	PO Qua	O	C	Deliv. Date	C	Plnt	Stor. Location
		10		U	100-100	Gehäuse	4	PC	D	17.09.2013	EUR	Werk Hamburg	Materiallager

Header

In a stock transport order, you choose the document type UB, and the supplying plant. Note that you do not specify the vendor.

Items

Specify item category U. In this scenario, no delivery is to be created in the supplying plant; hence you will not have a **Shipping** tab for the item in the purchase order.

8.5.4 Goods Issue

Process Step

You issue goods from the supplying plant to **Stock in Transit** of the receiving plant.

Transaction

MB11—Goods Movement

Initial Screen

Document Date	07.09.2013	Posting Date	07.09.2013
Material Slip			
Doc.Header Text		GR/GI Slip No.	

Defaults for Document Items

Movement Type	351	Special Stock	
Plant	1100	Reason for Movement	
Storage Location	0001	☐ Suggest Zero Lines	

GR/GI Slip

☑ Print

○ Individual Slip
◉ Indiv.Slip w.Inspect.Text
○ Collective Slip

Plant and storage location are that of the supplying plant.

Reference Purchase Order

Click ☐ New Item to enter the purchase order details.

Reference: Purchase Order ☒

Movement Type	351
Plant	1100
Storage Location	0001

Purchase Orders

PO	Item
	🔁

Find POs

Material	
Supplying Plant	

✔ 🗍 Adopt + Details ✖

Item

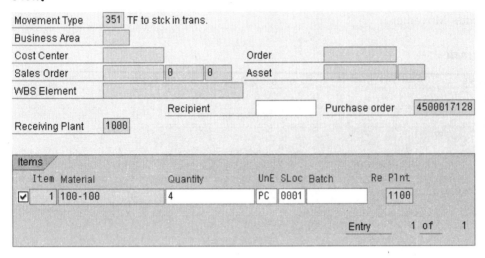

Posting Goods Issue

After the goods issue is entered, post it by clicking 🖫.

Material Document

The material document can be displayed using transaction MB02 or MB03.

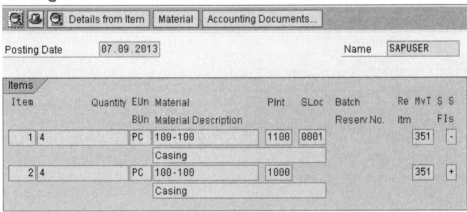

Note that the system automatically creates an item for receiving plant because it has to put the material in Stock in Transit in that plant.

Accounting Documents

List of documents in accounting

In transaction MB02 or MB03 click [Accounting Documents...] in the item overview of the material document to see the accounting documents.

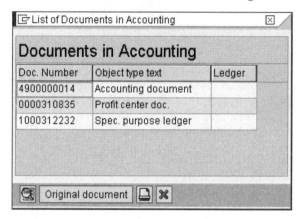

Accounting entries

Double-click the [Accounting document] to open it.

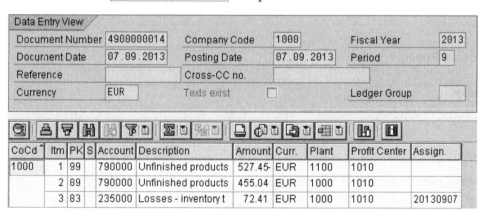

The material may have different prices in different plants. The value of transfer is equal to the value of stock in the issuing plant. Difference is posted in the receiving plant as gain or loss from inventory transfer.

Stock of Material in Receiving Plant after Transfer Out

Run transaction MM02 to see the stock of the material in the receiving plant.

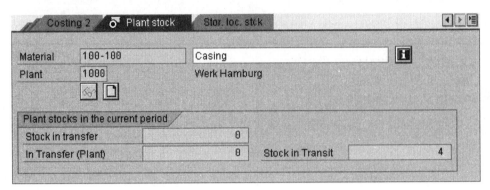

Note the Stock in Transit in the receiving plant.

Stock in Transit Report

You can also run transaction MB5T to see the stock in transit.

Material Purch.Doc	Item SPlt S	Material Description Quantity BUn Amount in LC Crcy	Plnt Name 1 Order Quantity OUn	Net Order Value Crcy
100-100 4500017128	10 1100	Casing 4 PC 0.00 EUR	1000 Werk Hamburg 4 PC	0.00 EUR

8.5.5   Goods Receipt

Process Step

You receive goods from Stock in Transit of the receiving plant to a storage location.

Transaction

MIGO—Goods Movement (MIGO)

Selection

Item Overview

Line	Mat. Sh.	OK	Qt.	E.	SLoc	M.	D	Stock Type	Plnt	Vendor	Purchase	Item
1	Gehäuse	☑	4	PC	Material	101	+	Unrestr	Werk Berlin		4500017128	10

Posting Goods Receipt

After the goods receipt is entered, post it by clicking 💾.

Goods Receipt Slip

You can see/print the GR/GI slip and labels using transaction MB90. Choose `Processing mode` `2` for `Repeat processing`. If GR/GI slip and/or labels are not generated, print indicator may not have been set in the goods movement screen, or printing may not be enabled in Output Determination (see Chapter 24).

```
G O O D S   R E C E I P T   S L I P        5000000022/0001
------------------------------------------------------------
Goods receipt date : 07.09.2013
Current date       : 07.09.2013
------------------------------------------------------------
Plant       : 1000
Description : Werk Hamburg

Iss. Plant  : 1100             Delivery note:
Name        : Berlin
PO          : 4500017128/00010
Pur. group  : 000   Chef,H.    Telephone    : 069/5510
------------------------------------------------------------
Material    : 100-100
Batch       :
Description : Gehäuse

Quantity    :                  4  PC
------------------------------------------------------------
W A R E H O U S E   I N F O R M A T I O N

Storage loc.: 0001
Storage bin :
------------------------------------------------------------

Issued by   : SAPUSER   S I G N A T U R E
```

Goods Receipt Labels

```
Material: 100-100             Material: 100-100
Vendor: Berlin                Vendor: Berlin
Plant/SL: 1000 0001           Plant/SL: 1000 0001
GR/ GI Number: 5000000022     GR/ GI Number: 5000000022
GR/ GI Date: 07.09.2013       GR/ GI Date: 07.09.2013
```

Material Document

The material document can be displayed using transaction MB02 or MB03.

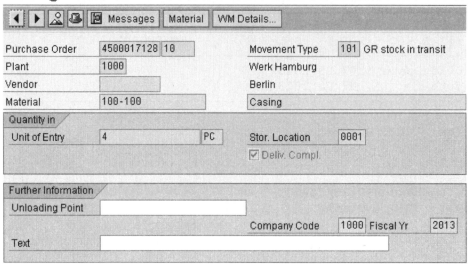

Change Material Document 5000000022 : Details 0001 / 0001

Accounting Documents

List of documents in accounting

In transaction MB02 or MB03 click | Accounting Documents... | in the item overview of the material document to see the accounting documents. Since accounting entries were already passed during transfer in, there is no accounting document now.

Stock of Material in Receiving Plant after Transfer In

Run transaction MM02 to see the stock of the material in the receiving plant.

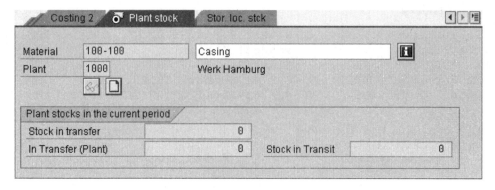

Note that after transfer in, the Stock in Transit in the receiving plant becomes zero.

Stock in Transit Report

You can also run transaction MB5T to see the stock in transit.

Material	Material Description	Plnt Name 1		
Purch.Doc.	Item SPlt S	Quantity BUn Amount in LC Crcy	Order Quantity OUn	Net Order Value Crcy
List contains no data				

Note that after transfer in, there is no stock in transit.

8.6 STOCK TRANSFER USING STO WITH DELIVERY VIA SHIPPING

Functional Consultant	User	Business Process Owner	Senior Management	My Rating	Understanding Level
A	B	C	X		

8.6.1 Scenario

Some companies prefer a mechanism wherein the ordering plant raises a formal purchase order on the supplying plant and delivery takes place using shipping functionality. Stock transport orders are a type of purchase order. In a stock transport order, instead of ordering the material on a vendor, you order it on one of your plants.

8.6.2 Prerequisites

The system must be able to determine the delivery type, shipping point, sales area (sales organization, distribution channel and division) and customer. Configuration for determining all these values is explained in Sections 8.4.6 and 8.4.7. The purchase order generated in this scenario has a Shipping tab, which contains all these values.

8.6.3 Stock Transport Order

Process Step

The ordering plant orders the material on the supplying plant using a stock transport order (a type of purchase order). This method can be used even if the supplying plant and receiving plants are in different company codes.

Transaction

ME21N—Create Purchase Order

Screen

| 🛒 | UB Stock transport ord. 📄 | | | Supplying Plant | 1100 Berlin | Doc. date | 07.09.2013 |
| 📄 | Header | | | | | | |

	S	It	A	I	Material	Short Text	PO Qua	O.	C	Deliv. Date	C.	Plnt	Stor. Location
		10		U	100-100	Gehäuse	4	PC	D	17.09.2013	EUR	Werk Hamburg	Materiallager

Header

In a stock transport order, you choose the document type UB, and the supplying plant. Note that you do not specify the vendor.

Items

Specify item category U. In this scenario, a delivery is to be created in the supplying plant; hence you will have a **Shipping** tab for the item in the purchase order.

8.6.4   Delivery

Process Step

In the supplying plant you create delivery of the material to be transferred.

Transaction

VL10B—Delivery for Purchase Orders

Initial Screen

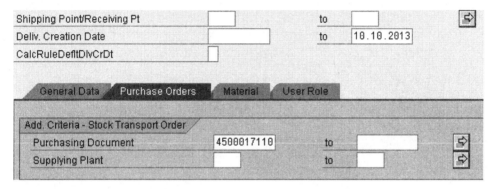

Shipping Point/Receiving Pt		to	
Deliv. Creation Date		to	10.10.2013
CalcRuleDefltDlvCrDt			

General Data | Purchase Orders | Material | User Role

Add. Criteria - Stock Transport Order

Purchasing Document	4500017110	to	
Supplying Plant		to	

List of Purchase Orders

	Light	GI Date	DPrio	Ship-to	Route	OriginDoc.	Gross	WUn	Volume	VUn
	●○○			1185	R00050	4500017127				

The red light does not prevent you from creating the delivery; it merely indicates that the delivery should have been created earlier.

Delivery Creation

Select the item and click [☐ Background] to create the delivery.

	Light	GI Date	DPrio	Ship-to	Route	OriginDoc.	Gross	WUn	Volume	VUn	SD Doc.
	●○○			1185	R00050	4500017127					
	○○○			1185		4500017127					80014990

The system displays the delivery number.

Delivery Status

Click the SD document number. This takes you to transaction VL03N, where you can see the delivery details. Click the Status Overview tab to see the status.

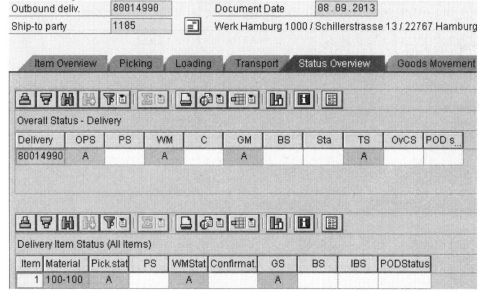

8.6.5 Picking

Process Step

After creating delivery, you pick the material to be issued.

Transaction

VL06P—Picking via Outbound Delivery Monitor

Pick List

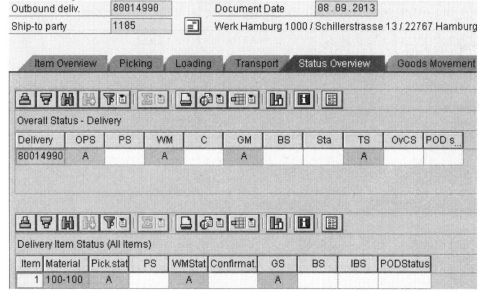

Transfer Order for Delivery Note

Select the delivery and click TO in Foreground .

Initial screen

The system gives initial screen for transfer order creation.

Warehouse Number	011
Plant	
Delivery	0080014990
Group	

Control
- ☑ Activate Item
- Foreground/Backgrnd — H Foreground
- Adopt Pick Quantity
- Adopt putaway qty
- Putaway TO proc.

List

Warehouse Number	011		Delivery Priority	0
Delivery	80014990		Picking Date	17.09.2013
Shipping Point	1100		Loading Date	17.09.2013

Active Worklist | Inactive items | Processed items

Items

Delivery	Item	Material	Description	SLoc	Plant	Picking quantity	Sa	2	T	Shi	D	Picking D
80014990	1	100-100	Gehäuse	0001	1100	4	PC		☐		0	

Generate transfer order item

Click ⟨ Generate TO Item ⟩. The delivery is shifted to the ▓Processed items▓ tab.

Warehouse Number	011		Delivery Priority	0
Delivery	80014990		Picking Date	17.09.2013
Shipping Point	1100		Loading Date	17.09.2013

Active Worklist | Inactive items | **Processed items**

Items

Delivery	Item	Material	Description	Plant	SLoc	Withdrawal quantity	Sa	2	T	Sh	D	Picking D
80014990	1	100-100	Gehäuse	1100	0001	4	PC		☑		0	

Save the transfer order

⊘ Transfer order 0000000041 created

8.6.6 Goods Issue

Process Step

After picking, you issue the material.

Transaction

VL02N—Post Goods Issue Outbound Delivery Single Document

Delivery Status

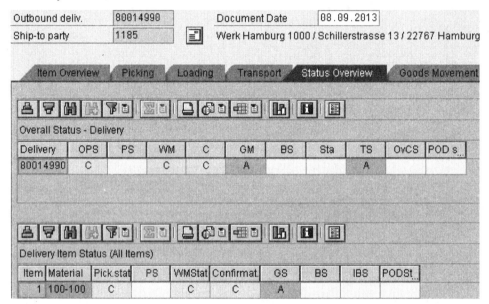

Goods Issue

Click Post Goods Issue .

✅ Replenishment dlv. 80014990 has been saved

Document Flow

Click 🔁 . The system shows the document flow.

Document	Qua...	Unit	Ref. ...	Cur...	On	Status
▽ 📄 Purchase order 4500017127 / 10	4 PC				07.09.2013	
▽ 📄 ➡ Replenishment dlv. 0080014990 / 1	4 PC				08.09.2013	Completed
📄 WMS transfer order 0000000041 / 1	4 PC				08.09.2013	Completed
📄 TF to stck in trans. 4900000031 / 1	4 PC			527.45 EUR	08.09.2013	complete

Material Document

The material document can be displayed using transaction MB02 or MB03.

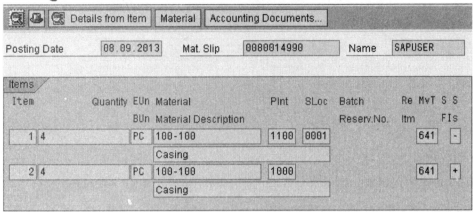

Note that the system automatically creates an item for receiving plant because it has to put the material in Stock in Transit in that plant.

Accounting Documents

List of documents in accounting

In transaction MB02 or MB03 click Accounting Documents... in the item overview of the material document to see the accounting documents.

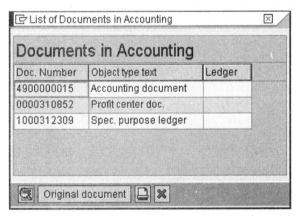

Accounting entries

Double-click the Accounting document to open it.

Data Entry View						
Document Number	4900000015	Company Code	1000	Fiscal Year		2013
Document Date	08.09.2013	Posting Date	08.09.2013	Period		9
Reference	0080014990	Cross-CC no.				
Currency	EUR	Texts exist	☐	Ledger Group		

CoCd	Itm	PK	S	Account	Description	Amount	Curr.	Tx	Cost Ctr	Profit Center	Assign.
1000	1	99		790000	Unfinished products	527.45-	EUR			1010	
	2	89		790000	Unfinished products	455.04	EUR			1010	
	3	83		235000	Losses - inventory t	72.41	EUR			1010	20130908

Goods in Transit

You can see the goods in transit in the material master of the receiving plant.

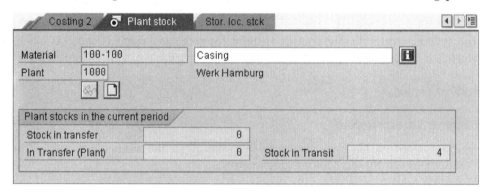

8.6.7 Goods Receipt

Process Step

You receive goods in the receiving plant.

Transaction

MIGO—Goods Movement (MIGO)

Selection

Header

You create goods receipt with reference to outbound delivery using movement type 101. You will see the delivery note number in the header of the goods receipt document.

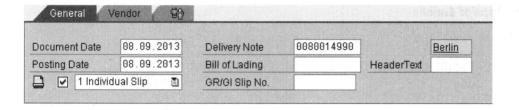

Item

Line	Mat. Short Text	OK	Qty	E	SLoc	M	D	Stock Type	Plnt	Vendor
1	Gehäuse	☑	4	PC	Materiallager	101	+	Unrestricted☐	Werk Hambu	Berlin

Posting Goods Receipt

After the goods receipt is entered, post it by clicking [Post]. The system posts only those items for which ☑ Item OK indicator is set.

Goods Receipt Slip

You can see/print the GR/GI slip and labels using transaction MB90. Choose [Processing mode 2] for Repeat processing. If GR/GI slip and/or labels are not generated, print indicator may not have been set in the goods movement screen, or printing may not be enabled in Output Determination (see Chapter 24).

```
G O O D S   R E C E I P T   S L I P      5000000031/0001
-----------------------------------------------------------
Goods receipt date : 08.09.2013
Current date       : 08.09.2013
-----------------------------------------------------------
Plant       : 1000
Description : Werk Hamburg

Iss. Plant  : 1100              Delivery note: 0080014990
Name        : Berlin
PO          : 4500017127/00010
Pur. group  : 000   Chef,H.     Telephone    : 069/5510
-----------------------------------------------------------
Material    : 100-100
Batch       :
Description : Gehäuse

Quantity    :              4  PC
-----------------------------------------------------------
W A R E H O U S E   I N F O R M A T I O N

Storage loc.: 0001
Storage bin :
-----------------------------------------------------------

Issued by   : SAPUSER   S I G N A T U R E
```

Goods Receipt Labels

Material: 100-100	Material: 100-100
Vendor: Berlin	Vendor: Berlin
Plant/SL: 1000 0001	Plant/SL: 1000 0001
GR/ GI Number: 5000000031	GR/ GI Number: 5000000031
GR/ GI Date: 08.09.2013	GR/ GI Date: 08.09.2013

Material Document

The material document can be displayed using transaction MB02 or MB03.

Change Material Document 5000000031 : Details 0001 / 0001

| ◀ | ▶ | 🗊 | 🖨 | 🖹 Messages | Material | WM Details... |

Purchase Order	4500017127 10	Movement Type	101 GR stock in transit
Plant	1000	Werk Hamburg	
Vendor		Berlin	
Material	100-100	Casing	

Quantity in

Unit of Entry	4	PC	Stor. Location	0001
Del. Note Qty	4	PC	☑ Deliv. Compl.	

Further Information

Unloading Point			
		Company Code	1000 Fiscal Yr 2013
Text			

Accounting Documents

List of documents in accounting

In transaction MB02 or MB03 click [Accounting Documents...] in the item overview of the material document to see the accounting documents. Since accounting entries were already passed during goods issue, there is no accounting document now.

Plant Stock

Costing 2	Plant stock	Stor. loc. stck		◄ ► 📋

Material	100-100	Casing	🛈
Plant	1000	Werk Hamburg	

Plant stocks in the current period

Stock in transfer	0		
In Transfer (Plant)	0	Stock in Transit	0

Note that after goods receipt the Stock in Transit has become zero.

8.7 STOCK TRANSFER USING PURCHASE ORDER

Functional Consultant	User	Business Process Owner	Senior Management	My Rating	Understanding Level
A	B	C	X		

8.7.1 Scenario

You transfer stock from a plant belonging to one company code to another belonging to a different company code. The process mimics the normal buyer seller relationship and provides all the features of such a process. The receiving plant raises a purchase order on the supplying plant. The supplying plant creates a delivery, issues goods, and creates billing document. The receiving plant receives goods and processes invoice.

8.7.2 Purchase Order

Process Step

The ordering plant orders the material on the supplying plant using a purchase order.

Transaction

ME21N—Create Purchase Order

Screen

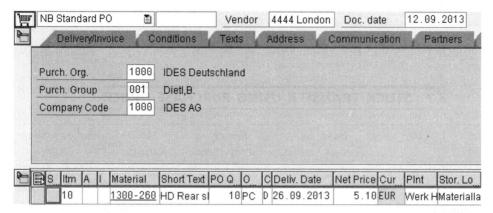

Note that the order type is NB, which is used for purchase orders raised on vendors and item category is blank.

8.7.3 Stock/Requirement List in the Receiving Plant

Process Step

You can check the stock/requirement list in the receiving plant.

Transaction

MD04—Stock/Requirements List

Screen

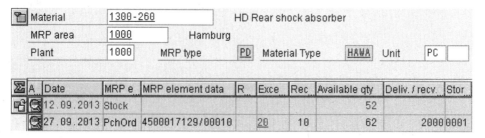

8.7.4   Delivery

Process Step

In the supplying plant you create delivery of the material to be transferred.

Transaction

VL10B—Delivery for Purchase Orders

Initial Screen

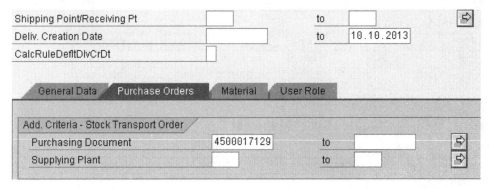

List of Purchase Orders

	Light	GI Date	DPrio	Ship-to	Route	OriginDoc.	Gross	WUn	Volume	VUn
	OOO			1185		4500017129				

Delivery Creation

Select the item and click ☐ Background to create the delivery.

	Light	GI D...	DPrio	Ship-to	Route	OriginDoc.	Gross	WUn	Volume	VUn	Document
	OOO			1185		4500017129					
	OOO			1185		4500017129					80014991

The system displays the delivery number.

Delivery Status

Click the SD document number. This takes you to transaction VL03N, where you can see the delivery details. Click the Status Overview tab to see the status.

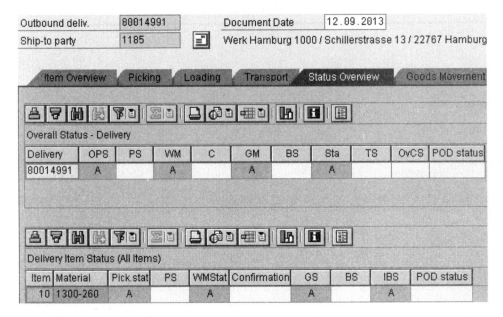

8.7.5 Picking

Process Step

After creating delivery, you pick the material to be issued.

Transaction

VL06P—Picking via Outbound Delivery Monitor

Pick List

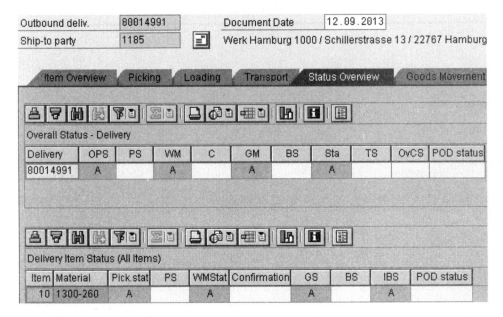

Transfer Order for Delivery Note

Select the delivery and click 🗋 TO in Foreground .

Initial screen

The system gives initial screen for transfer order creation.

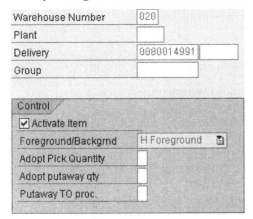

List

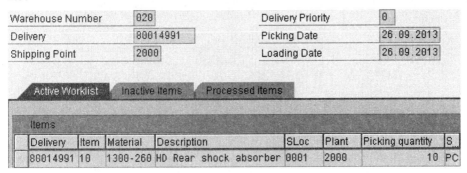

Generate transfer order item

Click Generate TO Item . The delivery is shifted to the Processed items tab.

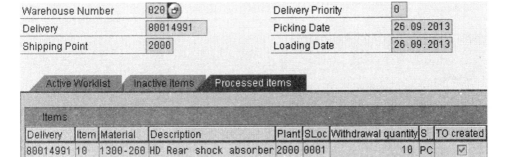

Save the transfer order

Transfer order 0000000001 created

8.7.6 Goods Issue

Process Step

After picking, you issue the material.

Transaction

VL02N—Post Goods Issue Outbound Delivery Single Document

Delivery Status

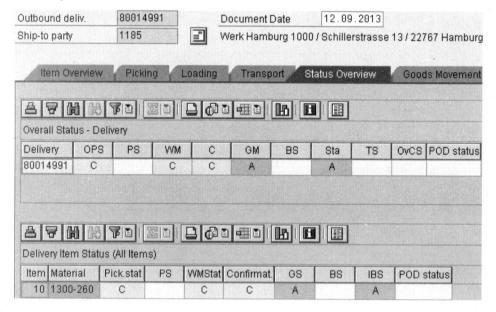

Goods Issue

Click Post Goods Issue .

Replen.Cross-company 80014991 has been saved

Document Flow

Click 🗗. The system shows the document flow.

Document	Qu	U	Ref.	Cu	On	Status
▽ 🗋 Purchase order 4500017129 / 10	10 PC				12.09.2013	
▽ 🗋 ➡ Replen.Cross-company 0080014991 / 10	10 PC				12.09.2013	Completed
🗋 WMS transfer order 0000000001 / 1	10 PC				12.09.2013	Completed
🗋 TF to cross company 4900000050 / 1	10 PC			54.30 GBP	16.09.2013	complete

Material Document

The material document can be displayed using transaction MB02 or MB03.

Change Material Document 4900000050 : Details 0001 / 0001

◀ ▶ 🔍 🖨 📧 Messages | Material | WM Details...

Movement Type	643 TF to cross company		
Material	1300-260	HD Rear shock absorber	

Quantity in

Unit of Entry	10	PC	Plant	2000	Stor. Loc. 0001
Purchase Order	4500017129	10			

Account Assignment

G/L Account	893010	
Cost Center		Order
WBS Element		
		Business Area 3000
		Sales Order 0 0
		Goods recipient 0000001185
Text		

Accounting Documents

List of documents in accounting

In transaction MB02 or MB03 click Accounting Documents... in the item overview of the material document to see the accounting documents.

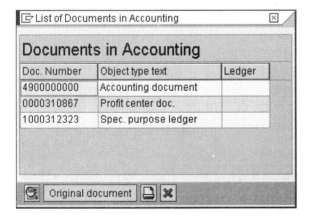

🖝 List of Documents in Accounting   ☒

Documents in Accounting

Doc. Number	Object type text	Ledger
4900000000	Accounting document	
0000310867	Profit center doc.	
1000312323	Spec. purpose ledger	

🔍 Original document 🖨 ✖

Accounting entries

Double-click the Accounting document to open it.

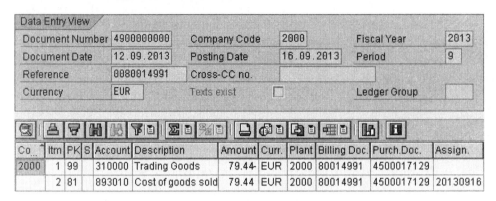

8.7.7 Stock in Receiving Plant after Goods Issue

Process Step

After goods issue, you can see the stock in the receiving plant.

Transaction

MMBE—Stock Overview

Screen

Select plant 1000 Werk Hamburg and click Detailed Display. The system displays the stock in transit (cross company) Stock in trans.CC 10.000.

8.7.8 Billing

Process Step

After goods issue, the supplying plant bills the receiving plant.

Transaction

VF04—Process Billing Due List

Initial Screen

Billing Data

Billing Date from		to	16.09.2013
Billing Type		to	
SD Document		to	

Selection | Default Data | Batch and Update

Organizat. Data

Sales Organization			
Distribution channel		to	
Division		to	
Shipping point		to	

Customer Data

Sold-To Party	1185	to	
Destination country		to	
Sort Criterion		to	

Documents to be selected

- ☐ Order-related
- ☑ Delivery-related
- ☐ Rebate-related
- ☑ Intercompany Billing
- ☐ No docs with billing block
- ☐ Docs with SES Status

List

S	BIC	SOrg.	Billing Date	Sold-to pt	BillT	DstC	Document	DChl	Dv	Doc	A	Name of sold-to party
X	I	2000	16.09.2013	1185	IV	DE	80014991	12	00	J		Werk Hamburg 1000

Bill

Select the item and click 🖫.

Maintain Billing Due List

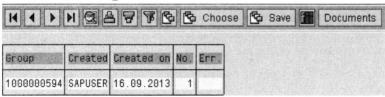

Group	Created	Created on	No.	Err.
1000000594	SAPUSER	16.09.2013	1	

Display Documents in the Group

Select the line and click | Documents |. The system shows the documents in the group.

Group	Document	Billing Date	Description
1000000594	90036099	16.09.2013	Intercompany billing

Display Billing Document

Click on a document to display it.

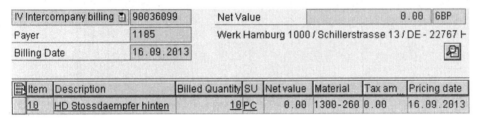

	Item	Description	Billed Quantity	SU	Net value	Material	Tax am	Pricing date
	10	HD Stossdaempfer hinten	10	PC	0.00	1300-260	0.00	16.09.2013

Document Flow

Click [icon]. The system shows the document flow.

Document	Qu	U	Ref.	Cu	On	Status
▽ 📄 Purchase order 4500017129 / 10	10	PC			12.09.2013	
▽ 📄 ➡ Replen.Cross-company 0080014991 / 10	10	PC			12.09.2013	Completed
📄 WMS transfer order 0000000001 / 1	10	PC			12.09.2013	Completed
📄 TF to cross company 4900000050 / 1	10	PC	54.30	GBP	16.09.2013	complete
📄 Intercompany billing 0090036099 / 10	10	PC	0.00	GBP	16.09.2013	

8.7.9 Goods Receipt

Process Step

You receive goods in the receiving plant.

Transaction

MIGO—Goods Movement (MIGO)

Selection

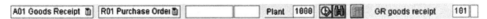

Item Detail

Where

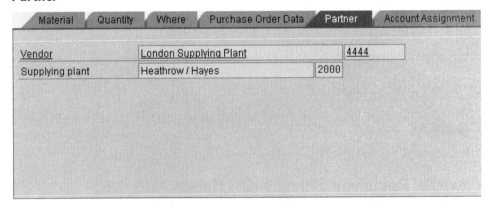

Partner

Note that the Partner tab shows the Supplying plant in addition to the Vendor.

Posting Goods Receipt

After the goods receipt is entered, post it by clicking Post. The system posts only those items for which ☑ Item OK indicator is set.

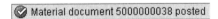

Goods Receipt Slip

You can see/print the GR/GI slip and labels using transaction MB90. Choose Processing mode 2 for Repeat processing. If GR/GI slip and/or labels are not generated, print indicator may not have been set in the goods movement screen, or printing may not be enabled in Output Determination (see Chapter 24).

```
G O O D S    R E C E I P T    S L I P        5000000038/0001
------------------------------------------------------------
Goods receipt date : 16.09.2013
Current date       : 16.09.2013
------------------------------------------------------------
Plant       : 1000
Description : Werk Hamburg

Vendor      : 0000004444           Delivery note:
Name        : London Supplying Plant
PO          : 4500017129/00010
Pur. group  : 001   Dietl,B.       Telephone: 069/5511
------------------------------------------------------------
Material    : 1300-260
Batch       :
Description : HD Rear shock absorber

Quantity    :              10   PC
------------------------------------------------------------
W A R E H O U S E    I N F O R M A T I O N

Storage loc.: 0001
Storage bin :
------------------------------------------------------------

Issued by   : SAPUSER    S I G N A T U R E
```

Material Document

The material document can be displayed using transaction MB02 or MB03.

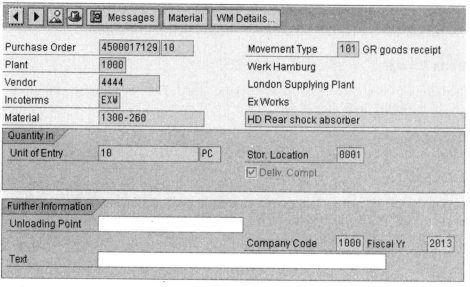

Change Material Document 5000000038 : Details 0001 / 0001

Accounting Documents

List of documents in accounting

In transaction MB02 or MB03 click Accounting Documents... in the item overview of the material document to see the accounting documents.

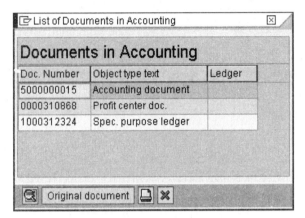

Accounting entries

Double-click the Accounting document to open it.

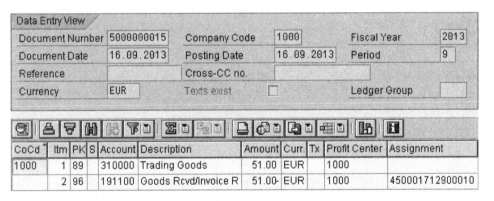

8.7.10 Stock in Receiving Plant after Goods Receipt

Process Step

After goods receipt, you can see the stock in the receiving plant.

Transaction

MMBE—Stock Overview

Screen

Select plant [📖 1000 Werk Hamburg] and click [🔍 Detailed Display]. The system displays the stock in transit (cross company) [Stock in trans.CC .... 0.000]. Note that the stock has now become zero.

8.7.11 Invoice Posting

Process Step

When you receive the invoice from the supplying plant, you enter it in the system.

Transaction

MIRO—Enter Invoice

Screen

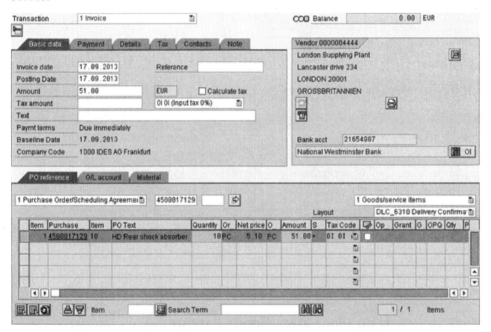

Post the Invoice

After creating the invoice with purchase order reference, post it.

Document no. 5105608672 created

Accounting Documents

List of documents in accounting

Run transaction MIR4 to display the invoice document. Click | Follow-On Documents ... | to display the accounting documents.

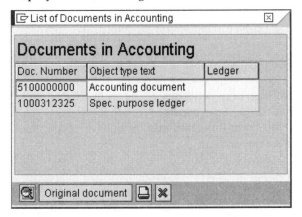

Accounting entries

Double-click the | Accounting document | to open it.

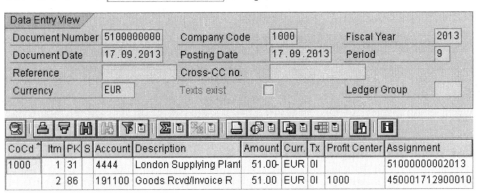

8.8 STOCK TRANSFER BETWEEN STORAGE LOCATIONS USING STO

Functional Consultant	User	Business Process Owner	Senior Management	My Rating	Understanding Level
B	X	X	X		

8.8.1 Scenario

You use stock transport order to transfer stock from one storage location to another within the same plant. This may be needed if your plant covers a wide geographic area.

8.8.2 Activating Stock Transfer between Storage Locations using STO

If you wish to do stock transfer between storage locations using stock transport orders or stock transport scheduling agreements, activate it in view V_TCURM_SUPPSLOC.

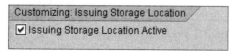

If you set this indicator, you can enter issuing storage locations in stock transport orders and stock transport scheduling agreements.

After this activation you can do stock transfer between storage locations using stock transport orders and stock transport scheduling agreements. No other configuration explained in this section is required unless you want determination of delivery type, sales area, or shipping point to be storage location dependent.

8.8.3 Delivery Type

The delivery type is determined based on the supplying plant in view VV_161V_VF (Section 8.4.7). However, if you want the delivery type also to depend on the issuing storage location, you specify it in view V_161VN.

Doc. Category

	Type	Desc.	SPlt	IStLoc	DlvTy	Desc.	C	Desc.	Ship.	Route	Deli	Deli	DTC	A	Req.
									☐	☐					
									☐	☐					
									☐	☐					

Stock Transfer Data with Issuing Storage Location

8.8.4 Sales Area and Shipping Point

The sales area (sales organization, distribution channel, division) and shipping point are determined based on the receiving plant in view V_T001W_L (Section 8.4.6). However, if you want the sales area and shipping point also to depend on the issuing storage location, you specify it in view V_T001L_L.

Plnt	SLoc	Sales Org.	Distr. Channel	Shipping Point	Division	Vendor	Customer	HU reqmnt
0001	0001							☐
0001	0002							☐
0001	0088							☐

8.8.5 Purchase Order

Process Step

The ordering storage location orders the material on the supplying storage location using a purchase order.

Transaction

ME21N—Create Purchase Order

Screen

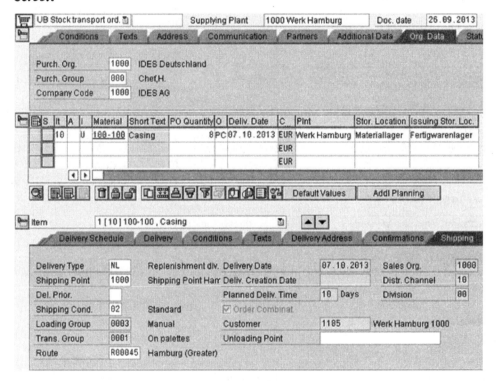

Specify the same plant in the Supplying Plant and the Plnt. Also enter the Stor. Location and the Issuing Stor. Loc.. Note that the Issuing Stor. Loc. field is available in item overview only when storage location based stock transfer is activated. Create and save the purchase order.

By default, the issuing storage location is not determined by MRP during the creation of stock transfer requisitions or stock transfer orders. For that purpose, the BAdI MD_EXT_SUP was delivered on the standard system. BAdI MD_EXT_SUP allows you to create your own logic to determine the issuing storage location and a sample code is provided, which can be used as a basis for your own implementation.

8.8.6 Delivery

Process Step

The issuing storage location creates delivery of the material to be transferred.

Transaction

VL10B—Delivery for Purchase Orders

Initial Screen

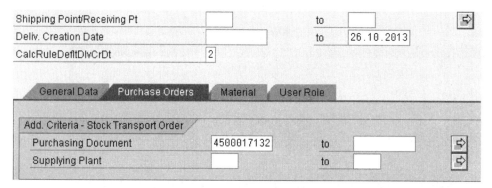

List of Purchase Orders

	Light	GI Date	DPrio	Ship-to	Route	OriginDoc.	Gross	WUn	Volume	VUn
	⬡⬡⬡			1185	R00045	4500017132				

The yellow light does not prevent you from creating the delivery; it merely indicates that the delivery should have been created earlier.

Delivery Creation

Select the item and click [🗋 Background] to create the delivery.

	Light	GI Date	DPrio	Ship-to	Route	OriginDoc.	Gross	WUn	Volume	VUn	SD Doc.
	⬡⬡⬡			1185	R00045	4500017132					
	⬡⬡⬡			1185		4500017132					80014992

Delivery Status

Click the SD document number. This takes you to transaction VL03N, where you can see the delivery details. Click the Status Overview tab to see the status.

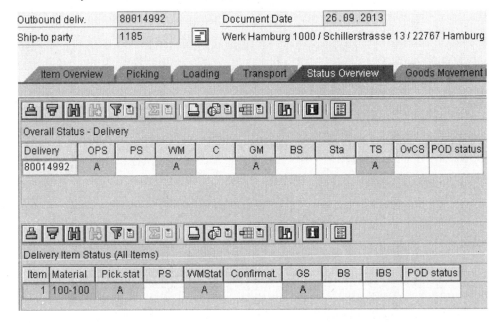

8.8.7 Picking

Process Step

After creating delivery, you pick the material to be issued.

Transaction

VL06P—Picking via Outbound Delivery Monitor

Pick List

Transfer Order for Delivery Note

Select the delivery and click ☐ TO in Foreground .

Initial screen

The system gives initial screen for transfer order creation.

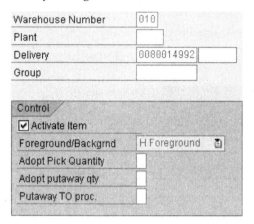

List

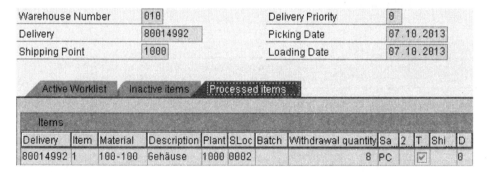

Generate transfer order item

Click [Generate TO Item]. The delivery is shifted to processed items tab.

Save the transfer order

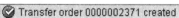

8.8.8   Goods Issue

Process Step

After picking, you issue the material.

Transaction

VL02N—Post Goods Issue Outbound Delivery Single Document

Delivery Status

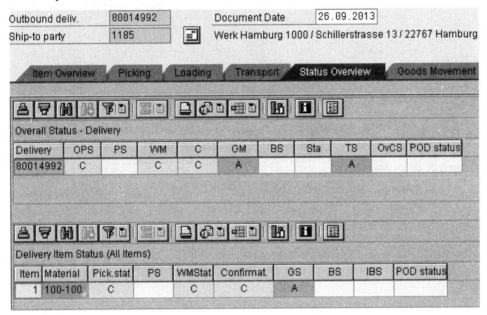

Post Goods Issue

Click   Post Goods Issue .

Replenishment dlv. 80014992 has been saved

Document Flow

Click 🔃. The system shows the document flow.

Document	Qua	Unit	Ref.	Cu	On	Status
▽ 🗋 Purchase order 4500017132 / 10	8 PC				26.09.2013	
▽ 🗋 ➡ Replenishment dlv. 0080014992 / 1	8 PC				26.09.2013	Completed
🗋 WMS transfer order 0000002371 / 1	8 PC				26.09.2013	Completed
🗋 TF to stck in trans. 4900000062 / 1	8 PC			0.00 EUR	26.09.2013	complete

Material Document

The material document can be displayed using transaction MB02 or MB03.

Change Material Document 4900000062 : Overview

Posting Date	26.09.2013	Mat. Slip	0080014992	Name	SAPUSER

Items

Item	Quantity	EUn	Material	Plnt	SLoc	Batch	Re	MvT	S	S
		BUn	Material Description			Reserv.No.	Itm			FIs
1	8	PC	100-100	1000	0002			641		-
			Casing							
2	8	PC	100-100	1000				641		+
			Casing							

Accounting Documents

List of documents in accounting

In transaction MB02 or MB03 click [Accounting Documents...] in the item overview of the material document to see the accounting documents. Since the material is being transferred in the same plant, no accounting document is created.

ⓘ Material document 4900000062 does not include an accounting document

Goods in Transit

You can see the goods in transit in the material master of the receiving plant.

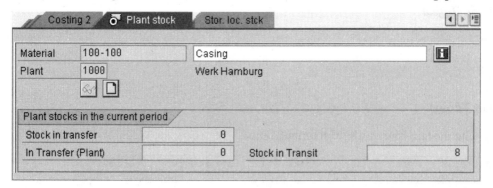

8.8.9   Goods Receipt

Process Step

You receive goods in the receiving storage location.

Transaction

MIGO—Goods Movement (MIGO)

Selection

Header

You create goods receipt with reference to outbound delivery using movement type 101.
You will see the delivery note number in the header of the goods receipt document.

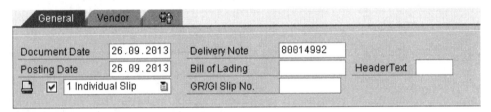

Item

Line	Mat. S	OK	Qt	E	SLoc	M	D	Stock Ty	Vendor	Purchase	Plant	Stor
1	Casing	✓	8	PC	Materiallager	101	+	Unrest	Werk Hambu	4500017132	1000	0001

Posting Goods Receipt

After the goods receipt is entered, post it by clicking [Post]. The system posts only those
items for which ☑ Item OK indicator is set.

Goods Receipt Slip

You can see/print the GR/GI slip and labels using transaction MB90. Choose Processing mode 2 for Repeat processing. If GR/GI slip and/or labels are not generated, print indicator may not have been set in the goods movement screen, or printing may not be enabled in Output Determination (see Chapter 24).

```
G O O D S   R E C E I P T   S L I P         5000000042/0001
--------------------------------------------------------------
Goods receipt date : 26.09.2013
Current date       : 26.09.2013
--------------------------------------------------------------
Plant        : 1000
Description : Werk Hamburg

Iss. Plant  : 1000              Delivery note: 80014992
Name         : Werk Hamburg
PO           : 4500017132/00010
Pur. group  : 000   Chef,H.     Telephone   : 069/5510
--------------------------------------------------------------
Material     : 100-100
Batch       :
Description : Casing

Quantity     :               8  PC
--------------------------------------------------------------
W A R E H O U S E   I N F O R M A T I O N

Storage loc.: 0001
Storage bin :
--------------------------------------------------------------
Issued by   : SAPUSER   S I G N A T U R E
```

Goods Receipt Labels

```
Material: 100-100                Material: 100-100
Vendor: Werk Hamburg             Vendor: Werk Hamburg
Plant/SL: 1000 0001              Plant/SL: 1000 0001
GR/ GI Number: 5000000042        GR/ GI Number: 5000000042
GR/ GI Date: 26.09.2013          GR/ GI Date: 26.09.2013
```

Material Document

The material document can be displayed using transaction MB02 or MB03.

Change Material Document 5000000042 : Details 0001 / 0001

| ◀ | ▶ | 🔍 | 🖶 | 🔧 | Messages | Material | WM Details... |

Purchase Order	4500017132 10		Movement Type	101 GR stock in transit
Plant	1000		Werk Hamburg	
Vendor			Werk Hamburg	
Material	100-100		Casing	

Quantity in

Unit of Entry	8	PC	Stor. Location	0001
Del. Note Qty	8	PC	☑ Deliv. Compl.	

Further Information

Unloading Point	
	Company Code 1000 Fiscal Yr 2013
Text	

Accounting Documents

List of documents in accounting

In transaction MB02 or MB03 click [Accounting Documents...] in the item overview of the material document to see the accounting documents. Since the material is being transferred in the same plant, no accounting document is created.

ⓘ Material document 5000000042 does not include an accounting document

Plant Stock

| Costing 2 | Plant stock | Stor. loc. stck | | ◀ ▶ 📋 |

Material	100-100	Casing	🛈
Plant	1000	Werk Hamburg	

Plant stocks in the current period

Stock in transfer	0		
In Transfer (Plant)	0	Stock in Transit	0

Note that after goods receipt the Stock in Transit has become zero.

Transfer Posting

9.1 GOODS TRANSFER FROM ONE STOCK TYPE TO ANOTHER

Functional Consultant	User	Business Process Owner	Senior Management	My Rating	Understanding Level
B	X	X	X		

9.1.1 Scenario

You transfer goods from one stock type to another. Following movement types are available.

Movement type	Description
321	Quality Inspection Stock to Unrestricted Use Stock
343	Blocked to Unrestricted Use
349	Blocked to quality inspection

9.1.2 Transaction

MIGO_TR—Transfer Posting (MIGO)

9.1.3 Selection

| Transfer Posting 📄 | Other 📄 | | TF quality to unrest | 321 |

9.1.4 Item Detail

Transfer Posting

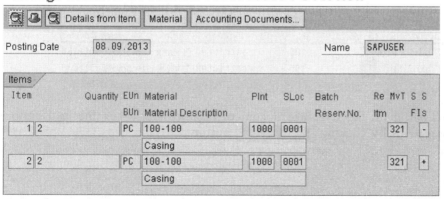

9.1.5 Posting Goods Transfer

After the goods transfer is entered, post it by clicking | Post |.

9.1.6 Goods Transfer Slip

You can see/print the GR/GI slip and labels using transaction MB90. Choose Processing mode 2 for Repeat processing . If GR/GI slip and/or labels are not generated, print indicator may not have been set in the goods movement screen, or printing may not be enabled in Output Determination (see Chapter 24).

9.1.7 Material Document

The material document can be displayed using transaction MB02 or MB03.

9.1.8 Accounting Documents

List of documents in accounting

In transaction MB02 or MB03 click | Accounting Documents... | in the item overview of the material document to see the accounting documents. Since goods are transferred between stock types within same storage location, there are no accounting entries.

> ⓘ Material document 4900000030 does not include an accounting document

9.2 GOODS TRANSFER FROM GR BLOCKED STOCK TO WAREHOUSE

Functional Consultant	User	Business Process Owner	Senior Management	My Rating	Understanding Level
B	X	X	X		

9.2.1 Scenario

Material is held in GR blocked stock temporarily. It is either returned to the vendor, or moved into the company's stock. This process explains the later scenario. In this process the GR blocked stock is identified through the purchase order number.

9.2.2 Transaction

MIGO—Goods Movement (MIGO)

9.2.3 Selection

| A01 Goods Receipt ▼ | R01 Purchase Order▼ | | Plant | | ⊕⋈ | GR from blocked stck | 105 |

9.2.4 Item Overview

When you select a purchase order, the system inserts goods movement of movement type 103 as possible candidates for movement of goods from GR blocked stock to warehouse.

Line	Mat. Sho	OK	Qty	E	S	SLoc	M	D	Stock Type	Plnt	Ref. Doc.
1	Gehäuse	☐	1	PC	🖼		105	+	Unrestricted ▤	Werk Hambu	5000011836
2	Gehäuse	☐	6	PC	🖼		105	+	Unrestricted ▤	Werk Hambu	5000011837
3	Gehäuse	☑	1	PC		Materiallag	105	+	Unrestricted ▤	Werk Hambu	5000000011

Select the items based on the reference document number and select the | OK | button. Delete remaining items by clicking | 🗑 Delete | button.

9.2.5 Item Detail

Where

Movement type

Movement type should be 105.

Stock type

Enter the stock type.

Storage location

Enter the storage location.

Purchase Order Data

Purchase order

The system shows the purchase order number against which the goods were received in GR blocked stocks, which are now being moved to the warehouse.

Reference document

This field contains the document number that moved the material in the GR blocked stock.

9.2.6 Posting Goods Transfer

After the goods transfer is entered, post it by clicking Post . The system posts only those items for which ☑ Item OK indicator is set.

9.2.7 Goods Transfer Slip

You can see/print the GR/GI slip and labels using transaction MB90. Choose Processing mode 2 for Repeat processing . If GR/GI slip and/or labels are not generated, print indicator may not have been set in the goods movement screen, or printing may not be enabled in Output Determination (see Chapter 24).

9.2.8 Material Document

The material document can be displayed using transaction MB02 or MB03.

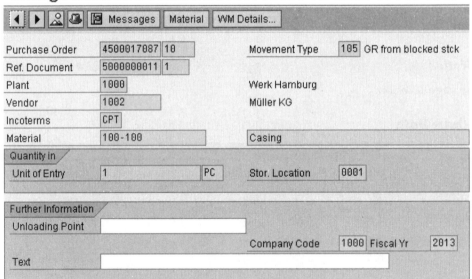

9.2.9 Accounting Documents

List of documents in accounting

In transaction MB02 or MB03 click Accounting Documents... in the item overview of the material document to see the accounting documents.

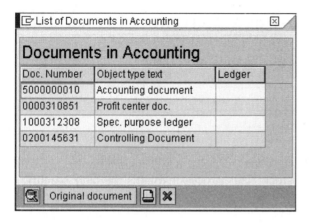

Accounting entries

Double-click the [Accounting document] to open it.

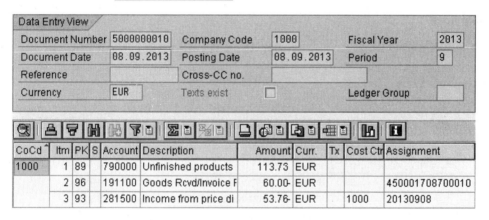

GR blocked stock are not valuated and they do not become a part of your inventory. But when you move the material from GR blocked stock to company's stock, accounting entries are created.

9.2.10 Releasing GR Blocked Stock

You can also release GR blocked stock by referring to the material document number under which it was received in the GR blocked stock. You can identify goods receipts into GR blocked stock using transaction MB51, movement type 103.

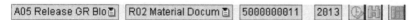

The system automatically selects movement type 105. Quantity proposed is that in the material document.

9.3 GOODS TRANSFER FROM VALUATED GR BLOCKED STOCK TO WAREHOUSE

Functional Consultant	User	Business Process Owner	Senior Management	My Rating	Understanding Level
B	X	X	X		

9.3.1 Scenario

Material is held in valuated GR blocked stock temporarily. It will either be returned to the vendor, or moved into the company's stock. This process explains the later scenario. In this process the valuated GR blocked stock is identified through purchase order.

9.3.2 Transaction

MIGO—Goods Movement (MIGO)

9.3.3 Selection

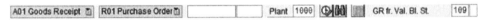

9.3.4 Item Overview

When you select a purchase order, the system inserts goods movement of movement type 107 as possible candidates for movement of goods from valuated GR blocked stock to warehouse.

Line	Mat. Sho	OK	Qt	E.	SLoc	M	D	Stock Type	Plnt	Vendor	Ref. Doc.
1	Gehäuse	☐	1	PC		109	+	Unrestricted	Werk Hambu	Müller KG	5000011836
2	Gehäuse	☐	6	PC		109	+	Unrestricted	Werk Hambu	Müller KG	5000011837
3	Gehäuse	☑	3	PC	Material	109	+	Unrestricted	Werk Hambu	Müller KG	5000000015

9.3.5 Item Detail

Where

Material	Quantity	Where	Purchase Order Data	Partner	Account Assignment

Movement Type	109	+ GR fr. Val. Bl. St.	Stock type	Unrestricted use	

Plant	Werk Hamburg	1000	
Storage Location	0001		
Goods recipient			
Unloading Point			

Text		

Movement type

Movement type should be 109.

Stock type

Enter the stock type.

Storage location

Enter the storage location.

Purchase Order Data

Purchase order

The system shows the purchase order number against which the goods were received in valuated GR blocked stock, which are now being moved to the warehouse.

Reference document number

Note that the reference document number refers to the material document number that created the valuated GR blocked stock. This reference material document was created in Section 5.4.8.

9.3.6 Posting Goods Transfer

After the goods transfer is entered, post it by clicking Post . The system posts only those items for which ☑ Item OK indicator is set.

9.3.7 Goods Transfer Slip

You can see/print the GR/GI slip and labels using transaction MB90. Choose Processing mode 2 for Repeat processing . If GR/GI slip and/or labels are not generated, print indicator may not have been set in the goods movement screen, or printing may not be enabled in Output Determination (see Chapter 24).

```
G O O D S   R E C E I P T   S L I P        5000000032/0001
-----------------------------------------------------------------
Goods receipt date : 08.09.2013
Current date       : 08.09.2013
-----------------------------------------------------------------
Plant       : 1000
Description : Werk Hamburg

Vendor      : 0000001002          Delivery note:
Name        : Müller KG
PO          : 4500017087/00010
Pur. group  : 000   Chef,H.       Telephone    : 069/5510
-----------------------------------------------------------------
Material    : 100-100
Batch       :
Description : Gehäuse

Quantity    :                 3  PC
-----------------------------------------------------------------
W A R E H O U S E    I N F O R M A T I O N

Storage loc.: 0001
Storage bin :
-----------------------------------------------------------------

Issued by   : SAPUSER    S I G N A T U R E
```

Movement out of valuated GR blocked stock not mentioned

Note that the goods receipt slip does not indicate that the item has been moved out of the valuated GR blocked stock. You may want to modify the goods receipt slip to include this.

9.3.8 Goods Transfer Labels

```
Material: 100-100              Material: 100-100
Vendor: Müller KG              Vendor: Müller KG
Plant/SL: 1000 0001            Plant/SL: 1000 0001
GR/ GI Number: 5000000032      GR/ GI Number: 5000000032
GR/ GI Date: 08.09.2013        GR/ GI Date: 08.09.2013
```

9.3.9 Material Document

The material document can be displayed using transaction MB02 or MB03.

Change Material Document 5000000032 : Details 0001 / 0001

| ◄ | ► | 🔲 🕮 | 🖳 Messages | Material | WM Details... |

Purchase Order	4500017087	10	Movement Type	109	GR fr. Val. Bl. St.
Ref. Document	5000000015	1		
Plant	1000		Werk Hamburg
Vendor	1002		Müller KG
Incoterms	CPT		
Material	100-100		Casing

Quantity in

| Unit of Entry | 3 | PC | Stor. Location | 0001 |

Further Information

Unloading Point		
	Company Code	1000	Fiscal Yr	2013
Text		

9.3.10 Accounting Documents

List of documents in accounting

In transaction MB02 or MB03 click │ Accounting Documents... │ in the item overview of the material document to see the accounting documents. No accounting document is generated as accounting entries were already passed when the material was received in valuated GR stock.

9.3.11 Stock Overview

Run transaction MMBE to see the stock overview of a material. Valuated GR blocked stock is a special type of stock, where accounting entries are passed but the material does not become a part of the company's inventory. When the material is moved from valuated GR blocked stock to standard stock, inventory is shown in the appropriate column (unrestricted use, quality inspection or blocked stock) and valuated GR blocked stock becomes zero. Click │ 🔍Detailed Display │. The system shows this quantity: │ Val. GR Bl. Stock │ 0.000 │.

9.3.12 Releasing Valuated GR Blocked Stock

You can also release valuated GR blocked stock by referring to the material document number under which it was received in the valuated GR blocked stock. You can identify goods receipts into valuated GR blocked stock using transaction MB51, movement type 107.

│ A05 Release GR Blo🔽 │ R02 Material Docum🔽 │ 5000000015 │ 2013 │ 🔄🕮 🔲

The system automatically selects movement type 109. Quantity proposed is that in the material document.

9.4 GOODS TRANSFER FROM MATERIAL TO MATERIAL

Functional Consultant	User	Business Process Owner	Senior Management	My Rating	Understanding Level
B	X	X	X		

9.4.1 Scenario

Sometimes properties of material change during storage. For example, 5-year old wine may become 10-year old wine. You need to transfer material from one material number to another. This is done using movement type 309. Both materials must have the same valuation class.

9.4.2 Transaction

MIGO_TR—Transfer Posting (MIGO)

9.4.3 Selection

| Transfer Posting | Other | | TF tfr.ps.mat.to mat | 309 |

9.4.4 Item Detail

Transfer Posting

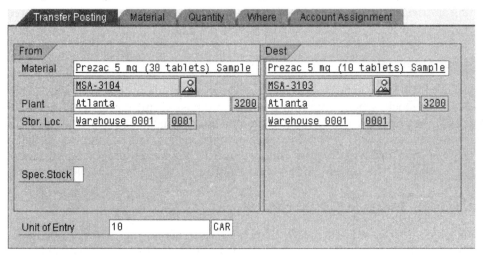

9.4.5 Posting Goods Transfer

After the goods transfer is entered, post it by clicking Post .

9.4.6 Goods Transfer Slip

You can see/print the GR/GI slip and labels using transaction MB90. Choose Processing mode 2 for Repeat processing . If GR/GI slip and/or labels are not generated, print indicator may not have been set in the goods movement screen, or printing may not be enabled in Output Determination (see Chapter 24).

9.4.7 Material Document

The material document can be displayed using transaction MB02 or MB03.

Change Material Document 4900000048 : Overview

| | Details from Item | Material | Accounting Documents... |

| Posting Date | 11.09.2013 | | | Name | SAPUSER |

Items

Item	Quantity	EUn	Material		Plnt	SLoc	Batch		Re	MvT	S	S
		BUn	Material Description				Reserv.No.		Itm			FIs
1	10	CAR	MSA-3104		3200	0001				309		-
			Prezac 5 mg (30 tablets) Sample									
2	10	CAR	MSA-3103		3200	0001				309		+
			Prezac 5 mg (10 tablets) Sample									

9.4.8 Accounting Documents

List of documents in accounting

In transaction MB02 or MB03 click Accounting Documents... in the item overview of the material document to see the accounting documents.

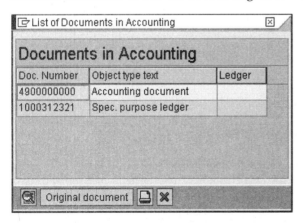

List of Documents in Accounting ☒

Documents in Accounting

Doc. Number	Object type text	Ledger
4900000000	Accounting document	
1000312321	Spec. purpose ledger	

Original document

Accounting entries

Double-click the [Accounting document] to open it.

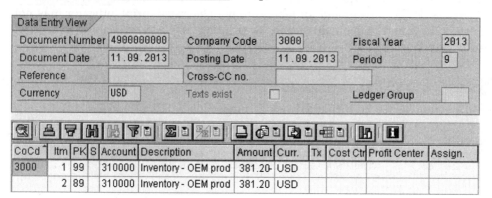

CoCd	Itm	PK	S	Account	Description	Amount	Curr.	Tx	Cost Ctr	Profit Center	Assign.
3000	1	99		310000	Inventory - OEM prod	381.20-	USD				
	2	89		310000	Inventory - OEM prod	381.20	USD				

Customer Returns

10.1 CUSTOMER RETURNS

Functional Consultant	User	Business Process Owner	Senior Management	My Rating	Understanding Level
A	A	B	X		

10.1.1 Scenario

Sometimes customers return goods to you. You receive them in your warehouse. The stock is separately maintained.

10.1.2 Transaction

MIGO—Goods Movement (MIGO)

10.1.3 Selection

10.1.4 Item Detail

Where

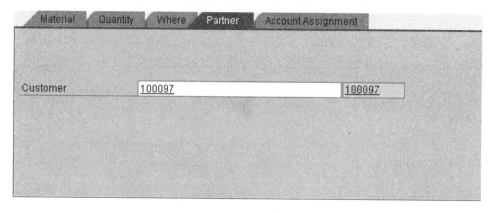

Partner

10.1.5 Posting Goods Receipt

After the goods receipt is entered, post it by clicking Post . The system posts only those items for which ☑ Item OK indicator is set.

10.1.6 Goods Receipt Slip

You can see/print the GR/GI slip and labels using transaction MB90. Choose Processing mode 2 for Repeat processing . If GR/GI slip and/or labels are not generated, print indicator may not have been set in the goods movement screen, or printing may not be enabled in Output Determination (see Chapter 24).

10.1.7 Material Document

The material document can be displayed using transaction MB02 or MB03.

Change Material Document 4900000033 : Details 0001 / 0001

| ◀ | ▶ | 👤 | 🖨 | 📋 Messages | Material | WM Details... |

Movement Type	451 GI returns	
Material	100-100	Casing

Quantity in

| Unit of Entry | 5 | PC | Plant | 1000 | Stor. Loc. | 0001 |

Account Assignment

Business Area	1000
Customer	100097
Text	

10.1.8 Accounting Documents

List of documents in accounting

In transaction MB02 or MB03 click Accounting Documents... in the item overview of the material document to see the accounting documents. When customer returns are received, no accounting entries are passed. When they are moved to the company's own stock, accounting entries are generated.

(!) Material document 4900000033 does not include an accounting document

10.1.9 Stock Overview after Customer Returns

Run transaction MMBE to see the stock overview of a material.

Client/Company Code/Plant/Storage Location/Batch/	Unrestricted use	Qual. inspection	Returns
▽ 📦 Full	1,131.000	23.000	5.000
▽ 📑 1000 IDES AG	1,131.000	23.000	5.000
▽ 🏭 1000 Werk Hamburg	1,131.000	23.000	5.000
🗄 0001 Materiallager	1,101.000	23.000	5.000
🗄 0002 Fertigwarenlager	20.000		
🗄 0088 Zentrallager WM	10.000		

10.2 GOODS TRANSFER FROM CUSTOMER RETURNS TO OWN STOCK

Functional Consultant	User	Business Process Owner	Senior Management	My Rating	Understanding Level
A	A	B	X		

10.2.1 Scenario

You transfer goods returned by customers to your warehouse stock using the following movement types.

Movement type	Type of stock created
453	Unrestricted use
457	Quality inspection
459	Blocked

10.2.2 Transaction

MIGO_TR—Transfer Posting (MIGO)

10.2.3 Selection

10.2.4 Item Detail

Transfer Posting

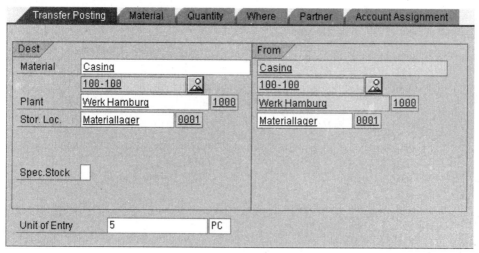

10.2.5 Posting Goods Transfer

After the goods transfer is entered, post it by clicking Post .

10.2.6 Goods Transfer Slip

You can see/print the GR/GI slip and labels using transaction MB90. Choose Processing mode 2 for Repeat processing . If GR/GI slip and/or labels are not generated, print indicator may not have been set in the goods movement screen, or printing may not be enabled in Output Determination (see Chapter 24).

10.2.7 Material Document

The material document can be displayed using transaction MB02 or MB03.

Overview

Change Material Document 4900000034 : Overview

	Details from Item	Material	Accounting Documents...

| Posting Date | 09.09.2013 | | Name | SAPUSER |

Items

Item	Quantity	EUn BUn	Material Material Description	Plnt	SLoc	Batch Reserv.No.	Re Itm	MvT	S	S FIs
1	5	PC	100-100	1000	0001			453		+
			Casing							
2	5	PC	100-100	1000	0001			453		-
			Casing							

Goods Transfer from Customer Returns to Own Stock results in two goods movements.

Item 1

Item 1 is for receipt of goods in the company's warehouse.

Change Material Document 4900000034 : Details 0001 / 0002

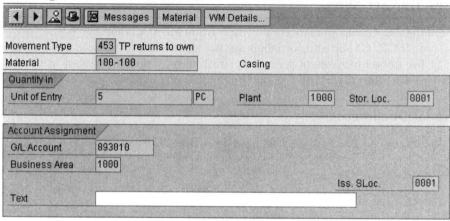

Item 2

Item 2 is for reducing the stock in customer returns, which was increased when customer returns were posted.

Change Material Document 4900000034 : Details 0002 / 0002

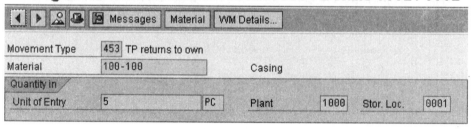

10.2.8   Accounting Documents

List of documents in accounting

In transaction MB02 or MB03 click | Accounting Documents... | in the item overview of the material document to see the accounting documents.

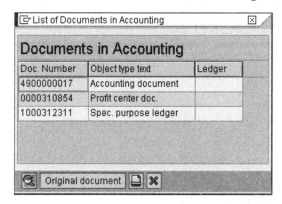

Accounting entries

Double-click the | Accounting document | to open it.

Note that accounting entries are passed only when the goods are transferred to the company's stock.

10.2.9   Stock Overview after Transfer from Customer Returns

Run transaction MMBE to see the stock overview of a material.

Client/Company Code/Plant/Storage Location/Batch/	Unrestricted use	Qual. inspection	Returns
▽ 📦 Full	1,136.000	23.000	
▽ 🏢 1000 IDES AG	1,136.000	23.000	
▽ 🏭 1000 Werk Hamburg	1,136.000	23.000	
🏬 0001 Materiallager	1,106.000	23.000	
🏬 0002 Fertigwarenlager	20.000		
🏬 0088 Zentrallager WM	10.000		

Subcontracting

11.1 OVERVIEW

Functional Consultant	User	Business Process Owner	Senior Management	My Rating	Understanding Level
A	A	A	B		

11.1.1 Subcontracting

Sometimes you order a component on a vendor for which you provide raw or semi-finished material; or an assembly for which you supply the components. The vendor finishes the component or assembly and supplies it to you.

In the purchase order you use item category 'Subcontract'. If the bill of material is not maintained for this item, a screen is displayed in which you enter the components the subcontractor requires from you to produce the ordered assembly. When you dispatch the parts to the vendor, your inventory does not reduce, as you still own the material supplied.

When you create goods receipt of the ordered material, the material document reduces the inventory of the supplied components, while it increases the inventory of the received material. Accounting entries are appropriately passed.

11.1.2 Bill of Material

You maintain BOM for the part/assembly supplied by the vendor using transaction CS01 or CS02.

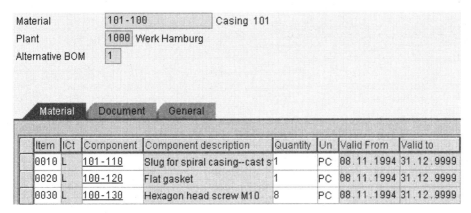

This specifies the material you need to supply to the vendor in order to receive the subcontracted item.

11.1.3 Purchase Order

You create purchase order on the vendor for parts to be procured using transaction ME21N.

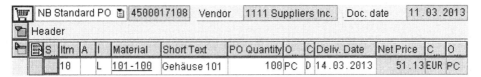

For subcontracted item, the item category is L.

11.1.4 Subcontract Stock with Vendor

Check whether the vendor has been given parts for supplying the ordered item using transaction ME2O.

Vendor	1111	Suppliers Inc.		NILES		
Material		Plnt Short Text				SC Stock
				Reqt qty	Available SC Stock	
☐ 100-120		1000 Flat gasket				10 PC ⊞
⊞ Requirements via SC Orders				90 PC ⊖	80- PC	
☐ 101-110		1000 Slug for spiral casing				10 PC ⊞
⊞ Requirements via SC Orders				90 PC ⊖	80- PC	

11.1.5 Stocks at Subcontractor

If you are interested in knowing total value of stock lying with subcontractors, rather than knowing their ability to supply goods, you can use transaction MBLB.

Vendor	Name 1		City						
Material		Plnt	Batch	Unrestricted	In Quality Insp.	Restricted-Use	BUn	Total Value	Crcy
1111	Suppliers Inc.		NILES						
100-120		1000		10	0	0	PC	117.74	EUR
101-110		1000		10	0	0	PC	34.84	EUR

11.2 GOODS TRANSFER TO VENDOR

Functional Consultant	User	Business Process Owner	Senior Management	My Rating	Understanding Level
A	A	B	X		

11.2.1 Scenario

In subcontracting, the vendor supplies the assembly, for which you supply components to the vendor. This process is used to supply components to the vendor.

11.2.2 Transaction

MB1B—Transfer Posting

11.2.3 Initial Screen

Document Date	09.09.2013	Posting Date	09.09.2013
Material Slip			
Doc.Header Text		GR/GI Slip No.	

Defaults for Document Items

Movement Type	541	Special Stock	
Plant	1000	Reason for Movement	
Storage Location	0001	☐ Suggest Zero Lines	

GR/GI Slip

☑ Print

◉ Individual Slip
○ Indiv.Slip w.Inspect.Text
○ Collective Slip

11.2.4   Reference Purchase Order

Click   To Purchase Order... . The system gives you the dialog box to enter details of the reference purchase order.

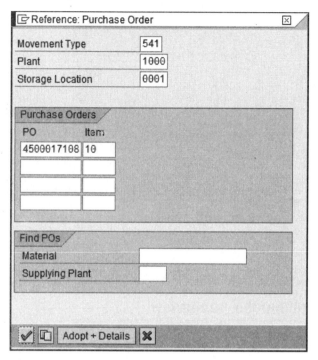

11.2.5   Proposed Items

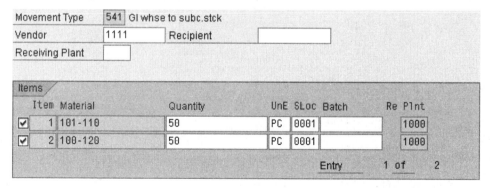

11.2.6   Copy Items to Goods Transfer Screen

Select the items and click 🗐 to copy the items to goods transfer screen.

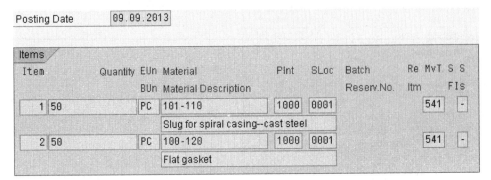

11.2.7   Posting Goods Transfer

After the goods transfer is entered, post it by clicking 🖫.

11.2.8   Material Document

The material document can be displayed using transaction MB02 or MB03.

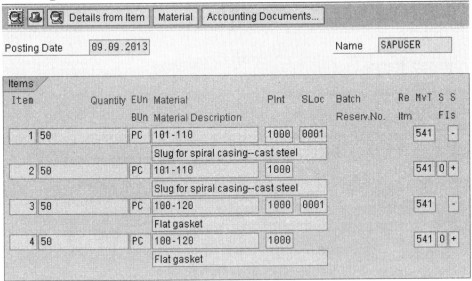

Note that the material is credited to the storage location and debited from the special stock, thus creating two entries for each item. Since there are two items, there are four entries in the material document.

11.2.9 Accounting Documents

List of documents in accounting

In transaction MB02 or MB03 click | Accounting Documents... | in the item overview of the material document to see the accounting documents. No accounting document is generated because the material still belongs to you.

11.2.10 Subcontract Stock with Vendor

The material transferred to vendor is reflected in the subcontract stock with vendor report generated using transaction ME2O.

```
Vendor    1111        Suppliers Inc.                    NILES

 Material            Plnt Short Text                      SC Stock
      Date         Document   Item  Deliv. Date Reqt Qty  Available SC Stock

□ 100-120            1000 Flat gasket                       60  PC
   Requirements via SC Orders                  90 PC ⊖     30- PC
      08.03.2013    4500017108 00010 14.03.2013  90 PC

□ 101-110            1000 Slug for spiral casinc            60  PC
   Requirements via SC Orders                  90 PC ⊖     30- PC
      08.03.2013    4500017108 00010 14.03.2013  90 PC
```

The report also shows quantity of material still to be supplied to the subcontractor so that he can fulfill the order.

11.3 GOODS RECEIPT FROM VENDOR

Functional Consultant	User	Business Process Owner	Senior Management	My Rating	Understanding Level
A	A	B	X		

11.3.1 Scenario

In subcontracting, the vendor supplies the assembly, for which you supply components to the vendor. This process is used to receive goods from the vendor.

11.3.2 Transaction

MIGO—Goods Movement (MIGO)

11.3.3 Selection

Receive the goods with reference to a subcontracting purchase order.

11.3.4   Item Overview

Click ⊞ to display the supplied parts which are received along with subcontracted item.

Line	⏚	Mat. Short Text	OK	Qt	E	SLoc	M	D	Stock Ty	Plnt	S	Purchase	Item
1	▤	Gehäuse 101	☑	10	PC	Materia	101	+	Unrest🖹	Werk Ham|		4500017108	10
1		Flat gasket	☑	10	PC		543	-	Unrest🖹	Werk Ham	0		
1		Slug for spiral casi	☑	10	PC		543	-	Unrest🖹	Werk Ham	0		

Note that the components used in the supplied assembly have special stock type O.

11.3.5   Posting Goods Receipt

After the goods receipt is entered, post it by clicking Post . The system posts only those items for which ☑ Item OK indicator is set.

11.3.6   Goods Receipt Slip

You can see/print the GR/GI slip and labels using transaction MB90. Choose Processing mode 2 for Repeat processing . If GR/GI slip and/or labels are not generated, print indicator may not have been set in the goods movement screen, or printing may not be enabled in Output Determination (see Chapter 24).

```
G O O D S     R E C E I P T     S L I P          5000000033/0001
------------------------------------------------------------------
Goods receipt date : 09.09.2013
Current date        : 09.09.2013
------------------------------------------------------------------
Plant        : 1000
Description : Werk Hamburg

Vendor       : 0000001111        Delivery note:
Name         : Suppliers Inc.
PO           : 4500017108/00010
Pur. group   : 004   Eiffel,J.      Telephone    : 069/1300
------------------------------------------------------------------
Material     : 101-100
Batch        :
Description : Gehäuse 101

Quantity     :                10   PC
------------------------------------------------------------------
W A R E H O U S E     I N F O R M A T I O N

Storage loc.: 0001
Storage bin :
------------------------------------------------------------------

Issued by    : SAPUSER    S I G N A T U R E
```

11.3.7 Material Document

The material document can be displayed using transaction MB02 or MB03.

Change Material Document 5000000033 : Overview

| | | Details from Item | Material | Accounting Documents... |

| Posting Date | 09.09.2013 | | | Name | SAPUSER |

Items

Item	Quantity	EUn	Material	Plnt	SLoc	PO	Item	S	DCI
		BUn	Material Description			Batch	R	MvT	S S
1	10	PC	101-100	1000	0001	4500017108	10		☐
			Casing 101				101	+	
2	10	PC	100-120	1000		4500017108	10		0
			Flat gasket				543	-	
3	10	PC	101-110	1000		4500017108	10		0
			Slug for spiral casing--cast steel				543	-	

11.3.8 Accounting Documents

List of documents in accounting

In transaction MB02 or MB03 click Accounting Documents... in the item overview of the material document to see the accounting documents.

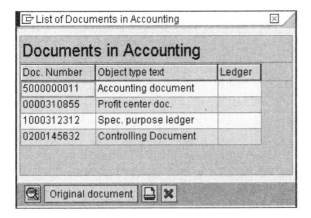

Doc. Number	Object type text	Ledger
5000000011	Accounting document	
0000310855	Profit center doc.	
1000312312	Spec. purpose ledger	
0200145632	Controlling Document	

Accounting entries

Double-click the | Accounting document | to open it.

Data Entry View								
Document Number	5000000011		Company Code	1000		Fiscal Year		2013
Document Date	09.09.2013		Posting Date	09.09.2013		Period		9
Reference			Cross-CC no.					
Currency	EUR		Texts exist	☐		Ledger Group		

CoCd	Itm	PK	S	Account	Description	Amount	Curr.	Tx	Cost Ctr	Assignment
1000	1	89		790000	Unfinished products	384.60	EUR			
	2	96		191100	Goods Rcvd/Invoice F	511.30-	EUR			450001710800010
	3	91		893010	Cost of goods sold	384.60-	EUR			20130909
	4	86		417001	Purchased services	511.30	EUR		1000	5000000112013
	5	99		300000	Inventory - Raw Mate	117.74-	EUR			
	6	81		400020	Raw materials consu	117.74	EUR			20130909
	7	99		790000	Unfinished products	34.84-	EUR			
	8	81		893020	Inventory change - a	34.84	EUR		4200	20130909

11.3.9 Subcontract Stock with Vendor

The material received from vendor is reflected in the subcontract stock with vendor report generated using transaction ME2O.

```
Vendor    1111       Suppliers Inc.                      NILES

Material            Plnt Short Text                        SC Stock
        Date         Document   Item  Deliv. Date Reqt Qty   Available SC Stock

☐ 100-120            1000 Flat gasket                         50  PC ⊞
  🗐 Requirements via SC Orders                    80 PC ⊖      30- PC
     08.03.2013   4500017108 00010 14.03.2013      80 PC

☐ 101-110            1000 Slug for spiral casing             50  PC ⊞
  🗐 Requirements via SC Orders                    80 PC ⊖      30- PC
     08.03.2013   4500017108 00010 14.03.2013      80 PC
```

11.4 SUBSEQUENT ADJUSTMENT

Functional Consultant	User	Business Process Owner	Senior Management	My Rating	Understanding Level
B	C	X	X		

11.4.1 Scenario

The parts required to produce a material may be exact, or approximate. In the later case, a subcontractor may report that he used more, or less, parts in producing the material supplied by him. If this information is available when subcontracted goods are received, you can make the change in quantity of parts consumed during the goods receipt itself. However, if this information becomes available subsequently, you can make subsequent adjustment.

11.4.2 Transaction

MIGO_GS—Subsequent Adjustment in Subcontracting (MIGO)
MB04—Subsequent Adjustment in Subcontracting

11.4.3 Selection

| A11 Subsequent Adj | R01 Purchase Order | | | Plant | 1000 |

11.4.4 Item Overview

Line		Mat. Short Text	OK	Qty	E	Underconsumption	M	D	Stock Type	Plnt	Sp
1		Gehäuse 101	✓	8	PC		121	-		Werk Ham	
1		Flat gasket	✓	5	PC	☐	543	-	Unrestricted	Werk Ham	0
1		Slug for spiral ca	✓	10	PC	☐	543	-	Unrestricted	Werk Ham	0

11.4.5 Posting Goods Receipt

After the goods receipt is entered, post it by clicking Post . The system posts only those items for which ✓ Item OK indicator is set.

11.4.6 Material Document

The material document can be displayed using transaction MB02 or MB03.

Change Material Document 5000000034 : Overview

Details from Item	Material	Accounting Documents...

Posting Date   09.09.2013   Name   SAPUSER

Items

Item	Quantity	EUn	Material	Plnt	SLoc	PO	Item	S	DCI
		BUn	Material Description			Batch	R	MvT	S S
1			101-100	1000		4500017108	10		
			Casing 101				121	+	
2	5	PC	100-120	1000		4500017108	10		0
			Flat gasket				543	-	
3	10	PC	101-110	1000		4500017108	10		0
			Slug for spiral casing--cast steel				543	-	

Item 1 is the material supplied by the vendor. In subsequent adjustment, the quantity of material supplied by the vendor does not change. Hence the quantity is zero. This entry is kept only for recording the material supplied by the vendor against which subsequent adjustment was made.

Items 2 and 3 are for the quantities adjusted in the vendor stock. Note that the company has not received any material, hence there are no entries to that effect.

11.4.7 Accounting Documents

List of documents in accounting

In transaction MB02 or MB03 click ⎮ Accounting Documents... ⎮ in the item overview of the material document to see the accounting documents.

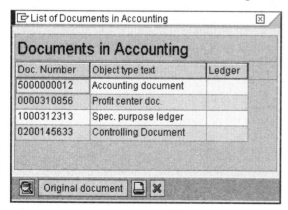

Doc. Number	Object type text	Ledger
5000000012	Accounting document	
0000310856	Profit center doc.	
1000312313	Spec. purpose ledger	
0200145633	Controlling Document	

Accounting entries

Double-click the | Accounting document | to open it.

Data Entry View							
Document Number	5000000012	Company Code	1000		Fiscal Year		2013
Document Date	09.09.2013	Posting Date	09.09.2013		Period		9
Reference		Cross-CC no.					
Currency	EUR	Texts exist	☐		Ledger Group		

CoCd	Itm	PK	S	Account	Description	Amount	Curr.	Tx	Cost Ctr	Profit Center	Assign.
1000	1	99		300000	Inventory - Raw Mate	58.87-	EUR			1010	
	2	81		400020	Raw materials consu	58.87	EUR			1010	20130909
	3	99		790000	Unfinished products	34.84-	EUR			1010	
	4	81		893020	Inventory change - a	34.84	EUR		4200	1000	20130909

Since the material held by the subcontractor belongs to you, if that quantity is reduced/ increased, the value of inventory is reduced/increased. The offsetting entry debits/credits a consumption account. This is done for each item.

11.4.8 Subcontract Stock with Vendor

The quantity of material adjusted in vendor stock is reflected in the subcontract stock with vendor report generated using transaction ME2O.

```
Vendor    1111      Suppliers Inc.                   NILES


 Material           Plnt Short Text                       SC Stock
       Date          Document   Item  Deliv. Date Reqt Qty   Available SC Stock

☐100-120             1000 Flat gasket                         45  PC
 Requirements via SC Orders                    80 PC ⊟        35- PC
    08.03.2013   4500017108 00010 14.03.2013   80 PC

☐101-110             1000 Slug for spiral casing             40  PC
 Requirements via SC Orders                    80 PC ⊟        40- PC
    08.03.2013   4500017108 00010 14.03.2013   80 PC
```

Consignment Stock of Vendor

12.1 GOODS RECEIPT FOR CONSIGNMENT STOCK

Functional Consultant	User	Business Process Owner	Senior Management	My Rating	Understanding Level
B	C	X	X		

12.1.1 Scenario

Consignment goods are materials that vendors keep at their own cost on the orderer's premises. There is goods receipt for consignment items. The orderer is responsible for the stock, only he does not pay for it until he uses it. There is no invoice receipt. Payment is made on withdrawal of the material.

Although the stock belongs to the vendor, the company is responsible for its safekeeping. It carries out physical inventory to reconcile book inventory with actual stock.

12.1.2 Transaction

MIGO—Goods Movement (MIGO)

12.1.3 Selection

12.1.4   Item Detail

Where

Material	Quantity	Where	Purchase Order Data	Partner	Account Assignment

Movement Type	101	K	+	GR for consgt. stock	Stock type	Unrestricted use
Vendor	C.E.B. BERLIN		1000	
Plant	Werk Hamburg		1000	
Storage Location	Materiallager		0001	
Goods recipient				
Unloading Point				
Text				

You receive consignment goods by referencing a purchase order and selecting an item having item category K. The system automatically determines the special stock indicator K based on the item category of the purchase order item and it cannot be changed. Consignment goods may be received in any stock type: unrestricted use, quality inspection, or blocked stock.

12.1.5   Posting Goods Receipt

After the goods receipt is entered, post it by clicking Post . The system posts only those items for which ☑ Item OK indicator is set.

12.1.6   Goods Receipt Slip

You can see/print the GR/GI slip and labels using transaction MB90. Choose Processing mode 2 for Repeat processing. If GR/GI slip and/or labels are not generated, print indicator may not have been set in the goods movement screen, or printing may not be enabled in Output Determination (see Chapter 24).

```
G O O D S   R E C E I P T   S L I P       5000000035/0001
-------------------------------------------------------------
Goods receipt date : 09.09.2013
Current date       : 09.09.2013
-------------------------------------------------------------
Plant       : 1000
Description : Werk Hamburg

Vendor      : 0000001000          Delivery note:
Name        : C.E.B. BERLIN
PO          : 4500017107/00010
Pur. group  : 000   Chef,H.       Telephone    : 069/5510
-------------------------------------------------------------
Material    : 1300-550
Batch       :
Description : Sensor-Bauteil

Quantity    :                20   PC
-------------------------------------------------------------
W A R E H O U S E   I N F O R M A T I O N

Storage loc.: 0001
Storage bin :
-------------------------------------------------------------

Issued by   : SAPUSER    S I G N A T U R E
```

12.1.7 Material Document

The material document can be displayed using transaction MB02 or MB03.

Change Material Document 5000000035 : Details 0001 / 0001

| ◀ | ▶ | 👤 | 🖨 | 🗎 Messages | Material | WM Details... |

Purchase Order	4500017107	10		Movement Type	101	GR for consgt. stock

Plant	1000		Werk Hamburg
Vendor	1000		C.E.B. BERLIN
Incoterms	EXW		
Material	1300-550		Sensor assembly

Quantity in

| Unit of Entry | 20 | PC | Stor. Location | 0001 |

Further Information

Unloading Point		
		Company Code	1000	Fiscal Yr	2013
Text		

12.1.8   Accounting Documents

List of documents in accounting

In transaction MB02 or MB03 click | Accounting Documents... | in the item overview of the material document to see the accounting documents. Since the material still belongs to the vendor, no accounting entries are generated.

12.1.9   Stock Overview

Run transaction MMBE to see the stock overview of a material.

Client/Company Code/Plant/Storage Location/Batch/Special Stock	Unrestricted use
▽ 🗄 Full	
▽ 🗄 1000 IDES AG	
▽ 🏢 1000 Werk Hamburg	
▽ 🏢 0001 Materiallager	
Vendor Consignment	58.000

Detailed display

Select Vendor Consignment and click | 🔍Detailed Display | to see the details of that stock.

Stock Vendor Consignment
Plnt 1000
SLoc 0001

Vendor no.	Supplier name	Stock Type	Stock
0000001000	C.E.B. BERLIN	Unrestricted use	58.000
		Qual. inspection	0.000
		Blocked	0.000
		Restricted-use	0.000

12.1.10   Consignment Stock of Vendor

Run transaction MB54 to see consignment stocks.

Material		Material Description				Plnt Name 1				
Vendor	SLoc	Batch	Unrestr. Consgt	BUn	Cnsgt price	Curre	per	Total Value	Curre
1300-550		Sensor assembly				1000 Werk Hamburg				
1000	0001		58	PC	6.37	EUR	1	369.46	EUR

12.1.11   Consignment and Pipeline Settlement

Run transaction MRKO to display consignment and pipeline withdrawals that are not yet settled and are therefore a liability.

CoCd	Vendor	Mat. Doc.	MatYr	Item	Doc. Date	Plant	Material	Qty Withdr	Un	Amount	Crcy
1000	1000	4900000036	2013	1	09.09.2013	1000	1300-550	10	PC	63.65	EUR
1000	1000	4900000037	2013	1	09.09.2013	1000	1300-550	5	PC	31.82	EUR
1000	1000	4900000038	2013	1	09.09.2013	1000	1300-550	4	PC	25.46	EUR
1000	1000	4900000043	2013	1	10.09.2013	1000	1300-800	10	L	7.22	EUR

You can also settle them by choosing the ⦿ Settle option in the selection screen of this report.

12.2 GOODS ISSUE FROM CONSIGNMENT STOCK TO A COST CENTER

Functional Consultant	User	Business Process Owner	Senior Management	My Rating	Understanding Level
B	C	X	X		

12.2.1 Scenario

Consignment stock belongs to a vendor. When you issue consignment stock to a cost center, it is equivalent to goods receipt from the vendor.

12.2.2 Prerequisites

When you issue consignment material to a cost center, the following conditions must be met.

Purchasing info record

For consignment stock, there is no invoice. Payment is credited to the vendor on goods issue. In order to valuate the goods issued, a purchasing info record must be maintained for material, vendor combination for information category Consignment using transactions ME11 or ME12.

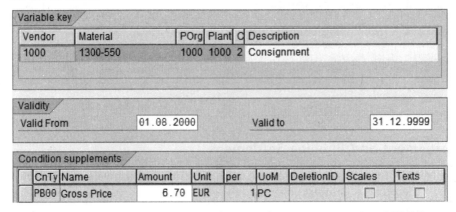

You can also view a purchasing info record using transaction ME1M.

Stock

There must be stock of the material which you may see using transaction MMBE.

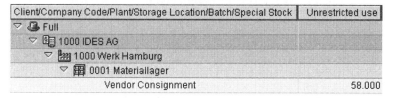

Client/Company Code/Plant/Storage Location/Batch/Special Stock	Unrestricted use
▽ 📖 Full	
▽ 📗 1000 IDES AG	
▽ 🏭 1000 Werk Hamburg	
▽ 📦 0001 Materiallager	
Vendor Consignment	58.000

12.2.3 Transaction

MIGO_GI—Goods Issue (MIGO)

12.2.4 Selection

A07 Goods Issue	R10 Other	GI cst.cnt.fm.consgt	201 K

12.2.5 Item Detail

Where

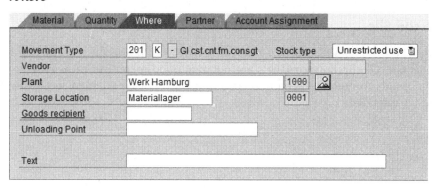

Material	Quantity	Where	Partner	Account Assignment

Movement Type	201 K - GI cst.cnt.fm.consgt	Stock type	Unrestricted use
Vendor		
Plant	Werk Hamburg	1000
Storage Location	Materiallager	0001
Goods recipient		
Unloading Point		
Text		

Partner

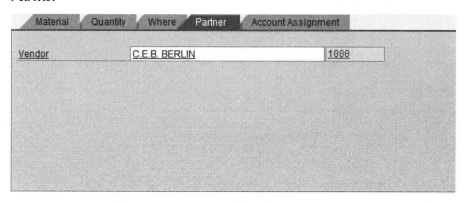

Material	Quantity	Where	Partner	Account Assignment

Vendor	C.E.B. BERLIN	1000

Account Assignment

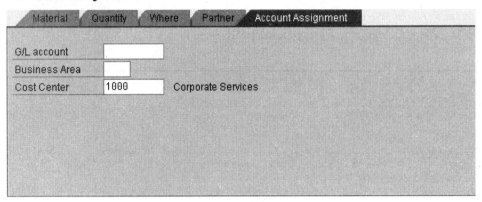

In order to issue goods from consignment stock to cost center, you must specify the cost center.

12.2.6 Posting Goods Issue

After the goods issue is entered, post it by clicking Post . The system posts only those items for which ☑ Item OK indicator is set.

12.2.7 Goods Issue Slip

You can see/print the GR/GI slip and labels using transaction MB90. Choose Processing mode 2 for Repeat processing. If GR/GI slip and/or labels are not generated, print indicator may not have been set in the goods movement screen, or printing may not be enabled in Output Determination (see Chapter 24).

```
G R / G I   S L I P                     4900000036/0001
-----------------------------------------------------------
Posting date  : 09.09.2013
Current date  : 09.09.2013

Plant         : 1000
Description   : Werk Hamburg
-----------------------------------------------------------
Material      : 1300-550
Batch         :
Description   : Sensor assembly

Quantity      :                10   PC
-----------------------------------------------------------

Storage loc.  : 0001
Storage bin   :

Cost center   : 0000001000
```

12.2.8 Material Document

The material document can be displayed using transaction MB02 or MB03.

Change Material Document 4900000036 : Details 0001 / 0001

| ◀ | ▶ | 🖂 | 🖨 | 🖹 Messages | Material | WM Details... |

Movement Type	201 GI cst.cnt.fm.consgt	Special Stock	K
Material	1300-550	Sensor assembly	

Quantity in

Unit of Entry	10	PC	Plant	1000	Stor. Loc.	0001

Account Assignment

G/L Account	400010	
Business Area	9900	
Cost Center	1000	Corporate Services
		Goods recipient
Vendor	1000	
Text		

12.2.9 Accounting Documents

List of documents in accounting

In transaction MB02 or MB03 click | Accounting Documents... | in the item overview of the material document to see the accounting documents.

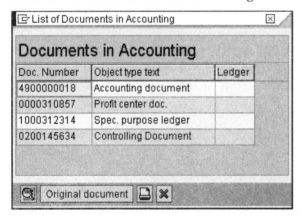

List of Documents in Accounting

Documents in Accounting

Doc. Number	Object type text	Ledger
4900000018	Accounting document	
0000310857	Profit center doc.	
1000312314	Spec. purpose ledger	
0200145634	Controlling Document	

| Original document | 🖨 | ✖ |

Accounting entries

Double-click the | Accounting document | to open it.

Data Entry View								
Document Number	4900000018		Company Code	1000		Fiscal Year		2013
Document Date	09.09.2013		Posting Date	09.09.2013		Period		9
Reference			Cross-CC no.					
Currency	EUR		Texts exist	☐		Ledger Group		

CoCd	Itm	PK	S	Account	Description	Amount	Curr.	Tx	Cost Center	Assignment
1000	1	91		169900	Accounts Payable - c	63.65-	EUR			49000000362013
	2	81		400010	Raw material 2 cons.	63.65	EUR		1000	20130909

Note that the cost center is debited and accounts payable is credited. Credit is not posted to GR/IR clearing account.

12.3 GOODS ISSUE FROM CONSIGNMENT STOCK TO A PROJECT

Functional Consultant	User	Business Process Owner	Senior Management	My Rating	Understanding Level
B	C	X	X		

12.3.1 Scenario

You issue goods from consignment stock to a project.

12.3.2 Prerequisites

When you issue consignment material to a project, the following conditions must be met.

Purchasing info record

For consignment stock, there is no invoice. Payment is credited to the vendor on goods issue. In order to valuate the goods issued, a purchasing info record must be maintained for material, vendor combination for information category Consignment using transactions ME11 or ME12.

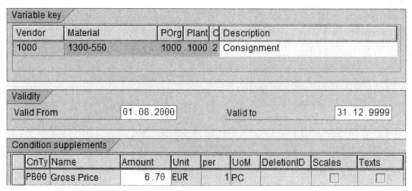

You can also view a purchasing info record using transaction ME1M.

Stock

There must be stock of the material which you may see using transaction MMBE.

Client/Company Code/Plant/Storage Location/Batch/Special Stock	Unrestricted use
▽ 🗄 Full	
▽ 🗄 1000 IDES AG	
▽ 🏭 1000 Werk Hamburg	
▽ 🗄 0001 Materiallager	
Vendor Consignment	48.000

12.3.3 Transaction

MIGO_GI—Goods Issue (MIGO)

12.3.4 Selection

Goods Issue 🗐	Other 🗐		GI consgt.f. project	221	K

12.3.5 Item Detail

Where

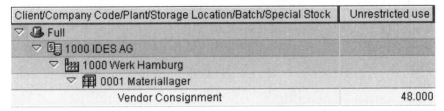

| Material | Quantity | Where | Partner | Account Assignment |

Movement Type	221	K	- GI consgt.f. project	Stock type	Unrestricted use 🗐
Vendor	C.E.B. BERLIN			1000	
Plant	Werk Hamburg		1000	🖾	
Storage Location	Materiallager		0001		
Goods recipient					
Unloading Point					
Text					

Specify movement type 221, special stock indicator K.

Account Assignment

Material	Quantity	Where	Partner	Account Assignment

G/L account   [   ]

Business Area   [   ]

WBS Element   [T-20301   ]   Network   [   ] [   ]

Specify the WBS element.

12.3.6 Posting Goods Issue

After the goods issue is entered, post it by clicking [Post]. The system posts only those items for which ☑ Item OK indicator is set.

12.3.7 Goods Issue Slip

You can see/print the GR/GI slip and labels using transaction MB90. Choose Processing mode [2] for Repeat processing. If CR/GI slip and/or labels are not generated, print indicator may not have been set in the goods movement screen, or printing may not be enabled in Output Determination (see Chapter 24).

```
G R / G I   S L I P                         4900000037/0001
--------------------------------------------------------------
Posting date  : 09.09.2013
Current date  : 09.09.2013

Plant         : 1000
Description   : Werk Hamburg
--------------------------------------------------------------
Material      : 1300-550
Batch         :
Description   : Sensor assembly

Quantity      :                   5   PC
--------------------------------------------------------------

Storage loc.  : 0001
Storage bin   :

Project       : T-20301
```

12.3.8 Material Document

The material document can be displayed using transaction MB02 or MB03.

Change Material Document 4900000037 : Details 0001 / 0001

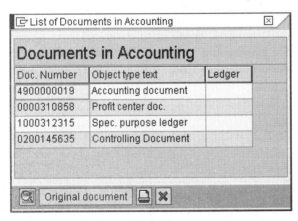

| ◄ ► 🔍 🖨 📋 Messages | Material | WM Details... |

Movement Type	221 GI consgt.f. project	Special Stock	K	
Material	1300-550	Sensor assembly		

Quantity in

| Unit of Entry | 5 | PC | Plant | 1000 | Stor. Loc. | 0001 |

Account Assignment

G/L Account	400010		
Business Area	2000		
WBS Element	T-20301	Network	
		Goods recipient	
Vendor	1000		
Text			

12.3.9 Accounting Documents

List of documents in accounting

In transaction MB02 or MB03 click Accounting Documents... in the item overview of the material document to see the accounting documents.

List of Documents in Accounting

Documents in Accounting

Doc. Number	Object type text	Ledger
4900000019	Accounting document	
0000310858	Profit center doc.	
1000312315	Spec. purpose ledger	
0200145635	Controlling Document	

 Original document 🖨 ✖

Accounting entries

Double-click the Accounting document to open it.

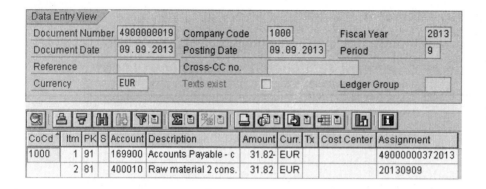

12.4 GOODS ISSUE FROM CONSIGNMENT STOCK TO A SALES ORDER

Functional Consultant	User	Business Process Owner	Senior Management	My Rating	Understanding Level
B	C	X	X		

12.4.1 Scenario

You issue consignment stock to a sales order.

12.4.2 Prerequisites

When you issue consignment material to a sales order, the following conditions must be met.

Purchasing info record

For consignment stock, there is no invoice. Payment is credited to the vendor on goods issue. In order to valuate the goods issued, a purchasing info record must be maintained for material, vendor combination for information category Consignment using transactions ME11 or ME12.

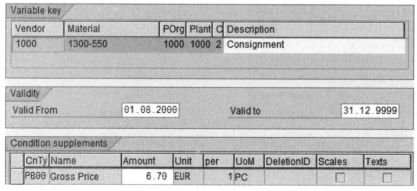

You can also view a purchasing info record using transaction ME1M.

Stock

There must be stock of the material which you may see using transaction MMBE.

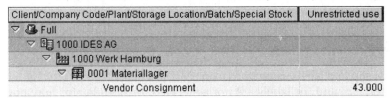

12.4.3   Transaction

MIGO_GI—Goods Issue (MIGO)

12.4.4   Selection

| Goods Issue 📇 | Other 📇 | | GI sls.ord.fm.consgt | 231 | K |

12.4.5   Item Detail

Where

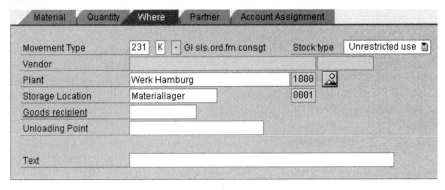

Account Assignment

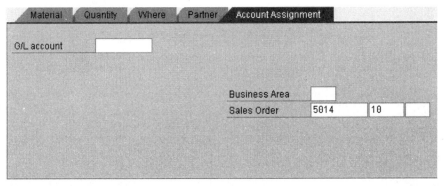

Specify the sales order number, item and year.

12.4.6 Posting Goods Issue

After the goods issue is entered, post it by clicking ⸢Post⸣. The system posts only those items for which ☑ Item OK indicator is set.

12.4.7 Goods Issue Slip

You can see/print the GR/GI slip and labels using transaction MB90. Choose ⸢Processing mode 2⸣ for ⸢Repeat processing⸣. If GR/GI slip and/or labels are not generated, print indicator may not have been set in the goods movement screen, or printing may not be enabled in Output Determination (see Chapter 24).

```
G R  /  G I   S L I P                        4900000038/0001
--------------------------------------------------------------.
Posting date  : 09.09.2013
Current date  : 09.09.2013

Plant         : 1000
Description   : Werk Hamburg
--------------------------------------------------------------.
Material      : 1300-550
Batch         :
Description   : Sensor assembly

Quantity      :                    4   PC
--------------------------------------------------------------.

Storage loc.  : 0001
Storage bin   :

Sales order   : 00000050140000100000
```

12.4.8   Material Document

The material document can be displayed using transaction MB02 or MB03.

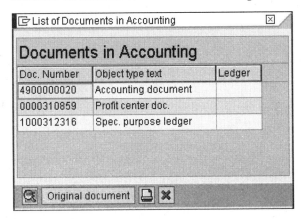

Change Material Document 4900000038 : Details 0001 / 0001

Movement Type	231 GI sls.ord.fm.consgt
Material	1300-550

Special Stock K

Sensor assembly

Quantity in

| Unit of Entry | 4 | PC | Plant | 1000 | Stor. Loc. | 0001 |

Account Assignment

G/L Account   894010

Business Area
Sales Order   5014   10   0
Goods recipient

Vendor   1000

Text

12.4.9   Accounting Documents

List of documents in accounting

In transaction MB02 or MB03 click Accounting Documents... in the item overview of the material document to see the accounting documents.

🗗 List of Documents in Accounting   ⊠

Documents in Accounting

Doc. Number	Object type text	Ledger
4900000020	Accounting document	
0000310859	Profit center doc.	
1000312316	Spec. purpose ledger	

Original document

Accounting entries

Double-click the Accounting document to open it.

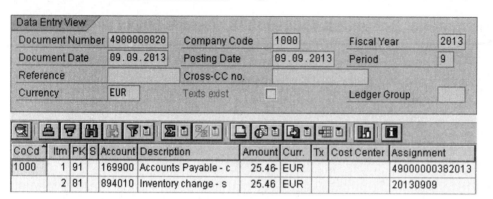

13 Consignment Stock with Customer

13.1 GOODS LENDING TO CONSIGNMENT STOCK WITH CUSTOMER

Functional Consultant	User	Business Process Owner	Senior Management	My Rating	Understanding Level
B	C	X	X		

13.1.1 Scenario

You transfer goods from your own stock to consignment stock held with the customer. The goods are still owned by you; hence no accounting entries are generated. The customer is responsible for receiving and safe keeping of the goods. Physical inventory can be carried out for consignment stock maintained with the customer.

13.1.2 Stock Overview

Run transaction MMBE to see the stock overview of a material.

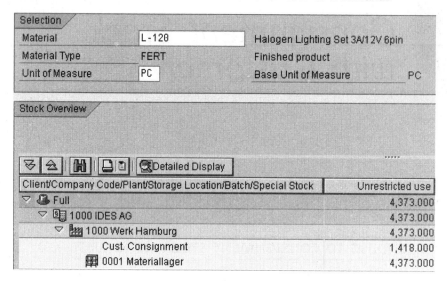

13.1.3 Transaction

MB11—Goods Movement

13.1.4 Initial Screen

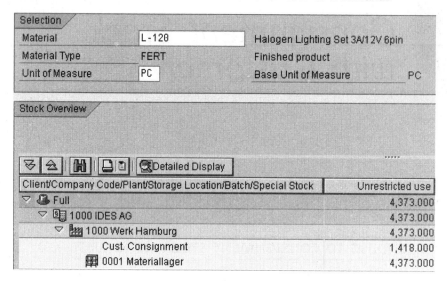

Do not specify special stock W in the initial screen.

13.1.5 Item

Add an item by clicking 🗋 New Item .

Movement Type	631	GI consgmt: lending				
Material	L-120					

Quantity in

Unit of Entry	5		PC	Plant	1000	Stor. Loc.	0001
				Batch			

Account Assignment

		Goods recipient	
		Receiving Plant	
Receiving Batch			
Customer	1171		
No. Containers			
Text			

13.1.6   Posting Goods Lending

After the goods lending is entered, post it by clicking 🖫.

13.1.7   Goods Issue Slip

You can see/print the GR/GI slip and labels using transaction MB90. Choose `Processing mode` `2` for `Repeat processing`. If GR/GI slip and/or labels are not generated, print indicator may not have been set in the goods movement screen, or printing may not be enabled in Output Determination (see Chapter 24).

13.1.8   Material Document

The material document can be displayed using transaction MB02 or MB03.

Change Material Document 4900000039 : Overview

🔍 🖨 🔍	Details from Item		Material		Accounting Documents...	

Posting Date	10.09.2013			Name	SAPUSER

Items

Item	Quantity	EUn	Material	Plnt	SLoc	Batch	Re	MvT	S	S
		BUn	Material Description			Reserv.No.	Itm			FIs
1	5	PC	L-120	1000	0001			631	-	
			Halogen Lighting Set 3A/12V 6pin							
2	5	PC	L-120	1000				631	W	+
			Halogen Lighting Set 3A/12V 6pin							

Note that the quantity of goods in your store is debited, while that in consignment stock held with customer (special stock W) is credited.

13.1.9 Accounting Documents

List of documents in accounting

In transaction MB02 or MB03 click | Accounting Documents... | in the item overview of the material document to see the accounting documents. Since the material is still owned by you, no accounting document is generated.

13.1.10 Stock Overview

Run transaction MMBE to see the stock overview of a material.

Client/Company Code/Plant/Storage Location/Batch/Special Stock	Unrestricted use
▽ 🦴 Full	4,368.000
▽ 📇 1000 IDES AG	4,368.000
▽ 📇 1000 Werk Hamburg	4,368.000
Cust. Consignment	1,423.000
🏢 0001 Materiallager	4,368.000

Detailed display

Select Cust. Consignment and click | 🔍Detailed Display | to see the details of that stock.

Stock Cust. Consignment
Plnt 1000

Customer	Name	Stock Type	Stock
0000001171	Hitech AG	Unrestricted use	89.000
		Qual. inspection	0.000
		Restricted-use	0.000
0000001175	Elektromarkt Bamby	Unrestricted use	1,334.000
		Qual. inspection	0.000
		Restricted-use	0.000

13.1.11 Consignment at Customer

Run transaction MB58 to generate a list of consignment stocks and stocks of returnable packaging at customer's site.

Customer Material	Name 1 Batch	Unrestricted	In Quality Insp.	Restricted-Use	BUn
1171 L-120	Hitech AG	89	0	0	PC
1175 L-120	Elektromarkt Bamby	1,334	0	0	PC

13.2 GOODS ISSUE FROM CONSIGNMENT STOCK TO CUSTOMER

Functional Consultant	*User*	*Business Process Owner*	*Senior Management*	*My Rating*	*Understanding Level*
B	C	X	X		

13.2.1 Scenario

You hold consignment stock at customer's site so that the customer will consume it and pay for it. This process is discussed here.

13.2.2 Transaction

MB11—Goods Movement

13.2.3 Initial Screen

Document Date	10.09.2013	Posting Date	10.09.2013
Material Slip			
Doc.Header Text		GR/GI Slip No.	

Defaults for Document Items

Movement Type	633	Special Stock	W
Plant	1000	Reason for Movement	
Storage Location		☐ Suggest Zero Lines	

GR/GI Slip

☑ Print

○ Individual Slip
◉ Indiv.Slip w.Inspect.Text
○ Collective Slip

Do not specify a storage location, as the material is not being moved out of a storage location. Specify special stock W.

13.2.4   Item

Add an item by clicking 🗋 New Item .

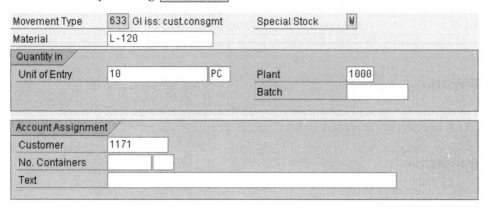

13.2.5   Posting Goods Issue

After the goods issue is entered, post it by clicking 💾.

13.2.6   Goods Issue Slip

You can see/print the GR/GI slip and labels using transaction MB90. Choose Processing mode 2 for Repeat processing. If GR/GI slip and/or labels are not generated, print indicator may not have been set in the goods movement screen, or printing may not be enabled in Output Determination (see Chapter 24).

13.2.7   Material Document

The material document can be displayed using transaction MB02 or MB03.

Change Material Document 4900000041 : Details 0001 / 0001

| ◀ | ▶ | 🖎 | 🖨 | 📧 Messages | Material | WM Details... |

| Movement Type | 633 GI iss: cust.consgmt | Special Stock | W |
| Material | L-120 | Halogen Lighting Set 3A/12V 6pin |

Quantity in
| Unit of Entry | 10 | PC | Plant | 1000 |

Account Assignment
G/L Account	894010
Customer	1171
Text	

13.2.8 Accounting Documents

List of documents in accounting

In transaction MB02 or MB03 click $\boxed{\text{Accounting Documents...}}$ in the item overview of the material document to see the accounting documents.

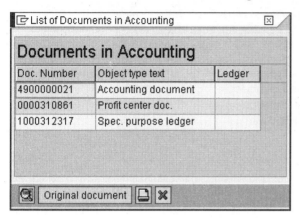

Accounting entries

Double-click the $\boxed{\text{Accounting document}}$ to open it.

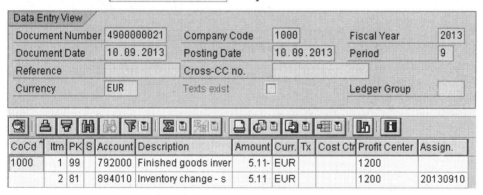

13.2.9 Stock Overview

Run transaction MMBE to see the stock overview of a material.

Client/Company Code/Plant/Storage Location/Batch/Special Stock	Unrestricted use
▽ 🗂 Full	4,368.000
▽ 🏢 1000 IDES AG	4,368.000
▽ 🏭 1000 Werk Hamburg	4,368.000
Cust. Consignment	1,413.000
🏬 0001 Materiallager	4,368.000

Detailed display

Select Cust. Consignment and click 🔍Detailed Display to see the details of that stock.

Stock Cust. Consignment
Plnt 1000

Customer	Name	Stock Type	Stock
0000001171	Hitech AG	Unrestricted use	79.000
		Qual. inspection	0.000
		Restricted-use	0.000
0000001175	Elektromarkt Bamby	Unrestricted use	1,334.000
		Qual. inspection	0.000
		Restricted-use	0.000

13.2.10 Consignment at Customer

Run transaction MB58 to generate a list of consignment stocks and stocks of returnable packaging at customer's site.

Customer	Name 1					
Material		Batch	Unrestricted	In Quality Insp.	Restricted-Use	BUn
1171	Hitech AG					
L-120			79	0	0	PC
1175	Elektromarkt Bamby					
L-120			1,334	0	0	PC

Project Stock

14.1 GOODS RECEIPT IN PROJECT STOCK

Functional Consultant	User	Business Process Owner	Senior Management	My Rating	Understanding Level
B	C	X	X		

14.1.1 Scenario

You maintain stock of material separately for projects.

➤ You may buy materials for specific projects.

➤ Such materials may be used on goods receipt or may be stored under Project stock in the warehouse.

➤ Project stock is shown below a storage location in the stock overview.

➤ Project stock is identified by special stock indicator Q.

➤ Project stock may be classified into unrestricted use, quality inspection, or blocked.

➤ Project stock is always reserved by specified WBS elements. You can maintain projects using transactions CJ01, CJ02 and CJ03.

14.1.2 Prerequisite

In order to receive goods in project stock, you should have a purchase order with account assignment specifying a WBS element. You can create a purchase order using transaction ME21N.

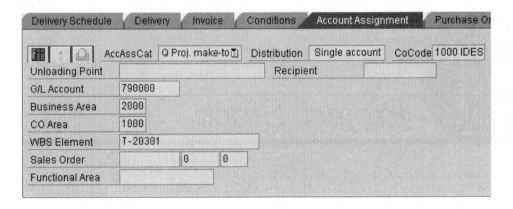

Account assignment categories

In order to receive material in project stock, you must use account assignment category Q or O and specify WBS element. Note that material received for purchase order items having account assignment categories N and P is received in the standard stock, and not in the project stock.

WBS element

You should specify WBS elements having following characteristics:

➤ Special stock valuation indicator should be M or A.

➤ Deletion indicator should be null.

➤ Technical completion date should be null.

Release purchase order

If required, release the purchase order using transaction ME28.

14.1.3   Transaction

MIGO—Goods Movement (MIGO)

14.1.4   Selection

14.1.5 Item Detail

Where

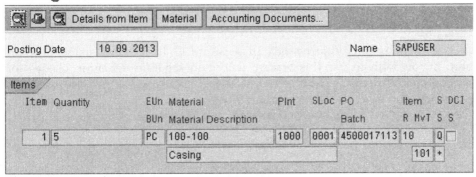

Note that you cannot specify that you want to receive material in project stock. It is determined by the system automatically using the account assignment in the purchase order.

14.1.6 Posting Goods Receipt

After the goods receipt is entered, post it by clicking Post. The system posts only those items for which ☑ Item OK indicator is set.

14.1.7 Goods Receipt Slip

You can see/print the GR/GI slip and labels using transaction MB90. Choose Processing mode 2 for Repeat processing. If GR/GI slip and/or labels are not generated, print indicator may not have been set in the goods movement screen, or printing may not be enabled in Output Determination (see Chapter 24).

14.1.8 Material Document

The material document can be displayed using transaction MB02 or MB03.

Change Material Document 5000000036 : Overview

| | Details from Item | Material | Accounting Documents... |

| Posting Date | 10.09.2013 | | | Name | SAPUSER |

Items										
Item	Quantity	EUn	Material	Plnt	SLoc	PO		Item	S	DCI
		BUn	Material Description		Batch			R	MvT	S S
1	5	PC	100-100	1000	0001	4500017113	10		Q	
			Casing					101	+	

The material document also shows that the goods are received in project stock.

14.1.9 Accounting Documents

List of documents in accounting

In transaction MB02 or MB03 click | Accounting Documents... | in the item overview of the material document to see the accounting documents.

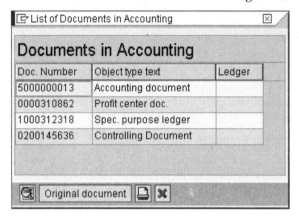

Accounting entries

Double-click the | Accounting document | to open it.

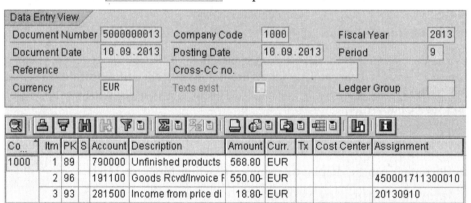

Separate valuation class for project stock

SAP allows you to maintain project stock in separate G/L accounts using account determination. If you wish to use this feature, maintain separate valuation classes for project stock and specify them in the material master.

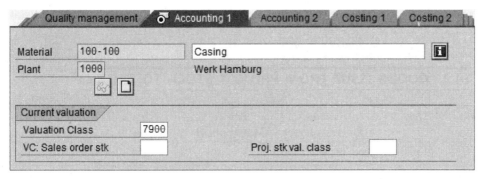

If you do not specify a separate valuation class for project stock, valuation class used for standard stock is used for project stock as well.

14.1.10 Stock Overview

Run transaction MMBE to see the stock overview of a material.

Client/Company Code/Plant/Storage Location/Batch/Special Stock	Unrestricted use
▽ 🍥 Full	1,136.000
▽ 🗐 1000 IDES AG	1,136.000
▽ 🏭 1000 Werk Hamburg	1,136.000
▽ 🎛 0001 Materiallager	1,106.000
Project Stock	5.000

Detailed display

Note that the project stock is stored in a storage location. Select Project Stock and click 🔍 Detailed Display to see the details of that stock.

Stock Project Stock
Plnt 1000
SLoc 0001

Project	Stock Type	Stock
T-20301	Unrestricted use	5.000
	Qual. inspection	0.000
	Blocked	0.000
	Restricted-use	0.000

14.1.11 Project Stock Report

Run transaction MBBS to see the report of project stock.

Material	ValA	Val. Type	S	WBS Element	Total Stock	BUn	Total Value	Crcy
100-100	1000		Q	T-20301	5	PC	568.80	EUR

This provides further confirmation that the material is received in project stock, and not in standard stock.

14.2 GOODS ISSUE FROM PROJECT STOCK TO PROJECT

Functional Consultant	User	Business Process Owner	Senior Management	My Rating	Understanding Level
B	C	X	X		

14.2.1 Scenario

You issue material from project stock to a project.

14.2.2 Transaction

MIGO_GI—Goods Issue (MIGO)

14.2.3 Selection

A07 Goods Issue	R10 Other		GI project for proj.	221	Q

14.2.4 Item Detail

Where

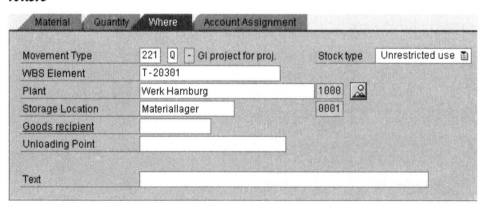

You can issue material to the same WBS element for which you have stored it. If you specify some other WBS element, you get an error. You can issue partial quantity, but not more than what is stored.

14.2.5   Posting Goods Issue

After the goods issue is entered, post it by clicking Post . The system posts only those items for which ☑ Item OK indicator is set.

14.2.6   Goods Issue Slip

You can see/print the GR/GI slip and labels using transaction MB90. Choose Processing mode 2 for Repeat processing . If GR/GI slip and/or labels are not generated, print indicator may not have been set in the goods movement screen, or printing may not be enabled in Output Determination (see Chapter 24).

```
G R / G I   S L I P                      4900000042/0001
-----------------------------------------------------------
Posting date   : 10.09.2013
Current date   : 10.09.2013

Plant          : 1000
Description    : Werk Hamburg
-----------------------------------------------------------
Material       : 100-100
Batch          :
Description    : Casing

Quantity       :                   2   PC
-----------------------------------------------------------
Storage loc.   : 0001
Storage bin    :

Project        : T-20301
```

14.2.7   Material Document

The material document can be displayed using transaction MB02 or MB03.

Change Material Document 4900000042 : Details 0001 / 0001

| ◀ ▶ ⬛ ⬛ ⬛ Messages | Material | WM Details... |

Movement Type	221 GI project for proj.	Special Stock	Q
Material	100-100	Casing	
		WBS Element	T-20301

Quantity in

| Unit of Entry | 2 | PC | Plant | 1000 | Stor. Loc. | 0001 |

Account Assignment

| G/L Account | 890000 |
| Business Area | 2000 |

| Network | | |
| Goods recipient | | |

| Text | |

14.2.8 Accounting Documents

List of documents in accounting

In transaction MB02 or MB03 click Accounting Documents... in the item overview of the material document to see the accounting documents.

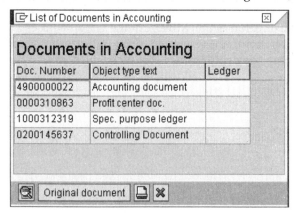

Accounting entries

Double-click the Accounting document to open it.

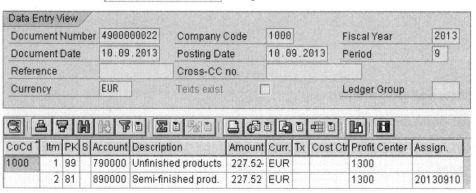

Separate valuation class for project stock

SAP allows you to maintain project stock in separate G/L accounts using account determination. If you wish to use this feature, maintain separate valuation classes for project stock and specify them in the material master.

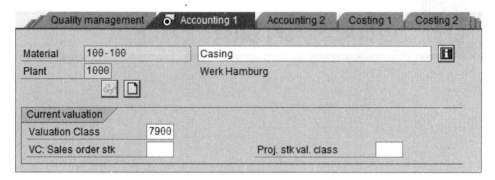

If you do not specify a separate valuation class for project stock, valuation class used for standard stock is used for project stock as well.

14.2.9 Stock Overview

Run transaction MMBE to see the stock overview of a material.

Client/Company Code/Plant/Storage Location/Batch/Special Stock	Unrestricted use
▽ 📦 Full	1,136.000
▽ 🗄 1000 IDES AG	1,136.000
▽ 🏭 1000 Werk Hamburg	1,136.000
▽ ⊞ 0001 Materiallager	1,106.000
Project Stock	3.000

After goods issue, the project stock is reduced. If it becomes zero, it does not appear in the stock overview.

Sales Order Stock

15.1 GOODS RECEIPT INTO SALES ORDER STOCK

Functional Consultant	User	Business Process Owner	Senior Management	My Rating	Understanding Level
B	C	X	X		

15.1.1 Scenario

You maintain stock of material separately for sales orders.

➤ You may buy materials for specific sales orders by specifying them in purchase orders.

➤ Such materials may be used on goods receipt, or may be stored under Sales order stock in the warehouse.

➤ Sales order stock is shown below a storage location in the stock overview.

➤ Sales order stock is identified by special stock indicator E.

➤ Sales order stock may be classified into unrestricted use, quality inspection, or blocked.

15.1.2 Prerequisites

Sales Order

Run transaction VA01 to create a sales order. The system gives you the initial screen.

Order Type	OR	Standard Order

Organizational Data		
Sales Organization	1000	Germany Frankfurt
Distribution Channel	10	Final customer sales
Division	00	Cross-division
Sales Office		
Sales Group		

Click [🔏 Sales] to enter sales order details.

Standard Order		Net value	2,000.00 EUR
Sold-to party	1171	Hitech AG // 21015 Hamburg	▯
Ship-to party	1171	Hitech AG // 21015 Hamburg	
PO Number		PO date	

Sales | Item overview | Item detail | Ordering party | Procurement | Shipping | R

Req. deliv.date	D 02.10.2013	Deliver.Plant		
☐ Complete dlv.		Total Weight	60 KG	
Delivery block		Volume	0.000	
Billing block		Pricing date	21.09.2013	
Payment card		Exp.date		
Payment terms	ZB01 14 Days 3%, 30/2%,	Incoterms	CPT Hamburg	
Order reason				
Sales area	1000 / 10 / 00	Germany Frankfurt, Final customer sales, Cross-division		

All items

Item	Material	Order	S	Description	S	ItCa	First date	Plnt	CnTy	Amount	Crcy	Net valu
10	100-100	20	PC	Gehäuse	☑	TAB	02.10.2013	1000	PR00	100.00	EUR	2,000

Click 🖫 to save the sales order.

✅ Standard Order 11763 has been saved

Purchase Requisition

Purchase requisition generation

When you save the sales order, the purchase requisition is generated automatically. You can see the purchase requisition by specifying the material and account assignment category in transaction ME5A.

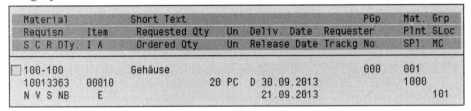

Purchase requisition display

You can display the purchase requisition using transaction ME53N.

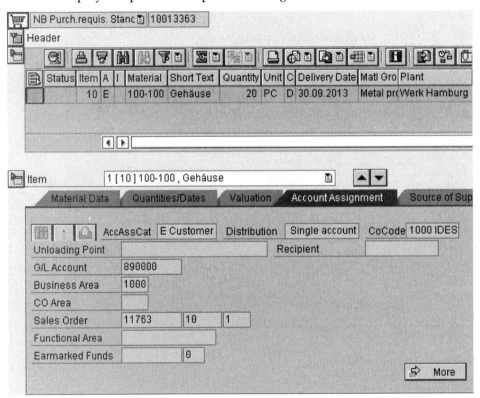

Note that the account assignment category is E and the account assignment object is the sales order. You may need to release the purchase requisition using transaction ME54N.

Purchase Order

You can create purchase order with reference to the purchase requisition. In transaction ME21N you select the purchase requisition in the document overview and click 🔳.

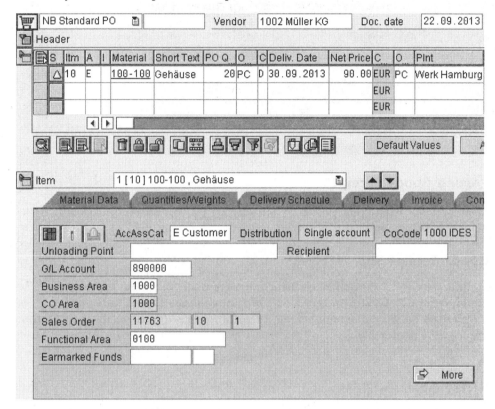

Save the purchase order.

✅ Standard PO created under the number 4500017130

15.1.3 Transaction

MIGO—Goods Movement (MIGO)

15.1.4 Selection

15.1.5   Item Detail

Where

| Material | Quantity | Where | Purchase Order Data | Partner | Account Assignment |

Movement Type	101 E + GR for sales ord. st	Stock type Unrestricted use
Sales Order	11763 10	
Plant	Werk Hamburg	1000
Storage Location	0001	
Goods recipient		
Unloading Point		
Text		

15.1.6   Posting Goods Receipt

After the goods receipt is entered, post it by clicking Post . The system posts only those items for which ☑ Item OK indicator is set.

15.1.7   Goods Receipt Slip

You can see/print the GR/GI slip and labels using transaction MB90. Choose Processing mode 2 for Repeat processing . If GR/GI slip and/or labels are not generated, print indicator may not have been set in the goods movement screen, or printing may not be enabled in Output Determination (see Chapter 24).

```
G O O D S    R E C E I P T    S L I P      5000000040/0001
-----------------------------------------------------------
Goods receipt date : 23.09.2013
Current date       : 23.09.2013
-----------------------------------------------------------
Plant       : 1000
Description : Werk Hamburg

Vendor      : 0000001002        Delivery note:
Name        : Müller KG
PO          : 4500017130/00010
Pur. group  : 000   Chef,H.     Telephone    : 069/5510
-----------------------------------------------------------
Material    : 100-100
Description : Gehäuse

Quantity    :             10  PC
-----------------------------------------------------------
C O N S U M P T I O N / U S A G E  I N F O R M A T I O N

Recipient    :
Unloadg. point:
Sales order  : 0000011763000010
-----------------------------------------------------------

Issued by   : SAPUSER   S I G N A T U R E
```

15.1.8   Material Document

The material document can be displayed using transaction MB02 or MB03.

Change Material Document 5000000040 : Details 0001 / 0001

| ◀ | ▶ | 🔍 | 🖨 | 📧 Messages | Material | WM Details... |

Purchase Order	`4500017130` `10`	Movement Type `101` GR for sales ord. st
Ref. Document	`5000000040` `1`	
Plant	`1000`	Werk Hamburg
Vendor	`1002`	Müller KG
Incoterms	`CPT`	
Material	`100-100`	Casing

Quantity in

Unit of Entry	`10`	`PC`	Stor. Location	`0001`

Further Information

Unloading Point	
	Acct Assgt Cat. `*`
	Company Code `1000` Fiscal Yr `2013`
Text	

15.1.9   Accounting Documents

List of documents in accounting

In transaction MB02 or MB03 click [Accounting Documents...] in the item overview of the material document to see the accounting documents.

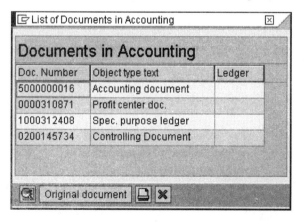

🗁 List of Documents in Accounting   ⊠

Documents in Accounting

Doc. Number	Object type text	Ledger
5000000016	Accounting document	
0000310871	Profit center doc.	
1000312408	Spec. purpose ledger	
0200145734	Controlling Document	

| 🔍 | Original document | 🖨 | ✖ |

Accounting entries

Double-click the | Accounting document | to open it.

Data Entry View			
Document Number 5000000016	Company Code 1000	Fiscal Year	2013
Document Date 23.09.2013	Posting Date 23.09.2013	Period	9
Reference	Cross-CC no.		
Currency EUR	Texts exist ☐	Ledger Group	

CoCd	Itm	PK	S	Account	Description	Amount	Curr.	Tx	C	Profit Center	Assignment
1000	1	81		890000	Semi-finished prod.	900.00	EUR			1010	20130923
	2	96		191100	Goods Rcvd/Invoice F	900.00-	EUR			1010	450001713000010

Separate valuation class for sales order stock

SAP allows you to maintain sales order stock in separate G/L accounts using account determination. If you wish to use this feature, maintain separate valuation classes for sales order stock and specify them in the material master.

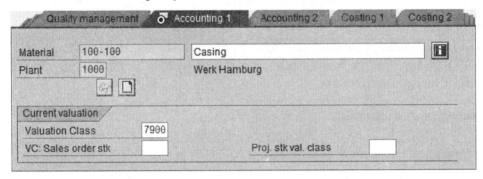

| Quality management | Accounting 1 | Accounting 2 | Costing 1 | Costing 2 |

Material	100-100	Casing	ℹ
Plant	1000	Werk Hamburg	

Current valuation			
Valuation Class	7900		
VC: Sales order stk		Proj. stk val. class	

If you do not specify a separate valuation class for sales order stock, valuation class used for standard stock is used for sales order stock as well.

15.1.10 Stock Overview

Run transaction MMBE to see the stock overview of a material.

Client/Company Code/Plant/Storage Location/Batch/Special Stock	Unrestricted use
▽ 🎛 Full	1,131.000
▽ 📑 1000 IDES AG	1,131.000
▽ 🏭 1000 Werk Hamburg	1,131.000
▽ 🎛 0001 Materiallager	1,101.000
Sales Order Stock	10.000
Project Stock	3.000
🎛 0002 Fertigwarenlager	20.000
🎛 0088 Zentrallager WM	10.000

Detailed display

Select  Sales Order Stock and click |Detailed Display| to see the details of that stock.

SD Doc.	Item (SD)	Stock Type	Stock
11763	10	Unrestricted use	10.000
	10	Qual. inspection	0.000
	10	Blocked	0.000
	10	Restricted-use	0.000

15.1.11 Sales Order Stock Report

Run transaction MBBS to see the report of sales order stock.

✓ No stock exists for specified data

You may wonder why the report does not show any data when the stock overview shows the stock. This is because if you have defined that valuated sales order stock is to be valuated together with the anonymous warehouse stock in one valuation class (indicator KZBWS=A), you can no longer use this report to display the value of this stock.

15.2 GOODS ISSUE FROM SALES ORDER STOCK TO A SALES ORDER

Functional Consultant	User	Business Process Owner	Senior Management	My Rating	Understanding Level
B	C	X	X		

15.2.1 Scenario

You issue goods from sales order stock to a sales order.

15.2.2 Transaction

MIGO_GI—Goods Issue (MIGO)

15.2.3 Selection

| A07 Goods Issue | R10 Other | | GI sls.or.fm.sls.or. | 231 | E |

15.2.4 Item Detail

Where

Material	Quantity	Where	Account Assignment

Movement Type	231	E	-	GI sls.or.fm.sls.or.	Stock type	Unrestricted use
Sales Order	11763	10				
Plant	Werk Hamburg		1000			
Storage Location	Materiallager		0001			
Goods recipient						
Unloading Point						
Text						

15.2.5 Posting Goods Issue

After the goods issue is entered, post it by clicking [Post]. The system posts only those items for which ☑ Item OK indicator is set.

15.2.6 Goods Issue Slip

You can see/print the GR/GI slip and labels using transaction MB90. Choose Processing mode [2] for Repeat processing. If GR/GI slip and/or labels are not generated, print indicator may not have been set in the goods movement screen, or printing may not be enabled in Output Determination (see Chapter 24).

```
G R / G I   S L I P                        4900000060/0001
-------------------------------------------------------------.
Posting date  : 23.09.2013
Current date  : 23.09.2013

Plant         : 1000
Description   : Werk Hamburg
-------------------------------------------------------------.
Material      : 100-100
Batch         :
Description   : Casing

Quantity      :                     5   PC
-------------------------------------------------------------.

Storage loc.  : 0001
Storage bin   :

Sales order   : 0000000000

-------------------------------------------------------------.

Mvt. type : 231 GI sls.or.fm.sls.or.    Issued by: SAPUSER

-------------------------------------------------------------.
```

15.2.7 Material Document

The material document can be displayed using transaction MB02 or MB03.

Change Material Document 4900000060 : Details 0001 / 0001

◀ ▶ 🔏 🖨 📋 Messages	Material	WM Details...	

Movement Type	231	GI sls.or.fm.sls.or.	Special Stock	E	
Material	100-100		Casing		
			Sales Order	11763	10

Quantity in

Unit of Entry	5	PC	Plant	1000	Stor. Loc.	0001

Account Assignment

	Business Area	1000
	Goods recipient	
Text		

15.2.8 Accounting Documents

List of documents in accounting

In transaction MB02 or MB03 click [Accounting Documents...] in the item overview of the material document to see the accounting documents.

> ⓘ Material document 4900000060 does not include an accounting document

When the material is received in the project stock, it is debited to unfinished products. When it is issued to a specific project, it is moved to semi-finished products. In contrast, when the material is received in the sales order stock, it is directly debited to semi-finished products. Therefore, no accounting entries are generated when it is issued to a specific sales order.

Separate valuation class for sales order stock

SAP allows you to maintain sales order stock in separate G/L accounts using account determination. If you wish to use this feature, maintain separate valuation classes for sales order stock and specify them in the material master.

Quality management	🔘 Accounting 1	Accounting 2	Costing 1	Costing 2

Material	100-100	Casing	ℹ
Plant	1000	Werk Hamburg	

Current valuation

Valuation Class	7900		
VC: Sales order stk		Proj. stk val. class	

If you do not specify a separate valuation class for sales order stock, valuation class used for standard stock is used for sales order stock as well.

15.2.9 Stock Overview

Run transaction MMBE to see the stock overview of a material.

Client/Company Code/Plant/Storage Location/Batch/Special Stock	Unrestricted use
▽ 🗄 Full	1,131.000
▽ 🗐 1000 IDES AG	1,131.000
▽ 🏭 1000 Werk Hamburg	1,131.000
▽ ⊞ 0001 Materiallager	1,101.000
Sales Order Stock	5.000
Project Stock	3.000
⊞ 0002 Fertigwarenlager	20.000
⊞ 0088 Zentrallager WM	10.000

16

Pipeline Material

16.1 GOODS ISSUE FROM PIPELINE MATERIAL

Functional Consultant	User	Business Process Owner	Senior Management	My Rating	Understanding Level
B	C	X	X		

16.1.1 Scenario

Pipeline material

Pipeline materials are materials that are supplied through pipelines.

Special stock

Pipeline materials are maintained using special stock indicator P.

Stock

Pipeline materials are always available and they do not have any stock.

Standard stock

The same material may also be available as stock material. For example, petrol may be available both as pipeline material as well as stock material. Petrol is supplied through pipeline from the special stock whereas it is supplied from tanks from the standard stock. For standard stock of the material inventory is maintained in terms of quantity and value like any other material. Price of a material from standard stock and from pipeline may be different.

Pipeline mandatory and pipeline allowed

For a material type in a valuation area, you specify whether materials of this type are always pipeline materials or whether they can be both pipeline as well as standard stock. This is specified in view VT134M of view cluster MTART.

Val.	Matl	Qty updating	Value Upda	Pipe.mand.	PipeAllowd
1000	PIPE	☐	☐	☑	☐
1000	PLAN	☐	☐	☐	☐
1000	PLM	☑	☑	☐	☐
1000	PROC	☐	☐	☐	☐

Purchase order

You cannot raise a purchase order for pipeline materials.

Purchasing info record

Price of a pipeline material must be maintained in purchasing info records using transaction ME11 or ME12.

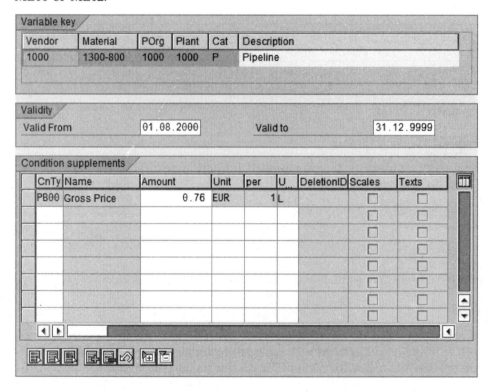

Variable key

Vendor	Material	POrg	Plant	Cat	Description
1000	1300-800	1000	1000	P	Pipeline

Validity

Valid From	01.08.2000	Valid to	31.12.9999

Condition supplements

CnTy	Name	Amount	Unit	per	U	DeletionID	Scales	Texts
PB00	Gross Price	0.76	EUR	1	L		☐	☐
							☐	☐
							☐	☐
							☐	☐
							☐	☐
							☐	☐
							☐	☐
							☐	☐
							☐	☐

You can also view a purchasing info record using transaction ME1M.

16.1.2 Transaction

MIGO_GI—Goods Issue (MIGO)

16.1.3 Selection

16.1.4 Item Overview

Enter appropriate item data and post.

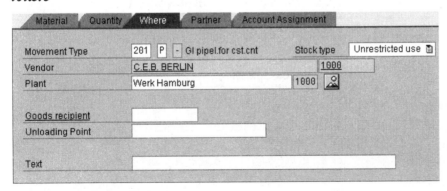

Note that the special stock indicator is P.

16.1.5 Item Detail

Where

Material	Quantity	Where	Partner	Account Assignment

Movement Type	201 P - GI pipel.for cst.cnt	Stock type	Unrestricted use
Vendor	C.E.B. BERLIN	1000	
Plant	Werk Hamburg	1000	
Goods recipient			
Unloading Point			
Text			

16.1.6 Posting Goods Issue

After the goods issue is entered, post it by clicking Post . The system posts only those items for which ☑ Item OK indicator is set.

16.1.7 Goods Issue Slip

You can see/print the GR/GI slip and labels using transaction MB90. Choose Processing mode 2 for Repeat processing. If GR/GI slip and/or labels are not generated, print indicator may not have been set in the goods movement screen, or printing may not be enabled in Output Determination (see Chapter 24).

```
G R / G I   S L I P                        4900000043/0001
-----------------------------------------------------------------
Posting date  : 10.09.2013
Current date  : 10.09.2013

Plant         : 1000
Description   : Werk Hamburg
-----------------------------------------------------------------
Material      : 1300-800
Batch         :
Description   : Gas 95 octane

Quantity      :                  10   L
-----------------------------------------------------------------

Storage loc.  :
Storage bin   :

Cost center   : 0000001000
```

16.1.8 Material Document

The material document can be displayed using transaction MB02 or MB03.

Change Material Document 4900000043 : Details 0001 / 0001

| ◀ ▶ 🔏 🕮 🖻 Messages | Material | WM Details... |

| Movement Type | 201 GI pipel.for cst.cnt | Special Stock | P |
| Material | 1300-800 | Gas 95 octane | |

Quantity in
| Unit of Entry | 10 | L | Plant | 1000 |

Account Assignment
G/L Account	400000	
Business Area	9900	
Cost Center	1000	Corporate Services
		Goods recipient
Vendor	1000	
Text		

16.1.9   Accounting Documents

List of documents in accounting

In transaction MB02 or MB03 click ⌷Accounting Documents...⌷ in the item overview of the material document to see the accounting documents.

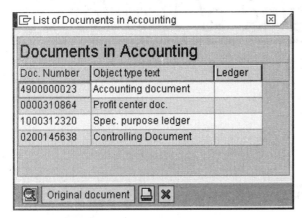

Accounting entries

Double-click the ⌷Accounting document⌷ to open it.

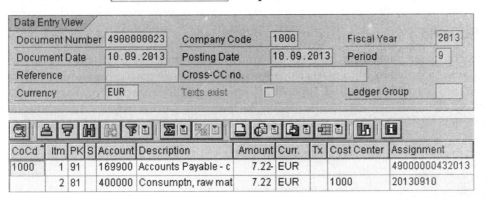

Cost center is debited the value of the consumption and vendor is credited by the same amount.

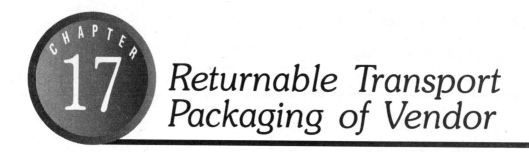

Returnable Transport Packaging of Vendor

17

17.1 RECEIVING RETURNABLE TRANSPORT PACKAGING FROM VENDOR

Functional Consultant	User	Business Process Owner	Senior Management	My Rating	Understanding Level
B	C	X	X		

17.1.1 Scenario

Returnable transport packaging is used for transporting material from the vendor to your company. In order to minimize cost, returnable transport packaging is returned to the vendor. SAP provides material type LEIH for returnable transport packaging. You keep track of returnable transport packaging so that they can be returned to vendors. Run transaction MMBE to see the stock of returnable transport packaging from vendor.

Selection			
Material	TCC-C-A	Cylinder Type A	
Material Type	LEIH	Returnable packaging	
Unit of Measure	EA	Base Unit of Measure	EA

Stock Overview	

Client/Company Code/Plant/Storage Location/Batch/Special Stock	Unrestricted use
Full	34.000
3000 IDES US INC	34.000
3000 New York	34.000
Cust.Ret.Pkg	6.000
0001 Warehouse 0001	
0002 Warehouse 0002	34.000
RT Packaging	8.000

17.1.2 Transaction

MIGO—Goods Movement (MIGO)

17.1.3 Selection

| Goods Receipt 🗎 | Other 🗎 | | GI receipt to RTP | 501 | M |

17.1.4 Item Detail

Material

| Material | Quantity | Where | Partner | Account Assignment | Serial Numbers |

| Material | Cylinder Type A | TCC-C-A |

| Material Group | 00804 |

| Equipment | |

Where

| Material | Quantity | Where | Partner | Account Assignment | Serial Numbers |

Movement Type	501	M	+	GI receipt to RTP	Stock type	Unrestricted use 🗎
Vendor				
Plant	New York	3000	🗺
Storage Location	Warehouse 0002	0002
Goods recipient	
Unloading Point	
Text	

Partner

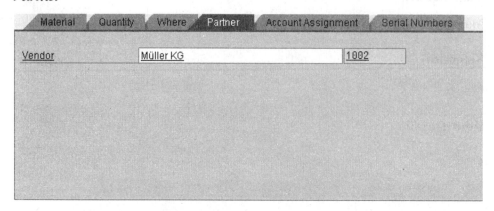

Serial Numbers

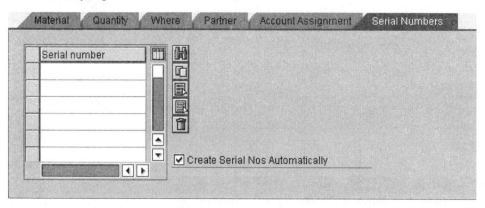

17.1.5 Posting Goods Receipt

After the goods receipt is entered, post it by clicking Post . The system posts only those items for which ☑ Item OK indicator is set.

17.1.6   Goods Receipt Slip

You can see/print the GR/GI slip and labels using transaction MB90. Choose `Processing mode` `2` for `Repeat processing`. If GR/GI slip and/or labels are not generated, print indicator may not have been set in the goods movement screen, or printing may not be enabled in Output Determination (see Chapter 24).

```
G R / G I   S L I P                           4900000044/0001
--------------------------------------------------------------
Posting date  : 10.09.2013
Current date  : 10.09.2013

Plant         : 3000
Description   : New York
--------------------------------------------------------------
Material      : TCC-C-A
Batch         :
Description   : Cylinder Type A

Quantity      :                   2   EA
--------------------------------------------------------------

Storage loc.  : 0002
Storage bin   :
```

17.1.7   Material Document

The material document can be displayed using transaction MB02 or MB03.

Change Material Document 4900000044 : Details 0001 / 0001

17.1.8 Accounting Documents

List of documents in accounting

In transaction MB02 or MB03 click | Accounting Documents... | in the item overview of the material document to see the accounting documents. Since the returnable transport packaging is still owned by the vendor, no accounting document is generated.

17.1.9 Stock Overview

Run transaction MMBE to see the stock overview of a material.

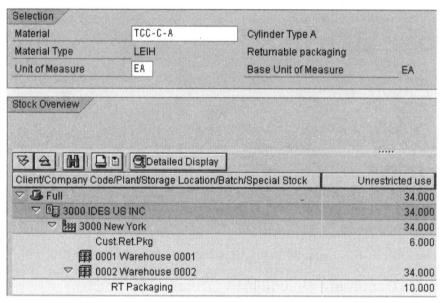

Detailed display

Select RT Packaging and click | Detailed Display | to see the details of that stock.

Stock	Returnable Trans.Packagin		
Plnt	3000		
SLoc	0002		

Vendor no.	Supplier name	Stock Type	Stock
0000001002	Müller KG	Unrestricted use	10.000
		Qual. inspection	0.000
		Blocked	0.000
		Restricted-use	0.000

17.2 RETURNING RETURNABLE TRANSPORT PACKAGING TO VENDOR

Functional Consultant	User	Business Process Owner	Senior Management	My Rating	Understanding Level
B	C	X	X		

17.2.1 Scenario

After the returnable transport packaging becomes free, you return them to vendor.

17.2.2 Transaction

MIGO—Goods Movement (MIGO)

17.2.3 Selection

| Goods Issue | 📋 | Other | 📋 | | GI consgt.f. project | 502 | M |

17.2.4 Item Detail

Material

| Material | Quantity | Where | Partner | Serial Numbers |

| Material | Cylinder Type A | TCC-C-A |

| Material Group | 00804 |

| Equipment | |

Where

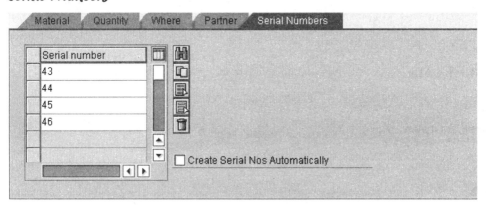

Material	Quantity	Where	Partner	Serial Numbers

Movement Type	502 M - RE receipt to RTP	Stock type	Unrestricted use
Vendor	Müller KG	1002	
Plant	New York	3000	
Storage Location	Warehouse 0002	0002	
Goods recipient			
Unloading Point			
Reason for Movement			
Text			

Serial Numbers

Material	Quantity	Where	Partner	Serial Numbers

Serial number
43
44
45
46

☐ Create Serial Nos Automatically

17.2.5 Posting Goods Issue

After the goods issue is entered, post it by clicking ⟨Post⟩. The system posts only those items for which ☑ Item OK indicator is set.

17.2.6 Goods Issue Slip

You can see/print the GR/GI slip and labels using transaction MB90. Choose Processing mode 2 for Repeat processing. If the GR/GI slip and/or labels are not generated, print indicator may not have been set in the goods movement screen, or printing may not be enabled in Output Determination (see Chapter 24).

17.2.7 Material Document

The material document can be displayed using transaction MB02 or MB03.

Change Material Document 4900000045 : Details 0001 / 0001

◀ ▶ 🔍 🖨 🔯 Messages | Material | WM Details...

Movement Type	502 RE receipt to RTP	Special Stock	M
Material	TCC-C-A	Cylinder Type A	

Quantity in

Unit of Entry	4	EA	Plant	3000	Stor. Loc.	0002

Account Assignment

Goods recipient [ ]

Vendor	1002
Text	

17.2.8   Accounting Documents

List of documents in accounting

In transaction MB02 or MB03 click ⌷Accounting Documents...⌷ in the item overview of the material document to see the accounting documents. There is no accounting entry when returnable transport packaging is received. Consequently, there is no accounting entry when returnable transport packaging is returned to the vendor.

17.2.9   Stock Overview

Run transaction MMBE to see the stock overview of a material.

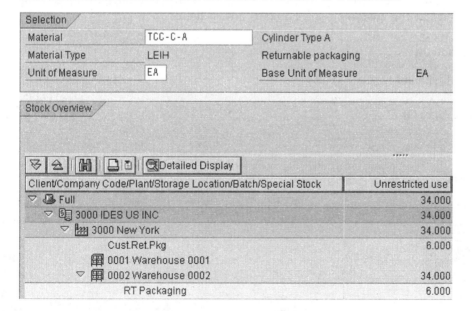

Selection

Material	TCC-C-A	Cylinder Type A	
Material Type	LEIH	Returnable packaging	
Unit of Measure	EA	Base Unit of Measure	EA

Stock Overview

▽ △ 🔍 🖨 🔍Detailed Display

Client/Company Code/Plant/Storage Location/Batch/Special Stock	Unrestricted use
▽ 📦 Full	34.000
▽ 📇 3000 IDES US INC	34.000
▽ 🏭 3000 New York	34.000
Cust.Ret.Pkg	6.000
🏢 0001 Warehouse 0001	
▽ 🏢 0002 Warehouse 0002	34.000
RT Packaging	6.000

Returnable Transport Packaging with Customer

18.1 LENDING RETURNABLE TRANSPORT PACKAGING TO CUSTOMER

Functional Consultant	User	Business Process Owner	Senior Management	My Rating	Understanding Level
B	C	X	X		

18.1.1 Scenario

You deliver goods to your customers in returnable transport packaging. Although they are not charged to customers, but an account is kept of the returnable transport packaging with each customer as the customers are liable to return them.

18.1.2 Transaction

MB11—Goods Movement

18.1.3 Initial Screen

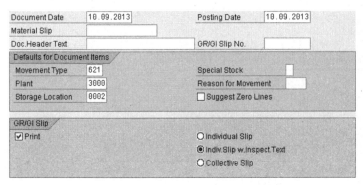

18.1.4 Item

Click ☐ New Item . The system gives the screen below.

Movement Type	621	GI ret.pack.:lending					
Material	TCC-C-A						
Quantity in							
Unit of Entry	2			Plant	3000	Stor. Loc.	0002
				Batch			
Account Assignment							
				Goods recipient			
				Receiving Plant			
Receiving Batch							
Customer	3000						
Text							

18.1.5 Serial Numbers

Click ☐ New Item . The system gives you the following dialog box to enter the serial numbers.

⌐ Maintain Serial Numbers			⊠
Material doc.	$	/ 1	GI ret.pack.:lending
Material	TCC-C-A		
No.serial no	0	/ 2	

	Serial number	Eqpt
☐	6	☑
☐	8	☑

✓ 🔍 🏛 ☐ 🗐 🗑 ✗

18.1.6 Posting Goods Issue

After the goods issue is entered, post it by clicking 🖫.

18.1.7 Goods Issue Slip

You can see/print the GR/GI slip and labels using transaction MB90. Choose Processing mode 2 for Repeat processing . If the GR/GI slip and/or labels are not generated, print indicator may not have been set in the goods movement screen, or printing may not be enabled in Output Determination (see Chapter 24).

18.1.8 Material Document

The material document can be displayed using transaction MB02 or MB03.

Change Material Document 4900000046 : Overview

| | | | Details from Item | Material | Accounting Documents... |

| Posting Date | 10.09.2013 | | Name | SAPUSER |

Items

Item	Quantity	EUn	Material	Plnt	SLoc	Batch	Re	MvT	S	S
		BUn	Material Description			Reserv.No.	Itm			FIs
1	2	EA	TCC-C-A	3000	0002			621		-
			Cylinder Type A							
2	2	EA	TCC-C-A	3000				621	V	+
			Cylinder Type A							

Note that the returnable transport packaging is transferred from storage location to special stock.

18.1.9 Accounting Documents

List of documents in accounting

In transaction MB02 or MB03 click Accounting Documents... in the item overview of the material document to see the accounting documents. No accounting entries are generated for returnable transport packaging as they move to customers and back.

18.1.10 Stock Overview

Run transaction MMBE to see the stock overview of a material.

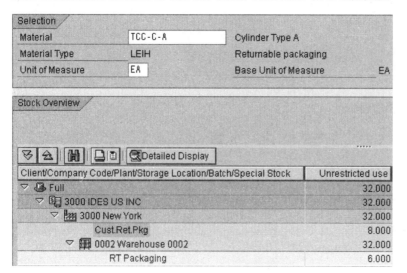

Detailed display

Select RT Packaging and click [🔍Detailed Display] to see the details of that stock.

Stock Cust.Ret.Pkg
Plnt 3000

Customer	Name	Stock Type	Stock
0000003000	Thomas Bush Inc.	Unrestricted use	8.000
		Qual. inspection	0.000
		Restricted-use	0.000

18.2 RECEIVING RETURNABLE TRANSPORT PACKAGING FROM CUSTOMER

Functional Consultant	User	Business Process Owner	Senior Management	My Rating	Understanding Level
B	C	X	X		

18.2.1 Scenario

You deliver goods to your customers in returnable transport packaging. Although they are not charged to customers, but an account is kept of the returnable transport packaging with each customer as the customers are liable to return them. This chapter describes the process of receiving returnable transport packaging from customers.

18.2.2 Transaction

MB11—Goods Movement

18.2.3 Initial Screen

Document Date	10.09.2013		Posting Date	10.09.2013
Material Slip				
Doc.Header Text		GR/GI Slip No.		

Defaults for Document Items

Movement Type	622	Special Stock	
Plant	3000	Reason for Movement	
Storage Location	0002	☐ Suggest Zero Lines	

GR/GI Slip

☑ Print

○ Individual Slip
◉ Indiv.Slip w.Inspect.Text
○ Collective Slip

18.2.4   Item

Click ☐ New Item . The system gives the screen below.

Movement Type	622	GI ret.pack:ret.del.

Material	TCC-C-A

Quantity in

Unit of Entry	1	EA	Plant	3000	Stor. Loc.	0002
			Batch			

Account Assignment

		Goods recipient	
		Issuing Plant	
Issuing Batch			
Customer	3000		
Text			

18.2.5   Serial Numbers

Click ☐ New Item . The system gives you the following dialog box to enter the serial numbers.

☞ Maintain Serial Numbers			⊠
Material doc.	$	/ 1	GI ret.pack:ret.del.
Material	TCC-C-A		
No.serial no	0	/ 1	

	Serial number	Eqpt
☐	6	☑

✓ ⊠ ▦ ⬚ ▤ 🗑 ✖

18.2.6   Posting Goods Receipt

After the goods receipt is entered, post it by clicking 🖫.

18.2.7   Goods Receipt Slip

You can see/print the GR/GI slip and labels using transaction MB90. Choose Processing mode 2 for Repeat processing . If GR/GI slip and/or labels are not generated, print indicator may not have been set in the goods movement screen, or printing may not be enabled in Output Determination (see Chapter 24).

18.2.8   Material Document

The material document can be displayed using transaction MB02 or MB03.

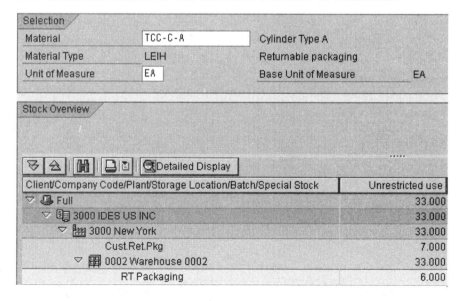

18.2.9   Accounting Documents

List of documents in accounting

In transaction MB02 or MB03 click Accounting Documents... in the item overview of the material document to see the accounting documents. No accounting entries are generated for returnable transport packaging as they move to customers and back.

18.2.10   Stock Overview

Run transaction MMBE to see the stock overview of a material.

Detailed display

Select RT Packaging and click 🔍Detailed Display to see the details of that stock.

Stock	Cust.Ret.Pkg
Plnt	3000

Customer	Name	Stock Type	Stock
0000003000	Thomas Bush Inc.	Unrestricted use	7.000
		Qual. inspection	0.000
		Restricted-use	0.000

19 Goods Movement Reversal

19.1 REVERSAL OF GOODS MOVEMENT

Functional Consultant	User	Business Process Owner	Senior Management	My Rating	Understanding Level
A	A	B	C		

19.1.1 Scenario

You want to reverse a goods receipt. When a goods receipt is reversed, the warehouse stock is reduced and material document and corresponding accounting documents are created. A return delivery slip is also printed.

When you select a purchase order, the system inserts the original goods movements in the item overview. However, the following goods movements cannot be reversed.

➢ Goods movements that are already reversed.

➢ Goods that are returned to vendor.

➢ Goods that have been moved further, e.g. from GR blocked stock to warehouse.

If the above has happened for partial quantity, the item is inserted with the balance quantity. All goods receipt reversals work much in the same way.

19.1.2 Transaction

MIGO—Goods Movement (MIGO)

19.1.3 Movement Type

When you receive goods, you use a movement type. For reversing the goods receipt, you use a movement type which is 1 more than the goods receipt movement type.

19.1.4 Selection

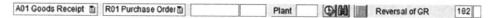

You can enter the purchase order number, item and plant in the selection subscreen given above, or double-click a purchase order number in the document overview.

19.1.5 Item Overview

When you select a purchase order, the system inserts goods movement of movement type 101 as possible candidates for goods movement reversal. However, you cannot reverse the following goods movements.

➢ The document has already been reversed using movement type 102.

➢ The material received has been returned to the vendor using movement type 122.

If the above has happened for partial quantity, you can reverse the balance quantity.

Line	Mat. Sho	OK	Qty	E	SLoc	M	D	Stock Type	Plnt	Vendor	Ref. Doc.
1	Gehäuse	☐	10	PC		102	-	Unrestr	Werk Hamburg	Müller KG	5000011811
2	Gehäuse	☐	25	PC		102	-	Unrestr	Werk Hamburg	Müller KG	5000011814
3	Gehäuse	☐	10	PC		102	-	Unrestr	Werk Hamburg	Müller KG	5000011815

You may select the item to be reversed based on the number of the material document generated which is shown in the Ref. Doc. column. Select ☑ Item OK of the line to be reversed.

19.1.6 Item Detail

Quantity

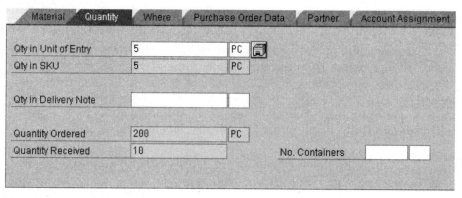

If you are reversing a goods movement for partial quantity, enter the quantity.

Where

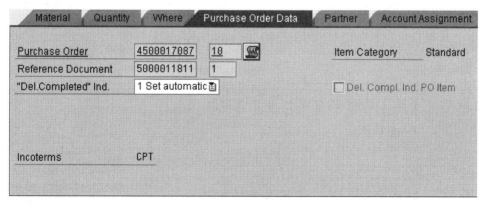

Stock type

Enter the stock type.

Storage location

Enter the storage location.

Reason for movement

You can select from the reasons for movement configured for this movement type. Configuration for a movement type also specifies whether reason for movement is mandatory, or optional, or whether the field is hidden.

Purchase Order Data

Reference document

The reference document shows the material document number of the goods movement being reversed.

Item OK

Select ☑ Item OK . Only those items for which this indicator is selected are checked and posted. No action is taken on other items.

19.1.7 Posting Goods Movement Reversal

After the goods movement reversal is entered, post it by clicking Post . The system posts only those items for which ☑ Item OK indicator is set.

19.1.8 Return Delivery Slip

You can see/print the GR/GI slip and labels using transaction MB90. Choose Processing mode 2 for Repeat processing . If GR/GI slip and/or labels are not generated, print indicator may not have been set in the goods movement screen, or printing may not be enabled in Output Determination (see Chapter 24).

```
R E T U R N   D E L I V E R Y   S L I P   5000000037/0001
---------------------------------------------------------------
Goods receipt date : 11.09.2013
Current date       : 11.09.2013
---------------------------------------------------------------
Plant       : 1000
Description : Werk Hamburg

Vendor      : 0000001002        Delivery note:
Name        : Müller KG
PO          : 4500017087/00010
Pur. group  : 000   Chef,H.     Telephone    : 069/5510
---------------------------------------------------------------
Material    : 100-100
Batch       :
Description : Gehäuse

Quantity    :                5   PC
---------------------------------------------------------------
W A R E H O U S E   I N F O R M A T I O N

Storage loc.: 0001
Storage bin :
---------------------------------------------------------------

Issued by   : SAPUSER   S I G N A T U R E
```

Reference document not mentioned

The goods receipt slip does not mention the reference document number and date. Reference document is the material document against which the material was originally received.

19.1.9 Return Delivery Labels

Material: 100-100   Material: 100-100
Vendor: Müller KG   Vendor: Müller KG
Plant/SL: 1000 0001   Plant/SL: 1000 0001
GR/ GI Number: 5000000037 GR/ GI Number: 5000000037
GR/ GI Date: 11.09.2013   GR/ GI Date: 11.09.2013

19.1.10 Material Document

The material document can be displayed using transaction MB02 or MB03.

Change Material Document 5000000037 : Details 0001 / 0001

◀ ▶ | ⊠ ⬛ | ☒ Messages | Material | WM Details...

Purchase Order	4500017087 10	Movement Type	102	Reversal of GR
Ref. Document	5000011811 1		
Plant	1000	Werk Hamburg
Vendor	1002	Müller KG
Incoterms	CPT	
Material	100-100	Casing

Quantity in

Unit of Entry   5   PC   Stor. Location   0001

Further Information

Unloading Point

Company Code   1000   Fiscal Yr   2013

Text

19.1.11 Accounting Documents

List of documents in accounting

In transaction MB02 or MB03 click | Accounting Documents... | in the item overview of the material document to see the accounting documents.

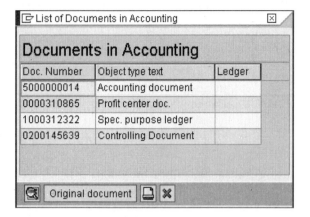

Accounting entries

Double-click the | Accounting document | to open it.

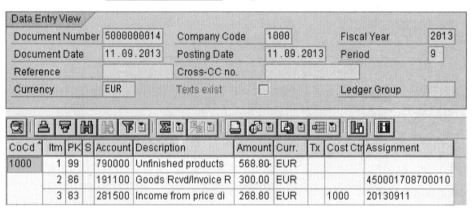

19.1.12 Purchase Order History

Run transaction ME22N or ME23N to see the purchase order history.

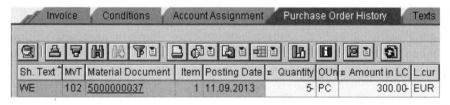

The purchase order history for goods receipt reversal shows that both quantity and amount have negative values.

20 Screen Layout

20.1 PERMITTED EVENTS AND REFERENCE DOCUMENTS

Functional Consultant	User	Business Process Owner	Senior Management	My Rating	Understanding Level
A	X	X	X		

20.1.1 Purpose

When you run transaction MIGO, or MIGO_GI etc., you specify several parameters in the top line.

`A01 Goods Receipt` `R01 Purchase Order` [   ] Plant [   ] ⊕ 🔳 🔳 GR goods receipt [101]

Here you define the possible values for field `A01 Goods Receipt` and `R01 Purchase Order`. You can also define valid combinations of these two fields and default movement type in field `101` for each combination.

20.1.2 IMG Node

SM34 ➤ MIGO_LISTBOX

20.1.3 Transaction

SAP provides the following MIGO transactions as shown in view V_MIGO_TCODE.

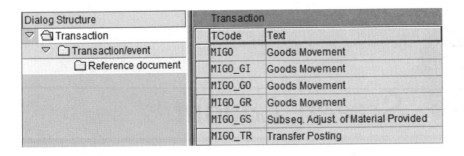

20.1.4 Event

When you run transaction MIGO, you specify several parameters in the top tine.

In the first field 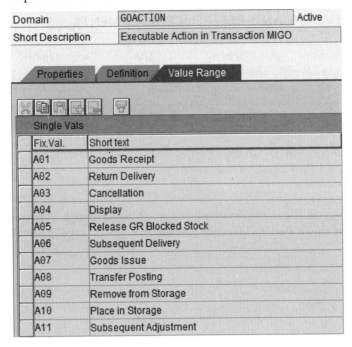 of transaction MIGO you enter event. The list of events is predefined.

Domain	GOACTION	Active
Short Description	Executable Action in Transaction MIGO	

Properties | Definition | **Value Range**

Single Vals

Fix.Val.	Short text
A01	Goods Receipt
A02	Return Delivery
A03	Cancellation
A04	Display
A05	Release GR Blocked Stock
A06	Subsequent Delivery
A07	Goods Issue
A08	Transfer Posting
A09	Remove from Storage
A10	Place in Storage
A11	Subsequent Adjustment

20.1.5 Permitted Events

For each transaction, you can specify the permitted events. These are available in the Executable action field to choose from.

MIGO			MIGO_GR		
Transaction/event			**Transaction/event**		
Promotion		Active	Promotion		Active
A01 Goods Receipt	🗒	☑	A01 Goods Receipt	🗒	☑
A02 Return Delivery	🗒	☑	A02 Return Delivery	🗒	☑
A03 Cancellation	🗒	☑	A03 Cancellation	🗒	☑
A04 Display	🗒	☑	A04 Display	🗒	☑
A05 Release GR Blocked Stock	🗒	☑	A05 Release GR Blocked Stock	🗒	☑
A06 Subsequent Delivery	🗒	☑	A06 Subsequent Delivery	🗒	☑
A07 Goods Issue	🗒	☑	A07 Goods Issue	🗒	☐
A08 Transfer Posting	🗒	☑	A08 Transfer Posting	🗒	☐
A09 Remove from Storage	🗒	☑	A09 Remove from Storage	🗒	☐
A10 Place in Storage	🗒	☑	A10 Place in Storage	🗒	☑
A11 Subsequent Adjustment	🗒	☑	A11 Subsequent Adjustment	🗒	☐

Transaction MIGO is the most general goods movement transaction which permits all 11 executable actions. Transaction MIGO_GR, in contrast, does not allow some of these events.

20.1.6   Reference Document

When you run transaction MIGO, you specify several parameters in the top tine.

In the second field `R01 Purchase Order 🗒` of transaction MIGO you enter reference document. The list of reference documents is predefined.

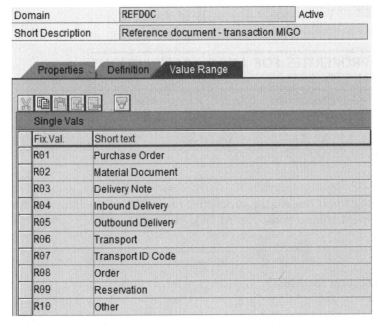

Domain	REFDOC		Active
Short Description	Reference document - transaction MIGO		

Properties | Definition | **Value Range**

Single Vals	
Fix.Val.	Short text
R01	Purchase Order
R02	Material Document
R03	Delivery Note
R04	Inbound Delivery
R05	Outbound Delivery
R06	Transport
R07	Transport ID Code
R08	Order
R09	Reservation
R10	Other

20.1.7 Permitted Reference Documents

For each combination of transaction and event, SAP has specified permitted reference documents.

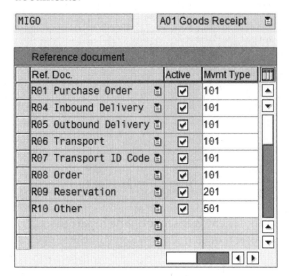

If you do not want to allow some reference documents, you can deactivate it. You can also define a default movement type. You can also define user specific default values by selecting Settings ➢ Default Values inside the MIGO transaction.

Action	Reference Document	Movement Type
A01 Goods Receipt 🗎	R01 Purchase Order 🗎	101
A01 Goods Receipt 🗎	R04 Inbound Delivery 🗎	101

20.2 FIELD PROPERTIES FOR MIGO TRANSACTIONS

Functional Consultant	User	Business Process Owner	Senior Management	My Rating	Understanding Level
A	X	X	X		

20.2.1 Purpose

In screen group Field selection MIGO you can set the properties of fields and pushbuttons for items in MIGO goods movement transactions, e.g. MIGO, MIGO_GI, etc.

20.2.2 IMG Node

Transaction OMJX—Field Selection for MIGO

20.2.3 Modifiable Fields

On running transaction OMJX, you will get the following screen.

Screen group	Field selection MIGO						

Modifiable fields							
Modifiable field	Field name	Input	Req.	Disp.	Hide	HiLi	
"Del.Completed" Ind.	GOITEM-MIGO_ELIKZ	⦿	◯	◯	◯	☐	▲
🗑 Delete	OK_NOT_OK	⦿	◯	◯	◯	☐	▼
📲	OK_NOT_ORDERED	⦿	◯	◯	◯	☐	
📇 Contents	OK_TAKE_VALUE	⦿	◯	◯	◯	☐	
🔯	OK_CONTAINER	⦿	◯	◯	◯	☐	
💾	OK_DETERMINE_ALL	⦿	◯	◯	◯	☐	
💾	OK_DETERMINE	⦿	◯	◯	◯	☐	
🖧	OK_EXPAND_BOM	⦿	◯	◯	◯	☐	
🗐	OK_LINKED_DOCUMENT	⦿	◯	◯	◯	☐	
✂	OK_SPLIT_QUANTITY	⦿	◯	◯	◯	☐	
Base Unit of Measure	GOITEM-EANME	⦿	◯	◯	◯	☐	
Base Unit of Measure	GOITEM-MEINS	⦿	◯	◯	◯	☐	
Batch Restricted	GOITEM-ZUSTD	⦿	◯	◯	◯	☐	▲
Bill of Lading	GOHEAD-FRBNR	⦿	◯	◯	◯	☐	▼

If you are in some other screen, click [Modifiable] to get to this screen. If you are in some other screen group, click [Screen groups] and select Field selection MIGO .

20.2.4 Unconditional Change in Field Properties

In this screen you can change the properties of a field. By default, all fields are Input input fields. You can change them to Req. , or Disp. , or Hide . You can also HiLi a field. If your company does not need the Bill of Lading field, you can hide it.

Modifiable field	Field name	Input	Req.	Disp.	Hide	HiLi
Bill of Lading	GOHEAD-FRBNR	◯	◯	◯	⦿	☐

Click [Influences] to see the changes.

```
List of All Influences for Screen Group

Settings without influencing field

  Modified field        In     Mand    Displ    Hide    Hilite

   Bill of Lading                                  X



Settings with influencing field (field 1 influences field 2)

  Influencing field     Modified field      In      Mand     Displ     Hide



Settings with influencing field (field 1 influenced by field 2)

  Modified field        Influencing field     In     Mand     Displ     Hide
```

20.2.5   Conditional Change in Field Properties

SAP also lets you modify the field properties conditionally through the concept of influencing fields. The properties of a field can depend on a value of the influencing field. The list of influencing fields can be seen by clicking [⚹ Influencing]. In screen group [Field selection MIGO], there are no influencing fields. Hence the system does not show the list of influencing fields; instead, it takes you to the list of [Modified fields].

Screen group   Field selection MIGO
Influencing field
Contents   [   ]

Modified fields							
Modifiable field	Field name	Input	Req.	Disp.	Hide	HiLi	
"Del.Completed" Ind.	GOITEM-MIGO_ELIKZ	◉	○	○	○	☐	▲
🗑 Delete	OK_NOT_OK	◉	○	○	○	☐	▼
📑	OK_NOT_ORDERED	◉	○	○	○	☐	
📖 Contents	OK_TAKE_VALUE	◉	○	○	○	☐	
📦	OK_CONTAINER	◉	○	○	○	☐	
💾	OK_DETERMINE_ALL	◉	○	○	○	☐	
💾	OK_DETERMINE	◉	○	○	○	☐	
🔗	OK_EXPAND_BOM	◉	○	○	○	☐	
🔲	OK_LINKED_DOCUMENT	◉	○	○	○	☐	
✂	OK_SPLIT_QUANTITY	◉	○	○	○	☐	
Base Unit of Measure	GOITEM-EANME	◉	○	○	○	☐	▲
Base Unit of Measure	GOITEM-MEINS	◉	○	○	○	☐	▼

Since there are no influencing fields, conditional change in properties of a field in screen group `Field selection MIGO` is not possible.

20.2.6　Field Properties based on Movement Type

The field properties defined above are for all movement types. But in MIGO transactions, some fields may be mandatory or optional depending on the movement type. For example, for goods issue to cost center (movement type 201), cost center is mandatory. You define that in view MIGO_CUST_FIELDS.

Mvmt Type	Field Name	Required Entry	Optional Entry
201	GSBER	○	◉
201	KONTO	○	◉
201	KOSTL	◉	○
201	SGTXT	○	◉
201	WEMPF	○	◉

20.3　FIELD PROPERTIES FOR HEADER FIELDS

Functional Consultant	User	Business Process Owner	Senior Management	My Rating	Understanding Level
A	X	X	X		

20.3.1　Purpose

In screen group `Goods Movements: Initial/Header Screens` you can set the properties of fields in the initial screen and header of non-MIGO goods movement transactions, e.g. MB04, MB1A, MB1B, MB1C, MB31, etc.

20.3.2　IMG Node

Transaction OMJN—Field Selection for Goods Movements Initial/Header Screens

20.3.3　Modifiable Fields

On running transaction OMJN, you will get the following screen.

Screen group   Goods Movements: Initial/Header Screens

Modifiable fields

Modifiable field	Field name	Input	Req.	Disp.	Hide	HiLi	
Bill of Lading	MKPF-FRBNR	●	○	○	○	☐	▲
Collective Slip	RM07M-WVERS3	●	○	○	○	☐	▼
Create Delivery	RM07M-XDELIV	●	○	○	○	☐	
Delivery	RM07M-VLIEF	●	○	○	○	☐	
Delivery	RM07M-GWELF	●	○	○	○	☐	
Delivery	RM07M-VBELN	●	○	○	○	☐	
Delivery Note	RM07M-LFSNR	●	○	○	○	☐	
Delivery Note No.	RM07M-GWELS	●	○	○	○	☐	
Document Date	MKPF-BLDAT	●	○	○	○	☐	
Document Header Text	MKPF-BKTXT	●	○	○	○	☐	
EAN/UPC	RM07M-EAN11	●	○	○	○	☐	
Goods Receipt/Issue Slip	RM07M-XABLN	●	○	○	○	☐	
Indiv.Slip w.Inspect.Text	RM07M-WVERS2	●	○	○	○	☐	▲
Individual Slip	RM07M-WVERS1	●	○	○	○	☐	▼

If you are in some other screen, click [👤 Modifiable] to get to this screen.

20.3.4 Unconditional Change in Field Properties

In this screen you can change the properties of a field. By default, all fields are [Input] fields. You can change them to [Req.], or [Disp.], or [Hide]. You can also [HiLi] a field. If your company does not need the [Bill of Lading] field, you can hide it.

Modifiable field	Field name	Input	Req.	Disp.	Hide	HiLi
Bill of Lading	MKPF-FRBNR	○	○	○	●	☐

Click [👤 Influences] to see the changes.

List of All Influences for Screen Group

Settings without influencing field

Modified field	In	Mand	Displ	Hide	Hilite
Bill of Lading				X	

Settings with influencing field (field 1 influences field 2)

Influencing field	Modified field	In	Mand	Displ	Hide

Settings with influencing field (field 1 influenced by field 2)

Modified field	Influencing field	In	Mand	Displ	Hide

20.3.5 Conditional Change in Field Properties

Influencing Fields

SAP also lets you modify the field properties conditionally through the concept of influencing fields. The properties of a field can depend on a value of the influencing field. The list of influencing fields can be seen by clicking [👤 Influencing].

Screen group	Goods Movements: Initial/Header Screens

Influencing fields	
Influencing field	Field name
Document Type	T158-BLART
Print Active	RM07M-XNAPR
Print Version	T158-WEVER
Suggest Zero Lines	RM07M-XNUVO
Transaction Code	T158-TCODE

Determination of Influencing Field Values

Influencing field	Determination of influencing field value
Transaction Code	When you select a menu item, the system runs the transaction code associated with it. Alternatively, you could enter the transaction code directly in the command field 🔘 [🗎].
Document Type	Determined from table T158 based on the transaction code.
Print Version	Determined from table T158 based on the transaction code.
Print Active	You specify this value in the ☑ Print field in the header.
Suggest Zero Lines	You specify this value in the ☑ Suggest Zero Lines field in the header of order related transactions, e.g. MB31. In some transactions, e.g. MB1A, MB1B, MB1C etc., ☑ Suggest Zero Lines field is XNUVR, not XNUVO.

Header of Goods Issue Transaction MB1A

The header of goods issue transaction MB1A in the standard system is given below.

| Document Date | 01.10.2013 | Posting Date | 01.10.2013 |

| Material Slip | | | |

| Doc.Header Text | | GR/GI Slip No. | |

Defaults for Document Items

Movement Type		Special Stock	
Plant		Reason for Movement	
Storage Location		☐ Suggest Zero Lines	

GR/GI Slip

☑ Print

       ○ Individual Slip

       ⊙ Indiv.Slip w.Inspect.Text

       ○ Collective Slip

Business Scenario

In SAP, the document date is the date on which the business transaction, in this case the goods issue, took place. If your company's policy is that goods issue must be recorded when they are issued, you want the document date to be the current date, which is the default value of the document date field. You do not want the user to change this value. This can be achieved by making the document date a display field for transaction MB1A. But for other transactions the company wants the document date to remain input field.

Conditional Change in Field Properties

Select ⬚Document Date and click 🔍 Modified .

| Screen group | Goods Movements: Initial/Header Screens |
| Modifiable field | Document Date |

Influencing fields

Influencing field	Contents	Input	Req.	Disp.	Hide	HiLi	
Document Type		⊙	○	○	○	☐	▲
Print Active		⊙	○	○	○	☐	▼
Print Version		⊙	○	○	○	☐	
Suggest Zero Lines		⊙	○	○	○	☐	
Transaction Code		⊙	○	○	○	☐	
							▲
							▼

Select ⬚Transaction Code and click New values ... .

Contents	Input	Req	Disp	Invis	HiLi	
MB1A	○	○	◉	○	☐	
	◉	○	○	○	☐	
	◉	○	○	○	☐	
	◉	○	○	○	☐	
	◉	○	○	○	☐	
	◉	○	○	○	☐	
	◉	○	○	○	☐	
	◉	○	○	○	☐	
	◉	○	○	○	☐	
	◉	○	○	○	☐	

Field Selection: Modified Field

Influencing field   Transaction Code

✔ Continue   Cancel

Enter the transaction code, change field properties and click ✔ Continue .

Screen group   Goods Movements: Initial/Header Screens

Modifiable field   Document Date

Influencing fields

Influencing field	Contents	Input	Req.	Disp.	Hide	HiLi	
Document Type		◉	○	○	○	☐	
Print Active		◉	○	○	○	☐	
Print Version		◉	○	○	○	☐	
Suggest Zero Lines		◉	○	○	○	☐	
Transaction Code		◉	○	○	○	☐	
Transaction Code	MB1A	○	○	◉	○	☐	

Click ⚬ Influences . The system displays all influences.

```
List of All Influences for Screen Group
```

Settings without influencing field

Modified field	In	Mand	Displ	Hide	Hilite
Bill of Lading				X	

Settings with influencing field (field 1 influences field 2)

Influencing field	Modified field	In	Mand	Displ	Hide	Hilite	Onfluencing value
Transaction Code	Document Date			X			MB1A

Settings with influencing field (field 1 influenced by field 2)

Modified field	Influencing field	In	Mand	Displ	Hide	Hilite	Influencing value
Document Date	Transaction Code			X			MB1A

Note that the document date is a display field for transaction MB1A.

Modified Header of Goods Issue Transaction MB1A

Document Date	01.10.2013	Posting Date	01.10.2013
Material Slip			
Doc.Header Text		GR/GI Slip No.	

Defaults for Document Items

Movement Type		Special Stock	
Plant		Reason for Movement	
Storage Location		☐ Suggest Zero Lines	

GR/GI Slip

☑ Print

- ◯ Individual Slip
- ◉ Indiv.Slip w.Inspect.Text
- ◯ Collective Slip

Multiple Influences

A field may be subject to multiple influences. In that case the property with the highest priority is selected. The priority of field properties is given below.

Priority	Property
1	Hide
2	Display
3	Required
4	Input

20.4 FIELD PROPERTIES FOR ITEM FIELDS

Functional Consultant	User	Business Process Owner	Senior Management	My Rating	Understanding Level
A	X	X	X		

20.4.1 Purpose

Here you can change properties of fields for non-MIGO goods movement screens. Field properties can depend on movement type and special stock indicator. Field properties cannot be defined for movement types starting with 1.

20.4.2 IMG Node

Transaction OMBW—Screen Layout for Goods Issue/Transfer Postings
Transaction OMCJ—Screen Layout for Goods Receipt
Transaction OMJA—Screen Layout for Automatic Movements

20.4.3 Field Selection Overview

	MvT	Movement Type Text	S	Special stock descr.	Spec. Ind. Stock Tfr
	201	GI for cost center			
	201	GI cst.cnt.fm.consgt	K	Consignment (vendor)	
	201	GI pipel.for cst.cnt	P	Pipeline material	
	202	RE for cost center			
	202	RE cst.cnt.fm.consgt	K	Consignment (vendor)	
	202	RE pipel.for cst.cnt	P	Pipeline material	

Special stock indicator for physical stock transfer

This indicator is used, for example, in the case of the physical transfer of a consignment material and when consignment material is transferred from the vendor's stock to the company's own stock. It specifies the special stock indicator in the second posting line of a document item.

20.4.4 Field Status Groups

In the field selection overview, select a line and click 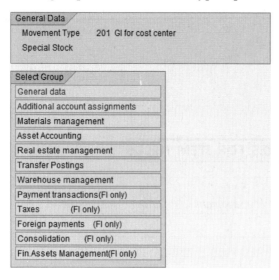. The system shows the field status groups for a movement type, special stock indicator combination.

General Data	
Movement Type	201 GI for cost center
Special Stock	

Select Group

General data
Additional account assignments
Materials management
Asset Accounting
Real estate management
Transfer Postings
Warehouse management
Payment transactions(FI only)
Taxes   (FI only)
Foreign payments   (FI only)
Consolidation   (FI only)
Fin.Assets Management(FI only)

20.4.5 Field Properties

You select a group and click 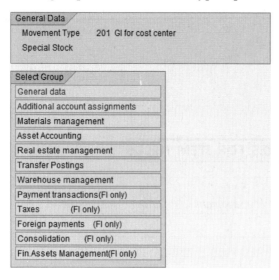. The system shows you the fields in a field status group.

General Data		Page 1 / 3
Movement Type	201 GI for cost center	
Special Stock		

Additional account assignments

	Suppress	Req. Entry	Opt. entry
Calculation period (FI only)	●	○	○
Material number (FI only)	●	○	○
Cost center	○	●	○
CO/PP order	●	○	○
Project	●	○	○
Sales order	●	○	○
Personnel number (FI only)	●	○	○
Network	●	○	○
Commitment item	●	○	○
Plant (FI only)	●	○	○
Business area	○	○	●
Trad.partn.bus.area (FI only)	●	○	○
Quantity (FI only)	●	○	○
Profit Center	●	○	○
Profitability segment	●	○	○
Cost object	●	○	○
Joint venture acct assgnmt(FI)	●	○	○

The above screenshot shows that for `Movement Type` `201 GI for cost center` without `Special Stock` , the `Cost center` field is mandatory. You can change the properties of fields here.

20.4.6 Changing Field Property

You change the field property by selecting the appropriate radio button.

Additional account assignments	Suppress	Req. Entry	Opt. entry
Business area	◉	○	○

Save the change.

20.4.7 Change in Field Property in non-MIGO Transactions

Run the appropriate transaction (MB1A in this case).

Screen before change

Account Assignment	
G/L Account	
Business Area	
Cost Center	☑
	Goods recipient
No. Containers	
Text	

Screen after change

Account Assignment	
G/L Account	
Cost Center	☑
	Goods recipient
No. Containers	
Text	

Note that the `Business Area` field has disappeared.

20.4.8 Change in Field Property in MIGO Transactions

Screen before and after change

Material	Quantity	Where	Account Assignment

G/L account

Business Area

Cost Center

The `Business Area` field remained unchanged even after making the change.

20.5 SUBSCREEN FOR ACCOUNT ASSIGNMENT BLOCK

Functional Consultant	User	Business Process Owner	Senior Management	My Rating	Understanding Level
B	X	X	X		

20.5.1 Purpose

SAP has a number of screens for account assignment. For an account assignment category you define a set of fields. When entering account assignment data for an item, based on the account assignment category, the system needs to show you a screen. The system selects the most suitable subscreen from a number of predefined subscreens. If there is no subscreen that contains all the necessary fields, you have to enter the additional fields in a separate dialog box.

For the subscreens provided by SAP, you can only change priority and active flag. However, you can define your own subscreens. This means you can structure your subscreens to suit your own requirements and thus avoid having to enter account assignment fields in an additional dialog box. To be able to maintain subscreens, you must have authorization to maintain cross-client tables in authorization object S_TABU_CLI.

20.5.2 IMG Node

Transaction OXK1—Coding Block: Maintain Subscreens

20.5.3   List of Subscreens

SAP Subscreens

No.	Description	Priority	Active	Lines
1001	BusArea/CCtr	3	X	5
1002	BusArea Cost ctr Order Cost object	7	X	5
1003	BusArea/Order	4	X	5
1004	BusArea Cost ctr ProfitCtr Order Funct. Area	7	X	5
1005	BusArea/ProfitCtr/PftblySeg	3	X	5
1006	BusArea Cost ctr Order ProfitCrt PrfObj WBS	8	X	5
1007	Bus.area Cost ctr Order Sales ord Asset WBS	8	X	5
1010	BusArea Asset Cost ctr Order Material Pla	8	X	5
1011	BusArea G/L acct ProfitCtr	3	X	5
1012	BusArea Material Plant ValtnType MatWBS Mat	6	X	5
1013	FinMstr FundsResv ComItmH Funds CCtr	6	X	5
1014	Cost ctr Sales ord WBS el. ProfSegm G/Lacct Bu	8	X	5
1015	Cost ctr Sales ord WBS el. ProfSegm Asset Coc	1	X	5
1101	Large subscreen with all account assignments	8	X	20

Customer Subscreens

No.	Description	Priority	Active	Lines
9000	Test	9	X	5
9002	Additional Test	9	X	5
9003	Arrow Coding Block	1	X	5
9015		1	X	5

20.5.4   SAP Subscreens

Subscreen	1001	BusArea/CCtr
Priority	3	☑ Active

Field Name	Position	With Text
Accounting Indicator	0	☐
Activity Type	5	☐
Asset	0	☐
Business Area	1	☐

20.5.5   Customer Subscreens

Subscreen	9003	Arrow Coding Block
Priority	1	☑ Active

Field Name	Position	With Text
Accounting Indicator		☐
Activity Type		☐
Asset		☐
Business Area		☐

20.5.6 Subscreen Definition

Subscreen

SAP provides a number of pre-defined subscreens. You can't change the content of a subscreen, except priority and active flag. However, you can define your own subscreens, using the number range given below.

9999	0000	Reserved for customer: Subscreen for "All assignments" popup
0001	8999	SAP standard
9000	9998	Reserved for customer: Subscreens

Priority

The coding block searches through the existing subscreens for the one which fulfills most requirements. The "Priority" serves to fine tune the search procedure: 1 is the highest priority, 9 the lowest. The system searches for the most suitable subscreen according to the following strategy:

First, it searches for subscreens containing all the account assignment fields required. If there is more than one, it selects the one with the highest priority.

If this is unsuccessful, the system then looks for subscreens containing all of the obligatory fields, or as many of them as possible. The subscreen containing the most obligatory fields is selected.

Active indicator

A subscreen can only be used in the individual account assignment transactions if the ☑ Active indicator is set.

Lines

In a subscreen, there are fields in multiple lines. Number of lines in a subscreen is defined here.

Field name

A screen usually contains multiple fields.

Item

The positions of the account assignment fields on the subscreens are numbered 1 (1st line left) to 10 (5th line right). If this column contains zero, the field is not shown on the subscreen.

With text

If you tick this checkbox, and enter data in the subscreen which has a text (e.g. cost center), short description of the field content is shown.

21 Movement Type and Other Configurations

21.1 MOVEMENT TYPES

Functional Consultant	User	Business Process Owner	Senior Management	My Rating	Understanding Level
A	B	C	C		

21.1.1 Overview

Movement type

When you enter a goods movement, you must always enter the movement type. The movement type has important control functions in Inventory Management, including determination of screen layout. It determines what you can or cannot do. It also determines what happens internally in the system.

Deciding the movement type to use

Chapters 5–19 of this book help you determine the movement type you should use in a given scenario. If you have a rare business scenario, look at the descriptions of the movement types which are in business language. In case of doubt, ask a knowledgeable colleague, or the consultant supporting your installation. In course of time, you will remember important movement types, and will need to look for the movement types rarely.

Reversal movement type

You can reverse the action of a goods movement, by another goods movement using reversal movement type. The reversal movement type is the original movement type + 1 (reversal of movement type 101 is movement type 102).

Types of posting

Goods movements can be classified by types of posting.

Type of posting	Description
Blank	Normal posting, e.g. goods receipt or goods issue
1	Return posting
2	Reversal posting
3	Transfer posting

For each movement type, types of postings are specified in view V_156N_VC.

Special stock indicators

Sometimes a goods movement involves special stocks. The special stock is specified along with the movement type and determines the system behavior including screen layout.

E	Orders on hand
K	Consignment (vendor)
M	Ret.trans.pkg vendor
O	Parts prov. vendor
P	Pipeline material
Q	Project stock
V	Ret. pkg w. customer
W	Consignment (cust.)
Y	Shipping unit (whse)

21.1.2 IMG Node

SM34 ➤ MB_156

Transaction OMJJ—Copy, Change Movement Types

Both these methods give the following screen.

▽ 📁 Movement Type
    ☐ Short Texts
    ☐ Allowed Transactions
    ☐ Help Texts
    ☐ Field selection (from 201)/Batch search procedure
    ☐ Field selection (Enjoy)
    ☐ Update control / WM movement types
    ☐ Account Grouping
    ☐ Reversal/follow-on movement types
    ☐ Reason for Movement
    ☐ Deactivate QM inspection / delivery category
    ☐ LIS Statistics Group

21.1.3 Properties of a Movement Type

In transaction OMJJ you get the screen showing the properties of the specified movement type. In view cluster MB_156 you select a movement type and click 🔍. The system shows you the screen containing the properties of the selected movement type (view V_156_VC). The properties are grouped in logical subscreens (rectangular boxes). The discussion below is also similarly organized. Each subscreen is discussed with its image and related field descriptions.

Movement Type

Movement Type	101 GR goods receipt

When you enter a goods movement in the system, you must enter a movement type to differentiate between the various goods movements. Examples of movement types are:

MvT	Movement Type Text
101	GR goods receipt
102	Reversal of GR
103	GR into blocked stck
104	Rev. GR to blocked

Entry Control

Entry Control			
Print item	1	Check SLExpir.date	1
Selection parameter	WE101	Account control	
Classif.batches	3	Control Reason	-
Create New Batch		Stck determation rule	
☐ Ext.classific.		☐ RevGR despite IR	

Print item indicator

The print indicator gets associated with a goods movement item based on the movement type. It determines the type of document to be printed for the item (or if no document is to be printed). The output determination takes into account several parameters (as explained in Chapter 24), one of which is the print item indicator. Master list of print items is defined in view V_159Q.

	No Document Printout
1	Material Document Printout
2	Return Delivery
3	GR/GI Slip for Subcontracting
4	Inventory List W/o Sales Price
5	Inventory List w. Sales Price
6	Matl Doc. Printout for GR/GI

Print item indicators 4 and 5 are for physical inventory.

Selection parameter

In Inventory Management, selection parameter is used for goods receipt to search the purchase orders.

Classify batches

If you work with batch classification, set this indicator for all receipt-specific movement types so that all existing batches are classified.

	No branching to batch classification
1	Classification carried out in background (all batches)
2	Classification only in foregr.for mand.charac. (all batches)
3	Classification always in foreground (all batches)
4	Classification in foreground for new batches only

Create new batch

Here you specify whether new batches are created automatically/manually, with or without check etc.

	Automatic / manual without check
A	Automatic / manual and check against external number range
B	Automatic / manual and check in USER EXIT
C	Automatic / no manual creation
D	Manual without check
E	Manual and check against external number range
F	Manual and check in USER EXIT
G	No creation

Extended classification

You can use a Customer Function Call (CFC) to assign values to characteristics of a batch to be specified, as a background job, if this indicator is set.

Check shelf life expiry date

If you deal with products with expiry date, you may want to check it at the time of goods receipt and goods issue. Shelf life check is meaningful only for materials that are maintained with batch information; there cannot be an expiry date for a material. This functionality works if the expiration date check is active for the given plant in view V_159L_MHD and a minimum remaining shelf life has been maintained in the material master record in Plant data / stor. 1 view or in the purchase order item. You specify whether such a check is carried out for a movement type.

	No check
1	Enter and check
2	Enter only
3	No check at goods issue

Account control

Here you can specify whether G/L account field is hidden, optional or mandatory when a goods movement is posted and whether or not the manual entry of a cost account ("manual account assignment") is possible.

	Entry in this field is optional.
+	Entry in this field is required.
-	Field is suppressed.
.	Entry in this field is optional.

If you want to maintain only this field for all movement types, you can do so in view V_156_K. You can use manual account assignment to override automatic account assignment.

MvT	Movement Type Text	Account control
101	GR goods receipt	
102	Reversal of GR	
103	GR into blocked stck	
104	Rev. GR to blocked	

Control reason

For some movement types you may want to maintain reason for a goods movement. For example, for returning material to vendor, you may want to specify reason. Reasons for movement are maintained in view V_157D_VC (Section 21.1.12). For a movement type, you can control entry in the field 'Reason for movement'.

	Entry in this field is optional.
+	Entry in this field is required.
-	Field is suppressed.
.	Entry in this field is optional.

In this field you specify this control. If you want to maintain only this field for all movement types, you can do so in view V_156_G.

MvT	Movement Type Text	Reas.	Control reason
101	GR goods receipt	-	Field is suppressed.
102	Reversal of GR	.	Entry in this field is optional.
103	GR into blocked stck	.	Entry in this field is optional.
104	Rev. GR to blocked	-	Field is suppressed.

Stock determination rule

Here you specify the stock determination rule which is used in stock determination when this movement type is used. Stock determination rules are discussed in Section 27.3.

Reverse GR despite IR

Here you can specify that in the case of GR-based invoice verification you can enter a reversal in respect of the purchase order, or a return delivery, even though the corresponding invoice for the goods receipt document has already been posted.

If you want to maintain only this field for all movement types, you can do so in view V_156_R.

	MvT	Movement Type Text	RevGR desp. IR
	102	Reversal of GR	☑
	106	Rev.GR from blocked	☐
	122	RE return to vendor	☑
	162	GR rtrns reversal	☑

Updating Control

Updating Control	
☑ Create SLoc. automat.	Statistically relev. [2]
☑ Ind. rqmts reduction	Consumption posting [G]
☐ Generate ph.inv.doc.	☐ Store
☑ Automatic PO	

Create storage location automatically

The material master specifies the storage locations where that material is stored. If you try to receive a material in a storage location where that material is not stored, the system will give error. SAP provides a facility of creating this master data automatically provided that it is allowed for the movement type (this field) as well as for the plant.

Indicator for requirements reduction

In make-to-stock planning scenario, you create planned independent requirements against which goods are produced. When goods are received in storage location from production facility, the requirement is reduced. This indicator determines whether that happens or not.

Generate physical inventory document

If a movement type involves posting of inventory difference, you tick this checkbox so that physical inventory documents are generated automatically. It only makes sense to set this indicator in connection with those goods movements that are automatically generated with the inventory difference posting in the Warehouse Management System (movement types 711 to 718).

If you want to automatically generate physical inventory documents for goods movements for a plant, you should enter transaction/event type WV (inventory difference from Warehouse Management System) in view V_159L_V.

Automatic PO

Sometimes you may receive goods without purchase order. Here you can specify whether automatic purchase order generation is enabled for this movement type or not. Section 5.6 illustrates creation of automatic purchase order during goods receipt.

Statistically relevant

Here you specify whether the movement type leads to an update of the statistics (inventory controlling) and whether this update is carried out online or in batch mode.

	Not relevant
2	Document evaluations and standard analyses (update)
3	Standard analyses only (update)

Consumption posting

If a stock withdrawal is a planned withdrawal, only total consumption is updated. If the withdrawal is unplanned, unplanned consumption as well as total consumption are updated. You may also specify that no consumption is updated.

	No consumption update
G	Planned withdrawal (total consumption)
R	Planned, if ref. to reservation, otherwise unplanned
U	Unplanned withdrawal (unplanned consumption)

Store

This indicator specifies whether storage for goods receipts is active.

Internal Control

Internal Control (Please Do Not Change)		
☐ Rev. mvmnt type ind.	Debit/Credit Ind.	S
☐ CostElem account	Reserv. cat.	
Mvt type category	GR blocked stock	
	Direction Indicator	

These fields are used by SAP for internal control of the system and cannot be changed.

Reversal movement type indicator

You can reverse the action of a goods movement, by another goods movement using reversal movement type. The reversal movement type is the original movement type + 1 (reversal of movement type 101 is movement type 102). Last digit of all reversal movement types is an even number.

Debit/credit indicator

This indicator specifies whether the goods movement is an inward movement (debit posting, S) or an outward movement (credit posting, H).

Cost element accounting

This indicator specifies the account assignment of the cost element. It is only relevant if a goods movement has been generated automatically by another application e.g. Shipping, Quality Management etc.

Reservation category

When you create a reservation, you specify the movement type. Depending on this movement type, the system determines the account assignment data required. If this indicator has not been set, the movement type cannot be used to generate a reservation.

Reserv. cat.	Short text
A	Asset
U	Stock transfer
W	Without account assignment
K	Cost center
P	Project
V	Sales document
F	Order
N	Network

Reservation category	Description	Movement types
A	Asset	241, 242
U	Stock transfer	301, 302, 311, 312, 411, 412, 413, 414, 415, 416
W	Without account assignment	501, 502, 503, 504, 505, 506, 841, 842, 843, 844
K	Cost center	201, 202, 251, 252, 291, 292, 901
P	Project	221, 222, 533, 534
V	Sales document	231, 232, 535, 536, 571, 572, 573, 574, 575, 576
F	Order	261, 262, 521, 522, 523, 524, 525, 526, 531, 532
N	Network	281, 282, 581, 582

Movement type category

This category determines whether or not a movement type is allowed for a certain transaction or event. The indicator also specifies the transaction or event for which the movement type can be used. For example, this indicator is used for the withdrawal of material in conjunction with a stock transport order (movement type 351).

GR blocked stock

This field controls goods movements involving GR blocked stock.

Indicator	Description	Movement types
S	Goods receipts and return deliveries in respect of purchase orders	103, 104, 107, 108, 124, 125
X	Movements between the segregated GR blocked stock and standard stock held in the warehouse or stores	105, 106, 109, 110, 805, 806, 815, 816, 825, 826

Direction indicator

This indicator is used for cross-system flows of goods, i.e., goods movement performed across a system boundary.

	Integrated Case
S	Issuing System
R	Receiving System

Indicator	Description	Movement types
S	Issuing system	6A1, 6A2, 6A3, 6A4, 6A5, 6A6, 6A7, 6A8, 6W5, 6W6
R	Receiving system	6B1, 6B2, 6B3, 6B4, 6B5, 6B6, 6B7, 6B8, 6K5, 6K6

21.1.4 Short Texts

Purpose

Here you maintain the description of movement types. The description can depend on other parameters, as is evident from the screenshot below. Movement type text explains the movement type from a business perspective. You will repeatedly find the following acronyms in the text.

Acronym	Description
GI	Goods issue
GR	Goods receipt
GD	Goods movement with reference to a delivery
RE	Return
TP	Transfer to company's own stock
TF	Transfer posting
TR	Reversal of transfer posting

Possible Values of Special Stock Indicators for a Movement Type

This view V_156T_VC also specifies possible values of special stock indicators for a movement type. In fact, in a goods movement, the entire key must be found in this view.

IMG Node

SM30 ➢ V_156T_VC

Screen

La	MvT	Spec.Stock	Mvt ind.	Receipt	Consumpt.	Movement Type Text
EN	101		B			GR goods receipt
EN	101		B		A	GR for asset
EN	101		B		E	GR for sales order
EN	101		B		P	GR for sales ord. st

Primary Key

Language Key
Movement Type (Inventory Management)
Special Stock Indicator
Movement Indicator
Receipt Indicator
Consumption Posting

Important Fields

Language

You can specify the movement type text in any language.

Movement type

You specify the movement type text for a movement type.

Special stock

Movement type text can depend on the special stock indicator.

Movement indicator

Movement indicator specifies the type of document (such as purchase order or delivery note) that constitutes the basis for the movement. This indicator is necessary, for example, to enable a distinction to be made between a goods receipt for a purchase order and a goods receipt for a production order. These two goods movements result in different data and account updates in the system. The movement indicator is derived from the transaction code in table T158 which is maintained by SAP.

Movement indicator	Short text
	Goods movement w/o reference
B	Goods movement for purchase order
F	Goods movement for production order
L	Goods movement for delivery note
K	Goods movement for kanban requirement (WM - internal only)
O	Subsequent adjustment of "material-provided" consumption
W	Subsequent adjustment of proportion/product unit material

Receipt

Receipt indicator indicates the order type if this requires different accounting treatment (for example, stock transport order).

	Normal receipt
X	Stock transport order
L	Tied empties

Consumption

Consumption posting specifies the type of account to which the consumption is to be posted.

	No consumption
V	Consumption
A	Asset
E	Sales order
P	Project

This indicator is used in the case of goods receipts for purchase orders and is derived from the account assignment category of the purchase order item.

Movement type text

The description of a movement type can be different for any combination of the above fields.

21.1.5   Allowed Transactions

Purpose

The movement types you can use in a transaction are defined in table T158B. This view presents the reverse perspective: transaction codes that can use a movement type.

JMG Node

SM30 ➤ V_158B_VC

Screen

	MvT	TCode	Transaction Text	Proposal
	101	MB01	Post Goods Receipt for PO	3
	101	MB0A	Post Goods Receipt for PO	3
	101	MB31	Goods Receipt for Production	
	101	ME23	Display Purchase Order	

Primary Key

Transaction Code
Movement Type (Inventory Management)

Important Fields

Movement type, transaction code and text

The proposal value is specified for a combination of movement type and transaction code.

Proposal

Propose movement type despite different movement type indicator is used for internal program control. You should not change the entry in this field.

	Not Relevant
1	Manual input allowed
2	Manual input not allowed
3	Manual input allowed + GR with automatically generated PO
4	Manual input allowed + GR with auto. generated returns order

21.1.6   Help Texts

Purpose

Here you can specify help text in different languages for each combination of movement type, special stock indicator and transaction code.

IMG Node

SM30 ➤ V_157H_VC

Screen

	La	MvT	Spec	TCode	Text
	EN	101		MB01	Goods receipt for purchase order into warehouse/stores
	EN	101		MB0A	Goods receipt for purchase order into warehouse/stores
	EN	101		MB31	Goods receipt for order into warehouse
	EN	101		MIGO	Goods receipt for purchase order into warehouse/stores

Primary Key

Language Key
Transaction Code
Movement Type (Inventory Management)
Special Stock Indicator

21.1.7   Field Selection (From 201)/Batch Search Procedure

Purpose

Here you specify search procedure and batch check for a movement type and special stock indicator. You can also define screen layout, which is discussed in Section 20.4.

IMG Node

SM30 ➤ V_156B_VC

Screen

	MvT	Movement Type Text	S	Special stock descr.	Search proced.	Check batch
	201	GI for cost center			Z00001	☐
	201	GI cst.cnt.fm.consgt	K	Consignment (vendor)		☐
	201	GI pipel.for cst.cnt	P	Pipeline material		☐

Primary Key

Movement Type (Inventory Management)
Special Stock Indicator

Important Fields

Movement type and special stock indicator

Search procedure and batch check depends on the movement type and special stock indicator.

Search procedure

Here you specify the search procedure for batch determination.

Check batch

This indicator controls that batches that are entered manually during a business transaction, are checked against the selection criteria stored for batch determination.

Field status group

If you select a line and click ⬛, the system shows you the field selection group. This is discussed in Section 20.4.

21.1.8   Field Selection (Enjoy)

This view MIGO_CUST_FIELDS is discussed in Section 20.2.6.

21.1.9   Update Control/Warehouse Management Movement Types

Purpose

Here you specify whether the system checks for availability in goods movement and reservation. Checking for missing parts is also specified here. Controls related to Warehouse Management and SAP's internal control are also specified here.

IMG Node

SM30 ➤ V_156SC_VC

Screen

Movement Type	101	GR for asset		
Special Stock			Movement indicator	B
☐ Value updating			Receipt indicator	
☐ Quantity updating			Consumption	A

Entry control

Dyn. avail. reserv.		ChckngRule: MssgPrts	
Dyn.avail.goods mvt.		Display rules	LE1

Updating Control

RefMvtType WM	999	Ref.mov.ty.post.chge	
☐ LIFO/FIFO-relevant		Ref.mov.ty.post.chge	

Internal control (not changeable)

Value string	WE06 ⬛	☐ Without value string	
Quantity string	ME02	☐ SLoc. necessary	
Inspect.lot origin	01	Trans./ev. serial no	****

Primary Key

Movement Type (Inventory Management)
Value Update in Material Master Record
Quantity Updating in Material Master Record
Special Stock Indicator
Movement Indicator
Receipt Indicator
Consumption Posting

Important Fields

Movement type

When you enter a goods movement in the system, you must enter a movement type to differentiate between the various goods movements.

Special stock

Special stock is stock of material that must be managed separately for reasons of ownership or location. An example is consignment stock from vendors.

Movement indicator

Movement indicator specifies the type of document (such as purchase order or delivery note) that constitutes the basis for the movement.

Value updating

This checkbox specifies that the material is managed on a value basis in the material master record for the valuation area concerned. The values are updated in the respective G/L accounts at the same time.

Quantity updating

This checkbox specifies that the material is managed on a quantity basis in the material master record for the relevant valuation area.

Receipt indicator

Receipt Indicator specifies the order type if this requires different accounting treatment (for example, stock transport order).

Consumption

Consumption posting specifies that the consumption is to be posted to a consumption account (V) or an asset account (A). This indicator is used in the case of goods receipts for purchase orders and is derived from the account assignment category of the purchase order.

Dynamic availability check for reservation

See Section 21.3.9.

Dynamic availability check for goods movement

See Section 21.3.8.

Checking rule for missing parts

See Section 21.4.5.

Display rules

Rule for display of goods movements controls the selection of the stock fields that are

> ➢ Included in the availability list in the event of a movement
> ➢ Displayed in the plant stock overview

Reference movement type for warehouse management

Reference movement type for warehouse management is used for determining the movement type in the Warehouse Management System from material movements. Each Inventory Management movement type that is relevant to the Warehouse Management System is allocated to a reference movement type, with which the system determines the corresponding movement type in the Warehouse Management System. Using the reference movement type, you can group together Inventory Management movement types that result in the same movement in the Warehouse Management System.

Inventory Management movement types that do not initiate any activity in the Warehouse Management System have the reference movement type 999.

LIFO/FIFO-relevant (Last-in, First-out/First-in, First-out-relevant)

This indicator determines whether the material or the movement type is relevant to LIFO and FIFO valuation.

Reference movement type for transfer in warehouse management

This reference movement type is necessary when a goods movement (stock transfer) in Inventory Management causes two transfers in the Warehouse Management System (stock removal from one storage type and stock placement in another).

Reference movement type for posting change in warehouse management

This reference movement type is necessary if a movement in the Inventory Management system (for example, release from quality inspection or takeover of consignment material into company stock) causes a stock posting change in the Warehouse Management System.

Internal control

These fields are only displayed here from view V_156SC_VC. They are not a part of this configuration view.

21.1.10   Account Grouping

For this view V_156X_VC see Section 26.7.

21.1.11   Reversal/Follow-on Movement Types

Purpose

After you have done a goods receipt, you may want to reverse it, or may want to transfer the material from quality inspection stock to unrestricted use stock. Here you specify all such valid combinations.

IMG Node

SM30 ➢ V_156N_VC

Screen

MvT	FCode	Description	MvT	Type of posting
101	RL	Return Delivery	122	1
101	SN		101	
101	SS	Reversal (Detail)	102	2
101	SSR	Return Del. (Detail)	122	1
101	ST	Reversal	102	2
101	WERE	Returns Item	161	

Primary Key

Function Code
Movement Type (Inventory Management)

Important Fields

Movement type

When you enter a goods movement in the system, you must enter a movement type to differentiate between the various goods movements.

Function code and description

Function code is passed on as a default value to the calling program for a standard action after the screen change.

Movement type

Here you specify the movement type of a reversal or follow-on document.

Type of posting

Here you specify whether the reversal or follow-on document is for a reverse posting, a return delivery or a release from GR blocked stock, for example.

	Neither return delivery nor reversal
1	Return deliv.(qty can be entered; no gener.of matchcode)
2	Reversal(qty cannot be entered; gener.of matchcode)
3	Transfer posting (qty can be entered; no gener.of matchcode)

21.1.12   Reason for Movement

Purpose

For some movement types you may want to maintain reasons for goods movement. For example, for returning material to vendor, you may want to specify reason.

JMG Node

SM30 ➤ V_157D_VC

Screen

MvT	Movement Type Text	Reason	Reason for Movement
122	RE return to vendor	1	Poor quality
122	RE return to vendor	2	Incomplete
122	RE return to vendor	3	Damaged
122	RE return to vendor	4	delivered wrong prod

Reason for Movement of all Movement Types

The reason for movement of all movement types can be maintained in V_157D.

MvT	Movement Type Text	Reason	Reason for Movement
103	GR into blocked stck	103	Spoiled
122	RE return to vendor	1	Poor quality
122	RE return to vendor	2	Incomplete
122	RE return to vendor	3	Damaged
122	RE return to vendor	4	delivered wrong prod
261	GI for order	261	Unplanned use
262	RE for order	262	Reversal Reason
543	GI issue sls.ord.st.	543	Damage in transport
544	GI receipt sls.or.st	544	Damage in ret.transp
551	GI scrapping	1	Shrinkage
551	GI scrapping	2	Spoiled
552	RE scrapping	1	Shrinkage
552	RE scrapping	2	Spoiled
922	RE return to vendor	1	Poor quality
922	RE return to vendor	2	Incomplete
922	RE return to vendor	3	Damaged

21.1.13   Deactivate QM Inspection/Delivery Category

Purpose

Here you can deactivate Quality Management for a movement type.

JMG Node

SM30 ➢ V_156Q_VC

Screen

Move	Spec	Move	Rece	Con	Stock type	QM not active	DelivCat
101	B				GR goods receipt	☐	ID
101	B		A		GR goods receipt	☐	ID
101	B		E		GR goods receipt	☐	
101	B		P		GR goods receipt	☐	

Primary Key

Movement Type (Inventory Management)
Special Stock Indicator
Movement Indicator
Receipt Indicator
Consumption Posting

Important Fields

Movement type

When you enter a goods movement in the system, you must enter a movement type to differentiate between the various goods movements.

Special stock

Special stock is stock of material that must be managed separately for reasons of ownership or location. An example is consignment stock from vendors.

Movement indicator

Movement indicator specifies the type of document (such as purchase order or delivery note) that constitutes the basis for the movement.

Receipt indicator

Receipt Indicator specifies the order type if this requires different accounting treatment (for example, stock transport order).

Consumption

Consumption posting specifies that the consumption is to be posted to a consumption account (V) or an asset account (A). This indicator is used in the case of goods receipts for purchase orders and is derived from the account assignment category of the purchase order.

Stock type

This field contains the description of movement type; disregard the heading.

QM not active

If you set this indicator for a movement type, no inspection lots are created for stock postings.

Delivery category

Delivery categories are assigned to movement types here. The delivery category dictates how the system determines a delivery type. The delivery type that is found depends on the delivery category (classification and goods movement) and the enterprise structures (plant, storage location).

ID	Delivery Category for Inbound Deliveries
OD	Delivery Category for Outbound Deliveries
TP	Delivery Category for Stock Transfer Delivs/Posting Changes
RL	Delivery Category for Return Delivery to Vendor
LB	Delivery Category for Subcontracting
RK	Delivery Category for Customer Returns

21.1.14 LIS Statistics Group

Purpose

Here you can define up to four statistics groups for Logistics Information System. These are defined at the level of movement type, special stock indicator and movement indicator.

JMG Node

SM30 ➤ V_MCA_VC

Screen

MvT	S	Mvt	Movement	STGRP1	STGRP2	STGRP3	STGRP4
101		B					
101		F					
101	E	B					
101	E	F					
101	K	B					
101	O	B					
101	Q	B					
101	Q	F					

Primary Key

Movement Type (Inventory Management)
Special Stock Indicator
Movement Indicator

21.2 COPY RULES FOR REFERENCE DOCUMENTS

Functional Consultant	User	Business Process Owner	Senior Management	My Rating	Understanding Level
B	X	X	X		

21.2.1 Goods Receipt

When you create a goods receipt with reference to a purchasing document, e.g. a purchase order, the system inserts the items of the purchasing document in the goods receipt transaction. You can then select the items you want to copy.

If you want the system can propose the items preselected, and you can manually deselect the items you do not want to copy. This setting is made in view V_158_E for every goods receipt transaction.

Transaction Code	Transaction Text	Proposed preselec.
MB01	Post Goods Receipt for PO	☑
MB0A	Post Goods Receipt for PO	☑
MB1C	Other Goods Receipts	☑
MB31	Goods Receipt for Production Order	☑
MBRL	Return Delivery for Matl Document	☑
MBSF	Release Blocked Stock via Mat. Doc.	☑
MBSL	Copy Material Document	☑
MBST	Cancel Material Document	☑

21.2.2 Goods Issue/Transfer Postings

When you create a goods issue or transfer posting for a reference document, the system inserts the items of the reference document in the goods movement transaction. You can then select the items you want to copy.

If you want the system can propose the items preselected, and you can manually deselect the items you do not want to copy. This setting is made in view V_158_A for every goods issue or transfer posting transaction.

Transaction Code	Transaction Text	Proposed preselec.
MB11	Goods Movement	☑
MB1A	Goods Withdrawal	☑
MB1B	Transfer Posting	☑

21.3 DYNAMIC AVAILABILITY CHECK

Functional Consultant	User	Business Process Owner	Senior Management	My Rating	Understanding Level
B	C	C	X		

21.3.1 Purpose

You can issue a material only if it is in stock. Such a check by the system is called availability check. In Inventory Management, availability checks are carried out automatically. The availability check prevents the book inventory balance of various physical stock types (for example, unrestricted-use stock) from becoming negative.

21.3.2 Overview

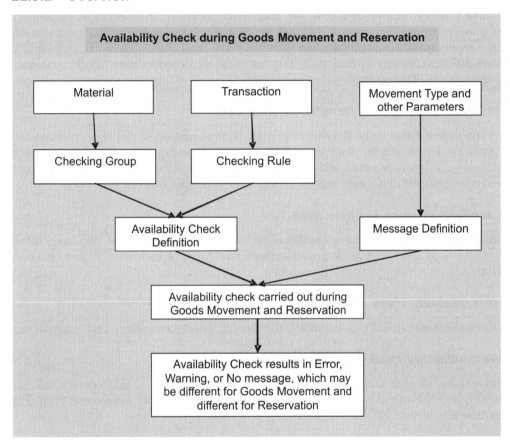

Availability check definition

Since there are different types of stocks, you need to define which stocks are to be considered as available. For example, do you want to consider only unrestricted use stock or quality inspection stock as well.

Multiple availability check definitions

Is there only one definition of availability in your organization? Some organizations may need multiple definitions. For example, you may transfer quality inspection stock of Paints from one plant to another, but in the case of Pharmaceutical goods you may not do so. Therefore, SAP lets you create multiple availability check definitions.

Different availability checks

SAP lets you define different availability checks for

➢ Different materials

➢ Different business processes, represented by transactions

Different availability checks for different materials

Availability checks can be different for different materials. For example, you may transfer quality inspection stock of Paints from one plant to another, but in the case of Pharmaceutical goods you may not do that. SAP lets you define different availability checks for different groups of materials. For the purpose of availability check, materials are grouped in checking groups.

Different availability checks for different transactions

SAP lets you define different availability checks for different business processes represented by transactions. For example, you may not mind transferring quality inspection stock to another storage location or plant, but may not want to issue it for consumption. Checking rules serve to group transactions whose availability is checked in the same way.

Which availability check is applicable?

Availability check is defined for a combination of checking groups and checking rules. Therefore, for a given material and transaction, you know which availability check is applicable.

When is availability check carried out?

Availability check is carried out automatically during goods movement and reservation.

Does the availability check give warning or error?

You may choose to give warning, error, or no message. You may also specify that no availability check be carried out. These are defined at the level of movement type and other parameters.

Different reactions to availability check for goods movement and reservation

SAP lets you specify one type of message (Error/Warning/No message) for goods movement and another for reservation.

21.3.3   Checking Group

In view V_TMVF you define the checking groups.

Av	Description	TotalSales	TotDlvReqs	Block QtRq	No check	Accumul.	Resp	RelC
01	Daily requirements	B	B	☑	☐			
02	Individual reqmt	A	A	☑	☐			
03	Repl Lead-time	A	A	☐	☐			
04	Current stock			☐	☐			

21.3.4   Assignment of Checking Group to Material

Checking group Availability check   02 is specified for a material in the MRP 3 view of the material master record.

21.3.5 Checking Rule

In view V_441R you define the master list of checking rules.

CRI	Description of Checking Rule
01	Checking rule 01
02	Checking rule 02
03	Checking rule 03
A	SD order
AE	SD order; make-to-order stock

In Inventory Management, checking rules are used for availability check and missing part check. Checking rules are also used in Sales & Distribution. SAP provides checking rule 03 for Inventory Management.

21.3.6 Assignment of Checking Rule to Transaction

Checking rules are assigned to transactions in view V_158_P.

TCode	Transaction Text	ChR	Checking Rule
MB01	Post Goods Receipt for PO	01	Checking rule 01
MB0A	Post Goods Receipt for PO		
MB1C	Other Goods Receipts	01	Checking rule 01
MB31	Goods Receipt for Production Order	03	Checking rule 03
MBNL	Subsequent Delivery f. Material Doc.	03	Checking rule 03
MBRL	Return Delivery for Matl Document		
MBSF	Release Blocked Stock via Mat. Doc.		
MBSL	Copy Material Document		
MBST	Cancel Material Document		
MIGO_GO	Goods Movement		
MIGO_GR	Goods Movement		

21.3.7 Availability Check Definition

Checking rules are defined in view V_441V.

Availability check	01	Daily requirements
Checking Rule	03	Checking rule 03

Stocks
- ☐ Include safety stock
- ☐ StockInTransfer
- ☐ Incl.quality insp. stock
- ☐ Incl. blocked stock
- ☐ Incl. restricted-use stock
- ☐ W/o subcontracting

Replenishment lead time
- ☐ Check without RLT

Storage location inspection
- ☐ No stor.loc. inspectn

Missing parts processing
Checking period: GR ☐

In/outward movements
- ☑ Incl.purchase orders
- ☐ Incl. purch.requisitions
- ☐ Incl. dependent reqs
- ☑ Include reservations
- ☑ Include sales reqmts
- ☑ Include deliveries
- ☐ Incl.ship.notificat.

Incl.depen.reservat.	☐	Do not check
Incl.rel.order reqs	☐	Do not check
Incl. planned orders	☐	Do not check
Incl. production orders	☐	Do not take into acc

Receipts in past ☐ Include receipts from past and future

21.3.8 Message for Goods Movement

Type of message

During goods movement depending on the availability, or non-availability, of the material, the system gives an error or warning message.

Dynamic avail. check	Short text
A	W mess. only issued in the case of non-availability
B	E mess. only issued in the case of non-availability
E	Message in any case: W mess. for non-avail., otherw. S mess.
F	Message in any case: E mess. for non-avail., otherw. S mess.
S	Availability check only with simulation

Assignment of type of message to movement type

The type of message you get can depend on the movement type and other parameters. Message type for a movement type and other parameters is specified in view V_156S_W. An availability check is only carried out if this indicator is set; otherwise, availability check is not carried out.

MvT	Movement Type Text	Val	Qua	S	Mvt	Rec	Cns	Dynamic avail. check
101	GR for asset	☐	☐	B		A		
101	GR for sales order	☐	☐	B		E		
101	GR for sales ord. st	☐	☐	B		P		·
101	GR for acct. assgt.	☐	☐	B		V		

Message type for a movement type and other parameters can also be specified in view V_156SC_VC where it is discussed in detail (see Section 21.1.9).

21.3.9 Message for Reservation

Type of message

During reservation depending on the availability, or non-availability, of the material, the system gives an error or warning message.

Dynamic avail. check	Short text
A	W mess. only issued in the case of non-availability
B	E mess. only issued in the case of non-availability
E	Message in any case: W mess. for non-avail., otherw. S mess.
F	Message in any case: E mess. for non-avail., otherw. S mess.
S	Availability check only with simulation

Assignment of type of message to movement type

The type of message you get can depend on the movement type and other parameters. Message type for a movement type and other parameters is specified in view V_156S_D. You should access this view through IMG node Materials Management ➤ Inventory Management and Physical Inventory ➤ Reservation ➤ Set Dynamic Availability Check. This access shows only the relevant movement types. An availability check is only carried out if this indicator is set; otherwise, availability check is not carried out.

MvT	Movement Type Text	Val	Qua	S	Mvt	Rec	Cns	Dynamic avail. check
201	GI pipel.for cst.cnt	☐	☐	P		☐		
201	GI for cost center	☐	☑			☐		A
201	GI cst.cnt.fm.consgt	☐	☑	K		☐		
201	GI pipel.for cst.cnt	☐	☑	P		☐		

Message type for a movement type and other parameters can also be specified in view V_156SC_VC where it is discussed in detail (see Section 21.1.9).

The availability check indicator that you see here is not the availability check indicator for goods movement. In Section 21.1.9, you can see that for the same key there are two fields: availability check indicator for goods movement and availability check indicator for reservations. This view refers to the latter field.

21.3.10 Availability Overview Report

Purpose

You can use this report to view the availability of a material in a plant.

Transaction

CO09—Availability Overview

Stock overview

Click ⚲ Stock to see the stock overview. Stock overview shows the total stock in the plant with storage location wise break up.

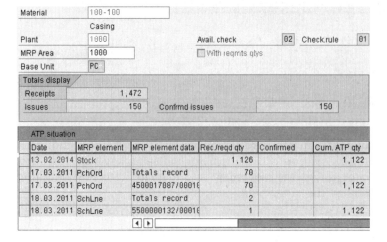

Stock details

Click ⚲ Stock to see the stock details. Stock details shows date-wise MRP element-wise breakup of the storage location stock.

Overview of totals records

Click 👤 Totals records to see the overview of totals records. If several deliveries of a material are expected on the same date, they are summarized in a totals record.

Material	100-100
	Casing

Plant	1000	Avail. check	02	Check.rule 01
MRP Area	1000	☐ With reqmts qtys		
Base Unit	PC			

Totals display

Receipts	1,472
Issues	150	Confrmd issues	150

ATP situation

Date	MRP element	MRP element data	Rec./reqd qty	Confirmed	Cum. ATP qty
13.02.2014	Stock		1,126		1,122
17.03.2011	PchOrd	Totals record	70		1,122
18.03.2011	SchLne	Totals record	2		1,122
19.03.2011	SchLne	Totals record	4		1,122
20.03.2011	SchLne	Totals record	3		1,122

Details of totals records

Click 🔍 Totals records to see the details of totals records.

Material	100-100
	Casing

Plant	1000	Avail. check	02	Check.rule 01
MRP Area	1000	☐ With reqmts qtys		
Base Unit	PC			

Totals display

Receipts	1,472
Issues	150	Confrmd issues	150

ATP situation

Date	MRP element	MRP element data	Rec./reqd qty	Confirmed	Cum. ATP qty
13.02.2014	Stock		1,126		1,122
17.03.2011	PchOrd	Totals record	70		
17.03.2011	PchOrd	4500017087/00016	70		1,122
18.03.2011	SchLne	Totals record	2		
18.03.2011	SchLne	5500000132/00016	1		1,122

All details

Click to move from any summary view to the view that shows details.

Period totals: day level

Click to see daily, weekly or monthly totals. Click Day level to see daily totals.

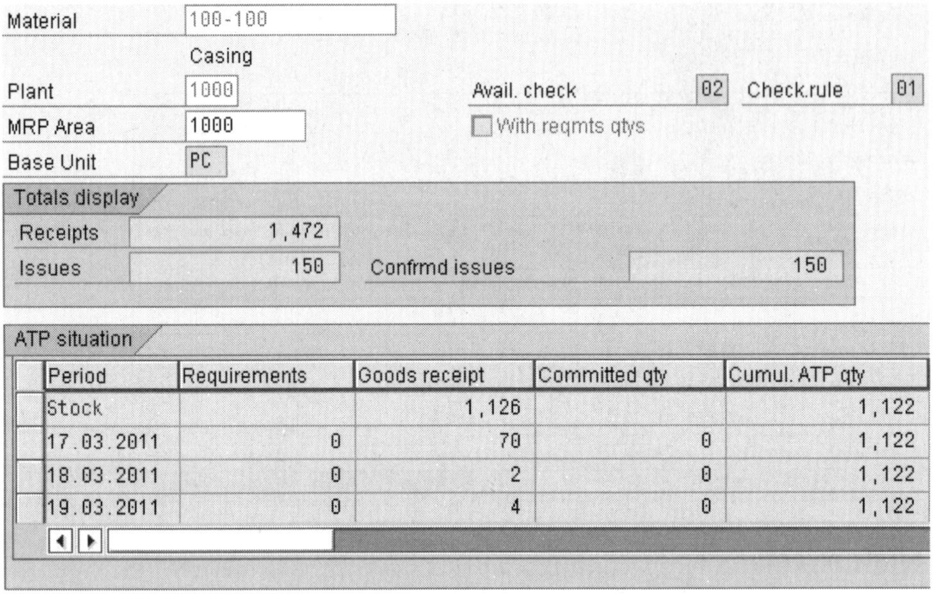

Period totals: week level

Click to see daily, weekly or monthly totals. Click Week level to see weekly totals.

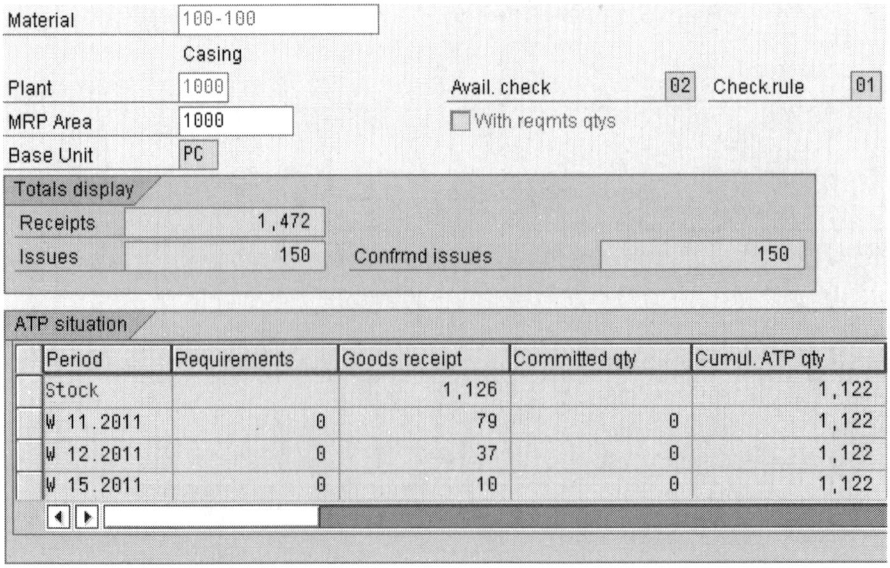

Period totals: month level

Click ⅀ to see daily, weekly or monthly totals. Click | Month level | to see monthly totals.

Material	100-100			
	Casing			
Plant	1000	Avail. check	02	Check.rule	01
MRP Area	1000	☐ With reqmts qtys		
Base Unit	PC			

Totals display

Receipts	1,472		
Issues	150	Confrmd issues	150

ATP situation

Period	Requirements	Goods receipt	Committed qty	Cumul. ATP qty
Stock		1,126		1,122
M 03.2011	0	116	0	1,122
M 04.2011	0	10	0	1,122
M 05.2011	30	0	30	1,122

Scope of check

Click | 👓 Scope of check | to see the definition of the checking rule that is generating all these numbers.

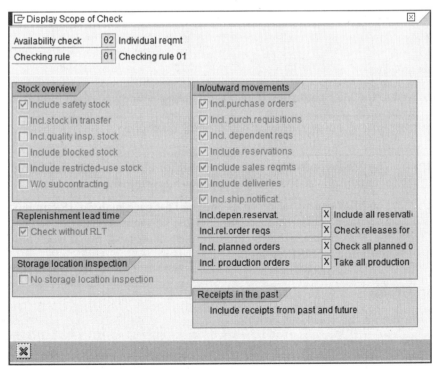

21.4 MISSING PARTS CHECK

Functional Consultant	User	Business Process Owner	Senior Management	My Rating	Understanding Level
B	C	C	X		

21.4.1 Purpose

In MRP, if requirement for a material exceeds the available quantity, that material is called a missing part. If the missing parts check function is active in the plant, the system checks whether the material posted as a receipt is a missing part. If it is a missing part, the system issues a warning message and sends an e-mail to the MRP controller responsible in the plant. It is possible to set the system messages M7 133 and M7 134 so that the person entering the goods receipt will not receive a warning message informing him/her of a missing parts scenario.

21.4.2 Activating Missing Parts Check

In view V_159L_F you define whether missing part check is active or not, and whether missing parts are to be summarized.

Plnt	Name 1	Miss. parts active	Summarize miss.parts
0001	Werk 0001	☐	☐
0005	Hamburg	☑	☑
0006	New York	☑	☑
0007	Werk Hamburg	☑	☑
0008	New York	☑	☑
1000	Werk Hamburg	☑	☑

The type of message sent to the MRP controller depends on the Summarize miss.parts indicator.

Summarize missing parts indicator	Type of message received by the MRP controller
Non-summarized	The MRP controller receives a mail for each material including a maximum of five MRP elements requiring the material.
Summarized	The MRP controller receives one mail for each material document and plant. This e-mail contains a list of the materials for which there are missing parts (missing part materials), but it does not contain any MRP elements.

21.4.3 Checking Group

In view V_TMVF you define the checking groups.

Av	Description	TotalSales	TotDlvReqs	Block QtRq	No check	Accumul.	Resp	RelC
01	Daily requirements	B	B	☑	☐			
02	Individual reqmt	A	A	☑	☐			
03	Repl Lead-time	A	A	☐	☐			
04	Current stock			☐	☐			

21.4.4   Assignment of Checking Group to Material

Checking group Availability check   02 is specified for a material in the MRP 3 view of the material master record.

21.4.5   Checking Rule

In view V_441R you define the master list of checking rules. If you use the same checking rules as for the availability check, you need not do anything. If you want to use different checking rules for the missing parts check than for the availability check, you create the Checking rule here.

CRI	Description of Checking Rule
01	Checking rule 01
02	Checking rule 02
03	Checking rule 03
A	SD order
AE	SD order; make-to-order stock

In Inventory Management, checking rules are used for availability check and missing part check. Checking rules are also used in Sales & Distribution. SAP provides checking rule 03 for Inventory Management.

21.4.6   Determination of Checking Rule

Assignment of checking rule to transaction

Checking rules are assigned to transactions in view V_158_P.

TCode	Transaction Text	ChR	Checking Rule
MB01	Post Goods Receipt for PO	01	Checking rule 01
MB0A	Post Goods Receipt for PO		
MB1C	Other Goods Receipts	01	Checking rule 01
MB31	Goods Receipt for Production Order	03	Checking rule 03
MBNL	Subsequent Delivery f. Material Doc.	03	Checking rule 03
MBRL	Return Delivery for Matl Document		
MBSF	Release Blocked Stock via Mat. Doc.		
MBSL	Copy Material Document		
MBST	Cancel Material Document		
MIGO_GO	Goods Movement		
MIGO_GR	Goods Movement		

Assignment of checking rule to movement type

If you want to use one checking rule for availability check and another for missing part check, you define that in view V_156S_F. This checking rule will get priority over the checking rule assigned to transaction in view V_158_P.

MvT	Movement Type Text	Val	Qua	S	Mvt	Rec	Cns	Check Rule
101	GR for asset	☐	☐		B	A		
101	GR for sales order	☐	☐		B	E		
101	GR for sales ord. st	☐	☐		B	P		
101	GR for acct. assgt.	☐	☐		B	V		

21.4.7 Checking Rule Definition

Checking rules are defined in view V_441V.

Availability check	01	Daily requirements
Checking Rule	03	Checking rule 03

Stocks
- ☐ Include safety stock
- ☐ StockInTransfer
- ☐ Incl.quality insp. stock
- ☐ Incl. blocked stock
- ☐ Incl. restricted-use stock
- ☐ W/o subcontracting

Replenishment lead time
- ☐ Check without RLT

Storage location inspection
- ☐ No stor.loc. inspectn

Missing parts processing

Checking period: GR ☐

In/outward movements
- ☑ Incl.purchase orders
- ☐ Incl. purch.requisitions
- ☐ Incl. dependent reqs
- ☑ Include reservations
- ☑ Include sales reqmts
- ☑ Include deliveries
- ☐ Incl.ship.notificat.

Incl.depen.reservat.	☐ Do not check
Incl.rel.order reqs	☐ Do not check
Incl. planned orders	☐ Do not check
Incl. production orders	☐ Do not take into acc

Receipts in past ☐ Include receipts from past and future

21.4.8   MRP Controllers for Plants

In view V_T399D_L you define the MRP controller for each plant. When a missing part is received, the MRP controller gets a mail.

Plnt	Name 1	MRP	Controller name	Recipient
0001	Werk 0001	001	PERSON 1	
0005	Hamburg	101	PP GENERAL	KUNITZ
0006	New York	001	MEIER	MEIER
0007	Werk Hamburg	101	PP GENERAL	KUNITZ
0008	New York	001	MEIER	MEIER
1000	Werk Hamburg	101	PP GENERAL	KUNITZ

21.4.9   Communication Details of MRP Controllers

In view V_T024D you define the communication details of MRP controllers. These are used for sending mail to the MRP controller when a missing part is received. You send these e-mails via the output function (output type MLFH).

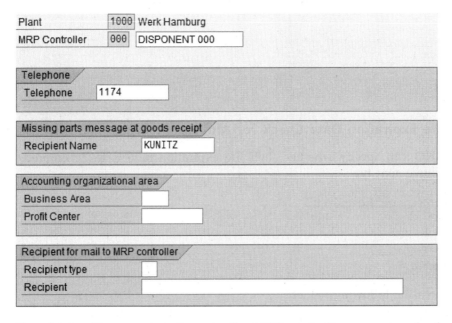

By selecting Document ➢ Execute, the MRP controller can access backorder processing of the missing part material in order to distribute the quantity received.

21.5 SHELF LIFE EXPIRATION DATE CHECK

Functional Consultant	User	Business Process Owner	Senior Management	My Rating	Understanding Level
B	C	C	X		

21.5.1 Purpose

You can check the shelf life of a material when you enter a goods receipt. You thereby ensure that you store only materials that are still usable. This functionality is possible only if the material is managed in batches.

21.5.2 Shelf Life Expiration Date Check for Plants

In view V_159L_MHD you can enable shelf life expiration date check for a plant.

Plnt	Name 1	BBD/ProdDt
0001	Werk 0001	☐
0005	Hamburg	☑
0006	New York	☑
0007	Werk Hamburg	☑
0008	New York	☑
1000	Werk Hamburg	☑

21.5.3 Shelf Life Expiration Date Check for Movement Types

In view V_156_MHD you specify whether shelf life expiration date is to be entered/ checked for each movement type.

MvT	Movement Type Text	Check SLExpDate
101	GR goods receipt	1
102	Reversal of GR	
105	GR from blocked stck	
106	Rev.GR from blocked	

You can choose from the following values.

	No check
1	Enter and check
2	Enter only
3	No check at goods issue

21.5.4 Shelf Life Data for a Material

Screen

You specify shelf life data in the `Plant data / stor. 1` tab of the material master.

Shelf life data			
Max. storage period		Time unit	
Min. Rem. Shelf Life	50	Total shelf life	200
Period Ind. for SLED	D	Rounding rule SLED	*
Storage percentage			

Plant Level Data

The data in the following fields is at plant level for a material. It is applicable to all storage locations.

Maximum storage period and time unit

Here you can specify the maximum period for which the material may be stored at plant level. This field is for information only; it is not used in any report.

Material Level Data

The data in the following fields is at material level. It is applicable to all plants and storage locations.

Minimum remaining shelf life

Minimum remaining shelf life is used to ensure that you have at least this much shelf life of the material left at the time of goods receipt. The time unit is specified in the `Period Ind. for SLED` field.

Total shelf life

Total shelf life is used to compute shelf life expiration date from the date of manufacturing. The time unit is specified in the `Period Ind. for SLED` field. At the time of goods receipt, if you do not enter the shelf life expiration date, that date is computed from the date of manufacturing and the total shelf life specified in this field. The shelf life expiration date is updated in the batch master record and in the material document.

Period indicator in SLED

Here you specify the time unit for `Min. Rem. Shelf Life` and `Total shelf life`.

Per.indic.	Date type descript.
D	Day
J	Year
M	Month
W	Week

Rounding rule SLED

In the material master, if the period indicator based on weeks, months or years has been selected for the total shelf life, you can round the shelf life expiration date (SLED), that has been calculated from the production date and total shelf life, to the first or last day of the period chosen.

Rounding rule SLED	Short text
	No rounding off
-	Start of chosen period (week, month or year)
+	End of chosen period (week, month or year)
F	Start of the following period (week, month, year)

Storage percentage

At the time of goods receipt the material must have `Min. Rem. Shelf Life`. At the time of goods issue or transfer it must have `Min. Rem. Shelf Life` × `Storage percentage`.

21.5.5 Remaining Shelf Life

Term	Definition
Total remaining shelf life	= Expiration date – System date
Minimum remaining shelf life for end-user	= `Min. Rem. Shelf Life` × `Storage percentage`
Remaining shelf life in the warehouse	= Expiration date – System date – Minimum remaining shelf life for end-user

21.5.6 Remaining Shelf Life in Purchase Order

In the purchase order you can specify the minimum remaining shelf life at the time of the goods receipt.

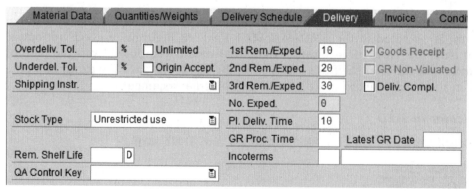

21.5.7 Entry and Check for Shelf Life Expiration Date during Goods Receipt

Entering date of manufacturing/shelf life expiration date

If the expiration date entry/check function is active, you must enter the shelf life expiration date or the production date of the material in the detailed data for an item at the time of the goods receipt. For each item you can enter the date of manufacturing in the `Date of Manuf.` field and/or shelf life expiration date/best before date in the `SLED/BBD` field.

Check for shelf life expiration date

If the movement type specifies that the shelf life expiration date should also be checked, the system does the following.

> If shelf life expiration date is not entered, it is computed from the date of manufacturing entered in the goods receipt and the total shelf life specified in the material master.

> The system determines the remaining shelf life from the shelf life expiration date and the system date.

> If the remaining shelf life is less that the remaining shelf life specified in the purchase order or the minimum remaining shelf life specified in the material master, the system gives warning or error depending on the category of message for application area 12, message number 07 and 08, in view V_160M (see Section 21.7).

Printout on goods receipt slip

The expiration date is printed on the goods receipt slip.

21.5.8 Check for Shelf Life Expiration Date during Goods Issue

Check for shelf life expiration date during goods issue

The system does not check for shelf life expiration date during goods issue.

Printout on goods issue slip

The expiration date is printed on the goods issue slip.

21.5.9 Expiration Date List

List of expired materials

Run transaction MB5M to see the list of expired material. In the selection screen, select `⊙ Tot. rem. shelf life` and do not specify the `Remaining shelf life` `(Days)`.

Material	Material Description		Plnt SLoc
⚠ RShLi	SLED/BBD Batch	Unrestricted BUn	
T-BCH	Color (Batches)		1000 0001
◑○○ 1,502- Days	31.12.2009 050798	250 L	
◑○○ 1,502- Days	31.12.2009 100798	225 L	
◑○○ 1,502- Days	31.12.2009 210798	120 L	
* T-BCH		595 L	
** Total		595 L	

List of materials about to expire

You can also use transaction MB5M to display the list of material about to expire. In the selection screen, select `⊙ Tot. rem. shelf life` and specify the `Remaining shelf life` `⃞` `(Days)`. The list displays the expired materials as well as materials that will expire in the specified number of days.

List of materials based on remaining shelf life in the warehouse

In the selection screen, if you choose `⊙ Rem.shelf life whse`, the report is based on the remaining shelf life in the warehouse.

Term	Definition
Remaining shelf life in the warehouse =	Expiration date – System date – Minimum remaining shelf life for end-user

The report then lists materials that have remaining shelf life in the warehouse less than `Remaining shelf life` `⃞` `(Days)` specified in the selection screen.

21.6 CREATION OF MATERIAL IN STORAGE LOCATION

Functional Consultant	User	Business Process Owner	Senior Management	My Rating	Understanding Level
B	X	X	X		

21.6.1 Manual Creation of Material in Storage Location

When you want to store a material in a storage location belonging to a plant, you have to first create appropriate master data. You can do so using transaction MMSC.

Material	100-100	Casing
Plant	1000	Werk Hamburg
Base Unit	PC	

Storage locations

SLoc	Copy from	Bin	MRP	Reorder Point	Fixed lot size	SPT
0001						
0088						

21.6.2 Automatic Creation of Material in Storage Location

Overview

During goods receipt the system may give you an error indicating that the master data for the material and storage location combination does not exist; hence goods receipt is not possible. You have to then first create the master data and then do the goods receipt.

SAP provides you an option whereby the essential part of this master data is created automatically during the first goods movement of a material in a storage location. The master data is created automatically only if the given quantity is posted to standard stock in storage location. They are not created upon receipts into any of the special stocks (such as the sales order stock).

This option can be controlled both at plant level and movement type level. Only if it is allowed at both levels, automatic creation of material in storage location will take place.

Plant level control

In view V_159L_X you can specify the plants for which this option is enabled.

Plant	Name 1	Create SLoc. automat.
0001	Werk 0001	☑
0005	Hamburg	☑
0006	New York	☑
0007	Werk Hamburg	☑
0008	New York	☑
1000	Werk Hamburg	☑

Movement type level control

In view V_156_X you can specify the movement types for which this option is enabled.

MvT	Movement Type Text	Create SLoc. automat.
101	GR goods receipt	☑
102	Reversal of GR	☐
103	GR into blocked stck	☐
104	Rev. GR to blocked	☐

Guidelines

From a business point of view, you may like to group the movement types as under and have a policy for each group. In SAP reference IMG, there is a node for each.

Business scenario	Guideline
Goods receipt	Automatic creation of material in storage location is advisable if you want to post a goods receipt without having to maintain the storage location view of the material master record in advance.
	The standard system is set in such a way that the storage location data is created automatically for all types of receipts (goods receipt with/without reference, stock transfers, initial entry of stock balances, reversal of goods issues, etc.).
Goods issue and transfer postings	Automatic creation of material in storage location is advisable if you work with negative stocks and a material's first movement may be an outward movement.
	Note that the reversal movement for a goods issue, for example, movement type 202 or 262, is not considered as an issue but as a receipt. If you only use the automatic creation of storage location data for reversals of goods issues, you do not have to allow negative stocks.
Automatic goods movements	Automatic creation of material in storage location is advisable for goods movements via Shipping or when you post physical inventory differences, for example.
	The standard system is set in such a way that the storage location data is created automatically for all types of receipts (goods receipt with/without reference, stock transfers, initial entry of stock balances, reversal of goods issues, etc.).

If your general policy is to allow automatic creation of material in storage location, the default settings at movement type level would be a good starting point. You make changes only based on a specific requirement. However, if your general policy is not to allow automatic creation of material in storage location, it is best to disable it at plant level.

21.7 ATTRIBUTES OF SYSTEM MESSAGES

Functional Consultant	User	Business Process Owner	Senior Management	My Rating	Understanding Level
B	X	X	X		

21.7.1 Purpose

When processing material master records, the system issues a number of system messages containing important user information. Here you define how the system handles these messages. You have the following options.

	No Message
W	Warning
E	Error Message

21.7.2 IMG Node

SM30 ➢ V_160M

Access this view through IMG node Materials Management ➢ Inventory Management and Physical Inventory ➢ Define Attributes of System Messages. This access gives only relevant messages.

21.7.3 Screen

Version	Appl.A.	No.	Message text	Cat
00	12	003	Date of production/SLED of batch &1 changed to &2/&3 in all items	P
00	12	004	Production date of bch &1 (&2) does not match the prod. date entered (&3)	W
00	12	005	SLED of batch &1 (&2) does not match the SLED of the current item (&3)	W
00	12	006	Existing SLED (&1) has been changed to &2 by the program	P
00	12	007	Shortfall of &3 days against remaining shelf life in current item (&1 &2)	E
00	12	008	Shortfall of &2 &3 against SLED in current item (&1)	E
00	12	010	The SLED (&1) must be after the date of production (&2)	W
00	12	013	Reference date (&1) must not be before date of production (&2)	W
00	12	015	SLED copied as default value from batch &1 - please check	W
00	12	016	Date of production copied as default value from batch &1 - please check	W
00	12	017	SLED and date of production copied as default fm bch &1 - please check	W
00	12	018	Enter the date of production	E
00	12	019	Enter the shelf life expiration date	E
00	12	154	Batch record does not exist (choose 'restricted' batch status)	S
00	M7			

21.7.4 Primary Key

| Message control version: Purchasing/Sales |
| Application Area |
| Message number |

21.8 NUMBER ASSIGNMENT FOR GOODS RECEIPT/ISSUE SLIPS

Functional Consultant	User	Business Process Owner	Senior Management	My Rating	Understanding Level
B	X	X	X		

21.8.1 Purpose

The GR/GI slip number has only been designed for use in those countries (Italy, for example) whose legislation requires specification of this number for goods that leave the plant and are transported on public roads.

In other countries, the material document number printed on the GR/GI slip (in the standard system) is sufficient. To enter external documents, you can use the field Material slip or Delivery note.

The goods receipt issue slip number can be assigned externally and internally. It is possible to define different number ranges for each plant, storage location, and movement type, or define the same number range for several plants, storage locations, and movement types.

21.8.2 Enabling GR/GI Slip Numbers for a Plant

In view V_159L_XA you enable the GR/GI slip number at plant level.

Plnt	Name 1	GR/GI slip number
0001	Werk 0001	☐
0005	Hamburg	☐
0006	New York	☐
0007	Werk Hamburg	☐
0008	New York	☐
1000	Werk Hamburg	☐

21.8.3 Assignment of Internal and External Number Range

You can group combinations of plant, storage location and movement type in such a way that they get GR/GI slip number from the same number range. For example, you may have a number range for each plant, or a number range for goods issue of all plants, or a number range for goods issue for each plant. In view V_159X you assign a number range grouping code to a combination of plant, storage location and movement type.

Plnt	Stor. Loc.	Movement Type	No. range grpg. code
0006	0001	101	49
0006	0001	261	50
0008	0001	101	49
0008	0001	261	50

In view V_159Z you assign an internal number range and an external number range to a number range grouping code.

No.rng.grpg.cde	Intern. number range	Extern. number range
49	01	
50		02

Taken together, you assign an internal number range and an external number range to a combination of plant, storage location and movement type.

Plnt	Stor. Loc	Movement Type	No.		No.	Intern. number range	Extern. number range
0006	0001	101	49		49	01	
0006	0001	261	50		50		02

21.8.4 Number Range Intervals

You define number range groups and number range intervals in transaction OMJ6.

Number range groups

Click ⊘ Groups to maintain the number range groups.

```
Number range object GR/GI Slip
Grouping..........


☐ Goods Issue Slip Numbers
   50

☐ Goods Receipt Slip Numbers
   49

☐ XAB group 0001

☐ XAB group 0002

☐ XAB group 0003

☐ XAB group 0004


Not assigned
```

Number range intervals for a group

Select a group and click ✐ to maintain number range intervals in the group.

NR Object	GR/GI Slip
Group............	Goods Issue Slip Numbers

Intervals

	Year	From number	To number	Current number	Ext
	2013	0020000000	0029999999		☑

Number range overview

Click ☒ to see the overview of number ranges.

Subobj.val	No	Year	From number			To number	Number Range Status	Ext	P
Element				No	No P				
	01	2013	0010000000			0019999999			
50				02					
49				01					
	02	2013	0020000000			0029999999		X	
50				02					
49				01					

21.9 TOLERANCE LIMITS

Functional Consultant	User	Business Process Owner	Senior Management	My Rating	Understanding Level
B	X	X	X		

21.9.1 Purpose

Tolerance limits

Here you can define the tolerance limits for the following.

	CoCd	Company Name	TlKy	Description
	1000	IDES AG	B1	Order price qty variance (GR)/E-MSG
	1000	IDES AG	B2	Order price qty variance (GR)/W-MSG
	1000	IDES AG	VP	Moving average price variance

Not the quantity variance for under-deliveries and over-deliveries

At the time of goods receipt, the quantity of goods received is compared with the quantity of goods ordered and warning or error messages are issued for under-deliveries and over-deliveries. The tolerance levels for this are specified in the purchase order itself, and this configuration is not meant for the above purpose.

21.9.2 IMG Node

SM30 ➢ V_169G

21.9.3 Order Price Quantity Variance (Error Message)

Tolerance key	B1	Order price qty variance (GR)/E-MSG
Company Code	1000	IDES AG
Amounts in	EUR	Euro (EMU currency as of 01/01/1999)

Lower limit

Percentage
- ○ Do not check
- ● Check limit
  - Tolerance limit %   50.00

Upper limit

Percentage
- ○ Do not check
- ● Check limit
  - Tolerance limit %   50.00

Scenario

The tolerance limits here are defined for the scenario where the order price unit differs from the order unit (unit of order quantity).

Conversion factor in purchase order

The conversion factor is defined in the purchase order item itself.

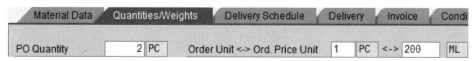

Material Data	Quantities/Weights	Delivery Schedule	Delivery	Invoice	Condi

| PO Quantity | 2 | PC | Order Unit <-> Ord. Price Unit | 1 | PC | <-> | 200 | ML |

Conversion factor in goods receipt

When you receive the material, you must enter the goods receipt in both units. Goods receipt quantity in the order price unit is needed for valuation of GR and invoice verification. Goods receipt quantity in the order unit is needed for updating the quantity of material in the storage location. The system computes the conversion factor in the goods receipt.

Tolerance for variance in conversion factor

The system compares the conversion factor in the goods receipt with the conversion factor in the purchase order. If the variance in the conversion factor exceeds the tolerance defined in tolerance key B2, you get a warning. If it exceeds the tolerance defined in tolerance key B1, you get an error.

21.9.4 Order Price Quantity Variance (Warning Message)

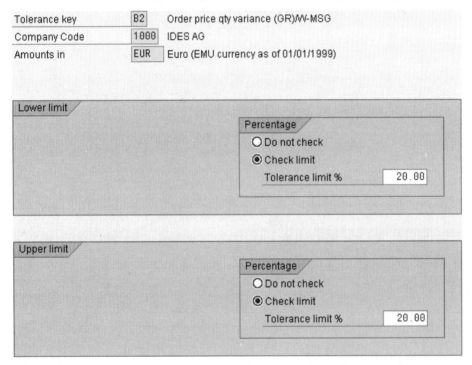

See the explanation above.

21.9.5 Moving Average Price Variance

Tolerance key	VP	Moving average price variance
Company Code	1000	IDES AG
Amounts in	EUR	Euro (EMU currency as of 01/01/1999)

Lower limit

Percentage
- ⦿ Do not check
- ◯ Check limit
  - Tolerance limit % [   ]

Upper limit

Percentage
- ◯ Do not check
- ⦿ Check limit
  - Tolerance limit % [25.00]

You can also set tolerance on rate using tolerance key VP. The rate of material in goods receipt is compared with the moving average rate, and if the tolerance is beyond the permissible limits you get a warning.

21.10   UNDER, OVER AND FINAL DELIVERIES

Functional Consultant	User	Business Process Owner	Senior Management	My Rating	Understanding Level
B	X	X	X		

21.10.1 Open Purchase Order Quantity

The open purchase order quantity is the quantity still to be delivered for an order item. It is calculated as the difference between the quantity ordered and the quantity delivered so far. If the entire order quantity or more has already been delivered, the open purchase order quantity equals zero. The open purchase order quantity is automatically adjusted whenever goods are received for an order item or when the order item is changed.

21.10.2 Quantity Check in Goods Receipt

During entry of goods receipt for a purchase order, the system proposes the item's open purchase order quantity as the quantity received. If the quantity delivered differs from the open order quantity, you can change the proposed quantity.

Whenever you enter a goods receipt item, the system compares the quantity delivered with the open order quantity. SAP can therefore determine and report under or over-deliveries immediately.

21.10.3 Under-delivery

If the quantity received is less than the open purchase order quantity, it is under-delivery. In the standard SAP System, under-deliveries are allowed. The system interprets the quantity received as a partial delivery and accepts it as such. The system issues a warning message indicating that there has been an under-delivery. It is also possible to enter an under-delivery tolerance percentage in the purchase order item.

When quantity of goods received lies within the under-delivery tolerance range, the quantity is interpreted as a partial delivery and is accepted as such. The system does not issue a warning message. If the quantity of goods received lies below the under-delivery tolerance, the system issues a warning message. If the under-delivery is not a partial delivery but a final delivery, you have to set the "Del.Completed" Ind. .

21.10.4 Over-delivery

If the quantity received is more than the open purchase order quantity, it is over-delivery. In the standard SAP System, over-deliveries are not allowed. In the event of an over-delivery, the system issues an error message. If over-deliveries are to be allowed, the following data can be maintained for the purchase order item.

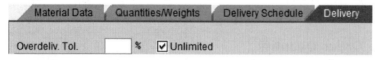

Over-delivery tolerance

In the purchase order, an over-delivery tolerance percentage can be specified. If a quantity of goods is received that is larger than the order quantity plus the over-delivery tolerance, it is not accepted by the system.

Unlimited over-delivery indicator

If this indicator is set, over-deliveries of any size are allowed. The system does not issue any message.

21.10.5 Partial Delivery

After the current delivery, if more material is expected from the vendor, the current delivery is partial delivery.

21.10.6 Final Delivery

After the current delivery, if no more material is expected from the vendor, the current delivery is final delivery.

21.10.7 Delivery Completed Indicator

Delivery completed indicator field

The Delivery tab of a purchase order item has the ☐ Deliv. Compl. field.

Delivery	Invoice	Conditions	Purchase Order History

1st Rem./Exped.	5	☑ Goods Receipt
2nd Rem./Exped.	10	☐ GR Non-Valuated
3rd Rem./Exped.	15	☐ Deliv. Compl.

Purpose of delivery completed indicator

The ☑ Deliv. Compl. specifies whether a purchase order item is considered closed. This means that no more goods receipts are expected for this item. If the ☑ Deliv. Compl. is set, the open purchase order quantity becomes zero, even if the full quantity has not been delivered. It is still possible to post goods receipts of remaining quantities, but these no longer change the open purchase order quantity.

Setting delivery completed indicator automatically

In view V_159L_E you can specify that the ☐ Deliv. Compl. be set automatically to ☑ Deliv. Compl. in the purchase order.

Plant	Name 1	Del. compl. default
0001	Werk 0001	☑
0005	Hamburg	☑
0006	New York	☐
0007	Werk Hamburg	☑
0008	New York	☐
1000	Werk Hamburg	☑

If the total quantity was delivered or the under-delivery or over-delivery lies within the tolerances, the system sets the ☐ Deliv. Compl. automatically to ☑ Deliv. Compl.. In this case, the system interprets any under-deliveries within the tolerances as final deliveries.

Setting delivery completed indicator manually

If an under-delivery lies outside the tolerances, you can set this indicator manually for the order item during entry of the goods receipt to indicate that delivery for the order item is to be considered complete. You can do this in the Purchase Order Data tab of the goods receipt.

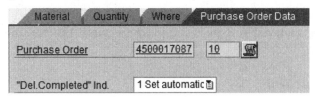

Return and reversal

If you enter a return delivery or reversal for an item whose ☑ Deliv. Compl. indicator has already been set, so that the delivered quantity falls below the under-delivery tolerance limit, the ☑ Deliv. Compl. is automatically reset to ☐ Deliv. Compl. and the system issues a warning message. If you are not expecting another delivery, you can reset ☐ Deliv. Compl. to ☑ Deliv. Compl. manually. After you do this, the system will no longer change the ☑ Deliv. Compl. automatically.

Effects of the delivery completed indicator

The ☑ Deliv. Compl. has the following effects:

➢ The purchase order item is considered closed, even though the total quantity may not have been delivered.

➢ Although a further delivery is not expected, it is still possible.

➢ At the time of the next goods receipt, the system suggests the item as unselected in the item selection list.

➢ The purchase order item can be deleted, even if the total quantity was not delivered.

Closed purchase order item

Although the ☐ Deliv. Compl. is not set, a purchase order item is still considered closed if the full quantity has been delivered. In this case, the ☐ Deliv. Compl. is not required.

21.11 PRICE DIFFERENCES FOR SUBCONTRACT ORDERS AT GOODS RECEIPT

Functional Consultant	User	Business Process Owner	Senior Management	My Rating	Understanding Level
C	X	X	X		

21.11.1 Purpose

Here you configure for each valuation area whether price differences are generated for a subcontract order at the time of a goods receipt if the manufactured material is managed at standard price and the standard price varies from the receipt value (externally performed service + value of components + delivery costs).

21.11.2 IMG Node

SM30 ➢ V_001K_LB

21.11.3 Screen

ValA	CoCd	Company Name	PrDiff. GR SC
0001	1000	IDES AG	☐
0005	0005	IDES AG NEW GL	☐
0006	0006	IDES US INC New GL	☐
0007	0007	IDES AG NEW GL 7	☐
0008	0008	IDES US INC New GL 8	☐
0099	1000	IDES AG	☐
1000	1000	IDES AG	☐

21.11.4 Primary Key

Valuation Area

21.12   STORAGE OF INCOMING DOCUMENTS

Functional Consultant	User	Business Process Owner	Senior Management	My Rating	Understanding Level
C	X	X	X		

21.12.1   Purpose

You can define the movement types and transactions in Inventory Management for which the storage of incoming documents is active. You can, therefore, decide the procedures in which a window for bar code entry is displayed in late input. You do not configure storage of documents here, but in Customizing for SAP ArchiveLink.

21.12.2   Activating Storage per Movement Type

In view V_156_OA you can activate storage of incoming documents for each movement type.

MvT	Movement Type Text	Store
101	GR goods receipt	☐
102	Reversal of GR	☐
103	GR into blocked stck	☐
104	Rev. GR to blocked	☐

21.12.3   Activating Storage per Transaction

In view V_158_OA you can activate storage of incoming documents for each transaction.

Transaction Code	Transaction Text	Store
		☐
BMBC	Batch Information Cockpit	☐
CAT5	Data Transfer CATS -> PS	☐
CAT9	Data Transfer CATS -> PM/CS	☐

21.13   PRINT FUNCTIONS FOR REPORTING

Functional Consultant	User	Business Process Owner	Senior Management	My Rating	Understanding Level
C	X	X	X		

21.13.1   Purpose

For the following programs, SAP lets you choose how your report should be printed.

Transaction	Program	Program Name
EW38	RM07MBST	EMU Conversion: MM Stock Value List
MB24	RM07RESL	Reservation List
MB25	RM07RESL	Reservation List
MB51	RM07DOCS	Material Doc. List
MB52	RM07MLBS	List of Warehouse Stocks on Hand
MB58	RM07MKON	Consgmt and Ret. Packag. at Customer
MB59	RM07DOCS	Material Doc. List
MB5L	RM07MBST	List of Stock Values: Balances
MB5OA	RM07MOA	Display Valuated GR Blocked Stock
MB5S	RM07MSAL	Display List of GR/IR Balances
MB5T	RM07MTRB	Stock in transit CC
MB5W	RM07MBST	List of Stock Values
MBGR	RM07MGRU	Display Material Docs. by Movement Reason
MBLB	RM07MLBB	Stocks at Subcontractor
MBPM	MMIM_PREDOC_MAINTAIN	Manage Held Data

21.13.2   IMG Node

SM30 ➤ V_MMIM_REP_PRINT

21.13.3 Screen

Program Name	Selections	Cover sheet	List info.	Grid Control	B/W
MMIM_PREDOC_MAINTAIN	☑	☐	☐	☑	☐
RM07DOCS	☑	☐	☐	☑	☐
RM07MBST	☑	☐	☐	☐	☐
RM07MGRU	☑	☐	☐	☑	☐
RM07MKON	☑	☐	☐	☑	☐
RM07MLBB	☑	☐	☐	☑	☐
RM07MLBS	☑	☐	☐	☐	☑
RM07MSAL	☑	☐	☐	☑	☐
RM07MTRB	☑	☐	☐	☑	☐
RM07RESL	☑	☐	☐	☑	☐

21.13.4 Primary Key

ABAP Program Name

21.13.5 Important Fields

Program name

You can specify different properties for different programs.

Selections

This checkbox indicates that the data entered on the report's selection screen is printed along with the output list on a separate page at the start of the printout.

Cover sheet

This checkbox specifies that the selection options and the list status are printed on a separate page. If you have set the Selections indicator or List info indicator, this information appears on a separate page at the start of the printout.

List information

You can set this indicator if you want the number of items in the output list, and the sort criteria, to be printed on a separate page at the start of the printout.

Grid control

This checkbox specifies that the report is formatted as a spread sheet, offering many advantages of the format, e.g. drag drop, adjustment of column width, computing totals etc.

B/W

In certain reports, positive numbers are highlighted green and negative numbers are highlighted red. This is specified in the report documentation. You can deactivate this feature to improve performance by selecting this checkbox.

21.14 CUSTOMER EXITS

Functional Consultant	User	Business Process Owner	Senior Management	My Rating	Understanding Level
C	X	X	X		

SAP provides the following customer exits

Customer exit	Description
MB_CF001	Updating of material document data upon posting
MBCF0002	Filling the item text in the material document
MBCFC003	Maintaining batch master data upon goods movements
MBCFC004	Maintaining batch specifications upon goods movements
MBCF0005	Filling the item data on goods receipt/ issue slips
MBCF0006	Transferring the number of the WBS element for subcontracting
MBCF0007	Posting a reservation
MBCF0009	Filling the Storage location field
IQSM0007	Serial numbers, user exit for goods movements
XMBF0001	Stock determination

21.15 BUSINESS ADD-INS

Functional Consultant	User	Business Process Owner	Senior Management	My Rating	Understanding Level
C	X	X	X		

SAP provides the following Business Add-Ins.

Business add-in	Description
MB_DOCUMENT_BADI	You can call this BAdI when creating a material document.
MB_MIGO_ITEM_BADI	This BAdI enables you to set the storage location and item text in the transaction for goods movements (MIGO).
MB_MIGO_BADI	With this BAdI you can add tabs in the header and the detail of the goods movements transaction (MIGO).
MB_RESERVATION_BADI	While maintaining reservations, with this BAdI you can populate screen fields, or check the data entered in the dialog according to your own defined rules.
MB_CHECK_LINE_BADI	You can use this BAdI to perform checks at item level when you post goods movements.
ARC_MM_MATBEL_WRITE	This BAdI is used in the programs RM07MARCS (write program for archiving material documents) and RM07MADES (deletion program for archiving material documents) and serves to write and delete additional data.
ARC_MM_MATBEL_CHECK	This BAdI is used in the program RM07MARCS (write program for archiving material documents) and serves to check your own archivability criteria.
ARC_MM_INVBEL_WRITE	You can use this BAdI to enhance the scope of the write program Archiving of Physical Inventory Documents (RM07IARCS) and the delete program Archiving of Physical Inventory Documents (RM07IDELS).
ARC_MM_INVBEL_CHECK	You can use this BAdI to enhance the archivability check of the write program Archiving of Physical Inventory Documents (RM07IARCS) by additional checks.

22 Material Document

22.1 MATERIAL DOCUMENT

Functional Consultant	User	Business Process Owner	Senior Management	My Rating	Understanding Level
A	A	A	A		

22.1.1 Automatic Generation of Material Document

In the Inventory Management system, when a goods movement is posted, a material document is automatically generated.

22.1.2 Purpose of Material Document

The material document serves as proof of the goods movement and as a source of information for any applications that follow.

22.1.3 Header and Items

A material document consists of a header and at least one item. The header contains general data about the movement, e.g., its date. Each item describes one movement.

22.1.4 Transaction

MB02—Change Material Document
MB03—Display Material Document

22.1.5 Initial Screen

Material Doc.	
Mat. Doc. Year	

22.1.6 Material Document List

In the initial screen you can specify the material document number and year directly. However, if you do not know the material document number, Click 🖸. The system gives you a selection screen.

Item Data

Material		to		⇨
Plant		to		⇨
Storage Location		to		⇨
Batch		to		⇨
Vendor		to		⇨
Customer		to		⇨
Movement Type		to		⇨
Special Stock		to		⇨

Header Data

Posting Date		to		⇨
User Name		to		⇨
Trans./Event Type		to		⇨
Reference		to		⇨

Display Options

Layout	

Data Source

☑ Database
☐ Short Documents
☐ Reread Short Docs In Archive
Archive Infostruct.

In the selection screen, you specify as much data as possible, so that the material document list is small.

Material				Material Description				Plnt Name 1	
SLoc	MvT	S	Mat. Doc.	Item	Pstng Date	Quantity in	UnE	EUn	
100-100				Casing				1000 Werk Hamburg	
	641		4900000062	2	26.09.2013	8	PC		
0002	641		4900000062	1	26.09.2013	8-	PC		
0001	101		5000000042	1	26.09.2013	8	PC		
0001	231	E	4900000060	1	23.09.2013	5-	PC		
0001	101	E	5000000040	1	23.09.2013	10	PC		
0001	102		5000000037	1	11.09.2013	5-	PC		
0001	221	Q	4900000042	1	10.09.2013	2-	PC		
0001	101	Q	5000000036	1	10.09.2013	5	PC		
0001	453		4900000032	1	09.09.2013	3	PC		
0001	453		4900000032	2	09.09.2013	3-	PC		
0001	451		4900000033	1	09.09.2013	5	PC		
0001	453		4900000034	1	09.09.2013	5	PC		
0001	453		4900000034	2	09.09.2013	5-	PC		

You can double-click on any material document to display or change it.

22.1.7 Material Document Header

After you select a material document, the system brings you back to the initial screen, in which the material document number is populated. Here you click 🔲 to display the header of the material document.

Change Material Document 5000000042 : Header

Document Date	26.09.2013	Posting Date	26.09.2013
Mat. Doc. Year	2013	Time of Entry	17:56:26
Entry Date	26.09.2013		

Transaction/Event

Trans./Ev. Type	WE	Goods Receipt for Purchase Order		
Doc.Header Text			Name	SAPUSER
Delivery Note	80014992			

☑ Print

◉ Individual Slip
○ Indiv.Slip w.Inspect.Text
○ Collective Slip

A material document represents a goods movement. The data you specify in the header of the goods movement is copied in the header of a material document and cannot be changed. You can only change or enter the document header text.

22.1.8 Material Document Items Overview

In the initial screen, or in the material document header, you can click ![icon] to display the items overview. A material document may contain multiple items.

Change Material Document 5000000042 : Overview

	Details from Item	Material	Accounting Documents...		
Posting Date	26.09.2013	Deliv.Note	80014992	Name	SAPUSER

Items

Item	Quantity	EUn	Material	PInt	SLoc	PO	Item	S DCI
		BUn	Material Description			Batch	R MvT	S S
1	8	PC	100-100	1000	0001	4500017132	10	☑
			Casing				101	+

22.1.9 Material Document Item Details

In items overview, you can select an item and click ![icon] to display item details.

Change Material Document 5000000042 : Details 0001 / 0001

◄	►				Messages	Material	WM Details...

Purchase Order	4500017132	10		Movement Type	101	GR stock in transit
Plant	1000			Werk Hamburg		
Vendor				Werk Hamburg		
Material	100-100			Casing		

Quantity in

Unit of Entry	8	PC	Stor. Location	0001
Del. Note Qty	8	PC	☑ Deliv. Compl.	

Further Information

Unloading Point				
		Company Code	1000	Fiscal Yr	2013
Text				

You can change only a few non-critical fields in a material document item, e.g. item text, unloading point, goods recipient etc.

22.1.10 Messages for a Material Document

In item details, you can click ![Messages] to see the message (output) generated for the goods movement.

Material Document... 5000000042 0001

	Status	Output	Description	Medium	Func	Partner	L	C	Processing	Time	D	Sa
	∞	WE01	GR Note Vers.1	1 Print🗐			EN	☐	26.09.2013	17:56:38	4	☑
	∞	WEE1	GR Label Vers.1	1 Print🗐			EN	☐	26.09.2013	17:56:38	4	☑

You can see more details of the message and perform various functions by clicking

| 📧 Communication method | 🖼 Processing log | Further data | Repeat output | Change output | ·

22.1.11 Printing/Displaying an Output Message

If you want to print/see the actual output, you can do so using transaction MB90. In the selection screen enter the material document year, material document number and select `Processing mode     2` if the message is already processed. You will get the message list.

Mat. Doc.	Item	Out.	Med	Material	Descr.	Plnt	SLoc
☐ 5000000042	1	WE01	1	100-100	Casing	1000	0001
☐ 5000000042	1	WEE1	1	100-100	Casing	1000	0001

Select a line and click 🗐 to see the actual output.

Goods receipt slip

```
G O O D S    R E C E I P T    S L I P        5000000042/0001
------------------------------------------------------------
Goods receipt date : 26.09.2013
Current date       : 26.09.2013
------------------------------------------------------------
Plant       : 1000
Description : Werk Hamburg

Iss. Plant  : 1000                   Delivery note: 80014992
Name        : Werk Hamburg
PO          : 4500017132/00010
Pur. group  : 000   Chef,H.          Telephone    : 069/5510
------------------------------------------------------------
Material    : 100-100
Batch       :
Description : Casing

Quantity    :                 8   PC
------------------------------------------------------------
W A R E H O U S E    I N F O R M A T I O N

Storage loc.: 0001
Storage bin :
------------------------------------------------------------
Issued by   : SAPUSER    S I G N A T U R E
```

Goods receipt labels

```
Material: 100-100              Material: 100-100
Vendor: Werk Hamburg           Vendor: Werk Hamburg
Plant/SL: 1000 0001            Plant/SL: 1000 0001
GR/ GI Number: 5000000042      GR/ GI Number: 5000000042
GR/ GI Date: 26.09.2013        GR/ GI Date: 26.09.2013
```

22.1.12 Material of an Item

For an item you can see the material details by clicking `Material`.

22.1.13 Accounting Documents

List of documents in accounting

In transaction MB02 or MB03 click `Accounting Documents...` in the item overview of the material document to see the accounting documents. In some cases, such as this, there may be no accounting documents.

> (!) Material document 5000000042 does not include an accounting document

22.2 MATERIAL DOCUMENT PROCESSES

Functional Consultant	User	Business Process Owner	Senior Management	My Rating	Understanding Level
A	A	B	C		

22.2.1 Creating a Material Document

Material documents are created automatically when a goods movement is posted. You cannot create a material document manually.

22.2.2 Changing a Material Document

See Section 22.1.

22.2.3 Displaying a Material Document

See Section 22.1.

22.2.4 Copying a Material Document

Purpose

You can copy a material document, thereby creating a goods movement.

Transaction

MBSL—Copy Material Document

Initial Screen

Posting Date	05.10.2013
Material Doc.	5000000010
Mat. Doc. Year	2013

GR/GI Slip

☑ Print

- ⦿ Individual Slip
- ○ Indiv. Slip w. Inspect. Text
- ○ Collective Slip

Material document number and year identify the material document you want to copy. You specify the posting date of the document that will be created. You also specify printing details.

Copying the Items

You can copy all the items by clicking 🗋, or copy the items selectively by clicking Adopt + Details .

Purchase Order	4500017087	10		Movement Type	101	GR goods receipt
Plant	1000			Werk Hamburg		
Vendor	1002			Müller KG		
Incoterms	CPT					
Material	100-100			Casing		
Ordered		200	PC	Material Group	001	
Received		120				

Quantity in

Unit of Entry	10		PC	Stor. Location	0001		Stock Type	
				Batch				
				Vendor Batch				
Del. Note Qty				☐ Deliv. Compl.				
				Manuf. Date/BBD		/		

Further Information

EAN in OUn				EAN Check			
Unloading Point							
				No. Containers			
No. of GR Slips	1						
Text							

Posting the Goods Movement

Save the document. A new material document is created.

Document 5000000050 posted

Displaying the Material Document Created by Copying

Run transaction MB02 or MB03 to display the newly created material document.

Display Material Document 5000000050 : Details 0001 / 0

| ◀ | ▶ | 🔍 | 🖨 | 🖹 Messages | WM Details... | Material |

Purchase Order	4500017087 10	Movement Type	101 GR goods receipt
Ref. Document	5000000050 1		
Plant	1000	Werk Hamburg	
Vendor	1002	Müller KG	
Incoterms	CPT		
Material	100-100	Casing	

Quantity in

| Unit of Entry | 10 | PC | Stor. Location | 0001 |

Further Information

| No. of GR Slips | 5 | Company Code | 1000 | Fiscal Yr | 2013 |

22.2.5 Cancelling/Reversing a Material Document

Purpose

You can cancel/reverse a material document. This process is equivalent to creating a goods movement. Note that you cannot use this process to return a partial quantity.

Transaction

MBST—Cancel/Reverse Material Document

Initial Screen

Posting Date	06.10.2013
Material Doc.	4900000000
Mat. Doc. Year	2013

Defaults for Document Items

Reason for Mvmt [ ]

GR/GI Slip

☑ Print

◉ Individual Slip
○ Indiv.Slip w.Inspect.Text
○ Collective Slip

Material document number and year identify the material document you want to cancel/reverse. You specify the posting date of the document that will be created. You also specify printing details.

Cancelling/Reversing the Items

You can copy all the items by clicking 🗐, or copy the items selectively by clicking Adopt + Details .

Movement Type	502 RE receipt w/o PO
Material	100-100 Casing

Quantity in

Unit of Entry	8	PC	Plant	1000	Stor. Loc.	0001

Account Assignment

		Goods recipient		
Vendor	1002			
Text				
Reason for Mvmt				

Note that the movement type is the reversal of original movement type. Also note that you cannot use this process to return a partial quantity.

Posting the Goods Movement

Save the document. A new material document is created.

✓ Document 4900000070 posted

Displaying the Material Document Created by Cancelling/Reversing

Run transaction MB02 or MB03 to display the newly created material document.

Change Material Document 4900000070 : Details 0001 / 0001

| ◀ | ▶ | 🔲 | 🖨 | 🖎 Messages | Material | WM Details... |

Movement Type	502	RE receipt w/o PO	
Material	100-100		Casing

Quantity in

| Unit of Entry | 8 | | PC | Plant | 1000 | Stor. Loc. | 0001 |

Account Assignment

G/L Account	893025		
		Goods recipient	
Vendor	1002		
Text			

22.2.6 Return Delivery

Purpose

You can return the material using a material document. This process is equivalent to creating a goods movement. You can use this process to return a partial quantity. If you want you can create an outbound delivery.

Transaction

MBRL—Return Delivery

Initial Screen

Posting Date	06.10.2013		
Material Doc.	5000000017		
Mat. Doc. Year	2013		
Delivery Note		Vendor	
☐ Create Delivery			

Defaults for Document Items

| Reason for Mvmt | 1 |

GR/GI Slip

☑ Print

○ Individual Slip
◉ Indiv.Slip w.Inspect.Text
○ Collective Slip

Material document number and year identify the material document whose material you want to return. You specify the posting date of the document that will be created. You also specify printing details.

If you want to create a delivery, select the ☑ Create Delivery field. If you want the system to assign the delivery note number, leave the Delivery Note field blank; otherwise enter the delivery note number in the Delivery Note field.

Returning the Items

You can copy all the items by clicking 🗍, or copy the items selectively by clicking
Adopt + Details .

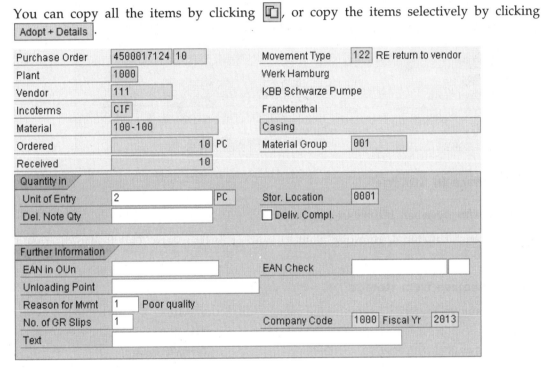

Note that for return delivery, the movement type is 122. Also note that you can use this process to return a partial quantity.

Posting the Goods Movement

Save the document. A new material document is created.

Document 5000000051 posted

Displaying the Material Document Created by Return Delivery

Run transaction MB02 or MB03 to display the newly created material document.

Change Material Document 5000000051 : Details 0001 / 0001

| ◀ | ▶ | 🔍 | 🖨 | 📋 | Messages | Material | WM Details... |

Purchase Order	4500017124 10	Movement Type	122 RE return to vendor
Plant	1000	Werk Hamburg	
Vendor	111	KBB Schwarze Pumpe	
Incoterms	CIF	Frankthenthal	
Material	100-100	Casing	

Quantity in

Unit of Entry	2	PC	Stor. Location	0001

Further Information

Unloading Point				
Reason for Mvmt	1	Poor quality		
No. of GR Slips	1		Company Code	1000 Fiscal Yr	2013
Text				

22.2.7 Place in Storage

Stock transfer between plants in two steps

You can transfer material from one plant to another in two steps. This is also discussed in Section 8.3.

Step 1: Remove from storage

You can remove material from storage using transaction MIGO_TR and the following selection.

| A09 Remove from St 🔽 | R10 Other 🔽 | TF rem.fm.stor.to pl | 303 |

Step 2: Place in storage

You can place material in storage using transaction MIGO_TR and the following selection.

| A10 Place in Storage 🔽 | R02 Material Docum 🔽 | | | ✔ 🔲 🔲 |

Transaction MBSU is an alternative transaction for this step.

22.3   MATERIAL DOCUMENT REPORTS

Functional Consultant	User	Business Process Owner	Senior Management	My Rating	Understanding Level
A	A	C	X		

22.3.1   Material Document List

Purpose

You can use this report to see the list of material documents. From the list you can also display a material document.

Transaction

MB51—Material Document List

Selection Screen

Item Data			
Material		to	
Plant		to	
Storage Location		to	
Batch		to	
Vendor		to	
Customer		to	
Movement Type		to	
Special Stock		to	

Header Data			
Posting Date		to	
User Name		to	
Trans./Event Type		to	
Reference		to	

Display Options	
Layout	

Data Source
☑ Database
☐ Short Documents
☐ Reread Short Docs In Archive
Archive Infostruct.

You can enter a number of selection criteria. The system shows you the list of material documents.

List of Material Documents

```
Material              Material Description              Plnt Name 1
SLoc MvT S Mat. Doc.  Item Pstng Date   Quantity in UnE EUn

100-100               Casing                            1000 Werk Hamburg
0001 101   5000000042   1 26.09.2013              8   PC
0001 101 E 5000000040   1 23.09.2013             10   PC
0001 231 E 4900000060   1 23.09.2013              5-  PC
```

Material document

Select a line and click [icon] to display a material document from the output list.

Stock overview

Select a line and click [icon] to display the stock overview of the material.

Accounting documents

Select a line and click [icon] to display the accounting documents.

Fields Available on Selection Screen and Output

For this report, you can specify the fields available on selection screen and output in view V_MMIM_REP_CUST.

Prog.name	Table	Field	Fld cont.	Selection field	Output field
RM07DOCS	MKPF	BKTXT	Document Header Text	☑	☑
RM07DOCS	MKPF	BLDAT	Document Date in Document	☐	☑
RM07DOCS	MKPF	BUDAT	Posting Date in the Document	☑	☑

Including Reference Documents in the Report

In standard SAP, this report does not show reference document for a material document. You may like to include it by specifying in view V_MMIM_REP_CUST.

Prog.name	Table	Field name	Fld cont.	Selection f	Output
RM07DOCS	MSEG	LFBNR	Document No. of a Reference Document	☐	☑
RM07DOCS	MSEG	LFPOS	Item of a Reference Document	☐	☑
RM07DOCS	MSEG	LFBJA	Fiscal Year of a Reference Document	☐	☑

22.3.2   Cancelled Material Documents

Purpose

You can use this report to see the list of cancelled material documents. From the list you can also display a material document.

Transaction

MBSM—Cancelled Material Documents

Selection Screen

Database Selections		
Material	to	⇨
Plant	to	⇨
Posting Date	to	⇨
User Name	to	⇨

Reversal Document		
Reversal Document	to	⇨
Year of Reversal Document	to	⇨

Original Document		
Original Document	to	⇨
Year of Original Document	to	⇨

Display Options	
Layout	

You can select the documents based either on the original documents, or on reversal documents.

List of Cancelled Material Documents

	Mat. Doc.	MatY	It	Material	MvT	Plnt	SLoc	D/C	Qua	EUn	Pstng Date	Mat. Doc.	It
☐	4900000070	2013	1	100-100	502	1000	0001	H	8	PC	06.10.2013	4900000000	1

Reversal and original material documents

You can select a line and click 🔳 to display the details of the reversal and original material documents.

```
              Mat. Doc. Pstng Date User Name
Item Material            Quantity in UnE EUn    Amount in LC Crcy  MvT
Material Description                     Batch   SLoc Plnt Item

Reversal Docume 4900000070 06.10.2013 SAPUSER
  1 100-100                       8  PC          910.08  EUR   502
Casing                                          0001 1000    1

Original Docume 4900000000 04.09.2013 SAPUSER
  1 100-100                       8  PC          910.08  EUR   501
Casing                                          0001 1000
```

Accounting documents

You can select a line and click 🔲 to display the accounting documents.

22.3.3 Material Documents by Movement Reason

Purpose

You can use this report to see the list of material documents. From the list you can also display a material document.

Transaction

MBGR—Display Material Documents by Movement Reason

Selection Screen

Search via material docmt			
Material		to	
Plant		to	
Reason for Movement		to	
Trans./Event Type		to	
Posting Date		to	
☐ No vendor			

Search via purch. docmt			
Vendor		to	
Purchasing Document		to	
Item		to	

Display options	
Layout	

If you want to see material documents for a specific reason for movement you can specify that. You can also see material documents having reason for movement for a specific vendor.

List of Material Documents

Material		Material Description				Vendor				
Rea Reason		MvT Quant OUn Quant OUn			% Amount L Crc Amount L Crc				%
500-130		Pyridin CDE 50%					1070			
		101 1800 KG				2604.51	EUR			
1 Poor quality 123	385	KG			548.22	EUR			
1 Poor quality 122			385- KG	17.62			548.22- EUR 17.39		

Material document

You can select a line and click ⊞ to display an ALV list of material documents with reason for movement.

Material	Material Description	Vendor	PO		Item	MvT	R	Reason	Material D	Plant	SLoc
500-130	Pyridin CDE 50%	1070	4500005836		20	122	1	Poor quality	50007613	1100	0001

You can select a line and click ⊞ to display the material document.

Stock overview

Select a line and click 🔲 to display the stock overview of the material.

22.4   NUMBER ASSIGNMENT FOR MATERIAL DOCUMENTS

Functional Consultant	User	Business Process Owner	Senior Management	My Rating	Understanding Level
A	A	C	X		

22.4.1   Purpose

Here you define different number ranges for material and physical inventory documents.

22.4.2   IMG Node

Transaction OMBT—Number Assignment for Material and Physical Inventory Documents

22.4.3 Groups

Click ✐ Groups .

> Number range object Material Document
> Grouping..........
>
> ☐ Phys. inventory documents
>   IB ID IN IZ WV
>
> ☐ Material documents for goods movements and inventory diffs.
>   WA WH WI WL WO WR WS WZ
>
> ☐ Material documents for goods receipts
>   WE WF WO WW
>
> ☐ Inventory sampling procedure number
>   SI

SAP provides four predefined groups as shown above. Each group is assigned a different number range. Thus, the material document number of goods receipt can come from one number range and the material document number of goods issue from another.

Transaction/event types in a group

When a goods movement takes place, the system determines its transaction/event type based on transaction code (table T158). These transaction/event types are grouped in a Group here and are shown in the screenshot above.

22.4.4 Number Range Intervals

After clicking ✐ Groups , select ☑ Material documents for goods receipts and click ✐ . You see the number range objects assigned to the group.

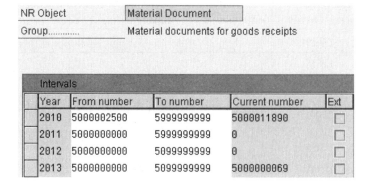

NR Object	Material Document
Group...........	Material documents for goods receipts

Intervals

	Year	From number	To number	Current number	Ext
	2010	5000002500	5999999999	5000011890	☐
	2011	5000000000	5999999999	0	☐
	2012	5000000000	5099999999	0	☐
	2013	5000000000	5099999999	5000000069	☐

22.4.5 Adding a Year in the Number Range

Put the cursor on a year in the above view and select `Edit` ➤ `Insert year` to add number range for a new year.

NR Object	Material Document
Group............	Material documents for goods receipts

Intervals

	Year	From number	To number	Current number	Ext
	2010	5000002500	5999999999	5000011890	☐
	2011	5000000000	5999999999	0	☐
	2012	5000000000	5099999999	0	☐
	2013	5000000000	5099999999	5000000069	☐
	2014	5000000000	5099999999	0	☐

Accounting Document

23.1 ACCOUNTING DOCUMENTS FOR GOODS MOVEMENT

Functional Consultant	User	Business Process Owner	Senior Management	My Rating	Understanding Level
A	A	A	A		

23.1.1 List of Documents in Accounting

You can see accounting documents for a material document by running transaction MB03. This method shows all accounting documents corresponding to a material document generated by a goods movement.

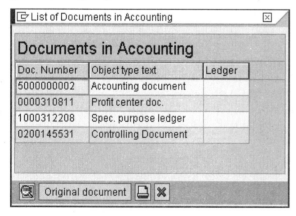

23.1.2 Accounting Document

The accounting document shows the general ledger accounts that have been debited and credited on the basis of the material document which was generated as a result of a goods movement.

Data Entry View						
Document Number	5000000002	Company Code	1000		Fiscal Year	2013
Document Date	03.09.2013	Posting Date	03.09.2013		Period	9
Reference		Cross-CC no.				
Currency	EUR	Texts exist	☐		Ledger Group	

CoCd	Itm	PK	S	Account	Description	Amount	Curr.	Tx	Cost Ctr	Assignment
1000	1	89		790000	Unfinished products	1,137.60	EUR			
	2	96		191100	Goods Rcvd/Invoice R	600.00-	EUR			450001708700010
	3	93		281500	Income from price di	537.60-	EUR		1000	20130903

23.1.3 Profit Center Document

You can divide a company code into profit centers that are independently managed. Both costs and revenues are posted to profit centers. You can thereby judge the profitability of each profit centre.

Ledger	8A
Controlling Area	1000
Company Code	1000
Posting Period	009
Fiscal Year	2013
Version	000

D	Ref.Doc.No.	Itm	Period	Profit Ctr	Partner PC	Account	Acc.Text	∑ In PCLC	Curr.
W	5000000010	1	9	1010		790000	Unfinished products	1,137.60	EUR
W	5000000010	3	9	1402		281500	Profit PD,int.prod.	537.60-	EUR
								▪ 600.00	EUR

23.1.4 Special Purpose Ledger

The Special Purpose Ledger allows you to report at various levels using the values from the various application components. The modules in the Special Purpose Ledger allow you to collect information, combine information, and create totals.

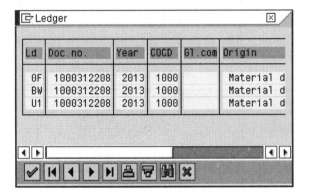

23.1.5 Controlling Document

Controlling provides you with information for management decision-making. Controlling has a cost element structure similar to G/L account structure in the Finance module. Goods movements result in posting in the Controlling module through the Controlling document.

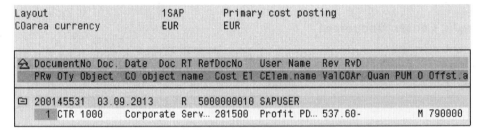

23.2 ACCOUNTING DOCUMENT FOR MATERIAL

Functional Consultant	User	Business Process Owner	Senior Management	My Rating	Understanding Level
A	A	C	X		

23.2.1 Purpose

You can see accounting documents generated during goods movements.

23.2.2 Transaction

MR51—Accounting Document for Material

23.2.3 Selection Screen

You can search for an accounting document based on various criteria.

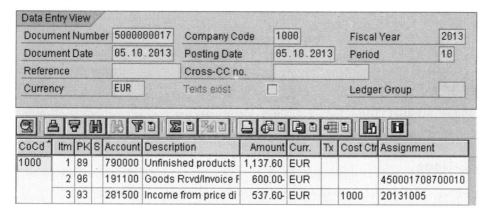

Database Selections				
Material		to		⇨
Company Code		to		⇨
Valuation Area		to		⇨
Posting Date		to		⇨
Document Date		to		⇨
Document Type		to		⇨

Display Options	
Layout	

23.2.4 Document List

The system displays the list of documents satisfying the selection criteria.

Material	Material Description		CoCd ValA	
Type DocumentNo Itm Pstng Date		Quantity BUn	Amount in LC Crcy	
100-100	Casing		1000 1000	
WE 5000000019 1 06.10.2013		2- PC	227.52- EUR	
WE 5000000018 1 06.10.2013		8- PC	910.08- EUR	
WE 5000000017 1 05.10.2013		10 PC	1,137.60 EUR	

Document display

You can select a document and click 🗐 Document to display the selected accounting document.

Data Entry View					
Document Number	5000000017	Company Code	1000	Fiscal Year	2013
Document Date	05.10.2013	Posting Date	05.10.2013	Period	10
Reference		Cross-CC no.			
Currency	EUR	Texts exist	☐	Ledger Group	

CoCd	Itm	PK	S	Account	Description	Amount	Curr.	Tx	Cost Ctr	Assignment
1000	1	89		790000	Unfinished products	1,137.60	EUR			
	2	96		191100	Goods Rcvd/Invoice F	600.00-	EUR			4500017087000010
	3	93		281500	Income from price di	537.60-	EUR		1000	20131005

Original document

Click Environment ➤ Document Environment ➤ Original Document to see the material document that resulted in the generation of this accounting document.

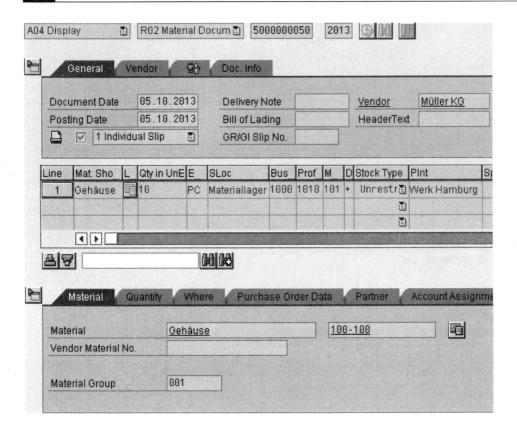

23.3 NUMBER ASSIGNMENT FOR ACCOUNTING DOCUMENTS

Functional Consultant	User	Business Process Owner	Senior Management	My Rating	Understanding Level
A	A	C	X		

23.3.1 Purpose

Here you maintain number ranges for accounting documents pertaining to goods movement for a company code.

23.3.2 IMG Node

Transaction FBN1—Define Number Assignment for Accounting Documents

23.3.3 Initial Screen

Company Code........ 1000

| Intervals | | Status |

| Intervals |

23.3.4 Number Range Intervals for Goods Receipt

Click [Intervals] to display intervals in change mode. Number range interval 50 is for goods receipt.

NR Object   Accounting document
Subobject   1000

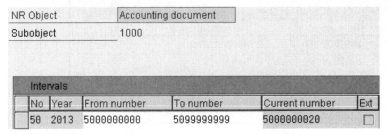

	No	Year	From number	To number	Current number	Ext
	50	2013	5000000000	5099999999	5000000020	☐

23.3.5 Number Range Intervals for Goods Issue and Transfer Posting

Click [Intervals] to display intervals in change mode. Number range interval 49 is for goods issue and transfer posting.

NR Object   Accounting document
Subobject   1000

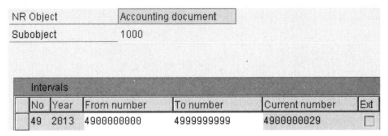

	No	Year	From number	To number	Current number	Ext
	49	2013	4900000000	4999999999	4900000029	☐

23.3.6 Adding Number Range for a Year

Click 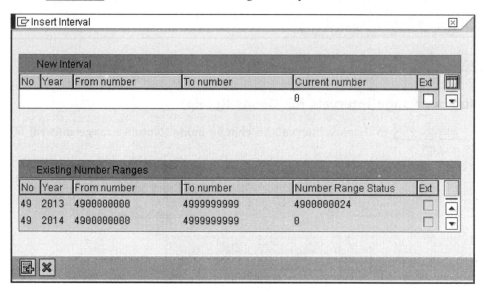 Interval to add the number range for a year.

Maintain From number and To number for every Year for No 49 (goods issue and transfer posting) and 50 (goods receipt).

Output Determination

24.1 FEATURES

Functional Consultant	User	Business Process Owner	Senior Management	My Rating	Understanding Level
A	A	A	A		

SAP has a feature rich process of output determination. These features are explained below.

Types of output

In Inventory Management you can get the following types of outputs.

➢ Goods receipt slips

➢ Goods issue slips

➢ Goods receipt labels

➢ Goods issue labels

➢ Kanban cards

➢ Mail for goods receipts and quantity deviation

➢ Mail for material that is urgently required

Content of the document

Goods receipt/goods issue slips can be designed as per your requirement, and can include data from the relevant material document and other sources.

Types of goods receipt/goods issue slips

In SAP you can print the following types of goods receipt/goods issue slips.

1 Individual Slip
2 Individual Slip with Inspection Text
3 Collective Slip

No documents for certain types of goods movement

For some movement types you do not want goods receipt/goods issue slips and labels to be printed. For example, when you move Quality Inspection Stock to Unrestricted Use Stock using movement type 321, there is no need to print goods receipt/goods issue slips and labels. For each movement type, you can specify whether goods receipt/goods issue slips are to be printed or not.

Print control at the time of goods movement

At the time of goods movement, you can specify if you do not want the documents to be printed.

Number of goods receipt slips

You can print just one goods receipt slip, or one goods receipt slip per pallet.

Medium

You may like to use a variety of transmission media to transmit your output. Most of the documents in Inventory Management are printed, but you may also want to send some messages through electronic media.

Time of printing

You can print a document immediately, or do it in a batch job.

Language

You can choose the language in which your output will be generated.

Printer

SAP supports a number of methods of determining the printer where your output will be printed.

24.2 CONDITIONS TECHNIQUE

Functional Consultant	User	Business Process Owner	Senior Management	My Rating	Understanding Level
A	C	C	X		

24.2.1 Standard Settings

SAP uses condition technique for output determination. This is a very powerful technique, which offers a lot of flexibility. Requirements of Inventory Management are, however, simple and do not need all the flexibility offered by the condition technique. SAP, therefore, offers a program that you can use to ensure that you have the right settings for Inventory Management. In your client, start the program RM07NCUS using transaction SA38. This copies all the standard settings from client 000. Although you may not need it, it is good to know the configuration that participates in the generation of your output.

24.2.2 Output Determination Procedure

In condition technique, output determination is driven by an output determination procedure. The output determination procedure for Inventory Management is ME0001 as shown in view cluster VVC_T683_XX_MB, view VV_T683_MB.

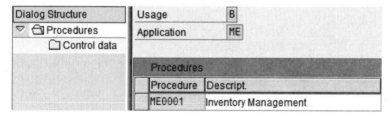

24.2.3 Steps in Output Determination Procedure

An output determination procedure has steps. The output determination procedure is executed step by step. The system reads the condition type (output type) specified in the step and accesses condition tables to determine if output of that type will be generated. The system also checks whether the requirement specified in the step is met, and the output is generated only if the requirement is met. The steps in the output determination procedure are maintained in view cluster VVC_T683_XX_MB, view V_T683S_XX.

Procedure   ME0001 Inventory Management

Reference Step Overview

Step	Counter	CTyp	Description	Requiremnt	Manual only
5	10	MLFH	GR Missing Parts Msg		☐
10	10	MLGR	GR Message	171	☐
20	10	MLMD	GR Qty Deviation	172	☐
25	10	MLUD	GR Qty Deviation	174	☐
30	10	WE01	GR Note Vers.1		☐
40	10	WE02	GR Note Vers.2		☐
50	10	WA01	GI Note Vers.1		☐
60	10	WA02	GI Note Vers.2		☐
70	10	WE03	GR Note Vers.3	173	☐
80	10	WA03	GI Note Vers.3	173	☐
90	10	WAE1	GI Label Vers.1		☐
100	10	WAE2	GI Label Vers.2		☐
110	10	WAE3	GI Label Vers.3		☐
120	10	WEE1	GR Label Vers.1		☐
130	10	WEE2	GR Label Vers.2		☐
140	10	WEE3	GR Label Vers.3		☐
150	10	WLB1	GI Note RP Vers.1		☐
160	10	WLB2	GI Note RP Vers.2		☐
170	10	WLB3	GI Note RP Vers.3	173	☐
180	10	WF01	GR Prod. Ord. Vers.1		☐
190	10	WF02	GR Prod. Ord. Vers.2		☐
200	1	ET01	Material label		☐
210	10	WEK1	Kanban Card 1		☐

Step, counter

An output determination procedure has a number of steps and sub-steps (counters) which are executed in the sequence of step and sub-step numbers. Counters are needed for manually inserted condition types and are used in pricing procedures, not in output determination.

Condition type and description

Each step has a condition type. When a step is executed, condition tables associated with that condition type are accessed to determine the output.

Requirement

If a step has a requirement, the step is executed only if the requirement is fulfilled. Requirements are maintained using transaction VOFM. Usually the requirements predefined by SAP are sufficient.

Manual only

Conditions, which are given this indicator, are only included in output determination either if they are entered manually or if they are transferred from an external process.

24.2.4 Output Type

In the previous section, a condition type was determined from a step in output determination procedure. This condition type (also called output type) is linked to an access sequence. This is specified in view VN_T685B.

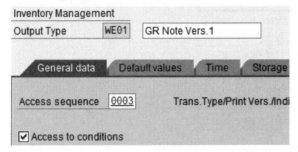

The link between output type and access sequence is stored in table T685 and the contents of this table are given below.

U	App	CTyp	AcSq	Name
☐ B	ME	ET01	0006	Material label
☐ B	ME	MLFH	0005	GR Missing Parts Msg
☐ B	ME	MLGR	0002	GR Message
☐ B	ME	MLMD	0002	GR Qty Deviation
☐ B	ME	MLUD	0002	GR Qty Deviation
☐ B	ME	WA01	0003	GI Note Vers.1
☐ B	ME	WA02	0003	GI Note Vers.2
☐ B	ME	WA03	0003	GI Note Vers.3
☐ B	ME	WAE1	0001	GI Label Vers.1
☐ B	ME	WAE2	0001	GI Label Vers.2
☐ B	ME	WAE3	0001	GI Label Vers.3
☐ B	ME	WE01	0003	GR Note Vers.1
☐ B	ME	WE02	0003	GR Note Vers.2
☐ B	ME	WE03	0003	GR Note Vers.3
☐ B	ME	WEE1	0001	GR Label Vers.1
☐ B	ME	WEE2	0001	GR Label Vers.2
☐ B	ME	WEE3	0001	GR Label Vers.3
☐ B	ME	WEK1	0007	Kanban Card 1
☐ B	ME	WF01	0003	GR Prod. Ord. Vers.1
☐ B	ME	WF02	0003	GR Prod. Ord. Vers.2
☐ B	ME	WLB1	0004	GI Note RP Vers.1
☐ B	ME	WLB2	0004	GI Note RP Vers.2
☐ B	ME	WLB3	0004	GI Note RP Vers.3

You should ensure that the checkbox ☑ Access to conditions is ticked for all output types.

24.2.5 Access Sequence

Access sequences are defined in view cluster VVC_T682_MB.

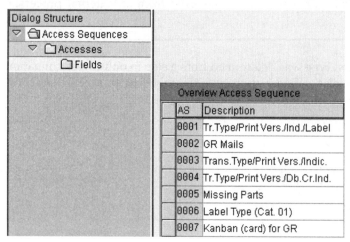

An access sequence is a sequence of condition tables.

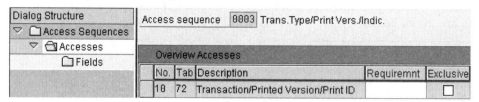

Table T682I shows the link between access sequences and condition tables.

U	App	AcSq	AcNo	Tab
☐ B	ME	0001	10	70
☐ B	ME	0002	10	71
☐ B	ME	0003	10	72
☐ B	ME	0004	10	73
☐ B	ME	0005	10	74
☐ B	ME	0006	1	16
☐ B	ME	0007	1	75

24.2.6 Condition Table

A condition table contains condition records that are maintained using transaction MN21, MN22, or MN23.

Trans./Event Type	WE	Goods Receipt for Purchase Order
Print Version	1	Individual Slip

Condition Recs.

	Print item	Name	Funct	Partner	Medium	Date/Time	Language
	1	Material Document Pr			1	4	EN
	2	Return Delivery			1	4	EN

A condition record consists of a condition and output parameters.

Condition   **Output parameters**

Trans./Event Type	WE
Print Version	1

Condition Recs.

	Print item	Name
	1	Material Document Pr
	2	Return Delivery

Funct	Partner	Medium	Date/Time	Language
		1	4	EN
		1	4	EN

A condition record is selected if the fields in the condition stub matches with the input parameters. If a match is found, output is created using both condition parameters and output parameters. How the system determines the input parameters before accessing condition records is discussed in the next section.

24.3 INPUT PARAMETERS FOR CONDITION RECORDS

Functional Consultant	User	Business Process Owner	Senior Management	My Rating	Understanding Level
A	C	C	X		

24.3.1 Input Parameters Required for Condition Records

Output types used in Inventory Management and the condition tables they access are given below:

Category of output	Output types	Access sequence	Condition table	Input parameters
Goods receipt/goods issue slips	WA01, WA02, WA03 WE01, WE02, WE03 WF01, WF02	0003	72	Output Type Transaction/Event Type Version for Printing GR/GI Slip Printing of document item

Category of output	Output types	Access sequence	Condition table	Input parameters
Goods issue slips for subcontracting	WLB1, WLB2, WLB3	0004	73	Output Type Transaction/Event Type Version for Printing GR/GI Slip Printing of document item Debit/Credit Indicator
Goods receipt/goods issue labels	WAE1, WAE2, WAE3 WEE1, WEE2, WEE3	0001	70	Output Type Transaction/Event Type Version for Printing GR/GI Slip · Printing of document item Label type Label form
Goods receipt message	MLGR, MLMD, MLUD	0002	71	Output Type Indicator: Goods Receipt Message
Goods receipt of missing parts message	MLFH	0005	74	Output Type Material is a missing part

Condition table 16 is for Industry Solution Retail, and condition table 75 for kanban process. Both these scenarios are out of scope of this book.

Different condition tables have different parameters. You need to understand what these parameters are, and how the system determines them.

24.3.2 Output Type

The process of output determination is driven by the output determination procedure. This procedure has steps and each step invokes an output type. This output type is passed to the condition records of the concerned condition table to determine if an output is generated. This is done for all output types, but a match is not found unless other input parameters match.

24.3.3 Transaction/Event Type

The transaction/event type determines the nature of event, e.g. an external goods receipt, an internal goods receipt, a goods issue, etc. The system uses this information to generate corresponding output, e.g. a goods receipt slip, or a goods issue slip. The transaction/ event type is determined from transaction in view V_158_ALL.

Transaction Code	TTyp	Type	DocTypeRev	TETy
MIGO	H	WE	PR	WE
MIGO_GI	H	WA	PR	WA
MIGO_GO	H	WE	PR	WF
MIGO_GR	H	WE	PR	WE
MIGO_GS	H	WE	PR	WO
MIGO_TR	H	WA	PR	WA

This table is maintained by SAP and customers cannot change it.

24.3.4 Print Version

When you receive goods, in the header you specify the type of slip.

1 Individual Slip
2 Individual Slip with Inspection Text
3 Collective Slip

Its default value can be set in view V_158_D.

TCode	Transaction Text	P	Print version
MIGO	Goods Movement	1	Individual Slip
MIGO_GI	Goods Movement	1	Individual Slip
MIGO_GO	Goods Movement	1	Individual Slip
MIGO_GR	Goods Movement	1	Individual Slip
MIGO_GS	Subseq. Adjust. of Material Provided		
MIGO_TR	Transfer Posting	2	Individual Slip with Inspection Tex

24.3.5 Print Item

Purpose

The Print item determines whether a goods movement slip is generated for a goods movement or not. It also provides additional information to determine the type of output produced.

Synonyms

For Print item , SAP also uses Item Print Indicator and Printing of document item . All these terms refer to the same data item.

Master List of Print Items

Run transaction OMBR and click Item Print Indicator to maintain the master list of Print item (view V_159Q).

Print item	Text
	No Document Printout
1	Material Document Printout
2	Return Delivery
3	GR/GI Slip for Subcontracting
4	Inventory List W/o Sales Price
5	Inventory List w. Sales Price
6	Matl Doc. Printout for GR/GI

Print item blank (no output)

One of the key uses of ⌐Print item⌐ is to determine whether or not to print goods movement slips and labels. For some movement types you do not want goods receipt/goods issue slips and labels to be printed. For example, when you move Quality Inspection Stock to Unrestricted Use Stock using movement type 321, there is no need to print goods receipt/ goods issue slips and labels. You can achieve this simply by making the ⌐Print item⌐ blank in view V_156_D.

Print item 1

This is the print item for normal material document printout.

Print item 2

This is the print item for return delivery.

Print item 3

When you transfer goods to subcontractor using movement type 541, for every item credited to the warehouse, the system creates one debited to the subcontract stock.

Change Material Document 4900000035 : Overview

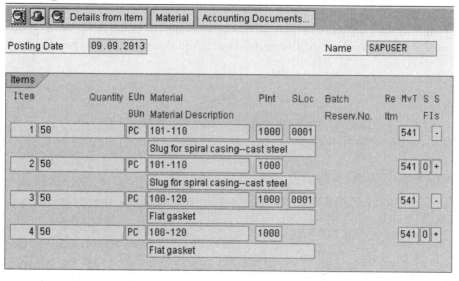

If you use |Print item| 1 for movement type 541, you will get four goods issue slips, whereas you actually want only two; one for each item transferred. This problem is solved by using |Print item| 3 and accessing condition table 73. In condition table 73, debit/credit indicator is also an input field and you create condition records only for credit entries. Therefore, output is generated only for credit entries (issue from warehouse), and not for debit entries (receipt in subcontract stock).

Print items 4 and 5

These values are used for determining forms in physical inventory in view V_159N.

Print item 6

This value is used for goods receipt where there is no purchase order, using movement types 501. When this print item is used, purchase order data is not printed in the goods receipt slip. If no movement type is linked to print item 6 in view V_156_D, you may not be using condition records having print item 6.

Determination of Print Item

|Print item| is determined from the movement type. It can be maintained in view V_156_D, or V_156_D_WA, or V_156_VC.

MvT	Movement Type Text	P	Print item
101	GR goods receipt	1	Material Document Printout
102	Reversal of GR	1	Material Document Printout
103	GR into blocked stck	1	Material Document Printout
104	Rev. GR to blocked	1	Material Document Printout

24.3.6 Debit/Credit Indicator

SAP has assigned a debit/credit indicator to each movement type, which can be seen in view V_156_VC.

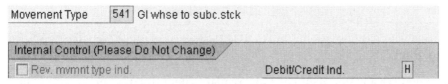

| Movement Type | 541 | GI whse to subc.stck |

| Internal Control (Please Do Not Change) | | |
| ☐ Rev. mvmnt type ind. | Debit/Credit Ind. | H |

This indicator is used to access condition table 73 for movement type 541.

24.3.7 Label Type and Label Form

Label type and label form for a material

Label type and label form are specified at the material level in the material master.

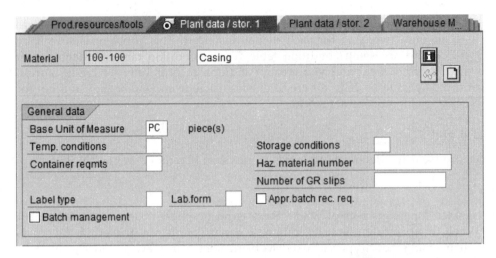

Although label type and label form are maintained in the Plant data / stor. 1 tab, they are valid for all plants and storage locations. Changing them for one plant and storage location changes it for all of them.

24.3.8 Goods Receipt Message

In the header of a purchasing document, in the ☐ GR Message checkbox, you can specify that a message should be sent to the buyer when goods are received.

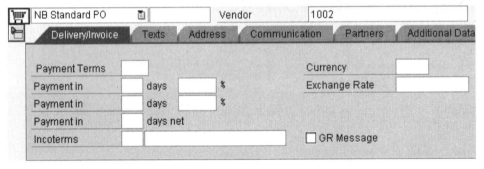

24.3.9 Missing Part

In MRP, if requirement for a material exceeds the available quantity, that material is called a missing part (see Section 21.4). When a part is received, the system checks if it is a missing part. Thus, whether a part is a missing part, or not, is automatically determined by the system, provided that the missing part check is active.

24.4 OUTPUT PARAMETERS OF CONDITION RECORDS

Functional Consultant	User	Business Process Owner	Senior Management	My Rating	Understanding Level
A	C	C	X		

24.4.1 Purpose

The system accesses a condition record with the following objectives.

Determine if an output is to be generated

Every condition record represents an output that is distinct from the output represented by other condition records. When a condition record is accessed, the system matches its condition part with the parameters it has determined earlier. If a match is found, the output represented by the condition record is generated.

Use output parameters

Every condition record stores a set of output parameters. If an output is generated because the condition of the condition record matches the input parameters, then the output parameters stored in the condition record are accessed and used in generating the output.

24.4.2 Architecture of a Condition Record

A condition record consists of a condition and output parameters. A condition record is selected if the fields in the condition stub matches with the input parameters. If a match is found, output is created in which output parameters are used.

Condition   **Output parameters**

Trans./Event Type	WE
Print Version	1

Condition Recs.	
Print item	Name
1	Material Document Pr
2	Return Delivery

Funct	Partner	Medium	Date/Time	Language
		1	4	EN
		1	4	EN

24.4.3 Condition

The condition contains fields that are matched with input parameters. Different output types have different fields in the condition part of the condition record. These have been discussed in the previous section.

24.4.4 Output Parameters

If a match is found in the condition stub, the system determines the output parameters. These output parameters are the same for all condition records and are stored in table NACH.

Partner function, partner

These fields are needed to determine the recipient of an electronic message. They are not needed for printed output.

Medium

The output may be communicated using various media. For goods receipt/goods issue slips and labels, usually you want print output (value 1).

```
1 Print output
2 Fax
4 Telex
5 External send
6 EDI
7 Simple Mail
8 Special function
9 Events (SAP Business Workflow)
A Distribution (ALE)
T Tasks (SAP Business Workflow)
```

Date/time

Here you specify when the goods receipt/goods issue slips and labels are printed.

```
1    Send with periodically scheduled job
2    Send with job, with additional time specification
3    Send with application own transaction
4    Send immediately (when saving the application)
```

Most people choose the value 4, in which the goods receipt/goods issue slips and labels are generated as soon as the transaction is saved.

Language

Here you can specify the language of the goods receipt/goods issue slips and labels.

Communication

In a condition record, click Communication .

Variabler Key			
Tr/Ev.Type	Version	Print item	Description
WE	1	1	Material Document Printout

Print output

Output Device	LP01	☐	Print immediately
Number of messages		☐	Release after output
Spool request name			
Suffix 1			
Suffix 2			
SAP cover page	Do Not Print		
Recipient			
Department			
Cover Page Text			
Authorization			
Storage Mode			

Print settings

Layout module	
Form	
SmartForm	

24.5 MAINTAINING CONDITION RECORDS

Functional Consultant	User	Business Process Owner	Senior Management	My Rating	Understanding Level
A	B	C	X		

You maintain condition records using transaction MN21, MN22, or MN23.

24.5.1 Condition Records in Table B072

Condition records for goods receipt slips

You need to maintain the following condition records for goods receipt slips.

App	Out.	TETy	Print Version	P
ME	WE01	WE	1	1
ME	WE02	WE	2	1
ME	WE03	WE	3	1

Condition records for goods return slips

You need to maintain the following condition records for goods return slips.

App	Out.	TETy	Print Version	P
ME	WE01	WE	1	2
ME	WE02	WE	2	2
ME	WE03	WE	3	2

Condition records for goods receipt slips for production order

You need to maintain the following condition records for goods receipt slips for production order.

App	Out.	TETy	Print Version	P
ME	WF01	WF	1	1
ME	WF02	WF	2	1

Condition records for goods return slips for production order

You need to maintain the following condition records for goods return slips for production order.

App	Out.	TETy	Print Version	P
ME	WF01	WF	1	2
ME	WF02	WF	2	2

Condition records for goods issue slips

You need to maintain the following condition records for goods issue slips.

App	Out.	TETy	Print Version	P
ME	WA01	WA	1	1
ME	WA02	WA	2	1
ME	WA03	WA	3	1

24.5.2   Condition Records in Table B073

Condition records for goods issue slips for subcontractors

You need to maintain the following condition records for goods issue slips for subcontractors.

App	Out.	TETy	Print Version	P	D/C
ME	WLB1	WA	1	3	H
ME	WLB2	WA	2	3	H
ME	WLB3	WA	3	3	H

24.5.3   Automatic Creation of Condition Records

The above condition records are recommended by SAP for output determination in Inventory Management. You can automatically create them by running program RM07NKON using transaction SA38. If no movement type is linked to 'Print item' 6 in view V_156_D, you may not be using the following condition records.

App	Out.	TETy	Print Version	P
ME	WA01	WA	1	6
ME	WA02	WA	2	6
ME	WA03	WA	3	6

App	Out.	TETy	Print Version	P
ME	WA01	WE	1	6
ME	WA02	WE	2	6
ME	WA03	WE	3	6

24.5.4   Condition Records in Table B070

These are discussed in Section 24.7.3.

24.5.5   Condition Records in Table B071

These are discussed in Section 24.10.4.

24.5.6   Condition Records in Table B074

These are discussed in Section 24.11.2.

24.6   GOODS MOVEMENT SLIPS

Functional Consultant	User	Business Process Owner	Senior Management	My Rating	Understanding Level
A	C	C	X		

24.6.1   Parameters from the Condition Technique

The condition technique determines whether an output is generated or not, and if generated, it provides the parameters required for generating the output.

24.6.2   Program

The output is generated by a program specified in view VV_TNAPR_ME.

Out.	Name	Med	Program	FORM routine	Form
WE01	GR Note Vers.1	1	SAPM07DR	ENTRY_WE01	WESCHEINVERS1
WE02	GR Note Vers.2	1	SAPM07DR	ENTRY_WE02	WESCHEINVERS2
WE03	GR Note Vers.3	1	SAPM07DR	ENTRY_WE03	WESCHEINVERS3

The program can be different for different output types and media. You can use the same program, but call different form routines, instead of calling different programs. The Form specifies the layout containing fixed and variable data items. Variable data items are determined by the form routine. The form can be modified to meet your requirement using transaction SE71 or by selecting the form and clicking [Form].

The program uses the input parameters passed to the condition records as well as the output parameters received from it. In addition, it takes the following into account.

24.6.3   Print via Output Control Checkbox

At the time of goods receipt/goods issue, you can specify whether you want the documents to be printed or not, in the ☑ checkbox in the document header.

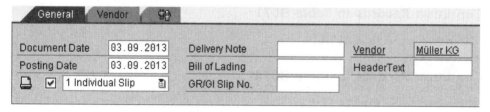

24.6.4   Number of GR Slips

Usually the system generates one goods receipt slip for an item regardless of the quantity received. However, the system allows you to generate multiple goods receipt slips, one per pallet for example. You specify the quantity of material for which one goods receipt slip is to be generated in the Number of GR slips field in the material master.

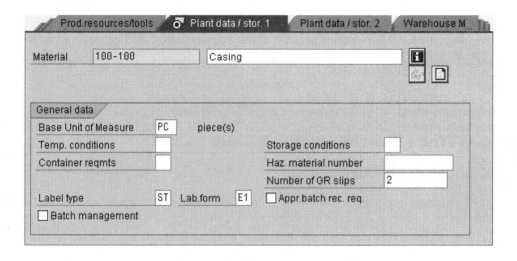

24.7 GOODS MOVEMENT LABELS

Functional Consultant	User	Business Process Owner	Senior Management	My Rating	Understanding Level
A	C	C	X		

24.7.1 Labels for a Material

You can print labels that can be stuck, or attached, to a material. Goods movement slips cannot be different for different materials, but labels can be. For a material, you can specify a label type and a label form that can be used to determine the content of the labels printed for that material.

Although label type and label form are maintained in the [Plant data / stor. 1] tab, they are valid for all plants and storage locations. Changing them for one plant and storage location changes it for all of them.

Label type

You can categorize labels in various types depending on their physical characteristics. You can maintain master list of label types in view V_6WP3, which you can also access using transaction OMCF and clicking [Label type   ].

Label type	Text
ST	Sticker
TG	Tag

Label form

If you have labels that are different from each other in content, you can have multiple label forms. You can maintain master list of label forms in view V_6WP4, which you can also access using transaction OMCF and clicking [Label form   ].

Label form	Text
E1	Label quantity in order quantity
E2	Label quantity in stock quantity
E3	Label quantity in order price quantity

No labels for a material

If you do not want to print labels for a material, e.g. Oxygen, keep the Label type and Lab.form fields blank in the material master.

24.7.2 Condition Records in Table B072

You usually maintain the following condition records in table B072.

Condition records for goods receipt slips

App	Out.	TETy	Print Version	P
ME	WE01	WE	1	1
ME	WE02	WE	2	1
ME	WE03	WE	3	1

Condition records for goods return slips

App	Out.	TETy	Print Version	P
ME	WE01	WE	1	2
ME	WE02	WE	2	2
ME	WE03	WE	3	2

Condition records for goods receipt slips for production order

App	Out.	TETy	Print Version	P
ME	WF01	WF	1	1
ME	WF02	WF	2	1

Condition records for goods return slips for production order

App	Out.	TETy	Print Version	P
ME	WF01	WF	1	2
ME	WF02	WF	2	2

Condition records for goods issue slips

App	Out.	TETy	Print Version	P
ME	WA01	WA	1	1
ME	WA02	WA	2	1
ME	WA03	WA	3	1

24.7.3 Condition Records in Table B070

Planning

Each record in table B072 represents a goods receipt/goods issue slip. For each of these goods receipt/goods issue slip, you need to decide whether labels are required or not. If labels are required, how many types of labels (combination of label type and label form) are required? You can plan your requirement of condition records for labels using the format given below. You also need to plan number of labels. This concept is explained in 'Maintaining number of labels' below.

Output type	Transaction/ event type	Print version	Print item	Label type, label form		
WAE1	WA	1	1	Label type	Label form	No. of labels
WAE2	WA	2	1	Label type	Label form	No. of labels

Output type	Transaction/ event type	Print version	Print item	Label type, label form		
WAE3	WA	3	1	Label type	Label form	No. of labels
WEE1	WE	1	1	Label type	Label form	No. of labels
WEE2	WE	2	1	Label type	Label form	No. of labels
WEE3	WE	3	1	Label type	Label form	No. of labels

The table above is only a format. Every record in table B072 must be included in this table. If no labels are to be printed for a record in table B072, indicate that.

Maintaining condition records

After planning, you maintain all these condition records in condition table B070 using transaction MN21, MN22, or MN23.

Trans./Event Type	WA		GI, Trsfr Posting, Other Goods Movement
Print Version	1		Individual Slip

	Print item	Label type	Label form	Name	Funct	Partner	Medium	Date/Time	Language
	1	ST	E1	Label quantity			1	4	EN
	1	ST	E2	Label quantity			1	4	EN
	1	ST	E3	Label quantity			1	4	EN
	1	TG	E1	Label quantity			1	4	EN
	1	TG	E2	Label quantity			1	4	EN
	1	TG	E3	Label quantity			1	4	EN

Condition Recs.

Maintaining number of labels

SAP prints a label for each unit of material. During a goods movement, quantity may be available in multiple units of measurement, e.g. stock keeping unit, order unit, order price unit etc. In view V_159E you can specify which quantity should be taken for label printing.

LT	LF	Cn	Field name	Short Description
ST	E1	1	MSEG-ERFMG	Quantity in Unit of Entry
ST	E2	1	MSEG-MENGE	Quantity
ST	E3	1	MSEG-BPMNG	Quantity in Purchase Order Price Unit
TG	E1	1	MSEG-ERFMG	Quantity in Unit of Entry
TG	E2	1	MSEG-MENGE	Quantity
TG	E3	1	MSEG-BPMNG	Quantity in Purchase Order Price Unit

The quantity field to be considered for label printing is specified for a combination of label type and label form, and thereby for a material. If the specified quantity field, e.g. quantity in order price unit, is not populated for a goods movement, the system will not know how many labels to print. SAP, therefore, lets you specify multiple quantity fields in the above view. The system accesses the fields in the sequence of Cn , until it finds non-zero quantity.

24.7.4 Program

The output is generated by a program specified in view VV_TNAPR_ME.

Out.	Name	Med	Program	FORM routine	Form
WAE1	GI Label Vers.1	1	SAPM07DR	ENTRY_ETIA	MM07ET
WAE2	GI Label Vers.2	1	SAPM07DR	ENTRY_ETIA	MM07ET
WAE3	GI Label Vers.3	1	SAPM07DR	ENTRY_ETIAS	MM07ET
WEE1	GR Label Vers.1	1	SAPM07DR	ENTRY_ETIE	MM07ET
WEE2	GR Label Vers.2	1	SAPM07DR	ENTRY_ETIE	MM07ET
WEE3	GR Label Vers.3	1	SAPM07DR	ENTRY_ETIES	MM07ET

Unlike other output types, the form specified for labels is not a form, but a sapscript application object. The form is derived from the application object as explained below.

Note that SAP provides only one Form : MM07ET . However, if you want to have different types of labels (and therefore different label content), you can have a different sapscript application objects assigned to output types.

24.7.5 Application Object

Run transaction OMCF, click Application Object to see view V_159O.

Object	Meaning
MM07ET	Goods receipt slip

Application object

Select an application object and click  to display details.

Form

Click `Form` and then `Page Windows`.

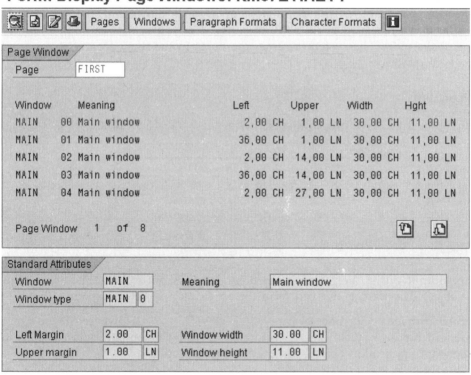

Note that the form name is the same as that specified in the application object `Form    RM07ETIKETT`.

This page has 8 windows (labels) of 30 characters width and 11 lines height. These windows are placed in two columns: the first column starts at character 2, and the second column starts at character 36.

24.7.6 Label Text

In transaction OMCF click [Maintain Label Text]. In the [Text object] [   ] field, enter the name of the application object [MM07ET] and click 🔾

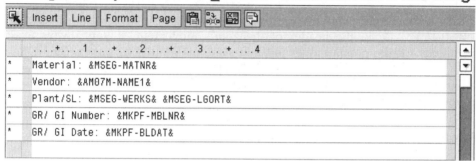

Note that the heading of the text is the same as [Text Name] [MM07_ETIKETT]. The system gives you the SAPscript editor for entering a label text. You can enter fixed text. You can enter standard text by clicking 🗗. You can enter data fields from several tables by click 🔲 and then [DDIC Fields].

24.8 PRINTER DETERMINATION

Functional Consultant	User	Business Process Owner	Senior Management	My Rating	Understanding Level
A	A	B	X		

24.8.1 Master List of Printers

In view V_159P you define all output devices used in Inventory Management and their print parameters.

Printer	Location	B.code	Multiple
LP01	Beispieldrucker. Mit SPAD anpassen.	☐	☑
$LT4F		☐	☑

Printer and location

Here you specify the printer that you propose to use in Inventory Management.

Bar code

This indicator specifies that the GR/GI slip is to be printed with a bar code. This indicator is only effective if the printer is capable of printing bar codes.

Multiple

If you want to print multiple GR/GI slips, e.g. a GR/GI slip for each pallet, tick this checkbox, and specify Number of GR slips in the material master.

24.8.2 Enabling Document Printing in Goods Movement

Documents for a goods movement are printed only if you select the check box 1 Individual Slip in the header of the goods movement. If you always want to print documents for the goods movement you post, maintain user parameter NDR = 'X' in System ➤ User Profile ➤ Own Data ➤ Parameters . If you maintain this parameter, the check box is selected by default. If you do not want to print documents for a goods movement, you can deselect it.

24.8.3 Printer Determination Sequence

SAP determines the printer in the following sequence.

1. Condition record
2. Output type

24.8.4 Printer Determination Based on the Condition Record

In a condition record, click Communication and specify the printer in the following dialog box.

Variabler Key			
Tr/Ev.Type	Version	Print item	Description
WE	1	1	Material Document Printout

Print output

Output Device	LP01	☐ Print immediately
Number of messages		☐ Release after output
Spool request name		
Suffix 1		
Suffix 2		
SAP cover page	Do Not Print	
Recipient		
Department		
Cover Page Text		
Authorization		
Storage Mode		

Print settings

Layout module	
Form	
SmartForm	

24.8.5   Printer Determination Based on Output Type

If the printer is not specified in the condition record, it is determined from the print parameter for the output type maintained in tab **Print** of view VN_T685B. You have the following options.

```
7  Plant/storage location
9  Plant/Storage location/User group
E  User exit
S  User parameters
U  User
```

Printer Determination By Storage Location

If you choose the option `7  Plant/storage location` , you specify the printer in transaction OMJ3, view V_TNAD7.

Condition Type	WA01	GI Note Vers.1
Plant	0001	Werk 0001
Stor. Location	0001	Lagerort 0001

Printing Information		
OutputDevice	$LT91	

Name		☐ Print immediately
Suffix 1		☐ Release after output
Suffix 2		
Recipient		
Department		
SAP cover page		
Cover Page Text		
Authorization		

Printer Determination By Storage Location/User Group

If you choose the option `9  Plant/Storage location/User group` , you specify the printer in transaction OMJ4, view V_TNAD9.

Condition Type	WA01	GI Note Vers.1
Plant	0001	Werk 0001
Stor. Location	0001	Lagerort 0001
User group	GROUP1	

Printing information

OutputDevice	$LT91	
Name		☐ Print immed.
Suffix 1		☐ Rel.after print
Suffix 2		
Recipient		
Department		
SAP cover page		
Cover Page Text		
Authorization		

You define user groups in System ➢ User Profile ➢ Own Data ➢ Parameters (parameter ND9), and use them here for printer determination.

Printer Determination By Output Type/User

If you choose the option U User , you specify the printer in transaction OMJR, view V_TNADU.

Application	ME
Condition Type	MLGR

User	☑

Printing Information

OutputDevice	☑	
Name		☐ Print immed.
Suffix 1		☐ Rel.after print
Suffix 2		
SAP cover page		
Recipient		
Department		
Cover Page Text		
Authorization		

Printer Determination by User

If you choose the option S User parameters, you specify the printer for a user in System ➤ User Profile ➤ Own Data ➤ Defaults ➤ OutputDevice .

User	SAPUSER					
Last Changed On	SAPUSER	29.03.2020	12:01:51	Status	Saved	

Address **Defaults** Parameters

Start menu	
Logon Language	EN
Decimal Notation	X 1,234,567.89
Date format	1 DD.MM.YYYY

Spool Control

OutputDevice	
☐ Output Immediately	
☐ Delete After Output	

Printer Determination by User Exit

If you choose the option E User exit , you specify the printer determination logic in user exit EXIT_SAPLV61B_002.

24.8.6 Changing the Printer

You can change the printer before printing, or reprinting, a document. In transaction MB90 generate the list of documents to be printed and select Edit ➤ Printer default . In the dialog box given below, change the printer.

☞ Printer default for output	☒
Output Device	LP01
	Beispieldrucker. Mit SPAD anpas
Number of messages	
Spool request name	
Suffix 1	
Suffix 2	
SAP cover page	Do Not Print
Recipient	SAPUSER
Department	
Cover Page Text	
Authorization	
☐ Print immediately	
☐ Release after output	

✓ ✗

24.9 OUTPUT PROCESSING

Functional Consultant	User	Business Process Owner	Senior Management	My Rating	Understanding Level
A	A	B	X		

24.9.1 Message Creation

Messages are created automatically, when the appropriate conditions arise, e.g. goods receipt. You can see the messages in a material document using transaction MB02 or MB03. In item details, click 🔲 Messages to see the message (output) generated for the goods movement.

24.9.2 Message Change

You can select a message and click Change output to change it.

24.9.3 Message Display

You can see the actual message using transaction MB90.

24.9.4 Message Transmission

Messages for goods movement may be transmitted using one of the following processes.

Immediate transmission

Messages may be transmitted immediately, if the date/time settings so require.

Batch transmission

Messages that are not transmitted immediately can be transmitted at predefined time intervals using a batch job. Usually, this is the preferred method, as this job can be run during lean hours. If the output is to be printed, the printing job can be done centrally, freeing the users from this task. To use this method, run transaction SA38, enter program RSNAST00, and create the appropriate variant. You then schedule the job using transaction SM36.

Manual transmission

The program RSNAST00, to process messages, can also be run manually using transaction SA38.

24.9.5   Message Retransmission

You can retransmit messages and reprint documents. For specific goods movements use material document transactions MB02 or MB03. For multiple material documents, use transaction MB90. Note that the system takes into account if any changes are made to the material document since it was last outputted, i.e., the system always outputs the current status of the document. If you wish to have old statuses available, you must optically archive the material document.

24.10   MAIL ON GOODS RECEIPT

Functional Consultant	User	Business Process Owner	Senior Management	My Rating	Understanding Level
A	C	C	X		

24.10.1   Purpose

When you receive goods, the system can automatically send a message to the buyer if the ☐ GR Message checkbox in the header of the purchasing document is ticked.

24.10.2   IMG Nodes

Transaction M706—Maintain Output Types: Inventory Management

SM34 ➤ VN_T685B

24.10.3   Output Types

SAP provides the following output types for this purpose.

Output type	Description
MLGR	Mail for goods receipt
MLMD	Mail for difference in order price quantity
MLUD	Mail for under-delivery or over-delivery

Unlike other outputs in Inventory Management, which are printed, these messages are sent by mail.

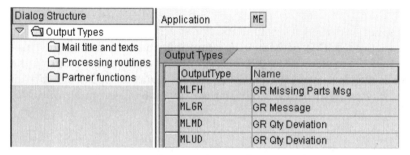

If you select an output type and click ![icon], the system shows you the properties of the output type (view VN_T685B). Among the most important attributes of an output type is the access sequence and the form.

24.10.4 Condition Records

For generation of mail on goods receipt also, SAP uses condition technique. You maintain the following condition record for each output type MLGR, MLMD, and MLUD in condition table B071 using transaction MN21, MN22, or MN23.

GR Message	Name	Funct	Partner	Medium	Date/Time	Languaye
X	Yes	ZP	Dummy recipient for output	7	4	EN

Note that the function you specify here is language dependent, and is converted in a language independent one using view V_TPAUM.

Partner function	Name	Lang-spec.part.func.
MP	Mail Partner	ZP

24.10.5 Mail Title and Texts

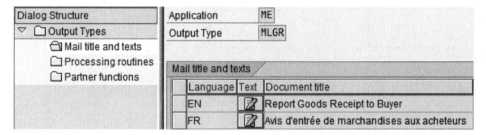

Dialog Structure	Application	ME
▽ ☐ Output Types	Output Type	MLGR
☐ Mail title and texts		
☐ Processing routines		
☐ Partner functions		

	Language	Text	Document title
	EN	📝	Report Goods Receipt to Buyer
	FR	📝	Avis d'entrée de marchandises aux acheteurs

In this view VN_TNATI you can specify the title and text of the mail in different languages.

Language

The system sends a mail in a language specified in the condition record. You maintain the mail title and text here in different languages.

Mail title

Here you specify the title of the mail in the specified language.

Mail text

You write the text of the mail by clicking 📝 . Mail texts are maintained by ABAP developers. The text can include data from the material document, the purchasing document, etc. If you change a mail text, you must delete the condition record and create a new one, as the mail text is copied into the condition record internally.

24.10.6 Processing Routines

Output Type	MLGR		GR Message
Application	ME		Inventory Management
Transm. Medium	7 Simple Mail		

Layout module

Processing routines

Processing 1

Program	RSNASTSO
Form Routine	SAPOFFICE_AUFRUF
Form	

PDF/Smartform Form		Form Type

Processing 2

Program	
Form Routine	
Form	

Processing 3

Program	
Form Routine	
Form	

Processing 4

Program	
FORM routine	
Form	

Processing 5

Program	
Form Routine	
Form	

In this view VN_TNAPR, for each medium you can specify the program, form routine, form, PDF/smart form and type (smart form or PDF). You can specify multiple forms.

24.10.7 Partner Functions

Dialog Structure	Application	ME	Inventory Management
▽ ☐ Output Types	Output Type	MLGR	GR Message
☐ Mail title and texts			
☐ Processing routines	**Partner functions**		
☐ Partner functions			

	Medium	Funct	Name
	7 Simple Mail ☷	ZP	Mail Partner

In this view VN_TNAPN, you specify which partner functions are allowed to receive an output of this type, and through which media. Note that the function you specify here is language dependent, and is converted in a language independent one using view V_TPAUM.

Partner function	Name	Lang-spec.part.func.
MP	Mail Partner	ZP

24.11 MAIL FOR MISSING PART

Functional Consultant	User	Business Process Owner	Senior Management	My Rating	Understanding Level
A	C	C	X		

24.11.1 Purpose

In MRP, if requirement for a material exceeds the available quantity, that material is called a missing part (see Section 21.4). If you receive a missing part, the system automatically sends a mail. This functionality is the same as that of the 'Mail on Goods Receipt'. The output type is MLFH.

24.11.2 Condition Record

For generation of mail on goods receipt also, SAP uses condition technique. You maintain the following condition record for output type MLFH in condition table B074 using transaction MN21, MN22, or MN23.

Miss. part	Name	Funct	Partner	Medium	Date/Time	Language
X	Yes	DC	Dummy recipient for output	7	4	EN

Note that the function you specify here is language dependent, and is converted in a language independent one using view V_TPAUM.

Partner function	Name	Lang-spec.part.func.
DP	PersResp for Shippng	DC

Material Valuation

25.1 MATERIAL VALUATION

Functional Consultant	User	Business Process Owner	Senior Management	My Rating	Understanding Level
A	A	A	A		

25.1.1 Valuation Area

Valuation of a material differs from company code to company code. However, if you want, you can choose to valuate materials at plant level instead of company code level. Material stocks within one material valuation area have the same value. Material stocks in different material valuation areas may have different values.

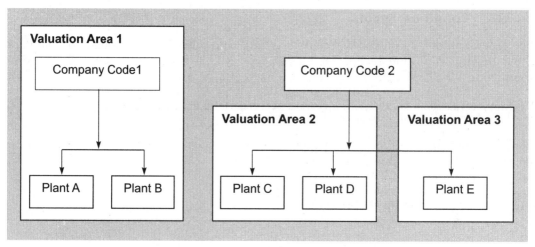

A valuation area may be a company code, a plant, or multiple plants in a company code. Valuation areas cannot be across the company codes. Materials within a valuation area have the same valuation.

25.1.2 Valuation Class

Value of materials in stock is maintained in G/L accounts. You can have different G/L accounts for different groups of materials, e.g. raw materials, finished products etc. The valuation class is used to determine the G/L accounts in which the stocks of different materials are maintained.

> The valuation class does not affect the valuation of material.

> It determines the G/L accounts.

Valuation class is discussed in detail in Section 26.8.

25.1.3 Split Valuation

Split valuation means managing a material as several partial stocks. Each partial stock is valuated separately. If a material is both externally procured as well as in-house produced, you may want to valuate them separately. Split valuation is discussed in Section 25.2.

> Materials may be valuated differently within a valuation area using split valuation.

> Each partial stock is identified by a valuation type.

25.1.4 Non-Valuated Materials

A company may not valuate certain materials, e.g. waste or low value materials. This can be specified for a combination of material type and valuation area in view VT134M.

Val.	Matl	Qty updating	Value Update	Pipe.mand.	PipeAllowd
0001	FERT	☑	☑	☐	☐
0005	FERT	☑	☑	☐	☐
0006	FERT	☑	☑	☐	☐
0007	FERT	☑	☑	☐	☐

If a material is subject to quantity update but not value update, its stock is maintained, but value is not.

> Some material types, and therefore materials belonging to those material types, may not be valuated.

25.1.5 Types of Material Valuation

> You can valuate a material at standard price or at moving average price.

Standard price

If you valuate a material at standard price, you specify the price of the material. You can change the price from a specified future date, using transaction CKMPRPN - Maintain Future Prices, thereby maintaining different prices for different periods. In goods receipt, valuation using standard price results in the following:

> ➤ GR/IR clearing account is credited by the goods receipt value.
> ➤ Inventory account is debited by the amount computed as quantity x standard price.
> ➤ Variances are posted to price difference accounts.

Even for material with standard price control, goods issues and transfer postings are at current price, i.e. moving average price.

Moving average price

If you valuate a material at moving average price, the system computes the price of the material. In goods receipt, valuation using moving average price has the following features:

> ➤ GR/IR clearing account is credited by the goods receipt value.
> ➤ Inventory account is debited by the goods receipt value.
> ➤ Total value and total quantity are updated in the material master and new price is computed as total value/total quantity.

Moving average price is always used for goods issues and transfer postings.

Price control for material

Whether the material is valuated at moving average price, or at standard price, is specified in the material master at valuation area level.

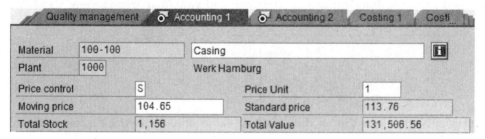

Price control for material types

In view V_134_P you specify whether the materials of a material type are valuated at standard price, or moving average price. You can further specify whether this choice can be changed at the material level or not.

Material Type	Material type description	Price control	Price ctrl mandatory
ABF	Waste	S	☑
AEM	Samples	V	☐
BLG	BLG Empties External	S	☑
BLGA	BLGAEmpties Fixed assets	S	☑

Price control

You can specify default price control for a material type in the `Price control` field.

Price control	Short text
S	Standard price
V	Moving average price/periodic unit price

The value you select here is defaulted when you create a material of this material type.

Price control mandatory

If you tick the checkbox `Price ctrl mandatory`, the type of price indicated in the `Price control` column cannot be changed in the material master. If you do not tick this checkbox, the type of price indicated in the `Price control` column is a default value and can be changed in the material master.

25.1.6 Account Determination

In a goods movement, the G/L accounts in which the values of the materials are updated is determined by the account determination process. If this process does not determine the G/L accounts to be updated, the values are not updated. Account determination is discussed in Chapter 26.

25.2 SPLIT VALUATION

Functional Consultant	User	Business Process Owner	Senior Management	My Rating	Understanding Level
A	C	C	X		

25.2.1 Split Valuation

Split valuation means managing a material as several partial stocks. Each partial stock is valuated separately. If a material is both externally procured as well as in-house produced, you may want to valuate them separately.

Each transaction, be it a goods receipt, goods issue, invoice receipt or physical inventory, is carried out at the level of the partial stock. When you process one of these transactions, you must always specify which partial stock is involved. This means that only the partial stock in question is affected by a change in value, the other partial stocks remain unaffected.

Alongside the partial stocks, the total stock is also updated. The calculation of the value of the total stock results from the total of the stock values and stock quantities of the partial stocks.

25.2.2 Overview

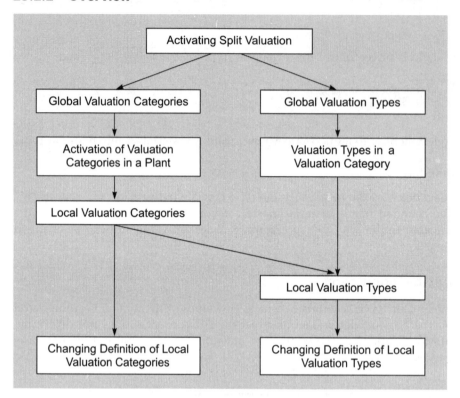

25.2.3 Activating Split Valuation

Purpose

You activate split valuation if some of your materials need to be valuated differently for different partial stocks.

IMG Node

Transaction OMW0—Activate Split Valuation

Activating Split Valuation

Material valuation
◉ Split material valuation active
○ Split material valuation not active

Select the radio button shown above and save.

25.2.4 Global Valuation Categories

Purpose

A valuation category specifies the criterion that should be used as the basis for differentiating between various partial stocks. Different groups of materials may be divided in partial stocks based on different criteria, or valuation categories.

When a global valuation category is activated for a plant, it becomes a local valuation category of that plant. Each material of the plant, which is split valuated, is assigned a local valuation category.

Here you define all valuation categories used by all plants.

IMG Node

Transaction OMWC—Configure Split Valuation

Global Valuation Categories

Click Global Categories to create, change, or delete valuation categories. Valuation categories are stored in table T149C.

Global Valuation Categories

Create	Change	Delete	Types -> Cat.

Valuation Cat.		DVT ExtPr	ExP	DVT InhPr	Inh	DVT Promo.	PrM	Autom.VTy
A		IAD1	☐	IAD2	☐		☐	☑
B	Inhse/ext.proc.	FREMD_HALB	☑	EIGEN_HALB	☑		☐	☐
C	Status	C1	☐	C2	☐		☐	☐
D	Grades	GRADE B	☐	GRADE A	☐		☐	☐
H	Origin	AUSLAND	☐	INLAND	☐		☐	☐
M	Remanufacturing	CORE	☑	REMAN	☑		☐	☐
R	Retail	RNORMAL	☐		☐	RAKTION	☐	☐
S			☐		☐		☐	☐
X	Automat.(batch)		☐		☐		☐	☑
Z	Containers	NEW	☐	REPAIRED	☐		☐	☐

Important Fields

Valuation category and description

You identify valuation categories by a code and a description.

Default/mandatory valuation type for external procurement

In column DVT InhP you specify the valuation type that is proposed automatically when purchase orders are entered. If column ExP is also set, the default valuation type is binding and cannot be changed by the user.

Default/mandatory valuation type for in-house production

In column DVT InhP you specify the valuation type that is proposed automatically when production orders are entered. If column Inh is also set, the default valuation type is binding and cannot be changed by the user.

Default/mandatory valuation type for promotional goods

In column DVT Promo. you specify the valuation type that is proposed automatically when inward or outward movements of promotional goods stocks occur. If column PrM is also set, the default valuation type is binding and cannot be changed by the user.

Indicator: valuation type is set automatically

The indicator causes the system to determine valuation type automatically at the time goods receipts are posted. The system will create a valuation record if no record with this valuation type exists yet for the material. This indicator is only useful for materials that are managed in batches. A valuation record is created automatically for each batch.

25.2.5   Activating Valuation Categories in a Plant

Purpose

You can activate, or deactivate, valuation categories at plant level.

JMG Node

Transaction OMWC—Configure Split Valuation

Activating Valuation Categories in a Plant

Click ⌊ Local Definitions ⌋, select a plant and click ⌊ Cats. -> OU ⌋. The system displays all the valuation categories and whether they are active in the plant, or not.

Plant 1000: Allocate Valuation Categories

Local Types	Local Categories

Allocation of Valuation Categories

Status		Valuation Cat.	DVT ExtPr	ExP	DVT InhPr	Inh	DVT Promo.	PrM	VT
	A		IAD1	☐	IAD2	☐		☐	☑
Active	B	Inhse/ext.proc.	FREMD_HALB	☑	EIGEN_HALB	☑		☐	☐
Active	C	Status	C1	☐	C2	☐		☐	☐
	D	Grades	GRADE B	☐	GRADE A	☐		☐	☐
Active	H	Origin	AUSLAND	☐	INLAND	☐		☐	☐
	M	Remanufacturing	CORE	☑	REMAN	☑		☐	☐
	R	Retail	RNORMAL	☐		☐	RAKTION	☐	☐
	S			☐		☐		☐	☐
	X	Automat.(batch)		☐		☐		☐	☑
	Z	Containers	NEW	☐	REPAIRED	☐		☐	☐

Activate	Deactivate	Entry	1 of 10

Activate

You can activate a valuation category by selecting it and clicking [Activate].

Deactivate

Similarly, you can deactivate an active valuation category by selecting it and clicking [Deactivate].

25.2.6   Local Valuation Categories

Purpose

A valuation category specifies the criterion that should be used as the basis for differentiating between various partial stocks. Different groups of materials may be divided in partial stocks based on different criteria, or valuation categories.

When a global valuation category is activated for a plant, it becomes a local valuation category of that plant. Each material of the plant, which is split valuated, is assigned a local valuation category.

IMG Node

Transaction OMWC—Configure Split Valuation

Local Valuation Categories

Click Local Categories . The system shows only those valuation categories that are active for the plant.

Plant 1000: Local Valuation Categories

| Change |

Valuation Cat.		DVT ExtPr	ExP	DVT InhPr	Inh	DVT Promo.	PrM	Autom.VTy
B	Inhse/ext.proc.	FREMD_HALB	☑	EIGEN_HALB	☑		☐	☐
C	Status	C1	☐	C2	☐		☐	☐
H	Origin	AUSLAND	☐	INLAND	☐		☐	☐
			☐		☐		☐	☐

25.2.7   Changing Definition of Local Valuation Categories

Purpose

By default a local valuation category has the same definition as the global valuation category of the same name. However, you can change the definition of a local valuation category in a plant.

IMG Node

Transaction OMWC—Configure Split Valuation

Changing Definition of Local Valuation Categories

Select a valuation category and click Change .

Plant 1000: Change Valuation Category

Change	Valuation Category +	Valuation Category -

Valuation cat   B Inhse/ext.proc.

Default: val.type ext.procure.   FREMD_HALB
Default: val.type ext.proc. mand   ☑

Default: val.type in-house prod   EIGEN_HALB
Default: val.type in-house mand.   ☑

Deflt val.type: action
Deflt val.type: obligat. action   ☐

Determine val. type automat.   ☐

Here you can make the change which is applicable only to the selected plant.

25.2.8 Global Valuation Types

Purpose

Valuation types divide the stock of a material in partial stocks which are valuated separately. Here you define all valuation types.

IMG Node

Transaction OMWC—Configure Split Valuation

Global Valuation Types

Click Global Types . The system shows global valuation types.

Global Valuation Types

Create	Change	Delete

Valuation Type	Ext. POs	Int. POs	ARef	Description
01	0	2	0001	Reference for raw materials
02	2	0	0001	Reference for raw materials
AUSLAND	2	1	0001	Reference for raw materials
BATCH NO.1	2	0	0001	Reference for raw materials
BATCH NO.2	2	0	0001	Reference for raw materials
C1	2	2	0003	Reference for spare parts
C2	2	2	0003	Reference for spare parts
C3	2	2	0003	Reference for spare parts
CORE	2	0	0008	Ref. for semifinished products

Important Fields

Valuation type

A valuation type splits the stock of a material into sub stocks which are valuated separately.

External purchase orders allowed

In column Ext. POs you specify whether external purchase orders are allowed, not allowed, or allowed with a warning.

Ext. Purchase Orders	Short text
0	No external purchase orders allowed
1	External purchase orders allowed, but warning issued
2	External purchase orders allowed

Internal purchase orders (in-house production orders) allowed

In column Int. POs you specify whether internal purchase orders (in-house production orders) are allowed, not allowed, or allowed with a warning.

Int. purchase orders	Short text
0	No internal purchase orders allowed
1	Internal purchase orders allowed, but warning issued
2	Internal purchase orders allowed

Account category reference and description

Account category reference is a group of valuation classes that the system uses to check whether the valuation class you have entered is allowed when you maintain accounting data in a material master record. By specifying an account category reference here you make the valuation type available to only those valuation classes.

25.2.9 Valuation Types in a Valuation Category

Purpose

A valuation category is a set of valuation types. Here you define valuation types in a valuation category.

JMG Node

Transaction OMWC—Configure Split Valuation

Valuation Types in a Valuation Category

Click | Global Categories |, select a valuation category and click | Types -> Cat. |.

Valuation Category B: Allocate Valuation Types

| Valuation Category + | Valuation Category - | Cat. -> OUs | Local Definitions | Local Definition: |

Valuation Cat. [B] Inhse/ext.proc.

Assignment

Status	Valuation Type	Ex	In	ARef	Description
Active	01	0	2	0001	Reference for raw materials
Active	02	2	0	0001	Reference for raw materials
	AUSLAND	2	1	0001	Reference for raw materials
	BATCH NO.1	2	0	0001	Reference for raw materials
	BATCH NO.2	2	0	0001	Reference for raw materials
	C1	2	2	0003	Reference for spare parts
	C2	2	2	0003	Reference for spare parts
	C3	2	2	0003	Reference for spare parts
	CORE	2	0	0008	Ref. for semifinished products
Active	EIGEN	0	2	0001	Reference for raw materials
Active	EIGEN_HALB	0	2	0008	Ref. for semifinished products
Active	FREMD	2	0	0001	Reference for raw materials
Active	FREMD_HALB	2	0	0008	Ref. for semifinished products

| Activate | Deactivate | Entry   1 of 31 |

Here you can activate, or deactivate, a valuation type in a valuation category.

25.2.10 Local Valuation Types

Purpose

A plant has local valuation categories. Each valuation category has active valuation types. All active valuation types in all active valuation categories of a plant are local valuation types. Stock in a plant can be maintained in one or more local valuation types.

JMG Node

Transaction OMWC—Configure Split Valuation

Local Valuation Types

Click Local Definitions , select a plant and click Local Types .

Plant 1000: Local Valuation Types

Change

Valuation Type	Ext. POs	Int. POs	ARef	Description
01	0	2	0001	Reference for raw materials
02	2	0	0001	Reference for raw materials
AUSLAND	2	1	0001	Reference for raw materials
C1	2	2	0003	Reference for spare parts
C2	2	2	0003	Reference for spare parts
C3	2	2	0003	Reference for spare parts
EIGEN	0	2	0001	Reference for raw materials
EIGEN_HALB	0	2	0008	Ref. for semifinished products
FRANKREICH	2	2	0008	Ref. for semifinished products
FREMD	2	0	0001	Reference for raw materials
FREMD_HALB	2	0	0008	Ref. for semifinished products
INLAND	2	1	0001	Reference for raw materials
ITALIEN	2	2	0008	Ref. for semifinished products
LAND 1	2	0	0001	Reference for raw materials
LAND 2	2	0	0001	Reference for raw materials

25.2.11 Changing Definition of Local Valuation Types

Purpose

By default a local valuation type has the same definition as the global valuation type of the same name. However, you can change the definition of a local valuation type in a plant.

JMG Node

Transaction OMWC—Configure Split Valuation

Changing Definition of Local Valuation Types

Select a valuation type and click | Change |.

Plant 0001: Change Valuation Type

| Change | Account Cat. Ref. | Valuation Type + | Valuation Type - |

Valuation Type | AUSLAND |

Local valuation

Ext. Purchase Orders	2
Int. purchase orders	1
Acct cat. reference	0001	Reference for raw materials

Here you can make the change which is applicable only to the selected plant.

25.3 SPLIT VALUATION OF A MATERIAL

Functional Consultant	User	Business Process Owner	Senior Management	My Rating	Understanding Level
A	C	C	X		

25.3.1 Materials not Subject to Split Valuation

Valuation category

Maintain the material master using transaction MM01, MM02, or MM03.

| Quality management | Accounting 1 | Accounting 2 | Costing 1 | Costing 2 |

| Material | 100-100 | Casing | |
| Plant | 1000 | Werk Hamburg |

General data

Base Unit of Measure	PC	piece(s)	Valuation Category	
Currency	EUR		Current period	12 2013
Division	01		Price determ.		☐ ML act.

If the Valuation Category field is blank in the material master, the material is not subject to split valuation.

Valuation type

For each tab in the material master, you specify organizational levels.

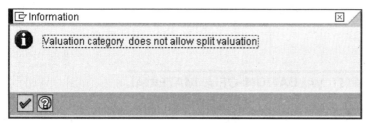

If a material is not subject to split valuation, and you try to specify the Valuation type, the system gives error.

25.3.2   Creating a Material Subject to Split Valuation First Time

When you create a material for the first time, you can specify the Valuation Category in Accounting 1 tab. You can also change it subsequently, if there is no stock of the material in the plant. For materials subject to split valuation, only Price control V (moving average price) is permitted.

25.3.3   Extending an Existing Material for a Valuation Type

Purpose

You can add a valuation type to an existing material. The material must have a Valuation Category.

Transaction

MM01—Create Material

Initial Screen

Material	100-302
Industry sector	M Mechanical Engine 📱
Material Type	HALB Semi-finished 📱
Change Number	

Copy from...	
Material	

Click Select view(s) , select ☐ Accounting 1 view and click ✔.

Organizational Levels

The system prompts you to enter organizational levels.

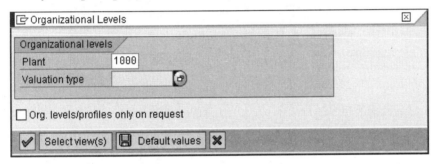

Enter the Plant . Click 🗗 to select the Valuation type .

Maint.	Val. Type
	01
	02
	EIGEN
X	EIGEN_HALB
	FREMD
X	FREMD_HALB

The system shows the list of permissible valuation types. Valuation types already in use are marked X. Select the valuation type you want to create. The system displays the Accounting 1 tab.

Accounting 1

Quality management	Accounting 1	Accounting 2	Costing 1	Costing 2

Material	100-302	Hollow shaft
Plant	1000	Werk Hamburg
Val. type	EIGEN	

General data

Base Unit of Measure	PC	piece(s)	Valuation Category	B
Currency	EUR		Current period	10 2013
Division	01		Price determ.	☐ ML act.

Current valuation

Valuation Class	☑			
VC: Sales order stk			Proj. stk val. class	
Price control	S		Price Unit	1
Moving price			Standard price	
Total Stock	0		Total Value	0.00
			☐ Valuated Un	
Future price			Valid from	

Previous period/year	Std cost estimate

Valuation category

You can do split valuation only if the material has a valuation category. If the valuation category for a material is blank, you cannot do split valuation.

ValCat	Description
B	Inhse/ext.proc.
C	Status
H	Origin

In the case of split valuation, the valuation category also determines which valuation types are allowed.

Valuation type

Valuation types divide the stock of a material in partial stocks which are valuated separately.

Valuation classes

Only valuation classes permitted for the valuation category can be used.

Price control

Only | Price control | V | (moving average price) is permitted.

25.4 STOCK OVERVIEW OF A MATERIAL HAVING SPLIT VALUATION

Functional Consultant	User	Business Process Owner	Senior Management	My Rating	Understanding Level
A	C	C	X		

Run transaction MMBE to see the stock overview of a material having split valuation.

Selection				
Material	100-302		Hollow shaft	
Material Type	HALB		Semi-finished product	
Unit of Measure	PC		Base Unit of Measure	PC

Stock Overview

Client/Company Code/Plant/Storage Location/Batch/Special Stock	Unrestricted use
▽ 📦 Full	1,000.000
▽ 🗐 1000 IDES AG	1,000.000
▽ 🏭 1000 Werk Hamburg	1,000.000
▽ 📦 0001 Materiallager	1,000.000
🧪 EIGEN_HALB	500.000
🧪 FREMD_HALB	500.000

Note that the stock for each valuation type 🧪 EIGEN_HALB and 🧪 FREMD_HALB is shown separately.

25.5 GOODS MOVEMENT OF A MATERIAL HAVING SPLIT VALUATION

Functional Consultant	User	Business Process Owner	Senior Management	My Rating	Understanding Level
A	C	C	X		

25.5.1 Purpose

You can issue goods of a material having split valuation to a cost center.

25.5.2 Transaction

MIGO_GI—Goods Issue (MIGO)

25.5.3 Selection

| A07 Goods Issue | R10 Other | GI for cost center | 201 |

25.5.4 Item Data without Valuation Type

Enter the data as you would in a normal case, and click Check . The system gives the following error.

```
┌─ Display logs ──────────────────────────────────── ⊠ ─┐

 Typ  Item  Message text                              LTxt

  ☢     1   Enter valuation type                       ⑦

 ✔ ⑦ ✂ ◄ ◄ ► ► ▼ ▤ ▼ ▣ ▢ ▦ ▦ ⓢ 0  ☢ 1  △ 0  ☐ 0
```

25.5.5 Item Detail

Material

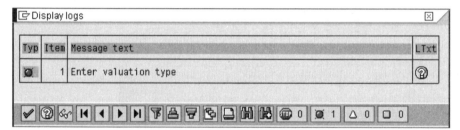

| Material | Quantity | Where | Account Assignment |

| Material | Hollow shaft | | 100-302 |

| Material Group | 001 | Valuation Type | EIGEN HALB |

| Equipment | | | |

You must enter the Valuation Type.

25.5.6 Posting Goods Issue

After the goods issue is entered, post it by clicking $\boxed{\text{Post}}$. The system posts only those items for which ☑ Item OK indicator is set.

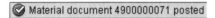

25.5.7 Goods Issue Slip

You can see/print the GR/GI slip and labels using transaction MB90. Choose Processing mode 2 for Repeat processing . If GR/GI slip and/or labels are not generated, print indicator may not have been set in the goods movement screen, or printing may not be enabled in Output Determination (see Chapter 24).

```
G R / G I   S L I P                        4900000071/0001
----------------------------------------------------------------
Posting date  : 09.10.2013
Current date  : 09.10.2013

Plant         : 1000
Description   : Werk Hamburg
----------------------------------------------------------------
Material      : 100-302
Batch         : EIGEN_HALB
Description   : Hollow shaft

Quantity      :                    5   PC
----------------------------------------------------------------

Storage loc.  : 0001
Storage bin   :

Cost center   : 0000001000
```

Note that the goods issue slip indicates that the material is issued from Batch   : EIGEN HALB.

25.5.8 Material Document

The material document can be displayed using transaction MB02 or MB03.

Change Material Document 4900000071 : Details 0001 / 0001

| ◄ | ► | 🧍 | 🖨 | 📇 Messages | Material | WM Details... |

Movement Type	201	GI for cost center
Material	100-302	Hollow shaft

Quantity in

Unit of Entry	5	PC	Plant	1000	Stor. Loc.	0001
			Batch	EIGEN_HALB		

Account Assignment

G/L Account	890000	
Business Area	9900	
Cost Center	1000	Corporate Services
		Goods recipient
Text		

25.5.9 Accounting Documents

List of documents in accounting

In transaction MB02 or MB03 click Accounting Documents... in the item overview of the material document to see the accounting documents.

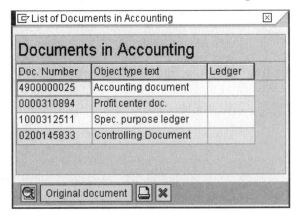

🖅 List of Documents in Accounting ☒

Documents in Accounting

Doc. Number	Object type text	Ledger
4900000025	Accounting document	
0000310894	Profit center doc.	
1000312511	Spec. purpose ledger	
0200145833	Controlling Document	

🔍 Original document 🖨 ☒

Accounting entries

Double-click the Accounting document to open it.

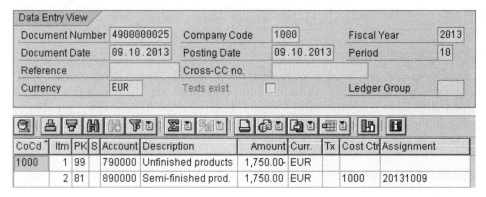

CoCd	Itm	PK	S	Account	Description	Amount	Curr.	Tx	Cost Ctr	Assignment
1000	1	99		790000	Unfinished products	1,750.00-	EUR			
	2	81		890000	Semi-finished prod.	1,750.00	EUR		1000	20131009

The cost center account is debited and inventory account is credited.

25.5.10   Stock Overview

Run transaction MMBE to see the stock overview of the material.

CoCd	Itm	PK	S	Account	Description	Amount	Curr.	Tx	Cost Ctr	Assignment
1000	1	99		790000	Unfinished products	1,750.00-	EUR			
	2	81		890000	Semi-finished prod.	1,750.00	EUR		1000	20131009

Note that the stock of valuation type EIGEN_HALB has reduced.

26

Account Determination

26.1 OVERVIEW

Functional Consultant	User	Business Process Owner	Senior Management	My Rating	Understanding Level
A	A	A	A		

When you receive goods, or issue goods, you need to pass accounting entries. SAP provides a sophisticated mechanism, called account determination, in which this process takes place automatically and consistently. Account determination depends on a number of factors. This section explains the overview of account determination. Subsequent sections explain each factor in detail.

26.1.1 Account Determination

Following the principle of double entry book keeping, each transaction requiring posting has a minimum of two entries in the books of accounts. For each entry you need to determine the G/L account and the posting key.

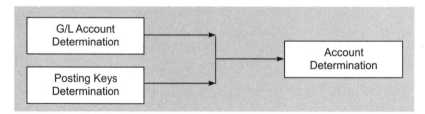

26.1.2 G/L Account Determination

The figure below shows a simplified view of the G/L account determination process.

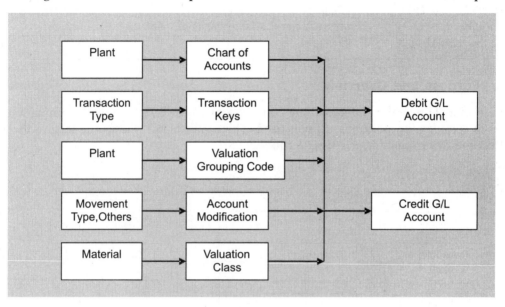

26.1.3 Posting Keys Determination

Posting keys determine the manner in which a G/L account is updated. Posting keys, and their determination, are predefined by SAP.

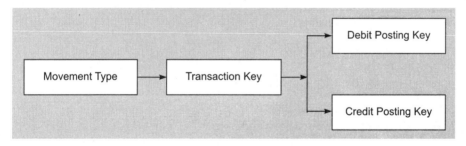

26.2 G/L ACCOUNTS

Functional Consultant	User	Business Process Owner	Senior Management	My Rating	Understanding Level
A	A	A	A		

26.2.1 Purpose and Overview

SAP gives a lot of flexibility in determining G/L accounts. Your G/L account determination may be as complex, or as simple, as you need. The figure below shows the factors that can affect the determination of a G/L account.

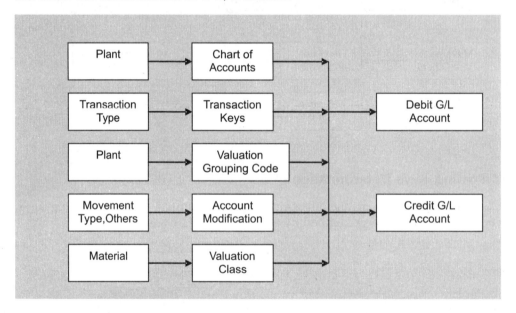

26.2.2 IMG Node

Transaction OMWB—Account Determination; click | Account Assignment |.

26.2.3 Simplest Scenario of Account Determination

Chart of Accounts	INT	Chart of accounts - international
Transaction	WRX	GR/IR clearing account

Account assignment		
Account		
191100		

The above screenshot shows the G/L account assigned to transaction key GR/IR clearing account. Since a G/L account is always defined within a chart of accounts, the chart of accounts is specified as well.

26.2.4 Most Complex Scenario of Account Determination

Chart of Accounts	INT	Chart of accounts - international
Transaction	GBB	Offsetting entry for inventory posting

Account assignment

Valuation modif.	General modification	Valuation class	Debit	Credit
0001	AUI	7920	895000	895000
0001	BSA	3000	399999	399999
0001	BSA	3001	399999	399999
0001	BSA	3030	399999	399999
0001	BSA	3040	399999	399999
0001	BSA	3050	399999	399999
0001	BSA	3100	399999	399999
0001	BSA	7900	799999	799999
0001	BSA	7920	799999	799999
0001	BSA	7925	799999	799999

In the most complex scenario, in addition to the transaction key, the G/L account also depends on the valuation area (valuation modification), general modification, and valuation class. It is also possible to post to one account if the amount to be posted is debit, and to another, if the amount to be posted is a credit.

26.2.5 Control of Factors

For each transaction key, you can decide the factors based on which the G/L account will be determined. To see or set the factors, click Rules . As shown below, for some transaction keys you can select any or all of the four factors.

Chart of Accounts	INT	Chart of accounts - international
Transaction	WRX	GR/IR clearing account

Accounts are determined based on

Debit/Credit	☐
General modification	☐
Valuation modif.	☐
Valuation class	☐

But, for some transaction keys you can select fewer factors as illustrated below.

Chart of Accounts	INT	Chart of accounts - international
Transaction	BSX	Inventory posting

Accounts are determined based on		
Debit/Credit	☐	Not changeable
Valuation modif.	☐	
Valuation class	☑	

26.2.6   Important Fields

Chart of accounts

Account determination always takes place in a chart of accounts. Another company, which uses a different chart of accounts, is free to specify its own G/L accounts. But if two company codes use the same chart of account, they also share the account determination process.

Transaction key

When a goods movement takes place, it may generate two or more accounting entries. In its simplest form, goods receipt debits an inventory account and credits a GR/IR clearing account. However, if the material is maintained at standard price, rather than at moving average price, a price difference account may also be posted to.

The system identifies each of these entries as a transaction key. These keys are automatically determined by the system. For each item in a goods movement, two or more transaction keys are involved. Important transaction keys are given below.

Goods issue

Credit	BSX	Inventory posting
Debit	GBB	Offsetting entry for inventory posting

Goods receipt in warehouse

Debit	BSX	Inventory posting
Credit	WRX	GR/IR clearing account
Dr/Cr	PRD	Cost (price) differences If inventory posting takes place at standard price

Goods receipt assigned to a project etc.

Debit	KBS	Account-assigned purchase order
Credit	WRX	GR/IR clearing account

Goods receipt for production orders

Debit	BSX	Inventory posting
Credit	GBB	Offsetting entry for inventory posting
Dr/Cr	PRD	Cost (price) differences If inventory posting takes place at standard price

Important transaction keys

Key	Description	Explanation
AKO	Expense/revenue from consumption of consignment material	This transaction is used in Inventory Management in the case of withdrawals from consignment stock or when consignment stock is transferred to own stock if the material is subject to standard price control and the consignment price differs from the standard price.
AUM	Expenditure/ income from transfer posting	This transaction is used for transfer postings from one material to another if the complete value of the issuing material cannot be posted to the value of the receiving material.
BSV	Change in stock	Changes in stocks are posted in Inventory Management at the time goods receipts are recorded or subsequent adjustments made with regard to subcontract orders.
BSX	Stock posting	This transaction is used for all postings to stock accounts in Inventory Management in the case of goods receipts to own stock and goods issues from own stock.
FRL	External service	The transaction is used for goods and invoice receipts in connection with subcontract orders.
FRN	External service, delivery costs	This transaction is used for delivery costs (incidental costs of procurement) in connection with subcontract orders.
GBB	Offsetting entry for stock posting	Offsetting entries for stock postings are dependent on the account modification to which each movement type is assigned.
KON	Consignment liabilities	Consignment liabilities arise in the case of withdrawals from consignment stock or from a pipeline or when consignment stock is transferred to own stock.
PRD	Price differences	Price differences arise for materials valuated at standard price in the case of all movements.
UMB	Revenue/expense from revaluation	This transaction key is used if the standard price of a material has been changed and a movement is posted to the previous period at the previous price.
WRX	GR/IR clearing	Postings to the GR/IR clearing account occur in the case of goods against purchase orders.

Valuation modification

If you do not want to specify different G/L accounts for different plants, you should switch off this column in Rules . Otherwise, you specify the valuation grouping code for which you are specifying G/L accounts. Valuation grouping code is a group of valuation areas. Valuation areas, in turn, are group of plants. Thus, you can post to different G/L accounts for goods movement in different plants.

General modification

For certain transaction keys, it is necessary to divide the posting transaction according to a further key: account modification. Account modification allows posting to different G/L accounts for different business scenarios. These keys are predefined by SAP and cannot be changed. These keys are used in account determination for transaction keys GBB, PRD, KON, etc. For more details see Section 26.7.

Valuation class

Valuation class allows you to post goods movement of different materials to different G/L accounts. Using this feature, you can post raw materials to one G/L account and bought out parts to another.

Debit account and credit account

If you are using standard price, and not moving average price, the price differences are posted to a price difference account. Usually you post both debit and credit entries to the same account. But some companies want to post debit entries to one G/L account and credit entries to another. SAP lets you do that.

26.3 POSTING KEYS

Functional Consultant	User	Business Process Owner	Senior Management	My Rating	Understanding Level
A	A	A	A		

26.3.1 Purpose and Overview

Another important use of transaction key is to determine posting keys. Posting keys determine the manner in which a G/L account is updated. Posting keys, and their determination, is predefined by SAP.

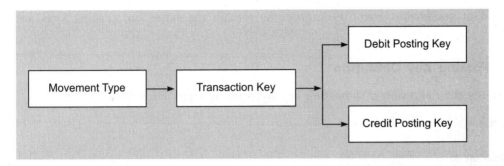

For determination of transaction key from movement type see Section 26.5.

26.3.2 IMG Node

Transaction OMWB—Account Determination
Click | Posting Key |.

26.3.3 Screen

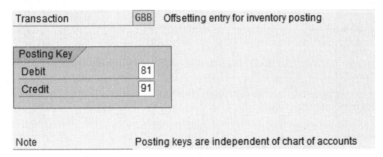

As the screenshot notes, posting keys are defined for a transaction key and are applicable to all charts of accounts.

26.3.4 Important Posting Keys

Transaction key	Transaction key name	Debit posting key	Credit posting key
BSX	Inventory posting	89	99
GBB	Offsetting entry for inventory posting	81	91
KBS	Account-assigned purchase order	81	91
KON	Consignment payables	81	91
PRD	Cost (price) differences	83	93
WRX	GR/IR clearing account	86	96

In reversal of goods movement, G/L accounts remain the same, but posting keys are different.

26.3.5 Posting Key Definition

You may see the definition of a posting key by running transaction OB41.

Posting Key	81	Costs

Debit/credit indicator
- ◉ Debit
- ○ Credit

Account type
- ○ Customer
- ○ Vendor
- ◉ G/L account
- ○ Assets
- ○ Material

Other attributes
- ☐ Sales-related
- ☐ Special G/L
- Reversal posting key [91]
- ☐ Payment transaction

26.4 CHART OF ACCOUNTS

Functional Consultant	User	Business Process Owner	Senior Management	My Rating	Understanding Level
A	A	A	A		

26.4.1 Purpose and Overview

All G/L accounts belong to a chart of account. All postings take place in a chart of accounts. The chart of accounts is assigned to a company code. Each plant is linked to a company code via valuation area.

Plant → Valuation area → Company code → Chart of accounts

26.4.2 Assignment of Plant to Company Code

After you create a plant, you can assign it to a company code in view V_T001K_ASSIGN, or using transaction OX18.

CoCd	Plnt	Name of Plant	Company Name	Status
0001	0001	Werk 0001	SAP A.G.	
0005	0005	Hamburg	IDES AG NEW GL	
0006	0006	New York	IDES US INC New GL	
0007	0007	Werk Hamburg	IDES AG NEW GL 7	
0008	0008	New York	IDES US INC New GL 8	
1000	0099	Werk für Customizing-Kurse SCM	IDES AG	
1000	1000	Werk Hamburg	IDES AG	

A plant is assigned to a company code through valuation area (not seen in this view). A plant has a valuation area, and a valuation area has a company code. Thus, a plant has a company code.

26.4.3 Assignment of Chart of Accounts to Company Code

In view V_001_S you can assign a chart of account to a company code.

CoCd	Company Name	City	Chrt/Accts	Cty ch/act
1000	IDES AG	Frankfurt	INT	GKR
1002	Singapore Company	Singapore		
2000	IDES UK	London	INT	CAGB
2100	IDES Portugal	Lisbon	INT	
2200	IDES France	Paris	CAFR	INT

26.4.4 Use of Chart of Accounts

All G/L accounts are defined within a chart of accounts. You, therefore, always specify chart of accounts in determination of G/L accounts.

26.5 TRANSACTION KEYS

Functional Consultant	User	Business Process Owner	Senior Management	My Rating	Understanding Level
A	C	C	X		

26.5.1 Purpose and Overview

Purpose

Transaction key is the most critical concept in account determination. The transaction keys, and their determination, are predefined by SAP and cannot be changed. The purpose of this section is to show you the underlying linkages so that you know how transaction keys are determined.

Transaction keys

When a goods movement takes place, it may generate two or more accounting entries. In its simplest form, goods receipt debits an inventory account and credits a GR/IR clearing account. However, if the material is maintained at standard price, rather than at moving average price, a price difference account may also be posted to.

The system identifies each of these entries as a transaction key. These keys are automatically determined by the system. For each item in a goods movement, two or more transaction keys are involved.

Determination of transaction keys

26.5.2 Posting String Reference

Movement types that are posted in the same way are grouped together in a posting string reference. This linkage is predefined by SAP and can be seen only in table T156. It is not available in any view in the IMG.

MvT	Posting string ref.
☐ 201	201
☐ 202	201
☐ 221	201
☐ 222	201
☐ 251	201
☐ 252	201
☐ 261	201
☐ 262	201
☐ 291	201
☐ 292	201
☐ 901	201

26.5.3 Posting String for Values

Posting of value is controlled by posting string for values (value string). Posting of quantity is controlled by posting string for quantities (quantity string). Both these posting strings are derived from posting string reference in view V_T156SY.

PstgStrRef	Val.Update	Qty update	Spec	Mvt ind.	Rece	Con	Value str.	Qty string
201	☑	☐					WA01	MA01
201	☑	☑					WA01	MA01
201	☑	☑	L				WA01	MA01
201	☑	☑	E				WA01	MAA1
201	☑	☑	E			E		MAA1
201	☑	☑	E			P		MAA1

Note that in certain business scenarios, where posting string for values is blank, no posting takes place. This table is SAP maintained; customers cannot change it. Important posting strings for values are given below.

Goods issue

Posting string reference	Posting string for values	Scenarios
201	No value string, hence no accounting entries.	Non-valuated materials. Materials with consumption indicator E (Sales order) and P (Project).
201	WA01	Standard stock and special stocks E, Q and W.
201	WA03	Special stocks P and K.

Goods receipt

Posting string reference	Posting string for values	Scenarios
101	No value string, hence no accounting entries.	Non-valuated materials.
101	WE01	Goods receipts for purchase orders with no consumption (without account assignment).
101	WE06	Goods receipts for purchase orders with consumption (with account assignment).
101	WF01	Goods receipts for production orders.

26.5.4 Transaction/Event Keys

Transaction/event keys are determined from the posting string for values in view V156W.

VStr	Cn	TEKey
WA01	1	BSX
WA01	2	GBB
WA01	3	PRD
WA01	5	BSX
WA01	6	UMB
WA01	97	GBB
WA01	98	GBB
WA01	99	BSX

A posting usually results in a debit and a credit entry. Sometimes there are more entries, e.g. exchange rate difference, price difference etc. All possible postings are defined here. Appropriate lines are selected by the system depending on the business scenario. This table is also SAP maintained; customers cannot change it.

Important transaction/event keys

Transaction/event keys are specified in table T156W for posting string reference. The table specifies all possible transaction/event keys.

WA01: Goods issue of standard stock and special stocks E, Q and W

Credit	BSX	Inventory posting
Debit	GBB	Offsetting entry for inventory posting

WA03: Goods issue of special stocks P and K

Credit	KON	Consignment payables
Debit	GBB	Offsetting entry for inventory posting

WE01: Goods receipts for purchase orders without account assignment

Debit	BSX	Inventory posting
Credit	WRX	GR/IR clearing account
Dr/Cr	PRD	Cost (price) differences If inventory posting takes place at standard price

WE06: Goods receipts for purchase orders with account assignment

Debit	KBS	Account-assigned purchase order
Credit	WRX	GR/IR clearing account

WF01: Goods receipts for production orders

Debit	BSX	Inventory posting
Credit	GBB	Offsetting entry for inventory posting
Dr/Cr	PRD	Cost (price) differences If inventory posting takes place at standard price

26.5.5 Transaction Key

There is one-to-one correspondence between the transaction/event key and transaction key. SAP has maintained the possibility of converting field VORSL to field KOTSL in table TCKMLBNKS, which is used for material ledger and has no records.

26.5.6 Use of Transaction Keys

G/L account determination

Transaction key selected from here is used in determining the G/L account in transaction OMWB (table T030).

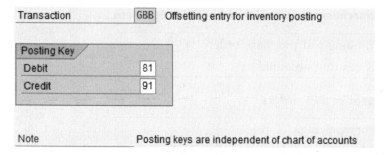

| Chart of Accounts | INT | Chart of accounts - international |
| Transaction | GBB | Offsetting entry for inventory posting |

Account assignment

Valuation modif.	General modification	Valuation class	Debit	Credit
0001	AUI	7920	895000	895000
0001	BSA	3000	399999	399999

Posting key determination

Transaction key selected from here is used in determining the posting keys in transaction OMWB (table T030B).

| Transaction | GBB | Offsetting entry for inventory posting |

Posting Key

| Debit | 81 |
| Credit | 91 |

| Note | Posting keys are independent of chart of accounts |

26.6 VALUATION MODIFICATION

Functional Consultant	User	Business Process Owner	Senior Management	My Rating	Understanding Level
A	C	C	X		

26.6.1 Purpose and Overview

Valuation area

Valuation area is a plant, or a group of plants, within which a material has the same value. For all the plants in a valuation area, the process of account determination is also the same.

Valuation grouping code

Whereas you may want to valuate material at plant level, you may want all plants to post to the same set of G/L accounts. If you use a common chart of accounts for multiple company codes, you may even want multiple company codes to post to the same set of G/L accounts. For this purpose, you can group multiple valuation areas into valuation grouping codes. Valuation grouping code is a group of valuation areas that follows the same process of account determination.

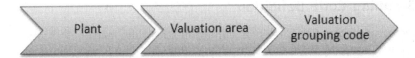

In account determination, valuation grouping code is called $\boxed{\text{Valuation modif.}}$.

Account determination

If different plants in your company want to follow different practices in determining G/L accounts for Materials Management, SAP caters to this need. Alternatively, many or all plants can follow a common account determination practice, which is defined at the level of valuation grouping code.

26.6.2 Valuation Area

Valuation of material

Some companies have the same price for a material in all plants of a company code, whereas other companies have different price for a material in different plants of a company code. SAP caters to this requirement by using a concept of valuation area, in which a material has the same price.

Levels of valuation area

SAP lets you define valuation areas as per your requirement. You have the following choices.

> If you want material valuation to be different for different plants, you define a valuation area for each plant.

> If you want material valuation for some plants to be different from other plants, you can define multiple valuation areas and assign one or more plants to each valuation area.

> If you want the same material valuation for the entire company code, you can define the valuation area at company code level.

Valuation area cannot be above company code level. Hence, you cannot ensure same price for a material across company codes.

26.6.3 Activating Valuation Grouping Code

If you want multiple valuation areas to post to the same G/L accounts, you activate the valuation grouping code using transaction OMWM.

Valuation grouping code

⊙ Valuation grouping code active

○ Valuation grouping code not active

26.6.4 Valuation Grouping Code Definition

In view V_001K_K you group valuation areas in valuation grouping codes. Valuation areas being grouped may belong to different company codes, but they must have the same chart of accounts. All valuation areas within a valuation grouping code post to the same set of G/L accounts.

Val. Area	CoCode	Company Name	Chrt/Accts	Val.Grpg Code
1000	1000	IDES AG	INT	0001
1100	1000	IDES AG	INT	0001
1200	1000	IDES AG	INT	0001
1300	1000	IDES AG	INT	0001
1400	1000	IDES AG	INT	0001
2000	2000	IDES UK	INT	0001
2010	2000	IDES UK	INT	0001
2100	2100	IDES Portugal	INT	0001
2200	2200	IDES France	CAFR	FR01

26.6.5 Use of Valuation Grouping Code

Valuation modification

Valuation modification is another name for valuation grouping code. In transaction OMWB it is used for determining the G/L account.

Chart of Accounts	INT	Chart of accounts - international
Transaction	GBB	Offsetting entry for inventory posting

Account assignment

Valuation modif.	General modification	Valuation class	Debit	Credit
0001	AUI	7920	895000	895000
0001	BSA	3000	399999	399999

26.7 GENERAL MODIFICATION/ACCOUNT MODIFICATION

Functional Consultant	User	Business Process Owner	Senior Management	My Rating	Understanding Level
A	C	C	X		

26.7.1 Purpose

Account modification is applicable only for transaction/event keys GBB, PRD and KON.

Offsetting entry for inventory posting (GBB)

Posting transaction "Offsetting entry for inventory posting" is used for different transactions (for example, goods issue, scrapping, physical inventory), which are assigned to different accounts (for example, consumption account, scrapping, expense/income from inventory differences), it is necessary to divide the posting transaction according to a further key: account modification. Under the posting transaction "Offsetting entry for inventory posting", you must assign G/L accounts for every account modification, that is, assign G/L accounts.

Price difference (PRD)

If you wish to post price differences to different price difference accounts in the case of goods receipts for purchase orders, goods receipts for orders, or other movements, you can define different account modifications for the transaction key.

Consignment and pipeline liabilities (KON)

Using account modification, you can also have different accounts for consignment liabilities and pipeline liabilities.

26.7.2   IMG Node

SM30 ≻ V_156X_KO

26.7.3   Screen

Overview screen

	MvT	S	Val.Update	Qty update	Mvt	Cns	Val.strng	Cn	TEKey	Acct modif	C
	101		☐	☐	B	A	WE06	1	KBS		☑
	101		☐	☐	B	E	WE06	1	KBS		☑
	101		☐	☐	B	P	WE06	1	KBS		☑
	101		☐	☐	B	V	WE06	1	KBS		☑
	101	E	☐	☐	B		WE01	3	PRD		☐
	101	E	☐	☐	B	E	WE06	1	KBS		☑
	101	E	☐	☐	B	P	WE06	1	KBS		☑
	101	Q	☐	☐	B		WE01	3	PRD		☐
	101	Q	☐	☐	B	P	WE06	1	KBS		☑

Detailed screen

Select a row and click 🔍 to see the following screen.

Movement Type	101 Goods receipt		Special Stock	
☑ Value Update			Movement ind.	F
☑ Quantity updating			Consumption	
Value string	WF01			

Current Entry

2	GBB	Offsetting entry for inventory posting	AUF	☑ Check

Trans./Event Key for String

TEKey	Description	Acct modif	Check
BSX	Inventory posting		☐
GBB	Offsetting entry for inventory posting	AUF	☑
PRD	Cost (price) differences	PRF	☐
AUM	Expense/revenue from stock transfer		☐
BSX	Inventory posting		☐
UMB	Gain/loss from revaluation		☐

Parts of the screen

This customizing interface shows the transaction/event keys that were explained by referring to SAP tables in Section 26.5. This screen can be divided in the following three parts.

Factors that determine transaction/event keys	This part contains the conditions in the goods movement that result in posting to different G/L accounts via transaction/event keys.

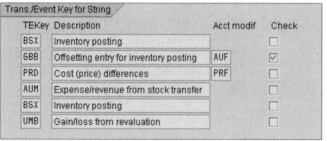

Transaction/event keys	This part of the screen shows the transaction/event keys that will result in posting to different G/L accounts specified by you for each key.

Trans./Event Key for String

TEKey	Description	Acct modif	Check
BSX	Inventory posting		☐
GBB	Offsetting entry for inventory posting	AUF	☑
PRD	Cost (price) differences	PRF	☐
AUM	Expense/revenue from stock transfer		☐
BSX	Inventory posting		☐
UMB	Gain/loss from revaluation		☐

Account modification	This part contains the account modification that will result in posting to different G/L accounts for the same transaction/event key, e.g. GBB, PRD, KON, etc.

Current Entry

2	GBB	Offsetting entry for inventory posting	AUF	☑ Check

26.7.4 Factors that Determine Transaction/Event Keys

This part of the screen contains the factors that determine the transaction/event keys. The values in these fields are matched with data coming from the goods movement to determine the set of transaction/event keys that are applicable for the goods movement.

Movement type

When you enter a goods movement in the system, you must enter a movement type to differentiate between the various goods movements.

Special stock

Special stock is stock of material that must be managed separately for reasons of ownership or location. If a goods movement involves movement of a special stock, it is specified in it.

Movement indicator

Movement indicator specifies the type of document (such as purchase order or delivery note) that constitutes the basis for the goods movement.

Value update and quantity updating in the materials master

If goods are received for consumption, their value and quantity are not updated in the materials master. The system determines values of both these fields and stores them in material documents table MSEG.

Consumption

Consumption posting specifies that the consumption is to be posted to a consumption account (V) or an asset account (A). This indicator is used in the case of goods receipts for purchase orders and is derived from the account assignment category of the purchase order.

Value string

Value string is derived from table T156SY based on the above fields and displayed here.

26.7.5 Account Modification

Account modification

This part shows if an account modification is applicable, and if so which one. You can change the account modification if there is a need.

Check account assignment

If ☑ Check indicator is set, the system checks whether a G/L account or an account assignment has been specified on the item screen. If so, the system copies this data to the posting line. If this indicator is not set, the system always uses the G/L accounts determined automatically.

26.7.6 Account Modification for Offsetting Entry for Inventory Posting

Account modifications for transaction/event key GBB are given below.

Account Modification	Description
AUF	Goods receipts for production orders with account assignment
BSA	Initial entries of stock balances
INV	Expense/revenue from inventory differences
VAX	Goods issues for sales orders without account assignment object
VAY	Goods issues for sales orders with account assignment object
VBO	Consumption from stock of material provided to vendor
VBR	Internal goods issues (e.g., for cost center)
VKA	Consumption for sales order without SD
VNG	Scrapping/destruction
VQP	Sampling
ZOB	Goods receipts without purchase orders
ZOF	Goods receipts without production orders

26.7.7 Account Modification for Cost (Price) Differences

If you also activate account grouping for transaction/event key PRD (price differences) when you make the settings for automatic postings, the following account groupings are already assigned to the relevant movement types in the standard.

Account Modification	Description
Blank	Goods receipts and invoice receipts for purchase orders
PRF	Goods receipts for production orders
PRA	Goods issues and other goods movements

26.7.8 Account Modification for Consignment Liabilities

If you also activate account grouping for transaction/event KON (consignment liabilities) when you make the settings for automatic postings, the following account groupings are already assigned to the relevant movement types in the standard.

Account Modification	Description
Blank	Consignment liabilities
PIP	Pipeline liabilities

26.7.9 Use of Account Modification

General modification is another name for account modification. In transaction OMWB it is used for determining the G/L account.

Chart of Accounts	INT	Chart of accounts - international
Transaction	GBB	Offsetting entry for inventory posting

Account assignment

Valuation modif.	General modification	Valuation class	Debit	Credit
0001	AUI	7920	895000	895000
0001	BSA	3000	399999	399999

26.8 VALUATION CLASS

Functional Consultant	User	Business Process Owner	Senior Management	My Rating	Understanding Level
A	C	C	X		

26.8.1 Classification of Inventory

Run transaction S_PL0_86000032 to see the account balances in structured form.

Commercial balance sheet

OL	Ledger
10	Currency type Company code currency
EUR	Amounts in Euro (EMU currency as of 01/01/1999)
2013.01 -2013.16	Reporting periods
2012.01 -2012.16	Comparison periods

F.S. item/account	Tot.rpt.pr
▽ ☐ A S S E T S	1,423.41
▽ ☐ Current assets	1,423.41
▽ ☐ Stocks	1,423.41
▽ ☐ Raw materials and supplies	198.14-
▷ 📂 0000300000 Inventory - Raw Material 1	198.14-
▽ ☐ Work in process	1,484.42
▷ 📂 0000790000 Unfinished products	2,622.02
▷ 📂 0000799999 Inventory (own goods)	1,137.60-
▽ ☐ Finished goods and merchandise	137.13
▷ 📂 0000310000 Trading Goods	142.24
▷ 📂 0000792000 Finished goods inventory	5.11-

Two-tier structure of account balances

A company usually has multiple G/L accounts that represent the stock of different types of materials. These accounts are usually grouped into categories as illustrated above.

Two-tier structure of material based account determination

SAP provides a two tier structure of material based account determination that may be considered to correspond to the structure of account balances.

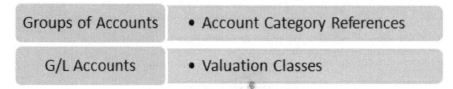

| Groups of Accounts | • Account Category References |
| G/L Accounts | • Valuation Classes |

26.8.2 Account Category References

You may design account category references on the lines of groups of inventory accounts. In view V_025K you maintain the master list of account category references.

ARef	Description
0001	Reference for raw materials
0002	Ref. for operating supplies
0003	Reference for spare parts
0004	Reference for packaging
0005	Reference for trading goods
0006	Reference for services
0007	Ref. for non-valuated material
0008	Ref. for semifinished products
0009	Ref. for finished products
0600	Ref for empties fixed
0700	Ref for empties current

26.8.3 Valuation Classes

In view V025 you define valuation classes.

ValCl	ARef	Description	Description
1210	0002	Low-value assets RU	Ref. for operating supplies
3000	0001	Raw materials 1	Reference for raw materials
3001	0001	Raw materials 2	Reference for raw materials
3002	0001	Raw materials 3	Reference for raw materials

In the two-tier structure, each account category reference has some valuation classes under it. That linkage is also defined here.

26.8.4   Account Category Reference for a Material Type

Valuation class for a material type

You would expect to determine valuation class of a material from its material type. However, it may so happen that your valuation classes are finer than the material types. In other words, you may want to post one material of a material type to one G/L account, and another material of the same material type to another G/L account.

Valuation class for a material

Therefore, you do not link a material type to a valuation class; you link a material to a valuation class.

Account category reference for a material type

However, you do not expect a material type to cross the boundary of an account category reference. Therefore, you link a material type to an account category reference in view V_134_K.

MTyp	Material type descr.	ARef	Description
DOCU	documentary batch	0008	Ref. for semifinished products
FHMI	Prod. resources/tools	0008	Ref. for semifinished products
HALB	Semi-finished product	0008	Ref. for semifinished products
KMAT	Configurable material	0008	Ref. for semifinished products
PROD	Product group	0008	Ref. for semifinished products
YCON	Configurable matl MPW	0008	Ref. for semifinished products

Valuation classes allowed for a material

This linkage restricts the valuation classes that can be assigned to a material.

26.8.5   Valuation Classes for a Material

Run transaction MM02 and select Accounting 1 view.

| Quality management | ⚙ Accounting 1 | Accounting 2 | Costing 1 | Costing 2 |

Material	100-302	Hollow shaft	🛈
Plant	1000	Werk Hamburg	
Val. type	EIGEN		

General data

Base Unit of Measure	PC	piece(s)	Valuation Category	B
Currency		EUR	Current period	10 2013
Division	01		Price determ.		☐ ML act.

Current valuation

Valuation Class	☑			
VC: Sales order stk			Proj. stk val. class	
Price control	S		Price Unit	1
Moving price			Standard price	
Total Stock	0		Total Value	0.00
			☐ Valuated Un	
Future price			Valid from	

| Previous period/year | Std cost estimate |

Valuation class

You specify valuation class for a material in a valuation area. If a valuation area consists of several plants, changing the valuation class for one plant will change it for all plants in the valuation area. Valuation classes possible for a material are restricted by the account category reference of the material type of the material.

Valuation class: sales order stock

If you want to post sales order stock of a material to an account different from the account to which the standard stock is posted, you can specify a valuation class here. Valuation classes possible for a material are restricted by the account category reference of the material type of the material.

Valuation class: project stock

If you want to post project stock of a material to an account different from the account to which the standard stock is posted, you can specify a valuation class here. Valuation classes possible for a material are restricted by the account category reference of the material type of the material.

26.8.6 Use of Valuation Class

Account assignment

In transaction OMWB you can use valuation class to determine the G/L account.

Chart of Accounts	INT	Chart of accounts - international
Transaction	BSX	Inventory posting

Account assignment

Valuation class	Account
3000	300000
3001	300010
3002	300010
3030	303000
3040	304000
3050	305000
3100	310000
3200	300000
7900	790000

You can see the effect of this account assignment in simulation of account determination.

Account determination of material 100–100

Run transaction OMWB. Click Simulation . Enter material number and movement type. Select a movement type description. Click Account Assignments .

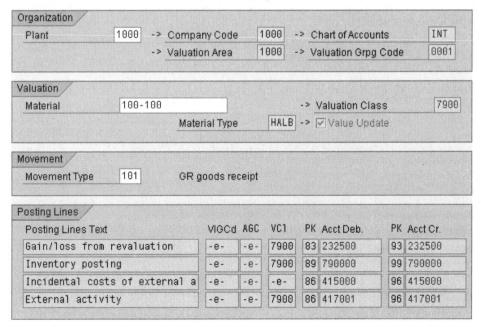

Organization

Plant	1000	-> Company Code	1000	-> Chart of Accounts	INT
		-> Valuation Area	1000	-> Valuation Grpg Code	0001

Valuation

Material	100-100			-> Valuation Class	7900
		Material Type	HALB	-> ☑ Value Update	

Movement

Movement Type	101	GR goods receipt

Posting Lines

Posting Lines Text	VIGCd	AGC	VC1	PK	Acct Deb.	PK	Acct Cr.
Gain/loss from revaluation	-e-	-e-	7900	83	232500	93	232500
Inventory posting	-e-	-e-	7900	89	790000	99	790000
Incidental costs of external a	-e-	-e-	-e-	86	415000	96	415000
External activity	-e-	-e-	7900	86	417001	96	417001

Account determination of material 100–110

Run transaction OMWB. Click | Simulation |. Enter material number and movement type. Select a movement type description. Click | Account Assignments |.

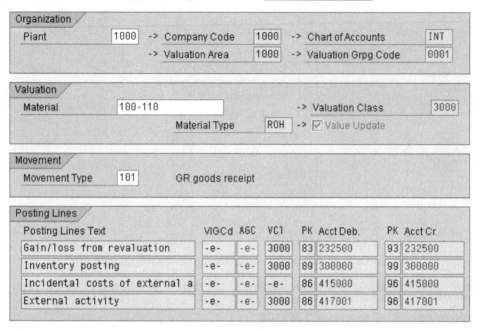

Posting Lines Text	VIGCd	AGC	VC1	PK	Acct Deb.	PK	Acct Cr.
Gain/loss from revaluation	-e-	-e-	3000	83	232500	93	232500
Inventory posting	-e-	-e-	3000	89	300000	99	300000
Incidental costs of external a	-e-	-e-	-e-	86	415000	96	415000
External activity	-e-	-e-	3000	86	417001	96	417001

Different valuation classes and accounts

Note that the two materials have different valuation classes and, as a result, post to different set of G/L accounts.

26.8.7 Features of Valuation Classes

Valuation classes are used for account determination, not for material valuation.

A valuation class groups materials that post to the same set of G/L accounts.

If a material is subject to split valuation, valuation classes for different valuation types of the same material can be different and can therefore post to different set of G/L accounts.

Project stock and sales order stock of a material can have different valuation classes and can therefore post to different set of G/L accounts.

Valuation classes are assigned to a material in a valuation area. It is therefore possible that the same material has different valuation classes in different valuation areas.

26.9 SIMULATION OF ACCOUNT DETERMINATION

Functional Consultant	User	Business Process Owner	Senior Management	My Rating	Understanding Level
A	C	C	X		

26.9.1 Purpose

Review Section 26.2 to understand account determination. Since account determination is a complex process, SAP provides a tool to simulate it.

26.9.2 IMG Node

Transaction OMWB—Account Determination

26.9.3 Simulation

Click Simulation , select GR goods receipt and click Account Assignments to see the screenshot below. This is the best way to understand account determination.

26.9.4 Screen

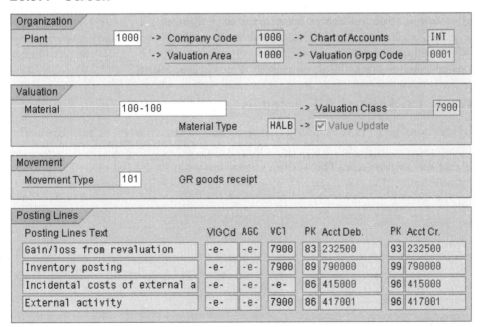

26.9.5 Factors Affecting Account Determination

This screenshot shows that the account determination is influenced by

➢ Plant

➢ Material

➢ Movement type

➢ Other factors, e.g. valuation area, valuation class etc.

26.9.6 Posting Lines

Posting lines show the postings that will take place depending on the business scenario.

26.10 SOURCES OF POSTING TO A G/L ACCOUNT

Functional Consultant	User	Business Process Owner	Senior Management	My Rating	Understanding Level
A	C	C	X		

26.10.1 Purpose

Since account determination automates the process of determining G/L accounts to which posting take place, business managers responsible for a G/L account may experience a loss of control over the entries being passed in that G/L account. They may want to know which business processes are passing entries to their G/L accounts.

26.10.2 Where Used List of G/L Accounts

For each G/L account in a chart of accounts, you can see the sources of posting in the Materials Management module. In transaction OMWB click ⟨ G/L Accounts ⟩ and specify the Company Code and the Valuation Area . The system shows the where used list of G/L accounts.

Company Code 1000	Chart of Accounts INT			
Valuation Area 1000	Valuatn Grouping Code 0001			

Ch.Acc. / Acc / ValClass / TEK/ AGCde	Description	Account	Val.Gr.Cde	Status
▽ 🗎 0000399999	Clearing account - stocktake resul...	Balance		
▽ 🗎 3000	Raw materials 1			
▽ 🗎 GBB	Offsetting entry for inventory posting			
🗎 BSA	Initial Entry of Stock Balances			
🗎 BSA	Initial Entry of Stock Balances	0001		
▽ 🗎 3001	Raw materials 2	0001		
▽ 🗎 GBB	Offsetting entry for inventory posting	0001		
🗎 BSA	Initial Entry of Stock Balances	0001		
▽ 🗎 3030	Operating supplies	0001		
▽ 🗎 GBB	Offsetting entry for inventory posting	0001		
🗎 BSA	Initial Entry of Stock Balances	0001		
▽ 🗎 3040	Spare parts	0001		
▽ 🗎 GBB	Offsetting entry for inventory posting	0001		
🗎 BSA	Initial Entry of Stock Balances	0001		
▽ 🗎 3050	(Returnable) packaging	0001		
▽ 🗎 GBB	Offsetting entry for inventory posting	0001		
🗎 BSA	Initial Entry of Stock Balances	0001		
▽ 🗎 3100	Trading goods	0001		
▽ 🗎 GBB	Offsetting entry for inventory posting	0001		
🗎 BSA	Initial Entry of Stock Balances	0001		
▽ 🗎 7900	Semifinished products			
▽ 🗎 GBB	Offsetting entry for inventory posting			
🗎 BSA	Initial Entry of Stock Balances			

26.10.3   Account Detective

Purpose

If you want to know other sources of posting to a G/L account, you can use the Account Detective.

Transaction

S_ALR_87101048—Account Detective.

Selection Screen

In the selection screen apart from other selection criteria, you specify the areas whose account determination entries are to be shown.

Area	Tables
☑ Output FI Account Assignments	T030C, T030D, T030G, T030H, T030K, T030S, T030U, T074
☑ Output MM/HR Account Assignmnt	T030
☑ Output Cost Element Categories	
☑ Output AA Account Assignments	T095, T095B, T095P
☑ Output SD/EK Account Assignmnt	C001, C002, C003, C004, C005

List of Tables Posting to an Account

G/L acct	Name				B/S acct	AT	AcGp	Crc
		Account Assignment	Account Assignment	Account Assignment	Account Assignment	Accou		
399999	Bestandsaufnahme				X		MAT	EUF
T030	GBB			BSA			3000	
T030	GBB			BSA			7900	
T030	GBB	0001		BSA			3000	
T030	GBB	0001		BSA			3001	
T030	GBB	0001		BSA			3030	
T030	GBB	0001		BSA			3040	
T030	GBB	0001		BSA			3050	
T030	GBB	0001		BSA			3100	
T095	02	00010000		BSA			3100	
T095	02	00020000		BSA			3100	
T095	03	00020000		BSA			3100	

Stock Determination

27.1 OVERVIEW

Functional Consultant	User	Business Process Owner	Senior Management	My Rating	Understanding Level
B	X	X	X		

27.1.1 Automatic Stock Determination

When planning your materials requirements, it is not always important that you define the stocks and storage locations from which the materials are later to be withdrawn. Automatic stock determination takes care of this decision for you, thus preventing you from defining these parameters too early and restricting your business processes unnecessarily.

27.1.2 Stock Determination Strategy

You may have a material in different storage locations. You may also have the same material with you as consignment material from several vendors. The prices of these materials might vary. You may want to withdraw material based on one of the following logics.

➢ Withdraw the cheapest material first, i.e. withdraw in ascending order of prices.

➢ Withdraw own material first, followed by vendors' material

➢ Withdraw vendors' material first, followed by own material

Each of this logic is called a stock determination strategy.

SAP does not require that you use the same logic for all materials. Further, it recognizes that the logic for stock transfer may be different from the logic of goods issue to production. It, therefore, lets you specify the stock determination strategy for a combination of material and movement type.

27.1.3 Determination of Stock Determination Strategy

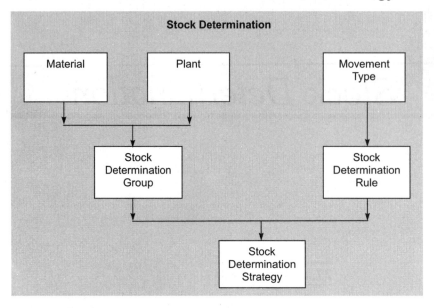

27.1.4 Stock Determination Group

Stock determination groups serve to group materials to which the same stock determination strategy is applied for a given movement type.

27.1.5 Stock Determination Rule

Stock determination rules form sets of movement types such that, for a material, each movement type from the set requires the same stock determination strategy.

27.1.6 Using Stock Determination

In a goods movement screen, in the ▨Quantity▨ tab, you can click 🗄 to do stock determination.

27.2 STOCK DETERMINATION GROUP

Functional Consultant	User	Business Process Owner	Senior Management	My Rating	Understanding Level
B	X	X	X		

27.2.1 Master List of Stock Determination Groups

For each plant you define the master list of stock determination groups in view V_T434G (view cluster VC_BEFI1)

Plnt	SDG	Description
1000	PP01	Stock determination group 01 for PP
1000	PP02	Stock determination group 02 for PP
1000	PP03	Stock determination grp 03 for pull list
1200	PP01	Stock determination grp 01 for pull list
5000	PP01	Stock determination strategy 01 for PP
CHP2	CHEM	CHEM DEMO
CPF5	PI78	Stock determination 178

27.2.2 Stock Determination Group for a Material in a Plant

The stock determination group is assigned to the material in the material master record at plant level.

27.3 STOCK DETERMINATION RULE

Functional Consultant	User	Business Process Owner	Senior Management	My Rating	Understanding Level
B	X	X	X		

27.3.1 Master List of Stock Determination Rules

Master list of stock determination rules is maintained in view V_T434R (view cluster VC_BEFI1)

StDR	Description
0001	Stock determination rule 0001
CHEM	Stock determination Rule Chem
MM01	
MM02	
PI78	Stock determination Rule 178
PP01	Stock determination rule 01 for PP
PP02	Stock determination rule 02 for PP
PP03	Stock determination rule 03 - pull list

27.3.2 Grouping Movement Types in Stock Determination Rules

Movement types are grouped in stock determination rules in view V_156_BF.

MvT	Movement Type Text	Stck determation rule
201	GI for cost center	MM01
202	RE for cost center	
221	GI for project	MM02
222	RE for project	

27.4 STOCK DETERMINATION STRATEGY

Functional Consultant	User	Business Process Owner	Senior Management	My Rating	Understanding Level
B	X	X	X		

27.4.1 Purpose

In a stock determination strategy you specify the priority of the following three parameters.

➤ Item table (see Section 27.5)
➤ Price
➤ Quantity

You may want stock determination to take place in such a way that you use the cheapest material first, and when the price is the same, use larger quantities first. This kind of logic is defined here.

27.4.2 IMG Node

SM34 ➤ VC_BEFI1 (view V_T434K)

27.4.3   Screen

Plant	1000	Werk Hamburg
Stock determ. group	PP01	Stock determination group 01 for PP
Stck determation rule	PP01	Stock determination rule 01 for PP
Description		Stock determination strategy 01 for PP

Sorting

	Item table	Price	Qty
	○ None	○ None	○ None
	● Ascending	● Ascending	● Ascending
	○ Descending	○ Descending	○ Descending
Rank.Ordr	1 Priority 1	2 Priority 2	3 Priority 3

Quantity Distribution

Qty proposal	1	✎		No. Splits	10

Other settings

WM processing   3   Stock determination has priority

☑ Stock determ. online

☑ Pipeline withdrawal

☐ User exit for item table

27.4.4   Primary Key

Plant
Stock determination group
Stock determination rule

27.4.5   Important Fields

Plant, stock determination group, stock determination rule

You can have multiple stock determination strategies for a plant. Stock determination strategies are combinations of stock determination groups and stock determination rules. In other words, stock determination strategies are chosen on the basis of the material and the movement type.

Ranking order and sorting

In stock determination, you can rank stocks by item table, price and quantity. Further, you specify whether each of them is to be sorted ascending, descending, or not to be sorted.

Quantity proposal

In the quantity distribution, you also have the option of defining a form routine. This is saved in the quantity proposal field. Enter one condition that controls how the system is to propose the quantity for this strategy record.

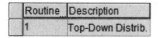

Routine	Description
1	Top-Down Distrib.

Number of splits

Here you specify the maximum number of partial quantities into which a requirements quantity may be divided by stock determination. If you leave the field blank, the number is unlimited.

Warehouse management processing

Here you define how the Warehouse Management System is to combine the withdrawal sequence determined by stock determination with its warehouse management strategies. This indicator only influences the creation of transfer orders in the Warehouse Management System. It is not relevant for stock determination at storage location level.

WM processing	Short text
1	WM has priority
2	WM storage type search has priority
3	Stock determination has priority

Stock determination online

This indicator controls whether stock determination is to run in the background or online.

Pipeline withdrawal

This indicator controls whether a pipeline withdrawal is allowed when the requirement cannot completely be covered by other stocks (according to the item table). The quantity withdrawn from the pipeline material is treated as a partial quantity according to the split criterion.

User exit for item table

This indicator specifies that the user exit EXIT_SAPLMDBF_002 of enhancement XMBF0001 is to be used for this strategy in the item table for Inventory Management.

27.5 STOCK DETERMINATION ITEM TABLE

Functional Consultant	User	Business Process Owner	Senior Management	My Rating	Understanding Level
B	X	X	X		

27.5.1 Purpose

Along with price and quantity, stock determination item table is one option in deciding which stocks are allocated in stock determination. In the item table, you can explicitly specify whether own stock, or consignment stock has priority. You can further specify the storage locations and valuation type for the stock type that has priority.

27.5.2 IMG Node

SM34 ➤ VC_BEFI1 (view V_T434P)

27.5.3 Screen

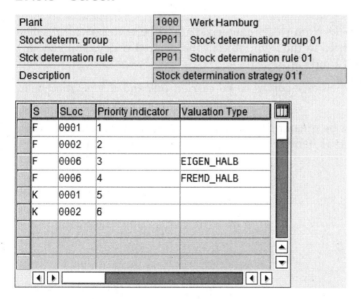

Plant	1000	Werk Hamburg
Stock determ. group	PP01	Stock determination group 01
Stck determation rule	PP01	Stock determination rule 01
Description		Stock determination strategy 01 f

S	SLoc	Priority indicator	Valuation Type	
F	0001	1		
F	0002	2		
F	0006	3	EIGEN_HALB	
F	0006	4	FREMD_HALB	
K	0001	5		
K	0002	6		

27.5.4 Primary Key

Plant
Stock determination group
Stock determination rule
Stock determination: Item number

27.5.5 Important Fields

Plant, stock determination group, stock determination rule

Priorities are defined at plant, stock determination group, stock determination rule level.

Special stock indicator

This indicator specifies the stock that stock determination should suggest for withdrawal.

Special Stock Indicator	Short text
K	Consignment
F	Unrestricted company's own stock

If this indicator is blank, both these stocks are considered,

Storage location

Priority indicator also determines the storage location from which material should be withdrawn.

Priority indicator

Priority indicator indicates the stocks from which material should be withdrawn first. The priority indicator arranges the entries in the item table in the desired order. You can sort the stocks found using the priority indicator.

In the header table, you define whether a sort is to be carried out and if yes whether in ascending or descending order.

The priority indicator must always be greater than or equal to 1. However, you can assign the same priority indicator to several items (same importance in sorting).

Valuation type

Valuation type uniquely identifies separately valued stocks of a material.

28

Reservation

28.1 RESERVATION

Functional Consultant	User	Business Process Owner	Senior Management	My Rating	Understanding Level
A	A	B	C		

28.1.1 Overview

Reservation

You can use reservation to request the warehouse to keep materials ready for withdrawal at a later date and for a certain purpose. A reservation for goods issue can be requested by various departments for various account assignment objects (such as cost center, order, asset, etc.). The purpose of a reservation is to ensure that a material will be available when it is needed. You can issue goods with reference to a reservation. Reservations are taken into account by Material Requirements Planning (MRP), which means that the required materials are procured in time if they are out of stock.

Manual reservations

Manual reservations are entered directly by the user using transaction MB21. They can be changed using transaction MB22 and displayed using transaction MB23.

Automatic reservations

Automatic reservations are generated automatically by the system. There are two types of automatic reservations.

➤ Reservations for orders, networks, WBS elements

➤ Stock transfer reservations

Reservations for orders, networks, WBS elements

When an order, a network, or a project is created, the components from the warehouse are reserved automatically.

Stock transfer reservations

You can plan stock transfers using stock transfer reservations. Stock transfer reservations are reservations that plan the goods issue from the issuing point. Stock transfer reservations are intended for one-step stock transfers only. They cannot be used for transfer postings because transfer postings are not planned in advance. Stock transfer reservations can be created manually using transaction MB21 with appropriate movement type. They can also be created automatically by MRP. The reserved quantity is managed in the unrestricted-use stock and in the reserved stock of the issuing point. In MRP, the reserved quantity reduces available stock in the issuing plant.

Changing automatic reservations

You cannot manually process automatic reservations. For example, it is not possible to change reservations for an order directly. You have to change the components in the order. The system then updates the reservation automatically.

Reservation for goods receipt

If you use purchase order and production order, you do not create reservations for goods receipt. The quantity expected to be received is shown in reports as open purchase order quantity and open order quantity. If you are expecting goods receipt without purchase order or production order, you can create reservation for goods receipt. The quantity expected to be received is shown in reports as planned receipts. Goods receipt can then take place with respect to reservation.

Effects of reservation

When a reservation is entered, the following events occur in the system:

➤ The system creates a reservation document, which serves as proof of the request.

➤ In the material master record, total stock and unrestricted-use stock of the material remain unchanged. Reserved stock is increased by the reserved quantity.

➤ In MRP, available stock is reduced by the reserved quantity. This is visible in the current stock/requirements list. The reservation causes an entry to be made in the requirements planning file.

28.1.2 Transaction

MB21—Create Reservation

28.1.3 Initial Screen

Create Reservation: Initial Screen

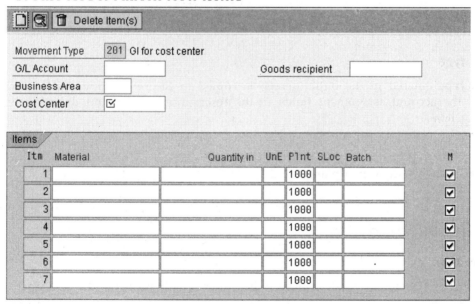

Base date	05.12.2013	☑ Check against cal.
Movement Type	201	
Plant	1000 ⊡	

Reference
Reservation [   ]

If you select the checkbox ☑ Check against cal. , the system checks the factory calendar to determine whether the dates in the reservation are valid workdays.

28.1.4 Collective Entry Screen

Click ⬜ to go to the collective entry screen.

Create Reservation: New Items

🗋 🔍 🗑 Delete Item(s)

Movement Type	201 GI for cost center		
G/L Account	[ ]	Goods recipient	[ ]
Business Area	[ ]		
Cost Center	☑		

Items

Itm	Material		Quantity in	UnE	Plnt	SLoc	Batch	M
1					1000			☑
2					1000			☑
3					1000			☑
4					1000			☑
5					1000			☑
6					1000		.	☑
7					1000			☑

Here you can enter reservation for several items. Movement type and account assignment fields are for all items.

28.1.5 Detailed Screen

Select a line, and click 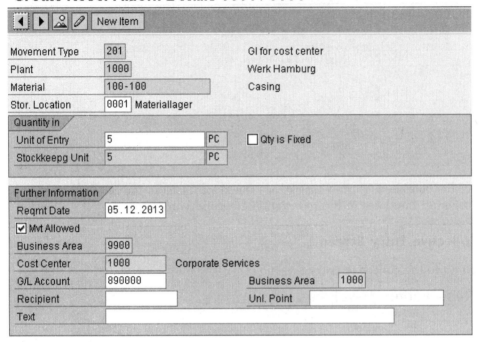 to go to the detailed screen.

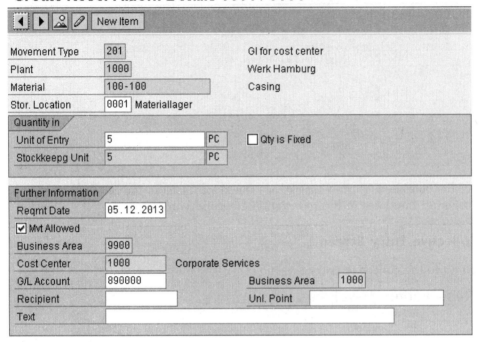

Movement type

Movement type entered in the initial screen is copied in the reservation header and determines the account assignment fields in the reservation header and debit/credit indicator for items.

Plant

Reservation is always done in a plant.

Material

This is the material being reserved.

Storage location

Here you specify the storage location from which the goods movement will take place.

Batch

If the material is to be issued from a batch, specify the batch.

Quantity, unit

You specify the quantity of material being reserved along with unit.

Quantity is fixed

This indicator causes the total quantity to be proposed for withdrawal every time there is a goods issue with reference to this reservation item (even if, in the extended selection, you enter a lower percentage as default value for the withdrawal).

Quantity in stock keeping unit, unit

Here the system shows the quantity in stock keeping unit.

Requirement date

Requirement date is defaulted from the base date entered in the initial screen, but may be changed in the detailed screen. Usually requirement dates are in future, but these reservations will not show in the stock overview until that date.

Movement allowed

This checkbox specifies that goods movements are allowed for the reservation item. Default value for this field is defined in Mvt column of view V_159L_R.

Plnt	Name 1	Mvt	Days m	Rete	MRA
1000	Werk Hamburg	☑	10	30	☐

Business area

When material is issued against this reservation, the debit entry will be posted to this business area.

Cost center

You specify the cost object for which reservation is done. Since the movement type was 201, the cost object is cost center.

G/L account

Normally the system automatically determines the G/L account that will get debited, but you can specify one if you want to. This G/L account is used as the offsetting entry for the inventory posting (usually a consumption account). When you create a goods movement with reference to a reservation, the G/L account entered here is copied.

Business area

When material is issued against this reservation, the credit entry will be posted to this business area.

Recipient

You may enter the recipient of an item in the collective entry screen, which is copied for all items. In the detailed screen, you may enter different recipients for different items.

Unloading point

Here you can specify the unloading point for an item.

Text

Here you can enter any text, e.g. reason for reservation, reference to instructions, etc.

28.1.6 Overview Screen

Click 🔍 to see the overview screen.

Create Reservation: Overview

Movement Type	201	GI for cost center
Business Area	9900	
Cost Center	1000	Corporate Services

Items

Itm	Reqmt Qty Qty Withdrawn	BUn	Material Material Description	Plnt	SLoc	Batch	Mvt	Reqmt Date FIs Del D/C
1	5	PC	100-100	1000	0001			05.12.2013
		PC	Casing				☑	☐ ☐ H

28.1.7 Posting a Reservation

Availability check

When you post (save) a reservation, the system carries out availability check and gives warning or error as described in Section 21.3.9. Availability check can also be carried out via Edit ➤ Additional Functions ➤ Check Availability.

Reservation number

The system assigns a reservation number to the reservation. The reservation number comes from an internal number range; it cannot be specified by the user. This number can be used to change or display a reservation. It is also used when you create a goods movement with reference to a reservation.

28.1.8 Reservation Document

When you create a reservation, the system creates a reservation document. It has a header and one or more items. This document can be displayed and changed. Goods movements can be posted with reference to a reservation document. A goods reservation document can also be deleted if reservation is no longer needed, or if goods movement corresponding to reservation has taken place.

28.2 RESERVATION PROCESSES

Functional Consultant	User	Business Process Owner	Senior Management	My Rating	Understanding Level
A	A	B	C		

28.2.1 Creating a Reservation

You can create a manual reservation using transaction MB21 as explained in Section 28.1.

28.2.2 Creating a Reservation with Reference to another Reservation

You can create a reservation with reference to another reservation by entering reference reservation number in the initial screen in transaction MB21. Entry of base date is mandatory. If movement type is entered in the initial screen, it is taken from the initial screen; otherwise it is taken from the reference reservation. The system shows the items of the reference reservation.

Create Reservation: Selection Screen

		Adopt + Details

Movement Type	221	GI for project
G/L Account		Goods recipient
Business Area	9900	
WBS Element	☑	Network

Items

Itm	Material	Quantity in	UnE	Plnt	SLoc	Batch	M
☑ 1	100-100	5	PC	1000	0001		☑

You can select the items you want to adopt and click 🗐 or Adopt + Details . In the former case, the items are copied in the reservation being created and you can change them there. In the latter case, you can change them before adopting them in the new reservation.

Copy rules for reference documents in reservation

When you create a reservation with reference to another, the system inserts all the items of the reference reservation in the current reservation. Before copying [⬚] or adopting [Adopt + Details] you select the items. You can specify that the items should be [Proposed preselec.] in view V_158_R.

Transaction Code	Transaction Text	Proposed preselec.
MB21	Create Reservation	☑

28.2.3 Importing Reservation Data from a File

Purpose

You can import reservation data from a file.

Transaction

MBBR—Create Session (Reservation)

Initial Screen

Batch Input: Create Reservation

Name of logical file	MM_INVENTORY_MANAGEMENT_RESERVATION
Max. number of items	20
User name in document	SAPUSER

Flow control ---

☑ Issue log
☐ Hold processed sessions
☐ Test data

Name of logical file

The data for the batch input session are imported from an external dataset as a sequential file. The structure of this sequential file is predefined in table BRESB and cannot be changed. See the program documentation on guidelines for preparing the file. Here you specify the name of logical file containing the inventory count data that you want to upload. The link between the logical file name and the physical file is maintained in view V_FILENACI, which is applicable to all clients. You can also maintain client specific file names using transaction SF01.

Issue log

Here you specify that a log be issued onscreen after processing.

Hold processed sessions

If this indicator is not set, sessions that do not have errors are deleted after they are processed. Sessions in which errors occurred are not deleted. Set this indicator if you do not want the processed sessions to be deleted. You can see the sessions using transaction SM35.

Test data

You can run this program with test data. To do so, set this indicator, maintain test data in view V_159A, and ensure that the specified file contains no productive data. When you run the program, test data is written from table T159A to the sequential file, before the sequential file is processed by the program to generate the batch session.

Default values for this initial screen

Default values for this initial screen are specified in view V_159B_MR.

```
Program Name
┌──────────┐
│ RM07RRES │ Batch Input: Create Reservation
└──────────┘

┌─ Default values ──────────────────────────────┐
│  Session                      [            ]   │
│  Maximum No. of Document Items  [20  ]         │
│  ☑ Batch Input                                 │
│  ☑ Issue Log                                   │
└────────────────────────────────────────────────┘
```

Generating Batch Input Session

Click 🕓 to generate a batch input session. The batch input session has the name specified in the initial screen.

Processing Batch Input Session

You can process the batch input session using transaction SM35. When the batch input session is processed, it updates count for the physical inventory document items.

28.2.4 Changing a Reservation

You can change a manual reservation using transaction MB22. In the initial screen enter the reservation number and click [✎].

Change Reservation 0000066136 : Collective Processing

| [🗋] [✎] [⊞] Details from Item |

Movement Type   201   GI for cost center

                                           Goods recipient

Business Area   9900

Cost Center   1000   Corporate Services

Items

Itm	Material		Quantity in	UnE	Plnt	SLoc	Batch	M	FIs	D
1	100-100	5		PC	1000	0001		☑	☐	☐

You cannot change automatic reservations. They are changed automatically, when the order creating it changes, for example.

Creating an Item

You can create an item by clicking [🗋]. The system gives the following dialog box.

| [🖉 Default Values | ⊠] |

Header information

Base date   05.12.2013

Suggestion for new items

Reqmt Date

Plant   ☑

| [✔] [🗋] New Item [✖] |

You enter the requirement date and plant, which are suggested for new items. If you click [✔] or [🗋], the system gives you collective entry screen. If you click [New Item], the system gives you details screen.

Changing an Item

Change Reservation 0000066136 : Collective Processing

Movement Type	201	GI for cost center		
Goods recipient				
Business Area	9900			
Cost Center	1000	Corporate Services		

Items

Itm	Material		Quantity in	UnE	Plnt	SLoc	Batch	M	FIs	D
1	100-100		5	PC	1000	0001		☑	☐	☐

You can change certain item details, e.g. quantity and storage location.

Updating Final Issue Indicator

The final issue indicator is used to mark a reservation item as completed. When you issue goods with reference to reservation, it is set automatically if the entire reserved quantity is withdrawn. It can also be set manually here, even if the full quantity is not withdrawn, if you have information that the remaining quantity is not required. If this indicator is set for a reservation item, the item will no longer be suggested when you issue goods with reference to reservation. This indicator can be reset here.

Deleting an Item

If a material no longer needs to be withdrawn, or if you entered an incorrect material number or plant, you can delete the item. You can delete an item either by updating the deletion indicator, or by choosing Edit ➤ Additional Functions ➤ Delete Item. After you save the data, the deletion indicator checkbox becomes gray and the item cannot be undeleted.

Data that cannot be Changed

You cannot change the movement type, or the account assignment. If the movement type or the account assignment is incorrect, you must delete the reservation and enter a new reservation. You also cannot change the material number or the plant for an item. If either of these entries is incorrect, you must delete the item and enter a new item.

28.2.5 Displaying a Reservation

You can display both manual and automatically reservations using transaction MB23.

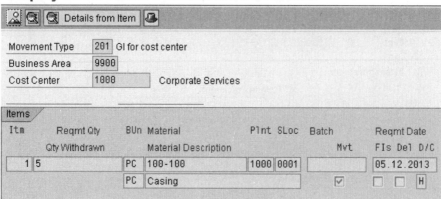

Display Reservation 0000066136 : Overview

28.2.6 Setting Movement Allowed Indicators

Purpose

When you create reservations, you may keep the movement allowed indicator blank to prevent accidental use of reservations. When the requirement date approaches, you want to set the movement allowed indicator.

Transaction

MBVR—Management Program: Reservations

Selection Screen

Base date

Select the base date that would determine the reservations for which movement allowed indicator is to be set.

Set goods movement to allowed

Select the checkbox ☑ Set Goods Movement to Allowed .

Configuration

Maintain view V_159L_R.

	Plnt	Name 1	MM	Days m	Rete	MRA
	1000	Werk Hamburg	☑	10	30	☐

In column ⟨Days m⟩ specify the period in calendar days for selecting reservations whose goods movement is to be allowed.

Execute

When you run transaction MBVR, movement allowed indicator is set for all reservations whose reservation requirement date is on or before `Base Date` + ⟨Days m⟩.

28.2.7   Posting Goods Movement based on Reservation

Purpose

You can perform goods movement with reference to a reservation.

Transaction

MIGO—Goods Movement (MIGO)

Selection

Item Detail

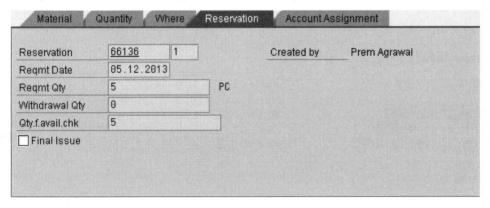

Posting Goods Issue

After the goods issue is entered, post it by clicking ⟨Post⟩. The system posts only those items for which ☑ Item OK indicator is set.

Goods Issue Slip

You can see/print the GR/GI slip and labels using transaction MB90. Choose `Processing mode` `2` for `Repeat processing`. If GR/GI slip and/or labels are not generated, print indicator may not have been set in the goods movement screen, or printing may not be enabled in Output Determination (see Chapter 24).

```
G R / G I   S L I P                         4900000080/0001
----------------------------------------------------------------
Posting date  : 05.12.2013
Current date  : 04.12.2013

Plant         : 1000
Description   : Werk Hamburg
----------------------------------------------------------------
Material      : 100-100
Batch         :
Description   : Casing

Quantity      :                  5   PC
----------------------------------------------------------------

Storage loc.  : 0001
Storage bin   :

Cost center   : 0000001000


----------------------------------------------------------------

Mvt. type   :    201 GI for cost center  Issued by : SAPUSER

----------------------------------------------------------------
```

Goods Issue Labels

```
Material: 100-100                  Material: 100-100
Vendor:                            Vendor:
Plant/SL: 1000 0001                Plant/SL: 1000 0001
GR/ GI Number: 4900000080          GR/ GI Number: 4900000080
GR/ GI Date: 05.12.2013            GR/ GI Date: 05.12.2013
```

Material Document

The material document can be displayed using transaction MB02 or MB03.

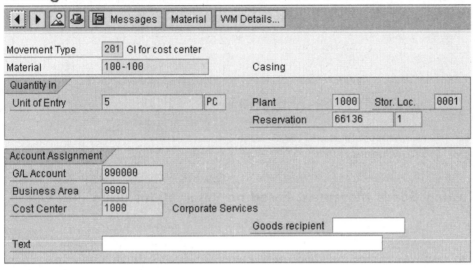

Accounting Documents

List of documents in accounting

In transaction MB02 or MB03 click | Accounting Documents... | in the item overview of the material document to see the accounting documents.

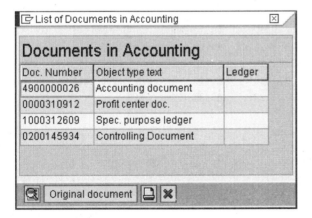

Accounting entries

Double-click the `Accounting document` to open it.

Data Entry View						
Document Number	4900000026	Company Code	1000	Fiscal Year		2013
Document Date	05.12.2013	Posting Date	05.12.2013	Period		12
Reference		Cross-CC no.				
Currency	EUR	Texts exist	☐	Ledger Group		

CoCd	Itm	PK	S	Account	Description	Amount	Curr.	Tx	Cost Ctr	Assignment
1000	1	99		790000	Unfinished products	568.80-	EUR			
	2	81		890000	Semi-finished prod.	568.80	EUR		1000	20131205

28.2.8   Posting Goods Movement based on Reservations using Pick List

Purpose

Pick list is an easy way of creating goods movement. You use existing data in the system, e.g. reservations and/or orders; enter the remaining data, e.g. storage location; change the proposed data, e.g. quantity; and post the goods movement.

Transaction

MB26—Picking list

Pick List

Material	Description	Q	U	Plant	RP	Stor	D	M	C	Reservati	Item	Co	Order
100-110	Slug for spiral casing	10	PC	1000	0	0001	H	261	☐	66118	1		60003225
100-120	Flat gasket	10	PC	1000	0	0001	H	261	☐	66118	2		60003225
100-130	Hexagon head screw	80	PC	1000	0	0001	H	261	☐	66118	3		60003225
100-100	Casing	5	PC	1000	0	0001	H	201	☐	66136	1	1000	

Filtering Items

You can filter the items according to different criteria using 🔽. However, when you post, even the filtered items get posted.

Deleting Items

If you do not want to post certain items, you should delete them from the pick list using 🗑. Note that deleting a reservation from the pick list does not delete the reservation itself.

Splitting Goods Movements

If you want to split goods movements for an item, for example, among various storage locations or vendors, choose `Edit` ➤ `Splitting`. A dialog box appears, in which you can distribute the quantity to be posted.

Posting Goods Movements

When you save, goods movements are posted.

28.2.9 Deleting a Reservation

Purpose

You can use this process to delete a specific reservation.

Transaction

MB22—Change Reservation

Initial Screen

| Reservation | |

Deleting a Reservation

After entering the reservation number in the initial screen, choose `Reservation` ➤ `Delete`. Confirm that you want to delete the reservation.

28.2.10 Deleting Completed and Unnecessary Reservations

Purpose

You should regularly delete completed, or unnecessary, reservations to keep the reservation list meaningful.

Completed reservations

When you issue the reserved quantity completely, the system sets the final issue indicator against the reservation item. Final issue indicator can also be set manually. Reservation items that are completed can be marked for deletion by the reservations management program. If all the items of a reservation are marked for deletion, the reservation is physically removed from the file.

Unnecessary reservations

Sometimes you make reservations for certain purpose, but later the scenario changes and you no longer need them. Ideally, you should delete these reservations as soon as they become unnecessary, but it may not always happen. SAP provides a facility to review the reservations whose requirement date is sufficiently in the past. After review, you can mark the unnecessary reservation items for deletion.

Transaction

MBVR—Administer Reservation

Selection Screen

Database selections

Database Selections				
Reservation		to		⇨
Base Date	10.02.2014			

Reservation

Here you can specify a range of reservations. Only those reservations which are in the specified range are selected. They may be further restricted by other selection criteria entered in the selection screen.

Base date

In this field, the system defaults the current date, which you can modify. This base date is used for computing the date for selecting reservations to be deleted.

Retention period

In column [Rete] of view V_159L_R you specify a retention period.

	Plnt	Name 1	Mvt	Days m	Rete	MRA
	1000	Werk Hamburg	☑	10	30	☐

The retention period signifies the period in calendar days for which completed reservation items are to be retained. It also signifies the period for which unused reservations are still considered needed. The system subtracts this period from the base date and all reservations whose base date is on or before this date are selected for setting deletion indicator/or for actual deletion if you have ticked ☑ Delete/Set Deletion Indicator . Note that when you create a reservation, you specify a base date in the initial screen. This base date is stored in the reservation header table RKPF.

Actions to be performed

Actions to be Performed
☑ Delete/Set Deletion Indicator
☑ Closed Items Only
☑ Set Goods Movement to Allowed
☑ Test Run
☑ Issue Log

Delete/set deletion indicator

If you select this checkbox, the system will check whether all the items of a reservation can be deleted. This is the case if the requirement date of the reservation item is earlier than the date calculated from 'base date–retention period'.

If all items of a reservation are marked as deleted, the entire reservation will be physically deleted. If this is not the case, those items that have fulfilled the deletion criteria will be marked with a deletion indicator. However, the reservation will remain in the system.

Closed items only

A closed item is one where quantity withdrawn is greater than or equal to reservation quantity, or the one which is marked with the 'final issue' indicator. If you set this indicator, only closed items are selected.

Set goods movement to allowed

You set this indicator to allow goods movement of selected reservation items as explained in Section 28.2.6. If you also select ☑ Delete/Set Deletion Indicator , the collective processing screen for the reservations to be deleted is displayed. Choose Goto ➤ Change Reservation Item to display the screen for the items to be changed.

Test run

You should select this field and the Issue log field if you want to start a test run. The system does not make any changes to the database, but issues a control list of the selected reservation items. You can select the items that are to be processed and then initiate the change to the database using the Save change function. If the indicator is not set, the database changes are made immediately.

Default value of this field is specified in the ☑ Batch Input field in view V_159B_MR where Program Name is RM07RVER Manage Reservations .

Program Name
RM07RVER Manage Reservations

Default values		
Session		
Maximum No. of Document Items		
☑ Batch Input		
☑ Issue Log		

Issue log

You tick this field to get a log of the actions carried out by the program.

Default value of the issue log field is specified in the ☑ Issue Log field in view V_159B_MR where Program Name is RM07RVER Manage Reservations .

Program Name

RM07RVER Manage Reservations

Default values

Session	
Maximum No. of Document Items	
☑ Batch Input	
☑ Issue Log	

Lock mode

Lock Mode

- ◉ Block Reservns Individually
- ○ Block Table of Reservations
- ○ Do Not Block Reservations

You can decide the lock mode you want to choose.

Block reservations individually

This option is suggested so that only the reservations that are actually changed are blocked. This can result in a number of lock entries.

Block table of reservations

To avoid this, you can select the Block Table of Reservations option. This means, however, that the update can only be carried out when no lock entries for reservations exist (regardless of whether these are suggested for change or not).

Do not block reservations

You should only choose the Do Not Block Reservations option if you have ensured that no one can make changes to manual reservations when the program is being run (using the function Change reservations or Goods movements with reference to reservations).

Restart report for blocked reservations

If the system finds that the reservations to be changed are blocked by other transactions, it issues an error log. For the blocked reservations, you must start the report again.

Account assignment

You can restrict the reservations selected to those having a specific account assignment.

Display options

In the list output, you can create/change layouts. You can select from these layouts here.

List Output

	Reserv.No.	Base date	To Delete
☐	66136	05.12.2013	X

Deletion in test mode

If you run the program in the test mode, you can select the reservations and delete them by clicking the save icon.

Deletion in non-test mode

If you do not select the test mode, all the selected reservations are deleted without any further input.

Issue log

If you have selected the Issue log indicator, you get a log of deleted reservations.

28.3 RESERVATION REPORTS

Functional Consultant	User	Business Process Owner	Senior Management	My Rating	Understanding Level
A	A	B	C		

28.3.1 Reservations List

Run transaction MB25 to display a list of reservations.

	Reserv.No.	Item	R	Reqmt Date	MvT	D	Material	Reqmt Qty	Difference qty	BUn	R	Account assign
	66118	1		15.07.2013	261	H	100-110	10	10	PC	F	000060003225
	66118	2		16.07.2013	261	H	100-120	10	10	PC	F	000060003225
	66118	3		16.07.2013	261	H	100-130	80	80	PC	F	000060003225
	66136	1		05.12.2013	201	H	100-100	5	5	PC	K	0000001000

From the output list, you can choose and display a reservation document. You can also see the stock overview of the material in the selected line.

28.3.2 Reservations in Stock Overview

Run transaction MMBE to see the stock overview of a material.

Client/Company Code/Plant/Storage Location/ ...	Unrestricted use	Qual. inspection	Reserved
▽ 🔷 Full	1,131.000	23.000	30.000
▽ 🔲 1000 IDES AG	1,131.000	23.000	30.000
▽ 🏭 1000 Werk Hamburg	1,131.000	23.000	30.000
▽ 🏢 0001 Materiallager	1,109.000	23.000	
Sales Order Stock	5.000		
Project Stock	3.000		
🏢 0002 Fertigwarenlager	12.000		
🏢 0088 Zentrallager WM	10.000		

This report also shows the reserved stock. If you create a reservation and run the report again, it shows the reserved quantity as well.

Client/Company Code/Plant/Storage Location/ ...	Unrestricted use	Qual. inspection	Reserved
▽ 🔷 Full	1,131.000	23.000	35.000
▽ 🔲 1000 IDES AG	1,131.000	23.000	35.000
▽ 🏭 1000 Werk Hamburg	1,131.000	23.000	35.000
▽ 🏢 0001 Materiallager	1,109.000	23.000	5.000
Sales Order Stock	5.000		
Project Stock	3.000		
🏢 0002 Fertigwarenlager	12.000		
🏢 0088 Zentrallager WM	10.000		

Note that the reserved quantity is not reduced from the unrestricted use quantity. It is listed for information. Also note that the reserved stock, whose requirement date is in future, is not shown. From the stock overview, you can click `Environment` ➤ `Reservations` to display a list of the reservations for the material.

28.3.3   Reservations in Current Stock/Requirements List

Run transaction MD04 to generate the list of stock and requirements at plant level.

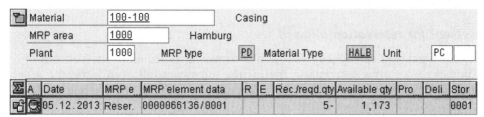

This report starts from stock and shows the expected receipts and requirements. In the partial screenshot above, it shows a `Rec./reqd.qty` of   5- on account of the reservation.

28.4   DEFAULT VALUES FOR RESERVATION

Functional Consultant	User	Business Process Owner	Senior Management	My Rating	Understanding Level
B	X	X	X		

28.4.1   Purpose

Here you set parameters for a plant, which are used in determining when the reservations can be deleted, when movements are allowed and whether the storage-location stock data is updated automatically when a reservation is posted for a material which does not exist in that storage location of the material master.

28.4.2   IMG Node

SM30 ➤ V_159L_R

28.4.3   Screen

Plnt	Name 1	Mvt	Days m	Rete	MRA
1000	Werk Hamburg	☑	10	30	☐

28.4.4   Primary Key

Plant

28.4.5   Important Fields

Plant, name 1

Default values for reservation are defined at plant level.

Goods movement for reservation allowed

For a reservation item you can specify that goods movements are allowed. You can only post a goods movement for a reservation item if the movement allowed indicator is set. Here you specify the default value of the movement allowed indicator of reservation items.

No. of days, if 'movement allowed' is set automatically

Transaction MBVR has the facility of setting movement allowed indicator as explained in Section 28.2.6.

Retention period

Transaction MBVR has the facility of deleting unnecessary reservations as explained in Section 28.2.10.

MRA

For a goods movement or reservation to take place in a storage location, the material master record for the storage location must exist. If the material master record for the storage location does not exist, reservation for the material in the storage location cannot be created. The system, however, has the functionality of automatic creation of the material master record for the storage location. When this indicator is set, the storage-location stock data is automatically created when a reservation is posted. This applies both to planned outward movements and planned receipts.

28.5   NUMBER ASSIGNMENT FOR RESERVATIONS

Functional Consultant	User	Business Process Owner	Senior Management	My Rating	Understanding Level
B	C	X	X		

28.5.1   Number Range Intervals for Reservations

You can use transaction OMJK to define number range intervals for reservations.

NR Object   MRES/DREQ

Intervals

No.	From number	To number	Current number	Ext
01	0000000001	0019999999	66055	☐
02	0020000000	0029999999		☑
10	0090000000	0099999999	90000059	☐
RS	0030000000	0039999999		☑

28.5.2   Number Range Assignment to Reservations

In transaction OMC2 you specify the number range for dependent requirements/reservations. You can choose only from the internal number range intervals defined in the node above.

No. range res/dep.rq
01

Physical Inventory

Functional Consultant	User	Business Process Owner	Senior Management	My Rating	Understanding Level
A	A	B	C		

29.1.1 Purpose

The purpose of physical inventory is to reconcile the physical stock with book stock. Physical inventory is a requirement for preparing the Balance Sheet. Physical inventory takes place at storage location level. If any differences are found, you may post the differences after proper investigation and approval.

29.1.2 Materials in a Storage Location

Physical inventory takes place at storage location level for the materials that belong to that storage location. Even if the book quantity for a material in a storage location is zero, you still check the physical balance. If the physical count is also zero, you update this information in the physical inventory document. If you actually find the material, you post the difference so that the information in the system tallies with the ground reality.

If, however, a material does not exist in a storage location, this means that no goods movement has ever taken place for the material in the storage location. The material, therefore, has never had any stock in this storage location. The material does not exist at stock management level in the storage location. It is therefore not possible to carry out a physical inventory for the material in this storage location.

29.1.3 Classification of Stocks

The stock you hold is classified in two ways.

General and special stocks

Stocks held for specific purposes, e.g. project stock or stock at non-company locations, e.g. at vendor or customer sites, are called special stocks. Stocks other than special stocks are called general stock. Each type of special stock and general stock are counted separately.

Stock types

Some of your stock may be under quality inspection. Similarly, some stock may be blocked because it is damaged etc. You count each of these stock types separately.

1	Warehouse
2	Quality inspection
3	Wrhse/QuInsp.(InvSa)
4	Blocked

29.1.4 Stock Management Unit

A company may have stock of a material in various plants, and within a plant in various storage locations. Further, there may be stock kept for a specific project or sales order. Considering all these factors, stock of a material is managed in stock management units. Stock management unit is a part of a stock of material which cannot be further subdivided and for which a separate book inventory exists. In transaction MI23 the inventory is reported at the level of stock management unit.

Material		Material Description		
Plnt Name 1				
SLoc Batch	S	Special stock descr. Assignmnt		STy
100-100		Casing		
1000 Werk Hamburg				
0001				1
0001				2
0001				4

As you can see, a stock management unit is a unique combination of the following.

➢ Material
➢ Plant
➢ Storage location
➢ Batch
➢ Special stock indicator
➢ Account assignment object for special stock, e.g. project, sales order etc.
➢ Stock type

Stock type has the following values.

STy	Stock type
1	Warehouse
2	Quality inspection
3	Wrhse/QuInsp.(InvSa)
4	Blocked

Stock type 3 is used in inventory sampling instead of stock types 1 and 2.

The book inventory is maintained at the level of stock management unit and counting in physical inventory also takes place at this level. In inventory sampling, the system decides which stock management units are counted and which are not.

29.1.5 Methods of Physical Inventory

SAP supports the following physical inventory procedures:

Periodic inventory

In a periodic inventory, all stocks of the company are physically counted on the balance sheet key date. In this case, every material must be counted. During counting, the entire warehouse must be blocked for material movements.

Continuous inventory

In the continuous inventory procedure, stocks are counted continuously during the entire fiscal year. In this case, it is important to ensure that every material is physically counted at least once during the year. Continuous inventory is used in Warehouse Management in SAP. In view V_T331_C you specify the type of inventory carried out for each storage type in a warehouse.

WNo	Typ	Invent.
001	001	PZ

You choose from the following options.

Inventory method	Short text
	No inventory
PZ	Continuous inventory
ST	Annual inventory

Cycle counting

Cycle counting is a method of physical inventory where inventory is counted at regular intervals within a fiscal year. These intervals (or cycles) depend on the cycle counting indicator set for the materials. You can use this method to count fast-moving items more frequently than slow-moving items. You may also count high value items more frequently than low value items.

Inventory sampling

In this method, randomly selected stocks of the company are physically counted on the balance sheet key date. If the variances between the result of the count and the book inventory balance are small enough, it is presumed that the book inventory balances for the other stocks are correct.

29.1.6 Process Steps

Typically, a physical inventory process has the following steps.

Creating physical inventory document

A physical inventory document is the document for carrying out physical inventory. It has a header and one or more items. The items are list of materials to be counted at stock management unit level. You can specify these materials yourself, but more likely, you will let the system specify the list of materials to be counted. A physical inventory document is at plant and storage location level. You may, therefore, create multiple physical inventory documents during a physical inventory process.

Printing physical inventory document

You print the physical inventory documents and give it to the persons who have to carry out the counting process. The printed document is also used for recording the result of the count.

Blocking materials for posting

Before you start counting, goods movement of the materials to be counted is frozen. This can be done either at the time of creating the physical inventory document, or just before starting the count.

Counting material and recording on the paper document

The persons responsible for counting count the material, and write it on the paper document. The document does not indicate what the count is expected to be, to prevent the possibility of someone adjusting his count.

Updating the count in the system

The count written on paper documents is updated in the system. The system shows the differences and gives a warning message if the difference exceeds the level defined in the initial screen of the count entry program. If you want a material to be recounted, you can specify that.

Viewing and investigating differences

After updating the count in the system, you can view the difference between the book inventory and the physical inventory. Some differences may be small in value and you may accept them without investigation, but some differences may be large in value or because of company policy may require further investigation, including recount.

Posting the difference

The counts updated in a physical inventory document remain in the document only and has no other effect. The physical inventory document can also be changed. You post the difference to create a goods movement with a material document and an accounting document. The material document adjusts the book inventory to bring it in line with the physical inventory count. The accounting document makes the required financial entries corresponding to the adjustment in the inventory. Posting the difference completes the physical inventory process and lifts the block on the movement of the material.

29.1.7 Documents in Physical Inventory

Physical inventory document

A physical inventory document is the document for carrying out physical inventory. It has a header and one or more items. The items are list of materials to be counted.

Material document

When you post the physical inventory difference, the system creates a material document that records the goods movement arising from posting the difference.

Accounting documents

When you post the physical inventory difference, the system creates a material document that records the goods movement arising from posting the difference and a set of accounting documents that contain the necessary accounting entries.

Accounting documents for inventory differences in company's own stock

When you post inventory differences, total stock is automatically adjusted to the counted quantity and the material master record shows the adjusted quantity. From the accounting point of view, this corresponds to a goods receipt or goods issue, meaning that when the inventory difference is posted, the stock account is debited or credited.

If the counted quantity is smaller than the book inventory balance, the stock account is credited with the value derived by multiplying inventory difference with price. The offsetting entry is made in the "Expense from physical inventory" account.

If the counted quantity is greater than the book inventory balance, the stock account is debited with the value derived by multiplying inventory difference with price. The offsetting entry is made to the "Income from physical inventory" account.

Since the amount posted is calculated on the basis of the current standard or moving average price, posting inventory differences does not lead to a price change.

Accounting documents for inventory differences in consignment stock

When you post inventory differences, the material master record is changed; the vendor consignment stock is automatically adjusted to the counted quantity. However, since the consignment stock belongs to the vendor, he must be paid if you reduce his stock. The offsetting entry is posted to the "Expenditure from inventory differences" account. Conversely, if you increase the consignment stock, accounting entries are the exact opposite.

29.2 CREATING A PHYSICAL INVENTORY DOCUMENT MANUALLY

Functional Consultant	User	Business Process Owner	Senior Management	My Rating	Understanding Level
A	A	C	X		

29.2.1 Purpose

Creating physical inventory document is the first step in physical inventory. You create a physical inventory document which contains the list of materials to be counted. You can specify these materials yourself as explained here. If you want the system to specify the list of materials to be counted, you can do so using transaction MI31 etc., as discussed in Section 29.3. A physical inventory document is at plant and storage location level. You may, therefore, create multiple physical inventory documents during a physical inventory process.

29.2.2 Transaction

MI01—Create a physical inventory document

29.2.3 Initial Screen

Document date	07.12.2013
Planned count date	07.12.2013

Loc.of phys.inv.

Plant	☑
Storage Location	
Special Stock	

Other information

- ☐ Posting Block
- ☐ Freeze book invntory
- ☑ Batches w. del. flag

Phys. inventory no.	
Phys. Inventory Ref.	
Grouping type	

When you create a physical inventory document, the data entered in the initial screen is copied in the header of the physical inventory document. Plant, storage location, special stock indicator, document date and grouping type fields are entered in the initial screen and cannot be modified in the header. Other fields can be modified in the header.

Batches with deletion flag

You select this field if you wish to include those batches of a material that are flagged for deletion in the physical inventory document. When you add an item in the physical inventory document, the system checks it according to this field.

29.2.4 Header

Click 🖫 to go to the physical inventory document header.

Loc. of phys.inv.		
Plant	1000	Werk Hamburg
Storage Location	0001	Materiallager
Special Stock		

Date and status			
Planned count date	07.12.2013	Posting period	0
Count date		Count status	
Posting Date		Adjustment status	
Document Date	07.12.2013	"Delete" status	
Created by	SAPUSER		

Other fields		
☐ Posting Block		
☐ Freeze book invntory		
Trans./Event Type	IB	Physical Inventory Document
Phys. inventory number		
Phys. inventory ref.		
Grouping type		
Grouping criterion		

Plant, storage location, special stock

To create a physical inventory document, you must enter the plant and the storage location. If you want to count special stock, you enter that too. These fields are copied from the initial screen in the document header and cannot be modified.

Planned count date

Planned count date is the date on which you plan to count the material. The planned count date determines the fiscal year in which the physical inventory document is posted. All postings involving this document must be effected during this fiscal year.

Count date

When you create the physical inventory document, this field is left blank. After the counting is done, you enter the actual counting date in transaction MI02.

Posting date

This field is automatically populated with the date on which you post the physical inventory document.

Document date

Document date is the date of the physical inventory document. It is copied from the initial screen.

Created by

This field is automatically populated by the system with the user name that created the physical inventory document.

Posting period

When you post the physical inventory document, the posting period is determined from the posting date.

Count status

The system determines the count status of the physical inventory document, based on the count status of the items in it.

Status	Description
Blank	No items have been counted
A	Some items have been counted
X	All items have been counted

Adjustment status

The system determines the adjustment status of the physical inventory document, based on the adjustment status of the items in it.

Status	Description
Blank	Differences have been posted for no items
A	Differences have been posted for some items
X	Differences have been posted for all items

Delete status

The system determines the delete status of the physical inventory document, based on the delete status of the items in it.

Status	Description
Blank	No items have been deleted
A	Some items have been deleted
X	All items have been deleted

Posting block, freeze book inventory

The timeline of physical inventory can be divided in the following parts.

Timeline	Goods movement	Method
Planning for physical counting	Optional	To block goods movement during this phase, set the ☐ Posting Block indicator while creating the physical inventory document.
		To allow goods movement during this phase, do not set the ☐ Posting Block indicator while creating the physical inventory document. Just before starting physical count, set the ☐ Posting Block indicator in the header of the physical inventory document using transaction MI02.
		The posting block indicator remains in the physical inventory document header even if the stock is unblocked through the posting of inventory differences. It then only indicates that a posting block was set for the documents.
Physical counting	Mandatory	During physical counting goods movement cannot be allowed.
Post processing of physical counting results	Optional	You should not set the ☐ Freeze book invntory indicator while creating the physical inventory document.
		To block goods movement during this phase, do not set the ☐ Freeze book invntory indicator during this phase.
		To allow goods movement during this phase, set the ☐ Freeze book invntory indicator in the header of the physical inventory document after completing physical count, using transaction MI02.
		When you set the ☐ Freeze book invntory indicator, a copy is made of the book stock and frozen. Physical inventory count is then compared with this frozen copy of the book stock. This method allows goods movements which change the book stock.

Transaction/event type

Transaction/event type is determined from transaction in view V_158_ALL.

Physical inventory number

During a physical inventory process, you will create multiple physical inventory documents. You can group them together using this field. This is an alphanumeric field and can be used to identify the physical inventory event, e.g. `Phys. inventory number` `PI on 1/4/2013` . You may also choose to divide the event and decide a physical inventory number for each department, for example.

Physical inventory reference

You can use this field to enter reference to an external document of any type.

Grouping type

Physical inventory documents can be created so that all items in the document have the same material group, or the same storage bin, depending on the value you choose in this field in the initial screen.

01	Material group
02	Storage bin

These are the only two grouping types, and they are defined in the domain of this field.

Grouping criterion

If you choose material group as the grouping type, you specify the material group here. When you enter items, the system ensures that you enter materials belonging to that material group only. Similarly, if you choose storage bin as the grouping type, you specify the storage bin here. When you enter items, the system ensures that you enter materials belonging to that storage bin only.

29.2.5 Items

You can add items in the physical inventory document by clicking 🗋.

Plant	1000	Werk Hamburg
Stor. Loc.	0001	Materiallager

Items

Itm	Material	Material Description	Batch	STy	AUn	BD	Del
1				1	☑	☑	☐
2				1	☑	☑	☐
3				1	☑	☑	☐
4				1	☑	☑	☐
5				1	☑	☑	☐
6				1	☑	☑	☐
7				1	☑	☑	☐
8				1	☑	☑	☐
9				1	☑	☑	☐
10				1	☑	☑	☐
11				1	☑	☑	☐

Plant, storage location and special stock

A physical inventory document is for a plant, storage location and special stock. In case you specify a special stock, e.g. stock for a project, you can also specify appropriate related field, e.g. WBS element. Physical inventory document items are stored in table ISEG.

Item number

A physical inventory document contains one or more items.

Material and description

Here you enter the material that is to be counted. You cannot do physical inventory of a material that does not have a material master record.

Batch

If a material is managed in batches, you enter the batch number here.

Stock type

You should count the material in warehouse, quality inspection and blocked stock separately. Here you enter the stock type that is to be counted.

1	Warehouse
2	Quality inspection
3	Wrhse/QuInsp.(InvSa)
4	Blocked

Alternative unit of measure

Normally counting in physical inventory takes place in the same unit as the stock keeping unit. However, for certain materials, it can take place in a different unit. Here you specify that. This can be done only if the system has the conversion factors necessary to convert quantities from one unit to another. These are kept in the material master and accessed by clicking ⇨ Additional data . You get additional tabs one of which is the Units of measure.

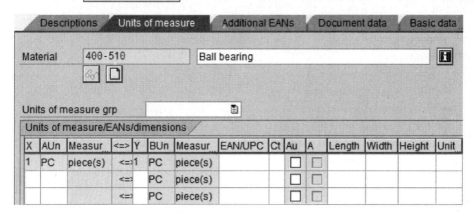

| Descriptions | Units of measure | Additional EANs | Document data | Basic data |

Material   400-510   Ball bearing

Units of measure grp

Units of measure/EANs/dimensions

X	AUn	Measur	<=>	Y	BUn	Measur	EAN/UPC	Ct	Au	A	Length	Width	Height	Unit
1	PC	piece(s)	<=>	1	PC	piece(s)			☐	☐				
			<=>		PC	piece(s)			☐	☐				
			<=>		PC	piece(s)			☐	☐				

Batch determination

If a material is managed in batches, you can enter the batch number in the batch field. If you do not enter the batch number, the system proposes the batches and you can manually select the batches to be counted.

If you set this indicator, all the batches of the material are automatically included as items in the physical inventory document. This process is carried out in the background, without any involvement of the user, adding items to the physical inventory document.

Delete indicator

If this checkbox is selected, the item is deleted from the physical inventory document.

29.2.6 Physical Inventory Document

You enter the materials and save. The system creates the physical inventory document. You can display it using transaction MI03 or change it using transaction MI02.

29.3 CREATING PHYSICAL INVENTORY DOCUMENTS FOR STANDARD STOCK

Functional Consultant	User	Business Process Owner	Senior Management	My Rating	Understanding Level
A	A	C	X		

29.3.1 Purpose

Although you can create physical inventory documents manually, you are unlikely to do so in normal circumstances. You would usually want to count all materials that have not been counted in the current period.

You can use transaction MI31 to create a batch input session, which creates physical inventory documents for standard stock without special stock. The system selects the materials based on the criteria entered in the initial screen and checks for each material whether the last physical inventory took place in the current period or in a previous period. If the last physical inventory has not been carried out in the current period, the system includes the material in the output list, which is used to create the physical inventory documents.

29.3.2 Transaction

MI31—Create Physical Inventory Documents without Special Stock

29.3.3 Initial Screen

Database Selections

Material		to	
Plant	1000	to	
Storage Location	0001	to	
Material Type		to	
Material Group		to	
Storage Bin Description		to	
☑ Materials Marked for Deletion			

Control

- ○ Select data and issue log
- ◉ Generate Batch Input   Name of Session   MB_MI01
- ○ Create dcmts directly   ☐ Hold processed sessions

- ☑ Issue Log
- Max. No. Items/Doc.   20
- No. Mtls to be Included

Selection Acc. to Stock Balance

▶   Acc. to Stck

Data in Phys. Inv. Docmt Header

Planned Count Date	07.12.2013	☐ Set posting block
Physical Inventory Number		☐ Freeze book inv.bal.
Phys. Inventory Ref.		

Sorting

▶   Sorting

Display Options

Layout

Database Selections

Here you specify the criteria for selection of materials for which physical inventory is to be carried out. If you do not select the 'Materials marked for deletion', materials marked for deletion at plant level are not included.

Control

Steps in creating physical inventory documents

```
Control
  ◉ Select data and issue log
  ○ Generate Batch Input
  ○ Create dcmts directly
```

You can create physical inventory documents in 3, 2, or 1 steps depending on the choice you make. The process is essentially the same and is described in Section 29.3.4. You can specify the name of the session. The default name comes from view V_159B. You should not change the default name, so that these sessions are easily identified in transaction SM35.

Hold processed sessions

If this indicator is not set, sessions that do not have errors will be deleted after they are processed. Sessions in which errors occurred are not deleted. You can display the sessions, using transaction SM35.

Issue log

You select this indicator to get a log onscreen after processing.

Maximum number of items per document

Here you can specify the maximum number of items per document. If the number of selected items is more than this number, the system generates multiple documents. All these documents can be linked through the physical inventory number specified in this screen.

Number of materials to be included

You can use this field to restrict the number of materials that are to be included in the physical inventory. However, you will have no knowledge of the materials that were not included as a result of this restriction.

Selection According to Stock Balance

Selection Acc. to Stock Balance

▼	Acc. to Stck		
Threshold Value for Stock		☐ Exclude from selectio
SP Threshold Value for VO Mat.		☐ Exclude from selectio
☐ Only Materials with Zero Stock		
☐ Only Materials W/o Zero Stock		
☐ Only Materials with Negative Stock		
Stock Types		
☑ Unrestricted Use	☐ Incl. Matls Subj. to Phys. Inv.
☑ In Quality Inspection	☐ Incl. Btchs Subj. to PhysInv
☐ Blocked	
☐ Value-Only Matls	

You can use various features of stock balance to select materials for which physical inventory is to be carried out. Many of these fields are self explanatory. Others are explained below.

Threshold value for stock, exclude from selection

Here you specify the maximum stock level in base unit of measure up to which materials are selected. Note that this is not the monetary value of stock. You can use the ☐ Exclude from selectio indicator to invert the selection.

Sales price threshold value for value-only material, exclude from selection

Here you specify the maximum stock level (at sales values) up to which value-only materials are selected. You can use the ☐ Exclude from selectio indicator to invert the selection.

Include materials subject to physical inventory

In continuous inventory, you would want to select only those items which have not been inventoried in the current fiscal year. If this indicator is not set, only the non-inventoried materials will be selected. However, if you want to select even those materials that have already been inventoried in the current fiscal year, you set this indicator.

Include batches subject to physical inventory

In continuous inventory, you would want to select only those batches which have not been inventoried (for example, batches that have been newly created since the last physical inventory). If this indicator is not set, only the non-inventoried batches will be selected. However, if you want to select even those batches that have already been inventoried, you set this indicator.

Data in Physical Inventory Document Header

Planned count date

Here you specify the date on which counting is planned. This date is copied in the headers of all physical inventory documents generated by this process.

Physical inventory number

You can use physical inventory number (a number or term of your choice) to group physical inventory documents that belong together. This allows you to display the physical inventory documents for a particular month or department directly without having to search the list of inventory differences.

Physical inventory reference

You can use this field to enter reference to an external document of any type.

Posting block

When you are counting a material, you do not want any goods movement to take place for that material. You can block goods movement of materials in the physical inventory document by selecting this indicator. The block is lifted when the count of physical inventory is posted. However, this indicator remains in the physical inventory document header even if the stock is unblocked through the posting of inventory differences. It then only indicates that a posting block was set for the documents.

If the counting is to take place at a later date, you may not create posting block when creating the physical inventory document. You can create the posting block later using transaction MI02 or via batch input.

Freeze book inventory

This indicator specifies that the book inventory balances of those items in a physical inventory document that have not yet been counted are frozen.

This indicator has the effect that the current book inventory balance is recorded in the physical inventory document. The system compares the counted stock with the frozen book inventory balance to determine any inventory differences.

If the count results are not entered immediately after the stock has been counted, it is useful to set this indicator so that any goods movements which may take place in the meantime will not change the book inventory balance relevant to the physical inventory.

Sorting

Sorting	
▼ Sorting	
◉ Plant - SLoc. - Material	
○ Plant - SLoc. - Stor. Bin Description - Material	
☐ Storage Bin Description -> Document Header	
○ Plant - StorLoc. - Matl Group - Material	
☐ Matl Group -> Docmt Header	
☐ New Document Created when Group Changed	

You can sort the content of a physical inventory document to facilitate the counting process. If you specify that the storage bin description or material group be in the document header, you should also select the 'new document created when group changed' indicator. Then, the physical inventory document is split when the storage bin description or material group changes. These multiple physical inventory documents are linked through the physical inventory number.

Diaplay Options

Layout

In the list output, you can create/change layouts. You can select from these layouts here.

29.3.4   Creating Physical Inventory Documents

After entering the data in selection screen, click ⊕.

Material list

The program selects the materials, carries out all checks and reports errors, if any.

Plnt	SLoc	Material	Batch	STy	Bin	Matl Group	PhysInvDoc	
Msg.	Note							Status
☐ 1000	0001	100-110		2		001		
☐ 1000	0001	100-120		1		001		
☐ 1000	0001	100-120		2		001		
☐ 1000	0001	100-130		1		001		
☐ 1000	0001	100-130		2		001		

Note that the list does not show material number 100-110 with stock type 1 because it has already been included in a physical inventory document. You can select the items manually, or select all items by clicking 📇.

Generate batch session

You can then generate batch session by clicking | Generate Session |.

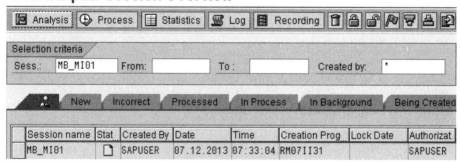

Plnt	SLoc	Material	Batch	STy	Bin	Matl Group	PhysInvDoc	
Msg.	Note						Status	
1000	0001	100-110		2		001		
							Batch Input	
1000	0001	100-120		1		001		
							Batch Input	
1000	0001	100-120		2		001		
							Batch Input	
1000	0001	100-130		1		001		
							Batch Input	
1000	0001	100-130		2		001		
							Batch Input	

Process batch session

You can | Process Session | to create the physical inventory documents.

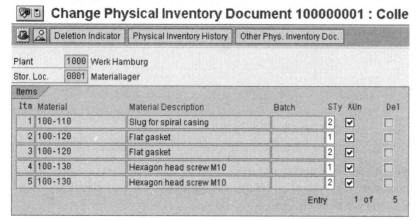

Batch Input: Session Overview

☒ Analysis	⊕ Process	▤ Statistics	☒ Log	▤ Recording	🗑 🔒 🔓 📝 🖨 📋

Selection criteria					
Sess.:	MB_MI01	From:	To :	Created by:	*

🔍	New	Incorrect	Processed	In Process	In Background	Being Created

	Session name	Stat	Created By	Date	Time	Creation Prog	Lock Date	Authorizat.
	MB_MI01	🗋	SAPUSER	07.12.2013	07:33:04	RM07II31		SAPUSER

Select the session and click | ⊕ Process |.

Display physical inventory document

You can display the physical inventory document so created using transaction MI02 or MI03.

📝📋 Change Physical Inventory Document 100000001 : Colle

🖨 👤	Deletion Indicator	Physical Inventory History	Other Phys. Inventory Doc.

Plant	1000 Werk Hamburg
Stor. Loc.	0001 Materiallager

Items						
Itm	Material	Material Description	Batch	STy	AUn	Del
1	100-110	Slug for spiral casing		2	☑	☐
2	100-120	Flat gasket		1	☑	☐
3	100-120	Flat gasket		2	☑	☐
4	100-130	Hexagon head screw M10		1	☑	☐
5	100-130	Hexagon head screw M10		2	☑	☐
			Entry	1 of	5	

29.4 CREATING PHYSICAL INVENTORY DOCUMENTS FOR SPECIAL STOCKS

Functional Consultant	User	Business Process Owner	Senior Management	My Rating	Understanding Level
A	A	C	X		

The previous section explained the functionality for material which does not belong to a special stock. All transactions for creating physical inventory document work in the same way. The selection screen has appropriate additional fields, e.g. vendor, customer, WBS element etc. Choices in sort order are also appropriately adjusted. Default name of the session differs from transaction to transaction.

29.4.1 Vendor Consignment

Run transaction MIK1 to create physical inventory documents for vendor consignment. The output contains special stock indicator and vendor.

Plnt	SLoc	Material	Batch	S	Vendor	STy	Bin	Matl Group	PhysInvDoc
Msg.	Note								Status
☐ 1000	0001	1300-550		K	1000	1		002	
☐ 1000	0001	1300-550		K	1000	2		002	
☐ 1000	0001	1300-550		K	1005	1		002	
☐ 1000	0001	1300-550		K	1005	2		002	

29.4.2 Sales Order

Run transaction MIE1 to create physical inventory documents for sales order. The output contains special stock indicator and sales order number.

Plnt	SLoc	Material	Batch	S	Document	Item	STy	Bin	Matl Group	PhysInvDoc
Msg.	Note									Status
☐ 1000	0001	1300-100		E	44	10	1			
☐ 1000	0001	1300-100		E	44	10	2			
☐ 1000	0001	1300-100		E	56	10	1			
☐ 1000	0001	1300-100		E	56	10	2			

29.4.3 Project

Run transaction MIQ1 to create physical inventory documents for project. The output contains special stock indicator and WBS element.

Plnt	SLoc	Material	Batch	S	WBS Element	STy	Bin	Matl Group	PhysInvDoc
Msg. Note							Status		
☐ 1000	0001	T-FP200	C1	Q	I/5001-1	1			00107
☐ 1000	0001	100-100		Q	T-20301	1			001
☐ 1000	0001	P-2002	C1	Q	I/5000-1-2-1	1			00107

29.4.4 Returnable Transport Packaging

Run transaction MIM1 to create physical inventory documents for returnable transport packaging. The output contains special stock indicator and vendor.

Plnt	SLoc	Material	Batch	S	Vendor	STy	Bin	Matl Group	PhysInvDoc
Msg. Note							Status		
☐ 3000	0002	TCC-C-A		M	1002	1			00804

29.4.5 Consignment at Customer

Run transaction MIW1 to create physical inventory documents for consignment at customer. The output contains special stock indicator and customer.

Plnt	Material	Batch	S	Customer	STy	Matl Group	PhysInvDoc
Msg. Note							Status
☐ 1000	L-120		W	1171	1	003	
☐ 1000	L-120		W	1175	1	003	

29.4.6 Returnable Packaging with Customer

Run transaction MIV1 to create physical inventory documents for returnable packaging at customer. The output contains special stock indicator and customer.

Plnt Material Msg. Note	Batch	S Customer	STy Matl Group PhysInvDoc	Status
☐ 3000 TCC-P-1		V 3000	1 00803	
☐ 3000 TCC-P-2		V 3000	1 00803	

29.4.7 Material Provided to Vendor

Run transaction MIO1 to create physical inventory documents for material provided to vendor. The output contains special stock indicator and vendor.

Plnt Material Msg. Note	Batch	S Vendor	STy Matl Group PhysInvDoc	Status
☐ 1000 100-120		O 1000	1 001	
☐ 1000 100-120		O 1111	1 001	

29.5 CHANGING A PHYSICAL INVENTORY DOCUMENT

Functional Consultant	User	Business Process Owner	Senior Management	My Rating	Understanding Level
A	A	C	X		

29.5.1 Purpose

You can change a physical inventory document after it has been created.

29.5.2 Transaction

MI02—Change Physical Inventory Document

29.5.3 Initial Screen

Phys. Inventory Doc.	☑
Fiscal Year	

29.5.4 Header

You can click 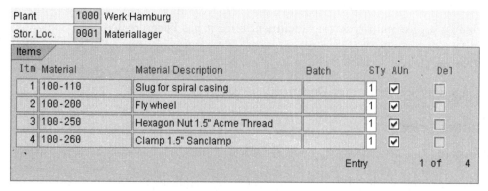 to display the header.

Loc.of phys.inv.		
Plant	1000	Werk Hamburg
Storage Location	0001	Materiallager
Special Stock		

Date and status			
Planned count date	07.12.2013	Posting period	0
Count date		Count status	
Posting Date		Adjustment status	
Document Date	07.12.2013	"Delete" status	
Created by	SAPUSER		

Other fields	
☐ Posting Block	
☐ Freeze book invntory	
Trans./Event Type	IB Physical Inventory Document
Phys. inventory number	
Phys. inventory ref.	
Grouping type	
Grouping criterion	

The system allows you to change only certain header fields.

29.5.5 Items

You can click 🖉 in the initial screen or 🖳 in the header to change the items in the physical inventory document.

Plant	1000	Werk Hamburg
Stor. Loc.	0001	Materiallager

Items						
Itm	Material	Material Description	Batch	STy	AUn	Del
1	100-110	Slug for spiral casing		1	☑	☐
2	100-200	Fly wheel		1	☑	☐
3	100-250	Hexagon Nut 1.5" Acme Thread		1	☑	☐
4	100-260	Clamp 1.5" Sanclamp		1	☑	☐

Entry   1 of   4

You can change the stock type and alternative unit of entry of the items.

Creating items

You can click [□] to create more items in the physical inventory document.

Deleting items

You can click [🗑] to update the deletion flag in the physical inventory document. If you set the deletion indicator for an item, the item remains in the document but cannot be processed. This will unblock the material.

Changing items

The system allows you to change the stock type and alternative unit indicator of an item.

Recounting items

You can choose Additional Functions ➤ Recount to call transaction MI11 to recount items.

29.5.6 Physical Inventory History

Uncounted items

Select an item and click Physical Inventory History to see its physical inventory history.

Material	100-110	Slug for spiral casing
Location of phys.inv.		
Plant	1000	Werk Hamburg
Stor. Location	0001	Materiallager
Stock type	Warehouse	

Promotions	
Phys.inv.status	Not yet counted

Counted items

If the item has been counted, the system shows the difference between book quantity and counted quantity.

Material	100-200	Fly wheel

Location of phys.inv.

Plant	1000	Werk Hamburg
Stor. Location	0001	Materiallager
Stock type	Warehouse	

Promotions

Phys.inv.status	Counted		
Count date	08.12.2013	Counted by	SAPUSER

Quantities and values

Quantity	902	PC		
Book quantity	900	PC	Ext.sales value	0.00
Difference qty	2.000	PC	Book value	0.00

29.6 DISPLAYING A PHYSICAL INVENTORY DOCUMENT

Functional Consultant	User	Business Process Owner	Senior Management	My Rating	Understanding Level
A	A	C		X	

You can display a physical inventory document using transaction MI03. This transaction works in the same way as transaction MI02 (Change Physical Inventory Document), except that you cannot change any data in this transaction.

29.7 DELETING A PHYSICAL INVENTORY DOCUMENT

Functional Consultant	User	Business Process Owner	Senior Management	My Rating	Understanding Level
A	A	C		X	

You can delete a physical inventory document using transaction MI02. In the initial screen you specify the physical inventory document number and the fiscal year and click 🗑. If you delete a document, it is physically deleted if there are no inventory difference postings for its items. If a difference has been posted, the document is proof of the posting. Therefore, it is simply flagged for deletion. This means it can then be displayed, but no longer processed. The document is physically deleted when the transaction MIAD is run next.

29.8 PRINTING A PHYSICAL INVENTORY DOCUMENT

Functional Consultant	User	Business Process Owner	Senior Management	My Rating	Understanding Level
A	A	C	X		

29.8.1 Purpose

You may print physical inventory document for different purposes. You may print uncounted items for giving them to persons who have to count the materials. You may print counted items for review by the person controlling the physical inventory process.

29.8.2 Transaction

MI21—Print Physical Inventory Document

29.8.3 Initial Screen

Physical Inventory Document		to		⇨
Fiscal Year		to		⇨
Plant		to		⇨
Storage Location		to		⇨
Planned Count Date		to		⇨
Physical Inventory Number		to		⇨
Phys. Inventory Ref.		to		⇨

Grouping Criterion

Material Group		to		⇨
Storage Bin		to		⇨

Status Selection for

☐ Phys. Inventory Documents
☐ Phys. Inventory Items

Setting

☐ Sort By Special Stock
Output Device
☐ New Spool Request
☐ Expand Value-Only Matls
Sorting of Serial Numbers

Status selection for physical inventory documents

If you select this checkbox, you can specify the status of physical inventory documents that should be selected for printing.

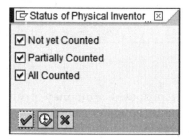

Status selection for physical inventory items

If you select this checkbox, you can specify the status of physical inventory items that should be selected for printing.

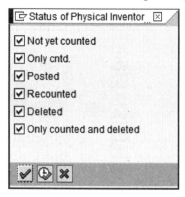

You can also select both these indicators.

29.8.4 Physical Inventory Document Printout

```
Plant              : 1000
Description        : Werk Hamburg
Phys. inv. doc.    : 100000000
Created by         : SAPUSER
Planned count date : 07.12.2013
Phys. inv. reference:
Phys. inv. no.     :
----------------------------------------------------------
Itm  Material            Batch      SLoc Stor. bin
     Mat. short text                Stock type
     Status of item                 Counted qty.    Un
----------------------
001  100-110                        0001
     Slug for spiral casing         Warehouse
     Not yet counted                _____  PC
002  100-200                        0001
     Fly wheel                      Warehouse
     Not yet counted                _____  PC
003  100-250                        0001
     Hexagon Nut 1.5" Acme Thread   Warehouse
     Not yet counted                _____  PC
004  100-260                        0001
     Clamp 1.5" Sanclamp            Warehouse
     Not yet counted                _____  PC


                   Date      Signature
```

You can change the format of the Physical Inventory Document Printout to suit your specific needs. For more details, see Section 29.36.

29.9 BLOCKING GOODS MOVEMENT DURING PHYSICAL INVENTORY

Functional Consultant	User	Business Process Owner	Senior Management	My Rating	Understanding Level
A	A	C	X		

29.9.1 Timeline of Physical Inventory

Timeline	Goods movement	Method
Planning for physical counting	Optional	To block goods movement during this phase, set the ☐ Posting Block indicator while creating the physical inventory document.
		To allow goods movement during this phase, do not set the ☐ Posting Block indicator while creating the physical inventory document. Just before starting physical count, set the ☐ Posting Block indicator in the header of the physical inventory document using transaction MI02.
		The posting block indicator remains in the physical inventory document header even if the stock is unblocked through the posting of inventory differences. It then only indicates that a posting block was set for the documents.
Physical counting	Mandatory	During physical counting goods movement cannot be allowed.
Post processing of physical counting results	Optional	You should not set the ☐ Freeze book invntory indicator while creating the physical inventory document.
		To block goods movement during this phase, do not set the ☐ Freeze book invntory indicator during this phase.
		To allow goods movement during this phase, set the ☐ Freeze book invntory indicator in the header of the physical inventory document after completing physical count, using transaction MI02.
		When you set the ☐ Freeze book invntory indicator, a copy is made of the book stock and frozen. Physical inventory count is then compared with this frozen copy of the book stock. This method allows goods movements which change the book stock.

29.9.2 Setting Posting Block for One Physical Inventory Document

When you are counting a material, you do not want any goods movement to take place for that material. You can block goods movement of materials in the physical inventory document by selecting the posting block indicator while creating the physical inventory document (transaction MI01, MI31 etc.) or while changing the physical inventory document (transaction MI02).

29.9.3 Setting Posting Block for Multiple Physical Inventory Documents

Although you can set posting block for one physical inventory document at a time, that is not what you usually do. Once you have completed preparation for physical inventory and printed all physical inventory documents, you set posting block for all items in all posting documents and go ahead with counting, entering and posting the count, and posting difference if any.

29.9.4 Transaction

MI32—Block Material for Multiple Physical Inventory Documents

29.9.5 Initial Screen

Status selection for physical inventory documents

If you select ☑ Phys. Inv. Documents , when you execute the program you get the following dialog box in which you can specify the status of physical inventory documents to be selected.

Grouping criterion

You may have created physical inventory documents by specifying material groups or storage bins. In that case, you may like to select physical inventory documents for blocking on the same basis.

Data in physical inventory header

If you specified a physical inventory number or a physical inventory reference while generating physical inventory documents, you can select them by specifying the same.

Set/reset posting block

You can use this report not only to set posting blocks, but also to reset them.

Batch input session

You can generate batch input session, whose name you specify. You can specify that a log be issued onscreen after processing.

29.9.6   Generating Batch Input Session

Click ⊕ to generate a batch input session. The batch input session has the name specified in the initial screen.

29.9.7   Processing Batch Input Session

You can process the batch input session using transaction SM35. When the batch input session is processed, it sets block for the physical inventory document items.

29.10   COUNTING THE MATERIAL

Functional Consultant	User	Business Process Owner	Senior Management	My Rating	Understanding Level
A	A	C	X		

After you have blocked the movement of materials, you count them and record the count on the physical inventory documents. After counting the material you enter the count in the system, view the difference, and post the difference. After the difference is posted, the system lifts the block on goods movement. If you want to start the goods movement at the earliest, you can freeze book inventory.

29.11   FREEZING BOOK INVENTORY FOR ONE PHYSICAL INVENTORY DOCUMENT

Functional Consultant	User	Business Process Owner	Senior Management	My Rating	Understanding Level
A	A	C	X		

29.11.1   Purpose

After you have counted the material, you want to restart goods movement without waiting for posting the difference in material count.

29.11.2   Timeline of Physical Inventory

The timeline of physical inventory can be divided in the following parts.

Timeline	Goods movement	Method
Planning for physical counting	Optional	To block goods movement during this phase, set the ☐Posting Block indicator while creating the physical inventory document.
		To allow goods movement during this phase, do not set the ☐Posting Block indicator while creating the physical inventory document. Just before starting physical count, set the ☐Posting Block indicator in the header of the physical inventory document using transaction MI02.
		The posting block indicator remains in the physical inventory document header even if the stock is unblocked through the posting of inventory differences. It then only indicates that a posting block was set for the documents.
Physical counting	Mandatory	During physical counting goods movement cannot be allowed.

Timeline	Goods movement	Method
Post processing of physical counting results	Optional	You should not set the ☐ Freeze book invntory indicator while creating the physical inventory document.
		To block goods movement during this phase, do not set the ☐ Freeze book invntory indicator during this phase.
		To allow goods movement during this phase, set the ☐ Freeze book invntory indicator in the header of the physical inventory document after completing physical count, using transaction MI02.
		When you set the ☐ Freeze book invntory indicator, a copy is made of the book stock and frozen. Physical inventory count is then compared with this frozen copy of the book stock. This method allows goods movements which change the book stock.

29.11.3   Allowing Freezing of Book Inventory

In view V_T001L_I you specify whether freezing of book inventory is permitted for a storage location.

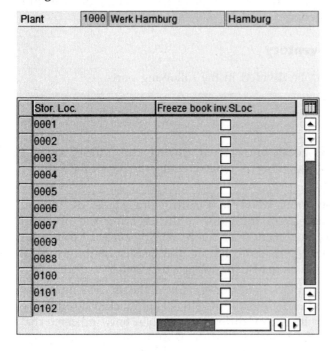

29.11.4   Transaction

MI02—Change Physical Inventory Document

29.11.5   Freezing Book Inventory

You can click 🔳 to display the header.

Loc.of phys.inv.		
Plant	1000	Werk Hamburg
Storage Location	0001	Materiallager
Special Stock		

Date and status			
Planned count date	07.12.2013	Posting period	0
Count date		Count status	
Posting Date		Adjustment status	
Document Date	07.12.2013	"Delete" status	
Created by	SAPUSER		

Other fields		
☐ Posting Block		
☐ Freeze book invntory		
Trans./Event Type	IB	Physical Inventory Document
Phys. inventory number		
Phys. inventory ref.		
Grouping type		
Grouping criterion		

Select ☐ Freeze book invntory and save to freeze book inventory for the physical inventory document. When book entries are frozen, the system updates the book quantity for all items in the physical inventory document. Book quantity is otherwise entered in the physical inventory document, when count for an item is saved.

29.12 FREEZING BOOK INVENTORY FOR MULTIPLE PHYSICAL INVENTORY DOCUMENTS

Functional Consultant	User	Business Process Owner	Senior Management	My Rating	Understanding Level
A	A	C	X		

29.12.1 Purpose

It may be too much effort to freeze book inventory one physical inventory document at a time. You can freeze book inventory of multiple documents simultaneously.

29.12.2 Transaction

MI33—Freeze Book Inventory

29.12.3 Initial Screen

Selection Criteria

Physical Inventory Document		to	
Fiscal Year		to	
Plant		to	
Planned Count Date		to	

Grouping Criterion

| Material Group | | to | |
| Storage Bin | | to | |

Changeable Data in Phys. Inv. Doc. Header

Physical Inventory Number

Phys. Inventory Ref.

Planned Count Date

◉ Freeze book inv. balances

◯ Reset book inv. balances

Batch Input Session

☐ Generate batch input   Name of Session   `MB_MI02`

☑ Issue log

29.12.4 Generating Batch Input Session

Click 🕒 to generate a batch input session. The batch input session has the name specified in the initial screen.

29.12.5   Processing Batch Input Session

You can process the batch input session using transaction SM35. When the batch input session is processed, it updates count for the physical inventory document items.

29.13   ENTERING THE INVENTORY COUNT

Functional Consultant	User	Business Process Owner	Senior Management	My Rating	Understanding Level
A	A	C	X		

29.13.1   Purpose

You count the material printed in the physical inventory document, and record it on the same document. You then enter the inventory count from the printed physical inventory document into the system.

29.13.2   Transaction

MI04—Enter Inventory Count

29.13.3   Initial Screen

Phys. Inventory Doc.	☑
Fiscal Year	2013

Date	
Count Date	08.12.2013

Other Information	
Variance in %	

Count date

The count date you enter here is copied in the header of the physical inventory document.

Variance in %

If you want to be notified of large inventory differences, enter a percentage value in this field. If the difference in the quantity of stock counted and book inventory is above this percentage, the system issues a warning message on entry of count results.

29.13.4 Header

Click 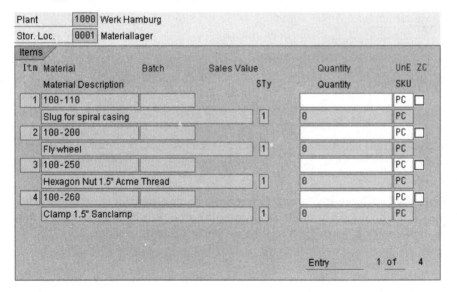 to go to the physical inventory document header.

Loc.of phys.inv.		
Plant	1000	Werk Hamburg
Storage Location	0001	Materiallager
Special Stock		

Date and status			
Planned count date	07.12.2013	Posting period	201312
Count date	08.12.2013	Count status	
Posting Date		Adjustment status	
Document Date	07.12.2013	"Delete" status	
Created by	SAPUSER		

Other fields	
☐ Posting Block	
☐ Freeze book invntory	
Trans./Event Type	IB Physical Inventory Document
Phys. inventory number	
Phys. inventory ref.	
Grouping type	
Grouping criterion	

29.13.5 Items

Click ⬅ to go back to the physical inventory document items.

Plant	1000	Werk Hamburg
Stor. Loc.	0001	Materiallager

Itm	Material	Batch	Sales Value		Quantity		UnE	ZC
	Material Description			STy	Quantity		SKU	
1	100-110						PC	☐
	Slug for spiral casing			1	0		PC	
2	100-200						PC	☐
	Fly wheel			1	0		PC	
3	100-250						PC	☐
	Hexagon Nut 1.5" Acme Thread			1	0		PC	
4	100-260						PC	☐
	Clamp 1.5" Sanclamp			1	0		PC	

Entry   1 of   4

Quantity in unit of entry and unit of entry

Here you enter the quantity in the unit of entry and the unit of entry. The system displays in quantity in the stock keeping unit as well as the stock keeping unit by doing the necessary conversion.

Setting zero count

If a quantity of zero was counted for an item, you enter this by setting the zero count indicator. It is not sufficient to enter 0 in the Quantity column because the system interprets a zero as "not yet counted".

If there are many items in a physical inventory document with zero quantity, you do not need to set the zero count indicator for each item individually. You first enter all non-zero quantities. You then click $\boxed{\text{Set Zero Count}}$ icon to set the zero count indicator for all remaining items. You can also use transaction MI35 to set zero count indicators for multiple physical inventory documents at the same time.

29.13.6 Posting the Count

After entering the count, you post (save) the data.

29.14 ENTERING THE INVENTORY COUNT IN BATCH MODE

Functional Consultant	User	Business Process Owner	Senior Management	My Rating	Understanding Level
A	A	C	X		

29.14.1 Purpose

Material is counted based on physical inventory documents and the count is recorded thereon. From these physical inventory documents, the count may be entered in the system using transaction MI04 as explained in the previous section. However, sometimes one finds it easier to create a file of inventory counts and upload in the system. This section describes this process. This program generates a batch input session (BI session) which, when processed, enters the inventory count results with reference to a physical inventory document.

29.14.2 Transaction

MI34—Enter Count

29.14.3 Initial Screen

Name of Logical File	MMIM_PHYSICAL_INVENTORY_DOCUMENTS

Processing Control

☑ Issue Log
☐ Hold Processed Sessions
☐ Test Data

Name of logical file

The data for the batch input session is imported from an external dataset as a sequential file. The structure of the sequential file is pre-allocated by the table BISEG. See the program documentation on guidelines for preparing the file. Here you specify the name of logical file containing the inventory count data that you want to upload. The link between the logical file name and the physical file is maintained in view V_FILENACI, which is applicable to all clients. You can also maintain client specific file names using transaction SF01.

Issue log

Here you specify that a log be issued onscreen after processing.

Hold processed sessions

If this indicator is not set, sessions that do not have errors are deleted after they are processed. Sessions in which errors occurred are not deleted. Set this indicator if you do not want the processed sessions to be deleted. You can see the sessions using transaction SM35.

Test data

You can run this program with test data. To do so, set this indicator, maintain test data in view V_159I, and ensure that the specified file contains no productive data. When you run the program, test data is written from table T159I to the sequential file, before the sequential file is processed by the program to generate the batch session.

29.14.4 Generating Batch Input Session

Click 🔄 to generate a batch input session. The batch input session has the name specified in the initial screen.

29.14.5 Processing Batch Input Session

You can process the batch input session using transaction SM35. When the batch input session is processed, it updates count for the physical inventory document items.

29.15   SETTING THE INVENTORY COUNT TO ZERO IN BATCH MODE

Functional Consultant	User	Business Process Owner	Senior Management	My Rating	Understanding Level
A	A	C	X		

29.15.1   Purpose

During physical inventory there may be many items that have no stock. It would be nice if the count for all these items can be set to zero in one go. This program is designed to do that. You first update the count for all items that have stock, and then run this program to set the stock of remaining items to zero.

29.15.2   Transaction

MI35—Set Zero Count

29.15.3   Initial Screen

Selection Criteria			
Physical Inventory Document		to	
Fiscal Year		to	
Plant		to	
Planned Count Date		to	
Physical Inventory Number		to	

Grouping Criterion			
Material Group		to	
Storage Bin		to	

Changeable Data in Phys. Inv. Doc. Header
Count Date

Batch Input Session
☐ Generate Batch Input   Name of Sess.   `MB_MI02`
☑ Issue Log

29.15.4   Generating Batch Input Session

Click ⊕ to generate a batch input session. The batch input session has the name specified in the initial screen.

29.15.5 Processing Batch Input Session

You can process the batch input session using transaction SM35. When the batch input session is processed, it sets the count to zero for those physical inventory document items whose count is not updated before running this program.

29.16 ENTERING COUNT WITHOUT DOCUMENT REFERENCE

Functional Consultant	User	Business Process Owner	Senior Management	My Rating	Understanding Level
A	A	C	X		

29.16.1 Purpose

Normally you create the physical inventory document, print it, count material, record it on the paper document and enter the count in the system. However, sometimes you count the material first, and want to update it in the system.

29.16.2 Transaction

MI09—Enter Inventory Count without Document Reference

29.16.3 Initial Screen

Count date	☑
Document date	☑

Loc.of phys.inv.	
Plant	☑
Storage Location	
Special Stock	

Other information	
Phys. inventory no.	
Phys. Inventory Ref.	
Variance in %	
Grouping type	

The data you enter here is copied in the header of the physical inventory document. If the difference in book count and physical count exceeds the value specified in the Variance in % field, the system gives warning.

29.16.4 Header

Loc.of phys.inv.

Plant	1000	Werk Hamburg
Storage Location	0001	Materiallager
Special Stock		

Date and status

Planned count date		Posting period	201310
Count date	31.10.2013	Count status	
Posting Date		Adjustment status	
Document Date	31.10.2013	"Delete" status	
Created by	SAPUSER		

Other fields

☐ Posting Block
☐ Freeze book invntory

Trans./Event Type	IZ	Phys. Inv. Doc. and Count
Phys. inventory number		
Phys. inventory ref.		
Grouping type		
Grouping criterion		

29.16.5 Items

Plant	1000	Werk Hamburg
Stor. Loc.	0001	Materiallager

Items

Itm	Material	Batch	Sales Value		Quantity	UnE	ZC
	Material Description			STy	Quantity	SKU	
1							☐
				1	0.000		
2							☐
				1	0.000		
3							☐
				1	0.000		
4							☐
				1	0.000		

Here you enter both the material as well as counted quantity along with unit of entry.

29.16.6 Posting the Count

When you save, the system generates a physical inventory document

⊘ Count entered for phys. inv. doc. 100000002 .

29.16.7 Displaying the Physical Inventory Document

You can display the physical inventory document using transaction MI03. Select the item and click | Physical Inventory History | .

🖫🗐 Display Physical Inventory History 100000002 / 001

| ◀ | ▶ | Other Item... | Display Material Document |

| Material | 100-100 | Casing |

Location of phys.inv.

Plant	1000	Werk Hamburg
Stor. Location	0001	Materiallager
Stock type	Warehouse	

Promotions

| Phys.inv.status | Counted | | |
| Count date | 08.12.2013 | Counted by | SAPUSER |

Quantities and values

Quantity	1,125	PC		
Book quantity	1,104	PC	Ext.sales value	0.00
Difference qty	21.000	PC	Book value	0.00

Note that the system has created a physical inventory document and entered the count in it.

29.17 ENTERING COUNT WITHOUT DOCUMENT REFERENCE USING BATCH INPUT

Functional Consultant	User	Business Process Owner	Senior Management	My Rating	Understanding Level
A	A	C	X		

29.17.1 Purpose

Normally you create the physical inventory document, print it, count material, record it on the paper document and enter the count in the system. However, sometimes you count the material first, and want to update it in the system. You can do so using transaction MI09 as explained in the previous section. However, sometimes you want to update the count from a file. This section describes this scenario.

29.17.2 Transaction

MI39—Document/Count

29.17.3 Initial Screen

Name of Logical File	MMIM_PHYSICAL_INVENTORY_NO_DOCUMENTS
Max. Number of Items	20
User Name in Document	SAPUSER

Processing Control
- ☑ Issue Log
- ☐ Hold Processed Sessions
- ☐ Test Data

Name of logical file

The data for the batch input session is imported from an external dataset as a sequential file. The structure of the sequential file is pre-allocated by the table BISEG. See the program documentation on guidelines for preparing the file. Here you specify the name of logical file containing the inventory count data that you want to upload. The link between the logical file name and the physical file is maintained in view V_FILENACI, which is applicable to all clients. You can also maintain client specific file names using transaction SF01.

Maximum number of items

Even though you are entering count without a physical inventory document, the system must create one in order to maintain the audit trail of the physical inventory activities. If the number of items are large, you may like to create multiple physical inventory documents, each containing a number of items not exceeding the value specified here.

User name in document

Here you specify the user name that will appear in the header of the physical inventory documents generated by this program.

Issue log

Here you specify that a log be issued onscreen after processing.

Hold processed sessions

If this indicator is not set, sessions that do not have errors are deleted after they are processed. Sessions in which errors occurred are not deleted. Set this indicator if you do not want the processed sessions to be deleted. You can see the sessions using transaction SM35.

Test data

You can run this program with test data. To do so, set this indicator, maintain test data in view V_159I, and ensure that the specified file contains no productive data. When you run the program, test data is written from table T159I to the sequential file, before the sequential file is processed by the program to generate the batch session.

29.17.4 Generating Batch Input Session

Click ⊕ to generate a batch input session. The batch input session has the name specified in the initial screen.

29.17.5 Processing Batch Input Session

You can process the batch input session using transaction SM35. When the batch input session is processed, it updates the count for the physical inventory document items.

29.18 RECOUNTING A PHYSICAL INVENTORY DOCUMENT ITEM

Functional Consultant	User	Business Process Owner	Senior Management	My Rating	Understanding Level
A	A	C	X		

29.18.1 Purpose

Sometimes it may be felt that certain items in a physical inventory document need to be recounted.

29.18.2 Transaction

MI11—Recount Physical Inventory Items

29.18.3 Initial Screen

Phys. Inventory Doc.	100000000
Fiscal Year	2013

Date

Planned count date	10.12.2013
Document Date	10.12.2013

Other Information

	☐ Posting Block
	☐ Freeze book invntory
Phys. Inventory No.	
Phys. Inventory Ref.	
Threshold Value	

Enter the data and click Selection Screen .

29.18.4 Items

Plant	1000	Werk Hamburg
Stor. Loc.	0001	Materiallager

Items

	Itm	Material	Batch	STy	Difference qty	BUn	Difference amt.
		Material Description			Diff. sales value		PhysInvDoc
☑	1	100-110		1	5.000-	PC	0.00
		Slug for spiral casing			0.00		100000000 1
☐	2	100-200		1	2.000	PC	114.96
		Fly wheel			0.00		100000000 2
☐	3	100-250		1	0.000	PC	0.00
		Hexagon Nut 1.5" Acme Thread			0.00		100000000 3
☐	4	100-260		1	4.000	PC	11.80
		Clamp 1.5" Sanclamp			0.00		100000000 4
						Entry	1 Of 4

Select the items you want to recount. Uncounted items or the items for which differences have been posted, cannot be selected. Post (save) the document. The system creates a new physical inventory document and displays its number ⊘ Physical inventory document 100000003 created .

29.18.5 New Document

Display the newly created physical inventory document using transaction MI02.

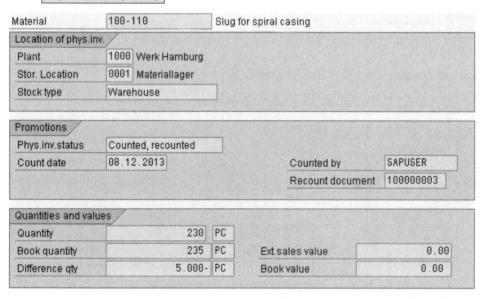

Note that it contains the item you want to recount.

29.18.6 Old Document

Display the old physical inventory document using transaction MI02. Select the item and click Physical Inventory History .

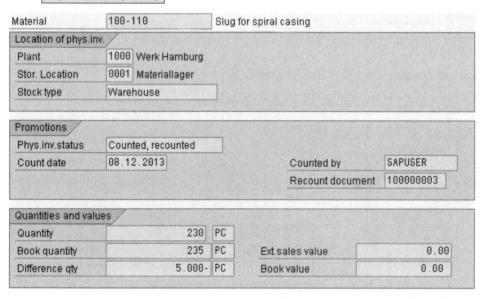

Note that the item shows Phys.inv.status   Counted, recounted   and Recount document   100000003 .
The recounted item is deactivated in the original document and can no longer be processed via that document.

29.19 CHANGING THE INVENTORY COUNT

Functional Consultant	User	Business Process Owner	Senior Management	My Rating	Understanding Level
A	A	C	X		

29.19.1 Purpose

You can change the count of an item. If difference is not posted, you can change the quantity or set/unset the zero count indicator.

29.19.2 Transaction

MI05—Change Inventory Count

29.19.3 Initial Screen

Phys. Inventory Doc.	100000000
Fiscal Year	2013

Other Information

Variance in %	

29.19.4 Items

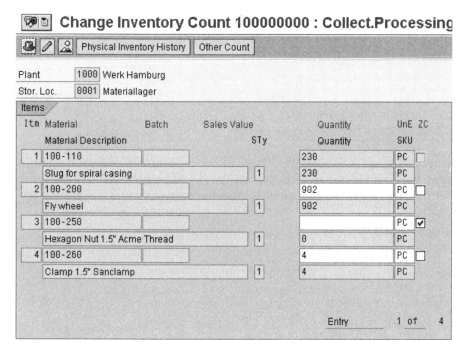

Change Inventory Count 100000000 : Collect.Processing

Physical Inventory History   Other Count

Plant	1000 Werk Hamburg
Stor. Loc.	0001 Materiallager

Items

Itm	Material	Batch	Sales Value		Quantity	UnE	ZC
	Material Description			STy	Quantity	SKU	
1	100-110				230	PC	☐
	Slug for spiral casing			1	230	PC	
2	100-200				902	PC	☐
	Fly wheel			1	902	PC	
3	100-250					PC	☑
	Hexagon Nut 1.5" Acme Thread			1	0	PC	
4	100-260				4	PC	☐
	Clamp 1.5" Sanclamp			1	4	PC	

Entry   1 of   4

Note that you cannot change the count of item number 1, for which recount has been ordered. That count must be entered in the new physical inventory document created for that purpose using transaction MI04.

You change inventory count only if you discover an error in counting either accidentally or while investigating the difference. If the difference is already posted, you must create a new physical inventory document, enter the count, and post the difference arising due to new count.

29.19.5 Effect of Changing the Count

Change the count of an item, save and display the document again using transaction MI05.

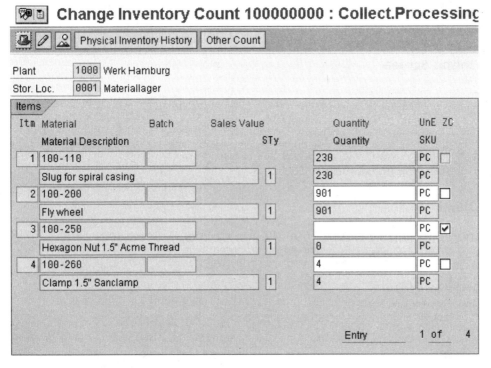

The physical inventory document shows the changed count. You can change it again if you want. Changing the count is just an error correction. If you want to maintain an audit trail of changes in physical inventory documents, you have to activate ☑ Change Document in view V_159L_EI.

29.20 DISPLAYING THE INVENTORY COUNT

Functional Consultant	User	Business Process Owner	Senior Management	My Rating	Understanding Level
A	A	C	X		

29.20.1 Purpose

You can display a physical inventory document with counted quantities.

29.20.2 Transaction

MI06—Display Inventory Count

29.20.3 Initial Screen

Phys. Inventory Doc.	100000000
Fiscal Year	2013

29.20.4 Header

Display Inventory Count 100000000: Header

Other Count

Loc.of phys.inv.

Plant	1000	Werk Hamburg
Storage Location	0001	Materiallager
Special Stock		

Date and status

Planned count date	07.12.2013	Posting period	201312
Count date	08.12.2013	Count status	X
Posting Date		Adjustment status	
Document Date	07.12.2013	"Delete" status	
Created by	SAPUSER		

Other fields

☐ Posting Block
☐ Freeze book invntory

Trans./Event Type	IB	Physical Inventory Document
Phys. inventory number		
Phys. inventory ref.		
Grouping type		
Grouping criterion		

29.20.5 Items

⚙️▣ Display Inventory Count 100000000: Overview

| 🔲 📇 Position... | Physical Inventory History | Statistics... | Other Phys. Inventory Doc. |

Plant   `1000` Werk Hamburg
Stor. Loc.   `0001` Materiallager

Items

Itm	Material	Batch	Sales Value		Quantity	UnE	ZC
	Material Description			STy	Quantity	SKU	
1	100-110				230	PC	☐
	Slug for spiral casing			1	230	PC	
2	100-200				901	PC	☐
	Fly wheel			1	901	PC	
3	100-250				0	PC	☑
	Hexagon Nut 1.5" Acme Thread			1	0	PC	
4	100-260				4	PC	☐
	Clamp 1.5" Sanclamp			1	4	PC	

Entry _____ 1 of 4

29.20.6 Statistics

You can display statistics by clicking | Statistics... |.

▣ Display Statistics	☒
Number of items	`4`
Open	`0`
Counted	`4`
Cleared	`0`
Recounted	`1`
Deleted	`0`

Cleared

This field shows the number of items for which adjustment postings have been made in respect of any differences found. For these items, the physical inventory process can be regarded as completed.

Recounted

Note that if an item is flagged for recounting, it also remains in the list of counted items.

29.20.7 Physical Inventory History

You can select an item and see its Physical Inventory History .

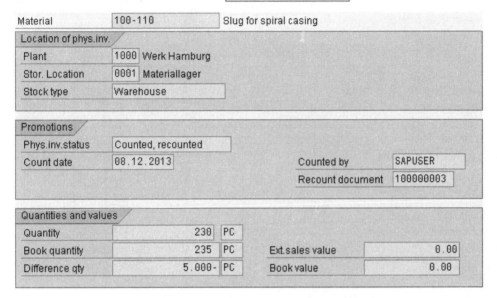

| Material | 100-110 | Slug for spiral casing |

Location of phys.inv.		
Plant	1000	Werk Hamburg
Stor. Location	0001	Materiallager
Stock type	Warehouse	

Promotions			
Phys.inv.status	Counted, recounted		
Count date	08.12.2013	Counted by	SAPUSER
		Recount document	100000003

Quantities and values			
Quantity	230 PC		
Book quantity	235 PC	Ext.sales value	0.00
Difference qty	5.000- PC	Book value	0.00

29.21 REVIEWING DIFFERENCES

Functional Consultant	User	Business Process Owner	Senior Management	My Rating	Understanding Level
A	A	C	X		

29.21.1 Purpose

You may like to see the inventory differences before posting.

29.21.2 Transaction

MI20—Difference List

29.21.3 Initial Screen

Database Selection

Material	to	⇨
Plant	to	⇨
Storage Location	to	⇨
Batch	to	⇨
Physical Inventory Document	to	⇨
Physical Inventory Number	to	⇨

Status Sel. for

☐ Phys. Inventory Documents

☐ Phys. Inventory Items

List Scope

Special Stock	to	⇨
Fiscal Year	to	⇨
Count Date	to	⇨
Planned Count Date	to	⇨
Phys. Inventory Ref.	to	⇨
Reason for Inventory Diff.	to	⇨
Threshold Value		

Display Options

Layout

List Display

◉ Single List

○ Group by Plant and Storage Location

○ Group by Physical Inventory Document

29.21.4 Difference List

PhysInvDoc	Item	Material	Plnt	SLoc	Book quantity	Qty Counted	Difference qty	BUn	Difference amt.	Crcy	S
☐ 100000002	1	100-100	1000	0001	1,104.000	1,125.000	21.000	PC	2,388.96	EUR	
☐ 100001160	1	100-100	1000	0001	1,105.000	1,075.000	30.000-	PC	3,412.80	EUR	
☐ 100001191	2	T-REL15	1000	0001	0.000	0.000	0.000	PC	0.00	EUR	
☐ 100001191	3	T-REL16	1000	0001	0.000	5.000	5.000	PC	255.65	EUR	
☐ 100001215	1	400-400	1000	0001	0.000	602.000	602.000	PC	21,184.38	EUR	

29.21.5 Actions in Difference List

Posting difference

You select the item and click Post Difference . The system takes you to transaction MI07, where you can post the difference.

Changing count

You select the item and click Change Count to change the count of the item. The system takes you to transaction MI05 in which you can change the count.

Entering count

If you have not entered the count for all items, you can select an item, and thereby the document, and click Enter Count . The system takes you to transaction MI04 in which you can enter the count.

List of un-posted documents

You may have old physical inventory documents where count was entered but difference was not posted. You can list these un-posted documents that cannot be posted now. Display all physical inventory documents; do not restrict your selection to exclude old physical inventory documents. Click List of Unposted Docs . The system lists un-posted documents that cannot be posted now.

Plnt	SLoc	PhysInvDoc	Doc. Date	Pstng Date	PBl	St.	ASt
1000	0001	100001160	09.05.2006			X	
1000	0001	100001191	19.05.2006	12.05.2006	X	A	A
1000	0001	100001215	14.05.2006			X	

It is only prudent to delete these documents using transaction MI02.

29.22 POSTING THE DIFFERENCE

Functional Consultant	User	Business Process Owner	Senior Management	My Rating	Understanding Level
A	A	C	X		

29.22.1 Purpose

You can post the difference between book quantity and physical inventory quantity. This step completes the physical inventory process and removes the block on the goods movement of the material. If there is a difference in the book quantity and the count of the material, it creates a goods movement for the difference and creates a material and an accounting document.

29.22.2 Transaction

MI07—Post the Difference

29.22.3 Initial Screen

Phys. Inventory Doc.	100000000
Fiscal Year	2013

Date

Posting Date	10.12.2013

Other Information

Threshold Value	

29.22.4 Header

Loc.of phys.Inv.

Plant	1000	Werk Hamburg
Storage Location	0001	Materiallager
Special Stock		

Date and status

Planned count date	07.12.2013	Posting period	201312
Count date	08.12.2013	Count status	X
Posting Date	10.12.2013	Adjustment status	
Document Date	07.12.2013	"Delete" status	
Created by	SAPUSER		

Other fields

☐ Posting Block
☐ Freeze book invntory

Trans./Event Type	IB	Physical Inventory Document
Phys. inventory number		
Phys. inventory ref.		
Grouping type		
Grouping criterion		

29.22.5 Items

Plant	1000	Werk Hamburg
Stor. Loc.	0001	Materiallager

	Itm	Material	Batch	ST	Difference qty	BUn	Difference Amnt	Reas.
							Diff. Sales Value	
☐	1	100-110		1	5.000-	PC	0.00	
							0.00	
☑	2	100-200		1	1.000	PC	57.48	
							0.00	
☑	3	100-250		1	0.000	PC	0.00	
							0.00	
☑	4	100-260		1	4.000	PC	11.80	
							0.00	

Entry   1 of   4

29.22.6 Pre-Selection of Proposed Items

When you run transaction MI07, the system inserts all the items of a physical inventory document in which there is a difference between book inventory and physical inventory count. You can select the items for which you want to post the difference. If you want, the system can give all these items preselected, and you can manually deselect items that you do not want to post. This setting is made in view V_158_I.

	Transaction Code	Transaction Text	Proposed preselec.
	MI07	Process List of Differences	☑

29.22.7 Entering Reason for Difference

SAP allows you to enter the reason for difference before you post the difference. The property of this field can be set in transaction OMJU.

Modifiable field	Field name	Input	Req.	Disp.	Hide	HiLi
Reason for inventory diff.	ISEG-GRUND	◉	○	○	○	☐

Posting of inventory difference generates goods movement (movement types 701 to 718). For each of these movement types, reasons can be configured in view V_157D_VC.

29.22.8 Posting the Difference

Click 🖫 to post the difference in selected items. The system creates a material document for goods movement resulting from the posting of difference.

✅ Diffs in phys. inv. doc. 100000000 posted with m. doc. 4900000081

29.22.9 Physical Inventory Document after Posting the Difference

Display the physical inventory document using transaction MI02. Select an item and click
Physical Inventory History .

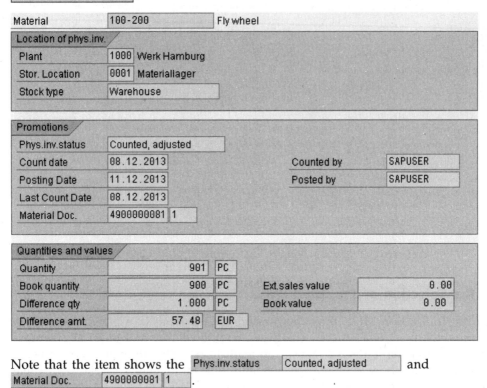

Note that the item shows the Phys.inv.status Counted, adjusted and
Material Doc. 4900000081 1 .

29.22.10 Material Document for Posting of Difference

You can see the material document using transaction MB03.

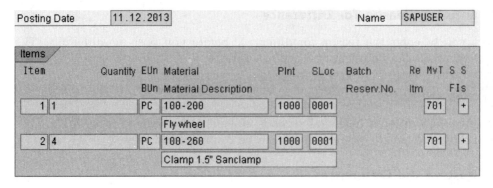

29.22.11 Accounting Documents for Posting of Difference

List of documents in accounting

In transaction MB02 or MB03 click | Accounting Documents... | in the item overview of the material document to see the accounting documents.

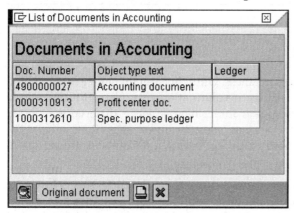

Accounting entries

Double-click the | Accounting document | to open it.

Data Entry View								
Document Number	4900000027	Company Code	1000		Fiscal Year		2013	
Document Date	07.12.2013	Posting Date	11.12.2013		Period		12	
Reference		Cross-CC no.						
Currency	EUR	Texts exist	☐		Ledger Group			

CoCd	Itm	PK	S	Account	Description	Amount	Curr.	Tx	Cost Ctr	Assignment
1000	1	89		790000	Unfinished products	57.48	EUR			
	2	91		283000	Gain - inventory dif	57.48-	EUR			20131211
	3	89		310000	Trading Goods	11.80	EUR			
	4	91		283000	Gain - inventory dif	11.80-	EUR			20131211

29.23 POSTING THE DIFFERENCE FOR MULTIPLE PHYSICAL INVENTORY DOCUMENTS

Functional Consultant	User	Business Process Owner	Senior Management	My Rating	Understanding Level
A	A	C	X		

29.23.1 Purpose

Physical inventory is an exercise that disrupts business. Until physical inventory is completed goods movement cannot take place. The exercise involves a large number of items. While the management definitely wants to investigate items having large difference in book versus physical inventory, it cannot and does not want to investigate items where the difference is small. It usually sets a threshold value up to which differences are accepted.

You can use transaction MI07 to post differences for items in one physical inventory document. You can also select the items where you want to post the difference. However, during physical inventory, management lacks patience. SAP therefore provides transaction MI37 where you can post differences up to specified threshold value in multiple physical inventory documents. This program generates a batch input session which, when processed, posts inventory differences.

Posting of inventory differences is not possible until a count has been performed for the items of the physical inventory document. The program only includes those physical inventory document items in the batch input session which have already been counted and for which the inventory differences have not yet been posted.

29.23.2 Transaction

MI37—Post Difference

29.23.3 Initial Screen

Selection Criteria				
Physical Inventory Document		to		⇨
Fiscal Year		to		⇨
Plant		to		⇨
Storage Location		to		⇨
Planned Count Date		to		⇨

Status Selection for
☐ Phys. Inv. Documents

Grouping Criterion				
Material Group		to		⇨
Storage Bin		to		⇨

PhysInvDoc.header				
Posting Date	03.12.2013			
Physical Inventory Number		to		⇨

Batch Input Session			
☑ Generate batch input	Name of Session	MB_MI07	
☑ Issue Log	Threshold Value		
☐ Hold Processed Sessions	Reason f. Difference		

29.23.4 Generating Batch Input Session

Click ⊕ to generate a batch input session. The batch input session has the name specified in the initial screen.

29.23.5 Processing Batch Input Session

You can process the batch input session using transaction SM35. When the batch input session is processed, it posts difference for the physical inventory document items.

29.24 ENTERING COUNT AND POSTING DIFFERENCE

Functional Consultant	User	Business Process Owner	Senior Management	My Rating	Understanding Level
A	A	C	X		

29.24.1 Purpose

You can enter the count and post the difference in a single step. The system lets you enter the quantity as well as the reason for difference, if any.

29.24.2 Transaction

MI08—Count/Difference

29.24.3 Initial Screen

Phys. Inventory Doc.	100000001
Fiscal Year	2013

Date	
Count Date	11.12.2013

Other Information	
Variance in %	

29.24.4   Header

Loc.of phys.inv.		
Plant	1000	Werk Hamburg
Storage Location	0001	Materiallager
Special Stock		

Date and status			
Planned count date	07.12.2013	Posting period	201312
Count date	11.12.2013	Count status	
Posting Date	11.12.2013	Adjustment status	
Document Date	07.12.2013	"Delete" status	
Created by	SAPUSER		

Other fields	
☐ Posting Block	
☐ Freeze book invntory	
Trans./Event Type	IB Physical Inventory Document
Phys. inventory number	
Phys. inventory ref.	
Grouping type	
Grouping criterion	

29.24.5   Items

Plant	1000	Werk Hamburg
Stor. Loc.	0001	Materiallager

Itm	Material	Batch	Sales Value		Quantity	UnE	ZC
	Material Description		STy	Reas.	Quantity	SKU	
1	100-110				1	PC	☐
	Slug for spiral casing		2		0	PC	
2	100-120				1420	PC	☐
	Flat gasket		1		0	PC	
3	100-120					PC	☑
	Flat gasket		2		0	PC	
4	100-130					PC	☐
	Hexagon head screw M10		1		0	PC	

Entry   1 of   5

Enter the count. It is not necessary to enter the count for all items.

29.24.6 Posting the Difference

Click 🖫 to post the difference in selected items. The system creates a material document for goods movement resulting from the posting of difference.

> ✓ Diffs in phys. inv. doc. 100000001 posted with m. doc. 4900000082

29.24.7 Material Document for Posting of Difference

You can see the material document using transaction MB03.

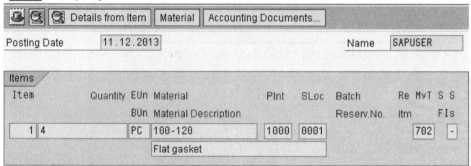

29.24.8 Accounting Documents for Posting of Difference

List of documents in accounting

In transaction MB02 or MB03 click [Accounting Documents...] in the item overview of the material document to see the accounting documents.

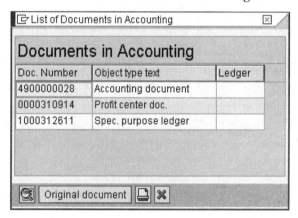

Accounting entries

Double-click the | Accounting document | to open it.

Data Entry View						
Document Number	4900000028	Company Code	1000	Fiscal Year		2013
Document Date	07.12.2013	Posting Date	11.12.2013	Period		12
Reference		Cross-CC no.				
Currency	EUR	Texts exist	☐	Ledger Group		

CoCd	Itm	PK	S	Account	Description	Amount	Curr.	Tx	Cost Ctr	Assignment
1000	1	99		300000	Inventory - Raw Mate	47.09	EUR			
	2	81		233000	Losses - inventory v	47.09	EUR			20131211

29.25 ENTERING COUNT AND POSTING DIFFERENCE IN BATCH MODE

Functional Consultant	User	Business Process Owner	Senior Management	My Rating	Understanding Level
A	A	C	X		

29.25.1 Purpose

You can use this program to enter count and post difference for one or more physical inventory documents using a batch input file. You can use this method only if the corresponding physical inventory documents have been created in the system.

29.25.2 Transaction

MI38—Count/Difference

29.25.3 Initial Screen

Name of Logical File	MMIM_PHYSICAL_INVENTORY_DOCUMENTS
Processing Control	
☑ Issue Log	
☐ Hold Processed Sessions	
☐ Test Data	

Name of logical file

The data for the batch input session is imported from an external dataset as a sequential file. The structure of the sequential file is pre-allocated by the table BISEG. See the program documentation on guidelines for preparing the file. Here you specify the name of logical file containing the inventory count data that you want to upload. The link between the logical file name and the physical file is maintained in view V_FILENACI, which is applicable to all clients. You can also maintain client specific file names using transaction SF01.

Issue log

Here you specify that a log be issued onscreen after processing.

Hold processed sessions

If this indicator is not set, sessions that do not have errors are deleted after they are processed. Sessions in which errors occurred are not deleted. Set this indicator if you do not want the processed sessions to be deleted. You can see the sessions using transaction SM35.

Test data

You can run this program with test data. To do so, set this indicator, maintain test data in view V_159I, and ensure that the specified file contains no productive data. When you run the program, test data is written from table T159I to the sequential file, before the sequential file is processed by the program to generate the batch session.

29.25.4 Generating Batch Input Session

Click 🔽 to generate a batch input session. The batch input session has the name specified in the initial screen.

29.25.5 Processing Batch Input Session

You can process the batch input session using transaction SM35. When the batch input session is processed, both the count and the difference are posted for the physical inventory document items.

29.26 ENTERING COUNT WITHOUT DOCUMENT REFERENCE AND POSTING THE DIFFERENCE

Functional Consultant	User	Business Process Owner	Senior Management	My Rating	Understanding Level
A	A	C	X		

29.26.1 Purpose

You can combine all the steps of physical inventory: creating a physical inventory document, posting count and posting difference. When you run transaction MI10, the system creates a physical inventory document with header and items. In the items screen, you can enter the material and the count in a single step and screen.

29.26.2 Transaction

MI10—Enter Difference w/o Document Reference

29.26.3 Initial Screen

Count date	11.12.2013
Document date	11.12.2013

Loc.of phys.inv.

Plant	1000
Storage Location	0001
Special Stock	

Other information

Phys. inventory no.	
Phys. Inventory Ref.	
Variance in %	
Grouping type	

29.26.4 Header

Loc.of phys.inv.

Plant	1000	Werk Hamburg
Storage Location	0001	Materiallager
Special Stock		

Date and status

Planned count date		Posting period	201312
Count date	11.12.2013	Count status	
Posting Date	11.12.2013	Adjustment status	
Document Date	11.12.2013	"Delete" status	
Created by	SAPUSER		

Other fields

☐ Posting Block		
☐ Freeze book invntory		
Trans./Event Type	ID	Phys. Inv. Doc., Count and Difference
Phys. inventory number		
Phys. inventory ref.		
Grouping type		
Grouping criterion		

29.26.5 Items

Click ⬚ to enter items and counted quantities.

Plant	1000	Werk Hamburg				
Stor. Loc.	0001	Materiallager				

Items

Itm	Material	Batch	Sales Value		Quantity		UnE ZC
	Material Description			STy Reas.	Quantity		SKU
1	100-101				140		☐
				1	0.000		
2							☐
				1	0.000		
3							☐
				1	0.000		
4							☐
				1	0.000		

29.26.6 Posting the Count and Difference

When you save 💾, both the count and difference are posted and goods movement and material document are created.

✓ Diffs in phys. inv. doc. 100000004 posted with m. doc. 4900000083

29.26.7 Physical inventory Document

In this transaction you entered count without a physical inventory document. The system, therefore, creates one and records the count and the difference. See the physical inventory document using transaction MI02. Select the item and click Physical Inventory History .

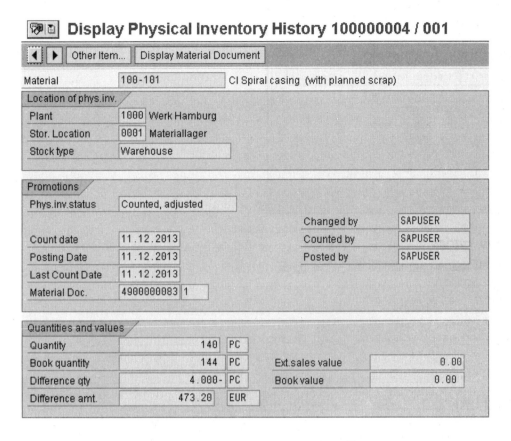

29.26.8 Material Document for Posting of Difference

You can see the material document using transaction MB03.

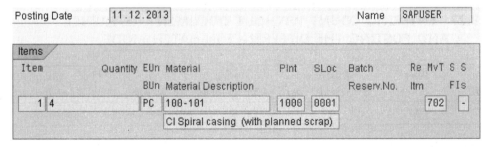

29.26.9 Accounting Documents for Posting of Difference

List of documents in accounting

In transaction MB02 or MB03 click Accounting Documents... in the item overview of the material document to see the accounting documents.

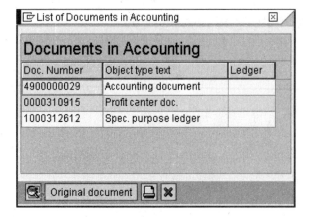

Accounting entries

Double-click the |Accounting document| to open it.

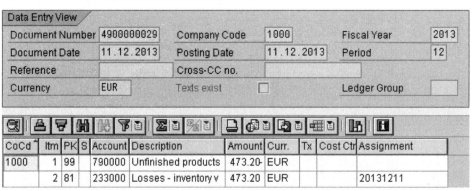

CoCd	Itm	PK	S	Account	Description	Amount	Curr.	Tx	Cost Ctr	Assignment
1000	1	99		790000	Unfinished products	473.20-	EUR			
	2	81		233000	Losses - inventory v	473.20	EUR			20131211

29.27 ENTERING COUNT WITHOUT DOCUMENT REFERENCE AND POSTING THE DIFFERENCE IN BATCH MODE

Functional Consultant	User	Business Process Owner	Senior Management	My Rating	Understanding Level
A	A	C	X		

29.27.1 Purpose

You can use this program to generate a batch input session that creates physical inventory documents, enters the count results and posts inventory differences simultaneously. The data for the batch input session is imported from an external dataset as a sequential file.

29.27.2 Transaction

MI40—Document/Count/Difference

29.27.3 Initial Screen

Name of Logical File	MMIM_PHYSICAL_INVENTORY_NO_DOCUMENTS
Max. Number of Items	20
User Name in Document	SAPUSER

Processing Control
- ☑ Issue Log
- ☐ Hold Processed Sessions
- ☐ Test Data

Name of logical file

The data for the batch input session is imported from an external dataset as a sequential file. The structure of the sequential file is pre-allocated by the table BISEG. See the program documentation on guidelines for preparing the file. Here you specify the name of logical file containing the inventory count data that you want to upload. The link between the logical file name and the physical file is maintained in view V_FILENACI, which is applicable to all clients. You can also maintain client specific file names using transaction SF01.

Maximum number of items

Even though you are entering count without a physical inventory document, the system must create one in order to maintain the audit trail of the physical inventory activities. If the number of items are large, you may like to create multiple physical inventory documents, each containing a number of items not exceeding the value specified here.

User name in document

Here you specify the user name that will appear in the header of the physical inventory documents generated by this program.

Issue log

Here you specify that a log be issued onscreen after processing.

Hold processed sessions

If this indicator is not set, sessions that do not have errors are deleted after they are processed. Sessions in which errors occurred are not deleted. Set this indicator if you do not want the processed sessions to be deleted. You can see the sessions using transaction SM35.

Test data

You can run this program with test data. To do so, set this indicator, maintain test data in view V_159I, and ensure that the specified file contains no productive data. When you run the program, test data is written from table T159I to the sequential file, before the sequential file is processed by the program to generate the batch session.

29.27.4 Generating Batch Input Session

Click ⊕ to generate a batch input session. The batch input session has the name specified in the initial screen.

29.27.5 Processing Batch Input Session

You can process the batch input session using transaction SM35. When the batch input session is processed, the system creates physical inventory documents, enters the count results and posts inventory differences simultaneously.

29.28 PHYSICAL INVENTORY REPORTS

Functional Consultant	User	Business Process Owner	Senior Management	My Rating	Understanding Level
A	A	C	X		

29.28.1 Physical Inventory Documents for Material

Run transaction MI22 to see physical inventory documents for one or more materials.

Material			Material Description			Plnt	SLoc	S	Special stock descr.	
PhysInvDoc	Item	Batch	Period	Plan. date	Count date	STy	Phys. inv. no.		Doc. Status	
100-100			Casing			1000	0001			
100000002	1		2013.12		08.12.2013	1			Doc. Active	
100-101			CI Spiral casing (with planned scrap)			1000	0001			
100000004	1		2013.12		11.12.2013	1				
100-110			Slug for spiral casing			1000	0001			
100000000	1		2013.12	07.12.2013	08.12.2013	1				
100000001	1		2013.12	07.12.2013	11.12.2013	2			Doc. Active	

29.28.2   Physical Inventory Data for Material

Run transaction MI23 to see physical inventory data for one or more materials.

```
Material           Material Description
Plnt Name 1
SLoc Batch S Descript.  Assignmnt  STy PIB PhyInvDate Unrest BUn Curr. Period

100-120            Flat gasket
1000 Werk Hamburg
0001                         1       11.12.2013 1,405  PC  To Be Executed
0001                         2                     0  PC

100-200            Fly wheel
1000 Werk Hamburg
0001                         1       08.12.2013   901  PC  To Be Executed
0001                         2                     0  PC
```

Here the report shows the stock of a material in all stock management units and the status of physical inventory for each.

29.28.3   Physical Inventory Overview

Run transaction MIDO to see physical inventory overview.

Selection screen

In the selection screen specify the physical inventory status for which you want the report.

```
Which physical inventory status?
  O Phys. inventory still to be executed
  O Phys. inventory still to be closed
  ● Phys. inv. executed
  O Phys. inv. is active again
```

List of materials undergoing physical inventory

```
Company Code        1000          Evaluation for     2013
Current Fiscal Year 2013          Current Period     12
Created on          11.12.2013    by                 SAPUSER
Plant               1000          Werk Hamburg        Warehouse Stock
Storage Location 0001             Materiallager
```

Material	Batch	S	Assignment	Unr.	Qual	Blck	Val	SL
100-101				D				
100-120				D				
100-200				D				
100-250				D				
100-260				D				

The report shows the physical inventory status of each material using the following codes.

Physical inventory status codes

Code	Description
___	Physical inventory still to be carried out
__D	Physical inventory carried out
A__	Physical inventory still to be completed
A_D	Physical inventory reactivated
S__	Sample-based physical inventory still to be completed
S_D	Sample-based physical inventory reactivated

29.28.4   Physical Inventory Documents List

Run transaction MI24 to see the list of physical inventory documents.

PhysInvDoc	Item	Material	Batch	Plnt	SLoc	Phys. inv. status	S	Stock type
☐ 100000002	1	100-100		1000	0001	Counted		Warehouse
☐ 100001160	1	100-100		1000	0001	Counted		Warehouse
☐ 100001161	1	100-100		1000	0001	Counted, adjusted		Quality inspecti

29.28.5   Changes to Physical Inventory Documents

You can change a physical inventory document using transaction MI02 or MI05. If you enable ☑ Change Document in view V_159L_EI, a change document is created every time a physical inventory document is changed using transaction MI02 or MI05. You can then run transaction MI12 to see the changes to physical inventory documents.

PhysInvDoc	Year	Doc. no.	Date	Time	Name	Transaction code

29.29   SETTINGS FOR PHYSICAL INVENTORY

Functional Consultant	User	Business Process Owner	Senior Management	My Rating	Understanding Level
B	X	X	X		

29.29.1   Purpose

Here you specify the system behavior for each plant for physical inventory.

29.29.2   IMG Node

SM30 ➤ V_159L_EI

29.29.3 Screen

Plant |1000| Werk Hamburg

General
☐ Change Document
Adj. Book Inventory   [ ]

Serial Numbers
☐ Display Serial Nos
Print Serial Numbers   [------------------]
No. Serial No. Lines   [ ]

29.29.4 Primary Key

Plant

29.29.5 Important Fields

Plant

Each plant can have its own setting for physical inventory.

Change document

You can change a physical inventory document using transaction MI02 or MI05. If you select this checkbox, a change document is created every time a physical inventory document is changed using transaction MI02 or MI05. You can then run transaction MI12 to see the changes to physical inventory documents.

Adjust book inventory

Before you start physical inventory, you should have entered all goods movements in the system. You then block goods movement and count the material. When you enter the count in the system, the book inventory is also recorded on the physical inventory document and you can perform goods movement. You have still not posted the difference.

If at such a point you enter a goods movement whose date is before the count date or same as the count date, should the system reduce the book inventory? This behavior is governed by the setting in this field.

	Not active
1	Active, if same date the phys. inv. was before goods mvt
2	Active, if same date the goods mvt was before the phys. inv.

Indicator	Description
Blank	Book inventory is not adjusted.
1	Book inventory is adjusted if goods movement is before the count date. For same date goods movements the system assumes that the physical inventory was before goods movement and does not adjust the book inventory.
2	Book inventory is adjusted if goods movement is before the count date. For same date goods movements the system assumes that the goods movement was before the physical inventory and adjusts the book inventory.

Serial numbers

Physical inventory with serial numbers is carried out for all materials that require serial numbers (serial number profile specified in material master record). When carrying out a physical inventory for materials that have serial numbers, you can enter the serial numbers while you are entering the results of the physical inventory count using transactions MI04, MI08, MI09 and MI10. You cannot enter the serial numbers first and then deduce the counted quantity from that number.

Display serial numbers

If you use serial numbers (a number assigned to each piece of the material), it is not enough to enter count during physical inventory. You have to enter serial number of each piece in the Maintain serial numbers dialog box. This task can become easier, if the system displays the existing serial numbers in the Maintain serial numbers dialog box. To enable this functionality, set this checkbox.

Print serial numbers

Here you can specify whether serial numbers are printed out along with the physical inventory documents and, if so, how many characters are printed out. Each material that has a serial number is printed on a page of its own.

Serial numbers have a maximum of 18 characters. In this field, you can define whether the whole serial number or only part of the serial number is printed, or whether it is not printed at all. For each character you specify whether it is to be printed (+) or not (–).

Number of printed serial number lines

If you are not printing serial numbers in the physical inventory document, you may want space so that you can write them during the counting process. Here you specify how many lines should be printed for each physical inventory document item involving serial numbers.

29.30   DEFAULT VALUES FOR PHYSICAL INVENTORY

Functional Consultant	User	Business Process Owner	Senior Management	My Rating	Understanding Level
B	X	X	X		

29.30.1   Purpose

Here you specify the default values for physical inventory for each plant. These indicators are suggested as default values when you enter a physical inventory document. But you can also change them there.

29.30.2   IMG Node

SM30 ➤ V_159L_I

29.30.3   Screen

Plnt   1000 Werk Hamburg

Details
Stock type   1 Warehouse
☑ Batch in background
☑ Alternative unit of measure
Reason f. difference

29.30.4   Primary Key

Plant

29.30.5   Important Fields

Plant

Default values are set for a plant.

Stock type

Here you can specify the default value of stock type.

STy	Stock type
1	Warehouse
2	Quality inspection
3	Wrhse/QuInsp.(InvSa)
4	Blocked

Batch in background

Here you specify the default value of batch determination in background.

Batch determination

In transaction MI01 you can select the field BD , batch determination in background.

Plant	1000	Werk Hamburg				
Stor. Loc.	0001	Materiallager				

Items							
Itm	Material	Material Description	Batch	STy	AUn	BD	Del
1				1	☑	☑	☐
2				1	☑	☑	☐
3				1	☑	☑	☐
4				1	☑	☑	☐

Batch determination in background

When you add a material that is managed in batches, if this indicator is selected, the system adds all the batches of the material.

Batch determination in foreground

When you add a material that is managed in batches, if this indicator is not selected, the system shows you the batches that exist for the material, and you can select the batches which are to be added.

Alternative unit of measure

Here you specify the default value of alternative unit of measure, shown in the above screenshot.

Reason for inventory difference

Here you can specify the default reason for inventory difference that should be suggested by the system when you want to post a difference without reference to a document. You should select from reasons for movement type 702.

29.31 DEFAULT VALUES FOR BATCH INPUT

Functional Consultant	User	Business Process Owner	Senior Management	My Rating	Understanding Level
B	X	X	X		—

29.31.1 Purpose

When you run a program, you get an initial screen. Here you define the default values that will appear in that screen for the following programs.

Program Name	Report title
RM07ICN1	Batch Input: Create Physical Inventory Documents For Cycle Counting
RM07IE31	Batch Input: Create Phys. Inventory Docs for Sales Order
RM07II31	Batch Input: Create Physical Inventory Documents for Normal Stock
RM07II32	Batch input: Block material for physical inventory
RM07II37	Batch Input: Post Differences
RM07IK31	Batch Input: Create Physical Inventory Docs for Vendor Consignment
RM07IM31	Batch Input: Create Physical Inventory Docs for Ret. Transp. Packaging
RM07IO31	Batch Input: Create Phys.Inventory Docs. for Mat. Prov. to Vendor
RM07IQ31	Batch Input: Create Phys.Inv. Docs. for Project
RM07IV31	Batch Input: Create Phys. Inventory Docs for Ret. Packaging at Cust.
RM07IW31	Batch Input: Create Phys. Inv. Docs for Consignment Stocks at Customer
RM07SVOR	Batch Input: Inventory Sampling

Transactions

Since you operate normally with transaction codes, here are the transactions corresponding to these programs.

TCode	Program	Transaction Text
MI31	RM07II31	Batch Input: Create Phys. Inv. Doc.
MI32	RM07II32	Batch Input: Block Material
MI37	RM07II37	Batch Input: Post Differences
MICN	RM07ICN1	Btch Inpt:Ph.Inv.Docs.for Cycle Ctng
MIE1	RM07IE31	Batch Input: Phys.Inv.Doc. Sales Ord
MIK1	RM07IK31	Batch Input: Ph.Inv.Doc.Vendor Cons.
MIM1	RM07IM31	Batch Input: Create Ph.Inv.Docs RTP
MIO1	RM07IO31	Batch Input: Ph.Inv.Doc.:Stck w.Subc
MIQ1	RM07IQ31	Batch Input: PhInvDoc. Project Stock
MIV1	RM07IV31	Batch I.:PhInDoc f.Ret.Pack.at Cust.
MIW1	RM07IW31	Batch I.;PhInDoc f. Consigt at Cust.

There is no transaction for program RM07SVOR, which is a dummy program.

29.31.2 IMG Node

SM30 ➤ V_159B

29.31.3 Screen

Program Name

| RM07II31 | Batch Input: Create Physical Inventory Documents f |

Batch Input Data

| Session | MB_MI01 |
| Maximum No. of Document Items | 20 |

☑ Batch Input
☑ Issue Log

Physical Inventory Data

Planned count date

☐ Phys. Inv. Block
☐ Incl. Inventoried Materials
☐ Include Inventoried Batches

Stock Types

☑ Unrestricted
☑ In Qual. Inspection
☐ Blocked Stock

Control

☐ Switch From Batch Input to Direct Posting (See F1 Help)

29.31.4 Default Values in Initial Screen

If you run transaction MI31 (program RM07II31), you will get the following selection screen.

Database Selections

Material		to		⇨
Plant		to		⇨
Storage Location		to		⇨
Material Type		to		⇨
Material Group		to		⇨
Storage Bin Description		to		⇨

☑ Materials Marked for Deletion

Control

○ Select data and issue log
◉ Generate Batch Input   Name of Session   `MB_MI01`
○ Create dcmts directly   ☐ Hold processed sessions

☑ Issue Log
Max. No. Items/Doc.   `20`
No. Mtls to be Included

Selection Acc. to Stock Balance

▶   Acc. to Stck

Data in Phys. Inv. Docmt Header

Planned Count Date	`11.12.2013`	☐ Set posting block
Physical Inventory Number		☐ Freeze book inv.bal.
Phys. Inventory Ref.		

Sorting

▶   Sorting

Display Options

Layout

Note the default values in this screen correspond to those set in view V_159B.

29.32 TOLERANCES FOR PHYSICAL INVENTORY DIFFERENCES

Functional Consultant	User	Business Process Owner	Senior Management	My Rating	Understanding Level
B	B	B	B		

29.32.1 Purpose

You may want to control the value of differences in physical inventory difference posting. You can control them at document level as well as at document item level. Further, you can allow senior officers to post larger differences than that allowed for junior officers.

29.32.2 IMG Node

SM30 ➢ V_T043I

29.32.3 Screen

Phys.inv.tolerance group	0001		
Company code	1000	IDES AG	Frankfurt
Currency	EUR		

Upper limits for inventory diff. postings	
Difference amount per phys. inv. doc.	1,000.00
Difference amount per phys. inv. item	150.00

29.32.4 Primary Key

Tolerance group for persons processing phys.inv. differences
Company Code

29.32.5 Important Fields

Physical inventory tolerance group

You can group your users in physical inventory tolerance groups such that members of each group have the same authorization in physical inventory difference posting. Users in a physical inventory tolerance group are defined in view V_043_B.

User name	Phys.inv.tolerance grp
BC_RFC	
JUTZE	
WEISSJ	

If you want to assign an inventory tolerance group to all existing users, you can enter *
in the user name field instead of having to enter the users individually.

Please note that table T043 underlying this view, has another view V_T043, which groups
users into 'Tolerance Groups for Financial Accounting Employees'. Therefore, do not delete
any User name , because it will get deleted from view V_T043 also.

Company code

Here you specify the company code for which the users are authorized to post physical
inventory difference.

Currency

Here you specify the currency for the authorized amounts.

Maximum difference amount per physical inventory document

Here you specify the maximum difference amount per physical inventory document in
the currency specified above.

Maximum difference amount per physical inventory document item

Here you specify the maximum difference amount per physical inventory document item
in the currency specified above.

29.33   INVENTORY SAMPLING

Functional Consultant	User	Business Process Owner	Senior Management	My Rating	Understanding Level
C	X	X	X		

29.33.1   Overview

Inventory sampling

The purpose of inventory sampling is to reduce the effort in counting physical inventory.
This is achieved by counting randomly selected samples, instead of all materials. If the
variances between the result of the count and the book inventory balance are small
enough, it is presumed that the book inventory balances for the other stocks are correct.

Stock management unit

Stock management unit is a part of a stock of material which cannot be further subdivided and for which a separate book inventory exists. In transaction MI23 the inventory is reported at the level of stock management unit.

Material		Material Description			
Plnt Name 1					
SLoc Batch		S Special stock descr. Assignmnt			STy
100-100		Casing			
1000 Werk Hamburg					
0001					1
0001					2
0001					4

As seen in the report above, a stock management unit is a unique combination of the following.

➢ Material
➢ Plant
➢ Storage location
➢ Batch
➢ Special stock indicator
➢ Account assignment object for special stock, e.g., project, sales order etc.
➢ Stock type

STy	Stock type
1	Warehouse
2	Quality inspection
3	Wrhse/QuInsp.(InvSa)
4	Blocked

The book inventory is maintained at the level of stock management unit and counting in physical inventory also takes place at that level. In inventory sampling, the system decides which stock management units are counted and which are not.

Stock management level

A stock management level is a combination of plant, storage location, material type and stock type.

Plnt	Stor. Loc.	Material Type	Stock type	InvSampl.allow.
0001	0001	ROH	1	☑

At stock management level, inventory sampling is either allowed or disallowed. Note that all materials of a material type are either included, or excluded, in inventory sampling. A stock management level has many stock management units.

Stock population

You select stock management levels and generate stock population. The stock population contains all stock management units in selected stock management levels, except those stock management units for which physical inventory is already on. The stock population is divided in the sampling area and the complete-count area.

Complete-count area

Even for stock management levels, for which inventory sampling is allowed, you can specify characteristics of materials for which you want to do complete-count. In an inventory sampling there are parameters, which are usually adopted from inventory sampling profile. There are five parameters through which you can specify that stock management units satisfying the relevant criteria be assigned to the complete-count area. These are:

➢ Deletion indicator of the material in the material master record

➢ Zero book inventory balance of the stock management unit

➢ ABC indicator of the stock management unit

➢ Price of the material in excess of the limit specified in the parameter

➢ Value of the stock management unit (material price x quantity) in excess of the limit specified in the parameter

You set these criteria before generating the stock population. When generating the stock population, the system automatically divides the stock population into the sampling area and complete-count area. In addition, if you have defined in the material master record that a material is a critical part, the material is always adopted to the complete-count area.

Sampling area

The sampling area contains all stock management units which will be subject to random selection, a process in which the system selects the stock management units to be counted.

Inventory sampling method

In inventory sampling profile you specify whether inventory sampling is to be carried out on a specific date or continuously during the year. When creating an inventory sampling, you can change the parameters.

1	Periodic inventory sampling
2	Continuous inventory sampling

Steps in inventory sampling

Inventory sampling is carried out in the following steps.

Step	Description
Creating inventory sampling	Creation of inventory sampling is the first step in the inventory sampling process. You specify the inventory sampling profile which determines the currency and defaults parameters for inventory sampling. You can change the parameters before saving the inventory sampling.
Selecting stock management levels	Combinations of plant, storage location, material type and stock type are called stock management levels. You perform inventory sampling for a set of stock management levels. The stock management levels can be across plants. You select the stock management levels from those allowed in customizing (see Section 29.33.2).
Creating stock population	This step inserts all stock management units in selected stock management levels in the inventory sampling. The stock management units are divided into complete-count area and sampling area. You can change the upper price limit and/or upper value limit to change the distribution of stock management units between complete-count area and sampling area. When stock population is created, the system classifies the stock management units into approximately 1000 classes based on the book value of stock management units.
Stratification	Stratification is the process of grouping individual consecutive classes to form various strata. The random selection and extrapolation are carried out for individual strata. This reduces the number of elements to be counted.
Random selection	For each stratum, the random selection is carried out with the aid of random numbers, which are generated in the system using an internal random number generator. The system performs the random selection on the basis of the transactions previously performed. Therefore, the stock management levels, stock population, and stratification can no longer be changed. However, when performing the random selection, the system does not automatically create the physical inventory documents. Therefore, at this point, you still have the option of deciding whether or not to carry out the physical inventory.
Plausibility check	The plausibility check gives you an idea of the quality of the random selection and thereby of the probable success of the inventory sampling. It also gives you an idea of how much work will be required. If the results of the plausibility check are not satisfactory, you can carry out a new random selection.
Creating physical inventory documents	When you perform random selection, the system also creates a batch input session for creating the physical inventory documents. The header of the displayed list contains the name of the session created. You can process this batch input session in transaction SM35 to create the physical inventory documents.

Step	Description
Updating physical inventory count	You count the inventory of stock management units and write it in the printed physical inventory documents. You then enter the count in the physical inventory documents in the system.
Posting inventory differences	After the counting results have been entered in the system, the inventory differences are posted in the physical inventory module. This also applies to items for which the difference between the book inventory balance and actual stock is zero.
Updating the result of physical count in inventory sampling	When random selection is done, initial book value and quantity of the stock management unit are stored for an inventory sampling. This initial book value forms the basis for classification and stratification. Then counting is done and entered in the physical inventory system. During the update process, book and actual values of the stock management units at the time of count are updated in inventory sampling and form the basis of extrapolation.
Extrapolating the Strata to Determine Inventory Balances	Inventory sampling is based on the principle that the system extrapolates the counting results for the stock management units that have been drawn at random to arrive at an estimated value for all stock management units of the sampling area. The counting results for the complete-count area are also considered in the overall calculation. The system uses both results to calculate the estimate for the stock population as a whole.

29.33.2 Allowing Inventory Sampling in Inventory Management

Purpose

Here you enable inventory sampling for stock management level.

JMG Node

Transaction OMCL—Define Stock Management Levels

SM30 ➤ V_064S_1

Screen

Plnt	Stor. Loc.	Material Type	Stock type	InvSampl.allow.	Group
1000	0001	ERSA	1	☐	
1000	0001	FERT	1	☐	
1000	0001	FHMI	1	☐	
1000	0001	HALB	1	☐	
1000	0001	HAWA	1	☐	
1000	0001	HIBE	1	☐	
1000	0001	LEER	1	☐	
1000	0001	ROH	1	☑	
1000	0001	UNBW	1	☐	
1000	0001	VERP	1	☐	

Primary Key

Plant
Storage Location
Material Type
Warehouse Number / Warehouse Complex
Storage Type

First three fields are used in Inventory Management; last two in Warehouse Management.

Important Fields

Plant, storage location, material type, stock type

Plant, storage location, material type and stock type together form the stock management level at which inventory sampling is allowed. The stock type can take the following values.

STy	Stock type
1	Warehouse
2	Quality inspection
3	Wrhse/QuInsp.(InvSa)
4	Blocked

Inventory sampling allowed

Here you specify whether inventory sampling is allowed for this stock management level.

Group

You can combine several stock management levels into a group. Groups can be used for generating inventory samplings for multiple stock management levels without having to specify them individually.

Regenerate

If new plants, storage locations, or material types have been added since last changing the setting, you first have to generate a new list.

29.33.3 Allowing Inventory Sampling in Warehouse Management

Purpose

If you are using Warehouse Management, you can enable inventory sampling from there.

IMG Node

Transaction OMCR—Define Stock Management Levels in WMS

SM30 ➤ V_064S_2

Screen

Warehouse No.	Storage Type	InvSampl.allow.	Group of stckMgtLvls
001	001	✔	
005	001	✔	
009	001	✔	
100	001	✔	

Primary Key

Plant
Storage Location
Material Type
Warehouse Number / Warehouse Complex
Storage Type

First three fields are used in Inventory Management; last two in Warehouse Management.

Important Fields

Warehouse number, storage type

Warehouse number and storage type together form the stock management level at which inventory sampling is allowed.

Inventory sampling allowed

Here you specify whether inventory sampling is allowed for this stock management level.

Group of stock management levels

You can combine several stock management levels into a group. Groups can be used for generating inventory samplings for multiple stock management levels without having to specify them individually.

Regenerate

If new plants, storage locations, or material types have been added since last changing the setting, you first have to generate a new list.

29.33.4   Inventory Sampling Profile

Purpose

When creating an inventory sampling, the user has to specify an inventory sampling profile. In an inventory sampling profile, the currency and the default values for the parameters of the inventory sampling are defined.

IMG Node

SM30 ➤ V_159G

Screen

Profile	01	Profile for Germany
Currency	EUR	Euro (EMU currency as of 01/01/1999)

Selection parameters

☑ Include deletion flag
☑ Consider zero stock balances
☐ Update

Consider ABC indicator	1
Upper price limit for sampling area	1,000.00 EUR

Procedure parameters

Inventory sampling method	1 Periodic inventory sampling
Extrapolation procedure	1 Mean-value estimation
Upper value limit for sampling area	10,000.00 EUR
Percentage upper value limit	
Lower number of strata for variation	1
Upper number of strata for variation	30
Minimum sample size per stratum	30

Statistical parameters

Probable degree of confidence	95.00 %
Relative statistical error	1.00 %
Rel. deviat. betw. book and act. value	2.00 %

Primary Key

Default key for inventory sampling profile

Important Fields

Profile

When creating an inventory sampling, the user has to specify an inventory sampling profile. In an inventory sampling profile, the currency and the default values for the parameters of the inventory sampling are defined.

Currency

Each inventory sampling profile has a currency which cannot be changed when you do inventory sampling.

Include deletion flag in complete-count area

If you select this field, all stock management units with a delete indicator are assigned to the complete-count area. If you do not select this field, all stock management units with a delete indicator are assigned to the sampling area.

Consider zero stock balances in complete-count area

If you select this field, all stock management units with zero stock balances are assigned to the complete-count area. If you do not select this field, all stock management units with zero stock balances are assigned to the sampling area.

Update

In inventory sampling, any count entered or difference posted is recorded in the relevant physical inventory document. However, this information is not updated automatically in the inventory sampling concerned. This will only be done during the update process.

When stratification is done, stock management units are assigned to strata based on their stock value. By the time you reach the extrapolation stage, stock values of some of the stock management units may have changed such that they should be placed in different strata. In parameter of an inventory sampling you use the update indicator to specify whether the strata of stock management units should be changed or not. The parameter of the inventory sampling received its default value from this field in the inventory sampling profile.

If you set this indicator, during the update process the system does not change the stratum of the stock management units that have been counted and for which inventory differences have been posted. The differences are used in the stratum to which the stock management unit was originally assigned.

If you do not set this indicator, during the update process the system changes the stratum of the stock management units that have been counted and for which inventory differences have been posted. The differences are used in the new stratum to which the stock management unit belongs at the current time. As a result, the remaining stock management units of the original stratum may not remain representative enough, and the system may have to advise further random selections.

Consider ABC indicator

Here you define that stock management units with specified ABC indicators are assigned to the complete-count area. Stock management units with other ABC indicators are assigned to the sampling area.

1	Indicator A for complete-count area
2	Indicators A and B for complete-count area
3	Indicators A, B, and C for complete-count area
4	Indicator B for complete-count area
5	Indicators B and C for complete-count area
6	Indicator C for complete-count area
7	Indicators A and C for complete-count area

Upper price limit for sampling area

Here you specify the maximum material price up to which stock management units are to be allocated to the sampling area. Materials whose price is more than the upper price limit are assigned to complete-count area.

Inventory sampling method

Here you specify whether inventory sampling is to be carried out on a specific date or continuously during the year.

1	Periodic inventory sampling
2	Continuous inventory sampling

Extrapolation procedure

At present SAP supports only the "mean-value estimation" procedure.

Upper value limit for sampling area

Here you specify the maximum material value up to which stock management units are to be allocated to the sampling area. Materials whose value is more than the upper value limit are assigned to complete-count area.

Percentage upper value limit

Here you can specify the percentage of the total value of all stock management units in the stock population that should be assigned to the sampling area. The system determines an upper value limit using the percentage of the total value.

If you enter a percentage value and an upper value limit at the same time, the upper value limit the system calculates from the percentage value overwrites the upper value limit that you enter manually.

Lower and upper number of strata for variation

To reduce the number of elements to be counted, the system divides the sampling area into classes, with each class containing elements of "approximately" the same value. Later, the system uses this classification as the basis for generating strata (stratification). For each stratum, the random selection and extrapolation is carried out separately.

When you carry out stratification, the system calculates the stratification for each number of strata, starting with the lowest number of strata up to and including the upper number of strata. The system lists all calculated stratifications and indicates the optimum stratification.

Here you define the minimum and maximum number of strata to be created.

Minimum sample size per stratum

In order to obtain usable extrapolation results, the mean values of possible samples must be normally distributed in each stratum. The greater the minimum sample size, the greater the probability that the mean values are normally distributed. On the other hand, a relatively large number of stock management units have to be counted if the size of the sample is large. In general, it can be assumed that the mean values are normally distributed if the sample size is 30.

Here you can specify the minimum number of elements to be counted in a stratum. If a stratum contains fewer elements than the predefined minimum sample size, all the stock management units of this layer have to be counted.

Statistical parameters

Statistical parameters define limits below which an inventory sampling can be considered successful. Statistical parameters in inventory sampling are shown below.

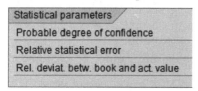

Statistical parameters
Probable degree of confidence
Relative statistical error
Rel. deviat. betw. book and act. value

Probable degree of confidence

Here you specify the degree of confidence expected of the extrapolation for an inventory sampling. With the probable degree of confidence specified, a possible error in the extrapolation result is less than the relative statistical error specified.

Relative statistical error

Here you specify the maximum error allowed for the extrapolation result. With the probable degree of confidence specified, a probable error in the extrapolation result is less than the relative statistical error specified.

Relative deviation between book and actual value

Here you specify the maximum relative deviation allowed between the book value and the actual value obtained by extrapolation.

29.33.5 Creating Inventory Sampling

Purpose

Creating an inventory sampling is the first step in the inventory sampling process.

Transaction

MIS1—Create Inventory Sampling
MIS2—Change Inventory Sampling
MIS3—Display Inventory Sampling

Initial Screen

Currency			Date	27.02.2014
Status	New		Count date	04.03.2014
Area	1 Inventory Management			
Text	Inventory Sampling 2014			

Parameter selection	
Inv.sampling profile	01

Currency

The currency is determined by the inventory sampling profile and cannot be changed.

Area

You can perform inventory sampling in the following areas.

Area	Short text
1	Inventory Management
2	Warehouse Management

Inventory sampling profile

In order to create an inventory sampling, you must specify an inventory sampling profile. The parameters for inventory sampling are defaulted from the profile.

Parameters

After you specify the inventory sampling profile you can click ⟨ Parameters ⟩. The system shows you the parameters defaulted from the inventory sampling profile.

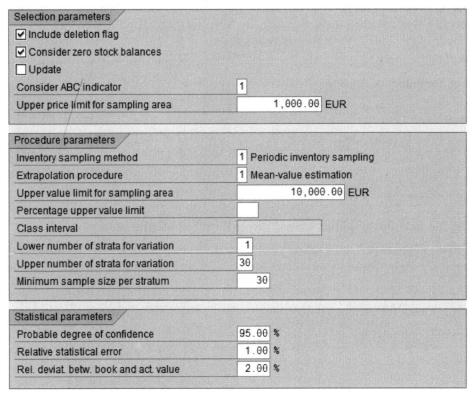

You can change these parameters and go back to ⟨ Header ⟩.

Creating Inventory Sampling

After entering the data in the initial screen, you save. The system creates a new inventory sampling and displays the inventory sampling number. It also freezes some of the parameters. After creating the inventory sampling, you may come out of the transaction, unless you want to create more inventory samplings.

29.33.6 Selecting Stock Management Levels

Purpose

After creating an inventory sampling, you select stock management levels for which you want to insert the stock management units in the inventory sampling.

Transaction

MIS2—Change Inventory Sampling

Initial Screen

Inventory sampling	2000010
Year	2014

Header

After entering the data in the initial screen, press 'Enter' to see the header.

Inventory sampling	2000010	ERP system		
Year	2014			
Currency	EUR		Date	27.02.2014
Status	In preparation		Count date	04.03.2014
Area	1 Inventory Management			
Text	Inventory Sampling 2014			

Transactions	
Stock mgmt levels	
Stock population	
Stratification	
Random selection	
Update	
Extrapolation	

Parameters

After creating an inventory sampling, you can always display or change parameters by clicking Parameters .

Selection parameters

☑ Include deletion flag

☑ Consider zero stock balances

☐ Update

Consider ABC indicator   `1`

Upper price limit for sampling area   `    1,000.00` EUR

Procedure parameters

Inventory sampling method	`1`	Periodic inventory sampling
Extrapolation procedure	`1`	Mean-value estimation
Upper value limit for sampling area		`    15,000.00` EUR
Percentage upper value limit	`  `	
Class interval		
Lower number of strata for variation	`1`	
Upper number of strata for variation	`30`	
Minimum sample size per stratum	`30`	

Statistical parameters

Probable degree of confidence	`95.00`	%
Relative statistical error	`1.00`	%
Rel. deviat. betw. book and act. value	`2.00`	%

Note that some of the parameters cannot be changed any more.

Status

After creating an inventory sampling, you can always check its status by clicking Status .

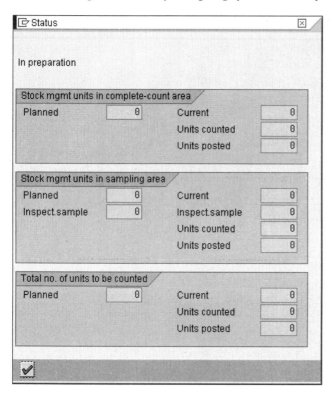

Categories of Stock Management Levels

Choose Transaction/Event ➢ Stock Mgmt Levels to see the categories of stock management levels.

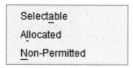

Non-Permitted Stock Management Levels

Choose Transaction/Event ➢ Stock Mgmt Levels ➢ Non-Permitted to see the non-permitted stock management levels.

Plnt	SLoc	MTy.	Stock type
1000	0001	ERSA	1
1000	0001	FERT	1
1000	0001	FHMI	1
1000	0001	HALB	1

You specify the stock management levels that are allowed or not allowed in view V_064S_1 (see Section 29.33.2). You can see these stock management levels here. If you want to permit some stock management levels, make the change in view V_064S_1.

Selecting Stock Management Levels

Choose Transaction/Event ➤ Stock Mgmt Levels ➤ Selectable to display the selectable stock management levels.

	Plnt	SLoc	MTy	StockType	Group
☐	0001	0001	ROH	1	
☐	0005	0001	ROH	1	
☐	0007	0001	ROH	1	
☐	1000	0001	ROH	1	
☐	1100	0001	ERSA	1	A
☐	1100	0001	FERT	1	A
☐	1100	0001	FHMI	1	B
☐	1100	0001	HALB	1	B

Select the stock management levels you want to insert in inventory sampling and click Copy . Note that the stock management levels can be across plants. The system gives a message and the header shows the change.

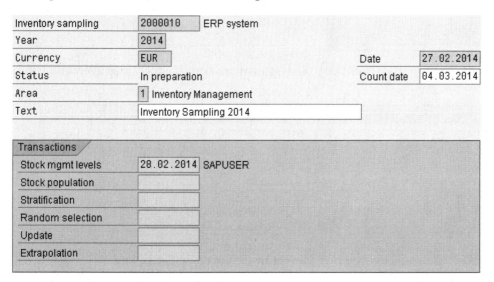

Deselecting Stock Management Levels

Choose Transaction/Event ➤ Stock Mgmt Levels ➤ Allocated to display the allocated stock management levels.

Plnt	SLoc	MTy.	StockType	CoCde	Crrency	Except.text
☑ 0001	0001	ROH	1	1000	EUR	
☑ 0005	0001	ROH	1	0005	EUR	
☑ 0007	0001	ROH	1	0007	EUR	
☑ 1000	0001	ROH	1	1000	EUR	
☑ 1100	0001	ERSA	1	1000	EUR	
☑ 1100	0001	FERT	1	1000	EUR	
☑ 1100	0001	FHMI	1	1000	EUR	
☑ 1100	0001	HALB	1	1000	EUR	
☑ 1100	0001	HAWA	1	1000	EUR	

If you want to remove a stock management level from inventory sampling, deselect the checkbox and click Copy . The stock management level is removed from the inventory sampling.

Selecting Stock Management Levels via Group

You can select the stock management levels manually, or you may select stock management levels belonging to a group by choosing Edit ➤ Selections ➤ Select Group .

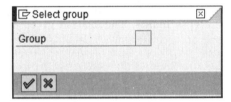

You enter the group and click ✔. The system marks all stock management levels belonging to the group.

Plnt	SLoc	MTy.	StockType	Group
☐ 0001	0001	ROH	1	
☐ 0005	0001	ROH	1	
☐ 0007	0001	ROH	1	
☐ 1000	0001	ROH	1	
☑ 1100	0001	ERSA	1	A
☑ 1100	0001	FERT	1	A
☐ 1100	0001	FHMI	1	B
☐ 1100	0001	HALB	1	B

You can Copy the stock management levels in the inventory sampling.

Displaying Stock Management Levels

You can see the stock management levels in inventory sampling by choosing Goto ➤ List ➤ Stock Mgmt Levels .

StockMgtLvlNo.	Plnt	SLoc	MTy	SType	Number	CoCde	Curr.	Book val.
1	0001	0001	ROH	1		1000	EUR	0.00
2	0005	0001	ROH	1		0005	EUR	0.00
3	0007	0001	ROH	1		0007	EUR	0.00
4	1000	0001	ROH	1		1000	EUR	0.00
5	1100	0001	ERSA	1		1000	EUR	0.00
6	1100	0001	FERT	1		1000	EUR	0.00
7	1100	0001	FHMI	1		1000	EUR	0.00
8	1100	0001	HALB	1		1000	EUR	0.00
Total								0.00

Freezing Stock Management Levels

You cannot change the allocation of stock management levels after you have performed random selection.

29.33.7   Creating Stock Population

Purpose

After selecting stock management levels, you create stock population. This step inserts all stock management units in the inventory sampling.

Transaction

MIS2—Change Inventory Sampling

Initial Screen

Inventory sampling	2000010	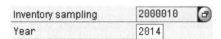
Year	2014	

Simulating Stock Population

Confirming formation of stock population

After allocating stock management levels, choose Transaction/Event ➤ Stock Population .

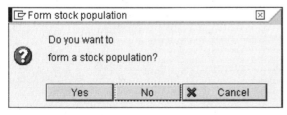

Click [Yes] to form the stock population.

Summary of stock population that will be created

The system gives you the summary of stock population that will be created.

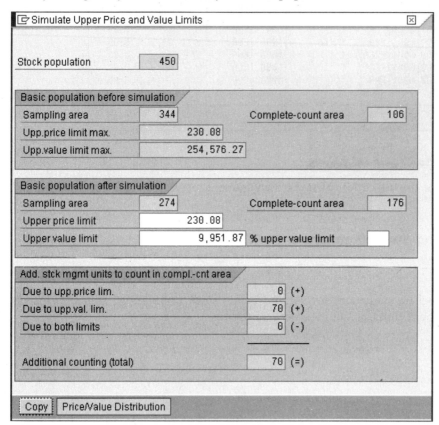

Note that 106 units are in complete-count area, to which 70 units are added due to upper value limit, taking the units in complete-count area to 176. This leaves 274 units in sampling area. If you want you can change the upper price limit and/or upper value limit and press 'Enter'. The system updates the counts on the screen.

Counting effort by upper price limit

If you click Price/Value Distribution , the system shows you how your counting effort will vary if you were to choose a different upper price limit or a different upper value limit.

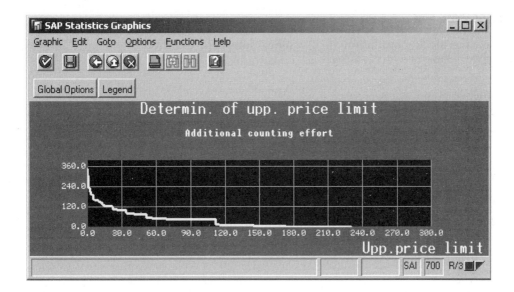

Counting effort by upper value limit

If you click | Price/Value Distribution |, the system shows you how your counting effort will vary if you were to choose a different upper price limit or a different upper value limit.

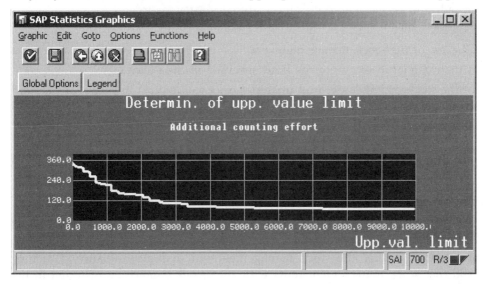

You can go back and change the upper price limit and/or upper value limit.

Creating Stock Population

When you are satisfied, click | Copy |. The stock population is formed. The header shows the change in status: Stock population   28.02.2014 SAPUSER.

Stock Population List

You can see the stock population in inventory sampling by choosing Goto ➤ List ➤ Stock Population ➤ Total.

Plant	1000	Stock type	1
Stor. location	0001	Currency	EUR
Material type	ROH		

Material	Batch	Val.type	CCA	DeI	Zer	ABC	STy	Ran	Cnt	Pst
100-120			X				1			
100-410							1			
100-420			X				1			
100-430							1			

This list contains all stock management units that are covered by this inventory sampling, according to the stock management levels allocated.

Complete-count area

This column shows whether the stock management unit is included in the complete-count area, i.e. the stock management unit must be counted and not subjected to selection by random sampling. Inclusion of a stock management unit in complete-count area may be caused by several factors.

➤ Deletion indicator of the material in the material master record

➤ Zero book inventory balance of the stock management unit

➤ ABC indicator of the stock management unit

➤ Price of the material in excess of the limit specified in the parameter

➤ Value of the stock management unit (material price x quantity) in excess of the limit specified in the parameter

➤ Material is a critical part in the material master

Deletion indicator

This column shows the delete indicator of the material in the material master. You may have specified that materials with delete indicator be included in the complete-count area.

Zero stock balances

This column shows whether the stock management unit has zero balance. You may have specified that stock management units with zero stock balance be included in the complete-count area.

ABC indicator

This column shows the ABC indicator of the material in the material master. You may have specified that materials having some of these indicators be included in the complete-count area.

Random selection

When random selection is carried out, the stock management units drawn in the random selection process will have an indicator in this column.

Counted

When a stock management unit is counted, this column will show that.

Posted

When difference for a stock management unit is posted, this column will show that.

Excluded Stock Management Units

You can also see the list of excluded stock management units by choosing Goto ➤ List ➤ Stock Population ➤ Excl. Stock Mgmt Units .

Plant	1000	Stock type	1
Stor. location	0001	Currency	EUR
Material type	ROH		

Material	Batch	Val.type	CCA	DeI	Zer	ABC	STy	Comment
100-110			A		X		1	Phys. inv. active
100-130			A		X		1	Phys. inv. active
100-210			A				1	Phys. inv. active
100-310			A				1	Phys. inv. active

Classification

Range of values

The sampling area of an inventory sampling usually contains a large number of stock management units with extremely differing values. The larger the value range between the smallest value and the largest value within the sampling area, the more stock management units must be counted, in order to obtain statistically correct results.

Classes

To reduce the number of elements to be counted, the system divides the sampling area into classes, with each class containing elements of "approximately" the same value. Later, the system uses this classification as the basis for generating strata (stratification). For each stratum, the random selection and extrapolation is carried out separately.

Consequently, a class is the quantity of stock management units (in the sampling area) whose values lie within a certain interval. These intervals (possibly with the exception of the last one) are of equal size, but generally contain a variable number of stock management units.

Automatic creation of classes

The classification of the sampling area is carried out automatically when the stock population is formed. Class interval is determined as the upper value limit for sampling area/1000 (rounded up to the next integer). On the basis of the class interval, the system then generates classes until the upper value limit is reached. Due to the rounding up process, usually less than 1000 classes are generated. The last class ends with the upper value limit.

List of classes

You can see the list of classes by choosing Goto ➤ List ➤ Classification . You can either see All Classes , or Only Classes w. Stock .

ClasNo	LowerVal.limit	UpperVal.limit	No.of SMUs	Book val.
1	0.00	10.00	4	8.29
2	10.01	20.00	2	29.98
3	20.01	30.00	4	103.68
4	30.01	40.00	2	74.46
5	40.01	50.00		0.00

29.33.8 Stratification

Purpose

The purpose of classification is to create classes of approximately same value. The purpose of stratification is to group individual consecutive classes and form a few strata. The random selection and extrapolation are carried out for individual strata.

Transaction

MIS2—Change Inventory Sampling

Initial Screen

Inventory sampling	2000010
Year	2014

Performing Stratification

To carry out stratification, you choose Transaction/Event ➤ Stratification . When you save, the system updates the status in the header Stratification   28.02.2014 SAPUSER .

List of strata

You can see the list of strata by choosing Goto ➤ List ➤ Stratification ➤ All Variants / Optimum Variant

No	LowerVal.limit	UpperVal.limit	Total	Select.	SMUs to cnt	CCA	Book val.
1	0.00	510.00	76	14	30		22,205.71
2	510.01	1,160.00	89	20	30		78,189.33
3	1,220.01	2,560.00	71	29	30		141,706.28
4	2,670.01	9,960.00	38	38	38	X	163,331.89
Total (optimum variation)			274	101	128		405,433.21

Stratum number

This column shows the stratum number. The number of strata is between the lower and upper number of strata specified in the parameter.

Lower and upper value limit

Stock management units are included in a stratum based on the book value of their inventory. The system creates the strata and determines the lower and upper limit of each stratum.

Total number of stock management units

This column shows the total number of stock management units in each stratum.

Number of stock management units to be selected

This column shows the number of stock management units to be selected for the stratum.

Number of stock management units to be counted

In a stratum, if the number of stock management units required for sampling is less than the 'Minimum sample size per stratum' specified in the parameter, this column shows the minimum number.

Complete-count area

If the total number of stock management units in the stratum is less than the minimum number specified in the parameter, all stock management units are counted. During stratification, the system issues a warning message (M7 641) if a stratum of the sampling area is going to be a complete-count stratum and subsequent random selection would thereby not be possible. The message long text explains what you have to do to prevent this. If you accept it, this indicator is updated.

Book value

This column shows the book value of all stock management units in the stratum.

29.33.9 Random Selection

Purpose

The stratification process determines the range of values for each stratum and the number of stock management units that need to be counted in it. The purpose of random sampling is to identify specific stock management units that will be counted. The random selection is carried out with the aid of random numbers, which are generated in the system using an internal random number generator.

Transaction

MIS2—Change Inventory Sampling

Initial Screen

Inventory sampling	2000010
Year	2014

Performing Random Selection

To perform random selection, you choose `Transaction/Event` ➤ Random Selection.

Batch Input for Physical Inventory

After random selection, you need to do physical inventory of stock management units selected in the random selection process. To facilitate this, the system automatically creates a batch input file for creating physical inventory documents.

```
Phys. inv. doc. reference number        SI20140002000010
Name of batch input session             SI0002000010

Phys. inv. docs. can be created for the following stock mgmt. units
```

Plnt	SLoc	Material	Batch	StockType
0001	0001	AS-RO		1
0001	0001	AS-ROH		1
1000	0001	100-120		1
1000	0001	100-410		1
1000	0001	100-420		1

The header of the list contains the name of the batch input session created that is to be processed using transaction SM35 to create the physical inventory documents. The header of inventory sampling shows the status: `Random selection` `28.02.2014` `SAPUSER`.

List of Randomly Selected Stock Management Units

You can see the list of stock management units randomly selected for counting by choosing Goto ➤ List ➤ Random Selection.

Plant   1000   Stock type   1
Stor. location 0001   Currency   EUR
Material type ROH

Material	Batch	Val.type	CCA	DeI	Zer	ABC	STy	Ran	Cnt	Pst
100-410							1	X		
100-430							1	X		
100-802							1	X		
100-804							1	X		

Freezing Earlier Transactions

The system performs the random selection on the basis of the transactions previously performed. Therefore, the stock management levels, stock population, and stratification can no longer be changed. However, when performing the random selection, the system does not automatically create the physical inventory documents; it only creates a batch input that can be processed using transaction SM35 to create the physical inventory documents. Therefore, at this point, you still have the option of deciding whether or not to carry out the physical inventory.

29.33.10   Plausibility Check

Purpose

The plausibility check gives you an idea of the quality of the random selection that has been carried out and thereby of the probable success of the inventory sampling. At the same time, the system provides you with an approximate overview of the expected subsequent random selections. If the results of the plausibility check are not satisfactory, you can carry out a new random selection.

Transaction

MIS2—Change Inventory Sampling

Initial Screen

Inventory sampling	2000010
Year	2014

Performing Plausibility Check

To run the plausibility check, choose Transaction/Event ➤ Plausibility Check.

Result of Plausibility Check

Plausibility check provides extrapolation result for each stratum, sampling area, complete-count area and total area. It may also specify subsequent random selection.

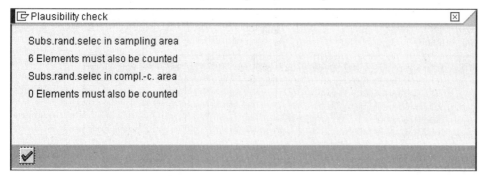

Extrapolation parameters

```
Extrapolation for inventory sampling       2000010    2014
  Planned on                               28.02.2014
  By                                       SAPUSER
  Updated on                               00.00.0000
  By
  Status                                   Completion successful

Procedure for Update:          Update the difference of posted elements (S)

                            Plausibility Check

Selection Parameters
  Deletion flags considered                X
  Zero stocks considered                   X
  ABC indicators considered                1
  Upper price limit for sampling area             230.08  EUR

Procedure Parameters
  Inventory sampling procedure             1
  Extrapolation procedure                  1
  Upper value limit for sampling area             9,951.87  EUR
  Minimum sample size per stratum          00030

Statistical Parameters
  Probable degree of certainty             95.00 %
  max. rel. deviation allowed               2.00 %
  max. rel. statist. error allowed          1.00 %
```

Extrapolation result of a sampling stratum

```
Sampling stratum:  01 :              0.00  EUR   to            510.00  EUR
```

Stock mgmt units	at time of planning	76	
	at time of update	76	
	Balance	0	
Book value	at time of planning	22,205.71	EUR
	at time of update	22,205.71	EUR
	Balance	0.00	EUR
Sample elements at	time of planning	30	
	at time of update	30	
	Balance	0	
	Elements counted	30	
	Elements posted	30	
Posted elements	Book value	8,089.70	EUR
	Actual value	8,089.70	EUR
	Phys. inv. diff. posted	0.00	EUR
Sampling stratum	Adjusted book value	22,205.71	EUR
	Estimate	20,493.91	EUR
	Phy.inv.diff. based on estimate	1,711.80-	EUR
	Weighted relative deviation	0.42-	%
	Weighted rel. statistical error	1.14	%

Extrapolation result of total area

```
Extrapolation result for total area
```

Stock mgmt units	at time of planning	450	
	at time of update	450	
	Balance	0	
	Elements counted	304	
	Elements posted	304	
Book value	at time of planning	3,462,161.04	EUR
	at time of update	3,461,831.04	EUR
	Balance	330.00-	EUR
Posted units	Book value	3,315,372.85	EUR
	Actual value	3,315,372.85	EUR
	Phys. inv. diff. posted	0.00	EUR
Total area	Adjusted book value	3,461,831.04	EUR
	Estimate	3,462,797.40	EUR
	Phy.inv.diff. based on estimate	966.36	EUR
	Relative deviation	0.03	%
	Relative statis. error	0.12	%

29.33.11 Creating Physical Inventory Documents

Purpose

When you perform random selection, the system also creates a batch input session for creating the physical inventory documents. The header of the displayed list contains the name of the session created.

```
Phys. inv. doc. reference number      SI20140002000010
Name of batch input session           SI0002000010
```

Transaction

SM35—Batch Input Monitoring

Screen

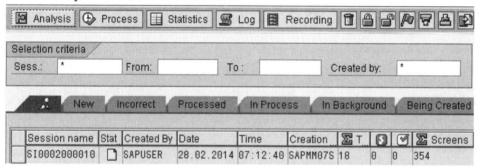

Processing

Select the batch input and click [⊕ Process] to update the system. You can see the list of items to be counted using transaction MI24.

PhysInvDoc	Item	Material	Batch	Plnt	SLoc	Phys. inv. status	S	Stock type
100000000	1	AS-RO		0001	0001	Not yet counted		Warehouse
100000000	2	AS-ROH		0001	0001	Not yet counted		Warehouse
100000001	1	100-120		1000	0001	Not yet counted		Warehouse
100000001	2	100-410		1000	0001	Not yet counted		Warehouse
100000001	3	100-420		1000	0001	Not yet counted		Warehouse
100000001	4	100-430		1000	0001	Not yet counted		Warehouse

29.33.12 Updating Count in Physical Inventory Document

You count the inventory of stock management units and write it in the printed physical inventory document. You then enter the count in the system using transaction MI04. See Section 29.13 for more details.

29.33.13   Posting Inventory Differences

After the counting results have been entered in the system, the inventory differences must be posted using transaction MI07. See Section 29.22 for more details.

29.33.14   Updating the Result of Physical Count in Inventory Sampling

Purpose

When random selection is done, initial book value and quantity of the stock management unit are stored for an inventory sampling. This initial book value forms the basis for classification and stratification.

Then counting is done and entered in the physical inventory documents.

These counts and differences need to be updated in the inventory sampling documents. This happens during the update process. During the update process, book and actual values of the stock management units at the time of count are updated in inventory sampling and form the basis of extrapolation. During an update, the system:

➢ Reads posted count results that have been added

➢ Determines changed book inventory balances and book values

➢ Determines whether subsequent random selection is required

Transaction

MIS2—Change Inventory Sampling

Initial Screen

Inventory sampling	2000010
Year	2014

Performing Update

You perform an update by choosing Transaction/Event ➢ Update. You do not have to wait for counting and difference posting of physical inventory documents to be completed for updating the inventory sampling. You can update the count and difference in the inventory sampling document whenever you want. Each time the system updates the counts and differences that have not been updated and takes consequent actions as required.

Updating Count and Difference

During inventory sampling process, physical inventory documents are created. Any count entered or difference posted is recorded in these physical inventory documents. This information is not updated automatically in the inventory sampling concerned. This happens during this update process. These differences are used for extrapolation.

Changing Strata of Stock Management Units

Goods movement and change in strata

During the stratification process, stock management units are assigned to different strata based on their book value. While the inventory sampling process is going on, goods movement may take place. Goods movement is allowed for all stock management units that are not to be counted. Even for stock management units that are to be counted, goods movement is blocked only during the physical inventory phase. If the book value of a stock management unit changes, should its stratum be changed? The system lets you decide.

The update indicator

In Parameters of an inventory sampling you use the ☐ Update indicator to specify whether the strata of stock management units should be changed or not. The parameter of the inventory sampling received its default value from the corresponding field in the inventory sampling profile.

Stratum of the stock management unit may not be changed

If this indicator is set, during the update process the system does not change the stratum of the stock management units that have been counted and for which inventory differences have been posted. The differences are used in the stratum to which the stock management unit was originally assigned.

Stratum of the stock management unit may be changed

If this indicator is not set, during the update process the system changes the stratum of the stock management units that have been counted and for which inventory differences have been posted. The differences are used in the new stratum to which the stock management unit belongs at the current time. As a result, the remaining stock management units of the original stratum may not remain representative enough, and the system may have to advise further random selections.

Determining whether Subsequent Random Selection is required

If the strata of stock management units change, the remaining elements that were selected for a stratum may no longer be representative of that stratum. In this case, further elements to be counted must be drawn for this stratum. The system performs this check for each stratum. If it determines that additional elements must be drawn, it proposes a subsequent random selection for the sampling area.

Status

You can see the updated status by choosing Goto ➤ Status .

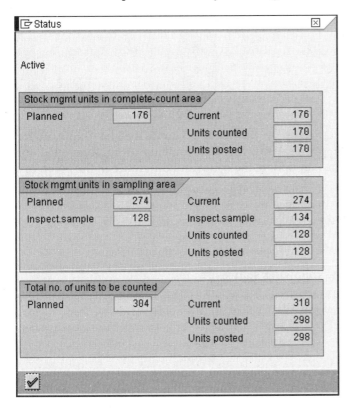

Stock Population

You can see the stock population in inventory sampling by choosing Goto ➤ List ➤ Stock Population ➤ Total .

Material	Batch	Val.type	CCA	DeI	Zer	ABC	STy	Ran	Cnt	Pst
100-120			X				1		X	X
100-410							1	X	X	X
100-420			X				1		X	X
100-430							1	X	X	X

After posting, the Pst column is updated.

29.33.15   Extrapolating the Strata to Determine Inventory Balances

Purpose

The purpose of extrapolation is to extrapolate the result of sampling count.

Transaction

MIS2—Change Inventory Sampling

Initial Screen

Inventory sampling	2000010	🕑
Year	2014	

Performing Extrapolation

You extrapolate by choosing Transaction/Event ➤ Extrapolation. You do not have to wait for counting and difference posting of physical inventory documents to be completed for updating the inventory sampling. You can update the count and difference in the inventory sampling document whenever you want.

Status of an Inventory Sampling

List of status values

An inventory sampling can have the following status:

Status	Short text
0	New
1	In preparation
2	Active
3	Inventory management units posted
4	Completion successful
5	Completion unsuccessful
2X	Active (completion partially successful)
G	Deleted
2Y	Completed (completion partially successful)

Explanation of status values

Status	Short text	Explanation
0	New	When creating an inventory sampling and before saving it
1	In preparation	After creating an inventory sampling and before making the random selection
2	Active	After the random selection and before the first counting result
3	Inventory management units posted	When entering the counting results
4	Completion successful	If all the stock management units have been counted and the extrapolation is completed successfully, the inventory sampling ends with this status.

Status	Short text	Explanation
5	Completion unsuccessful	If all the stock management units have been counted and the extrapolation is completed unsuccessfully, the inventory sampling ends with this status. In this case, it must be assumed that the deviations between the book inventory balances and the actual stock are too large. For this reason, a complete physical inventory must be carried out for all elements that have not been counted.
2X	Active (completion partially successful)	If all the stock management units have not been counted and the extrapolation is completed successfully, you can manually close an inventory sampling with this status if you are satisfied that the results of extrapolation are adequate.
G	Deleted	If an inventory sampling is deleted, its record remains in table SKPF with this status.
2Y	Completed (completion partially successful)	If you have set the status to Active (completion partially successful), and the auditor agrees with your judgment, you can manually set the status of inventory sampling to this. If the auditor does not agree with your judgment, you continue counting remaining randomly selected stock management units and perform another partial extrapolation, or final extrapolation.

Extrapolation determines whether the status of an inventory sampling is changed to 4, 5, 2X or 2Y.

Extrapolation

Extrapolation

Inventory sampling is based on the principle that the system extrapolates the counting results for the stock management units that have been drawn at random to arrive at an estimated value for all stock management units of the sampling area. The counting results for the complete-count area are also considered in the overall calculation. The system uses both results to calculate the estimate for the stock population as a whole.

Partial extrapolation

You can perform an extrapolation even if all the stock management units have not been counted. Such an extrapolation is called a partial extrapolation. If the relative statistical error and the maximum allowed deviation between the book value and the estimated value are already under the defined limit, you can assign the inventory sampling the status, Active (completion partially successful). You can perform as many extrapolations as you wish. Only the last one will be stored. If the auditor decides that the inventory sampling can be accepted at this stage, you can manually change the status of inventory sampling from Active (completion partially successful) to Completed (completion partially successful).

Partial unsuccessful completion

If all the stock management units have not been counted and the extrapolation is completed unsuccessfully, you should count the remaining stock management units in the physical inventory document to see whether the final completion is successful or unsuccessful.

Final extrapolation

An extrapolation is regarded as final once all randomly selected and complete-count stock management units are counted and inventory differences posted. This means all counting results have been taken into account in the calculation, and further subsequent random selection is not required. A final extrapolation can only be carried out once, since any new results cannot be added. The final extrapolation may be successful or unsuccessful.

Performing an Extrapolation

To perform extrapolation, in transaction MIS2 choose Transaction/Event ➤ Extrapolation. The system carries out the extrapolation and issues the message; 'Partial extrapolation has been carried out' or 'Final extrapolation has been carried out'. Whether the extrapolation is final or partial depends on whether all selected stock management units have been counted or not.

During a partial extrapolation, the status of the inventory sampling can be manually changed to Active (completion partially successful) and saved.

During the final extrapolation, the status of the inventory sampling is changed to 'Completion successful' or 'Completion unsuccessful'. You save the changes made to the inventory sampling.

Displaying the Result of an Extrapolation

To display the extrapolation result, choose Goto ➤ List ➤ Extrapolation. A list of the calculations performed by the system is displayed. After the extrapolation results for the individual strata, the system displays the extrapolation result for the entire sampling area, followed by the extrapolation result for the complete-count area. At the end, the result includes the whole area with the relative deviation and the relative statistical error.

Extrapolation parameters

```
Extrapolation for inventory sampling        2000010    2014
  Planned on                                28.02.2014
  By                                        SAPUSER
  Updated on                                28.02.2014
  By                                        SAPUSER
  Status                                    Active

Procedure for Update:         Update the difference of posted elements (S)

Selection Parameters
  Deletion flags considered                 X
  Zero stocks considered                    X
  ABC indicators considered                 1
  Upper price limit for sampling area              230.08  EUR

Procedure Parameters
  Inventory sampling procedure              1
  Extrapolation procedure                   1
  Upper value limit for sampling area            9,951.87  EUR
  Minimum sample size per stratum           00030

Statistical Parameters
  Probable degree of certainty              95.00 %
  max. rel. deviation allowed                2.00 %
  max. rel. statist. error allowed           1.00 %
```

Extrapolation result for total area

```
Extrapolation result for total area
────────────────────────────────────────────────────────────────────

Stock mgmt units   at time of planning                 450
                   at time of update                   450
                   Balance                               0
                   Elements counted                    298
                   Elements posted                     298

Book value         at time of planning         3,462,161.04  EUR
                   at time of update           3,460,864.08  EUR
                   Balance                         1,296.96- EUR

Posted units       Book value                  3,105,739.85  EUR
                   Actual value                3,104,772.89  EUR
                   Phys. inv. diff. posted           966.96- EUR

Total area         Adjusted book value         3,460,864.08  EUR
                   Estimate                    3,461,815.71  EUR
                   Phy.inv.diff. based on estimate   951.63  EUR
                   Relative deviation                  0.03  %
                   Relative statis. error              0.13  %
```

29.33.16 Deleting an Inventory Sampling

Purpose

You can delete an inventory sampling if you do not want to complete the inventory sampling process.

Transaction

MIS2—Change Inventory Sampling

Initial Screen

Inventory sampling	2000010
Year	2013

Deleting an Inventory Sampling

To delete an inventory sampling, choose `Inventory Sampling Procedure` ➢ `Delete` . The inventory sampling is deleted. The record of inventory sampling remains in table SKPF with `Inventory sampling status` G .

29.34 CYCLE COUNTING

Functional Consultant	User	Business Process Owner	Senior Management	My Rating	Understanding Level
B	C	X	X		

29.34.1 Purpose

Cycle counting

Cycle counting is a method of physical inventory where inventory is counted at regular intervals within a fiscal year.

Cycle counting indicators in a plant

You may want to count fast-moving items more frequently than slow-moving items or high value items more frequently than low value items. You can decide different counting frequencies required in your company and create a cycle counting indicator for each frequency.

Cycle counting indicator for a material

You then assign a cycle counting indicator to each material, thereby determining the frequency at which it is counted.

29.34.2 Cycle Counting Indicators in a Plant

You can define cycle counting indicators for each plant in view V_159C.

Plnt	CC phys. inv. ind.	No.of phys.inv.	Interval	Float time	Percentage
1000	A	12	20	5	56
1000	B	6	41	10	28
1000	C	3	83	20	14
1000	D	1	249		2

Plant

Physical inventory indicators for cycle counting can be different for different plants.

Cycle counting physical inventory indicator

For a plant, there can be multiple physical inventory indicators for cycle counting. This indicator groups the materials together into various cycle counting categories.

Number of physical inventories, interval

Here you specify the number of physical inventories per fiscal year for cycle counting. The system determines the count interval in workdays from this number.

Float time

Float time indicates the number of workdays by which the planned count date may vary from the current date. On expiration of the float time if the physical inventory has not yet been carried out, the material is parked for the next cycle counting run.

Percentage

In cycle counting, usually you count A class materials more often than B or C class materials. You can specify the percentage of value that constitutes A, B, C and D class here. You can then run transaction MIBC to update the cycle counting indicators for materials based on ABC analysis. Remember that the total of the percentages must be 100 if you want to assign the indicator to the individual materials as part of an ABC analysis.

29.34.3 Cycle Counting Indicator for a Material

In material master record maintenance (transactions MM01, MM02), you maintain the following data at plant level.

Cycle counting physical inventory indicator

Here you assign a physical inventory indicator for cycle counting to a material. This indicator can also later be updated automatically by the system using transaction MIBC.

Cycle counting fixed

Here you can specify that the cycle counting indicator cannot be changed by transaction MIBC (ABC analysis for cycle counting). Then the only way to change this indicator is through manual maintenance of the material master record.

29.34.4 Updating Cycle Counting Indicators through ABC Analysis

Purpose

In cycle counting, usually you count A class materials more often than B or C class materials. You can specify the percentage of value that constitutes A, B, C and D class in view V_159C. You can then run this transaction to update the cycle counting indicators for materials based on ABC analysis.

Transaction

MIBC—Set Cycle-Counting Indicator

Selection Screen

Area to Analyze					
Plant	☑				
Material Type			to		⇨
☐ Materials with Deletion Flag					
☐ All Materials Held in Stock					

Key Figure				
◉ Consumption/Usage	Dtd	13.09.2013	to	12.12.2013
○ Requirements	Dtd	12.12.2013	to	12.03.2014
☐ Change CC Percentages				

Processing
◉ Display List First
○ Update Without List

Plant

Here you specify the plant for which cycle counting indicator is to be updated.

Material type

You can update the cycle counting indicator for selected material types only.

Materials with deletion flag

Here you can specify that the cycle counting indicator is to be updated for materials with deletion flag also.

All materials held in stock

If the plant uses only cycle counting, you should select this checkbox. This program will then update the `CC phys. inv. ind.` for all materials. ABC indicator of materials having ☑ `CC fixed` will not be changed.

If the plant uses a combination of cycle counting and periodic inventory, you should not select this checkbox. This program will then update the `CC phys. inv. ind.` of only those materials that have a value in the `CC phys. inv. ind.` field. ABC indicator of materials having ☑ `CC fixed` will not be changed.

Usage/requirement

ABC analysis may be based either on usage or requirement. You also specify the period for which usage/requirement is considered.

Change cycle counting percentages

In view V_159C you specify the percentages for each cycle counting indicator. If you want to use a different percentage, you tick this checkbox. The system gives you a dialog box in which you can enter the percentages.

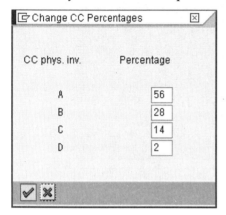

Display list first

Here you can specify that the system should display the list of materials with the newly determined cycle counting indicators. From this list, you can use Change CC Indicator to initiate the cycle counting indicator to be changed in the individual material master records.

Update without list

Here you can specify that the newly determined cycle counting indicators are updated directly into the material master records, without displaying the list.

Output

List

Material	Material Description	CC New	CC Old	Total Value	Total Stock	BUn	%	Cum. %	Inconsistent	CC Ind. Changed
L-40C	Light Bulb 40 Watt clear 220/235V	A	A	3,513,830.40	14,496	CAR	7.12	7.12		
M-08	Flatscreen MS 1575P	A		2,861,693.04	4,872	PC	5.84	12.96		
M-17	Jotachi SN4000	A		2,854,391.11	3,764	PC	5.79	18.75		
L-80C	Light Bulb 80 Watt clear 220/235V	A	A	2,432,236.53	8,806.070	CAR	4.93	23.68		
M-10	Flatscreen MS 1775P	A		2,245,561.10	3,059	PC	4.55	28.23		
L-60C	Light Bulb 60 Watt clear 220/235V	A	A	1,933,785.98	7,770.890	CAR	3.92	32.15		
L-60F	Light Bulb 60 Watt frosted 220/235V	A	A	1,767,640.26	7,782	CAR	3.58	35.74		
L-80F	Light Bulb 80 Watt frosted 220/235V	A	C	1,634,004.71	6,469	CAR	3.31	39.05		
L-40F	Light Bulb 40 Watt frosted 220/235V	A	B	1,604,376.69	6,469	CAR	3.25	42.30		
DPC1005	Harddisk 21.13 GB / ATA-2	A		1,362,637.92	18,167	PC	2.76	45.06		
M-03	Sunny Tetra13	A		1,357,186.94	2,715	PC	2.75	47.81		
DPC1004	Harddisk 42.94 GB / SCSI-2-Fast	A		1,340,266.82	5,166	PC	2.72	50.53		
YY-250	MDH 0.10000 mm bl.ggl	A	D	1,239,367.36	2,213,156	M	2.51	53.04		
M-06	Flatscreen MS 1460 P	A		1,168,856.95	3,422	PC	2.37	55.41		
M-07	Flatscreen LE 64P	A		1,137,433.33	2,791	PC	2.31	57.72		
YY-260	Current conveyor 3 piece	B	D	1,106,578.00	100,596,000	PC	2.24	59.96		
40-200C	Pistons A 40/33x128 clear EMG	B	D	1,015,104.00	9,952,000	PC	2.06	62.02		
DPC1002	Harddisk 10.80 GB / SCSI-2-Fast	B		932,881.42	18,102	PC	1.89	63.91		
L-60R	Light Bulb 60 Watt red 220/235V	B	A	923,613.75	3,625	CAR	1.87	65.78		
L-60Y	Light Bulb 60 Watt yellow 220/235V	B	A	906,873.27	3,881	CAR	1.84	67.62		

Change cycle counting indicator

You can select an item and click Change CC Indicator to change the cycle counting indicator manually.

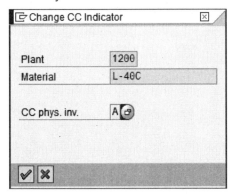

Counting effort

You can click Counting Effort... to estimate the counting effort per fiscal year.

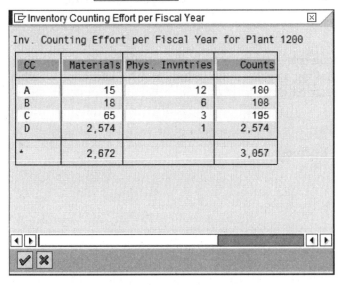

If you find the counting effort too much, you may reduce the percentages in the new analysis explained below.

New analysis

If you want to do the analysis again with changed percentages, click ⌑ New Analysis ⌑. The system gives you the dialog box, in which you can change the percentages.

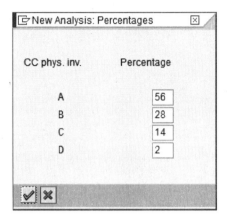

29.34.5 Creating Physical Inventory Documents for Cycle Counting

Purpose

You can run this transaction to create physical inventory documents for cycle counting. This program checks all materials having a cycle counting indicator to determine whether a physical inventory is due to be carried out.

Transaction

MICN—Create Physical Inventory Documents

Selection Screen

Selection criteria

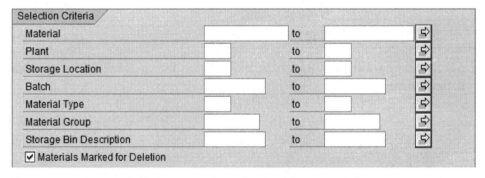

Here you can specify the criteria for selecting the materials.

Stock types

Stock Types
☑ Wareh
☐ Qual. Inspection
☐ Blocked

Apart from unrestricted stock, you can also select materials under quality inspection and blocked materials.

Stock level

Stock Level		
Threshold Value for Stock		☐ Exclude from Selectio
☐ Only Materials with Zero Stock		
☐ Only Materials W/o Zero Stock		
☐ Only Materials with Negative Stock		

Threshold value for stock

Here you specify the maximum stock level in base unit of measure up to which materials are selected. Note that this is the quantity and not the monetary value of stock.

Exclude from selection

If you select this checkbox, materials having stock up to the `Threshold Value for Stock` are excluded from selection.

Only materials with zero/positive/negative stock

If you do not select any checkbox above, all materials are selected. But if you want to select materials with zero/positive/negative values only, select the appropriate checkbox.

Data in physical inventory document header

Data in Phys. Inv. Docmt Header			
Planned Count Date From	12.12.2013	To	12.12.2013
Physical Inventory Number			
Phys. Inventory Ref.			
☐ Set Posting Block	☐ Freeze Book Inv.Bal.		

The values of these fields are copied in the physical inventory documents created by this process. These fields have been discussed in 'Creating a Physical Inventory Document Manually' (Section 29.2).

Batch input session

Batch Input Session		
☐ Generate Batch Input	Name of Session	MB_MI01_CN
☑ Issue Log	Max. No. of Items	20

Generate batch input, name of session

Here you can specify that a batch input be generated and the name of the batch input session. The batch input is processed using transaction SM35.

Issue log

You select this indicator to get a log onscreen after processing.

Maximum number of items per document

Here you can specify the maximum number of items per physical inventory document. If the number of selected items is more than this number, the system generates multiple physical inventory documents. All these documents can be linked through the physical inventory number specified in this screen.

Sort by

Sort by	
☐ Storage Bin Description	☐ New document created when group changed for sorting purposes
☐ Material Group	☐ Enter grouping criterion in document header

Storage bin description

You can sort the items by storage bin description.

Material group

You can sort the items by material group.

New document created on group changed for sorting purposes

Here you can specify that a new physical inventory document is to be created when the storage location description or the material group changes.

Enter grouping criterion in document header

Here you can specify that the grouping criterion (storage bin description or material group) is displayed in the header of the physical inventory document.

Output

List

The system issues a list containing the following data:

➤ It lists all stock management units for which no physical inventory documents can be created.

➤ It then lists the stock management units for which a physical inventory is already active, but has not been completed within the predefined float time and therefore must be completed urgently. These stock management units are not included when the batch input session is created because active physical inventory documents already exist.

➤ In addition, the list contains all materials for which cycle counting is required within the planned interval (specified interval for the planned count date). If a physical inventory had already been due prior to the planned interval, the planned count date would be highlighted.

The system calculates the planned count date for all stock types as follows: Date of last physical inventory of unrestricted-use stock + predefined interval.

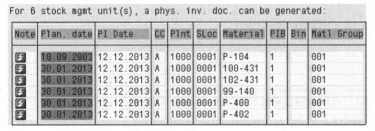

For 6 stock mgmt unit(s), a phys. inv. doc. can be generated:

Note	Plan. date	PI Date	CC	Plnt	SLoc	Material	PIB	Bin	Matl Group
	10.09.2003	12.12.2013	A	1000	0001	P-104	1		001
	30.01.2013	12.12.2013	A	1000	0001	100-431	1		001
	30.01.2013	12.12.2013	A	1000	0001	102-431	1		001
	30.01.2013	12.12.2013	A	1000	0001	99-140	1		001
	30.01.2013	12.12.2013	A	1000	0001	P-400	1		001
	30.01.2013	12.12.2013	A	1000	0001	P-402	1		001

Generate session

Click | Generate session | to create the batch input session for generating the physical inventory documents. The system displays the number of the batch input session: | ✅ BTCI session MB_MI01_CN created |.

Process session

Click | Process session |. The system takes you to transaction SM35.

Batch Input: Session Overview

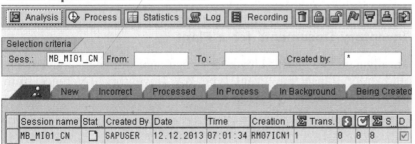

Session name	Stat.	Created By	Date	Time	Creation	∑ Trans.				S	D
MB_MI01_CN	🗋	SAPUSER	12.12.2013	07:01:34	RM07ICN1	1	0	0	0		☑

Select the session and click | ⊕ Process |. The system creates the physical inventory document.

Physical Inventory Document

Run transaction MI02 to display the physical inventory document created by processing the batch input session.

Plant	1000	Werk Hamburg
Stor. Loc.	0001	Materiallager

Items

Itm	Material	Material Description	Batch	STy	AUn	Del
1	P-104	Pump PRECISION 104		1	☑	☐
2	100-431	Mains adaptor 100 - 240 V		1	☑	☐
3	102-431	Mains adaptor 100 - 240 V		1	☑	☐
4	99-140	Ball bearing		1	☑	☐
5	P-400	Pump (Collective Order)		1	☑	☐
6	P-402	Pump standard IDESNORM 100-402		1	☑	☐

Entry   1 of   6

29.34.6 Posting Count and Difference

These processes are the same as those in normal physical inventory.

29.35 AUTOMATIC PHYSICAL INVENTORY DOCUMENTS FOR GOODS MOVEMENTS

Functional Consultant	User	Business Process Owner	Senior Management	My Rating	Understanding Level
C	X	X	X		

29.35.1 Purpose

If you post physical inventory differences in Warehouse Management using movement types 711–718, the system needs to generate physical inventory documents automatically. This section describes the settings required for that.

29.35.2 Physical Inventory Documents for a Plant

If you want to automatically generate physical inventory documents for goods movements for a plant, you should enter transaction/event type WV (inventory difference from Warehouse Management System) in view V_159L_V.

Plnt	Name 1	Trans./Event Type
0001	Werk 0001	WV
0005	Hamburg	WV
0006	New York	WV
0007	Werk Hamburg	WV
0008	New York	WV
1000	Werk Hamburg	WV

29.35.3 Number Range Assignment

In transaction OMBT (Section 22.4), you must include transaction/event type WV in the group physical inventory document.

```
☐ Phys. inventory documents
  IB ID IN IZ WV
```

You should also define number range intervals for this group.

NR Object	Material Document
Group............	Phys. inventory documents

Intervals

	Year	From number	To number	Current number	Ext
☐	1991	0100000000	0109999999	0	☐
☐	1999	0001000000	0001999999	1000064	☐
☐	2000	0100000000	0199999999	0	☐
☐	2001	0100000000	0199999999	0	☐
☐	2010	0100001000	0199999999	100001219	☐

29.35.4 Physical Inventory Documents for a Movement Type

If you want to automatically generate physical inventory documents for goods movements for a plant, you should tick Generate ph.inv.doc. in view V_156_I. In the standard SAP System, automatic generation of physical inventory documents is allowed for movement types 711 to 718.

MvT	Movement Type Text	Generate ph.inv.doc.
711	GI InvDiff.:whouse	☑
712	GR InvDiff.:wrhouse	☑
713	GI InvDiff.: QI	☑
714	GR InvDiff.: QI	☑
715	GI InvDiff.:returns	☑
716	GR InvDiff.:returns	☑
717	GI InvDiff.: blocked	☑
718	GR InvDiff.: blocked	☑

29.36 FORMS FOR PHYSICAL INVENTORY DOCUMENTS

Functional Consultant	User	Business Process Owner	Senior Management	My Rating	Understanding Level
A	X	X	X		

29.36.1 Purpose

For printing physical inventory document (program RM07IDRU), you can assign a form (layout set) of your choice. These lists are printed not via the output control, but directly from the report.

29.36.2 IMG Node

SM30 ➤ V_159N

29.36.3 Forms for Physical Inventory Documents

	Report	Report title	Version	P	Act
	RM07IDRU	Print Physical Inventory Document		4	☑
	RM07IDRU	Print Physical Inventory Document		5	☑

29.36.4 Inventory List without Sales Price

Program Name	RM07IDRU	Print Physical Inventory Document
Print Version		
Print item	4	Inventory List W/o Sales Price
☑ Form active		

Details		
Form	INVENT	Physical inventory document
	✎ Layout set	

Here you specify the form for inventory list without sales price.

29.36.5 Inventory List with Sales Price

Program Name	RM07IDRU	Print Physical Inventory Document
Print Version	☐	
Print item	5	Inventory List w. Sales Price
☑ Form active		

Details

Form	INVENT_VKBW

☆ Layout set

Here you specify the form for inventory list with sales price.

29.37 SERIAL NUMBERS

Functional Consultant	*User*	*Business Process Owner*	*Senior Management*	*My Rating*	*Understanding Level*
B	C	X	X		

29.37.1 Serial Numbers

There are some materials, e.g. cars, where each piece is identified by a unique serial number. Serial numbers are used in many modules of SAP.

Module	*Example*
Production	Each car produced may have a unique serial number.
Inventory Management	Bought out parts, e.g. fuel injection pump may have a serial number. These serial numbers may be external (assigned by the manufacturer of the fuel injection pump) or internal (assigned by the purchasing company).
Sales and Distribution	Cars may be custom-ordered and produced. They may only be sold to customers who ordered them.
Shipping	Cars shipped from Japan to the USA need to be offloaded on different ports based on their serial numbers.
Plant Maintenance	Each machine may be given a serial number that is referred in multiple applications.
Assets	Each asset may be given a serial number. Physical inventory may be carried out for assets as well.
Physical Inventory	For serialized materials and assets, it is not enough to count the material. Physical inventory needs to confirm existence of each individual item in the stock.

29.37.2 Serial Numbers for a Material

For each material, at plant level, you specify whether each piece is to be assigned a unique serial number. If so, you maintain its serial number profile and serialization level.

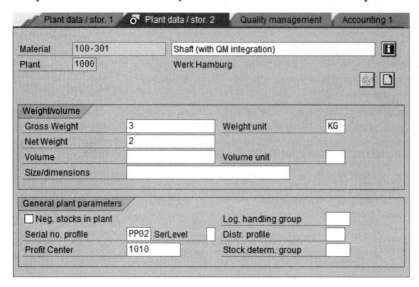

Serial number profile

Materials which are managed with serial numbers are assigned a serial number profile in the material master at plant level.

Serialization level

Serialization level	Short text
	Serialization within the stock material number
1	Keep equipment number and serial number synchronous

If serialization level is blank, serial numbers are unique within a material. If not, serial numbers are unique client wide.

29.37.3 Serial Number Profile

You maintain serial number profile in view V_T377P of view cluster SERIPROF.

	Profl.	Profile text	ExistReq.	Cat	Equipment category	StkCk
	0001	Serial profile 01	☐	S	Customer equipment	
	0002	Serial profile 02	☐	S	Customer equipment	
	0003	Inventory Management	☐	S	Customer equipment	2
	AM01	Automotive	☑	S	Customer equipment	

Profile

Serial number profile groups materials having same serialization characteristics.

Serial number existence requirement

If this indicator is set, the serial numbers must be created first as a master record in the system. If the indicator is not set, the serial numbers are created during a business transaction, e.g. production.

Equipment category

In this field you enter the equipment category for the profile that should be proposed as default when serial numbers are created automatically during serialization procedures. If equipment category is not maintained here, then the equipment category maintained in view V_T399J_SD is used. Master list of equipment categories is stored in table T370T. There are several views of this table which are used for different purposes.

Stock check

This indicator states whether the system should perform a stock check during serial number assignment. If it should, it can give a warning or error in the event of stock inconsistencies with Inventory Management.

Stock check	Short text
	No stock validation
1	Inconsistencies in stock data -> Warning
2	Inconsistencies in stock data -> Error

If the stock check is blank or 1, you can change the stock information in the serial number master record.

29.37.4 Serialization Procedures

You maintain serialization procedures for a serial number profile in view V_T377 of view cluster SERIPROF.

SerialNoProfile	0003
Profile text	Inventory Management

	Procd	Procedure descriptn	SerUsage	EqReq
	MMSL	Maintain goods receipt and issue doc.	03	01
	PPAU	Serial numbers in PP order	02	01
	PPRL	PP order release	03	01
	PPSF	Serial nos in repetitive manufacturing	03	01
	QMSL	Maintain inspection lot	03	01
	SDAU	Serial numbers in SD order	01	01
	SDCC	Completness check for delivery	03	01
	SDCR	Completion check IR delivery	03	01
	SDLS	Maintain delivery	02	01
	SDRE	Maintain returns delivery	02	01

Serialization procedure

Serialization procedure MMSL is for Inventory Management.

Serial number usage

This indicator determines whether serial number is optional, mandatory, etc.

Serial number usage	Short text
01	None
02	Optional
03	Obligatory
04	Automatic

If the serial numbers are automatically assigned during a transaction, the dialog box for creating serial numbers is not displayed.

Equipment requirement

This indicator determines whether or not an equipment master record should be created for each number when assigning serial numbers.

Equipment requiremt	Short text
01	Proposal: w/o equipment
02	always with equipment

Equipment requirement	Description
01	The user can later decide when assigning serial numbers in the dialog box, whether an equipment master record should still be created.
02	When assigning serial numbers in the dialog box, an equipment master record must be created.

29.37.5 Physical Inventory of Serialized Materials

Checking serial numbers

If a material has serial numbers, in physical inventory you must check that each serial number is present in physical stock.

Displaying serial numbers

If you use serial numbers (a number assigned to each piece of the material), it is not enough to enter count during physical inventory. You have to enter serial number of each piece in the Maintain serial numbers dialog box. This task can become easier, if the system displays the existing serial numbers in the Maintain serial numbers dialog box. To enable this functionality, set ☑ Display Serial Nos in view V_159L_EI.

Printing serial numbers in physical inventory documents

You may want to print serial numbers on physical inventory documents so that the persons verifying inventory can just tick them. This saves effort. If you want to do that, set `Print Serial Numbers` `+++++++++++++++++++` in view V_159L_EI. Each material that has a serial number is printed on a page of its own.

Serial numbers have a maximum of 18 characters. In `Print Serial Numbers` you can define whether the whole serial number or only part of the serial number is printed, or whether it is not printed at all. For each character you specify whether it is to be printed (+) or not (–).

Leaving blank lines for serialized materials

If you are not printing serial numbers in the physical inventory document, you may want to provide space so that the persons verifying inventory can write serial numbers during the counting process. In `No. Serial No. Lines` field in view V_159L_EI you can specify the number of lines to be left blank after each serialized material.

30

Financial Accounting

30.1 COMPANY CODE

Functional Consultant	User	Business Process Owner	Senior Management	My Rating	Understanding Level
A	A	A	A		

30.1.1 Purpose

All financial transactions take place in a company code. In Materials Management the company code is determined from the plant.

30.1.2 IMG Node

Transaction OBY6—Maintain company code

SM30 ➤ V_001_B

30.1.3 Screen

Change View "Company Code Global Data": Details

| | Additional Data | ◀ | ▶ | 🖨 |

Company Code	1000	IDES AG	Frankfurt
Country key	DE	Currency	EUR	Language Key	DE

Accounting organization

Chart of Accts	INT	Country Chart/Accts	GKR
Company	1000	FM Area	1000
Credit control area	1000	Fiscal Year Variant	K4
Ext. co. code	☐	Global CoCde	GL1000
Company code is productive	☑	VAT Registration No.	DE123456789

Processing parameters

Document entry screen variant		☑ Business area fin. statements	
Field status variant	1000	☑ Propose fiscal year	
Pstng period variant	1000	☑ Define default value date	
Max. exchange rate deviation	10 %	☐ No forex rate diff. when clearing in LC	
Sample acct rules var.		☐ Tax base is net value	
Workflow variant	1000	☐ Discount base is net value	
Inflation Method		☐ Financial Assets Mgmt active	
Crcy transl. for tax		☐ Purchase account processing	
CoCd->CO Area	2		
Cost of sales accounting actv.	2		
☑ Negative Postings Permitted		☐ Enable amount split	
☑ Cash Management activated			

30.1.4 Primary Key

| Company Code |

30.1.5 Important Fields

Company code

All properties are being defined for this company code.

Country key

This company code is a legal entity in this country.

Currency

This is the default currency of the company code.

Language key

This is the default language of the company code.

Chart of accounts

Accounting of a company code is done in G/L accounts which belong to a chart of accounts.

Fiscal year variant

The fiscal year variant defines the fiscal year, posting periods in a fiscal year, special periods and how the system determines the posting periods when posting. It is assigned to the company code.

Posting period variant

Posting period variant defines the beginning and end of posting periods.

30.2 CHART OF ACCOUNTS

Functional Consultant	User	Business Process Owner	Senior Management	My Rating	Understanding Level
A	A	A	A		

30.2.1 Purpose

Chart of accounts

A chart of accounts is a list of G/L accounts. For each G/L account, the chart of accounts contains the account number, account name, and control information, e.g., whether the account is a balance sheet account, or a P&L account.

Chart of accounts for a company code

Each company code is assigned one and only one chart of accounts. It may use some or all of the G/L accounts in the chart of accounts. Another company code may use the same chart of accounts, or a different chart of accounts.

Chart of accounts for a group of companies

Use of the same chart of accounts by several group companies helps in consolidation of the group's financial information.

30.2.2 IMG Node

Transaction OB13—Maintain Chart of Accounts
SM30 ➤ V_T004

30.2.3 Screen

Chart of Accts	INT
Description	Chart of accounts - international

General specifications

Maint.language	EN English
Length of G/L account number	10

Integration

Controlling integration	Manual creation of cost elements

Consolidation

Group Chart of Accts	CONS

Status

☐ Blocked

30.2.4 Primary Key

Chart of Accounts

30.3 G/L ACCOUNTS IN A CHART OF ACCOUNTS

Functional Consultant	User	Business Process Owner	Senior Management	My Rating	Understanding Level
A	B	B	B		

30.3.1 Purpose

Here you define the properties of G/L accounts that apply to all company codes using this chart of accounts.

30.3.2 IMG Node

Transaction FSP0—G/L Accounts in Chart of Accounts

30.3.3 Screen

| G/L Account | 300000 | Inventory - Raw Material 1 |
| Chart of Accts | INT | Chart of accounts - internatio |

Type/Description | Key word/translation | Information

Control in chart of accounts

| Account Group | MAT Materials management accoun |
| Sample account | |

○ P&L statement acct

Detailed control for P&L statement accounts

| P&L statmt acct type | |
| Functional Area | |

⦿ Balance sheet account

Description

| Short Text | Inventory - Raw Mate |
| G/L Acct Long Text | Inventory - Raw Material 1 |

Consolidation data in chart of accounts

| Trading Partner | |
| Group account number | 135100 | Raw Materials |

30.3.4 Primary Key

Primary key of table SKA1 is

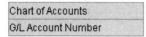

| Chart of Accounts |
| G/L Account Number |

30.3.5 Important Fields

G/L account number, chart of accounts

You specify the properties of this G/L account in this chart of accounts.

Account group

The account group determines the screen layout and number range of the G/L account. Account groups are maintained using transaction OBD4.

Sample account

The sample account contains data which will be transferred when you create a master record in the company code.

P&L statement account

P&L statement accounts contain revenues and expenditures of a company code. Every account is either a balance sheet account, or a P&L account.

P&L statement account type

P&L accounts are grouped in P&L statement account types, each of which is linked to a retained earning account.

ISA tpe	ChAc	Targ.acct	Short Text
X	INT	900000	Unap.ret.earnings py
Y	INT	10900000	AR60/Unap.ret.ear.py

Balance sheet account

Balance sheet accounts contain the assets and liabilities of a company code. Every G/L account is either a balance sheet account, or a P&L account.

Group account number

G/L accounts can be grouped in to group account number. A group account number is also a G/L account, which can be grouped further. In this way, G/L accounts can be structured in the form of a tree. Group accounts may be assigned to line items of the balance sheet and P&L statement.

30.3.6   Finding and Displaying a G/L Account

Purpose

In order to see details of a G/L account, you need to know its number. You can use this report to find a G/L account.

Transaction

S_ALR_87012326—Chart of Accounts

Selection Screen

You can narrow down the list of G/L accounts by specifying various selection criteria.

G/L account selection				
G/L account	300000	to	300999	⇨

Selection using search help		
Search help ID	☐	
Search String		
Complex search help	⇨	

Chart of accounts	INT	to		⇨
Charts of accts not assigned	1			

Account group	MAT	to		⇨
Sample account		to		⇨
Group account number	135100	to		⇨
P+L statement account type	☐	to	☐	⇨
Only with creation block	☐	to	☐	⇨
Only with planning block	☐	to	☐	⇨

Additional header	

List of G/L Accounts

After entering the selection criteria, click ⊕. The system gives the list of selected G/L accounts.

G/L acct	G/L Acct Long Text
300000	Inventory - Raw Material 1
300001	Value adjustment - other raw materials
300010	Inventory - Raw Material 2
300011	Depreciation - other raw materials 2
300100	Remaining Stock Raw Material 1
300200	Remaining Stock Raw Material 2
300550	Inventory - Raw Material SCM550

Display a G/L Account

Place cursor on a G/L account and click 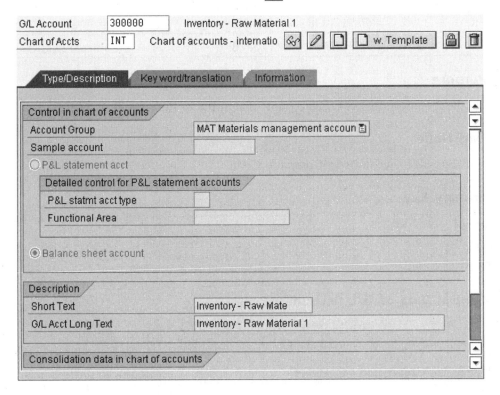 to display the G/L account.

G/L Accounts not assigned to any Company Code

You can also use this report to find G/L accounts that are not assigned to any company code by selecting `Charts of accts not assigned  2` in the selection screen.

```
IDES-ALE: Central FI Syst        Chart of Accounts      Date  15.10.2013
Frankfurt - Deutschland                                 Page         1
ChartofAccts CAES Chart of accounts - Spain

 G/L acct  G/L Acct Long Text

 100000    Capital ordinario
 100100    Capital privilegiado
 100200    Capital sin derecho a voto
 100300    Capital con derechos restringidos
 101000    Fondo social
 102000    Capital
```

30.4 G/L ACCOUNTS IN A COMPANY CODE

Functional Consultant	User	Business Process Owner	Senior Management	My Rating	Understanding Level
A	B	B	B		

30.4.1 Purpose

Here you define the properties of G/L accounts that apply to this specific company code.

30.4.2 IMG Node

Transaction FSS0—G/L Accounts in Company Code

30.4.3 Primary Key

Primary key of table SKB1 is

Company Code
G/L Account Number

30.4.4 Control Data of G/L Account

G/L account, company code

You specify the properties of this G/L account in this company code.

Account currency

If you specify a currency here, the account is maintained in this currency.

Only balances in local currency

This indicator indicates that balances are updated only in local currency when users post items to this account. You would set this indicator for accounts in which you do not want the system to update transaction figures separately by currency.

Tax category

In tax accounts, you can specify the type of tax on sales/purchases (input or output tax) that can be posted to the account.

Posting without tax allowed

Here you specify whether posting to accounting can take place when there is no tax calculation.

Reconciliation account for account type

For each vendor you maintain a sub-ledger account. Their totals are maintained in one or more reconciliation accounts in the general ledger. Here you specify whether this is a reconciliation account, and if so for which type of sub-ledger accounts.

```
A Assets
D Customers
K Vendors
V Contract accounts receivable
```

Alternative account number

You can use this field for keeping an account number that can be printed in the financial statement.

Account managed in external system

If you are working with distributed systems, you can specify that this account is managed in an external system.

Open item management

When a vendor supplies material, you create a credit entry; and when you pay, you make a debit entry. Having cleared a credit line item by matching debit line item, you would like both these items to vanish, and not clutter the account. This is called open line management. Here you specify whether this account is under open item management.

Line item display

Here you can specify that line items for this account can be displayed. This requires storage of detailed data, and should be specified only for those accounts for whom this feature is really important.

Sort key

Here you can specify the sort sequence for line items.

Authorization group

You can specify an authorization group here and use it for giving authorization to users.

Accounting clerk

The name of the accounting clerk specified here can be used in the payment program for correspondence and reporting.

Recovery indicator

This indicator is used in joint venture companies to share costs.

30.4.5   Create/Bank/Interest

| G/L Account | 300000 | Inventory - Raw Material 1 |
| Company Code | 1000 | IDES AG |

With Template

Control Data   **Create/bank/interest**   **Information**

Control of document creation in company code

| Field status group | G006 | Material accounts |

☑ Post automatically only

☐ Supplement auto. postings

Bank/financial details in company code

| Planning level | |
| Commitment Item | 9993 | Expense - Unclassifiable |

Interest calculation information in company code

Interest indicator	
Interest calc. frequency	0
Key date of last int. calc.	
Date of last interest run	

Field status group

Field status group determines the data entry characteristics. It specifies whether a field is optional, mandatory, or suppressed.

Post automatically only

When you receive goods, the system automatically posts debit to the stock account and credit to the GR/IR clearing account using account determination. Another method of posting is manual, where you specify the account and amount. If you select this checkbox, manual posting to the account is not allowed.

30.4.6 Information

G/L Account	300000	Inventory - Raw Material 1
Company Code	1000	IDES AG

Control Data | Create/bank/interest | **Information**

Information in company code

Created on	23.06.1992	
Created by	SAP	Change documents
Chart of Accounts	INT	Chart of accounts - international
Country Chart/Accts	GKR	German Joint Standard Accounting System
Country Key	DE	Germany
FM Area	1000	IDES AG
Controlling Area	1000	CO Europe

G/L Account texts in company code

X L	Meaning	First Line	T L	Cur	1 / 3
☐ EN	Account assignmen		☐☐		
☐ EN	Accounting note		☐☐		
☐ EN	Additional info		☐☐		

30.5 FISCAL YEAR VARIANT

Functional Consultant	User	Business Process Owner	Senior Management	My Rating	Understanding Level
A	C	C	C		

30.5.1 Fiscal Year

A fiscal year is usually a period of twelve months for which a company regularly creates financial statements and checks inventories. The fiscal year may correspond exactly to the calendar year, but this is not obligatory.

A fiscal year is divided into posting periods. Each posting period is defined by a start and a finish date. Before you can post documents, you must define posting periods, which in turn define the fiscal year. In addition to the posting periods, you can also define special periods for year-end closing.

In General Ledger Accounting, a fiscal year can have a maximum of twelve posting periods and four special periods. You can define up to 366 posting periods in the Special Purpose Ledger.

30.5.2 Fiscal Year Variant

The fiscal year variant defines the fiscal year, posting periods in a fiscal year, special periods and how the system determines the posting periods when posting. It is assigned to the company code.

30.5.3 IMG Node

Transaction OB29—Fiscal Year Variants

30.5.4 Screen

Dialog Structure							
▽ 🗁 Fiscal year variants	**Fiscal year variants**						
🗀 Periods	FV	Description	Year-depe	Calendar yr	Numb	No.of	
🗀 Period texts	01	Calendar year, 1 spec. pe	☐	☑	12	1	
🗀 Shortened Fisc	24	Half periods	☐	☐	24		
	AA	Short.fiscal year 1997 wit	☑	☐	12		
	AM	Short.fiscal year 1993 wit	☑	☐	12		
	C1	1st period (calendar year	☐	☐	1		
	F1	366 periods	☐	☐	366		
	K0	Calendar year, 1 spec. pe	☐	☑	12		
	K1	Calendar year, 1 spec. pe	☐	☑	12	1	
	K2	Calendar year, 2 spec. pe	☐	☑	12	2	
	K3	Calendar year, 3 spec. pe	☐	☑	12	3	
	K4	Calendar year, 4 spec. pe	☐	☑	12	4	
	MM	MM01-FISCAL YEAR	☐	☐	12	4	

30.5.5 Primary Key

Fiscal Year Variant

30.5.6 Important Fields

Fiscal year variant and description

The fiscal year variant defines the fiscal year, posting periods in a fiscal year, special periods and how the system determines the posting periods when posting.

Year-dependent

This indicator specifies that the allocation of posting periods to calendar days must be made individually for each year. This is necessary if the end of the period is not linked to a fixed calendar day.

Calendar year

If this indicator is selected, the fiscal year is a calendar year and the posting periods are the months of the calendar year.

Number of posting periods

The fiscal year can be divided into periods. These are divided into normal posting periods and special periods for closing purposes. This field contains the number of normal posting periods.

Number of special periods

Special posting periods subdivide the last regular posting period for closing operations. They represent an extension of the last normal posting period. When the posting date falls within the last normal posting period, then during document entry you can specify that the transaction figures be updated separately in one of the special periods.

30.5.7 Periods

If the calendar year indicator is not selected, you need to define the periods here.

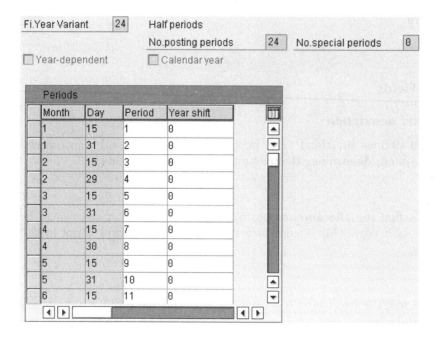

30.5.8 Period Texts

In period texts you can specify a name for each period.

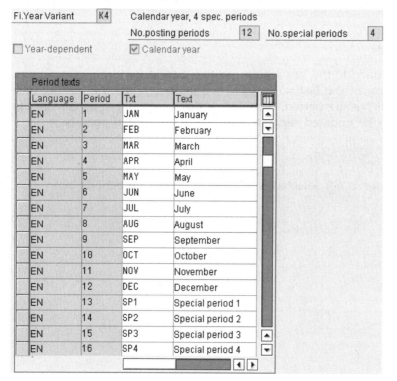

30.5.9   Shortened Fiscal Years

A shortened fiscal year is a fiscal year that contains less than twelve months. A shortened fiscal year can be defined for year-dependent fiscal year variants only.

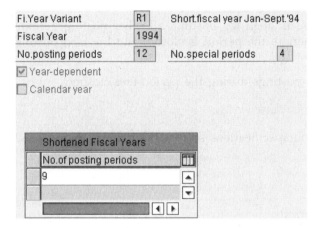

30.6   POSTING PERIOD VARIANT

Functional Consultant	User	Business Process Owner	Senior Management	My Rating	Understanding Level
A	C	C	C		

30.6.1   Posting Period Variants

Posting period variants are defined in view V_T010O.

Variant	Name
1000	Variant 1000

30.6.2   Assignment of Posting Period Variants to Company Code

Posting period variants are assigned to company code in view V_001_R.

CoCd	Company Name	City	Variant
1000	IDES AG	Frankfurt	1000

30.6.3   Opening and Closing Posting Periods

Overview

Opening and closing posting periods is usually controlled by senior users from the Finance department. This topic is included here so that if your goods movement fails because posting period is not open, you can see if the problem lies in these settings.

Opening posting periods

You define posting periods in your fiscal year variants. You can open and close these posting periods for posting. As many periods as you require can be open for posting simultaneously.

Usually, only the current posting period is open for posting, all other posting periods are closed. At the end of this posting period, the period is closed, and the next posting period is opened.

Special periods can be open for closing postings during the period-end closing.

Closing posting periods

You close periods by selecting the period specifications so that the periods to be closed are no longer contained.

IMG Node

Transaction OB52—Maintain Posting Periods
SM30 ➤ V_T001B

Screen

Var.	A	From acct	To account	From	Year	To	Year	From per.2	Year	To period	Year	AuGr
1000	+							9	2013	10	2013	
1000	A		ZZZZZZZZZZ					9	2013	10	2013	
1000	D		ZZZZZZZZZZ					10	2013	10	2013	
1000	K		ZZZZZZZZZZ					10	2013	10	2013	
1000	M		ZZZZZZZZZZ					10	2013	10	2013	
1000	S		ZZZZZZZZZZ					9	2013	10	2013	

Important Fields

Open period intervals 1 and 2

You can specify two period intervals during which posting are open. In each period, you specify the start period (including year) and end period (including year).

Open period interval 1

Open period interval 1 can be used to allow postings by users who belong to the authorization group specified in the field AuGr.

Open period interval 2

Open period interval 2 allows posting by all users.

Account type

You can differentiate the opening and closing of posting periods by account type. This means that for a specific posting period, postings can be permitted to customer accounts, but not to vendor accounts.

For each posting period that should be open, you must always specify at least account type + (valid for all account types). You can exercise more detailed control by specifying further account types.

Using the minimum entry, when you enter the posting date in the document header, the system checks whether the posting period determined in the posting period variant can be posted to. As soon as you then enter an account number, in a second step, the system checks whether the posting period is permitted for the account specified.

Account interval

You can differentiate the opening and closing of posting periods by account intervals. This means that you only open a posting period for posting to a specific account.

Account intervals always apply to G/L accounts. If you want to open sub ledger accounts, you have to enter the corresponding reconciliation account and the account type.

During the closing operations, you can, for example, use the reconciliation accounts to close customer and vendor accounts before G/L accounts. This allows you to prevent further postings to these accounts after you have confirmed the balances with your customers and vendors. Balance confirmation is one of the prerequisites for further closing operations.

Authorization group

You can open and close posting periods only for specific users. To do this, enter an authorization group at document header level. This authorization group is effective only in time period 1.

30.6.4   Open and Close Posting Periods According to G/L Account Assignment Objects

Purpose

You can allow posting for certain account assignment objects, while preventing posting for other objects. Here you can specify which posting periods are open for the posting for each posting period variant and account assignment object.

IMG Node

SM34 ➤ VC_T001B_PS

Screen

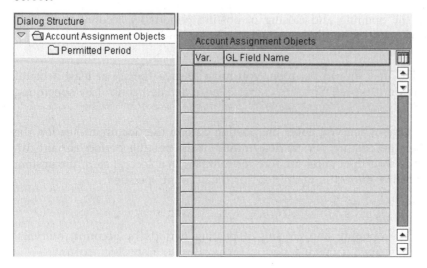

30.7 G/L ACCOUNTS REPORTS

Functional Consultant	User	Business Process Owner	Senior Management	My Rating	Understanding Level
A	A	A	A		

30.7.1 G/L Accounts List with Details

Run transaction S_ALR_87012328 to see the list of G/L accounts.

```
IDES-ALE: Central FI Syst                    G/L Account List
Frankfurt - Deutschland

  ChartofAccts:   INT = Chart of accounts - international
  Sort:           G/LAccount, CompanyCode

Name 1          Contents 1          Name 2           Contents 2      Name 3
G/L acct   0000001000 Company Code        Company Code Name
Section              GENERAL DATA
Long Text      Real estate and similar rights               Account Group
Section              STATUS IN CHART OF ACCTS
Creation block                      Posting Block            Planning block
G/L acct   0000001000 Company Code    0001  Company Code Name   SAP A.G.
Section              ACCOUNT CONTROL
Tax category     -                  Reconcil.ID    A          E/R diff. key
Balances in LC                      W/o tax                   Account exterr
Section              ACCOUNT MANAGEMENT
Line items                          OI management             Sort key
Section              DOCUMENT ENTRY CONTROL
Field status gp G007                Auto. posting             Supplement
```

On the selection screen you can specify the details that you want to see for the G/L accounts.

30.7.2 G/L Accounts in a Chart of Accounts

G/L accounts in a chart of accounts

Run transaction S_ALR_87012326 to see G/L accounts in a chart of accounts.

```
IDES-ALE: Central FI Syst           Chart of Accounts       Date   03.07.2013
Frankfurt - Deutschland                                     Page             1
ChartofAccts INT Chart of accounts - international
```

G/L acct	G/L Acct Long Text
1000	Real estate and similar rights
1010	Accum. depn - real estate and similar rights
1050	Appreciation land
2000	Buildings
2010	Accumulated depreciation-buildings
2050	Appreciation buildings
11000	Machinery and equipment
11002	Constructions
11010	Accumulated depreciation - machinery and equipment
11020	Accumulated depreciation-constructions
11050	Appreciation Plant & Machinery
12000	Low value assets
12010	Depreciation - Low value assets
13000	Vehicles
13010	Depreciation - motor vehicles

You can select an account and click 🔍 to see its details.

G/L accounts that are not assigned to any company code

You can also use this report to find G/L accounts that are not assigned to any company code by selecting `Charts of accts not assigned 2` in the selection screen.

```
IDES-ALE: Central FI Syst           Chart of Accounts       Date   15.10.2013
Frankfurt - Deutschland                                     Page             1
ChartofAccts CAES Chart of accounts - Spain
```

G/L acct	G/L Acct Long Text
100000	Capital ordinario
100100	Capital privilegiado
100200	Capital sin derecho a voto
100300	Capital con derechos restringidos
101000	Fondo social
102000	Capital

30.7.3 G/L Accounts in Company Codes

Run transaction S_ALR_87012333 to see the list of G/L accounts in one or more company codes.

G/L accounts list

ChAc	G/L account	CoCd	Long Text	D	D
INT	1000	1000	Real estate and similar rights		
INT	1010	1000	Accum. depn - real estate and similar rights		
INT	2000	1000	Buildings		
INT	2010	1000	Accumulated depreciation-buildings		
INT	11000	1000	Machinery and equipment		
INT	11010	1000	Accumulated depreciation - machinery and equipment		
INT	12000	1000	Low value assets		
INT	12010	1000	Depreciation - Low value assets		
INT	21000	1000	Fixtures and fittings		
INT	21010	1000	Accumulated depreciation - fixtures and fittings		
INT	22000	1000	Low value assets (fixtures and fittings)		
INT	22010	1000	Depreciation - LVA office equipment		

30.7.4 G/L Account Balances

Purpose

You can display balances in a G/L account and drill down to see its breakup.

Transaction

FS10N—Display Balances

Selection Screen

G/L account	191100
Company code	1000
Fiscal year	2013
Business area	
Currency type	

If you do not see Currency type on the selection screen, click 🔳.

G/L Account Balance Display

Account number	191100	Goods Rcvd/Invoice R
Company code	1000	IDES AG
Business area	*	
Fiscal year	2013	
All documents in currency	*	Display currency EUR

Period	Debit	Credit	Balance	Cum. balance
Balance Carryforward				288,344,325.16-
1				288,344,325.16-
2				288,344,325.16-
3		60.00	60.00-	288,344,385.16-
4				288,344,385.16-
5				288,344,385.16-
6		240.00	240.00-	288,344,625.16-
7				288,344,625.16-
8				288,344,625.16-
9	82.80	2,509.30	2,426.50-	288,347,051.66-
10		589.40	589.40-	288,347,641.06-
11				288,347,641.06-
12		20.00	20.00-	288,347,661.06-
13				288,347,661.06-
14				288,347,661.06-
15				288,347,661.06-
16				288,347,661.06-
Total	82.80	3,418.70	3,335.90-	288,347,661.06-

G/L Account Line Item Display

Select an item and click [image]. The system shows the accounting documents that added up to that total.

G/L Account	191100	Goods Rcvd/Invoice Rcvd (third party)
Company Code	1000	

Type	Doc. Date	Amount in local cur.	DocumentNo
WE	03.09.2013	600.00-	5000000002
WE	04.09.2013	180.00-	5000000004
WE	06.09.2013	120.00-	5000000007
WE	08.09.2013	60.00-	5000000010
WE	11.09.2013	300.00	5000000014
WE	09.09.2013	511.30-	5000000011
WE	10.09.2013	550.00-	5000000013
WE	04.09.2013	24.00-	5000000003
WE	05.09.2013	53.00-	5000000006
WE	06.09.2013	10.60	5000000008
WE	06.09.2013	21.20	5000000009
WE	16.09.2013	51.00-	5000000015
RE	17.09.2013	51.00	5100000000
WE	23.09.2013	900.00-	5000000016
* Account 191100		2,426.50-	
**		2,426.50-	

Accounting Document Line Item

We can select a line item and click 🔍 or 🖉 to display or change the line item in the document.

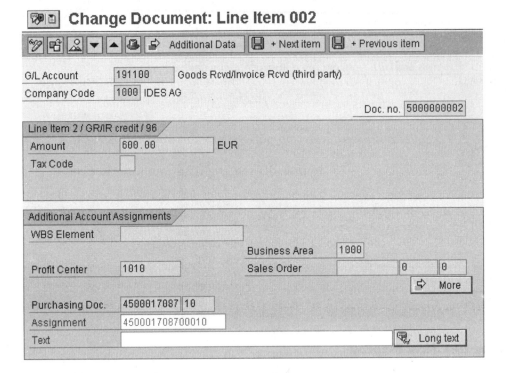

30.8 BALANCE SHEET AND PROFIT AND LOSS STATEMENT

Functional Consultant	User	Business Process Owner	Senior Management	My Rating	Understanding Level
A	A	A	A		

30.8.1 Structured Account Balances

Run transaction S_PL0_86000032 to see the account balances in structured form. In the selection screen you specify the `Financial statement version`.

Commercial balance sheet

OL   Ledger
10   Currency type Company code currency
EUR   Amounts in Euro (EMU currency as of 01/01/1999)
2013.01 -2013.16 Reporting periods
2012.01 -2012.16 Comparison periods

F.S. item/account	Tot.rpt.pr	tot.cmp.pr	Abs. diff.
▽ ☐ A S S E T S	2,388.92	0.00	2,388.92
▷ ☐ Current assets	2,388.92	0.00	2,388.92
▽ ☐ L I A B I L I T I E S	258.59-	0.00	258.59-
▷ ☐ Payables	258.59-	0.00	258.59-
▽ ☐ Profit and loss statement	1,185.57	0.00	1,185.57
▷ ☐ Inventory changes	1,598.07	0.00	1,598.07
▷ ☐ Raw materials and consumables	412.50-	0.00	412.50-
▽ ☐ Supplement	3,315.90-	0.00	3,315.90-
▷ ☐ GR/IR clearing (RM)	3,315.90-	0.00	3,315.90-

30.8.2 Financial Statement

A financial statement has both balance sheet and profit and loss statement. Run transaction S_ALR_87012284 to see the financial statement.

Commercial balance sheet

OL   Ledger
10   Currency type Company code currency
EUR   Amounts in Euro (EMU currency as of 01/01/1999)
2013.01 -2013.16 Reporting periods
2012.01 -2012.16 Comparison periods

FS Item	Text for B/S P&L item	Total report.per.	tot.cmp.pr	Abs. difference	Pct.Diff.
1000000	A S S E T S				
1000000	===========				
1040000	Current assets				
1040000	==============				
1041000	Stocks				
1041000	======				
1041010	Raw materials and supplies				
1041010	==========================				
1041010	0000300000 Inventory - Raw Material 1	151.05-	0.00	151.05-	
1041010		151.05-	0.00	151.05-	
1041020	Work in process				
1041020	===============				

The report shows the amount in reporting period, amount in comparison period, absolute difference and percentage difference for G/L accounts structured by the financial statement version.

30.8.3 Financial Statement Definition

Purpose

You can define the versions you need to create a balance sheet and profit and loss statement.

JMG Node

SM30 ➢ V_T011

Screen

Fin.Stmt.version	INT
Name	Commercial balance sheet

General specifications	
Maint. language	EN
Item keys auto.	☐
Chart of Accounts	INT
Group Account Number	☐
Fun.area perm.	☐

Balance Sheet Items

Click Goto > Fin.statement items, or run transaction FSE2, to define items in the financial statement.

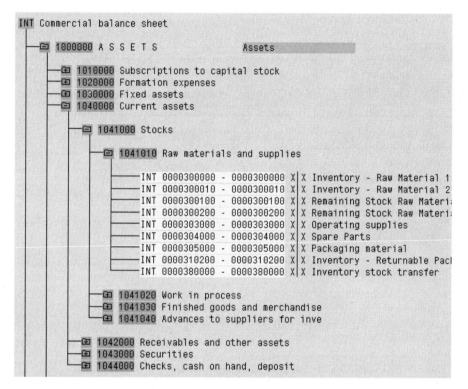

In this way you create the tree structure of G/L accounts.

30.9 ACCOUNTS PAYABLE REPORTS

Functional Consultant	User	Business Process Owner	Senior Management	My Rating	Understanding Level
A	A	A	A		

30.9.1 Accounts Payable: Balances

Purpose

You can display period wise amounts payable to vendors.

Transaction

FK10N—Accounts Payable: Display Balances

Account Payable: Balances

Vendor	4444	London Supplying Plant
Company Code	1000	IDES AG
Fiscal Year	2013	
Display crrncy	EUR	

Bals Special G/L

Period	Debit	Credit	Balance	Cum. balance	Sales/Purchases
Balance Carryforward					
1					
2					
3					
4					
5					
6					
7					
8					
9	51.00	51.00-	51.00-	51.00-	
10				51.00-	
11				51.00-	
12				51.00-	
13				51.00-	
14				51.00-	
15				51.00-	
16				51.00-	
Total	51.00	51.00-	51.00-	51.00-	

Account Payable: Line Items

You can select a period and click to display line items.

Vendor	4444
Company Code	1000
Name	London Supplying Plant
City	London

St	Assignment	DocumentNo	Type	Doc. Date	S	DD	Amount in doc.	Curr.
☐ ◉	51000000002013	5100000000	RE	17.09.2013		⚡	51.00-	EUR
* ◉							51.00-	EUR
** Account 4444							51.00-	EUR
***							51.00-	EUR

30.9.2   Accounts Payable: Line Items

Purpose

You can display the amount payable to various vendors.

Transaction

FBL1N—Accounts Payable: Display/Change Line Items

Account Payable: Line Items

```
Vendor                    4444
Company Code              1000

Name                      London Supplying Plant
City                      London
```

St	Assignment	DocumentNo	Type	Doc. Date	S	DD	Amount in doc.	Curr.
☐ 🔘	51000000002013	5100000000	RE	17.09.2013		🔲	51.00-	EUR
* 🔘							51.00-	EUR
** Account 4444							51.00-	EUR
***							51.00-	EUR

Controlling

31.1 OVERVIEW

Functional Consultant	User	Business Process Owner	Senior Management	My Rating	Understanding Level
A	A	A	A		

31.1.1 Controlling

Controlling area

A company code is a legal entity with statutory reporting requirements. Many corporate houses do their business under several company codes but have a single management. Controlling area is the organizational level for management control which can span several company codes.

Controlling business operations

Management controls the business by planning, recording the actual, comparing the two, and taking the necessary action.

Controlling for inventory management users

Consultants and users in the area of Inventory Management are not interested in the full functionality of the Controlling module. They would, however, be interested in understanding how the costs incurred in Inventory Management are reported.

31.1.2   Controlling Documents

Controlling document in inventory management

Costs are incurred during goods movement and recorded in a controlling document which may be seen in material document transaction MB02 or MB03.

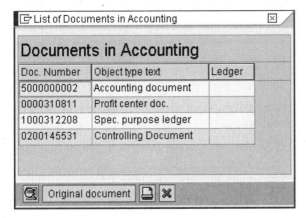

Cost documents report

If you want to see multiple cost documents, run transaction KSB5.

```
Layout                     /PKA        Primary cost posting
COarea currency            EUR         EUR
```

DocumentNo	Doc. Date	RT	RefDocNo	User Name	Rev	RvD						
PRw	OTy	Object	Obj. name	Cost El	CElem.name	ValCOArCur	Quant	PUM	O	Offst.		
200145531	03.09.2013	R	5000000010	SAPUSER								
1	CTR	1000	Corporate...	281500	Profit PD...	537.60-			M	790000		
200145536	04.09.2013	R	5000000014	SAPUSER								
1	CTR	1000	Corporate...	400000	Raw Mater...	24.00	10	L	S	191100		
200145537	04.09.2013	R	5000000015	SAPUSER								
1	CTR	1000	Corporate...	281500	Profit PD...	161.28-			M	790000		
200145538	04.09.2013	R	5000000016	SAPUSER								
2	ORD	60003225	Casing	895000	Factory o...	227.52-	2-	PC	M	790000		
200145539	05.09.2013	R	5000000017	SAPUSER								
1	CTR	1000	Corporate...	281500	Profit PD...	1,084.60-			M	790000		
200145540	05.09.2013	R	4900000002	SAPUSER								
1	CTR	4280	Quality C...	895000	Factory o...	2,275.20-	20-	PC	M	790000		

➢ An actual cost document is identified by a unique document number.

➢ In goods movements, the reference document number is the material document number.

> A document may have multiple line items that represent costs.
> A document line item is posted to a cost element.
> The cost in a document line item is collected in a cost object, which has an object number and an object type, e.g. cost center, order etc.
> A document line item has an offsetting account number which has an offsetting account type. Offsetting account type may be a material account (M), or a G/L account (S), etc.

31.1.3 Cost Objects

Cost objects

Cost objects are cost collectors, e.g. production orders, sales orders, projects, cost centers etc. They help you determine the cost of your output.

Cost object types

Production orders, sales orders, projects, cost centers etc. are cost object types.

Cost object ids

Cost objects are identified by a cost object type and cost object id; e.g. cost center 1000, cost center 2000, production order 85642319 etc.

Cost centers, overhead costs

Cost centers are also cost objects. Unlike other cost objects, e.g. an order which has a limited life, cost centers have a long life. Some costs, e.g. overhead costs, cannot be directly assigned to cost objects. These costs are assigned to cost centers or overhead cost orders. The system then allocates them using internal allocation techniques, according to their source.

31.1.4 Cost Elements

Cost elements

Cost elements in Controlling are similar to G/L accounts in Financial Accounting. There are two types of cost elements: primary cost elements and secondary cost elements.

Primary cost elements

A primary cost element in Controlling has a G/L account in Financial Accounting of the same number. Primary costs are transferred from Financial Accounting and classified according to managerial accounting perspectives. If the primary costs are direct costs, then they are assigned to cost objects.

Secondary cost elements

Secondary cost elements are used only in Controlling, and postings to these accounts take place within the Controlling module itself.

31.2 CONTROLLING AREA

Functional Consultant	User	Business Process Owner	Senior Management	My Rating	Understanding Level
A	A	A	A		

31.2.1 Purpose

A company code is a legal entity with statutory reporting requirements. Many corporate houses do their business under several company codes but have a single management. Controlling area is the organizational level for management control which can span over several company codes.

31.2.2 IMG Node

Transaction OKKP—Maintain Controlling Area

31.2.3 Basic Data

Controlling Area	1000		Distribution
Name	CO Europe		
Person Responsible			

Assignment Control

CoCd->CO Area	2 Cross-company-code cost accounting	

Currency Setting

Currency Type	30	Group currency	
Currency	EUR	Euro (EMU currency as of 01/0 ☑ Diff. CCode Currency	
Curr/Val. Prof.		☐ Active	

Other Settings

Chart of Accts	INT	Chart of accounts - international
Fiscal Year Variant	K4	Calendar year, 4 spec. periods
CCtr Std. Hierarchy	H1	** Standard Hierarchy CA1000

Reconciliation Ledger

☑ Recon.Ledger Active		
Document Type	SA	G/L account document

Setting for Authorization Hierarchies for Cost Centers

Do Not Use Std Hier.	☐	Alternative Hierarchy1	☐
		Alternative Hierarchy2	☐

Setting for Authorization Hierarchies for Profit Centers

Do Not Use Std Hier.	☐	Alternative Hierarchy1	☐
		Alternative Hierarchy2	☐

Company code to controlling area

A controlling area may be for a single company code or for multiple company codes.

```
1 Controlling area same as company code
2 Cross-company-code cost accounting
```

Currency setting

A controlling area may contain one or more company codes, which can operate in different currencies, if required.

Chart of accounts

The company codes within a controlling area must all use the same operational chart of accounts.

Fiscal year variant

The operative fiscal year variants in the company codes must match the fiscal year variants in the controlling area.

31.2.4 Active Components/Control Indicators

Select a controlling area and double-click Activate components/control indicators to see the active components.

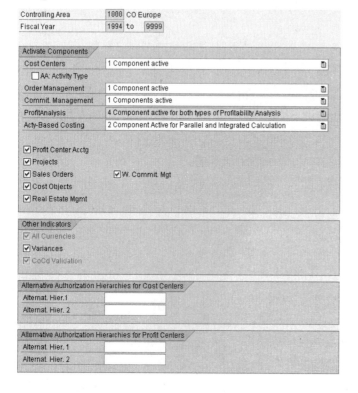

31.2.5   Assignment of Company Codes

Select a controlling area and double-click Assignment of company code(s).

Controlling Area   1000 CO Europe

Assigned Company Codes	
CoCd	Company Name
0005	IDES AG NEW GL
0007	IDES AG NEW GL 7
1000	IDES AG
2000	IDES UK
2100	IDES Portugal

31.3   COST ELEMENTS

Functional Consultant	User	Business Process Owner	Senior Management	My Rating	Understanding Level
A	B	B	B		

31.3.1   Cost Element

Overview

Cost elements

Cost elements in Controlling are similar to G/L accounts in Financial Accounting. There are two types of cost elements: primary cost elements and secondary cost elements.

Primary cost elements

A primary cost element in Controlling has a G/L account in Financial Accounting of the same number. Primary costs are transferred from Financial Accounting and classified according to managerial accounting perspectives. If the primary costs are direct costs, then they are assigned to cost objects.

Secondary cost elements

Secondary cost elements are used only in Controlling, and postings to these accounts take place within the Controlling module itself.

IMG Node

Transaction KA03—Display Cost Element

Screen

Cost Element	890000	Cons.semifin.product	
Controlling Area	1000	CO Europe	
Valid From	01.01.1994	to	31.12.9999

Basic Data | Indicators | Default Acct Assgnmt | History

Names

Name	Cons.semifin.product
Description	Consumption of semifinished product

Basic Data

CElem category	1	Primary costs/cost-reducing revenues
Attribute mix		
Functional Area		

31.3.2 Cost Element Groups

Purpose

You can combine similar cost elements into cost element groups. Similar cost element groups can be combined to form other cost element groups so as to build a cost element hierarchy. You can use cost element groups in reporting.

IMG Node

Transaction KAH3—Display Cost Element Group

Screen

```
CO-PC-MAT      Material cost
   ├─655100    655110
     655100    Overhead Surcharge - Raw Material
     655110    Overhead Surcharge - Other Materials
   ├─400000    Consumption, raw material 1
   ├─400002    414999
     400010    Consumption Raw Materials 2
     400080
     400444
     400550
     400666
     403000    Operating Supplies Consumed
     404000    Spare parts
     405000    Packaging materials consumption
     405100    Packing material purchase
     405200    Usage office supplies
     405201    Usage office supplies
     410000    OEM products consumed
     410001    OEM products scrapped
   ├─890000    892000
     890000    Consumption of semifinished product
     890001    Inventory change scrap own material
     891000    Change in work in process
     892000    Change in inventory: finished products
   └─893020    Inventory change-increase in own goods
```

31.3.3 Cost Elements Report: Breakdown by Object Type

Run transaction S_ALR_87013601 to display the report of cost elements broken down by object type.

```
Cost Elements: Brkdwn by obj.type    Date: 16.10.2013    Page:    2 /   2

Company Code             1000          Date
Reporting period         1 to  10 2013
```

Object types/cost elements	Period 10	Period 1 - 10
400000 Consumption, raw material 1		31
400010 Consumption Raw Materials 2		64
417001 Purchased services		511
890000 Cons.semifin.product	1,750	3,229
890001 Scrap own material		341
893020 Inv.Chg.Recv Int.Pro		70
895000 Factory output prod.		2,301-
* CTR Cost center	1,429	773
890000 Cons.semifin.product		228
* NWA Network activity		228
400000 Consumption, raw material 1		
895000 Factory output prod.		228-
* ORD Order		228-
281500 Profit PD,int.prod.		19-
400010 Consumption Raw Materials 2		32
890000 Cons.semifin.product		455

31.3.4 Cost Elements Report: Object Type in Columns

Run transaction S_ALR_87013602 to display cost elements where object types are in columns.

```
Cost Elements: Obj. type in columns    Date: 16.10.2013    Page:    2 /   2

Company Code             1000
Reporting period         1 to  10 2013
```

Cost elements	Total	Cost ctr	Orders	Projects	Others
237000 Exp.qual.contr.cons.	228	228			
281500 Profit PD,int.prod.	1,418-	1,400-		19-	
400000 Raw Materials 1	31	31			
400010 Raw Materials 2	95	64		32	
417001 Purchased services	511	511			
890000 Cons.semifin.product	4,584	3,229		455	900
890001 Scrap own material	341	341			
893020 Inv.Chg.Recv Int.Pro	70	70			
895000 Factory output prod.	2,528-	2,301-	228-		
* Total	1,914	773	228-	468	900

31.3.5 Cost Elements Report: Object Class in Columns

Run transaction S_ALR_87013600 to display cost elements where object classes are in columns.

```
Cost elem.: Obj. class in columns      Date: 16.10.2013   Page:    2 /   2

Company Code              1000          Date
Reporting period          1 to  10 2013
```

Cost elements		Overall	Overhead	Production
237000	Exp.qual.contr.cons.	228	228	
281500	Profit PD,int.prod.	1,418-	1,400-	19-
400000	Raw Materials 1	31	31	
400010	Raw Materials 2	95	64	32
417001	Purchased services	511	511	
890000	Cons.semifin.product	4,811	3,229	1,583
890001	Scrap own material	341	341	
893020	Inv.Chg.Recv Int.Pro	70	70	
895000	Factory output prod.	2,528-	2,301-	228-
* Total		2,141	773	1,368

31.4 COST CENTERS

Functional Consultant	User	Business Process Owner	Senior Management	My Rating	Understanding Level
A	B	B	B		

31.4.1 Purpose

Some costs, e.g. overhead costs, cannot be directly assigned to cost objects. These costs are assigned to cost centers and distributed later.

31.4.2 Transaction

KS03—Display Cost Center

31.4.3 Cost Center Screen

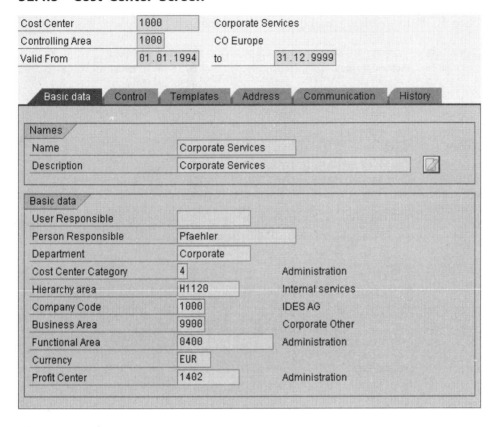

31.4.4 Cost Center Hierarchy

Cost centers are created as a hierarchy. You can see the cost center hierarchy using transaction OKEON.

Standard Hierarchy	Name	Acti...	Person ...	Company
▽ H1	** Standard Hierarchy CA1000			
▽ H1000	Company 1000 - Germany			
▽ H1010	Corporate			
▽ H1110	Executive Board			
1110	Executive Board	☐	Kuhn	1000
BOARD	BOARD	☐	Ms Pres...	1000
▷ H1120	Internal services			
▷ H1200	Administration & Financial			
▷ H1300	Marketing and Sales			
▷ H1400	Technical Area			
▷ H1800	BP Managers Self-Service			
▷ H1900	Offsetting Techn. Cost Ctr.			
▷ H2000	Company 2000 - UK			

31.4.5 Cost Center-Wise Cost Report

Run transaction KSB1 to display actual costs in cost centers.

Posting Date	Cost Elem.	Cost element name	DocTyp	Σ	Val.in rep.cur.	O	Offst.acct
08.09.2013	281500	Profit PD,int.prod.	WE		53.76-	M	790000
11.09.2013		Profit PD,int.prod.	WE		268.80	M	790000
05.10.2013		Profit PD,int.prod.	WE		537.60-	M	790000
06.10.2013		Profit PD,int.prod.	WE		216.92	M	790000
10.09.2013	400000	Raw Materials 1	WA		7.22	S	169900
09.09.2013	400010	Raw Materials 2	WA		63.65	S	169900
09.09.2013	417001	Purchased services	WE		511.30	S	191100
09.10.2013	890000	Cons.semifin.product	WA		1,750.00	M	790000
Cost Center 1000				▪	**2,226.53**		
				▪ ▪	**2,226.53**		

32

Periodic Processing

32.1 CLOSING PERIOD FOR MATERIAL MASTER RECORDS

Functional Consultant	User	Business Process Owner	Senior Management	My Rating	Understanding Level
A	B	B	B		

32.1.1 Purpose

You normally run the period closing program once a month at the beginning of a new period. This program sets the new period, making it possible to perform goods movements with reference to the new period. Depending on the settings in transaction OMSY (see Section 32.1.6), the system may still allow you to post to the immediately preceding previous period.

32.1.2 Transaction

MMPV—Close Periods

32.1.3 Initial Screen

From company code	☐
To company code	☐

Enter next period (including fiscal year) or a relevant date (but not both)

Period	☐
Fiscal year	☐

or

Date	☐

◉ Check and close period
○ Check period only
○ Close period only

☐ Allow neg. qties in prev. per.
☐ Allow neg. vals in prev. per.

Note that you do not enter the period you want to close, but the next period.

32.1.4 Closing Period

You enter the data in the initial screen and execute to close the period.

32.1.5 Log

The system closes the period and issues log confirming the action taken.

```
L O G

Mode: Check and close period

Client:800
Period entered (month/year):072013


Company code 1000 converted



Period closing complete; log issued.






E N D
```

32.1.6 Controlling Back Postings

Display current and previous periods

You can run transaction OMSY to maintain company codes for Materials Management.

CoCd	Company Name	Year	Pe	FYr	M	FYr	LM	ABp	DBp
1000	IDES AG	2013	7	2013	6	2012	12	☑	☐

In the screenshot above you can see the current period, the previous period, and the last period of the previous year. You should not change the current period here; run transaction MMPV to do so.

Allow back postings

If the `ABp` indicator is selected, posting to the previous period (back posting) is allowed. In this case, the previous period is the preceding month.

Default back postings

If the `DBp` indicator is not selected, when a new period is opened, back postings are allowed by default, i.e. the `ABp` indicator is selected. If you do not want back postings to be allowed by default, select this indicator.

32.2 ANALYSIS OF CONVERSION DIFFERENCES

Functional Consultant	User	Business Process Owner	Senior Management	My Rating	Understanding Level
C	X	X	X		

32.2.1 Purpose

You can analyze conversion differences that result during the conversion between a material's unit of entry and its base unit of measure. Conversion differences arise mainly due to rounding during conversion. Significant rounding differences may occur during conversion, in particular if a material's base unit of measure is not the lowest of all the alternative units of measure.

32.2.2 Transaction

MB5U—Analyze Conversion Differences

32.2.3 Selection Screen

Database Selections		
Posting Date		to
Material		to
Plant		to
Special Stock Indicator		

List Scope	
Threshold Value	
Reason for Movement	

32.2.4 Output

If there are no conversion differences, the system gives the following message.

⊘ No conversion differences exist for the specified data

32.3 COMPARISON OF BOOK VALUE AND STOCK VALUE

Functional Consultant	User	Business Process Owner	Senior Management	My Rating	Understanding Level
B	B	C	X		

32.3.1 Account-Wise Comparison

Run transaction MB5L to compare the value of stock in the books of accounts with the value determined by multiplying material stock with material price.

Bal. per G/L acct	CoCd	Materials Crcy		Stock Account Crcy		Variance Crcy	
01/2014	1000						
300000		6,345,971,228.09	EUR	6,345,971,228.09	EUR	0.00	EUR
300010		61,624.66	EUR	61,624.66	EUR	0.00	EUR
303000		763,288.26	EUR	763,288.26	EUR	0.00	EUR
304000		6,207,889.84	EUR	6,207,889.84	EUR	0.00	EUR
305000		5,267,704.04	EUR	5,267,704.04	EUR	0.00	EUR
310000		2,183,508,676.17	EUR	2,183,508,676.17	EUR	0.00	EUR
790000		97,332,642.46	EUR	97,332,642.46	EUR	0.00	EUR
790010		3,524.10	EUR	3,524.10	EUR	0.00	EUR
792000		32,932,646,607.69	EUR	32,932,646,607.69	EUR	0.00	EUR
* Total							
		41,571,763,185.31	EUR	41,571,763,185.31	EUR	0.00	EUR

You should run this report when no goods movements are taking place because the report does not lock the data and therefore may show false variance. You can run this report for the current period, the previous period, or the previous year.

32.3.2 Balance Transfer

At the end of each financial year, the Finance department of a company closes the preceding year and carries forward the account balances to the current year using transaction FAGLGVTR. If this activity is not performed for any preceding year, this report will show large variances.

32.3.3 Display Stocks

If you place the cursor on the G/L account and select Environment ➤ Display Stocks, the system displays an overview of all materials with their total stock and total value for the selected G/L account.

ValA	Material	Total Stock	BUn	Total Value	Crcy
1000	100-110	236	PC	0.00	EUR
1000	100-120	1,660	PC	19,544.04	EUR
1000	100-130	627	PC	0.00	EUR
1000	100-210	524	PC	9,555.70	EUR
1000	100-310	1,559	PC	16,366.07	EUR

32.3.4 Stock Overview

If you place the cursor on a material and select Environment ➤ Stock Overview, the system displays the stock overview of the material.

Selection			
Material	100-120	Flat gasket	
Material Type	ROH	Raw material	
Unit of Measure	PC	Base Unit of Measure	PC

Stock Overview

Client/Company Code/Plant/Storage Location	Unrestricted use	Qual. inspection	Reserved
▽ 📖 Full	1,410.000		20.000
▽ 📗 1000 IDES AG	1,410.000		20.000
▽ 📊 1000 Werk Hamburg	1,410.000		20.000
Stock Provided to Vendor	250.000		
▦ 0001 Materiallager	1,405.000		20.000
▦ MAM1 MAM Storage Loc1	5.000		

32.3.5   Periodic Check

You should run this transaction MB5L periodically and investigate variances if any.

32.4   STOCK CONSISTENCY CHECK

Functional Consultant	User	Business Process Owner	Senior Management	My Rating	Understanding Level
C	X	X	X		

32.4.1   Consistency Check

Run transaction MB5K to check the consistency of your stock data.

Material	ValA	Stock Qty Total Stock Comment/Incorrect Tables	UoM	Stock Value	LC	Price	PU
1300-230	1000	38	PC	3,541.17	EUR	93.19	V
		9	PC				
H4-LAMPE	1000	6,824	PC	17,445.28	EUR	2.56	S
		6,424	PC				

This report shows only those materials where the consistency check fails. After the price column, the system shows the price control indicator: Standard price (S) or Moving average price (V). If the material ledger is activated for the material, this indicator, together with the material's price determination indicator, determines whether the material is valuated at Standard price (S), Moving average price (V), Periodic unit price (V).

32.4.2   Consistency Check Logic

Anonymous stocks, valuated sales order stock, valuated project stock

For the table of stock values for anonymous stocks (MBEW), valuated sales order stock (EBEW), and valuated project stock (QBEW), the program checks if:

➤ The quantity of the total valuated stock matches the total of the individual subordinate stock segments.

➤ The price specified corresponds to the value/plant quotient.

➤ There is a negative price when you have a positive quantity of a material.

➤ A negative value exists for a material when negative stocks are not allowed in Customizing.

➤ There is a value when the relevant material has a stock level of zero.

Split valuation

In the case of split valuation, the program checks if:

➤ The quantity of the total valuated stock matches the total of the individual subordinate stock segments.

➤ The total valuated stock for each material matches the total of the valuation segments.

Cost estimate number

The program checks for each material whether a cost estimate number exists. This updates the index for the accounting documents for the material (table CKMI1).

Batch management

In the case of materials subject to batch management, the program checks if the quantity of storage location stock matches the total of the individual subordinate batches.

Material ledger

If the material ledger is active, the program checks if the tables in Inventory Management correspond to the material ledger tables.

32.4.3 Detail Screen

If you select a material, you can go to the detail screen by choosing Edit ➤ Choose.

```
Material          1300-230          HD GLAD BOY frame
Valuation Area    1000              Werk Hamburg
Cost. Est. No.    000100000558
Current period    09/1998           Valuation Class    7900
```

Stock Quantity		Correction	
Actual Quantity	38 PC	9 PC	
Total Stock	9 PC		

Stock Value			
Actual Value	3,541.17 EUR	838.70 EUR	

Valuation Price			
Price control	V		
Price Unit	1		
Moving price	93.19 EUR	93.19 EUR	
Value/Quantity	93.19 EUR		

```
500 Actual qty not equal to total of stocks
```

For a material with inconsistent stock, you can see [👤 Material documents] , [👤 Acctg docmts]
and [👤 Mat.ledger docs] .

32.4.4 Blocked Material

If a material was blocked at the time of the consistency check, the system issues a message that it was not included in the check. From the list, you can subsequently check a blocked material manually. To do this, select the material and choose Edit ➤ Check material . If the material is still blocked by a posting transaction, the system issues a message that the program was not able to block the material. In this case, you should repeat the manual check a few minutes later.

32.4.5 Periodic Check

You should run this transaction MB5K periodically and investigate variances if any.

32.5 MANAGING HELD DATA

Functional Consultant	User	Business Process Owner	Senior Management	My Rating	Understanding Level
A	A	B	X		

32.5.1 Creating Held Data

In MIGO series transactions one can create held data with the Hold pushbutton for continuing processing later. When you hold data, you enter a remark that is displayed in document overview.

32.5.2 Using Held Data

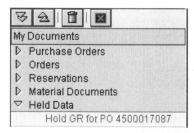

You can select and double-click held data to transfer it to the main area for further processing.

32.5.3 Managing Held Data

Run transaction MBPM to list and delete the held data that users have created.

	Age	Local date	Local Time	User Name	Lines	Notes
	0	29.12.2013	01:35:26	SAPUSER	1	Hold GR for PO 4500017087

You can select the entries manually or select all entries by clicking 🔳. You can then delete the 🗑 Selected Entries .

32.5.4 Deleting Held Data without Viewing

You can delete held data immediately by choosing ☑ Delete immediately in the selection screen. You can also schedule a job, with this indicator selected, to periodically delete held data without any manual intervention.

32.5.5 Deleting Own Held Data

You can delete your held data yourself in the MIGO transaction, by choosing Goods Receipt ➤ Held Data .

32.5.6 Periodic Processing

You should run this transaction MBPM at regular intervals so that you can delete held data that is no longer required.

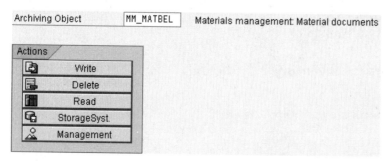

33 Archiving

33.1 ARCHIVE ADMINISTRATION

Functional Consultant	User	Business Process Owner	Senior Management	My Rating	Understanding Level
A	B	X	X		

33.1.1 Purpose

You archive material and physical inventory documents to free database space and to improve performance. In this section the general framework for archiving is discussed. Specific transactions for archiving material and physical inventory documents are discussed in subsequent sections.

33.1.2 Transaction

SARA—Create Archive

33.1.3 Control Screen

Archiving Object	MM_MATBEL	Materials management: Material documents

Actions
- Write
- Delete
- Read
- StorageSyst.
- Management

Archiving object

In transaction SARA you can specify the archiving object. The archiving object for material documents is MM_MATBEL. The archiving object for physical inventory documents is MM_INVBEL.

Write

In this step the archive file is created.

Delete

In this step the archived data is deleted from the database.

Read

In this step you can read the archived data from archive files.

Storage system

In this step the archive files are stored in content repository.

Management

In this step you can see the status of various archiving sessions.

Archiving object	MM_MATBEL Materials management: Material documents	
Sessions and Files for Archiving Object	Note	
▽ ◯◯◯ Incomplete Archiving Sessions		
▷ 787 - 788 (13.08.2003 - 13.08.2003)		
▽ ◯◯◯ Complete Archiving Sessions		
▷ 132 - 672 (22.07.1997 - 25.08.2000)		
▽ ⁝⁞ Invalid Archiving Sessions		
▷ 303 (19.05.1998)		

You can also see the above screen using transaction MBAV for material documents and transaction MIAV for physical inventory documents.

33.1.4 Archiving of Material Documents

SAP provides transaction MBAR for archiving material documents. When you use this transaction, deletion and storage may happen automatically if specified in 'Archiving Object-Specific Customizing' (Section 33.3).

33.1.5 Archiving of Physical Inventory Documents

SAP provides transaction MIAR for archiving physical inventory documents. When you use this transaction, deletion and storage may happen automatically if specified in 'Archiving Object-Specific Customizing' (Section 33.3).

33.2 ARCHIVING CUSTOMIZING

Functional Consultant	User	Business Process Owner	Senior Management	My Rating	Understanding Level
A	B	X	X		

33.2.1 Purpose

You can see customizing for data archiving.

33.2.2 Transaction

In archive administration transaction SARA, MBAR, or MIAR, click Customizing .

33.2.3 Screen

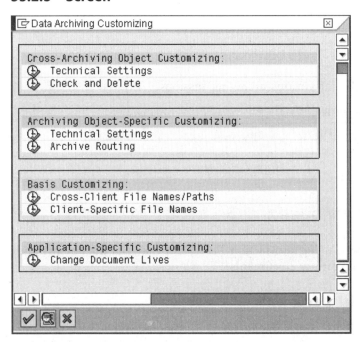

33.2.4 Customizing

Cross-archiving object customizing

This customizing is for all archiving objects. You should not change these settings without concurrence from other users.

Archiving object-specific customizing: technical setting

These settings are important for material documents and physical inventory documents. These are discussed in Section 33.3.

Archive routing

You can use this function to create rules and conditions, based on which archive files are automatically routed to specific areas in the file or storage system.

Cross client file names/paths

These cross-client settings are done by your Basis administrator to determine physical file names and paths from their logical counterparts. If there is a problem with these settings, storage of archive files may be affected.

Client-specific file names

These client-specific settings are done by your Basis administrator to determine physical file names from their logical counterparts. If there is a problem with these settings, storage of archive files may be affected.

Application specific customizing

For material documents you can define document life which is discussed in Section 33.4. There is no application-specific customizing for physical inventory documents.

33.3 ARCHIVING OBJECT-SPECIFIC CUSTOMIZING

Functional Consultant	User	Business Process Owner	Senior Management	My Rating	Understanding Level
A	B	X	X		

33.3.1 Purpose

After the data is archived, it is deleted from the database using the delete program, and the file is stored in the storage system. Both these activities can happen automatically after archiving.

33.3.2 IMG Node

SM30 ➤ V_ARC_USR

In archive administration transaction SARA, MBAR, or MIAR, click Customizing , and in
Archiving Object-Specific Customizing click ⊕ Technical Settings.

33.3.3 Screen

Object Name	MM_MATBEL	Materials management: Material documents
Logical File Name	ARCHIVE_DATA_FILE	

Archive File Size

Maximum Size in MB	1
Maximum Number of Data Objects	1,000

Settings for Delete Program

Test Mode Variant	TEST	Variant
Production Mode Variant	PROD	Variant

Delete Jobs

- ◯ Not Scheduled
- ⦿ Start Automatically
- ◯ After Event   Event
                    Parameter

Place File in Storage System

Content Repository	CD

☑ Start Automatically

Sequence

- ⦿ Delete Before Storing
- ◯ Store Before Deleting   ☐ Delete Program Reads from Storage System

33.3.4 Primary Key

Archiving Object

33.3.5 Important Fields

Object name

For archiving material document, the object is MM_MATBEL. For physical inventory documents, the object is MM_INVBEL. All other fields on the screen are the same.

Logical file name

At runtime, the logical file name is converted by the FILE_GET_NAME function module to a platform-specific path and file name. You can find out more about this setting in Basis customizing under Cross-Client Maintenance of File Names and Paths.

Maximum size in MB

This parameter controls the maximum size of an archive file. Before an object is written to an archive file, the system checks whether the maximum permitted size is exceeded. If so, the current archiving file is closed and another is opened to accommodate the object.

Maximum number of data objects

This parameter controls the maximum number of data objects per archive file. Before a data object is written to an archive file, the system checks whether the maximum number allowed would be exceeded. If this is the case, the current archive file is closed and a new one opened for the data object.

Test mode variant

If you run the delete program (transaction MBAD) in ☑ Test Mode, the system uses the variant specified here.

Production mode variant

If you run the delete program (transaction MBAD) in ☐ Test Mode, the system uses the variant specified here.

Delete jobs

Here you do settings for running the delete program.

Archiving program modes

When the archiving program (transaction MBAR), you specify a variant. In the variant you specify whether the program will be run in the ⦿ Test Mode, or in the ⦿ Production Mode.

Archiving program in test mode

When the archiving program (transaction MBAR) is run in test mode, objects are selected for archiving only for test purposes. No archive file is generated and, therefore, there is no deletion of the selected objects.

Archiving program in production mode

When the archiving program (transaction MBAR) is run in production mode, an archive file is generated and the selected objects get archived. The delete program may be run manually or automatically as explained below.

Delete jobs	Explanation
⦿ Not Scheduled	You can run the delete program (transaction MBAD) later, select the archive file, and schedule the deletion job.
⦿ Start Automatically	The deletion job starts immediately after archiving without any intervention from the user.
⦿ After Event	The deletion job starts without any intervention from the user after the specified event.

Content repository

Here you specify the storage repository of physical archive files.

Start automatically

This checkbox indicates that archive files, after successful processing, are automatically transferred to a connected storage system.

Delete before storing

This radio button indicates that the data is deleted from the database before the archive file is stored in the content repository.

Store before deleting

This radio button indicates that the data is deleted from the database after the archive file is stored in the content repository.

Delete program reads from storage system

If the archive file is stored before deleting, here you can specify that the deletion program should read the file from the storage system for deleting the data from the database.

33.4 ARCHIVING APPLICATION-SPECIFIC CUSTOMIZING

Functional Consultant	User	Business Process Owner	Senior Management	My Rating	Understanding Level
A	B	X	X		

33.4.1 Purpose

For material documents you can specify document life so that they are not accidentally archived and deleted.

33.4.2 IMG Screen

SM30 ➤ V_159R

In archive administration transaction SARA, MBAR, or MIAR, click Customizing , and in Application-Specific Customizing, click ⊕ Change Document Lives.

33.4.3 Screen

Plant	Trans./event type	Doc.life in days
####	##	200
0001	WA	200
0001	WE	200
0001	WI	200

33.4.4   Primary Key

Plant
Transaction/event type with masked entry

33.4.5   Important Fields

Plant

Document life can be different for different plants. Here you specify the plant. Enter #### if the document life is to apply to all plants.

Transaction/event type

Document life can be different for different transaction/event types. Here you specify the transaction/event type. Enter ## if the document life is to apply to all transaction/event types.

Document life in days

Here you specify document life in days. This gives the earliest time at which material documents can be archived.

33.5   ARCHIVING MATERIAL DOCUMENTS

Functional Consultant	User	Business Process Owner	Senior Management	My Rating	Understanding Level
A	B	X	X		

33.5.1   Purpose

You archive material and physical inventory documents to free database space and to improve performance. While archiving data the system ensures that the data can be read, analyzed and reloaded if required.

33.5.2   Transaction

MBAR—Create Archive (Material Documents)

33.5.3 Selection Screen

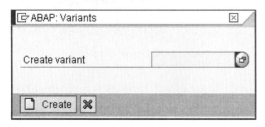

Selection parameters

Click 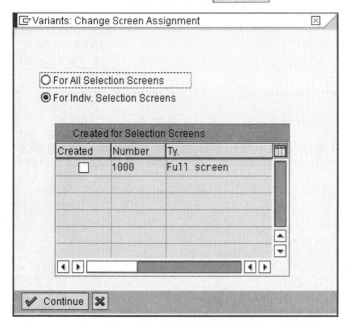 to specify the selection parameters in a variant.

Enter the variant name and click 🗋 Create .

Select the checkbox and click ✔ Continue .

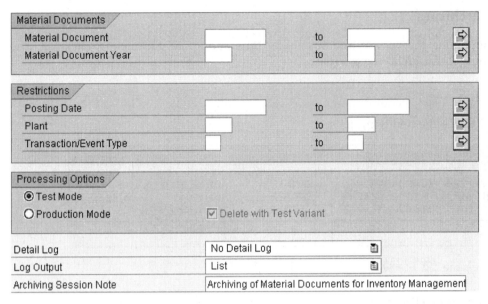

Specify the material documents to be archived.

Start date

Click [📇 Start Date] to define when you want processing to commence. You can specify [Immediate], [Date/Time], [After job] etc.

Spool parameters

Click [🖶 Spool Params.] to specify background print parameters.

Specify the output device and other parameters.

33.5.4 Archiving

After maintaining the variant and specifying time and spool parameters, click ⊕. The background job for archiving is created.

33.5.5 Job

Click 📋, to see the archiving jobs.

Job	Ln	Job CreatedBy	Status	Start date
☐ ARV_MM_MATBEL_SUB20131229000335		SAPUSER	Finished	29.12.2013
☐ ARV_MM_MATBEL_SUB20131229062409		SAPUSER	Released	
☑ ARV_MM_MATBEL_WRI20131229000349	🖥	SAPUSER	Finished	29.12.2013
*Summary				

You can see the 🖥 Spool and 📄 Job log.

33.5.6 Archive Directory

Click Archive Directory to see the archive directory and the space in it.

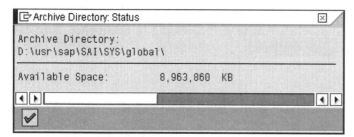

```
┌─ Archive Directory: Status ─────────────────[X]─┐
│ Archive Directory:                               │
│ D:\usr\sap\SAI\SYS\global\                       │
│                                                  │
│ Available Space:        8,963,860  KB            │
│ ◀▶ �_____██████_____◀▶        │
│ ✔                                                │
└──────────────────────────────────────────────────┘
```

33.5.7 Customizing

Click Customizing to see the customizing for archiving. For details, see Section 33.2.

33.5.8 Management

Click Management to see the status of various archiving sessions.

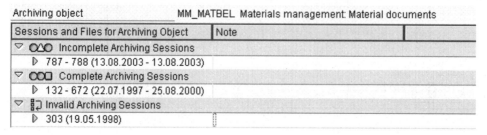

Archiving object		MM_MATBEL Materials management: Material documents	
Sessions and Files for Archiving Object	Note		
▽ ○⌀○ Incomplete Archiving Sessions			
▷ 787 - 788 (13.08.2003 - 13.08.2003)			
▽ ○○❑ Complete Archiving Sessions			
▷ 132 - 672 (22.07.1997 - 25.08.2000)			
▽ 🗐 Invalid Archiving Sessions			
▷ 303 (19.05.1998)			

You can also see the above screen using transaction MBAV for material documents and transaction MIAV for physical inventory documents.

33.5.9   Database Tables

Click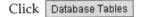

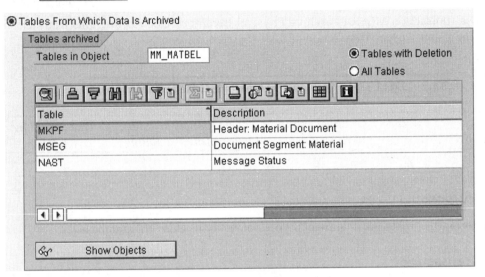

You can select a table and click [⚙ Show Objects] to show the objects through which that table is archived.

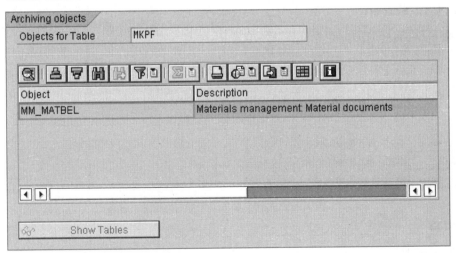

33.5.10   Information System

Click [Information System] to see information about archived data.

33.6 ARCHIVING PHYSICAL INVENTORY DOCUMENTS

Functional Consultant	User	Business Process Owner	Senior Management	My Rating	Understanding Level
A	B	X	X		

You can use transaction MIAR to archive Physical Inventory Documents. This transaction works in the same way as transaction MBAR (Section 33.5).

33.7 DELETING ARCHIVED MATERIAL DOCUMENTS

Functional Consultant	User	Business Process Owner	Senior Management	My Rating	Understanding Level
A	B	X	X		

33.7.1 Purpose

After archiving the material documents, you delete them from the database.

33.7.2 Transaction

MBAD—Delete Documents

33.7.3 Selection Screen

Archive selection

Click [⧉ Archive Selection].

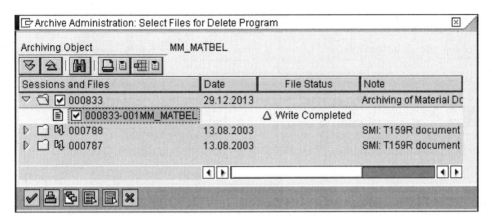

Select a file and click 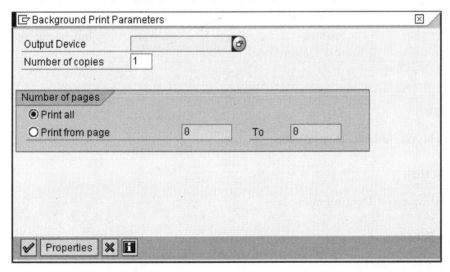.

Start date

Click ▥ **Start Date** to define when you want processing to commence. You can specify Immediate, Date/Time, After job etc.

Spool parameters

Click ▣ **Spool Parameters** to specify background print parameters.

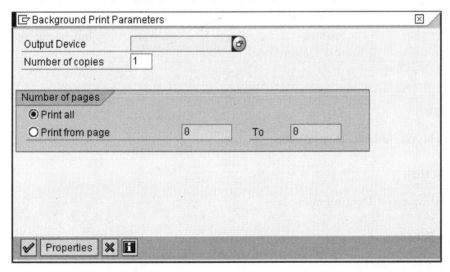

Specify the output device and other parameters.

33.7.4 Deleting Documents

After specifying the archive selection, time and spool parameters, click 🔱. The background job for deletion is created.

33.7.5 Job

Click [Job], to see the deletion jobs.

Job	Ln	Job CreatedBy	Status	Start date
☐ ARV_MM_MATBEL_DEL20131229071654	📋	SAPUSER	Finished	29.12.2013
☐ ARV_MM_MATBEL_DEL20131229091027	📋	SAPUSER	Finished	29.12.2013
☐ ARV_MM_MATBEL_DEL20131229092425	📋	SAPUSER	Finished	29.12.2013
☐ ARV_MM_MATBEL_DEL20131229122548	📋	SAPUSER	Finished	29.12.2013

33.8 DELETING ARCHIVED PHYSICAL INVENTORY DOCUMENTS

Functional Consultant	User	Business Process Owner	Senior Management	My Rating	Understanding Level
A	B	X	X		

You can delete archived physical inventory documents using transaction MIAD. This transaction works in the same way as transaction MBAD (Section 33.7).

33.9 READING ARCHIVED MATERIAL DOCUMENTS

Functional Consultant	User	Business Process Owner	Senior Management	My Rating	Understanding Level
A	B	X	X		

33.9.1 Purpose

You can read archived material documents.

33.9.2 Transaction

MBAL—Archived Material Documents

33.9.3 Initial Screen

Materials management: Material documents		
Background/Dialog	DIALOG	🔽
Read Program	RM07MAAU	🔽 Report for Material Document Archiving

33.9.4 Data Selection

Data Selection			
Archives			
Material Document		to	
Material Document Year		to	
Material Number		to	
Plant		to	
Posting Date		to	

33.9.5 Archive Files

You can specify a material document or click 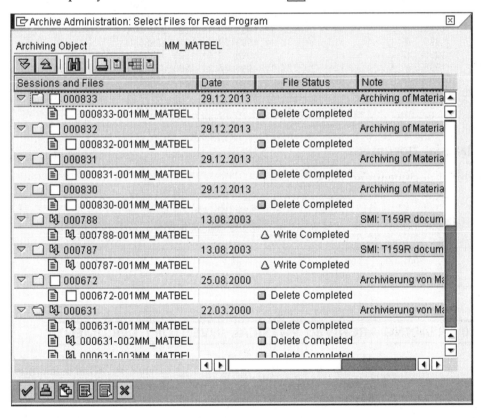 to select from the archive files.

Archive Administration: Select Files for Read Program			
Archiving Object	MM_MATBEL		

Sessions and Files	Date	File Status	Note
▽ ☐ ☐ 000833	29.12.2013		Archiving of Materia
☐ ☐ 000833-001MM_MATBEL		☐ Delete Completed	
▽ ☐ ☐ 000832	29.12.2013		Archiving of Materia
☐ ☐ 000832-001MM_MATBEL		☐ Delete Completed	
▽ ☐ ☐ 000831	29.12.2013		Archiving of Materia
☐ ☐ 000831-001MM_MATBEL		☐ Delete Completed	
▽ ☐ ☐ 000830	29.12.2013		Archiving of Materia
☐ ☐ 000830-001MM_MATBEL		☐ Delete Completed	
▽ ☐ ◪ 000788	13.08.2003		SMI: T159R docum
☐ ◪ 000788-001MM_MATBEL		△ Write Completed	
▽ ☐ ◪ 000787	13.08.2003		SMI: T159R docum
☐ ◪ 000787-001MM_MATBEL		△ Write Completed	
▽ ☐ ☐ 000672	25.08.2000		Archivierung von Ma
☐ ☐ 000672-001MM_MATBEL		☐ Delete Completed	
▽ ☐ ◪ 000631	22.03.2000		Archivierung von Ma
☐ ◪ 000631-001MM_MATBEL		☐ Delete Completed	
☐ ◪ 000631-002MM_MATBEL		☐ Delete Completed	
☐ ◪ 000631-003MM_MATBEL		☐ Delete Completed	

33.9.6 Material Documents in a File

Select a file and click ✅ to display material documents in the file.

Material Doc.	MYear	Tr./Ev.Type	Doc.Type	Doc.Date	Pstg Date	Name
49000306	1995	WQ	WA	08.03.1995	08.03.1995	VANDIJK
49000325	1995	WQ	WA	21.03.1995	21.03.1995	WESTERMANN
49001877	1995	WL	WL	04.12.1995	04.12.1995	TENNITY
49001878	1995	WL	WL	04.12.1995	04.12.1995	TENNITY
49001879	1995	WL	WL	04.12.1995	04.12.1995	TENNITY
49001886	1995	WL	WL	08.12.1995	08.12.1995	TENNITY
49001887	1995	WL	WL	08.12.1995	08.12.1995	TENNITY
49001888	1995	WL	WL	08.12.1995	08.12.1995	TENNITY
49001969	1995	WQ	WA	29.12.1995	29.12.1995	WESTERMANN
50000761	1995	WF	WE	22.11.1995	22.11.1995	JOHNSON
50000762	1995	WF	WE	22.11.1995	22.11.1995	JOHNSON
50000763	1995	WF	WE	22.11.1995	22.11.1995	JOHNSON
50000764	1995	WF	WE	22.11.1995	22.11.1995	JOHNSON
50000765	1995	WF	WE	22.11.1995	22.11.1995	JOHNSON
50000766	1995	WF	WE	27.11.1995	27.11.1995	JOHNSON
50000767	1995	WF	WE	27.11.1995	27.11.1995	JOHNSON
50000768	1995	WF	WE	27.11.1995	27.11.1995	JOHNSON
50000769	1995	WF	WE	27.11.1995	27.11.1995	JOHNSON
50000770	1995	WF	WE	27.11.1995	27.11.1995	JOHNSON

33.9.7 Material Document

Select a material document and click | Choose |.

Itm	Qty	in UnE	Material	Plnt	SLoc	Batch	MvT	S	V
		SKU	Mat. Short Text			ReservNo	Itm		FIs
0001	100	PC	100-400	3000	0001		101		+
			Electronic						

33.10 READING ARCHIVED PHYSICAL INVENTORY DOCUMENTS

Functional Consultant	User	Business Process Owner	Senior Management	My Rating	Understanding Level
A	B	X	X		

You can use transaction MIAL to read archived physical inventory documents in the same way as you use transaction MBAL.

Utilities

34.1 FUNCTIONALITY

Functional Consultant	User	Business Process Owner	Senior Management	My Rating	Understanding Level
A	A	A	B		

34.1.1 Users

Logging on

If you are going to work in SAP, your system administrator creates a SAP log on pad on your desktop/laptop. The log on pad can be accessed either through a shortcut on your desktop or through the Windows Start icon. When you open the SAP log on pad, you find one or more entries in it.

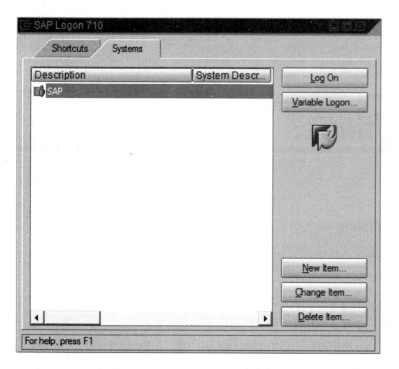

Each entry represents a server. Your system administrator tells you the purpose for which each server is to be used. You select the server you want to work on, and click the [Log On] icon. The system gives you the log on screen.

SAP

New password

Client		Information
User	☑	ℹ Welcome to IDES ECC 6.0
Password	∗∗∗∗∗∗∗∗∗∗∗∗	
Language		

You enter the details given to you by your system administrator. You can change your password or press 'Enter' to log on. The system gives you the SAP menu.

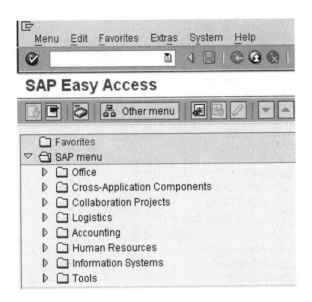

You can open the tree like structure of the SAP menu to reach the transaction you want to carry out. You can switch to user menu, if one has been set up for you. You can add transactions to the Favorites folder, which can have sub-folders.

Executing a transaction in the command field

An important part of all SAP screens is the command field, located in the top left corner of the screen. Here, you can enter a transaction directly, instead of going through a menu. If you are already in some transaction which you want to leave, prefix the transaction with /n, e.g. /nME21N. If you want to run the new transaction in a new session, prefix the transaction with /o, e.g. /oME21N.

Aborting the current transaction

You can abort the current transaction by entering /n in the command field.

Opening multiple sessions

You can open another session of SAP (same server and client) by clicking [icon] icon or by entering /o in the command field.

Closing a session

You can close a session by entering /i in the command line or by closing the window. If the session you are closing is the only session on a client, you are logged off. The system asks you to confirm that you want to log off.

Logging off

You can log off by entering /nend or /nex in the command line. In the former case, the system asks you to confirm that you want to log off. All the sessions on the client are closed.

Displaying transactions

You work in SAP either through menu, or through transactions. Experienced users often prefer the latter method. Therefore, they need to know the transaction codes of various transactions. You can display the transaction codes in the menu by ticking the checkbox ☑ Display technical names in Extras ➤ Settings . The menu display changes as shown below.

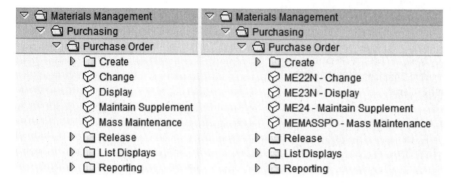

Business workplace

SAP provides a wide range of office functionality, e.g. mail, workflow, etc., in business workplace. You can access it using transaction SBWP or by clicking the icon as shown below.

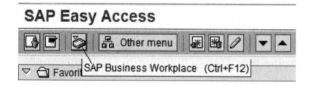

You can create and send a document by clicking 🖉 New message in business workplace. You can also do the same by running transaction SO00, or through menu System ➤ Short Message .

Maintaining own data

You can maintain your own data using transaction SU3 (System ➤ User Profile ➤ Own Data).

Running ABAP programs

You can run ABAP programs using transaction SA38 (System ➤ Services ➤ Reporting). It is recommended to avoid doing this by creating a transaction for every program.

Quick viewer

You can run quick viewer using transaction SQVI (System ➤ Services ➤ QuickViewer).

Output control

You can run transaction SP01 (System ➤ Services ➤ Output Control) to list the spool requests and output requests for a user id in a specific period. You can display their contents, print them and delete them. You can run transaction SP02 (System ➤ Own Spool Requests) to list your own spool requests.

Batch input

You can run transaction SM35 (System ➤ Services ➤ Batch Input ➤ Sessions) to monitor, process and analyze the batch input sessions. You can see the logs using transaction SM35P (System ➤ Services ➤ Batch Input ➤ Logs). You can do recording for batch input using transaction SHDB (System ➤ Services ➤ Batch Input ➤ Recorder).

Computer aided test tool

You can use transaction SECATT to perform computer aided testing.

Background jobs

You can use transaction SM36 to define and schedule a background job (System ➤ Services ➤ Jobs ➤ Define Job). You can use transaction SM37 (System ➤ Services ➤ Jobs ➤ Job Overview) to monitor and manage jobs. You can release a job, stop an active job, delete a job, display spool list, display job log and display step list. You can also check status, change status from released to scheduled, copy job, change job, repeat scheduling and move the job to a different server. You can also run transaction SMX to see your own jobs (System ➤ Own Jobs).

Queue

You can use transaction SM38 (System ➤ Services ➤ Queue) to display queue.

Reporting authorization problems

You can use transaction SU53 (System ➤ Utilities(H) ➤ Display Authorization Check) to see details of authorization problems and to report to the Basis team for resolution. Immediately after you encounter an authorization problem, enter /nSU53. The system shows a comparison between authorization available and authorization required.

Archived documents

You can use transaction OAAD to store and assign a new document in the content server. The transaction also provides a facility to search the archived documents.

Downloading file

You can use transaction CG3Y to download a file from the application server to your desktop.

Uploading file

You can use transaction CG3Z to upload a file from your desktop to the application server.

SAP query

You can start SAP queries using transaction SQ00.

34.1.2 Functional Consultants

Customizing

Transaction SPRO is used for accessing the customizing environment. You can customize the SAP system using the SAP Reference IMG or you can define projects for customization, e.g. adapting the SAP Reference IMG to the needs of your company and/or subdivide the customization task into different subprojects.

View maintenance

Transactions SM30 (System ➤ Services ➤ Table Maintenance ➤ Extended Table Maintenance) and SM31 are used for maintaining data in one or more tables through a maintenance view. This transaction also provides a facility to navigate to the underlying IMG node for a particular maintenance view. Transaction SM34 (System ➤ Services ➤ Table Maintenance ➤ View Cluster Maintenance) is used for maintaining view clusters.

Customizing comparison

You can compare customizing of two systems or two clients in the same system by using transaction SCMP. You can also create comparison runs involving multiple objects using transaction SCU0 or OY19.

Transport management

You can use transactions SE09 and SE10 for creating and releasing a customizing or workbench transport request.

Data migration, computer aided testing, BDC

You can use transaction LSMW to migrate legacy data to SAP. You can use transaction SCAT or SECATT for creating a test case by recording a transaction and creating and loading test data. You can record or modify a BDC and run it using transaction SHDB.

Viewing data in tables

You can view data in a table using transaction SE11, SE16, SE16N or SE17.

Logging on to OSS

You can use transaction OSS1 (System ➤ Services ➤ SAP Service) to log on to OSS. It is generally used to import and apply SAP notes.

Searching string in programs

You can use program RPR_ABAP_SOURCE_SCAN to search strings in programs.

Searching in SAP menu

You can use transaction SEARCH_SAP_MENU to search in SAP menu.

Searching in user menu

You can use transaction SEARCH_USER_MENU to search in user menu.

SAP query

You can use transaction SQ01 to maintain SAP queries, transaction SQ02 to maintain infoset and SQ03 to maintain user groups. You can start SAP queries using transaction SQ00.

Workflow builder

You can use transaction SWDD for creating and editing workflows.

System status

You can see versions of SAP, operating system and database by clicking System ➤ Status... . You can also see the transaction, program, and screen number.

Translation

You can use transaction SE63 to translate texts for various ABAP and non-ABAP objects.

34.1.3   ABAP

ABAP programs

You can create, modify, delete, and display source code of ABAP programs using transaction SE38. You can also execute ABAP programs using transaction SA38 or SE38. You can compare ABAP programs using transaction SE39.

Function modules

You can create, modify, delete, display and test function modules using transaction SE37. You can also maintain a function group.

Dialog modules

You can create, modify, delete, display and test dialog modules using transaction SE35. You can create menus using transaction SE41. Screens can be painted using transaction SE51 and its underlying flow logic defined.

Classes

You can create, modify, delete, display and test classes using transaction SE24.

Logical databases

You can create, modify, delete, display and test logical databases using transaction SE36. SAP provides several logical databases for materials, e.g. CKM and CMC. If you use logical databases in your ABAP programs, authorization checks are automatically taken care of; otherwise you must explicitly build authorization checks in your programs.

Enhancements

You can create enhancements through transaction CMOD. Enhancements are created in projects, which are logical groups of enhancements. You can test the enhancements using transaction SMOD.

BAdIs

You can use transaction SE19 to implement a Business Add-In. SAP provides predefined BAdIs for use by the customers. If you want to define your own BAdI, you can use transaction SE18.

Area menus

You can create area menus using transaction SE43. Area menus can be used in creating role menus in transaction PFCG.

Tables and views

You can create, modify, delete and display tables and table fields using transaction SE11. You can view data in a table using transaction SE11, SE16, SE16N or SE17. You can display/change technical settings of a table in transaction SE13.

Documentation

You can create documentation using transaction SE61.

SAP scripts

You can create SAP scripts using transaction SE71. Other transactions related to SAP script are SE72, SE73, SE74, SE75, SE75TTDTGC, SE75TTDTGD, SE76, SE77 and SO10.

Messages

You can maintain messages using transaction SE91. You can then call them in your own programs. You can also use SAP defined messages in your own programs.

Transactions

You can maintain transactions using transaction SE93. It is recommended that you have a transaction for every program so that the users are not required to run programs using transaction SA38 or SE38. This provides better control on authorizations. It is also recommended that you keep the transaction same as the program name.

Repository information

SAP has created lot of software objects. You can use transaction SE15/SE85/SE84 to find them.

BAPIs

You can see the BAPIs provided by SAP using transaction BAPI.

Object navigator

You use transaction SE80 to organize your programming in an integrated development environment. Development objects are arranged together in object lists. Each object list contains all of the objects in a certain category such as package, program and global class. From the object list, you can select an object by double-clicking it. When you open an object, the workbench calls up the development tool with which the object was created.

ABAP dump analysis

You can use transaction ST22 to see details of any runtime error or short dump. This helps in analyzing the root cause of the dump and finding its solution.

34.1.4   Basis

System administration

You can use transaction S002 to get the menu for system administration.

Users

You can maintain users using transaction SU01 or SU01_NAV. You can get a variety of information about users, roles and authorizations using transaction SUIM. You can view users' log on dates and password changes using transaction RSUSR200. You can use transaction SM04 to check the status of the users; for example, how many users are logged on and how many sessions a user is working on.

Roles

You can maintain roles using transaction PFCG. The system automatically inserts authorization objects based on transactions selected by you (These can be maintained using transaction SU22 or SU24). You update them with appropriate values. You can see change documents for roles using transaction RSSCD100_PFCG. The same program is called by transaction RSSCD100_PFCG_USER. Transaction S_BCE_68001403 gives the list of critical authorizations.

Transport management

You can manage transports using transactions SE01, SE03, SE09 and SE10. You can enable/disable transport using transaction SCC4.

SAP connect

You can use transaction SCOT for monitoring the status of the inbound and outbound traffic through SAPconnect.

ALE

Customizing of ALE can be done using transaction SALE. You can monitor ALE messages using transaction BD87.

Displaying and deleting locks

Transaction SM12 is used for checking and releasing lock entries.

Locking/unlocking transactions

You can use transaction SM01 to lock/unlock transactions.

Allowed menus for users

You can disable user menu or SAP menu at user level in view USERS_SSM.

34.2 TABLES AND VIEWS

Functional Consultant	User	Business Process Owner	Senior Management	My Rating	Understanding Level
A	A	A	B		

34.2.1 Data Dictionary

Domains

View DD01V contains the list of domains. View DD07V contains values for domains.

Data elements

View DD04V contains data elements and their descriptions.

Tables

View DD02V contains the list of tables.

Table fields

Table DD03L contains table fields and DD03T their descriptions. Table DD03M contains table fields with data elements, text, and domains. View DDVAL contains fixed values for table fields.

Foreign key fields

View DD08V contains foreign key relationship definitions.

Pool/cluster structures

View DD06V contains pool/cluster structures.

Technical settings of tables

Table DD09L contains technical settings of tables.

Matchcode objects

View DD20V contains matchcode objects. Table DD24S contains fields of a matchcode id.

Views

Table TVDIR contains directory of views. Table DD25T contains views, matchcode objects and lock objects. Table DD27S contains fields in a view, matchcode object or lock object.

34.2.2 Software Repository

Packages

All objects are developed under Packages (earlier called Development Classes), which are logical grouping of objects. Table TDEVC contains list of Packages. Package MB is for Inventory Management.

Repository objects

Table TADIR contains the directory of repository objects, along with their development class. Tables and structures are identified by object type TABL.

Objects

Objects are stored in OBJ series of tables.

ABAP programs

Table TRDIR contains list of ABAP programs. Table D010TAB contains the tables used by ABAP programs.

Transactions

View TSTCV contains list of transactions and programs associated with them.

34.2.3 Users, Roles and Authorization

User data

User data is stored in USR series of tables. Table USR01 stores the master list of users. Table USR04 contains the profiles attached to a user. A user's parameter IDs and their values are stored in table USR05.

Role maintenance

You can create, delete, or modify roles using transaction PFCG. Role related data is stored in tables starting with AGR.

Authorization objects

Authorization objects and their field names are in table TOBJ.

Authorization objects for roles

Table AGR_1250 contains authorization objects for a role which you see in transaction PFCG.

Master list of roles

Table AGR_DEFINE contains master list of roles.

Transactions for a role

Table AGR_TCODES contains transactions for roles.

Users having a role

Table AGR_USERS contains users for roles. Also see table AGR_USERT.

34.2.4 IMG Menu

Table CUS_IMGACH contains master list of IMG activities including documentation object and transaction.

34.2.5 SAP Scripts

SAP scripts

SAP scripts are stored in STX series of tables.

34.2.6 Others

Documentation

Documentation header is stored in table DOKHL and text in table DOKTL.

Reserved names

Reserved Names for Customizing Tables/Objects are stored in table TRESC.

34.2.7 Delivery Classes of Tables

SAP stores data in tables. The tables are classified in delivery classes that determine which tables are controlled by SAP and which tables are controlled by customers.

Code	Delivery class	Explanation
A	Application table (master and transaction data)	A Support Pack of SAP is not expected to update these tables in any client.
L	Table for storing temporary data, delivered empty	A Support Pack of SAP is not expected to update these tables in any client.
G	Customizing table, protected against SAP Upd., only INS all.	A Support Pack of SAP is not expected to update these tables in any client.
C	Customizing table, maintenance only by cust., not SAP import	A Support Pack of SAP updates these tables in client 000 only. In other clients, these tables have to be adjusted from client 000 to get these entries.
E	Control table, SAP and customer have separate key areas	A Support Pack of SAP updates these tables in all clients.
S	System table, maint. only by SAP, change = modification	A Support Pack of SAP updates these tables in all clients.
W	System table, contents transportable via separate TR objects	A Support Pack of SAP updates these tables in all clients.

34.2.8 Search Help

When SAP designs tables, for each column it tries to provide search help. If search help is provided, you can select a value from it. By assigning search help to table columns, the help becomes standardized. There are different types of search help. In transaction SE11 if you display a table and go to tab `Entry help/check` tab, you can see which columns have got entry help, and of which type in the column `Origin of the input help`. Different types of search help are listed below.

Fix.Val.	Short text
X	Explicit search help attachment to field
P	Input help implemented with check table
D	Explicit search help attachment to data element
F	Input help with fixed values
T	Input help based on data type
	No input help exists

Code	Search help	Explanation
X	Explicit search help attachment to field	Data integrity is checked against search help assigned to the field. There is no check table.
P	Input help implemented with check table	Data integrity is checked using a check table.
D	Explicit search help attachment to data element	Search help is attached to the data element assigned to the field.
F	Input help with fixed values	The field can take values only from a fixed list, which is defined in the Domain.
T	Input help based on data type	For example, Date (Calendar), Time.
Blank	No input help	There is no input help.

34.3 AUTHORIZATION

Functional Consultant	User	Business Process Owner	Senior Management	My Rating	Understanding Level
A	A	A	A		

34.3.1 Authorization Concepts

Authorization Objects

Creating a test role

The best way to understand how SAP controls authorizations is to create a test role for purchasing using transaction PFCG. After creating the role, you go to the Menu tab, and add a transaction, e.g. ME21N. You then go to the Authorizations tab, and click Change Authorization Data . You will see the following screen.

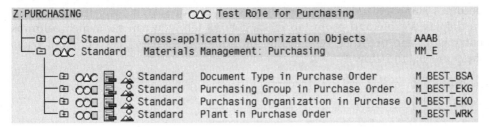

Object classes

The role has two object classes: AAAB and MM_E.

Authorization objects

The role has four authorization objects. Expand the authorization object M_BEST_BSA.

```
Z:PURCHASING                    OＡＣ Test Role for Purchasing

 ┌─囗 OＯＱ Standard   Cross-application Authorization Objects        AAAB
 └─囗 OＡＣ Standard   Materials Management: Purchasing               MM_E

       ┌─囗 OＡＣ 昼 叐 Standard   Document Type in Purchase Order        M_BEST_BSA
       └─囗 OＡＣ 昼 Standard   Document Type in Purchase Order   T-SI55039400

             ┌──── ⋇ ⌀ Activity                    01, 02, 03, 08, 09
             └──── ⋇ ⌀ Purchasing Document Type
```

Authorization fields

The screenshot above shows authorization fields in one authorization object. An authorization object groups up to ten authorization fields that are checked in an AND relationship. In this object you specify the authorization given to a role (or profile), which will become the authorization for one or more users through assignment of the role to users. In this object, you specify the activity that can be performed and the purchasing document type for which it can be performed.

If a user tries to create a purchase order of document type NB, the system will check whether the user has the authorization for `Activity 01(Create)` and `Purchasing Document Type NB`. If any of the tests fail, the user will not be able to carry out the action. In other words, the final result is determined by applying AND operation to the result of all tests within an authorization object.

Multiple copies of the same authorization object

But, what would you do if you want to give create authorization for purchasing document type NB and display authorization for purchasing document type UB? You can do that by creating two authorization objects in the same role, one for each purchasing document type. If the user satisfies any one authorization object fully, he will be able to perform the transaction.

Adding an authorization object manually

You can add an authorization object manually. If you do not know the technical name of the authorization object, click 🔣 Selection criteria . It opens the following screen.

```
Choose the authorizations you want to insert
 ┌─囗 Materials Management: Purchasing                      MM_E

     ┌─囗 ⊖ Approved Manufacturer Parts List              M_AMPL_ALL
     ├─囗 ⊖ Approved Manufacturer Parts List - Plant      M_AMPL_WRK
     ├─囗 ⊖ Document Type in RFQ                           M_ANFR_BSA
     ├─囗 ⊖ Purchasing Group in RFQ                        M_ANFR_EKG
     ├─囗 ⊖ Purchasing Organization in RFQ                 M_ANFR_EKO
     ├─囗 ⊖ Plant/Storage Location in RFQ                  M_ANFR_LGO
     └─囗 ⊖ Plant in RFQ                                   M_ANFR_WRK
```

This screenshot shows the authorization objects, grouped under object classes. You find the authorization object and add. The system shows the authorization objects that were manually added, and those, that were added by the system.

Default authorization objects and values

When you generated authorization profile, the system automatically added certain authorization objects, and in some cases, it also put values for the fields. SAP has created these defaults, but you can change the default settings if you want. You are advised not to do so, unless you have adequate mastery over the subject.

Authorization object for transactions

In authorization control, authorization object S_TCODE under object class AAAB is very important. This authorization object controls the transactions that a user can run.

```
☐ ○○☐ 🖪 ♂ Standard Transaction Code Check at Transaction Start   S_TCODE
  └─☐ ○○☐ 🖪 Standard Transaction Code Check at Transaction Start   T-SI55039500
         └──── ⧉ Transaction Code                    ME21N
```

Roles and Profiles

You can create a role using transaction PFCG. You can also create a menu for a role. This is displayed in user menu of all users who are assigned that role.

If you go to the authorizations tab and click `Change Authorization Data` , SAP proposes a set of authorization objects, along with their default values. You fill up the missing values, and check whether the proposed values are okay. If necessary, you may change them. Finally, when you save them, all authorization objects should be green, as only those authorization objects are active.

You can also see all users who have been granted the role in the `User` tab. If the `☐ User comparison` button on the `User` tab is not green, click it. Otherwise, the authorizations may not work correctly.

Authorization for User

You can use transaction SU01 to assign roles to users. You can assign him one or more roles, which govern user authorization in SAP. You can also specify a reference user, whose authorizations will be available to the current user. You can also assign a user one or more profiles, which also grant him authorization in SAP.

Troubleshooting Authorization Problems

When a user faces authorization failure, you need to know what authorization he required, and what authorization he had. This is displayed by executing transaction SU53 immediately after an authorization failure.

34.3.2 Authorization Design Challenge

In SAP, the users can only do what they are authorized to do. If they have less authorization than they need, they will not be able to perform the tasks they are required to perform. If they have more authorization than they need, they may do something they are not expected to do. Ensuring that the business is not overexposed becomes particularly important in the current environment with its emphasis on regulatory compliance. At the operating level, this business challenge manifests itself in the following ways.

Stability of roles

Despite constantly changing business needs, you need to provide a stable regime of authorizations. This is very important because there is nothing more irritating to a user than discovering that he cannot do today, what he could do till yesterday, particularly when he has not asked for any change.

This problem is faced by the members of your Basis team, who actually create authorizations in the system. When you add a transaction in an existing role, SAP adds a lot of authorization objects. These persons must look at each authorization object, decide whether it is needed or not and, if needed, what should be its values. Only those who have performed this task themselves would know what a terrible task it is. And, if by some chance, they delete an authorization object that is required or change its values inappropriately, they can be rest assured that all hell will break loose.

Number and complexity of roles

In a production environment, it is common to find a very large number of roles, each containing a large number of authorization objects. Remember that a role is a set of authorization objects, with values assigned to each authorization field. If two users are assigned a role, and one user needs a different value in one authorization object, you have to create another role. Typical culprits are organizational objects. Two persons perform identical tasks but for different plants, and one role becomes two roles. When the number of roles becomes too many, you lose control and give up.

Authorizers' understanding problem

The authorizers are business managers. They do not understand authorization objects. Usually, they are presented a paper document, which they sign with varied understanding level. This is then translated into roles by the members of the Basis team. Is this translation right? Can the members of the Basis team show authorization for each value they have assigned? These are uncomfortable questions, and no one asks them.

Role-based or person-based authorizations

Technically, every authorization you create is a role-based authorization. Here, the question is not from a technical viewpoint, but from the business perspective. In your organization, do you create role for Cashiers or do you create role for the person who is a cashier?

Somehow, it is fashionable and politically correct to say that 'authorizations should be role-based'. There are no votaries for person-based authorizations. What are the advantages and disadvantages of role-based authorizations and person-based authorizations? Is one inherently superior to the other? Is it possible that some authorizations are role-based whereas others are person-based? If yes, how do you decide which authorizations should be role-based and which should be person-based?

Generic access

There are some transactions which provide generic access. You can use transaction SA38 or SE38 to run any program. If a user has access to these transactions, he effectively has access to all transactions. Similarly, using SE16 or SE11, you can view data in tables. Access to these transactions exposes the data in your system.

Authorization control in Z programs

SAP builds authorization control in the programs it provides. The responsibility of doing the same in your own programs lies with you. If authorizations are not controlled properly in Z programs, your carefully created authorization control can come to naught.

34.3.3 Authorization Design Strategy

Fortunately, each of the problems listed above has a solution.

Authorization control in Z programs

Your ABAP development team needs to create a policy which ensures that no data can be accessed by a program without checking for authorizations. Walkthrough and testing of a program should ensure and document that the policy has indeed been followed.

Generic access

Use of transactions SA38, SE38, SE16, SE11, and their equivalents should be banned. For each Z program, there should be a transaction code (preferably same as the program name), and authorization to run any program should be given via its transaction code. By doing this, you can ensure that a user cannot run any programs other than those assigned to him through transaction codes.

Role-based or person-based authorizations

It is futile to argue for or against role-based authorization. No organization can have authorizations which are fully role-based or fully person-based. Whether an authorization should be role-based or person-based has a very simple intuitive answer. Thinking of an authorization, does the organization think role-based or does it think person-based? Users accessing Employee Self Service would have role-based authorization because you do not think of a specific employee for whom you are creating the authorization.

If the work content of positions in your organization is very precisely and firmly defined and a change in the person holding that position has little or no impact on its functioning, perhaps all your authorizations can be role-based. But many organizations are somewhat flexible in this. They allow the holder of a position to redefine his role to an extent. The emphasis is on results, and if one wants to do things differently, or even different things, he is allowed to do so. The Sales Manager of one zone may not work exactly in the same way as the Sales Manager of another zone. If this is the case, you should have person-based authorizations for them. You cannot, and do not want to, force them to work in the same manner. You cannot deny some authorization to one because the other does not want it. Nor should you give authorization to the other, even when he does not want it.

The critical attribute that should determine whether authorization should be role-based or person-based, is the number of persons who would use an authorization. If the number of persons is large, it is a clear candidate for role-based authorization. If the number of persons is small, it is better to have person-based authorization. Person-based authorization is easier to design and implement. It also results in better user satisfaction.

Separating transaction authorization object from other authorization objects

Even if you add a single transaction in an existing role, SAP adds a number of authorization objects. The process of cleaning up these authorization objects creates the stability problem. This problem can be solved by creating two roles: one which contains only transactions, and another which contains other authorization objects. You would add a transaction in the role that contains only transactions. The system will add a number of other authorization objects. You would review these authorization objects with the role that contains other authorization objects, to make changes in the latter as required. You then delete other authorization objects from the role that contain only transactions. By doing so, the role that contains other authorization objects remains clean. Addition and changes in authorizations are well considered; and so are deletions if any.

Separating utility authorization objects from other authorization objects

In a production environment, you will find that each role contains a large number of authorization objects under object class AAAB. These authorization objects are needed for a variety of utility transactions and actions. Typically, these authorization objects would have the same value in all roles. Since these authorization objects get repeated so many times, they make the task of maintaining roles appear very heavy and unmanageable. If all these authorization objects are grouped into two utility roles, one for utility transactions and the other for the remaining utility authorization objects, all other roles will become much lighter.

Separating organizational objects

Many a times, users have identical roles but different jurisdictions. One user may do purchasing activities for one plant, while another user may do the same activities for another plant. This affects only one authorization object, but the entire role gets replicated. It is, therefore, prudent to separate authorization objects involving organizational elements into a separate role.

Separation and simplification of roles

Considering the separation of authorization objects in different roles discussed above, each user will have at least five roles.

Role	Purpose
Utility transactions	This role will contain all utility transactions, e.g. SU53. This role will be assigned to all users. It will have no authorization objects other than transactions. Any user needing extra authorization will be given as person-based authorization.
Utility authorization objects	This role will contain all authorization objects other than transactions belonging to object class AAAB. This role will be assigned to all users and provide them authorization needed to run utility transactions. Any user needing extra authorization will be given as person-based authorization.
Business transactions	This role will contain all business transactions needed by a user to perform his business tasks. It will have no authorization objects other than transactions. If this authorization is role-based, extra authorization will be given as person-based authorization.
Business authoriza-tion objects	This role will contain all authorization objects other than transactions needed by a user to perform his business tasks. If this authorization is role-based, extra authorization will be given as person-based authorization.
Business organiza-tional objects	All organizational authorization objects will be compulsorily person-based authorizations.

It may sound contradictory that a strategy which requires five roles to be assigned to each user will actually reduce the number and complexity of roles. Note that the first two roles are common company-wide. Therefore, they are much better controlled. Also, they make all other roles much lighter.

The business role being bifurcated doubles the number of roles, but the roles are much lighter than your current composite role. The issue is not just the number of roles, but the complexity of roles, and your ability to comprehend it.

The key to reducing the number of roles lies in the roles containing organizational authorization objects. This ensures that a role is never duplicated because the organizational authorization objects are different. These roles will also be extremely light.

Solving the understanding problem

The strategy discussed above creates roles that are much lighter. The first two roles are utility roles and your CIO can understand and approve them. No other business authorizer needs to bother about them. The other three roles will be much lighter, but the authorizer still needs to understand them. Understanding authorizations is not very difficult, but the authorizers need to familiarize themselves with the basic concepts. It will then be easy for them to authorize with understanding.

34.3.4 Authorization Check for Storage Locations

Purpose

Here you can activate storage location authorization for individual storage locations. Storage location authorization means that a user has to have authorization for authorization object M_MSEG_LGO in order to enter a goods movement in the storage location, using a particular movement type. In the list of material documents, only the document items for which the user has a display authorization are displayed.

JMG Node

SM30 ➤ V_001L_B

Screen

Plnt	Name 1	SLoc	Description	Authoriztn
1000	Werk Hamburg	0001	Materiallager	☐
1000	Werk Hamburg	0002	Fertigwarenlager	☐
1000	Werk Hamburg	0003	WE-Lager Fertigu	☐
1000	Werk Hamburg	0004	FHM-Lager	☐

Primary Key

Plant
Storage Location

34.3.5 Authorization Check for G/L Accounts

Purpose

Here you can set the G/L accounts authorization check which is to be applied when goods movements and reservations are entered. If this check is active, the system checks for every G/L account entered whether the user has the authorization to make postings to the specified G/L account. The authorization check only applies to accounts that have been entered manually. The system does not perform this check for accounts determined through automatic account determination.

JMG Node

SM30 ➤ V_001_MB

Screen

CoCd	Company Name	Inventory mgmt
0001	SAP A.G.	☐
0005	IDES AG NEW GL	☐
0006	IDES US INC New GL	☐
0007	IDES AG NEW GL 7	☐

Primary Key

Company Code

34.4   PERSONALIZATION

Functional Consultant	User	Business Process Owner	Senior Management	My Rating	Understanding Level
A	A	A	A		

34.4.1   User Details

You can choose System ➤ User Profile ➤ Own Data to maintain your personal details.

User	SAPUSER				
Last Changed On	SAPUSER	29.03.2020	12:01:51	Status	Saved

Address   Defaults   Parameters

Person

Title	Mr.
Last name	Agrawal
First name	Prem
Academic Title	
Format	Prem Agrawal
Function	
Department	
Room Number	Floor	Building

Communication

Language	EN English		Other communication...
Telephone		Extension	
Mobile Phone			
Fax		Extension	
E-Mail			
Comm. Meth	RML Remote Mail		

Assign other company address...   Assign new company address...

Company

34.4.2   User Defaults

You can choose System ➤ User Profile ➤ Own Data to maintain your personal default values.

User	SAPUSER				
Last Changed On	SAPUSER	29.03.2020	12:01:51	Status	Saved

Address   Defaults   Parameters

Start menu	
Logon Language	EN
Decimal Notation	X 1,234,567.89
Date format	1 DD.MM.YYYY

Spool Control

OutputDevice

☐ Output Immediately

☐ Delete After Output

Personal Time Zone

of the User	
Sys. Time Zone	CET

CATT

☐ Check Indicator

34.4.3   User Parameters

You can choose System ➤ User Profile ➤ Own Data to maintain user parameters to personalize the system.

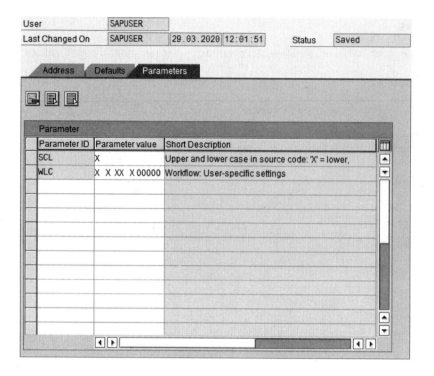

34.4.4 Customize Local Layout

You can click 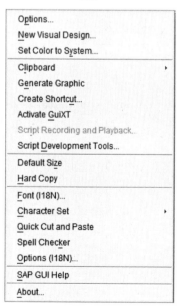 to customize the system to your liking. You choose from the following options.

Some important settings are explained here. You may explore the rest.

Options

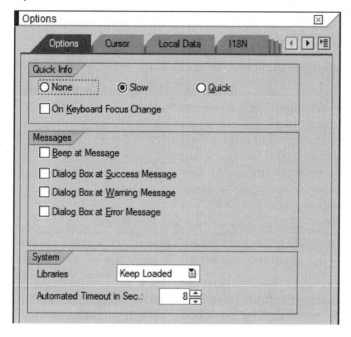

Messages

SAP gives you messages in the message bar. If you want the system to display the message in a dialog box, you can tick the appropriate checkbox. You can also get a beep at a message.

Cursor

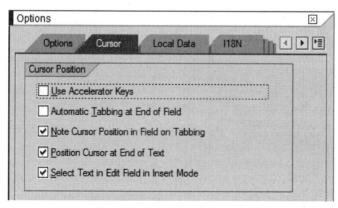

Cursor position	Selected	Not selected
Use Accelerator Keys	You can use numerous keys or key combinations to access frequently performed commands or operations quickly.	Accelerator keys are not enabled.
Automatic Tabbing at End of Field	The cursor automatically moves to the next input field when the maximum number of characters has been entered in a field. This function is useful when you are entering a large amount of data and you do not want to press the TAB key to move from field to field.	The cursor remains in the current input field.
Note Cursor Position in Field on Tabbing	Places the cursor exactly where you were when you last left an input field.	Places the cursor at the beginning of the input field.
Position Cursor at End of Text	Places the cursor at the end of a text in an input field when you click to the right of the text.	Places the cursor exactly where you click.
Select Text in Edit Field in Insert Mode	Selects and highlights the text when you tab to an input field. The session must be in insert mode. Any input in this field will clear the field.	When you tab to the next field, the text is not highlighted. The cursor appears at the end of any text already in the field.

Local Data

History

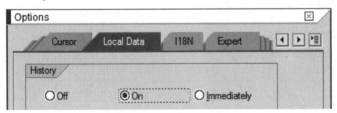

When you start entering data in a field, history shows you previously entered data matching your input as shown below.

User	s
Password	sapuser
	sap*

History	Description
Off	No input history is available.
On	Input history is available. Your input will be stored in the database locally. A list will be shown to the input field with focus when you make input or press the Backspace key.
Immediately	The history list will be shown immediately to the field with the focus before input is made.

Expert

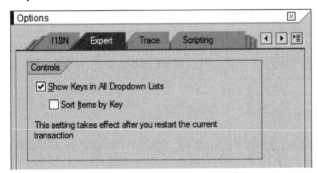

Displaying keys in drop down lists

In many fields, SAP provides a drop down list from which you can choose a value. These lists of values usually have a key and a description. Users who like to see the key in addition to the description can tick ☑ Show Keys in All Dropdown Lists . They can even sort the dropdown list by the key by ticking ☑ Sort Items by Key .

Quick Copy and Paste

SAP provides a method of quick copy and quick paste. You enable this by ticking ✔ Quick Cut and Paste in 🖿. After that, if you press the left button of the mouse, move the mouse on some text, and release it, the text gets copied to the clipboard. The text is not selected, as would be the case, if this feature is not enabled. Also, if you press the right button of the mouse in any field of SAP, the text is pasted from the clipboard. The text may have been copied on the clipboard from any application, e.g. Microsoft Word.

34.4.5   User Settings

Displaying transactions

You work in SAP either through menu or through transactions. Experienced users often prefer the latter method. Therefore, they need to know the transaction codes of various transactions. You can display the transaction codes in the menu by ticking the checkbox ☑ Display technical names in Extras ➤ Settings . The menu display changes as shown below.

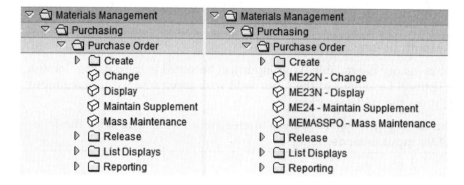

Menu settings

Through menu path Extras ➤ Settings , you can display or hide menu and display favorites at the top or at the bottom. You can also hide or display the picture.

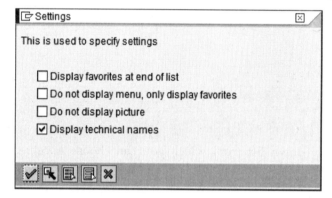

Set start transaction

You can also set a start transaction, which is executed automatically when you log on to the system through menu path Extras ➤ Set start transaction .

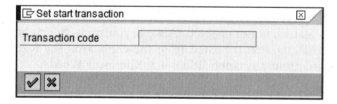

34.4.6 Defaults in the Material Master

You can set your own default values in the material master as explained in Sections 2.1.2 to 2.1.4.

34.4.7   Default Values and Copying Rules in MIGO Transactions

In a MIGO transaction you can set your own default values by selecting Settings ➢ Default Values . For more details, see Section 5.1.6. You can also set copying rules by selecting Settings ➢ Copying Rule Transfer Posting . For more details, see Section 5.1.8.

34.5   IMPLEMENTATION GUIDE

Functional Consultant	User	Business Process Owner	Senior Management	My Rating	Understanding Level
A	C	X	X		

When a consultant implements SAP MM Inventory Management for a client, how does the consultant determine the client requirement and do configuration, and how does the client know that the right configuration is done for him? The answers to these twin questions lie in the methodology you follow.

The consultant can use the structure of this book to guide the implementation. He can ask specific questions to the users, record their answers and use the answers to do the configuration. Having done the configuration, he can explain it to the users and get it approved. If the users do not have enough SAP knowledge to confirm the configuration, the consultant should record the user input and get it signed off. An auditor should then confirm that the configuration reflects the user input. The source of all configuration should be user input.

Whereas many factual inputs can come from a knowledgeable power user, policy inputs should come from senior management. In large companies, senior management is often surprised at the diversity of practices followed in different parts of the company. Implementation of SAP provides an opportunity to senior management to either commonize the practice, or approve diversity. Even when there is no diversity, decisions on policy should be approved by management.

Both user inputs and corresponding configuration should be recorded in a configuration manual. The configuration manual should explain what has been configured and, if necessary, why. If you use the following table as the Table of Content of your configuration manual, your configuration manual will be easy to understand. Apart from what you configure, you should also indicate what is not implemented (NR) and what is SAP standard (SS). You should also add all Z developments done by you in respective chapters. Feel free to add chapters in the table of contents, but do not delete any line which has configuration in it. The support team needs to know if something is not implemented. If some configuration is not implemented, you can keep the chapter number blank, instead of creating empty chapters in the configuration manual. The Reference column contains the chapter number in the book.

In the 'Approved by' column you should record the name of the person who has approved that particular configuration. If users are not knowledgeable enough to sign off the configuration, the users should sign off their input, and the auditor should sign off the configuration.

Chapter	Description	Configuration	NR/SS/ Done	Reference	Approved by
1	**Enterprise Structure**				
1.1	Company Code	V_T001		1.2	
1.2	Plant	V_T001W		1.3	
1.3	Assignment of Plant to Company Code	V_T001K_ASSIGN		1.3.6	
1.4	Factory Calendar for a Plant	V_001W_F		1.3.7	
1.5	Storage Location	VC_T001L		1.4	
2	**Material**				
2.1	External Material Group	V_TWEW		2.1.5	
2.2	Laboratory/Office	V_024L		2.1.5	
2.3	Basic Materials	TWSPR		2.1.6	
2.4	Units of Measure Groups	V_006M		2.1.8	
2.5	Temperature Conditions	V_143		2.1.10	
2.6	Storage Conditions	V_142		2.1.10	
2.7	Container Requirements	V_144		2.1.10	
2.8	Screen Sequence Determination	V_CM2		2.4.1	
2.9	Screen Sequence Definition	V_CM1		2.4.2	
2.10	Creating Your Own Subscreens	Transaction OMT3C		2.4.2	
2.11	Additional Screens	V_T133S_ZUORD		2.4.3	
2.12	Sequence of Main and Additional Screens	V_T133S_REIHF		2.4.4	
2.13	Field References for Industry Sectors	V137		2.4.5	
2.14	Field References for Plants	V_130W		2.4.5	
2.15	Assignment of Fields to Field Selection Group	V_130F		2.4.5	
2.16	Field Properties	V_T130A_FLREF		2.4.5	
2.17	Field Attributes	V_130F		2.4.6	
2.18	Lock-Relevant Fields	Transaction OMSFIX		2.4.7	
2.19	Maintenance Status of a Field	V_130F		2.5.5	
2.20	Maintenance Status Determination in Data Transfer	V_T133S		2.5.6	
2.21	Maintenance Status for Plants	V_130W		2.5.7	
2.22	Number Ranges for Material	Transaction MMNR		2.6	

Chapter	Description	Configuration	NR/SS/ Done	Reference	Approved by
2.23	Output Format of Material Numbers	V_TMCNV		2.6.10	
2.24	Material Type	MTART		2.7	
2.25	Material Creation Transactions for Specific Material Types	V_134K		2.7.13	
2.26	Material Group	V023		2.8.1	
2.27	Entry Aids for Items without a Material Master	V023_E		2.8.2	
2.28	Material Status	Transaction OMS4		2.9	
2.29	Purchasing Value Keys	V_405		2.10	
2.30	Shipping Instructions	VC_T027A		2.11	
3	**Goods and Accounts Movement**				
4	**Stock**				
4.1	Negative Stocks Allowed for a Valuation Area	Transaction OMJ1		4.2.3	
4.2	Negative Special Stocks Allowed for a Plant	V_159L_NEG		4.2.4	
4.3	Negative Stocks Allowed for Storage Locations	V_T001L_N		4.2.5	
4.4	Stock Overview: Detailed Display	V_136V		4.3.3	
4.5	Stock Overview: Display Versions	V_136A		4.3.3	
4.6	Stock Overview: Columns in a Display Version	V_136		4.3.3	
4.7	Movement Type Groups	V_156S_GR		4.3.8	
5	**Goods Receipt**				
5.1	Enabling Automatic Purchase Order for a Movement Type	V_156_AB		5.6.2	
5.2	Default Purchasing Organization	V_001W_E		5.6.3	
6	**Goods Issue**				
7	**Goods Return**				
7.1	Enabling Automatic Purchase Order for a Movement Type	V_156_AB		7.3.2	
7.2	Default Purchasing Organization	V_001W_E		7.3.3	
8	**Stock Transfer**				
8.1	Customer Number of Receiving Plant	V_001W_IV		8.4.6	
8.2	Shipping Point for Supplying Plant	V_T001W_L		8.4.6	

Chapter	Description	Configuration	NR/SS/ Done	Reference	Approved by
8.3	Delivery Type and Checking Rule	VV_161V_VF		8.4.7	
8.4	Activating Stock Transfer between Storage Locations using STO	V_TCURM_ SUPPSLOC		8.8.2	
8.5	Delivery Type and Checking Rule According to Storage Location	V_161VN		8.8.3	
8.6	Sales Area based on Storage Location	V_T001L_L		8.8.4	
9	**Transfer Posting**				
10	**Customer Returns**				
11	**Subcontracting**				
12	**Consignment Stock of Vendor**				
13	**Consignment Stock with Customer**				
14	**Project Stock**				
15	**Sales Order Stock**				
16	**Pipeline Material**				
17	**Returnable Transport Packaging Vendor**				
18	**Returnable Transport Packaging with Customer**				
19	**Goods Movement Reversal**				
20	**Screen Layout**				
20.1	Permitted Events and Reference Documents	MIGO_LISTBOX		20.1	
20.2	Field Properties for MIGO Transactions	Transaction OMJX		20.2	
20.3	Field Properties based on Movement Type	MIGO_CUST_ FIELDS		20.2.6	
20.4	Field Properties for Header Fields	Transaction OMJN		20.3	
20.5	Field Properties for Item Fields	Transactions OMBW, OMCJ, OMJA		20.4	
20.6	Subscreen for Account Assignment Block	Transaction OXK1		20.5	

Chapter	Description	Configuration	NR/SS/ Done	Reference	Approved by
21	**Movement Type and Other Configurations**				
21.1	Movement Types	V_156_VC		21.1.3	
21.2	Reason for Movement	V_157D		21.1.3	
21.3	Control Reason	V_156_G		21.1.3	
21.4	Short Texts	V_156T_VC		21.1.4	
21.5	Allowed Transactions	V_158B_VC		21.1.5	
21.6	Help Texts	V_157H_VC		21.1.6	
21.7	Field Selection (From 201)/ Batch Search Procedure	V_156B_VC		21.1.7	
21.8	Update Control/Warehouse Management Movement Types	V_156SC_VC		21.1.9	
21.9	Reversal/Follow-on Movement Types	V_156N_VC		21.1.11	
21.10	Reason for Movement	V_157D_VC		21.1.12	
21.11	Deactivate QM Inspection/ Delivery Category	V_156Q_VC		21.1.13	
21.12	LIS Statistics Group	V_MCA_VC		21.1.14	
21.13	Copy Rules for Reference Documents: Goods Receipt	V_158_E		21.2.1	
21.14	Copy Rules for Reference Documents: Goods Issue/ Transfer Postings	V_158_A		21.2.2	
21.15	Checking Group	V_TMVF		21.3.3	
21.16	Checking Rule	V_441R		21.3.5	
21.17	Assignment of Checking Rule to Transaction	V_158_P		21.3.6	
21.18	Availability Check Definition	V_441V		21.3.7	
21.19	Assignment of type of message to movement type	V_156S_W		21.3.8	
21.20	Assignment of type of message to movement type (Reservation)	V_156S_D		21.3.9	
21.21	Activating Missing Parts Check	V_159L_F		21.4.2	
21.22	Checking Group	V_TMVF		21.4.3	
21.23	Checking Rule	V_441R		21.4.5	
21.24	Assignment of Checking Rule to Transaction	V_158_P		21.4.6	
21.25	Assignment of checking rule to movement type	V_156S_F		21.4.6	

Chapter	Description	Configuration	NR/SS/ Done	Reference	Approved by
21.26	Checking Rule Definition	V_441V		21.4.7	
21.27	MRP Controllers for Plants	V_T399D_L		21.4.8	
21.28	Communication Details of MRP Controllers	V_T024D		21.4.9	
21.29	Shelf Life Expiration Date Check for Plants	V_159L_MHD		21.5.2	
21.30	Shelf Life Expiration Date Check for Movement Types	V_156_MHD		21.5.3	
21.31	Automatic Creation of Material in Storage Location: Plant Level Control	V_159L_X		21.6.2	
21.32	Automatic Creation of Material in Storage Location: Movement Type Level Control	V_156_X		21.6.2	
21.33	Attributes of System Messages	V_160M		21.7	
21.34	Enabling GR/GI Slip Numbers for a Plant	V_159L_XA		21.8.2	
21.35	Assignment of number range grouping code	V_159X		21.8.3	
21.36	Assignment of Internal and External Number Range	V_159Z		21.8.3	
21.37	Number Range for GR/GI Slip Numbers	Transaction OMJ6		21.8.4	
21.38	Tolerance Limits	V_169G		21.9	
21.39	Setting delivery completed indicator automatically	V_159L_E		21.10.7	
21.40	Price Differences for Subcontract Orders at Goods Receipt	V_001K_LB		21.11	
21.41	Activating Storage per Movement Type	V_156_OA		21.12.2	
21.42	Activating Storage per Transaction	V_158_OA		21.12.3	
21.43	Print Functions for Reporting	V_MMIM_REP_PRINT		21.13	
21.44	Updating of material document data upon posting	Customer Exit MB_CF001		21.14	
21.45	Filling the item text in the material document	Customer Exit MBCF0002		21.14	
21.46	Maintaining batch master data upon goods movements	Customer Exit MBCFC003		21.14	

Chapter	Description	Configuration	NR/SS/ Done	Reference	Approved by
21.47	Maintaining batch specifications upon goods movements	Customer Exit MBCFC004		21.14	
21.48	Filling the item data on goods receipt/issue slips	Customer Exit MBCF0005		21.14	
21.49	Transferring the number of the WBS element for subcontracting	Customer Exit MBCF0006		21.14	
21.50	Posting a reservation	Customer Exit MBCF0007		21.14	
21.51	Filling the Storage location field	Customer Exit MBCF0009		21.14	
21.52	Serial numbers, user exit for goods movements	Customer Exit IQSM0007		21.14	
21.53	Stock determination	Customer Exit XMBF0001		21.14	
21.54	BAdI: Creation of Material Document	MB_ DOCUMENT_ BADI		21.15	
21.55	BAdI: Changing of Item Data in Transaction MIGO	MB_MIGO_ ITEM_BADI		21.15	
21.56	BAdI: Maintenance of External Detail Subscreens for Transaction MIGO	MB_MIGO_ BADI		21.15	
21.57	BAdI: Checking/Supplementation of Dialog Data for Transactions MB21/MB22	MB_ RESERVATION_ BADI		21.15	
21.58	BAdI: Check Line Before Adoption in Blocking Tables	MB_CHECK_ LINE_BADI		21.15	
21.59	BAdI: Archiving of Add-On-Specific Data for MM_MATBEL	ARC_MM_ MATBEL_WRITE		21.15	
21.60	BAdI: Check Add-On-Specific Criteria for MM_MATBEL	ARC_MM_ MATBEL_CHECK		21.15	
21.61	BAdI: Enhancement of Scope of Archiving (MM_INVBEL)	ARC_MM_ INVBEL_WRITE		21.15	
21.62	BAdI: Enhancement of Archivability Check (MM_INVBEL)	ARC_MM_ INVBEL_CHECK		21.15	
22	**Material Document**				
22.1	Field Selection for Material Document List	V_MMIM_REP_ CUST		22.3.1	
22.2	Number Assignment for Material Documents	Transaction OMBT		22.4	

Chapter	Description	Configuration	NR/SS/ Done	Reference	Approved by
23	**Accounting Documents**				
23.1	Number Assignment for Accounting Documents	Transaction FBN1		23.3	
24	**Output Determination**				
24.1	Output Determination Procedure	VV_T683_MB		24.2.2	
24.2	Steps in Output Determination Procedure	V_T683S_XX		24.2.3	
24.3	Define Requirements	Transaction VOFM		24.2.3	
24.4	Output Type	VN_T685B		24.2.4	
24.5	Access Sequences	VVC_T682_MB		24.2.5	
24.6	Default Value of Print Version	V_158_D		24.3.4	
24.7	Master list of item print indicator	V_159Q		24.3.5	
24.8	Determination of print item	V_156_D		24.3.5	
24.9	Maintain Condition Records in Table B072	Transaction MN21, MN22		24.5.1	
24.10	Maintain Condition Records in Table B073	Transaction MN21, MN22		24.5.2	
24.11	Assign Forms and Programs	VV_TNAPR_ME		24.6.2	
24.12	Define Forms	SE71		24.6.2	
24.13	Label Type	V_6WP3		24.7.1	
24.14	Label Form	V_6WP4		24.7.1	
24.15	Maintain Condition Records in Table B070	Transaction MN21, MN22		24.7.3	
24.16	Maintain Number of Labels	V_159E		24.7.3	
24.17	Assign Forms and Programs for Label Printing	VV_TNAPR_ME		24.7.4	
24.18	Application Object	V_159O		24.7.5	
24.19	Label Text	Transaction OMCF		24.7.6	
24.20	Master List of Printers	V_159P		24.8.1	
24.21	Printer Determination Based on the Condition Record	Transaction MN21, MN22		24.8.4	
24.22	Printer Determination Based on Output Type	VN_T685B		24.8.5	
24.23	Printer determination by storage location	V_TNAD7		24.8.5	
24.24	Printer determination by storage location/user group	V_TNAD9		24.8.5	

Chapter	Description	Configuration	NR/SS/ Done	Reference	Approved by
24.25	Printer determination by output type/user	V_TNADU		24.8.5	
24.26	Printer determination by user exit	EXIT_ SAPLV61B_002		24.8.5	
24.27	Mail on Goods Receipt	VN_T685B		24.10	
24.28	Maintain Condition Records in Table B071	Transaction MN21, MN22		24.10.4	
24.29	Mail Title and Texts	VN_TNATI		24.10.5	
24.30	Processing Routines	VN_TNAPR		24.10.6	
24.31	Partner Functions	VN_TNAPN		24.10.7	
24.32	Maintain Condition Records in Table B074	Transaction MN21, MN22		24.11.2	
25	**Material Valuation**				
25.1	Price Control for Material Types	V_134_P		25.1.5	
25.2	Activating Split Valuation	Transaction OMW0		25.2.3	
25.3	Configure Split Valuation	Transaction OMWC		25.2	
26	**Account Determination**				
26.1	Account Determination	Transaction OMWB		26.2	
26.2	Activating Valuation Grouping Code	Transaction OMWM		26.6.3	
26.3	Valuation Grouping Code Definition	V_001K_K		26.6.4	
26.4	General Modification/Account Modification	V_156X_KO		26.7	
26.5	Account Category References	V_025K		26.8.2	
26.6	Valuation Classes	V025		26.8.3	
26.7	Account Category Reference for a Material Type	V_134_K		26.8.4	
27	**Stock Determination**				
27.1	Master List of Stock Determination Groups	V_T434G		27.2.1	
27.2	Master List of Stock Determination Rules	V_T434R		27.3.1	
27.3	Grouping Movement Types in Stock Determination Rules	V_156_BF		27.3.2	
27.4	Stock Determination Strategy	V_T434K		27.4	

Chapter	Description	Configuration	NR/SS/ Done	Reference	Approved by
27.5	Stock Determination Item Table	V_T434P		27.5	
28	**Reservation**				
28.1	Copy rules for reference documents in reservation	V_158_R		28.2.2	
28.2	Default Values for Batch Input	V_159B_MR		28.2.10	
28.3	Default Values for Reservation	V_159L_R		28.4	
28.4	Number Range Intervals for Reservations	Transaction OMJK		28.5.1	
28.5	Number Ranges for Reservations	Transaction OMC2		28.5.2	
29	**Physical Inventory**				
29.1	Allowing Freezing of Book Inventory	V_T001L_I		29.11.3	
29.2	Pre-Selection of Proposed Items	V_158_I		29.22.6	
29.3	Entering Reason for Difference	Transaction OMJU		29.22.7	
29.4	Settings for Physical Inventory	V_159L_EI		29.29	
29.5	Default Values for Physical Inventory	V_159L_I		29.30	
29.6	Default Values for Batch Input	V_159B		29.31	
29.7	Tolerances for Physical Inventory Differences	V_T043I		29.32	
29.8	Physical inventory tolerance group	V_043_B		29.32.5	
29.9	Allowing Inventory Sampling in Inventory Management	V_064S_1		29.33.2	
29.10	Allowing Inventory Sampling in Warehouse Management	V_064S_2		29.33.3	
29.11	Inventory Sampling Profile	V_159G		29.33.4	
29.12	Cycle Counting Indicators for a Plant	V_159C		29.34.2	
29.13	Physical Inventory Documents for Plant	V_159L_V		29.35.2	
29.14	Number Range Assignment	Transaction OMBT		29.35.3	
29.15	Physical Inventory Documents for Movement Type	V_156_I		29.35.4	
29.16	Forms for Physical Inventory Documents	V_159N		29.36	

Chapter	Description	Configuration	NR/SS/ Done	Reference	Approved by
29.17	Serial Number Profile	V_T377P		29.37.3	
29.18	Serialization Procedures	V_T377		29.37.4	
30	**Financial Accounting**				
31	**Controlling**				
32	**Periodic Processing**				
33	**Archiving**				
33.1	Archiving Object-Specific Customizing	V_ARC_USR		33.3	
33.2	Archiving Application-Specific Customizing	V_159R		33.4	
34	**Utilities**				
34.1	Authorization Check for Storage Locations	V_001L_B		34.3.4	
34.2	Authorization Check for G/L Accounts	V_001_MB		34.3.5	

34.6 TRANSACTIONS

Functional Consultant	User	Business Process Owner	Senior Management	My Rating	Understanding Level
A	X	X	X		

34.6.1 Inventory Management

Category	Transaction	Description	Page
User	CO09	Availability Overview	438
User	FBL1N	Vendor Line Items	779
User	FK10N	Vendor Balance Display	777
User	FS10N	Balance Display	772
User	J3RFLVMOBVED	Stock Overview (Russia)	104
User	KA03	Display Cost Element	785
User	KAH3	Display Cost Element Group	786
User	KS03	Display Cost Center	788
User	KSB1	Cost Centers: Actual Line Items	790
User	MB02	Change Material Document	469
User	MB03	Display Material Document	469

Category	Transaction	Description	Page
User	MB04	Subsequent Adjustment in Subcontracting	319
User	MB1A	Goods Withdrawal	178
User	MB1B	Transfer Posting	312
User	MB1C	Other Goods Receipts	154
User	MB21	Create Reservation	592
User	MB22	Change Reservation	600
User	MB23	Display Reservation	601
User	MB25	Reservation List	612
User	MB26	Picking List	606
User	MB31	Goods Receipt for Production Order	156
User	MB51	Material Document List	481
User	MB52	List of Warehouse Stocks on Hand	101
User	MB53	Display Plant Stock Availability	100
User	MB54	Consignment Stocks	325
User	MB58	Consignment and Ret. Packaging at Customer	342
User	MB5B	Stocks for Posting Date	101
User	MB5K	Stock Consistency Check	796
User	MB5L	List of Stock Values: Balances	794
User	MB5M	Expiration Date List	449
User	MB5S	Display List of GR/IR Balances	104
User	MB5T	Stock in Transit CC	102
User	MB5U	Analyze Conversion Differences	793
User	MB90	Output Processing for Material Documents	125
User	MBAD	Delete Material Documents	812
User	MBAL	Material Documents: Read Archive	814
User	MBAR	Archive Material Documents	807
User	MBAV	Manage Material Document Archive	811
User	MBBM	Batch Input: Post Material Document	169
User	MBBR	Batch Input: Create Reservation	598
User	MBBS	Display Valuated Special Stock	351
User	MBGR	Display Material Docs by Movement Reason	484
User	MBLB	Stocks at Subcontractor	312
User	MBPM	Manage Held Data	798
User	MBRL	Return Delivery for Material Document	478
User	MBSL	Copy Material Document	475

Category	Transaction	Description	Page
User	MBSM	Display Cancelled Material Documents	483
User	MBST	Cancel Material Document	476
User	MBSU	Place in Storage for Material Document	480
User	MBVR	Management Program: Reservations	602
User	MD04	Display Stock/Requirements Situation	266
User	ME23N	Display Purchase Order	129
User	ME33	Display Outline Agreement	
User	MI01	Create Physical Inventory Document	621
User	MI02	Change Physical Inventory Document	637
User	MI03	Display Physical Inventory Document	640
User	MI04	Enter Inventory Count with Document	651
User	MI05	Change Inventory Count	663
User	MI06	Display Inventory Count	665
User	MI07	Process List of Differences	670
User	MI08	Create List of Differences with Document	676
User	MI09	Enter Inventory Count w/o Document	656
User	MI10	Create List of Differences w/o Document	681
User	MI11	Recount Physical Inventory Document	660
User	MI12	Display Changes	688
User	MI20	Print List of Differences	667
User	MI21	Print Physical Inventory Document	641
User	MI22	Display Physical Inventory Docs. for Material	686
User	MI23	Display Physical Inventory Data for Material	687
User	MI24	Physical Inventory List	688
User	MI31	Batch Input: Create Phys. Inv. Doc.	628
User	MI32	Batch Input: Block Material	645
User	MI33	Batch Input: Freeze Book Inventory Balance	650
User	MI34	Batch Input: Enter Count	653
User	MI35	Batch Input: Post Zero Stock Balance	655
User	MI37	Batch Input: Post Differences	674
User	MI38	Batch Input: Count and Differences	679
User	MI39	Batch Input: Document and Count	659
User	MI40	Batch Input: Doc., Count and Diff.	685
User	MIAD	Delete Physical Inventory Documents	814
User	MIAL	Inventory Documents: Read Archive	816
User	MIAR	Archive Physical Inventory Documents	812

Category	Transaction	Description	Page
User	MIAV	Manage Physical Inventory Documents Archive	811
User	MIBC	ABC Analysis for Cycle Counting	736
User	MICN	Batch Input: Ph. Inv. Docs. for Cycle Counting	740
User	MIDO	Physical Inventory Overview	687
User	MIE1	Batch Input: Phys.Inv.Doc. Sales Order	635
User	MIGO	Goods Movement	106
User	MIGO_GI	Goods Movement	178
User	MIGO_GO	Goods Movement	156
User	MIGO_GR	Goods Movement	106
User	MIGO_GS	Subsequent Adjustment in Subcontracting	319
User	MIGO_TR	Transfer Posting	230
User	MIK1	Batch Input: Ph. Inv. Doc. Vendor Consignment	635
User	MIM1	Batch Input: Create Ph. Inv. Docs RTP	636
User	MIO1	Batch Input: Ph. Inv. Doc. Stock with Subcont.	637
User	MIQ1	Batch Input: Ph. Inv. Doc. Project Stock	636
User	MIS1	Create Inventory Sampling	708
User	MIS2	Change Inventory Sampling	708
User	MIS3	Display Inventory Sampling	708
User	MIV1	Batch Input: Ph. Inv. Doc. Ret.Pack.at Cust.	637
User	MIW1	Batch Input: Ph. Inv. Doc. Consign. at Cust.	636
User	MM03	Display Material	40
User	MMBE	Stock Overview	96
User	MMPV	Close Periods	791
User	MR51	Material Line Items	490
User	MRKO	Settle Consignment/Pipeline Liabilities	325
User	OKEON	Cost Center Standard Hierarchy	789
User	S_ALR_87012284	Balance Sheet/P+L Statement	775
User	S_ALR_87012326	Chart of Accounts	771
User	S_ALR_87012328	G/L Account List	770
User	S_ALR_87012333	G/L Accounts List	772
User	S_ALR_87013600	Cost Elements: Object Class in Columns	788
User	S_ALR_87013601	Cost Elements: Breakdown by Object Type	787
User	S_ALR_87013602	Cost Elements: Object Type in Columns	787
User	S_PL0_86000032	SAP Structured Balance List	774
User	XD03	Display Customer (Centrally)	
User	XK03	Display Vendor (Centrally)	243

34.6.2 Utility

Category	Transaction	Description	Page
ABAP	BAPI	Bapi explorer	825
Basis	BD87	Status monitor for ALE messages	826
User	CG3Y	Download file	821
User	CG3Z	Upload file	822
ABAP	CMOD	Enhancements	824
Consultant	LSMW	Legacy system migration workbench	822
User	OAAD	Archivelink administration documents	821
Consultant	OSS1	Log on to SAPNet	822
Consultant	OY19	Customizing cross-system viewer	822
Basis	PFCG	Role maintenance	830
Basis	RSSCD100_PFCG	Change documents for role admin.	825
Basis	RSSCD100_PFCG_USER	For role assignment	825
Basis	RSUSR200	List of users per login date	825
Basis	S_BCE_68001403	With critical authorizations	825
Basis	S002	Menu administration	825
User	SA38	ABAP reporting	820
Basis	SALE	Display ALE customizing	826
User	SBWP	SAP business workplace	820
Consultant	SCAT	Computer aided test tool	822
Basis	SCC4	Client administration	825
Consultant	SCMP	View/table comparison	822
Basis	SCOT	SAPconnect—administration	826
Consultant	SCU0	Customizing cross-system viewer	822
Basis	SE01	Transport organizer (extended)	825
Basis	SE03	Transport organizer tools	825
Consultant, Basis	SE09	Transport organizer	822
Consultant, Basis	SE10	Transport organizer	822
Consultant, ABAP	SE11	ABAP dictionary maintenance	822
ABAP	SE13	Maintain technical settings (tables)	824
ABAP	SE15	ABAP/4 repository information system	825
Consultant, ABAP	SE16	Data browser	822
Consultant, ABAP	SE16N	General table display	822

Category	Transaction	Description	Page
Consultant, ABAP	SE17	General table display	822
ABAP	SE18	Business add-ins: definitions	824
ABAP	SE19	Business add-ins: implementations	824
ABAP	SE24	Class builder	823
ABAP	SE35	ABAP/4 dialog modules	823
ABAP	SE36	Logical database builder	824
ABAP	SE37	ABAP function modules	823
ABAP	SE38	ABAP editor	823
ABAP	SE39	Splitscreen editor: (new)	823
ABAP	SE41	Menu painter	823
ABAP	SE43	Maintain area menu	824
ABAP	SE51	Screen painter	823
ABAP	SE61	SAP documentation	824
Consultant	SE63	Translation: initial screen	823
ABAP	SE71	SAPscript form	824
ABAP	SE72	SAPscript styles	824
ABAP	SE73	SAPscript font maintenance	824
ABAP	SE74	SAPscript format conversion	824
ABAP	SE75	SAPscript settings	824
ABAP	SE75TTDTGC	SAPscript: change standard symbols	824
ABAP	SE75TTDTGD	SAPscript: display standard symbols	824
ABAP	SE76	SAPscript: form translation	824
ABAP	SE77	SAPscript styles translation	824
ABAP	SE80	Object navigator	825
ABAP	SE84	Repository information system	825
ABAP	SE85	ABAP/4 repository information system	825
ABAP	SE91	Message maintenance	824
ABAP	SE93	Maintain transaction	824
Consultant	SEARCH_SAP_ MENU	Find in SAP menu	823
Consultant	SEARCH_USER_ MENU	Find in user menu	823
User, Consultant	SECATT	Extended computer aided test tool	821
User, Consultant	SHDB	Batch input transaction recorder	821
Consultant	SLG1	Application log: display logs	

Category	Transaction	Description	Page
Basis	SM01	Lock transactions	826
Basis	SM04	User list	825
Basis	SM12	Display and delete locks	826
Consultant	SM30	Call view maintenance	822
Consultant	SM31	Call view maintenance like SM30	822
Consultant	SM34	View cluster maintenance call	822
User	SM35	Batch input monitoring	821
User	SM35P	Batch input: log monitoring	821
User	SM36	Schedule background job	821
User	SM37	Job overview	821
User	SM38	Queue maintenance transaction	821
ABAP	SMOD	SAP enhancement management	824
User	SMX	Display own jobs	821
User	SO00	SAPoffice: short message	820
ABAP	SO10	SAPscript: standard texts	824
User	SP01	Output controller	821
User	SP02	Display spool requests	821
Consultant	SP11	TemSe directory	
Consultant	SPRO	Customizing - edit project	822
User, Consultant	SQ00	SAP query: start queries	823
Consultant	SQ01	SAP query: maintain queries	823
Consultant	SQ02	SAP query: maintain infoset	823
Consultant	SQ03	SAP query: maintain user groups	823
User	SQVI	Quickviewer	820
ABAP	ST22	ABAP dump analysis	825
Basis	SU01	User maintenance	825
Basis	SU01_NAV	User maintenance	825
Basis	SU21	Maintain the Authorization Objects	
Basis	SU22	Auth. object usage in transactions	825
Basis	SU24	Auth. object check under transactions	825
User	SU3	Maintain users own data	820
User	SU53	Display authorization check	821
Basis	SUIM	User information system	825
Consultant	SWDD	Workflow builder	823

Index

World Government
For a World Free from War, Terrorism and Poverty

Facts

- The world spends trillions of dollars every year on military and war equipment, while its people go hungry.
- Today the world is incapable of resolving any dispute through military actions.
- Terrorism thrives because of covert support of country governments.
- Enormous expenditure on militaries all over the world is not only a waste, but also extremely dangerous as it increases the destructive power of country governments.

We want

- A world free from war, terrorism and poverty.

How can it be done?

- Establish a world parliament, a world government and a world court.
- Disband militaries of all countries simultaneously.
- Use the savings to alleviate poverty.

Will all countries agree?

- Yes! When people of the countries want it.
- We have to awaken the people of the whole world.

How will it work?

- The world parliament will be formed through direct election of members of parliament all over the world. These members of parliament will form the world government.
- The world government will have limited but sufficient power to provide security to all countries, manage global environment and combat terrorism all over the world.
- The world government will secure the borders of all countries to ensure that there is no unauthorized entry or exit.
- The country governments will continue to manage their affairs.
- Disputes between countries will be resolved with the help of the world parliament and the world court.
- No country will disband its military first. All countries will disband their

militaries simultaneously in a phased manner, under the supervision of the world government, which will verify that the militaries are actually disbanded.

- Countries will retain their police to maintain law and order.
- Countries may have special forces to deal with terrorism and to provide relief in the event of natural disasters.

Is it possible?

- Many people say that this is an impossible task because other people will not agree.
- This task is possible if we talk only about ourselves, and not about others. This task is big but not impossible.
- We have only one world, we can't give up on it.
- We can succeed only if we try.

What should I do?

- Level 1: Register with WIII and become a world citizen. Even children can join.
- Level 2: Spread the message to your family, friends and neighbours. Convince five persons to join.

- Level 3: Convince five persons that each one of them would enroll five more persons.
- Level 4: Become an active volunteer.

Act now

- Act now. Don't give up because of enormity of the task.

You have nothing to lose

- There is no membership fee.
- You are not required to work unless you want to. But if you want, there is a lot of work to do.
- You are not required to follow any person or any belief.

Contact

World Integration and Improvement Initiative (WIII)
E-mail: agrawal.prem@gmail.com

World Language

Need for a World Language

Perhaps the most important gift of nature to mankind is the ability to communicate using a language. However, this gift is not unmitigated, because we have got too much of it. We do not have a single language, but a large number of them, which sometimes is as bad as not having any language.

Lack of a common world language can greatly handicap a person, as more and more people travelling around the world discover to their dismay. With the world becoming smaller and smaller, as a result of advances in transportation and communication, the need for a common world language is felt more and more acutely. One option to overcome this handicap is for a person to learn multiple languages, which is not only wasteful, but can be done only to a limited extent. Another way to overcome this handicap is through translation and inter-pretation, for which we pay a heavy price in terms of cost, time, and timeliness, and achieve at best partial communication. Scientific and technical literature available in one language cannot be used by people who do not know that language.

There is probably no one, who does not agree with the need for a world language. Only, people do not want to discuss it, fearing that accepting any language, other than their own, as world language will put them at a disadvantage. Also, people are strongly attached to their mother tongue, often considering it as revered as their mother, and feel a sense of guilt in accepting another language.

While there are some, who do not want to discuss this issue fearing that they may have to accept another language, there are others who do the same hoping that their language may become world language by default. This may well happen, but is it desirable even for them?

Importance of a good world language

A language is a tool for communication, and we must evaluate it as we would evaluate any other tool. How effective is it in meeting its objective; and how much resources does it consume in doing so? People who hope that their language may become world language, should think again. Do we just want a common language, or do we want a really good world language—a language which provides effective, unambiguous communication with minimum effort.

This article shows that existing languages score quite badly in a rational evaluation. Let us remember that many of us use almost our entire non-sleeping time in reading, writing, and thinking—activities which depend on the efficiency of language. If we can design a language, which is more efficient than our existing language, we will gain that much extra time, which can be used for productive or recreational purposes. It has also been well accepted that languages influence our thinking, making the role of language even more important.

We must, therefore, consider ourselves lucky that we do not have a single language in the world. This gives us a choice. It is possible for us to have a well designed world language. If we had only one language, we would not have this choice, as we have no choice today in numbering system, computer keyboard, etc. We must not squander this choice away, by letting an existing language become the world language. It will be like losing a fortune, just because we refused to decide. It is also important that we decide to develop a world language as early as possible. The more time we lose, the more will be the backlog of translation, which must necessarily be done.

Should an existing natural language be world language?

Some of the existing natural languages, particularly English, aspire to become world language. Their claim is based primarily on their widespread use in dominant segments of society all over the world, e.g. science, law, business, industry, government, etc. However, if we objectively examine their effectiveness and efficiency, they do not perform too well. Let us take a look at 'English'.

Let us start from the alphabet. English does not have a phonetic alphabet. The same letter is associated with different sounds in different words. This puts tremendous load on people learning the language. They have to learn both the pronunciation as well as the spelling. Many languages of the world have this problem, while many are free from it.

The length of the words in a language determines the effort in communication to a large extent. If the words are long, the communication time and effort is more. Natural languages being product of evolution, have not paid much attention to length of words. Consequently, the words tend to be long. The best proof of this defect in a language is the existence of short forms for long words. 'Info' for information, and 'ad' for advertisement, amply demonstrate that words can be shorter.

All languages use prefixes and suffixes to add additional meaning to the meaning of a word. By doing so, they avoid the need to define and learn a word. This practice is very good, but often there are exceptions, which are not desirable. Also, usually this concept is not utilized fully. We do not need separate words for boy and girl. We need only one word with a prefix or a suffix for gender.

The meanings of words is another area of concern. Many times the words have contextual meanings. This increases the learning effort, as all the meanings of the words have to be learnt. Also, the words often suffer from overprecision, and underprecision. There are many words which mean exactly, or nearly, the same. On the other hand there are some words, whose meaning is not precise enough.

Grammars of natural languages are usually quite complex. Agreement of number and gender between noun and verb is a case in point. Really speaking, there is no need to alter the verb for number and gender; they should be attributes of noun alone. If that was done, the language will become simpler. By unnecessarily modifying the verb for number and gender, we make the language complex, and introduce the possibility of making mistakes. Needless complexity of grammar is best understood by learners of a foreign language, who constantly compare the grammar of the new language with that of their mother tongues.

Ambiguity or lack of clarity in the meaning of a sentence also exists.

It might be argued that the defects of English may be removed to prepare it for the role of world language. However, the changes may be so many, that we may not recognise it as English at all. Also, however much we improve it, it can never be as good as a language designed from scratch. We are going to build the world language only once, and it must be the best. Evaluation of other natural languages is likely to bring us to the same conclusion.

Also, we must remember that adopting an existing language as world language will be more repugnant to the rest of the world, than adopting a newly designed language.

Should Esperanto be world language?

If natural languages do not qualify to be the world language, what about Esperanto? After all it was created precisely for this purpose. There is no doubt that Esperanto is better suited to be the world language, than any other natural language. However, the question remains: is it possible to design a language better than Esperanto? The answer would be in affirmative, primarily because even Esperanto is based on some natural languages, and has not exercised freedom of choice in design to the fullest. However, Esperanto has definitely proved

a major point—that it is possible to design a language.

How to develop a world language?

Designing a language is not a very difficult job, but designing a good language is. Designing a language involves making a large number of decisions. How much effort is put in arriving at these decisions will determine the quality of language. Also, the process should involve wide ranging consultations with experts in various fields. After an initial decision is made based on expert opinion, it should be widely publicized, and feedback and comments of all the people should be considered, before finalizing the decision. Even then, if there is a good reason to alter a decision previously made, it should be done. In no case should we compromise on the quality of the world language. Some ideas are discussed here to illustrate the kind of improvements possible. Obviously, they are at best the tip of the iceberg.

Objectives of the world language

Some of the objectives of the world language would be as under. These need to be debated and enlarged. They also need to be interpreted for each sub-activity.

1. Achieve effective and unambiguous communication
   1.1 Between humans
   1.2 Between humans and machines
2. Minimize effort in communication
   2.1 Minimize effort in speaking and hearing
   2.2 Minimize effort in writing and reading
3. Minimize effort in learning the language
   3.1 Minimize the length and number of words
   3.2 Maximize the use of rules to form words and sentences. Have no exceptions.

Designing alphabet and script

One of the most fundamental components of a language is its alphabet. The alphabet is in two forms—written and spoken. While designing the alphabet, the spoken alphabet should be designed first. The sounds produced by human beings are not discrete. From a continuous spectrum, we have to select a set of sounds. If we select too few sounds, the alphabet will be small and words will be longer. On the other hand, too many sounds may cause problems in distinguishing between them. Fortunately, this science, called phonetics, is well developed, and can be used for selecting a set of sounds. The sounds should be selected in such a way that we get the maximum distinction between sounds, and the effort required in production of sound is minimum. In addition, pleasantness of sound in hearing may also be considered. The ability of machines to produce these sounds, and distinguish between them on hearing may also be considered.

In order to minimize learning effort, each sound should be assigned a character. Frequently occurring sound combinations may also be assigned an additional character, as in shorthand. The language should be phonetic. We already have natural languages which are phonetic, and they demonstrate the advantages offered by a phonetic language.

The script for the world language should be designed keeping in mind the ability of human hand for writing, and human eye for reading. In writing, the script should provide continuity. There should be no dotting the 'i', or cutting the 't'. This will minimize the movement of hand, and save effort. Each character should be independent, and combined sequentially. In some scripts, a part of the character is outside the main writing area, e.g. a part of 'g' is below the main line of writing. This should be avoided to conserve space. Characters should be as uniform in size as possible. Each character should be written in only one way. There should be no concept of upper and lower case, wherein the same character is written in two ways.

The effort in writing can be greatly reduced, if natural movements of body are used in the design of characters. Research should be conducted to determine which movements are easy for human hands, and which are not. For example, it is common experience that people find it easier to write 'u' than to write 'n'. So much so, that often 'n' looks like 'u'. This is not accidental, because its opposite never happens. This is an interesting example, because the two characters are mirror images of one another. It can perhaps be said that human hand can turn in quickly, but cannot turn out as quickly. Perhaps it has a natural tendency to move towards the chest as observed in case of an electric shock. Similarly, research should be conducted to determine if the human eye has any preferences in pattern recognition. We should also consider, whether the writing will be from left to right, right to left, top to bottom, or bottom to top. The suitability of the script for machine production and recognition should also be considered.

Designing words

Words, even in natural languages, consist of parts which have independent meaning. For example, both 'un' and 'well' in unwell have independent meanings, which determine the meaning of unwell. These parts are called morphemes by linguists; we may call them roots. All languages use the concepts of roots, prefixes, suffixes, etc. But they do not use it to the fullest. For example, the word 'bad' is not needed; 'ungood' could be used in its place.

We should design word roots in such a way that their meanings are, as far as possible, independent of each other. For the same meaning there should not be more than one word root. If word roots are well defined, the learning effort will greatly reduce. Let me illustrate.

We need word roots to indicate the number and the gender. We may decide that there will be three genders—masculine, feminine, and unknown or unspecified. Similarly, we may decide that there will be three numbers—singular, plural, and unknown or unspecified. We may combine both these attributes, and assign a vowel to each of the nine combinations. We then use these vowels to suffix nouns and pronouns. Let us see the power of this simple design. We now need only one word for father, mother, and parent. Similarly, only one word will be needed for brother, sister, and sibling. Not only that the number of words will be reduced, some new words will become available, e.g. a word for either son or daughter. Speakers of Hindi, will find new words like parent and sibling, which they never had before. Also, we do not often know the sex of a bird, and use masculine, feminine, or neuter gender, depending on convention. In the new scheme, we can use the unspecified gender most of the time, and can specify it if we know the gender. Also, legal documents often use words like person(s). This is because there is no concept of unknown, or unspecified, number. We can, thus, see the power of a simple well-defined word root.

The above example is not an isolated one. By defining just three morphemes, for parent, child, and spouse, hundreds of existing and non-existing words for family relations can be eliminated. A large number of words describing young members of a species can be eliminated by using a single prefix with the word for species. Also, we can have a prefix each for first half, second half, first quarter, second quarter etc. of age, and so on. Thus, the communicator can choose the precision with which he wants to convey the age.

Word roots will be formed by assigning a sequence of characters to each concept. This should be done, using principles of classification and codification. In many branches of science, e.g. zoology and botany, such classification already exists. These should be used, so that there is no need to have a separate scientific name. Also, the frequency of their use should be considered. Highly used roots should be identified by few characters, so that the words are short.

Rules should be defined to combine roots into words. Where classification and codification gives a large word, but the frequency of use requires a small word, a synonym may be defined. Thus, synonyms will exist only for the purpose of making the language more efficient.

Designing grammar

Grammar defines how to combine words into sentences. These rules should be as simple as possible, and there should be no exceptions. The sequence of words in a sentence should not affect its meaning. Also, preferably the sequence of words should not change, as it happens in English, where changing a sentence from affirmative to inquisitive requires a change in the sequence of words.

In many existing languages, attributes which should affect only words, are defined at the level of sentence. Number and gender are attributes of noun, and they have nothing to do with verb. Similarly, tense is an attribute of verb, and should not affect the noun. We think that a sentence is affirmative, or inquisitive (asks a question). Let us consider a simple sentence, "Are you going?". This may be interpreted as, "Are you going? (or not going)", or as "Are you? (or someone else) going". Here we can see that the question is an attribute of word, and not of sentence. Research will be needed to determine whether enquiry is always at word level, or sometimes at word level, and sometimes at sentence level.

What do we do next?

There is no doubt that it is possible to develop a language, which is far superior to existing languages. The development of such a language will be an iterative process. It will go through several cycles of improvement, before it becomes reasonably good. If we can assign even 1% of resources being spent in linguistic research, we can easily build such a language. Then it can be improved, and compared with existing languages. Only after its superiority is clearly demonstrated, do we have to think of adopting it. This project is definitely worthy of research, and I call upon the world community to take it up.

Good Governance

Many countries of the world face a number of problems. Are there any solutions? I believe that there are. Here are some ideas that could be helpful in solving some of our problems. There could be a structured public debate on these, and those which meet public approval could be implemented.

Minimize government functions

- Often governments try to do too many things.
- It is not government's job to provide goods and services. It should facilitate their production and distribution and ensure competitiveness, efficiency and non-exploitation of customers.
- Government should not be looked upon to provide direct employment. It should ensure a vibrant economy in which people are gainfully engaged.

Minimize government expenditure

- Whatever functions the government must perform, must be performed in the most efficient way, thereby reducing the cost of governance to a minimum.

- Methods of governance should be regularly reviewed, debated in public, and benchmarked with other countries and states to ensure that they are most effective and efficient.

Taxation

- There should be a single authority in each country which can levy taxes. No one else should be allowed to collect tax from any one. However, governments should be allowed to sell specific goods and services, which the citizens should be free to buy, or not to buy.
- The taxes collected by the taxation authority should be distributed among country, state and local governments as per a pre-defined agreed formula.
- The distribution of revenue from taxes should consider both the needs of governments and their contribution to revenue.
- The needs should be determined by estimating the cost of functions the governments are expected to provide.
- It will be citizens' right to get the services for which money is provided by the tax authority.

- The tax structure should be simplified. There should be only two forms of taxes. Excise for all goods and services produced in the country, and Custom for all goods and services brought in a country from outside.
- Sales tax, octroi, income tax, etc. should be abolished.
- Collection of excise and custom should be made effective by allocating more resources which would become available because of abolition of other taxes. In addition, the penalty for tax evasion should be very heavy, and corruption should be severely dealt with.
- It may be argued that income tax is applicable to only affluent sections of population. But, the same effect can be achieved by levying more excise on items which are consumed by these sections.

Norm-based governance

- People have started thinking that what the government does for them is charity. As a result, while some people get too much, others don't get even the basic minimum.
- This tendency is clearly visible. Constituencies of VIPs, e.g. prime minister, railway minister, etc. get generous allocation, which suddenly dries up if the concerned minister no longer holds office.
- This tendency is often justified by saying that at least somewhere something is getting done. This argument shows how little we have come to expect from our governments.
- In order to ensure that justice is done to all, we must define the functions of government, the levels in each function, and the entitlement criteria.
- For example we may say that all villages with population between 100 and 1000

will be linked with brick road, while those with a population of more than 1000, will be linked with tar road.
- Such norms will ensure fairness to all.
- Along with norms, the mechanism to redress grievances arising from not following the norms should be specified. In case of deliberate victimization, those responsible should be punished.

Government as service provider

- Where the government provides service, e.g. water, health care, education, roads, etc. it should be paid by the government treasury to the concerned government department for quantity and quality of service provided. This mechanism should replace the current mechanism of budgetary allocation.
- Government departments should be run as business. Their units should earn revenue, pay bills, and make profit or loss. The employees of each individual unit should be rewarded based on the financial performance of the unit.
- Citizens should be treated as customers and given bills for the service provided, showing the amount payable by them and the subsidies.
- Where possible, the quantity and quality of service should be certified by the individual customers. Where it is not possible, it should be certified by customer bodies.
- If private parties offer to provide service at a cheaper rate, the job should be given to them.

Accountability

- Government functionaries seem to have all power but no accountability.
- For example, the encroachment department of a municipal corporation has powers to demolish an illegal building.

But such powers are often exercised selectively to demolish some and leave others. The municipal corporation is not accountable to people as to why rules are being applied selectively.

- Lack of accountability breeds corruption.
- Whenever someone is given power, he should also be made accountable, preferably to the public.
- For example, if an illegal construction is found in the jurisdiction of an anti-encroachment department, its officers should be punished.

Citizens role in governance

- Governance can be much better and easier if citizens are involved in it.
- Schemes to involve citizens in governance should clearly specify how the citizens are going to contribute.
- Citizens can contribute by providing information, monitoring situations and taking action.
- The schemes involving citizens' role should be planned keeping their convenience in mind and should utilize their contribution in a most effective way.
- For example, 'Each one teach one' is not a viable and effective method; but asking a citizen to teach for two hours in a week is both convenient to the citizen and also effective in spreading education.
- Citizens should be able to see the effect of their contribution.
- One way of involving citizens would be to have a well publicised telephone number, which citizens can use to report situations such as street lights being kept on in daytime, engine of a parked bus running, leakage in a water pipe, etc. The person manning such a telephone should contact the concerned officer, who in turn should remedy the situation. Only when citizens see their involvement resulting in action, they would participate more and more.
- Another way to involve citizens would be to assign them a small neighbourhood, which they will look after to ensure its cleanliness and orderliness. If someone digs up a road in their area, they will ensure that it is mended. They will also ensure that conservancy staff keeps their area clean. There can be many ways in which citizens can help.

Innovation

- Innovation can greatly help in good governance. Chronic problems faced by government can be solved by innovative methods.
- For example, a municipal corporation should never award a contract merely for building roads. It should always be a contract to build and maintain roads. Then the contractor will do a good job in building the road, as he will have to spend less on its maintenance. This will benefit everyone.

Political system

- In many countries, political system is corrupt because politics is not an economically viable profession.
- Every profession, except politics, offers a regular income.
- It is futile to argue that MLAs and MPs are paid a salary. These are the highest levels to which people reach in politics. The corruptionalisation is completed much before such levels are reached.
- We cannot expect to have politicians for free. If we do, we pay through our nose.
- Unless politics can attract young men and women and provide them a descent secure career, it is futile to expect politicians to be honest.

- Many countries have administrative or civil services. They should also create a political service in which young men and women should be recruited in an open competition. This service should conduct competitive examinations on the lines of the administrative or civil services.
- Those qualifying in the competitive examination should be trained and given pay and perks at par with the administrative or civil services.
- Those selected for political service, should be barred from taking up any other job, or doing any business.
- They should not be given any regular work. They should do political or social work of their choice.
- Their work should be monitored by Judiciary to ensure that they do adequate amount of work. If the quantum of their work is found inadequate, they must be withdrawn from political service and assigned administrative work. If they are found to be corrupt, their services should be terminated.
- They will contest election like any other person, and if they get elected, they will be entitled to only one salary, either of the service or of the elected office.
- Only if we can attract young students, and allow them to make an honest career in politics, can we hope to end corruption some day.

Education

- The objective of the education system is not clearly defined.
- People claim that education system has failed without even defining what education is expected to achieve.
- The objective of primary and secondary education should be to impart skills in languages and mathematics, and to create general awareness and scientific temperament.

- The objective of higher level education should be to impart skills and knowledge which a person will need in his career.
- The availability of different courses should be based on the manpower needs of a country. Consequently, in a country like India a large number of students should be educated in agriculture, horticulture, fishery, cattle rearing, etc.
- Education should not be fashionable; it should be need based and add value. It should also be easy to obtain, preferably without sacrificing the earning capacity of students.

Judiciary

- The effectiveness of judiciary determines how civilized a society is.
- The objective of judiciary is not merely to hear cases and pronounce judgement, but also to create confidence in people that if they are wronged, judiciary will help remedy the problem. It should also create the impression that no one can do wrong and get away with it.
- From the above point of view, judiciary in many countries has failed miserably.
- Failure of judiciary is the primary reason of corruption in society.
- Judiciary must work out and implement a strategy to achieve the above objectives. Judicial management should be a part of judiciary.
- Judiciary must get its workload studied to see what part of it can be eliminated by improving the rules governing those situations. For example, Judiciary handles a large number of cases related to motor vehicle accident compensation. If rules are framed to determine this compensation based on relevant factors like age, earning capacity, number of dependants, etc. insurance companies will be able to settle most of the cases, and the number of such cases going to court will drastically reduce.

- Judiciary should work on cases in a time bound manner. It should fix time norms for different types of cases and endeavour to finish a case in the allotted time.
- Judiciary can work in a time bound manner only if it has a reasonable number of cases in hearing. Therefore, new cases should go in a queue from which they should be taken for hearing. The cases may not be taken for hearing on a first-come first-served basis, but based on some guidelines which take into account the importance and urgency of a case.
- Judiciary must augment its capacity to meet the workload. The major resource that the judiciary requires is manpower. It is ironic that even in countries with excess manpower, this function is poorly performed due to lack of resources.
- Judiciary may take help of retired citizens to augment its capacity.
- Judiciary should review its policies to ensure that they are concomitant with speedy and effective justice.

E-Governance

- Information Technology (IT) is having a major impact on governance. Many country and state governments are changing their business processes to take advantage of the benefits that IT offers. However, if we have to get the most efficient e-governance at minimum cost, we need to do two things: commonize business processes and develop soft IT infrastructure.

Commonize business processes

- At present, the same business process gets computerized by different agencies in different ways. This creates islands of information which cannot talk to each other.

- A case in point is the computerization of RTO (Regional Transport Office) operations in India. Initially, different RTOs created their systems independently, and now it is proposed to scrap all those systems and replace them with a common central system. Needless to say the expenditure in independent systems could have been avoided.

Develop soft IT infrastructure

- We are aware of the importance of IT infrastructure in the development of IT. However, we usually think only of hardware infrastructure. It is high time we start thinking of soft IT infrastructure as well, and understand its importance in the development of IT. Let me explain.
- Any computerization project requires creation of master data, e.g. citizens, business entities, real estate properties, etc. At present each system creates its own master data. In India, a citizen has one id for income tax department, another for his driving licence, and yet another for his bank. He also has an id in each of the hospitals he visits, and so on. Obviously, these systems cannot talk to each other. If each person in the world were to be given a unique person id, that id would get used by all these systems, instead of trying to create their own. This not only would save development effort but also would enable diverse systems to talk to each other.
- It is not only the persons we need to identify uniquely but also every legal entity such as businesses, each piece of land and real estate, etc. The list is endless and so are the benefits of creating such unique identities.
- Wherever possible, we should look for natural attributes in giving id to an entity. For example, we can give a number to land and real estate based on its longitude, latitude and altitude. Similarly, we can

codify the primary relation between two persons as Father (F), Mother (M), Brother (B), Sister (C), Husband (H), Wife (W), Son (S) and Daughter (D). All other relations can be derived by combining these primary relations.

- It is important that standards for master data creation and codification are discussed and agreed in international bodies such as International Standards Organization. If this is not done, the world will have to incur additional cost later either in changing the systems, or in building interfaces.

- The benefits of unique identification are enormous. If each person is given a unique numeric id, we can store a telephone number and an e-mail id against him. For calling a person, you would make the call on his person id with a prefix, say 1. The prefix will indicate to the telephone system that the following number is a person id which has to be converted into telephone number. If the person's telephone number changes, only the link needs to be changed. The callers will still call the same number. Similarly, a person can be contacted on the same e-mail id, even if he changes his service provider.

- E-governance should not be creating islands of computer systems. We must

have a clear vision, strategy and master plan. We must understand what to do and what not to do, if we are not to waste our precious time and resources.

Pledge your time (samay daan)

- We citizens only criticize. We do nothing concrete.
- Things are not going to change if we expect others to change them. They will change if we act to change them.
- Those who want to change the world for better should pledge 1% of their time for society. This works out to less than 15 minutes a day and less than two hours a week.
- They can spend this time to pursue the cause of their choice. They can join an NGO, or form local groups to discuss and debate what can be done.
- Even if they just meet once a week to discuss what can be done, ideas will emerge and things will begin to happen.
- Their own efforts will shape their actions and organizations.
- The key thing is commitment and doing; not idle criticism.
- Register your time pledge (samay daan) with World Integration and Improvement Initiative (agrawal.prem@gmail.com)

City without Traffic Lights

Are you fed up with traffic lights? Traffic lights at every junction. Stop, start. Stop, start. Stop, start. Do you sometimes wish that the roads of your city were like expressway. Where your car would compete with the wind and you would reach your destination in minutes.

Fortunately, this is possible. In order to use this plan, the main roads of the city need to be like a grid, as shown in Figure 1.

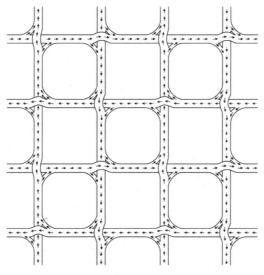

Figure 1

All roads will be one-way. When one road meets another at an intersection, there are two possibilities; you may either continue on your road, or you may turn on the other road in the direction of the traffic on that road. This is shown in Figure 2.

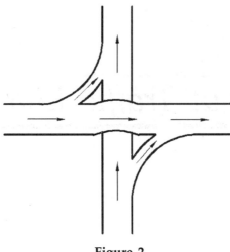

Figure 2

If you turn on the other road, there is no problem. But if you continue on your road, you will run into the traffic going straight on the other road. This is solved by a flyover or grade separator. Traffic on one road will go above the flyover, and the traffic on the other road will go under the flyover. This will ensure smooth flow of traffic without traffic light. This will be done on all intersections. Figure 1 shows this arrangement.

Sounds like a good idea. But how will the pedestrians cross the road? If the traffic moves at a fast speed, it will become impossible for the pedestrians to cross the road. The solution to this is in Figure 3.

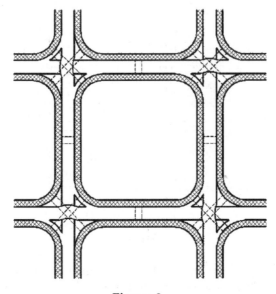

Figure 3

There will be a ring road for pedestrians and cyclists in each sector (the area bounded by main roads on all four sides). This pedestrian ring road will be connected to the pedestrian ring roads of adjoining sectors through subways. Thus, no pedestrian or cyclist will ever come on the main roads, allowing the vehicles to move freely on the main roads. Pedestrian roads will not be one-way. Pedestrians and cyclists will move on the pedestrian roads in both directions.

But how will a person take public transport, e.g. bus or taxi? This is explained in Figure 4.

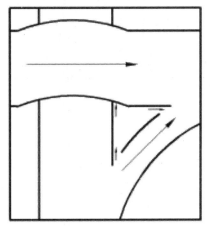

Figure 4

At each intersection, there are two triangular areas. Buses and taxis will go inside these triangular areas. There they will drop and pickup the passengers and come out of the triangle on the road they wish to take. These triangular areas will be connected to the pedestrian roads through subways.

Figure 5 shows the vehicle ring roads inside the sectors. This ring road will be connected to all the four main roads as well as to the internal roads of the sector. These roads will be two-way.

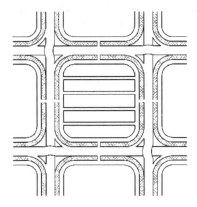

Figure 5

Figure 6 shows how the vehicles will move from one sector to another sector. Draw a horizontal and a vertical line from the source sector to the destination sector. You can do this in two ways. You can take either of these two ways to travel to your destination. You come out of the source sector taking the exit according to your travel path, move to the destination sector and enter it.

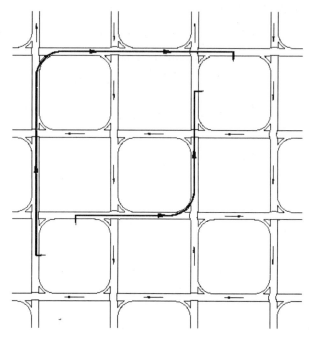

Figure 6

The main roads will be fenced on both sides so that no one can enter or exit them except through designated entry and exit roads. No pedestrian or cyclist will enter these roads. The vehicles will enter these roads, move to their destination and exit. Vehicles will neither stop on the main roads, nor be parked on it. Public transport will not stop on the main roads. There will be no shops or vendors on the main roads. Main roads will be like expressways. Enter, Move, Exit. No stoppage. The road network can be further modified to accommodate a parallel metro rail network.

For further information, contact

P K Agrawal
E-mail: agrawal.prem@gmail.com

INDEX
(863–872)